Frequently Used Symbols in Essentials of Managerial Finance

a	periodic level payment or annuity
b	proportion of net income (NI) retained by the firm
B	the market value of the firm's debt
β (beta)	beta of a security, a measure of its riskiness
c	coupon payment for a bond
CV	coefficient of variation
$CVIF$	compound value interest factor
$CVIF_a$	compound value interest factor for an annuity
d	dividend payment per share of common equity
D	total dividend payments of the firm for common equity
Dep	depreciation
EPS	earnings per share; also e
F	net after-tax cash flows for capital budgeting analysis of projects
g	growth rate or growth factor
i	interest rate
I	amount of investment
k	in general, the discount factor; more specifically, the weighted average cost of capital
k_b	cost of debt
k_c	cost of a convertible issue
k_j	returns to firm j or on security j
k_s	cost of common equity for the levered firm
k_{ps}	cost of senior equity, e.g., preferred stock
k_u	cost of capital for the unlevered firm
k_M	return on the market portfolio
λ (lambda)	slope of the security market line $= (\bar{k}_M - R_F)/\sigma^2_M$
n	number of shares outstanding
N	life of a project; also terminal year of decision or planning horizon
p	price of a security
P	sales price per unit of product sold
P_s	probability for state of the world s
$PVIF$	present value interest factor
$PVIF_a$	present value interest factor for an annuity
Q	quantity produced or sold
r	rate of return on new investments; also internal rate of return (IRR)
R_F	risk-free rate of interest
s	subscript referring to alternative states of the world
S	market value of a firm's common equity
σ (sigma)	standard deviation
σ^2	variance
t	time period
T	the marginal corporate income tax rate
TR	total revenues $\equiv$ sales $\equiv PQ$
V	market value of a firm
w	weights in capital structure or portfolio proportions
X	net operating income of the firm; also equals EBIT $\equiv$ NOI

ESSENTIALS OF MANAGERIAL FINANCE

J. FRED WESTON
UNIVERSITY OF CALIFORNIA
LOS ANGELES

EUGENE F. BRIGHAM
UNIVERSITY OF FLORIDA

FIFTH EDITION

THE DRYDEN PRESS
HINSDALE, ILLINOIS

Copyright © 1979 by The Dryden Press
A division of Holt, Rinehart and Winston
Library of Congress Catalog Card Number: 78-56194
ISBN: 0-03-045446-8

Printed in the United States of America
9 032 987654321

Cover and text design by James Buddenbaum
Copy edited by Jo-Anne Naples

PREFACE

Managerial finance continues to reflect important new developments. The changing values of the U.S. dollar dramatize the increased importance of international finance. Strong inflationary pressures have pushed interest rates to unprecedented heights, and the resulting high cost of capital has led to profound changes in corporate financial policies and practices. Academic researchers have made significant advances, especially in the areas of capital budgeting and the cost of capital. At the same time, business practitioners are making increasing use of financial theory, and feedback from the "real world" has led to revisions in this theory. These trends have dictated the revisions made in this edition of *Essentials of Managerial Finance.*

The changes reflect our experience and that of others in teaching business finance. Organizational changes have been made to provide for smoother flow and greater continuity; points that have proved troublesome to students have been clarified; errors have been corrected; and, of course, descriptive materials have been updated.

Much of the book's content is the result of our experience in executive development programs and in consulting with business firms on financial problems and policies over a number of years. This experience has helped us identify the significant responsibilities of financial managers, the fundamental problems facing firms, and the most feasible approaches to practical decision making. Some topics are conceptually difficult, but so are the issues faced by financial managers. These managers must be prepared to handle complex problems, and solving the problems necessarily involves the use of advanced tools and techniques.

Although we could have simplified the text in many places by avoiding difficult issues, we prefer to provide a basic framework based on the received doctrine, then to present materials on a number of important but controversial issues. We hope that our presentation will stimulate the reader to further inquiry.

We acknowledge that the level and difficulty of the material is somewhat uneven. Certain sections are simply descriptions of the institutional features of the financial environment and are not difficult to understand. Others—notably the material on capital budgeting, uncertainty, and the cost of capital—are by nature rather abstract and difficult for those not used to thinking in abstract terms. In some of the more complex sections, we simply outline procedures in the text and refer interested readers to more advanced works.

Changes in the Fifth Edition

The fifth edition of *Essentials* differs from the fourth in several respects. Some of the more significant alterations are itemized below:

1. The discussion of the finance function (Chapter 1) has been streamlined, and the goals of the firm have been placed in a broader perspective.
2. The impact and results of inflation are discussed throughout the book.
3. A section on the financial system (Chapter 2) has been added to give an overview of financial institutions and instruments. This section provides a framework of terminology and background on long- and short-term in-

terest rate patterns needed to handle issues in the chapters on working capital management.

4. The materials on the cost of capital and valuation (Chapters 14 to 17) have been moved forward so the concepts can be employed in the chapters dealing with alternative forms and sources of financing. This change provides increased opportunity for students to use these basic concepts and to master them.

5. The subject of international business finance has been added (Chapter 26), and international aspects of a number of individual topics are treated throughout the book.

6. The capital asset pricing material is introduced early in Chapter 13 with simple explanations and applications. Along with other approaches, it can help financial managers make judgmental decisions.

7. The section on leasing (Chapter 21) incorporates the important developments in recent articles.

8. The end-of-chapter problems have been substantially reworked and augmented. Usually, five to seven problems per chapter are presented in a sequence from relatively basic to relatively difficult. The instructor can thus select problems at levels to match the students' backgrounds and the available time.

9. Materials have been thoroughly updated, particularly in the areas of interest rates, stock prices, and the money and capital markets in general.

10. A listing of frequently used symbols has been provided. Some symbols in specialized areas have been changed from previous editions so the reader can be assured that each set of symbols is used consistently in the main conceptual flow of the book.

11. Answers to selected problems have been provided (Appendix B). They are intended to resolve students' uncertainty about the correctness of their own answers.

12. Particular attention has been given to the glossary and index. Their completeness will ease any problems occurring when instructors assign chapters out of sequence.

Ancillary Materials

Several items are available as supplements. Many students will find the *Study Guide* useful, since it highlights the key points of the text and presents a comprehensive set of problems similar to those at the end of each chapter. The problems are solved in detail, so students who have difficulty with the end-of-chapter problems can be helped by reviewing them.

Note to instructors: For those instructors who adopt the textbook, the publisher has prepared a set of supplementary problems and solutions to be included in the instructor's manual and a set of transparencies. These are all available directly from Dryden Press.

Acknowledgments In its many revisions, *Essentials* has been worked on and critically reviewed by numerous individuals. We have also received detailed comments and suggestions from instructors and students using the book. We are deeply indebted to them and to the following individuals in particular: M. Adler, E. Altman, J. Andrews, R. Aubey, P. Bacon, W. Beranek, V. Brewer, W. Brueggeman, R. Carleson, S. Choudhury, P. Cooley, C. Cox, L. Dann, H. DeAngelo, D. Fischer, R. Gray, J. Griggs, R. Haugen, S. Hawk, R. Hehre, J. Henry, A. Herrmann, G. Hettenhouse, R. Himes, C. Johnson, R. Jones, D. Kaplan, M. Kaufman, D. Knight, H. Krogh, R. LeClair, W. Lee, D. Longmore, J. Longstreet, H. Magee, P. Malone, R. Masulis, R. Moore, T. Morton, T. Nantell, R. Nelson, R. Norgaard, J. Pappas, R. Pettit, R. Pettway, J. Pinkerton, G. Pogue, W. Regan, F. Reilly, R. Rentz, R. Richards, C. Rini, R. Roenfeldt, W. Sharpe, K. Smith, P. Smith, D. Sorenson, M. Tysseland, P. Vanderheiden, D. Woods, J. Yeakel, and D. Ziegenbein for their careful reviews of this and previous editions.

For providing us with detailed reviews of this edition's manuscript we owe special thanks to B. J. Campsey, R. D. Hollinger, J. N. Morse, D. L. Stevens, A. M. Tuberose, and G. J. Wells. Considerable help was also provided by C. B. McNutt, R. L. Smith, G. A. Woodward, H. Johnson, M. McElroy, and L. Hickman.

We would also like to thank C. Barngrover, S. Mansinghka, W. Eckardt, H. Rollins, H. Alwan, D. Wort, and J. Zumwalt for their assistance in developing the transparency program. Special thanks to Bob LeClair and The American College for their help as well.

The Universities of California and Florida and our colleagues on these campuses have provided us with intellectual support in bringing the book to completion. Finally, we are indebted to the Dryden Press staff—principally Paul Jones and Daniel Tomcheff—and to Jo-Anne Naples for their special efforts in getting the manuscript into production and for following through to the bound book.

The field of finance will continue to experience significant changes. It is stimulating to participate in these developments, and we hope that *Essentials* will contribute to a better understanding of the theory and practice of finance.

J. Fred Weston
Graduate School of Management
University of California
Los Angeles, California

January 1979

Eugene F. Brigham
University of Florida
Gainesville, Florida

CONTENTS

Part One   **The Environment of Managerial Finance**   **1**

Chapter 1   **Scope and Nature of Managerial Finance**   **2**

The Finance Function 3   Goals of the Firm 4   Changing Role of Financial Management 8   Financial Decisions: Risk-Return Tradeoff 11   Organization and Structure of This Book 12

Chapter 2   **The Financial Sector of the Economy**   **16**

Financial Markets 17   The Federal Reserve System 21   Fiscal Policy 21   Securities Markets 22   Interest-Bearing Business Securities 29   International Markets 32   Summary 34

Chapter 3   **The Tax Environment and Forms of Business Organization**   **38**

Corporate Income Tax 39   Personal Income Tax 46   Choices among Alternative Forms of Business Organization 49   Summary 54   Appendix 3A: Depreciation Methods 56   Straight Line 57   Double Declining Balance 57   Sum-of-Years'-Digits 58   Units of Production 58   Effect of Depreciation on Taxes Paid 59   Changing the Depreciable Life of an Asset 59

Part Two   **Financial Analysis, Planning, and Control**   **61**

Chapter 4   **Ratio Analysis**   **62**

Basic Financial Statements 63   Basic Types of Financial Ratios 67   du Pont System of Financial Analysis 79   Rates of Return in Different Industries 81   Sources of Comparative Ratios 83   Use of Financial Ratios in Credit Analysis 86   Use of Financial Ratios in Security Analysis 87   Some Limitations of Ratio Analysis 87   Summary 88   Appendix 4A: Impact of Inflation on Financial Ratios 95   Inflation and the Measurement of Profitability 96   Inflation and Inventory Valuation Methods 97   Procedures in Replacement Cost Accounting 99   General Purchasing Power Reporting (GPPR) 102

Chapter 5   **Profit Planning**   **105**

Breakeven Analysis 106   Sources and Uses of Funds Statement 119   Summary 123

Chapter 6   **Financial Forecasting**   **127**

Cash Flow Cycle 128   Financing Patterns 131   Percent-of-Sales Method 131   Scatter Diagram, or Simple Regression Method 137   Multiple Regression Method 138   Comparison of Forecasting Methods 139   Summary 141

Chapter 7   **Financial Planning and Control Budgeting**   **148**

Budgeting 149   Nature of the Budgeting Process 149   Financial Control Policies 151
Problems of Budgeting 158   Use of Financial Plans and Budgets 158   Divisional Control
in a Decentralized Firm 159   Effects of Inflation on Required Returns 162   External Uses
of Financial Forecasts and Budgets 165   Summary 165

Part Three   **Working Capital Management**   **171**

Chapter 8   **Working Capital Policy**   **172**

Importance of Working Capital Management 173   Original Concept of Working
Capital 174   Extending the Working Capital Concept 174   Long-Term versus Short-Term
Debt 177   Relationship of Current Assets to Fixed Assets 186   Combining Current Asset
and Current Liability Management 189   Summary 190

Chapter 9   **Current Asset Management**   **196**

Cash Management 197   Determining the Minimum Cash Balance 204   Marketable
Securities 206   Management of Accounts Receivable: Credit Policy 210   Inventory 216
Generality of Inventory Analysis 217   Cash Management as an Inventory Problem 221
Recent Restructuring of Current Asset Management 222   Summary 222

Chapter 10   **Major Sources and Forms of Short-Term Financing**   **227**

Trade Credit 228   Concept of Net Credit 230   Short-Term Financing by Commercial
Banks 231   Commercial Paper 236   Use of Security in Short-Term Financing 237
Financing Accounts Receivable 238   Inventory Financing 242   Summary 245

Part Four   **Investment Decisions**   **253**

Chapter 11   **The Interest Factor in Financial Decisions**   **254**

Compound Value 255   Present Value 257   Compound Value versus Present Value 259
Compound Value of an Annuity 261   Present Value of an Annuity 261   Annual Payments
for Accumulation of a Future Sum 264   Annual Receipts from an Annuity 264
Determining Interest Rates 265   Linear Interpolation 265   Present Value of an Uneven
Series of Receipts 266   Semiannual and Other Compounding Periods 268   A Special
Case of Semiannual Compounding: Bond Values 270   Appropriate Compounding or
Discounting Rates 272   Summary 273

Chapter 12   **Capital Budgeting Techniques**   **280**

Significance of Capital Budgeting 281   A Simplified View of Capital Budgeting 283

Application of the Concept 284   Administrative Details 286   Analysis: Choosing among Alternative Proposals 286   Importance of Good Data 287   Ranking Investment Proposals 288   Basic Differences between the NPV and IRR Methods 295   Capital Budgeting Project Evaluation 298   Alternative Capital Budgeting Worksheet 304   Capital Rationing 304   Public Expenditure Decisions 307   Summary 308   Appendix 12A: Accelerated Depreciation 313

Chapter 13   **Investment Decisions under Uncertainty 318**

Risk in Financial Analysis 319   Traditional Measures of Risk of Individual Projects 324   Risk Analysis in a Portfolio Context 332   The Capital Asset Pricing Model 338   The Use of Risk Adjusted Discount Rates: An Example 342   Summary 343

Part Five   **Valuation and the Cost of Capital 349**

Chapter 14   **Valuation and Rates of Return 350**

Definitions of Value 351   The Required Rate of Return 353   Bond Valuation 355   Preferred Stock Valuation 360   Common Stock Valuation and Rates of Return 361   Factors Leading to Changes in Market Prices 365   Marketability and Rates of Return 366   Summary 366   Appendix 14A: Multi-Period Stock Valuation Models 372   Expected Dividends as the Basis for Stock Values 372   Stock Values with Zero Growth 373   Normal, or Constant, Growth 373   Supernormal Growth 375   Comparing Companies with Different Expected Growth Rates 376

Chapter 15   **Financial Leverage and Risk 380**

Basic Definitions 381   Theory of Financial Leverage 381   Analysis of Alternative Methods of Financing 388   Breakeven Analysis 394   Relationship of Financial Leverage to Operating Leverage 395   Variations in Financial Structure 399   Factors Influencing Financial Structure 400   Summary 404

Chapter 16   **The Cost of Capital 410**

The Cost of Capital 411   Composite, or Overall, Cost of Capital 411   Basic Definitions 412   Before-Tax Component Cost of Debt (k_b) 413   Preferred Stock 415   Tax Adjustment 416   Cost of Retained Earnings (k_r) 417   Cost of New Common Stock, or External Equity Capital (k_e) 419   Finding the Basic Required Rate of Return on Common Equity 420   Effects of Risky Leverage 422   Effect of Leverage on the Component Cost of Debt 424   Combining Debt and Equity: Weighted Average, or Composite, Cost of Capital 425   Calculating the Marginal Cost of Capital for an Actual Company 428   Large Firms versus Small Firms 437   Summary 438

Chapter 17   **Dividend Policy and Internal Financing 445**

Factors Influencing Dividend Policy 446   Dividend Policy Decisions 449   Rationale for Stable Dividends 450   Alternative Dividend Policies 451   Residual Theory of Dividends 452   Long-Run Viewpoint 455   High and Low Dividend Payout Industries 455 Conflicting Theories on Dividends 456   Dividend Payments 457   Stock Dividends and Stock Splits 458   Stock Repurchases as an Alternative to Dividends 460   Summary 463

Part Six   **Long-Term Financing   471**

Chapter 18   **Obtaining External Long-Term Funds   472**

Direct Financing 474   Investment Banking 480   Investment Banking Operation 482 Costs of Flotation 487   Regulation of Security Trading 489   Appraisal of Regulation of Security Trading 491   Summary 491

Chapter 19   **Common Stock   498**

Apportionment of Income, Control, and Risk 499   Common Stock Financing 501 Evaluation of Common Stock as a Source of Funds 505   Use of Rights in Financing 506 Theoretical Relationships of Rights Offerings 507   Effects on Position of Stockholders 510 Advantages of Use of Rights in New Financing 514   Choosing among Alternative Forms of Financing 515   Summary 523

Chapter 20   **Fixed Income Securities: Debt and Preferred Stock   530**

Instruments of Long-Term Debt Financing 531   Secured Bonds 535   Unsecured Bonds 536   Characteristics of Long-Term Debt 539   Decisions on the Use of Long-Term Debt 540   Nature of Preferred Stock 541   Major Provisions of Preferred Stock Issues 542 Evaluation of Preferred Stock 545   Decision Making on the Use of Preferred Stock 547 Rationale for Different Classes of Securities 547   Refunding a Bond or a Preferred Stock Issue 549   Summary 552

Chapter 21   **Lease Financing 561**

Types of Leases 562   Accounting for Leases 564   Cost Comparison between Lease and Purchase 567   Alternative Approaches to Leasing Decisions 572   Use of an Internal Rate of Return Analysis 575   Additional Influences on the Leasing versus Owning Decision 576   Summary 581

Chapter 22   **Warrants and Convertibles 586**

Warrants 587   Convertibles 591   Analysis of Convertible Debentures 593   Decisions

Contents

on the Use of Warrants and Convertibles 601   Reporting Earnings If Convertibles or Warrants Are Outstanding 603   Summary 603

Part Seven   **Integrated Topics in Financial Management   611**

Chapter 23   **Timing of Financial Policy   612**

Significance to Financial Management 613   Historical Patterns in Interest Rate Movement 614   Interest Rates as an Index of Availability of Funds 617   Costs of Different Kinds of Financing over Time 617   Characteristic Patterns in Cost of Money 619   Interest Rate Forecasts 620   Implications of Interest Rate Patterns for Financial Timing 625 Summary 626

Chapter 24   **External Growth: Mergers and Holding Companies   633**

Mergers versus Internal Growth 635   Terms of Mergers 636   Holding Companies 643 Summary 652   Appendix 24A: Financial Accounting Policies in Mergers 657

Chapter 25   **Failure, Reorganization, and Liquidation   665**

The Firm's Life Cycle 666   Failure 667   Causes of Failures 667   The Failure Record 668   Extension and Composition 669   Reorganization in General 671 Financial Decisions in Reorganization 671   Liquidation Procedures 677 Bankruptcy 678   Summary 684

Chapter 26   **International Business Finance   689**

Introduction 690   The Development of an International Firm 691   Impact of Exchange Rate Fluctuations 694   Risk Position of the Firm in Foreign Currency Units 695   Methods of Dealing with the Risk of a Decline in Foreign Currency Values 695   Protection against Rising Values of Foreign Currencies 697   Monetary Balance 699   International Financing 702   Working Capital Management in International Enterprise 706 Summary 707

Appendix A   **Interest Tables**

Appendix B   **Answers to Selected End-of-Chapter Problems**

Glossary

Index

x

PART 1 THE ENVIRONMENT OF MANAGERIAL FINANCE

Part 1 consists of three chapters. Chapter 1, which describes the scope and nature of managerial finance, serves as an introduction to the book. Chapter 2 develops an overview of the total financial framework within which decisions are made. It deals with the role of the money and capital markets—their international dimensions and their major financing sources. It views the functions of financial managers in the perspective of this broad social framework. Chapter 3 examines the tax system. It emphasizes that since a high percentage of business income is paid to the government, taxes have an important influence on many kinds of business decisions—particularly the form of business organization chosen (proprietorship, partnership, or corporation). As a group, the three chapters in Part 1 provide a necessary background and framework for the financial planning and control processes discussed in Part 2 as well as for the analytical decision areas covered in the remainder of the book.

1

CHAPTER   SCOPE AND NATURE
OF MANAGERIAL FINANCE

What is managerial finance? What is the finance function in the firm? What specific tasks are assigned to financial managers? What tools and techniques are available to them, and how can their performance be measured? On a broader scale, what is the role of finance in the U.S. economy, and how can managerial finance be used to further national goals? Providing at least tentative answers to these questions is the principal purpose of this book.

The Finance Function

Financial management is defined by the functions and responsibilities of financial managers. While the specifics vary among organizations, some finance tasks are basic. Funds are raised from external financial sources and allocated for different uses. The flow of funds involved in the operations of an enterprise is monitored. Benefits to the financing sources take the form of returns, repayments, products, and services. These key financial functions must be performed in all organizations—from business firms to government units or agencies, aid groups such as the Red Cross or Salvation Army, and other nonprofit organizations such as art museums and theater groups.

The main functions of financial managers are planning for, acquiring, and utilizing funds in ways that maximize the efficiency of the organization's operation. This requires knowledge of the financial markets from which funds are drawn and of how sound investment decisions are made and efficient operations stimulated. Managers must consider a large number of alternative sources and uses of funds in making their financial decisions. They must choose, for example, internal or external funds, long-term or short-term projects, long-term or short-term fund sources, and higher or lower rates of growth.

Up to this point, the discussion of the finance function has applied to all types of organizations. What is unique about business organizations is that they are directly and measurably subject to the discipline of the financial markets. These markets are continuously determining the valuations of business firms' securities, thereby providing measures of the firms' performance.[1] A consequence of this reassessment of managerial performance by the capital markets is the change in relative valuation levels of business firms. That is, changes in valuations signal changes in performance. Therefore, valuations stimulate efficiency and provide incentives to business managers to improve their performance. It is difficult to test the efficiency and performance of organizations other than business firms because of the lack of financial markets for continuously placing valuations on them and assessing their performance.

---

1. The financial markets discussed in Chapter 2 provide valuations of firms whose shares are traded. The relationships between return and risk also provide the basis for the valuation of smaller companies whose ownership shares are not actively traded.

Goals of the Firm

The objectives of financial management have been formulated in the context of the valuation processes of the financial markets. The primary goal of financial management is to maximize shareholder wealth. By formulating the firm's objectives in terms of the shareholders' interest, the discipline of the financial markets is implemented. Thus firms that perform better than others have higher stock prices and can raise additional funds under more favorable terms. When funds go to firms with favorable stock price trends, the economy's resources are directed to their most efficient uses. Hence, throughout this book we operate on the assumption that management's primary goal is to maximize the wealth of its shareholders.

Most of the finance literature has adopted the basic postulate of maximizing the price of the firm's common stock. From this postulate, theories have been developed that receive considerable support from empirical tests. Shareholder wealth maximization also provides a basis for rational analysis and actions with respect to a wide range of financial decisions to be made by the firm. However, some other goals have also been proposed.

Managers' versus Stockholders' Goals

A considerable number of people in the field of financial management argue that managers substitute their own objectives and welfare in place of those of the stockholders (the owners of the firm). They hold that managers come to know more about the firm than its shareholders do and that they control the machinery for electing the board of directors, thereby dominating the board (which in theory is supposed to represent the shareholders). In addition, they argue that managers are interested in the firm's growth or bigness because managers' salaries and other benefits are related to the size of the firm as measured by sales or total assets. They further allege that the larger the firm the greater the opportunity for managers' perquisites in the form of spacious offices, luxurious furniture, numerous secretaries, company cars, and so on. Finally, they claim that managers operate the firm they control in a way that avoids much risk, since managers' reputations are closely tied to their firm's reputation.

While there is some basis for this view of managerial control, the predominant evidence is that managers operate in the interests of their firm's owners. One reason is that the compensation arrangements for managers include bonuses tied to profits and stock options tied to the increasing value of the firm's common stock. A second reason is that the shareholders have the ultimate power to replace management and do in fact exercise this power. Just the threat of its use is enough to keep managers oriented to the best interests of the firm's owners. But even assuming that managers operate on behalf of the shareholders, a number of alternative measures of performance have been proposed.

Profit versus Wealth Maximization

Suppose management is interested primarily in stockholders, making its decisions so as to maximize their welfare. Is profit maximization best for stockholders?

Total Profits In answering this question, we must consider the matter of total corporate profits versus earnings per share. Suppose a firm raises capital by selling stock and then invests the proceeds in government bonds. Total profits will rise, but more shares will be outstanding. Earnings per share will probably decline, pulling down the value of each share of stock and, hence, the existing stockholders' wealth. Thus, to the extent that profits are important, management should concentrate on earnings per share rather than on total corporate profits.

Earnings per Share Will maximizing earnings per share also maximize stockholder welfare, or should other factors be evaluated? Consider the timing of the earnings. Suppose one project will cause earnings per share to rise by $.20 per year for five years, or $1 in total, while another project has no effect on earnings for four years but increases earnings by $1.25 in the fifth year. Which project is better? The answer depends on which project adds the most to the value of the stock, and this in turn depends on the time value of money to investors. In any event, timing is an important reason to concentrate on wealth as measured by the price of the stock rather than on earnings alone.

Risk Still another issue relates to risk. Suppose one project is expected to increase earnings by $1 per share while another is expected to increase them by $1.20 per share. The first project is not very risky; if it is undertaken, earnings will almost certainly rise by about $1 per share. The other project is quite risky, so while the best guess is that earnings will rise by $1.20 per share, the possibility exists that there may be no increase whatever. Depending on how averse stockholders are to risk, the first project may be preferable to the second.

Recognizing all these factors, managers interested in maximizing stockholder welfare seek to maximize the value of the firm's common stock. The price of the stock reflects the market's evaluation of the firm's prospective earnings stream over time, the riskiness of this stream, and a host of other factors. The higher the price of the stock, the better management's performance from the standpoint of the stockholders. Thus, market price provides a performance index by which management can be judged.[2]

2. A firm's stock price might, of course, decline because of factors beyond management's control. Accordingly, it is useful to look at comparative statistics; even though a firm's stock declines by 10 percent, management has performed well if the stock of other firms in the industry declines by 20 percent.

5

Maximizing Stockholder Wealth versus Other Goals

In theory, stockholders own the firm and elect the management team. In turn management is supposed to operate in the best interests of the stockholders and seek to maximize shareholder wealth. But there are other goals also, and they will now be evaluated.

Maximizing versus Satisficing Consider *maximizing,* which involves seeking the best possible outcome, versus *satisficing,* which involves a willingness to settle for something less.[3] A firm on the brink of bankruptcy may be forced to operate as efficiently as possible. But some argue that the management of a large, well-entrenched corporation can work to keep stockholder returns at a fair or "reasonable" level and then devote part of its efforts and resources to public service activities, employee benefits, higher management salaries, or golf.

Similarly, an entrenched management can avoid risky ventures even when the possible gains to stockholders are high enough to warrant taking the gamble. The theory here is that stockholders are generally well-diversified (holding portfolios of many different stocks), so if one company takes a chance and loses, the stockholders lose only a small part of their wealth. Managers, on the other hand, are not diversified, so setbacks affect them more seriously. Accordingly, some argue that the managers of widely held firms tend to play it safe rather than aggressively seeking to maximize the prices of their firms' stocks.

It is impossible to definitively answer these questions. Several studies have suggested that managers are not completely stockholder-oriented, but the evidence is cloudy.[4] More and more firms are tying management's compensation to the company's performance, and research suggests that this motivates management to operate in a manner consistent with stock price maximization.[5] Additionally, in recent years tender offers and proxy fights have removed a number of supposedly entrenched managements; the recognition that such actions can take place has doubtless stimulated many

---

3. J. Fred Weston, *The Scope and Methodology of Finance* (Englewood Cliffs, N.J.: Prentice-Hall, 1966), chap. 2; and Herbert A. Simon, "Theories of Decision Making in Economics and Behavioral Science," *American Economic Review,* June 1959.

4. W. J. Baumol, *Business Behavior, Value, and Growth* (New York: Macmillan, 1959), argues that firms may seek to maximize sales subject to a minimum profit constraint. J. W. Elliott, "Control, Size, Growth, and Financial Performance in the Firm," *Journal of Financial and Quantitative Analysis,* January 1972, concludes that firms managed by the owners hold fewer liquid assets; this suggests a greater propensity to take risks. On the other hand, W. G. Lewellen, "Management and Ownership in the Large Firm," *Journal of Finance,* May 1969, concludes that top managers of large firms have most of their wealth tied to their firms' fortunes; hence they behave more like owners than earlier literature would suggest.

5. See R. T. Masson, "Executive Motivations, Earnings, and Consequent Equity Performance," *Journal of Political Economy,* November 1971.

firms to attempt to maximize share prices.[6] Finally, a firm operating in a competitive market, or almost any firm during an economic downturn, is forced to undertake actions that are reasonably consistent with shareholder wealth maximization. Thus, while managers may not seek only to maximize stockholder wealth, there are reasons to view this as a dominant goal for most firms. And even though a management group may pursue other goals, stockholder wealth is bound to be of considerable importance.

Maximizing Wealth versus Utility In many formulations, the objective is stated in terms of utility—the satisfactions enjoyed by individuals that result in a set of preferences. But the utility patterns or utility functions of individuals vary greatly. For example, some individuals receive positive gratification from the excitement of exposure to risks; for other individuals even moderate risks cause nervousness or illness. Who is to determine or to interpret the risk attitudes of individual investors? What can the financial manager do if shareholders have widely divergent utility preferences?

Again the capital markets come to the rescue. Whatever the individual attitudes toward risk, the market returns in relation to various measures of risk establish that investors on the average exhibit risk aversion; they consider risk a "bad" rather than a "good." Furthermore, capital market relationships make it possible to quantify the relationships between required returns and measures of risk. Methods of valuation are provided from these relationships.

Therefore, the decision criteria and decision rules for financial management are more operational and usable when the analysis is formulated in terms of the objective of shareholder wealth maximization rather than utility maximization.

Social Responsibility Another viewpoint that deserves consideration is social responsibility. Should businesses operate strictly in stockholders' best interests, or are they also partly responsible for the welfare of society? This is a complex issue with no easy answers. As economic agents whose actions have considerable impact, business firms should take into account the effects of their policies and actions on society as a whole. No one— least of all large firms—can ignore the obligations of responsible citizenship. Furthermore, it may even help long-run wealth maximization to be viewed as a "good corporate citizen" making substantial contributions to social welfare. Even more fundamentally, some amount of social responsi-

6. A tender offer is a bid by one company to buy the stock of another, while a proxy fight involves an attempt to gain control by getting stockholders to vote a new management group into office. Both actions are facilitated by low stock prices, so self-preservation can lead management to try to keep the stock value as high as possible.

bility on the part of business firms may be required for the survival of a private enterprise system in which they can operate.

But many different views exist on what is best for society. By what authority do businesses have the right to allocate funds in terms of their own views of the social good? In addition, if some firms attempt to be socially responsible and their costs thereby increase substantially, they will be at a disadvantage if their competitors do not incur the same additional costs. Because of these considerations, an argument can be made that social programs should be formulated through the processes of representative government in our democracy. This implies that most cost-increasing programs should be enacted by the government and put on a mandatory rather than a voluntary basis, at least initially, to ensure that their burden rests uniformly on all businesses.[7]

It is critical that industry and government cooperate in establishing rules for corporate behavior and that firms follow the spirit as well as the letter of the law in their actions. Thus the rules of the game become constraints, and firms should strive to maximize shareholder wealth within these constraints. Throughout the book, we shall assume that managements operate in this manner.

Changing Role of Financial Management

As with many things in the contemporary world, financial management has undergone significant changes over the years. When finance first emerged as a separate field of study in the early 1900s, the emphasis was on legalistic matters such as mergers, consolidations, the formation of new firms, and the various types of securities issued by corporations. Industrialization was sweeping the country, and the critical problem faced by firms was obtaining capital for expansion. The capital markets were relatively primitive, and transfers of funds from individual savers to businesses were quite difficult. Accounting statements of earnings and asset values were unreliable, and stock trading by insiders and manipulators caused prices to fluctuate wildly; consequently, investors were reluctant to purchase stocks and bonds. In this environment, it is easy to see why finance concentrated so heavily on legal issues relating to the issuance of securities.

The emphasis remained on securities through the 1920s; however, radical changes occurred during the depression of the 1930s. Business failures during that period caused finance to focus on bankruptcy and reorganization, corporate liquidity, and government regulation of securities markets. Fi-

---

7. What is first imposed by government may be too much and too fast, and after some experience the requirements may be modified. An example is the initial requirement of seat belts interlocked so that a car could not be started until the seat belts were fastened. This requirement was later modified.

nance was still a descriptive, legalistic subject, but the emphasis shifted to survival rather than expansion.

During the 1940s and early 1950s, finance continued to be taught as a descriptive, institutional subject, viewed from the outside rather than from within the firm's management. However, some effort was devoted to budgeting and other internal control procedures, and, stimulated by the work of Joel Dean, capital budgeting began to receive attention.[8]

The evolutionary pace quickened during the late 1950s. While the right-hand side of the balance sheet (liabilities and capital) had received more attention in the earlier era, increasing emphasis was placed on asset analysis during the last half of that decade. Mathematical models were developed and applied to inventories, cash, accounts receivable, and fixed assets. Increasingly, the focus of finance shifted from the outsider's to the insider's point of view, as financial decisions within the firm were recognized to be the critical issues in corporate finance. Descriptive, institutional materials on capital markets and financing instruments were still studied, but these topics were considered within the context of corporate financial decisions.

The emphasis on decision making has continued in recent years. First, there has been increasing belief that sound capital budgeting procedures require accurate measurements of the cost of capital. Accordingly, ways of quantifying the cost of capital now play a key role in finance. Second, capital has been in short supply, rekindling the old interest in ways of raising funds. Third, there has been continued merger activity, which has led to renewed interest in take-overs. Fourth, accelerated progress in transportation and communications has brought the countries of the world closer together; this in turn has stimulated interest in international finance. Fifth, inflation is now recognized as a critical problem, as so much of the financial manager's time is presently devoted to coping with high wages, prices, and interest rates while stock prices are relatively low. Finally, there is an increasing awareness of social ills such as air and water pollution, urban blight, and unemployment among minorities. Finding the firm's realistic role in efforts to solve these problems demands much of the financial manager's attention.

The Impact of Inflation on Financial Management

During the 1950s and 1960s prices rose at an average rate of about $1\frac{1}{2}$ to 2 percent per year, but in the 1970s the rate of inflation in some years has been more than 10 percent. This "double digit inflation" has had a tremendous impact on business firms, especially on their financial operations. As a result, many established financial policies and practices are undergoing dramatic changes, some of which are outlined here.

8. Joel Dean, *Capital Budgeting* (New York: Columbia University Press, 1951).

1. *Interest rates.* The rate of interest on U.S. government securities (called the default-free rate) consists of a "real rate of interest" of 1 to 3 percent plus an "inflation premium" that reflects the expected long-run rate of inflation. Accordingly, an increase in the rate of inflation is quickly translated into higher default-free interest rates. The cost of money to firms is the default-free rate plus a risk premium, so inflation-induced increases in the default-free rate are also reflected in business borrowing rates.

2. *Planning difficulties.* Businesses operate on the basis of long-run plans. For example, a firm builds a plant only after making a thorough analysis of expected costs and revenues over the life of the plant. Reaching such estimates is not easy under the best of conditions, but during rapid inflation, when labor and materials costs are changing dramatically, accurate forecasts are especially important yet exceedingly hard to make. Efforts are, of course, being made to improve forecasting techniques, and financial planning must include more flexibility to reflect the increased level of uncertainty in the economy. The increased uncertainty in many industries tends to raise the risk premiums for firms in those industries, driving their costs of capital still higher.

3. *Demand for capital.* Inflation increases the amount of capital required to conduct a given volume of business. When inventories are sold, they must be replaced with more expensive goods. The costs of expanding or replacing plants are also greater, while workers demand higher wages. All these things put pressure on financial managers to raise additional capital. At the same time, in an effort to hold down the rate of inflation, the Federal Reserve System tends to restrict the supply of loanable funds. The ensuing scramble for limited funds drives interest rates still higher.

4. *Bond price declines.* Long-term bond prices fall as interest rates rise, so, in an effort to protect themselves against such capital losses, lenders are beginning (a) to put more funds into short-term than into long-term debt, and (b) to insist upon bonds whose interest rates vary with "the general level of interest rates" as measured by an index of interest rates. Brazil and other inflation-plagued South American countries have used such index bonds for years. Unless inflation in the United States is controlled, their use is likely to increase in this country.

5. *Investment planning.* High interest rates, as well as a general shortage of capital, are causing firms to be especially wary in planning long-term investment outlays. Indeed, headlines such as "ITT Cuts '74 Spending Plan $106 Million Because of Difficulties in Raising Funds" or "Detroit Edison to Fight Cash Shortage by Sale-Leaseback of Coal Equipment" have become commonplace.[9]

6. *Accounting problems.* With high rates of inflation, reported profits are

---

9. *Wall Street Journal,* July 18, 1974.

distorted. The sale of low-cost inventories results in higher reported profits, but cash flows are held down as firms restock with higher-cost inventories. Similarly, depreciation charges are inadequate, since they do not reflect the new costs of replacing plant and equipment. If a firm is unaware of the "shakiness" of profits that reflect inventory valuation and inadequate depreciation charges, and if it plans dividends and capital expenditures on the basis of such figures, then it can develop serious financial problems.

Inflation is a disturbing and challenging new experience for United States financial managers. If it continues, financial policies and practices will continue to be modified.

Organization of a Firm's Finance Department

In the typical firm, the chief financial officer (who has the title of vice-president for finance) reports to the chief executive officer and has accountable to him two key officers, the treasurer and the controller. The treasurer's staff is responsible for raising capital, dealing with suppliers of capital, and forming the firm's credit policy. The controller's staff is responsible for the accounting and budgeting systems, including capital budgeting. In a sense, the treasurer handles the outside finance functions and the controller the inside functions, while the vice-president for finance has the overall responsibility for both.

Financial Decisions: Risk-Return Tradeoff

Financial decisions affect the value of a firm's stock by influencing both the size of the earnings stream, or profitability, and the riskiness of the firm. These relationships are diagrammed in Figure 1.1. Policy decisions, which are subject to government constraints, affect both profitability and risk; these two factors jointly determine the value of the firm.

The primary policy decision is that of choosing the industry in which to operate—the product-market mix of the firm. When this choice has been made, both profitability and risk are determined by decisions relating to the size of the firm, the types of equipment used, the extent to which debt is employed, the firm's liquidity position, and so on. Such decisions generally affect both risk and profitability. An increase in the cash position, for instance, reduces risk; however, since cash is not an earning asset, converting other assets to cash also reduces profitability. Similarly, the use of additional debt raises the rate of return, or the profitability, on the stockholders' net worth; at the same time, more debt means more risk. The financial manager seeks to strike the particular balance between risk and profitability that will maximize the wealth of the firm's stockholders—called the *risk-return tradeoff*. Most financial decisions involve such tradeoffs.

**Figure 1.1
Valuation as the Central Focus of
the Finance Function**

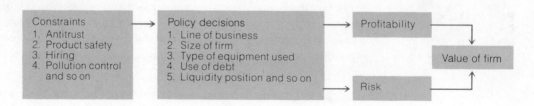

| Constraints
1. Antitrust
2. Product safety
3. Hiring
4. Pollution control
and so on | → | Policy decisions
1. Line of business
2. Size of firm
3. Type of equipment used
4. Use of debt
5. Liquidity position and so on | → | Profitability

Risk | → | Value of firm |

Organization and Structure of This Book

The optimal structure for a finance text, if one exists, is elusive. On the one hand, it is desirable to set out a theoretical structure first, then use the theory in later sections to explain behavior and to attack real-world decision problems. On the other hand, it is easier to understand the theoretical concepts of finance if one has a working knowledge of certain institutional details. Given this conflict, which should come first—theory or institutional background? We have wrestled with this problem, experimenting with both approaches in our own classes, and the following outline of the seven parts of the book reflects our own experience and that of others who shared their ideas and preferences with us.

1. The Environment of Managerial Finance
2. Financial Analysis, Planning, and Control
3. Working Capital Management
4. Investment Decisions
5. Valuation and the Cost of Capital
6. Long-Term Financing
7. Integrated Topics in Managerial Finance

The content of each part is discussed briefly to provide an overview of both the book and the field of managerial finance.

Part 1: The Environment of Managerial Finance

Part 1 provides the setting for the analysis of financial decisions. The scope and nature of managerial finance has been set forth in Chapter 1. Chapter 2 presents an overview of the financial framework within which financial managers make decisions. Chapter 3 seeks to outline the essentials of taxation as it affects financial decisions.

Part 2: Financial Analysis, Planning, and Control

Part 2, which consists of Chapters 4 to 7, develops certain key concepts and commonly used tools of financial analysis. Included are topics such as ratio analysis, operating leverage, sources and uses of funds analysis, financial forecasting, and financial planning and control techniques. The material provides a useful overview of finance, and the ideas and terminology developed facilitate an understanding of all the other parts of the book.

Part 3: Working Capital Management

Financial management involves the acquisition and use of assets, and to a large extent these actions are reflected in the firm's balance sheet. Accordingly, to a degree, the book has a balance sheet orientation. Part 3, which consists of Chapters 8 to 10, focuses on the top part of the balance sheet—the "working capital" section. *Working capital* refers to the firm's short-term, or current, assets and liabilities, and emphasis is placed on determining optimal levels for these items. Chapter 8 deals with the theory of working capital, Chapter 9 concerns current assets, and Chapter 10 discusses current liabilities. Chapter 8 sets forth a rational framework in which to consider decisions affecting the specific balance sheet items that comprise working capital. Firms make two kinds of working capital decisions: *strategic* decisions about target working capital levels and *tactical* decisions about day-to-day operations. The strategic decisions are fundamentally related to the tradeoff between risk and return, to alternative sources of capital, to management's view of the term structure of interest rates, to the effectiveness of internal control procedures (inventory control), to credit policy decisions, and so on. The tactical operating decisions involve short-run adjustments in current assets and current liabilities to meet temporary conditions. The most obvious short-run adjustment is that of changing sales levels; fixed assets and long-term liabilities are inflexible in the short run, so changes in market demand must be met by working capital adjustments. Working capital is also adjusted from the target levels to reflect changes in long- and short-run interest rates and other changes in the availability of and need for funds.

Chapter 9 discusses some factors bearing on target levels of each kind of current asset and methods for economizing on the investment in each one. For example, the target inventory level is determined jointly by costs of stock-outs and of carrying and ordering inventories, order lead times and usage rates, and the probability distributions of each. The discussion of inventories is thus based on the standard EOQ-plus-safety-stock inventory model. Finally, Chapter 10 examines the sources and forms of short-term credit.

Part 4: Investment Decisions

Part 4, which consists of Chapters 11 to 13, moves into an analysis of investment decisions. The time value of money is basic to investment decisions, so compound interest concepts are developed in Chapter 11. These concepts are then used in presenting capital budgeting principles and procedures in Chapter 12. Working capital management, which was discussed in Part 3, also involves investments; but the earlier presentation emphasizes adjusting to changes in the firm's level of activity.

With the use of compound interest and capital budgeting concepts, Part 4 extends the analysis of working capital decisions to include investment aspects as well. Most financial decisions involve an uncertain future, so Chapter 13 presents approaches for dealing with uncertainty. These include the basic concepts of probability distribution, the trade-off between risk and return, decision trees, and simulation.

Part 5: Valuation and the Cost of Capital

Part 5, which consists of Chapters 14 to 17, provides a bridge between the investment decisions discussed in Part 4 and the long-term financing decisions discussed in Part 6. Investment decisions require the use of cost of capital for taking the time value of money into account. Since risk and expected return are affected by financial structure, Part 5 analyzes the influence of financial structure on estimates of the cost of capital. Principles useful in guiding a firm to make financial structure decisions are developed. The application of these concepts in estimating the cost of capital required for making fixed asset decisions is set forth. Part 5 also shows how investment opportunities and cost of capital considerations interact in influencing the formulation of the firm's overall capital budget and of the targets for the growth rate of its investments in assets to support potential sales.

Part 6: Long-Term Financing

Part 6, which consists of Chapters 18 to 22, treats decisions with respect to specific forms of debt and equity financing. It begins with a consideration of the important role played by investment bankers in the operation of the capital markets. It then moves on to a consideration of the major instruments of long-term financing, including common stock, bonds and preferred stock, term loans, and leases. It concludes with an analysis of the nature and use of warrants and convertibles. The analytic framework previously developed helps Part 6 focus on the use of alternative forms and sources of financing in a decision framework.

Part 7: Integrated Topics in Managerial Finance

Part 7, the final section of the book (comprising Chapters 23 to 26), draws on the concepts developed in earlier sections to illustrate their application in a number of specialized but important decision areas. Chapter 23 introduces dynamics into the decision process, showing how financial managers react to changing conditions in the capital markets. Chapter 24 discusses the external growth of firms through mergers and holding companies along with the factors affecting this development. Most of the text deals with growing and successful firms; however, since many firms face financial difficulties, the causes of and possible remedies for these difficulties are discussed in Chapter 25. Finally, Chapter 26 deals with managerial finance in the increasingly important dimension of international finance.

Questions

1.1 What are the main functions of financial managers?

1.2 Why is wealth maximization a better operating goal than profit maximization?

1.3 What role does utility maximization perform in finance theory?

1.4 What role does social responsibility have in formulating business and financial goals?

1.5 What have been the major developmental periods in the field of finance, and what circumstances led to the evolution of the emphasis in each period?

1.6 What is the nature of the risk-return tradeoff faced in financial decision making?

2

CHAPTER   THE FINANCIAL SECTOR
OF THE ECONOMY

An important part of the environment within which financial managers function is the financial sector of the economy, which consists of financial markets, financial institutions, and financial instruments. This chapter will discuss each of the three aspects of the sector.

Financial Markets

In Figure 2.1, the financial manager is shown as linking the financing of an organization to its financing sources via the financial markets. The major parts of this figure will be explained throughout the discussion of the finance function. Funds for conducting organizational operations are obtained from a wide range of financial institutions in forms such as loans, bonds, and common stocks. The financial manager has primary responsibility for acquiring funds and participates in allocating them among alternative projects and specific uses, such as inventories, plant, and equipment. The cash flow cycle must be managed. Payments must be made for labor, materials, and capital goods purchased from the external markets. Products and services that generate fund inflows must be created. In the management of cash inflows and outflows, some cash is recycled and some is returned to financing sources.

The financial manager functions in a complex financial network because the savings and investment functions in a modern economy are performed by different economic agents. For savings surplus units, savings exceed their investment in real assets, and they own financial assets. For savings deficit units, current savings are less than investment in real assets so they issue financial liabilities. The savings deficit units issue a wide variety of financial claims, including promissory notes, bonds, and common stocks.

The transfer of funds from a savings surplus unit or the acquisition of funds by a savings deficit unit involves the creation of a financial asset and a financial liability. For example, when a person places funds in a savings account in a bank or savings and loan association, the deposit represents a financial asset on the personal balance sheet, along with real assets such as automobiles or household goods. The savings deposit is a liability account for the financial institution, representing a financial liability. When the funds are loaned to another person for, say, the purchase of a home, the loan by the financial institution represents a financial asset on its balance sheet. The borrower incurs a financial liability, represented by the loan owed to the financial institution. Consider another example. When a person buys goods on credit from a department store, the purchase price is added to "accounts receivable" on the store's books. The amount payable by the person who has purchased goods on credit represents a financial liability incurred by that person.

A financial transaction results in the simultaneous creation of a financial

Figure 2.1
Financial Markets, the Financial
Manager, and the Firm

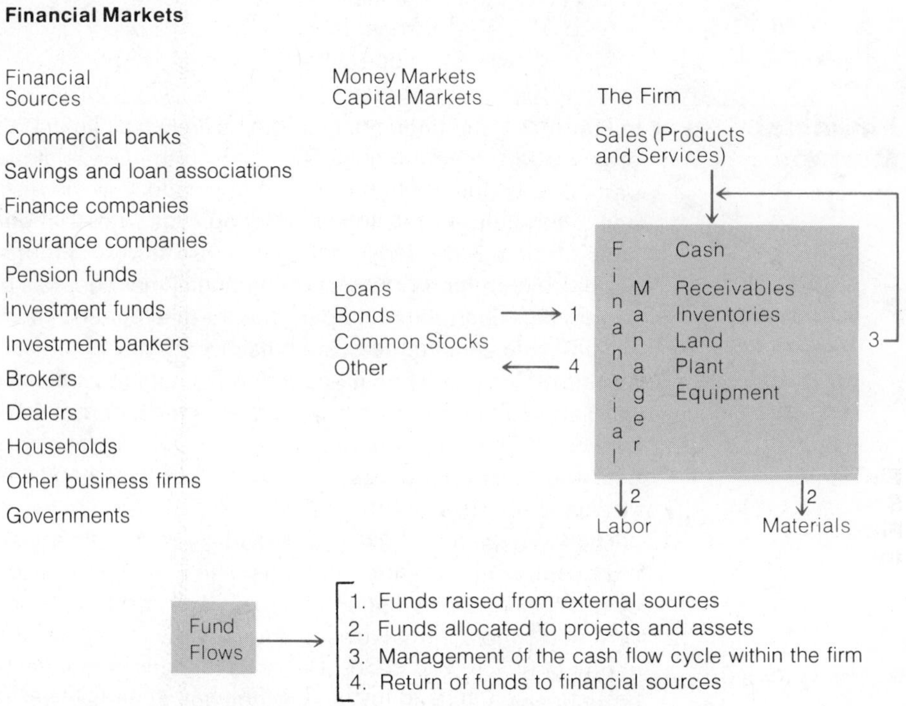

Financial Markets

Financial
Sources

Money Markets
Capital Markets

The Firm

Commercial banks

Savings and loan associations

Finance companies

Insurance companies

Pension funds

Investment funds

Investment bankers

Brokers

Dealers

Households

Other business firms

Governments

Sales (Products
and Services)

Loans
Bonds
Common Stocks
Other

1

4

Financial Manager

Cash
Receivables
Inventories
Land
Plant
Equipment

3

2
Labor

2
Materials

Fund
Flows

1. Funds raised from external sources
2. Funds allocated to projects and assets
3. Management of the cash flow cycle within the firm
4. Return of funds to financial sources

asset and a financial liability. The creation and transfer of such assets and liabilities constitute *financial markets.* The nature of financial markets can be further explained by analogy to the market for actual goods, such as automobiles. The "automobile market" is defined by all transactions in automobiles, whether they occur at the auto dealer's showroom, at wholesale auctions of used cars, or at individuals' homes. These transactions all constitute the automobile market because they make up part of the total demand and supply curves for autos.

Similarly, financial markets are comprised of all trades that result in the creation of financial assets and financial liabilities. Some trades are made through organized institutions such as the New York Stock Exchange or the regional stock exchanges. A large number are made through the thousands of brokers and dealers who buy and sell securities (comprising what is called the "over-the-counter market"). Individual transactions with department stores, savings banks, or other financial institutions also create financial assets and financial liabilities. Thus financial markets are not specific physical structures; nor are they remote. Everyone is involved in them to some degree.

Continuing the auto analogy, just as a distinction is made between a new car market and a used car market because somewhat different demand and supply influences are operating in each, different segments of the financial markets are also categorized and named. When the financial claims and obligations bought and sold have a maturity of less than one year, the transactions constitute *money markets.* When the maturities of the instruments traded are more than one year, the markets are referred to as *capital markets.* The latter term is somewhat confusing because real capital in an economy is represented by things such as plants, machinery, and equipment. But long-term financial instruments are regarded as ultimately representing claims on the real resources in an economy, and for that reason the markets in which these instruments are traded are referred to as capital markets.

Financing Sources and Financial Intermediation

The financial markets, composed of money markets and capital markets, provide a mechanism through which the financial manager obtains funds from a wide range of financing sources (shown in Figure 2.1).

Commercial banks are defined by their ability to accept demand deposits subject to transfer by depositors' checks. Such checks represent a widely accepted medium of exchange, accounting for over 90 percent of the transactions that take place. Savings and loan associations receive funds from passbook savings and invest them primarily in real estate mortgages representing long-term borrowing (mostly by individuals). Finance companies are business firms whose main activity is making loans to other business firms and to individuals. Life insurance companies sell protection against the loss of income from premature death or disability. The insurance policies they sell typically have a savings element in them. Pension funds collect contributions from employees and/or employers to make periodic payments upon employees' retirement. Investment funds or mutual funds sell shares to investors and use the proceeds to purchase already existing equity securities.

Investment bankers are financial firms that buy new issues of securities from business firms at a guaranteed agreed-upon price and seek immediately to resell the securities to other investors. Related financial firms that function simply as agents linking buyers and sellers are called investment brokers. Investment dealers are those who purchase for their own account from sellers and ultimately resell to other buyers. While investment bankers (discussed in Chapter 18) operate in the new issues market, brokers and dealers engage in transactions in already issued securities. Other sources of funds are households, other business firms, and governments. At any point in time some of these will be borrowers and others lenders.

Financial intermediation is accomplished through transactions in the financial markets that bring the savings surplus units together with the savings deficit units so that savings can be redistributed into their most productive uses. The specialized business firms whose activities include the creation of financial assets and liabilities are called financial intermediaries. Without these intermediaries and the processes of financial intermediation, the allocation of savings into real investment would be limited by whatever the distribution of savings happened to be. With financial intermediation, savings are transferred to economic units that have opportunities for profitable investment. In the process, real resources are allocated more effectively, and real output for the economy as a whole is increased.

Financial managers have important responsibilities in the financial intermediation process. They are the part of the process by which funds are allocated to their most productive uses. Therefore, the functions of financial managers can now be restated in the perspective of this broader social framework. In the aggregate, business firms are savings deficit units that obtain funds to make investments to increase the supply of goods and services. Financial managers utilize financial markets to obtain external funds. How should the funds be acquired efficiently? What is the most economical mix of financing to be obtained? From what alternative sources and in what specific forms should the funds be raised? What should be the timing and forms of returns and repayments to financing sources?

Since funds are acquired as part of the process by which resources are allocated to their most productive uses, financial managers have responsibility for effectively using funds. To what projects and products should the funds be allocated? What assets and resources should the organization acquire in order to produce its products and services? What standards and controls should monitor the effective utilization of funds allocated among the segments of operating activities? How should the planning and control of funds be managed so the organization will produce and sell its products and services most efficiently? The financial manager's major responsibility is to implement these choices in the various financial markets to meet the firm's capital requirements.

Financial institutions make use of three major types of financial assets: money, stock, and debt. *Money* is issued by the U.S. Treasury as coins and paper currency. The central bank, the Federal Reserve System, interacts with the commercial banking system in creating the demand deposits (the familiar checking accounts) by which about 90 percent of commercial transactions are conducted. *Stock* generally means common stock, which represents ownership of a firm. *Debt* represents a promise to pay to the creditor a specified amount plus interest at a future date.

The Federal Reserve System

Fundamental to an understanding of the behavior of the money and capital markets is an analysis of the role of the Federal Reserve System. The Fed, as it is called, has a set of instruments with which to influence the operations of commercial banks, whose loan and investment activities in turn have an important influence on the cost and availability of money. The most powerful of the Fed's instruments, hence the one used most sparingly, is changing reserve requirements (the percentage of deposits that must be kept in reserve with the Fed). The one most often used is changing the pattern of open-market operations (the Fed's buying and selling of securities, which expands and contracts the amount of funds in the public's hands).

Changes in the discount rate (the interest rate charged to commercial banks when they borrow from Federal Reserve Banks) are likely to have more psychological influence than direct quantitative effect. These changes represent an implicit announcement by Federal Reserve authorities that a change in economic conditions has occurred and that the new conditions call for a tightening or easing of monetary conditions. The data demonstrate that increases in the Federal Reserve Bank discount rate have been followed by rising interest rate levels and decreases by lowered levels. When the Federal Reserve System purchases or sells securities in the open market, makes changes in the discount rate, or varies the reserve requirement, this procedure changes interest rates on most securities.

Fiscal Policy

The fiscal policy of the federal government has great impact on movements in interest rates. A cash budget deficit represents a stimulating influence by the federal government, and a cash surplus exerts a restraining influence. However, this generalization must be modified to reflect the way a deficit is financed and the way a surplus is used. To have the most stimulating effect, a deficit should be financed by a sale of securities through the banking system, particularly the central bank; this provides a maximum amount of bank reserves and permits a multiple expansion in the money supply. To have the most restrictive effect, the surplus should be used to retire bonds held by the banking system, particularly the central bank, thereby reducing bank reserves and causing a multiple contraction in the supply of money.

The impact of Treasury financing programs varies. Ordinarily, when the Treasury needs to draw funds from the money market, it competes with other potential users of funds; the result may be a rise in interest rate levels. However, the desire to hold down interest rates also influences Treasury and Federal Reserve policy. To ensure the success of a large new offering, Federal Reserve authorities may temporarily ease money conditions—a procedure that tends to soften interest rates. If the Treasury encounters resistance in selling securities in the nonbanking sector, it may sell them in large volume to the commercial banking system, which expands its reserves

21

and thereby increases the monetary base. This change in turn tends to lower the level of interest rates.

Securities Markets

Within the framework of the broad functions of financial intermediation and the monetary and fiscal policies briefly summarized in the preceding sections is another important institution in the operation of the financial system—the securities markets. One basis for classifying securities markets is the distinction between *primary markets,* in which stocks and bonds are initially sold, and *secondary* markets, in which they are subsequently traded. Initial sales of securities are made by investment banking firms, which purchase them from the issuing firm and sell them through an underwriting syndicate or group. Subsequent transactions take place on organized securities exchanges or in less formal markets. The operations of securities markets provide a framework within which the nature of investment banking and the new issues market (discussed in Chapter 15) can be understood. Accordingly, the organized security exchanges, the over-the-counter markets, the third market, and the fourth market will be discussed in this section.

The major exchange is the New York Stock Exchange (NYSE), on which about 1,500 common stocks are listed, accounting for over 80 percent of the almost $200 billion of annual dollar volume of trading and somewhat less than 80 percent of the over 6 billion annual share volume of trading. The American Stock Exchange, with 1,300 stocks traded, is second in volume, accounting for under 10 percent of dollar volume and somewhat over 10 percent of share volume. Some 350 stocks are traded on one or more of the eleven registered regional exchanges, accounting for about 2 to 5 percent of volume in the three largest regional exchanges and less than 1 percent of total volume in the remaining ones.

The organized security exchanges are tangible physical entities. Each of the larger ones occupies its own building and has specifically designated members and an elected governing body—its board of governors. Members are said to have "seats" on the exchange, although everybody stands up. These seats, which are bought and sold, represent the right to trade on the exchange. In 1968 seats on the NYSE sold at a record high of $515,000; in 1974 they sold for about $85,000. During 1977 they ranged between $35,000 and $95,000.[1]

Most of the larger stockbrokerage firms own seats on the exchanges and designate one or more of their officers as members of the exchange. The exchanges are open daily, and the members meet in a large room equipped

---

1. New York Stock Exchange, *1978 Fact Book* (New York: New York Stock Exchange, 1977), p. 58.

with telephones and telegraphs that enable each brokerage house member to communicate with the firm's offices throughout the country.

Like other markets, a security exchange facilitates communication between buyers and sellers. For example, Merrill Lynch, Pierce, Fenner & Smith (the largest brokerage firm), may receive an order in its Atlanta office from a customer who wants to buy 100 shares of General Motors stock. Simultaneously, a brokerage house in Denver may receive an order from a customer wishing to sell 100 shares of GM stock. Each broker communicates by wire with the firm's representative on the NYSE. Other brokers throughout the country are also communicating with their own exchange members. Members with sell orders offer the shares for sale, and they are bid for by members with buy orders. Thus, the exchanges operate as *auction markets.*[2]

Benefits Provided by Security Exchanges

Organized security exchanges are said to provide at least four important benefits to businesses.

1. Security exchanges facilitate the investment process by providing a marketplace in which to conduct efficient and relatively inexpensive transactions. Investors are thus assured that they will have a place in which to sell their securities if they decide to do so. The increased liquidity provided by the exchanges makes investors willing to accept a lower rate of return on securities than they would otherwise require. This means that exchanges lower the cost of capital to businesses.
2. By providing a market, exchanges create an institution in which continuous transactions test the values of securities. The purchases and sales of securities record judgments on the values and prospects of companies. Those whose prospects are judged favorably by the investment community have higher values, which facilitate new financing and growth.
3. Security prices are relatively more stable because of the operation of the security exchanges. Organized markets improve liquidity by providing continuous markets that make for more frequent but smaller price changes. In the absence of organized markets, price changes are less frequent but more violent.
4. The securities markets aid in the digestion of new security issues and facilitate their successful flotation.

Although these benefits are important, not all firms can use them. However, some firms that cannot utilize the exchanges can get many of the same benefits by having their securities traded in the over-the-counter market.

The securities markets are in a state of flux. After four years of research

2. This discussion is highly simplified. The exchanges have members, known as "specialists," who facilitate the trading process by keeping an inventory of shares of the stocks in which they specialize. If a buy order comes in at a time when no sell order arrives, the specialist may sell off some inventory. Similarly, if a sell order comes in, the specialist will buy and add to inventory.

and investigation, Congress enacted the Securities Acts Amendments of 1975.[3] This new law departs from the concept of self-regulation that had previously been followed in the relationships between the government and the securities industry. It states that no national securities exchange can impose a schedule of minimum fixed commission rates. While it is still too early to judge its impact, one likely effect of the law is the "unbundling" of joint services such as research reports from the buying and selling activities provided by brokerage firms.

The new law also provides for the development of a national market system. Two concepts of a central market system have emerged. One, sponsored by the NYSE, envisions a single trading exchange. The other sees competitive trading in a number of places linked together by a system of communications, including clearing and settlement facilities. The SEC is empowered to exercise leadership in developing a central market system.

Over-the-Counter (OTC) Security Markets

Over-the-counter security markets is the term used for all the buying and selling activity in securities that does not take place on a stock exchange. The OTC market includes stocks of all types and for all sizes of U.S. corporations, as well as some foreign issues. In the OTC market there are approximately 30,000 common stocks of public corporations, but only about 10,000 are actively traded. This is about three times the number of companies listed on the organized exchanges. In addition, the OTC market is where transactions take place in (1) almost all bonds of U.S. corporations; (2) almost all bonds of federal, state, and local governments; (3) open-end investment company shares of mutual funds; (4) new issues of securities; (5) most secondary distributions of large blocks of stock, regardless of whether they are listed on an exchange; and (6) stocks of most of the country's banks and insurance companies.

The exchanges operate as auction markets; the trading process is achieved through agents making transactions at one geographically centralized exchange location. On an exchange, firms known as specialists are responsible for matching buy and sell orders and for maintaining an orderly market in a particular security. In contrast, the OTC market is a dealer market—that is, business is conducted across the country by broker/dealers known as market makers. These dealers stand ready to buy and sell securities in a manner similar to wholesale suppliers of goods or merchandise. The exchanges are used to match buy and sell orders that come in more or less simultaneously. But if a stock is traded less frequently, perhaps because it is a new or a small firm, matching buy and sell orders might require

3. The original Securities Acts of 1933 and 1934 are discussed in Chapter 16.

an extended period of time. To avoid this problem, some broker/dealer firms maintain an inventory of stocks. They buy when individual investors want to sell and sell when investors want to buy. At one time these securities were kept in a safe; when they were bought and sold, they were literally passed "over the counter."

The brokers and dealers operating in the OTC markets communicate through a network of private wires and telephone lines and, since 1971, by an electronic quotation system called NASDAQ, whose letters stand for the National Association of Securities Dealers Automated Quotation system. NASDAQ is a computerized system that enables current price quotations to be displayed on terminals in subscribers' offices.

The term *third market* refers to OTC trading in listed securities by nonmembers of an exchange. It generally represents trades of large blocks of listed stocks off the floor of the exchange, with a brokerage house acting as intermediary between two institutional investors.

The *fourth market* refers to direct transfers of blocks of stock among institutional investors without an intermediary broker. A well-known example is the arrangement between the Ford Foundation and the Rockefeller Foundation to exchange the common stocks of the Ford Motor Co. and Standard Oil of New Jersey. Such transactions have led to the development of *Instinet,* a computerized quotation system with display terminals to provide communications among major institutional investors.

The development of the third and fourth markets reflects the increased importance of institutional investors in stock trading. During the decade of the 1960s, for example, the equity holdings of private, noninsured pension funds rose by over 500 percent, of state and local retirement funds by over 2,800 percent, and of investment companies (mutual funds) by over 300 percent. New York Stock Exchange studies indicate that by the mid-1970s these institutions held a third of NYSE-listed stocks and accounted for over half the dollar volume on the NYSE.

In terms of numbers of issues, the majority of stocks are traded over the counter. However, because the stocks of larger companies are listed on the exchanges, it is estimated that two-thirds of the dollar volume of stock trading takes place on the exchanges. The situation is reversed in the bond market. Although the bonds of a number of the larger companies are listed on the NYSE bond list, over 95 percent of bond transactions take place in the OTC market. The reason for this is that bonds typically are traded among the large financial institutions (for example, life insurance companies and pension funds), which deal in very large blocks of securities. It is relatively easy for the OTC bond dealers to arrange the transfer of large blocks of bonds among the relatively few holders of the bonds. It would be impossible to conduct similar operations in the stock market among the literally millions of large and small stockholders.

**Decision to List
Stock**

The exchanges have certain requirements that firms must meet before their stock can be listed; these requirements relate to size of company, number of years in business, earnings record, number of shares outstanding and their market value, and the like. In general, requirements become more stringent as we move from the regional exchanges toward the NYSE.

The firm itself makes the decision on whether to seek to list its securities on an exchange. Typically, the stock of a new and small company is traded over the counter; there is simply not enough activity to justify the use of an auction market for such stocks. As the company grows and establishes an earnings record, expands the number of shares outstanding, and increases its list of stockholders, it may decide to apply for listing on one of the regional exchanges. For example, a Chicago company may list on the Midwest Stock Exchange and a West Coast company on the Pacific Coast Exchange. As the company grows still more and its stock becomes distributed throughout the country, it may seek a listing on the American Stock Exchange, the smaller of the two national exchanges. Finally, if it becomes one of the nation's leading firms, it may switch to the Big Board, the New York Stock Exchange—if it qualifies.

Many people believe that listing is beneficial to both the company and its stockholders. Listed companies receive a certain amount of free advertising and publicity, and the status of being listed enhances their prestige and reputation. This probably has a beneficial effect on the sales of the firms' products, and is advantageous in terms of lowering the required rate of return on the common stock. Investors respond favorably to increased information, increased liquidity, and increased prestige; by providing investors with these services in the form of listing their companies' stocks, financial managers lower their firms' costs of capital.[4]

**Stock Market
Reporting**

Securities traded on the organized security exchanges are called listed securities; they are distinguished from unlisted securities, which are traded in the over-the-counter market.

Considerable information is available on transactions among listed securities, and the very existence of this information reduces the uncertainty inherent in security investments. This reduction of uncertainty, of course,

---

4. Two industries, banking and insurance, have a tradition against listing their stocks. The historic reason given by banks is that they were afraid a falling market price of their stocks would lead depositors to think the bank itself was in danger, and this would cause a run on the bank. Some basis for such fears may have existed before the creation of the Federal Deposit Insurance Corporation in 1935, but the fear is no longer justified. The other reason for banks' not listing has to do with the reporting of financial information. The exchanges require that quarterly financial statements be sent to all stockholders; banks have been reluctant to provide financial information. Increasingly, bank regulatory agencies are requiring public disclosure of additional financial information. As this trend continues, it is expected that banks will increasingly seek to list their securities on exchanges. A notable first is the Chase Manhattan Bank, which was listed on the New York Stock Exchange in 1965.

makes listed securities relatively attractive to investors, and it lowers the cost of capital to firms.[5] We cannot delve deeply into the matter of financial reporting (which is more properly the field of investment analysis), but we will attempt to explain the most widely used service—the New York Stock Exchange reporting system.

Figure 2.2 is a section of the "stock market page" taken from the *Wall Street Journal* reporting of NYSE-Composite Transactions, which include trades on five regional exchanges and those reported by the National Association of Securities Dealers and Instinet. Stocks are listed alphabetically, with those whose names consist of capital letters listed first. The items are explained by reference to the information on Abbott Labs, a drug company. The two columns on the left show the highest and the lowest prices at which the stocks have sold during the year; Abbott has traded in the range from $42\frac{1}{4}$ to $49\frac{1}{8}$ (or $42.25 to $49.125). The figure just to the right of the com-

Figure 2.2
Stock Market Transactions

—1977—		Stocks	Div.	P-E Ratio	Sales 100s	High	Low	Close	Net Chg.
High	Low			—A—A—A—					
$37\frac{1}{2}$	$32\frac{3}{8}$	ACF Ind	1.80	9	41	$36\frac{1}{4}$	36	$36\frac{1}{4}$.......	
$23\frac{1}{4}$	$19\frac{3}{4}$	AMF	1.24	10	164	$20\frac{3}{4}$	$20\frac{1}{2}$	$20\frac{5}{8}$.......	
$15\frac{3}{8}$	$13\frac{1}{2}$	APL Cp	1	5	1	$13\frac{3}{4}$	$13\frac{3}{4}$	$13\frac{3}{4}+$	$\frac{1}{8}$
$50\frac{3}{4}$	$38\frac{1}{8}$	ARASv	1.32	10	53	$42\frac{3}{4}$	$41\frac{1}{4}$	$41\frac{3}{8}-$	$1\frac{1}{8}$
$23\frac{5}{8}$	$17\frac{1}{4}$	ASALtd	.80	..	183	$19\frac{3}{4}$	$19\frac{1}{2}$	$19\frac{1}{2}-$	$\frac{3}{8}$
$10\frac{3}{4}$	$9\frac{3}{8}$	ATOInc	.40	6	101	10	$9\frac{7}{8}$	$9\frac{7}{8}-$	$\frac{1}{4}$
$49\frac{1}{8}$	$42\frac{1}{4}$	AbbtLab	1	13	247	$43\frac{3}{4}$	$42\frac{1}{2}$	$42\frac{7}{8}-$	1
$3\frac{1}{2}$	$2\frac{3}{4}$	AdmDg	.04	5	3	$2\frac{7}{8}$	$2\frac{7}{8}$	$2\frac{7}{8}$.......	
$13\frac{1}{4}$	$11\frac{5}{8}$	AdmEx	1.15e	..	55	$12\frac{3}{8}$	$12\frac{1}{4}$	$12\frac{3}{8}$.......	
5	$3\frac{7}{8}$	AdmMil	.05e	8	6	$4\frac{1}{8}$	4	$4\frac{1}{8}+$	$\frac{1}{8}$
$14\frac{3}{8}$	$10\frac{1}{2}$	Addrssg	.10e	17	94	11	$10\frac{5}{8}$	$10\frac{7}{8}-$	$\frac{1}{8}$
$35\frac{3}{4}$	$28\frac{3}{8}$	AetnaLf	1.20	8	547	$32\frac{3}{8}$	$31\frac{1}{2}$	$31\frac{3}{4}+$	$\frac{1}{2}$
51	$44\frac{5}{8}$	AetnaLf	pf 2	..	3	48	$47\frac{1}{2}$	48 +	3
$14\frac{1}{2}$	$10\frac{1}{2}$	Aguirre		..	47	$13\frac{3}{4}$	$13\frac{1}{2}$	$13\frac{5}{8}-$	$\frac{1}{8}$
20	$15\frac{1}{8}$	Ahmans	.40	6	104	$19\frac{1}{8}$	$18\frac{7}{8}$	19 −	$\frac{1}{4}$
$3\frac{7}{8}$	3	Aileen		60	55	$3\frac{1}{8}$	3	3	
$35\frac{7}{8}$	25	AirProd	.20b	11	245	$26\frac{1}{2}$	26	$26\frac{1}{4}-$	$\frac{1}{4}$
$15\frac{1}{2}$	$12\frac{7}{8}$	AirbnFrt	.60	11	27	$14\frac{1}{4}$	$13\frac{7}{8}$	$13\frac{7}{8}-$	$\frac{1}{2}$
$32\frac{3}{8}$	$28\frac{1}{4}$	Airco	1.15	7	40	$31\frac{5}{8}$	$31\frac{1}{8}$	$31\frac{5}{8}+$	$\frac{3}{8}$
$19\frac{1}{8}$	16	Akzona	1.20	78	31	$18\frac{3}{8}$	$17\frac{5}{8}$	18 −	$\frac{1}{4}$
$16\frac{7}{8}$	$14\frac{3}{8}$	AlaGas	1.28	7	2	$15\frac{3}{8}$	$15\frac{1}{8}$	$15\frac{1}{8}-$	$\frac{1}{4}$

Source: *Wall Street Journal*, April 20, 1977 (reporting transactions on April 19, 1977). Reprinted by permission of The Wall Street Journal, © Dow Jones & Company, Inc. 1977. All rights reserved.

5. If the stock markets today seem risky, imagine what it was like in the era before the existence of the SEC, routine reporting, and the like!

pany's abbreviated name is the dividend rate based on the most recent regular quarterly payment. Abbott Labs was expected to pay $1 a share in 1977. Next comes the price/earnings (P/E) ratio, or the current price of the stock divided by its earnings per share during the last year. (Price/earnings ratios are discussed at some length in Chapter 14.)

After the P/E ratio comes the volume of trading for the day; 24,700 shares of Abbott Labs stock were traded on April 19, 1977. Following the volume are the high and low prices for the day and the closing price. On April 19 Abbott traded as high as $43^3/_4$ and as low as $42^1/_2$, while the last trade was at $42^7/_8$. The last column gives the change from the closing price on the previous day. Abbott Labs was down $1, so the previous close must have been $43^7/_8$ (since $43^7/_8 - \$1 = \$42^7/_8$, the indicated closing price on April 18). A set of footnotes giving additional information about specific issues always accompanies the stock market quotes.

Margin Trading and Short Selling

Margin trading and short selling are two practices that contribute to the securities markets' efficiency. *Margin trading* involves the buying of securities on credit. For example, when margin requirements are 80 percent, 100 shares of a stock selling for $100 a share can be bought by putting up, in cash, only $8,000, or 80 percent of the purchase price, and borrowing the remaining $2,000. The stockbroker lends the margin purchaser the funds, retaining custody of the stock as collateral. Margin requirements are determined by the Federal Reserve Board. When the Fed judges that stock market activity and prices are unduly stimulated by easy credit, it raises margin requirements and thus reduces the amount of credit available for the purchase of stocks. On the other hand, if the Fed wants to stimulate the market as part of its overall monetary policy operations, it reduces margin requirements.

Short selling is somewhat more complicated. Suppose you own 100 shares of ZN, which is currently selling for $80 a share. If you become convinced that ZN is overpriced and that it is going to fall to $40 within the next year, you will probably sell your stock. Now suppose you do not own any ZN, but you still think the price will fall from $80 to $40. If you are really convinced that this drop will occur, you can *go short* in ZN, or *sell ZN short*.

Short selling means selling a security that is not owned by the seller. To effect a short sell, you borrow, say, 100 shares of ZN from your broker, then sell these shares in the normal manner for $80 a share, or $8,000 in total. Suppose you are correct and ZN declines to $40 a share. You can buy 100 shares and repay the loan from your broker, recording a $4,000 profit. Of course, if ZN goes up to $150 instead of declining, you will have to pay $15,000 to replace the stock you borrowed and sold for $8,000, so you will lose $7,000. The advantages claimed for short selling are that it increases the number of participants in the market and makes a more "continuous" market, thereby reducing fluctuations in stock prices. It is, however, a controversial subject.

Insofar as margin trading and short selling do make a more continuous market, they encourage stock ownership and have two other beneficial effects: (1) they broaden ownership of securities by increasing the ability of people to buy them, and (2) they provide for a more active market—and more active trading makes for narrower price fluctuations. However, when a strong speculative psychology grips the market, margin trading can be a fuel that feeds the speculative fervor, while short selling can aggravate pessimism on the downside. The downside effects of short selling are somewhat restricted, however, in that a short sale cannot be made at a price lower than that of the last previously recorded sale. If a stock is in a continuous decline, short selling cannot occur; hence it cannot be used to push the stock down. In the 1920s, before this rule was put into effect, market manipulators could and did use short sales to drive prices down. Today most short selling occurs when stocks are rising rapidly, and this has a stabilizing influence.

Interest-Bearing Business Securities

Within the framework of the financial markets and financial institutions we have described, financial managers have a wide range of possibilities with respect to financial instruments in which they can invest or forms of financing by which they can raise funds. The range of business financial instruments is set forth in Table 2.1, which is organized by issuer, maturity, and other such characteristics.

Short-Term Financial Instruments

Federal Funds Trading in federal funds has developed as a way of adjusting the reserve position of commercial banks. Commercial banks that are members of the Federal Reserve System account for over three-fourths of the bank deposits in the United States. Their required reserves are held on deposit in the Federal Reserve Banks. In the ebb and flow of commercial transactions throughout the United States from day to day, funds are withdrawn from some sectors and accumulate in others. Some banks accumulate more deposits with the Federal Reserve Banks then they need to meet their reserve requirements, while others need to increase their deposits to meet their reserve requirements.

The federal funds market represents purchases and sales of member bank deposits held at the Federal Reserve Banks. A sale of federal funds is a loan by one bank to another. The basic trading unit is $1 million, and the volume of such loans can be in excess of $20 billion per day. Transactions in federal funds can be accomplished within minutes by wire. The loans are for overnight or over the weekend.

Table 2.1
Overview of Business Securities
Traded in Financial Markets

I. Corporate Issues
A. Short-term
1. Commercial banks
   a. Federal funds
   b. Certificates of deposit (CDs)
   c. Banker's acceptances
   d. Prime rate loans
2. Finance companies
   a. Direct commercial paper
   b. Dealers' commercial paper
3. Other corporations
   a. Commercial paper
   b. Bank loans
B. Long-term (utilities and industrials)
1. Term loans
2. Bonds
3. Mortgages

II. International Instruments
A. Eurocurrency deposits
B. Eurocurrency CDs
C. Euromarket bonds

The interest rate on federal funds is the most sensitive of money market rates. It is not unusual for it to fluctuate as much as 25 percent on either side of its average level for the day. The federal funds rate reflects the many changes taking place in the economy and in the financial markets. It provides a highly sensitive index of the impact the Fed has on the money markets. Sharp movements in the rate may reflect the market's judgment that the Fed has embarked on a shift in its policies with regard to tightening or relaxing conditions in the money markets.

Certificates of Deposit In early 1961 major New York commercial banks began to issue interest-bearing negotiable certificates of deposit (CDs) to domestic business corporations. These certificates are a form of savings deposit, except that they cannot be withdrawn before their maturity date. However, since they are negotiable, they can be sold in the money market prior to maturity—and there is an active secondary market for them. CDs give banks an opportunity to compete for corporate and other funds that in the past were invested in Treasury bills and other types of short-term paper. They bear rates of interest in line with money rates at the time of issuance. However, during periods of tight money market conditions, when banks are aggressively seeking to add to their deposits, CD rates may rise sharply.

Banker's Acceptances A banker's acceptance is a debt instrument created by the creditor and arising out of a self-liquidating business transaction. It arises mainly from import and export activity. For example, a U.S. coffee processor may arrange with his U.S. commercial bank for the issuance of an irrevocable letter of credit in favor of a Brazilian exporter with whom he has negotiated a transaction. The letter of credit covers the details of the shipment and states that the Brazilian exporter can draw a time draft for a specified amount on the U.S. bank. On the basis of the letter of credit the exporter draws a draft on the bank and negotiates the draft with his local Brazilian bank, receiving immediate payment. The Brazilian bank then forwards the draft to the United States for presentation to the bank that issued the letter of credit. When this bank stamps the draft "accepted," it accepts the obligation to pay the draft at maturity, thereby creating an acceptance. Typically the acceptance is then sold to an acceptance dealer, and the proceeds are credited to the account of the Brazilian bank. The shipping documents are released to the U.S. importer against a trust receipt, enabling him to process and sell the coffee.

The proceeds of the coffee sales are deposited by the importer at the accepting bank in time to meet the required payment on the draft at maturity. The holder of the acceptance at maturity presents it to the accepting bank for payment, which completes the transaction. The cost of the acceptance reflects the discount in the dealer's bid plus the accepting bank's commission rate. The cost can be paid by either of the parties to the transaction in accordance with the agreement made with the accepting bank. It reflects the tradeoffs involved in the selling price of the goods (which is related to provisions for bearing the risks that may be involved in the transaction) and the payment of fees for various instruments created by the transaction (such as the acceptance itself).

Prime Rate Loans Prime rate loans are loans made by commercial banks to customers who qualify for the best rate available on short-term bank lending. The result of direct negotiation between the bank and the borrower, they usually are part of a continuing financial relationship. Commercial bank rates to borrowers other than those qualifying for the prime rate are usually higher than that rate. Prime rate loans compete on a rate basis with commercial paper borrowing.

Commercial Paper Commercial paper is unsecured promissory notes issued by firms to finance short-term credit needs. In recent years the issuance of commercial paper has become an increasingly important source of short-term financing for many types of corporations, including utilities, finance companies, insurance companies, bank holding companies, and manufacturing companies. It is used increasingly not only to finance seasonal working capital needs but also as a method of interim financing of major projects such as bank buildings, ships, pipelines, nuclear fuel cores, and plant expansion.

Some commercial paper—especially the large volume of it issued by finance companies—is sold directly to investors, including business corporations, commercial banks, insurance companies, and state and local government units. At the end of 1976 about 60 percent of the commercial paper outstanding had been sold directly to investors. The remainder represented that sold through commercial paper dealers, who function as intermediaries in the commercial paper market.

The commercial paper market is generally available only to the best credits. Commercial paper sold through dealers is rated as to quality by Moody's or Standard & Poor's. Surprises do occur, however; witness the Penn Central bankruptcy in 1970, which happened with over $80 million of commercial paper outstanding. In March 1978, when Standard & Poor's reduced its rating on the senior long-term debt of Chrysler Corporation from BBB to BBB−, S&P maintained its existing ratings on the company's short-term instruments, including commercial paper. While commercial paper rates are generally somewhat higher than the rates on Treasury bills, they are somewhat lower than the prime bank loan rate.

Long-Term Corporate Borrowing

Like government units and financial institutions, nonfinancial business firms issue various forms of long-term debt. Some forms are arranged with financial institutions such as banks or insurance companies; others are sold with the help of investment bankers to a wider range of buyers. The many different kinds of corporate bonds are discussed in Chapter 18.

Technically, bonds are any form of long-term debt. When secured by real estate, they are referred to as mortgage bonds or simply mortgages. The long-term loans on individual residences are referred to as mortgages, but mortgage financing exists for commercial properties as well. The federal government has established a number of organizations that provide a secondary market in mortgages by purchasing them from the financial institutions that originally made the loans. In the mortgage and related fields considerable interaction exists between private financial institutions and government agencies.

International Markets

Next we turn to increasingly important international dimensions of financial markets and the instruments that have been developed. The international dimension of financial markets has been stimulated through the mechanism of the Eurocurrency market. The Eurocurrency deposit is created when a banking office in one country accepts a deposit denominated in the currency of another country. The development of this market began in the late

1950s, and by the mid-1970s the volume of Eurocurrency accounts had grown to over $250 billion, at least three-fourths of it in U.S. dollars. The Eurocurrency market denominated in dollars is referred to as the Eurodollar market. While the main instrument of the Eurocurrency market is the deposit, other forms include certificates of deposit, banker's acceptances, commercial paper, and loans of various maturities.

A bank, corporation, or government unit owning foreign currency in excess of its working needs will seek to earn interest on these temporary surplus funds. If the amount is large, it is worthwhile for the financial manager to seek the best rate available. This may include the use of a banking office in a foreign country and the deposit of funds denominated in the currency of that country. When foreign money markets provide more favorable terms than U.S. markets, the lender and the banking office that accepts the deposit exchange letters detailing the terms of the deposit, and the transfer of funds is acknowledged. The normal deposit unit is 1 million currency units. The lender who needs short-term funds prior to the maturity of the deposit can become a borrower for the necessary period by initiating an offsetting transaction in the Eurocurrency market.

The rate paid on these deposits among the largest and best-known international banks is called the London Inter-Bank (LIBO) rate. Deposit rates are generally fixed for shorter-term deposits but may float on longer-term deposits. Floating rates are usually adjusted semiannually in response to changes in the LIBO short-term rate to which they are tied.

The Eurocurrency market has participants located throughout the world; transactions are negotiated by Telex, cable, and telephone. Trading is normally done for settlement on the second business day following the trade date. Funds are transferred either directly through correspondent banks in the home country of the currency involved or according to the broker's instructions against delivery of the required instrument.

In addition to conventional interbank deposits, there are Eurodollar certificates of deposit (similar to the CDs in our domestic market), negotiable instruments that enjoy an active secondary trading market. Many branches of U.S. banks compete for Eurodollar funds through the issuance of Eurodollar certificates of deposit.

Besides placing temporary surplus funds in Eurocurrency deposits or Eurodollar CDs, many U.S. firms utilize the Euromarket as borrowers. The rates on long-term borrowing in the Euromarket are sometimes below the rates on comparable securities in the United States. The relative rates depend on supply and demand conditions in the U.S. capital market as compared with conditions in the Euromarket. A situation that illustrates this point developed at the end of 1976: "Fierce competition among banks across the Atlantic for loan business is driving down the cost of credit to the point where U.S. corporations and their overseas subsidiaries can now borrow five-year money in Europe for nearly the same price that they have to pay for short-term bank loans at home."[6] Of course, if interest rates are relatively lower in Europe, the increased borrowing abroad tends to bring other rates back into balance. Sometimes foreign firms find it attractive to sell " 'Yankee' bonds—bonds issued by foreign governments and corporations but sold in the U.S. and denominated in U.S. dollars."[7]

Increasingly the financial manager (whether in the United States or in a foreign country) is looking at the whole world as a relevant financial market. With the ebb and flow of changing economic and financial conditions throughout the world, the financial manager is sometimes an investor and sometimes a borrower abroad. Transportation and communication systems now link nations together directly and closely. For this reason further analysis of the international dimensions of financial markets will be developed later in the book (see Chapter 26).

Summary

The financial sector of the economy, an important part of the financial manager's environment, is comprised of financial markets, financial institutions, and financial instruments.

Financial markets involve the creation and transfer of financial assets and liabilities. The financial manager uses these markets to obtain needed funds for the operation and growth of the business and to employ funds temporarily not needed by the business. Funds are provided by savings surplus units to be used by savings deficit units. This transfer of funds creates a financial asset for the surplus unit and a financial liability for the deficit unit. Transfers can be directly between a surplus and a deficit unit or can involve a financial intermediary, such as a bank. Intermediaries take on financial liabilities in order to create financial assets, typically profiting from their expertise in packaging these assets and liabilities. The operations of intermediaries and financial markets in general bring about a more efficient allocation of real resources.

The money markets involve financial assets and liabilities with maturities of less than one year, and the capital markets involve transfers for longer periods. Since most businesses are savings deficit units, the financial manager is concerned with the choice of financial markets, the intermediaries, and instruments best suited to the needs of the firm and with the decision of how best to employ excess funds for short periods.

The initial sale of stocks and bonds is known as the primary market; subsequent trading takes place in the secondary market—the organized exchanges. The over-the-counter market, the third market, is a dealer market

6. "Big Loan Bargains in the Euromart," *Business Week,* December 13, 1976, pp. 10–11.
7. "'Yankee' Bonds Are Doing Just Dandy," *Business Week,* December 6, 1976, pp. 76–77.

where broker-dealers throughout the country act as market makers. Sometimes large blocks of stock are traded directly among institutional investors, which represent the fourth market.

In addition to the ordinary purchase or sale of stocks or bonds, margin trading involves borrowing to increase the size of the investment. Margin requirements, set by the Fed, change from time to time. Short selling is the practice of borrowing securities and selling them immediately, while anticipating an opportunity to repurchase them later at a lower price to repay the loan. (That is, the short seller benefits if the price of the stock falls.) Short selling and margin trading make the stock market more active and thus may contribute to the ability to buy or sell securities with smaller price swings than otherwise would occur.

Two major forms of financing are used by business firms: equity financing through common stock and various forms of debt financing. There are numerous alternative types of debt instruments; they differ in duration and in the degree of risk of the borrower (the issuer of the debt) being unable to meet the obligation.

International financial markets extend the range of alternatives available to financial managers. Surplus funds can be invested at advantageous rates in the many different types of international financial instruments. Financing can be obtained in the Eurocurrency market for short-term borrowing or in the Eurobond market for longer-term debt financing.

Questions

2.1 What activities of financial managers are depicted by Figure 2.1?

2.2 What are financial intermediaries, and what economic functions do they perform?

2.3 How could each tool of the Fed be used to slow down expansion?

2.4 Evaluate each of the arguments in favor of organized securities exchanges relative to OTC markets a hundred years ago versus today.

2.5 One day the New York Stock Exchange reporting system showed XYZ Corporation as follows:

49   27   XYZ   1.20   8   60   33   30   32 + 1

a. Is XYZ trading near its high or its low for the year?

b. What was yesterday's closing price?

c. In terms of the closing price, what is the expected dividend yield on XYZ stock?

d. Based on the information given in the report, what would you estimate XYZ's annual earnings to be?

2.6. Why might an investor want to sell short?

2.7 As the financial manager of a business, what factors would you want to consider in deciding how to invest some temporary surplus funds?

2.8 If your firm needs more long-term capital, can you think of a situation where you might want to use a short-term source of funds?

Problems

2.1 Walter Jones buys a hundred shares of XYZ Corporation common stock at a price of $20 per share and holds the stock for one year. Brokerage costs and transfer taxes are 2 percent of the transaction value. What is the percentage gain or loss on the funds he has invested if the stock pays a single year-end dividend of $1? The brokerage firm charges him 10 percent on his unpaid balance for the year. If he does not invest the full $2,000, he is able to earn 6 percent on the funds not invested in the XYZ stock.

  a. What is the percentage gain or loss on the funds invested by Jones if the stock is sold for $25 per share and the cash he provides is
    1. 100 percent of the sum of the purchase price plus brokerage expenses?
    2. 70 percent of the sum of the purchase price plus brokerage expenses?
    3. 50 percent of the sum of the purchase price plus brokerage expenses?

  b. What is the percentage gain or loss on the funds invested by Jones if the stock is sold for $15 per share under the same three margin percentages?

  c. What is the effect of using debt on the percentage gain or loss to Jones?

2.2 Assume the same facts as in Problem 2.1 except that Jones sells the stock short. Answer the same questions as in Problem 2.1.

2.3 In a recent issue of the *Federal Reserve Bulletin,* locate the table giving information on margin requirements for margin stocks, convertible bonds, and short sales.

  a. Does *margin requirements* refer to the percentage of borrowing to market value of the collateral or to the percentage of funds provided by the investor?

  b. Are the requirements always the same for the three types of securities?

  c. What has been the trend in margin requirements since March 11, 1968?

  d. What are current margin requirements?

2.4 Using a recent issue of the *Wall Street Journal,* answer the following questions with respect to General Electric Company common stock:

  a. On what exchange is it listed?

  b. What is the annual dollar amount of dividends based on the last quarterly or semiannual distribution?

  c. What percentage yield is represented by this dollar amount of dividend based on the closing price of the stock?

  d. How does this compare with the rate of interest the same funds could earn in a savings account?

  e. What is the indicated price/earnings ratio of the stock based on the closing price and the most recent twelve months' earnings?

  f. By what percentage is the closing price below the high price for the previous fifty-two weeks?

  g. By what percentage is the closing price above the low price for the previous fifty-two weeks?

  h. Would you say that the common stock of General Electric has experienced high, low, or moderate volatility during the previous fifty-two weeks?

2.5 Using a recent issue of the *Wall Street Journal,* answer the following questions about the 8 $^{7}/_{8}$ percent bonds of the Dow Chemical Company:

a. On what exchange are they listed?

b. What is their maturity date?

c. What is their current yield?

d. What was their closing price?

e. Was their closing price below or above their par value of 100?

CHAPTER **3** THE TAX
ENVIRONMENT AND FORMS OF BUSINESS
ORGANIZATION

The federal government is often called the most important stockholder in the U.S. economy. This is not literally true, since the government does not "own" corporate shares in the strict sense of the word; it is, however, by far the largest recipient of business profits. Income of unincorporated businesses is subject to tax rates ranging up to 70 percent (50 percent on earned income), while corporate income in excess of $100,000 is taxed at a 46 percent rate. Furthermore, dividends received by stockholders are subject to personal income taxes at the stockholders' individual tax rates. State and sometimes city or county taxes must be added to these federal taxes.

With such a large percentage of business income going to the government, it is not surprising that taxes play an important role in financial decisions. To lease or to buy, to use common stock or debt, to make or not to make a particular investment, to merge or not to merge—all these decisions are influenced by tax factors. This chapter summarizes some basic elements of the tax structure relating to financial decisions.

Corporate Income Tax

The tax law of 1978 adopted the following rates, effective 1979, for the corporate income tax:

Rate Structure

First $25,000	17%
Second $25,000	20%
Third $25,000	30%
Fourth $25,000	40%
Over $100,000	46%

For example, if in 1979 a corporation has a taxable net income of $110,000, its tax will be computed as follows:

$$
\begin{aligned}
0.17(\$25,000) &= \$\ 4,250 \\
0.20(\$25,000) &= \ \ \ 5,000 \\
0.30(\$25,000) &= \ \ \ 7,500 \\
0.40(\$25,000) &= \ \ 10,000 \\
0.46(\$10,000) &= \underline{\ \ \ 4,600} \\
\text{Total tax} &= \$31,350
\end{aligned}
$$

Thus the corporation's effective tax rate will be $31,350 ÷ $110,000 = 28.5 percent. However, on any amount over $100,000, the tax rate on this incremental income will be 46 percent. Table 3.1 shows that the average

This chapter has benefited from the assistance of R. Wendell Buttrey, tax attorney and lecturer on taxation at the University of California, Los Angeles.

Table 3.1
Marginal and Average Corporate
Tax Rates, 1979

Taxable Corporate Income (in Dollars)	Marginal Tax Rate (Percent)	Incremental Taxes Paid	Total Taxes Paid	Average Tax Rate (Percent)[a]
0–25,000	17	4,250	4,250	17.00
25,001–50,000	20	5,000	9,250	18.50
50,001–75,000	30	7,500	16,750	22.33
75,001–100,000	40	10,000	26,750	26.75
100,001–200,000	46	46,000	72,750	36.38
200,001–1,000,000	46	368,000	440,750	44.08
1,000,001–11,000,000	46	4,600,000	5,040,750	45.82
11,000,001–111,000,000	46	46,000,000	51,040,750	45.98

[a] Based on upper limit of income range.

corporate income tax is moderately progressive up to $11 million, after which it becomes virtually a flat 46 percent.

This relatively simple tax structure has wide implications for business planning. Because the tax rate increases sharply when corporate income rises above $100,000, it clearly will seem advantageous to break moderate-sized companies into two or more separate corporations in order to make the lower corporate income tax rates applicable. This was, in fact, done for many years by a number of firms, with some groups (such as retail chains and small loan companies) having literally thousands of separate corporations. However, the Tax Reform Act of 1969 eliminated the advantages of multiple corporations from a tax standpoint.

Accelerated Depreciation

Depreciation charges are deductible in computing federal income taxes; the larger the depreciation charge, the lower the actual tax liability. The tax laws specify the methods for calculating depreciation for purposes of computing federal income taxes. When tax laws are changed to permit more rapid, or accelerated, depreciation, this reduces tax payments and stimulates business investments.[1]

A number of different depreciation methods are authorized for tax purposes: (1) straight line, (2) units of production, (3) sum-of-years'-digits, and (4) double declining balance. These methods are explained in the appendix to this chapter. The last two methods listed are generally referred to as accelerated depreciation methods; ordinarily, they are more favorable than straight line depreciation from a tax standpoint.

1. Federal tax statutes also consider the time over which assets must be depreciated. A reduction in that period has the same stimulating effect on the economy as does a change in permitted depreciation methods that speeds up depreciation expenses for tax purposes.

The fiscal policy implications of depreciation methods stem from two factors: (1) accelerated depreciation reduces taxes in the early years of an asset's life, thus increasing corporate cash flows and making more funds available for investment; and (2) faster cash flows increase the profitability, or rate of return, on an investment. The second point is discussed in Chapter 12 in the context of capital budgeting.

Depreciation methods, like tax rates, are determined by Congress and are occasionally altered to influence the level of investment and thereby to stimulate or retard the economy. The most sweeping changes were made in 1954, when the accelerated depreciation methods listed above were first permitted, and in 1962 and 1970, when the depreciable lives of assets for tax purposes were reduced.

Investment Tax Credit

The concept of an investment tax credit was first incorporated into the federal income tax laws in 1962. Under the investment tax credit program, business firms could deduct, as a credit against their income tax, a specified percentage of the dollar amount of new investment in each of certain categories of assets. Under the rules existing in 1978, the tax credit amounted to 10 percent of the amount of new investment in assets having useful lives of seven years or more, two-thirds of 10 percent for assets having lives of five or six years, one-third of 10 percent for assets having lives of three or four years, and no tax credit for assets having useful lives of fewer than three years. Thus, if a firm that otherwise will have a $100,000 tax bill purchases an asset costing $200,000 and having a twenty-year life, it will receive a tax credit of $20,000 (10 percent of $200,000), and its adjusted tax bill will be $80,000.

The investment tax credit, like tax rates and depreciation methods, is subject to congressional changes. During the boom in the early part of 1966, the investment tax credit was suspended in an effort to reduce investment; it was reinstated later that year, then removed again in 1969 and reinstated in 1971. The Revenue Act of 1978 makes the investment tax credit, including a $100,000 used-property limitation, permanent. The amount of tax liability that can be offset is the first $25,000 plus a fraction of the amount over $25,000 that rises from 50 percent by 10 percentage points a year beginning in 1979, reaching 90 percent by 1982. The provisions are somewhat more liberal for railroad and airline companies and some utilities.

Corporate Capital Gains and Losses

Corporate taxable income consists of two components: profits from the sale of capital assets and all other income (defined as *ordinary income*). *Capital assets* (for example, security investments) are defined as assets not bought and sold in the ordinary course of a firm's business. Gains and losses on the sale of capital assets are defined as capital gains and losses, and under certain circumstances they receive special tax treatment.[2] Real and depreciable property used in the business is not defined as a capital asset, although the Internal Revenue Code specifies that such property is treated as a capital asset in the event of a net gain. (However, the recapture of depreciation provisions may eliminate much of this benefit.) If there is a net loss, the full amount can be deducted from ordinary income without any of the limitations described below for capital loss treatment.[3]

Until 1977, the distinction between short-term and long-term capital gains was based on a six-month holding period. Assets held six months or less gave rise to short-term capital gains or losses on their sale. If held more than six months, the gain or loss was considered long-term. The Tax Reform Act of 1976 increased the period assets must be held for purposes of determining long-term capital gain or loss from six months to nine months in 1977 and to twelve months thereafter. Thus, from 1978 on, the sale of a capital asset held for twelve months or less gives rise to a short-term capital gain or loss. When held for more than twelve months, its disposal produces a long-term gain or loss. Short-term capital gains less short-term capital losses equals net short-term gains, which are added to the firm's ordinary income and taxed at regular corporate income tax rates. For net long-term capital gains (long-term gains less long-term losses), the tax is limited to 28 percent plus a minimum tax factor on part of a corporation's gains, which makes the maximum rate on corporate capital gains slightly higher. For example, if a corporation holds the common stock of another corporation as an investment for more than twelve months and then sells it at a profit, the gain is subject to a maximum tax of 28+ percent. Of course, if income is below $50,000, regular tax rates of 17 or 20 percent apply.

Depreciable Assets

If a building is subject to depreciation, its tax cost is defined as the original purchase price less allowable accumulated depreciation. To illustrate, suppose a building cost $100,000, and $40,000 of (allowable) depreciation has been taken on it. Its book value, by definition, is $100,000 − $40,000 = $60,000.

A building cannot be depreciated by an accelerated method to transfer ordinary income to capital gains. Thus a problem may arise when it is bought, depreciated by an accelerated method, and subsequently sold. If

2. Corporate capital gains and losses (as well as most other tax matters) are subject to many technical provisions. This section and the others dealing with tax matters include only the most general provisions. For special cases see *Federal Tax Course* (Englewood Cliffs, N.J.: Prentice-Hall, 1979).
3. The special treatment of depreciable properties should be kept in mind in connection with the material in Chapter 12 on capital budgeting. The difference between the book value of an asset and its salvage or abandonment value (if lower than book value) can be deducted from ordinary income; thus the full amount of this difference is a deductible expense.

the sale is at a price above book value, the difference between straight line and accelerated depreciation is not allowable for determining the capital gain or loss. To illustrate: In the above example, if straight line depreciation had been $25,000, then $15,000 of the $40,000 depreciation would be recaptured. Thus the tax cost for figuring a capital gain would be $75,000 ($100,000 − $25,000). If the asset were sold for $85,000, a long-term capital gain of $10,000 ($85,000 − $75,000) would result. The $15,000 difference between allowable depreciation and depreciation claimed would be taxed as ordinary income. This rule is intended to prevent firms from converting regular income to capital gains by accelerated depreciation, thus avoiding payment of some income tax.

In the case of personal property such as machinery, the entire gain is recaptured as ordinary income up to the amount of the depreciation taken, regardless of the method employed. In the case of depreciation of buildings, the recapture provisions apply only to the excess of depreciation deducted over straight line depreciation.

Deductibility of Capital Losses

A corporation's net capital loss is not deductible from ordinary income. For example, if in 1979 a corporation had ordinary income of $100,000 and a net capital loss of $25,000 (that is, capital losses for the year exceeded capital gains for the year by $25,000), it still paid a tax of $26,750 on the $100,000 ordinary income. The net capital loss, however, can be carried back three years and forward five years and can be used to offset capital gains during that period.

Dividend Income

Another important rule is that 85 percent of the dividends received by one corporation from another are exempt from taxation.[4] For example, if Corporation H owns stock in Corporation J and receives $100,000 in dividends from that corporation, it must pay taxes on only $15,000 of the $100,000. Assuming H is in the 46 percent tax bracket, the tax is $6,900 or 6.9 percent of the dividends received. The reason for this reduced tax is that to subject intercorporate dividends to the full corporate tax rate would eventually lead to triple taxation. First, Corporation J would pay its regular taxes. Then, Corporation H would pay a second tax. Finally, H's own stockholders would be subject to taxes on their dividends. The 85 percent dividend deduction thus reduces the multiple taxation of corporate income.

4. If the corporation receiving the dividends owns 80 percent or more of the stock of a dividend-paying firm, it can file a consolidated tax return. In this situation there are no dividends as far as the Internal Revenue Service is concerned, so there is obviously no tax on dividends received. The internal books of the related corporations may show an accounting entry entitled "dividends," which is used for transferring funds from the subsidiary to the parent; but this is of no concern to the IRS.

Deductibility of Interest and Dividends

Interest payments made by a corporation are a deductible expense to the firm, but dividends paid on its own stock are not. Thus, if a firm raises $100,000 and contracts to pay the suppliers of this money 7 percent, or $7,000 a year, the $7,000 is deductible if the $100,000 is debt. It is not deductible if the $100,000 is raised as stock and the $7,000 is paid as dividends.[5] This differential treatment of dividends and interest payments has an important effect on the manner in which firms raise capital, as later chapters will show.

Payment of Tax in Installments

Firms must estimate their taxable income for the current year and, if reporting on a calendar year basis, pay one-fourth of the estimated tax on April 15, June 15, September 15, and December 15 of that year. The estimated taxes paid must be identical to the previous year or at least 80 percent of actual tax liability for the current year, or the firm will be subject to penalties. Any differences between estimated and actual taxes are payable by March 15 of the following year. For example, if a firm expects to earn $100,000 in 1979 and to owe a tax of $26,750 on this income, then it must file an estimated income statement and pay $6,688 on the 15th of April, June, September, and December of 1979. By March 15, 1980, it must file a final income statement and pay any shortfall (or receive a refund for overages) between estimated and actual taxes.

Net Operating Carry-Back and Carry-Forward

Any ordinary corporate operating loss can be carried back three years and forward seven. Previous to the Tax Reform Act of 1976 the carry-forward was only five years, and the loss had to be carried back to the earliest year. But now operating losses do not have to be carried back. For example, an operating loss in 1978 can be used to reduce taxable income from 1975 through 1985 or 1979 through 1985.

The purpose of permitting this loss averaging is to avoid penalizing corporations whose incomes fluctuate widely. To illustrate: Suppose the Ritz Hotel made $100,000 before taxes in all years except 1978, when it suffered a $600,000 operating loss. The Ritz could utilize the carry-back feature to recompute its taxes for 1975, using $100,000 of the operating losses to reduce the 1975 profit to zero and recovering the amount of taxes paid in that year; that is, in 1979 the Ritz would receive a refund of its 1975 taxes because of the loss experienced in 1978. Since $500,000 of unrecovered losses would still be available, it could do the same thing for 1976 and 1977. Then, in 1979, 1980, and 1981, it could apply the carry-forward loss to reduce its

---

5. Limits have been placed on the deductibility of interest payments on some forms of securities issued in connection with mergers.

profits to zero in each of these years. Alternately, the Ritz could have chosen to start this procedure in 1979.

The Tax Reform Act of 1976 limits the use of a company's net operating losses in periods following a change in its ownership. If the prior owners of the loss company do not receive at least 40 percent ownership in the acquiring company, or if its fifteen largest stockholders have acquired more than 60 percent ownership in the loss company by purchase, the loss carry-over allowable after the change of ownership will be reduced. (There are other important restrictions on the acquisition of a loss company, but they are too complex to be covered in this brief summary.)

Improper Accumulation

A special surtax on improperly accumulated income is provided for by Section 531 of the Internal Revenue Code, which states that earnings accumulated by a corporation are subject to penalty rates *if the purpose of the accumulation is to enable the stockholders to avoid the personal income tax.* The penalty rate is 27.5 percent on the first $100,000 of improperly accumulated taxable income for the current year and 38.5 percent on all amounts over $100,000. Of income not paid out in dividends, a cumulative total of $150,000 (the balance sheet item of retained earnings) is prima facie retainable for the reasonable needs of the business; this benefits small corporations. Of course, most companies have legitimate reasons for retaining earnings over $150,000, and they are not subject to the penalty.

Retained earnings are used to pay off debt, to finance growth, and to provide the corporation with a cushion against possible cash drains caused by losses. How much a firm should properly accumulate for uncertain contingencies is a matter of judgment. Fear of the penalty taxes that can be imposed under Section 531 may cause a firm to pay out a higher rate of dividends than it otherwise would.[6]

Sometimes Section 531 stimulates mergers. A clear illustration is provided by the purchase of the Toni Company (home permanents) by the Gillette Safety Razor Company.[7] The sale was made at a time when Toni's sales volume had begun to level off. Since earnings retention might have been difficult to justify, Toni's owners—the Harris brothers—were faced with the alternatives of paying penalty rates for improper accumulation of earnings or of paying out the income as dividends. Toni's income after corporate

6. See materials in James K. Hall, *The Taxation of Corporate Surplus Accumulations* (Washington, D.C.: U.S. Government Printing Office, 1952), especially app. 3.
7. See J. K. Butters, J. Lintner, and W. L. Cary, *Effects of Taxation on Corporate Mergers* (Boston: Harvard Business School, 1951), pp. 96–111. The lucid presentation by these authors has been drawn on for the general background, but the data have been approximated to simplify the illustration. The principle involved is not affected by the modifications of the facts.

taxes was $4 million a year; with the Harris brothers' average personal income tax of 75 percent, only $1 million a year would have been left after they had paid personal taxes on dividends. By selling Toni for $13 million, they realized a $12 million capital gain (their book value was $1 million). After paying the 25 percent capital gains tax on the $12 million—$3 million —the Harrises realized $10 million after taxes ($13 million sale price minus $3 million tax). Thus Gillette paid the equivalent of three and one-quarter years' after-corporate-tax earnings for Toni, while the Harris brothers received ten years' after-personal-income-tax net income for it. The tax factor made the transaction advantageous to both parties.

The broad aspects of the federal corporate income tax have now been covered. Because the federal income tax on individuals is equally important for many business decisions, the individual tax structure will now be examined and compared with the corporate tax structure. This will provide a basis for making an intelligent choice as to which form of organization a firm should elect for tax purposes.

Personal Income Tax

Of some 5 million firms in the United States, over 4 million are organized as sole proprietorships or partnerships. The income of these firms is taxed as personal income to the owners or the partners. The net income of a proprietorship or partnership provides a basis for determining the individual's income tax liability. Thus, as a business tax, the individual income tax can be as important as the corporate income tax.

The personal income tax is conceptually straightforward, although many taxpayers find it confusing. Virtually all the income a person or family receives goes into determining the tax liability. For tax purposes income is classified as earned (wages or salary) and nonearned (primarily capital gains, rents, interest, and dividends). Under existing tax laws different kinds of income may be taxed in different ways or at different rates.

Total income from all sources is called gross income. All taxpayers are permitted to deduct part of their gross income before computing any tax. These deductions are of two types: standard deductions and personal exemptions.

Deductions State and local taxes, medical expenses, interest payments, and charitable contributions are tax deductible expenses. The standard deduction can be claimed in lieu of these actual expenses. Effective in 1979 the standard deduction is $3,400 for joint returns of married couples and $2,300 for single taxpayers. Taxpayers with actual expenses in excess of the standard deduction reduce the amount of taxable income by itemizing their deductible expenses.

Personal Exemptions A $1,000 deduction is allowed for the taxpayer and each of that person's dependents. The deduction is doubled for any taxpayer who is over sixty-five years old or blind. In 1979, a family of four—husband, wife, and two dependent children, none blind or over sixty-five—have personal exemptions totaling $4,000. The apparent intent of the personal exemption is to exempt the first part of income from taxation, thereby enabling the family to obtain the basic necessities of life, such as food and shelter. The same intent appears in the form of the graduated income tax, where the highest tax rates are levied against "discretionary" income.

The following classifications are used in connection with calculating an individual's income tax liability:

Income
Wages, salaries, tips, and so on
Interest income
Dividends less exclusion
Business income
Applicable capital gains or losses
Pensions, annuities, rents, royalties, partnerships, and so on
Alimony received
Several other categories

Total income (the sum of the above)

Adjustments to income
Moving expenses
Employee business expenses
Payments to an individual retirement arrangement
Alimony paid
Several other categories

Total adjustments (the sum of the above)

Adjusted gross income =
Total income less adjustments to income

Less: number of personal exemptions times $1,000

Less: excess itemized deductions (itemized deductions in excess of the applicable standard deduction)

Equals taxable income

A number of aspects of tax liability have significance for corporate financial policy. Among the itemized deductions that enable gross income to be reduced is interest paid on borrowings by individuals. Thus, for both corporations and individuals, interest expenses paid are deductible for tax purposes.

Tax Rates for the Personal Income Tax Tax rates that became effective with the Revenue Act of 1978 are indicated in Table 3.2. The tax rates presented are for the joint return of a married couple or surviving spouse. The taxable income is adjusted gross income less personal exemptions less the excess of itemized deductions over the applicable standard deduction. The average tax rate rises relatively slowly, but the marginal rate reaches 49 percent for taxable income of $60,000. For other than earned income, the marginal tax goes up to a maximum of 70 percent on income of $215,400. Table 3.2 will be used in subsequent comparisons of sole proprietorships, partnerships, and corporations.

Table 3.2
Marginal and Average Personal
Income Tax Rates, 1979

Taxable Income		Tax Liability		Average
Over (1)	Not over (2)	Tax (3)	Percent of Excess over column (1) (4)	Percent Tax on Upper Limit of Bracket (5)
$ 3,400	$ 5,500	$ 0	14	5.35
5,500	7,600	294	16	8.29
7,600	11,900	630	18	11.80
11,900	16,000	1,404	21	14.16
16,000	20,200	2,265	24	16.20
20,200	24,600	3,273	28	18.31
24,600	29,900	4,505	32	20.74
29,900	35,200	6,201	37	23.19
35,200	45,800	8,162	43	27.77
45,800	60,000	12,720	49	32.80
60,000	85,600	19,678	54	39.14
85,600	109,400	33,502	59	43.46
109,400	162,400	47,544	64	50.16
162,400	215,400	81,464	68	54.55
215,400	and over	117,504	70	—[a]

The table shows a joint return for a married couple or surviving spouse.
[a] Not calculable.
Source: *Revenue Act of 1978* (Washington, D.C.: Government Printing Office, 1978).

Individual Capital Gains and Losses As with corporations, the distinction between short-term and long-term gains and losses is the twelve-month holding period. Net short-term gains are taxed at regular rates. The tax on net long-term capital gains is computed by deducting 60 percent of the amount, with the remaining 40 percent subject to tax at the marginal tax rate on ordinary income.

Dividend Income

The first $100 of dividend income received by an individual stockholder is excluded from taxable income. If stock is owned jointly by a husband and wife, the exclusion is $200. If only one spouse owns stock, however, the total exclusion is generally only $100.

To illustrate, if a family's gross income consists of $12,000 of salary and $500 of dividends on stock owned by the husband, the gross taxable income (before deductions) is $12,400. However, if the stock is jointly owned, the gross taxable income is $12,300, because $200 of the dividend income is excluded.

Choices among Alternative Forms of Business Organization

Taxes are an important influence in choosing among alternative forms of business organization. In the following sections the nature of the alternatives and their advantages and disadvantages will be described. Then, the tax aspects will be considered.

From a technical and legal standpoint, there are three major forms of business organization: the sole proprietorship, the partnership, and the corporation.[8] In terms of numbers, 70 percent of business firms are operated as sole proprietorships, 8 percent are partnerships, and 14 percent are corporations. By dollar value of sales, however, about 80 percent of business is conducted by corporations, about 13 percent by sole proprietorships, and about 7 percent by partnerships. The remainder of this section describes and compares the characteristics of these alternative forms of business organization.

Sole Proprietorship

A sole proprietorship is a business owned by one individual. Going into business as a sole proprietor is very simple; a person merely begins business operations. However, cities or counties may require even the smallest establishments to be licensed or registered. There may also be state licenses required.

The proprietorship has key advantages for small operations. It is easily and inexpensively formed, requires no formal charter for operations, and is subject to few government regulations. Further, it pays no corporate income taxes, although all earnings of the firm are subject to personal income taxes, regardless of whether they are reinvested in the business or withdrawn from it.

The proprietorship also has important limitations. Most significant is its

---

8. Other less common forms of organization include business trusts, joint stock companies, and co-operatives.

inability to obtain large sums of capital. Further, the proprietor has unlimited personal liability for business debts; creditors can look to both business assets and personal assets to satisfy their claims. Finally, the proprietorship is limited to the life of the individual who creates it. For all these reasons, the sole proprietorship is limited primarily to small business operations. However, businesses frequently are started as proprietorships and converted to corporations when their growth causes the disadvantages of the proprietorship form to outweigh its advantages.

Partnership

When two or more persons associate to conduct a business enterprise, a partnership is said to exist. Partnerships can operate under different degrees of formality, ranging from an informal oral understanding to a written partnership agreement to a formal agreement filed with the secretary of state. Like the proprietorship, the partnership has the advantages of ease and economy of formation as well as freedom from special government regulations. Partnership profits are taxed as personal income in proportion to the partners' claims, whether or not they are distributed to them.

One of the advantages of the partnership over the proprietorship is that it makes possible a pooling of various types of resources. Some partners contribute particular skills or contacts, while others contribute funds. However, there are practical limits to the number of co-owners who can join in an enterprise without destructive conflict, so most partnership agreements provide that the individual partners cannot sell their share in the business unless all the partners agree to accept the new partner (or partners).

If a new partner comes into the business, the old partnership ceases to exist and a new one is created. The withdrawal or death of any of the partners also dissolves the partnership. To prevent disputes under such circumstances, the articles of the partnership agreement should include terms and conditions under which assets are to be distributed upon dissolution. Of course, dissolution of the partnership does not necessarily mean the end of the business; the remaining partners may simply buy out the one who left the firm. To avoid financial pressures caused by the death of one of the partners, it is a common practice for each partner to carry life insurance naming the remaining partners as beneficiaries. The proceeds of such policies can be used to buy out the investment of the deceased partner.

A number of drawbacks stemming from the characteristics of the partnership limit its use. They include impermanence, difficulty of transferring ownership, and unlimited liability (except for limited partners). Partners risk their personal assets as well as their investments in the business. Further, under partnership law, the partners are jointly and separately liable for business debts. This means that if any partner is unable to meet the claims resulting from the liquidation of the partnership, the remaining partners must take over the unsatisfied claims, drawing on their personal assets if necessary.[9]

Corporation

A corporation is a legal entity created by a state.[10] It is a separate entity, distinct from its owners and managers. This separateness gives the corporation three major advantages: (1) it has an unlimited life—it can continue after its original owners and managers are dead; (2) it permits limited liability—stockholders are not personally liable for the debts of the firm; and (3) it permits easy transferability of ownership interest in the firm—ownership interests can be divided into shares of stock, which can be transferred far more easily than partnership interests.[11]

While a proprietorship or a partnership can commence operations without much paperwork, the chartering of a corporation involves a complicated, but routinized, process. First, a certificate of incorporation is drawn up; in most states it includes the following information: (1) name of proposed corporation, (2) purposes, (3) amount of capital stock, (4) number of directors, (5) names and addresses of directors, and (6) duration (if limited). The certificate is notarized and sent to the secretary of the state in which the business seeks incorporation. If it is satisfactory, the corporation officially exists.

The actual operations of the firm are governed by two documents, the charter and the bylaws. The corporate charter technically consists of a certificate of incorporation and, by reference, the general corporation laws of the state. Thus the corporation is bound by the general corporation laws of the state as well as by the unique provisions of its certificate of incorporation. The bylaws are a set of rules drawn up by the founders of the corporation to aid in governing the internal management of the company. Included are such points as (1) how directors are to be elected (all elected each year or, say, one-third each year, and whether cumulative voting will be used); (2) whether the preemptive right is granted to existing stockholders in the event new securities are sold; and (3) provisions for management committees, such as an executive committee or a finance committee, and their duties. Also included is the procedure for changing the bylaws themselves should conditions require this.

---

9. However, it is possible to limit the liabilities of some partners by establishing a limited partnership, wherein certain partners are designated general partners and others limited partners. Limited partnerships are quite common in the area of real estate investment.
10. Certain types of firms (for example, banks) are also chartered by the federal government.
11. In the case of small corporations, the limited liability feature is often a fiction, since bankers and credit managers frequently require personal guarantees from the stockholders of small, weak businesses.

Tax Aspects of the Forms of Organization

To a small, growing firm, the advantage of the corporate form of organization is that the tax rate is low for income up to $100,000. There is "double taxation" of dividends, but salaries paid to the principals in the corporation are a tax-deductible expense and so are not subject to double taxation. The income of a proprietorship or partnership is subject to the personal tax at rates up to 70 percent unless it is paid out in salaries qualifying as earned income, which is subject to a maximum tax rate of 50 percent (a rate only 4 percent higher than the highest corporate tax rate). Thus the influence of taxes involves more than just a comparison of the personal tax rates with the corporate tax rates.

A specific example will illustrate the application of the several factors influencing the amount of taxes under alternative forms of business organization. Craig Vernon, a married man with two children, is planning to start a new business, CV Manufacturing. He is trying to decide between a corporation or a sole proprietorship as the form of organization. Under either form, he will initially own 100 percent of the firm. Tax considerations are very important to him because he plans to finance the expected growth of the firm by drawing a salary sufficient for living expenses for his family (about $30,000) and plowing the remainder back into the enterprise.

Vernon will have no outside income, since he is liquidating all his investments in order to initially finance CV Manufacturing. He estimates that his itemized deductions will be $5,800 in excess of the standard deduction. He expects the following income before deducting his salary:

1979	$ 50,000
1980	80,000
1981	100,000

To determine whether Vernon should form the new business as a corporation or a proprietorship, we will first calculate the total taxes to be paid if it is organized as a corporation (see Table 3.3). Then we will calculate total taxes on the basis of a proprietorship (see Table 3.4).

The taxes are lower for a corporation in each of the years. The reason is that the corporate form of ownership enables Vernon to split his income so it is taxed at low marginal rates (most of it at less than 30 percent). But under the single proprietorship, much of the income is subject to higher rates.

To a certain extent, the advantage to the corporate form of organization is somewhat illusory. The figures shown for the corporation deal with dollars that have not yet come into the hands of the shareholders. If the earnings are distributed as a dividend, there will be further taxes to be borne by the shareholders individually. If a shareholder sells his or her stock and gets the benefit of corporate earnings in the form of a capital gain, the person will have to pay a capital gains tax. The extent of the ultimate additional tax is currently unknown, but the shareholder does benefit from having at least temporary use of the tax dollars saved.

Table 3.3
Total Taxes for CV as a
Corporation

	1979	1980	1981
Income before salary and tax	$50,000	$80,000	$100,000
Less salary	−30,000	−30,000	−30,000
Taxable income, corporate	$20,000	$50,000	$ 70,000
Corporate taxes:			
$25,000 at 17%	3,400	4,250	4,250
$25,000 at 20%	0	5,000	5,000
Balance at 30%	0	0	6,000
Total corporate tax	$ 3,400	$ 9,250	$ 15,250
Salary	$30,000	$30,000	$ 30,000
Less exemptions	−4,000	−4,000	−4,000
Total	$26,000	$26,000	$ 26,000
Less excess deductions	−5,800	−5,800	−5,800
Taxable income, personal	$20,200	$20,200	$20,200
Total personal tax	$ 3,273	$ 3,273	$ 3,273
Combined total tax	$ 6,673	$12,523	$ 18,523

Table 3.4
Total Taxes for CV as a
Sole Proprietorship

	1979	1980	1981
Total income	$50,000	$80,000	$100,000
Less exemptions	−4,000	−4,000	−4,000
Total	$46,000	$76,000	$96,000
Less excess deductions	−5,800	−5,800	−5,800
Taxable income	$40,200	$70,200	$ 90,200
Tax liability	$10,312	$25,186	$ 36,216

We can now compare the results:

	1979	1980	1981
Taxes paid as a proprietorship	$10,312	$25,186	$36,216
Taxes paid as a corporation	6,673	12,523	18,523
Advantage as a corporation	$ 3,639	$12,663	$17,693

Of course, for a large enterprise with income of several hundred million dollars, the "tax splitting" effect does not have as great an influence. However, in that case, the corporation's effectiveness in raising large sums of capital from a large number of sources becomes the major consideration in selecting the corporate form of organization.

While broad generalizations are not possible, these are factors that should at least be taken into account in making the decision about the form of organization for any business enterprise.

Summary

This chapter provides some basic background on the tax environment within which business firms operate. The corporate tax rate structure is relatively simple. The tax rate is 17 percent on income up to $25,000; 20, 30, and 40 percent respectively on the next three increments of $25,000; and 46 percent on all income over $100,000. Estimated taxes are paid in quarterly installments during the year in which the income is earned; when the returns are filed, the actual tax liability results either in additional payments or in a refund due. Any operating loss incurred by the corporation can be carried back three years and forward seven years against income in those years. The firm can elect not to employ the carry-back provision.

Assets that are not bought and sold in the ordinary course of business are subject to capital gains tax on disposition. If an asset is held more than twelve months, any gain on the sale is classified as long-term and taxed at a maximum rate of 28+ percent. Gains on assets held fewer than twelve months are subject to taxation at the company's regular rate. Capital losses can be offset against capital gains to arrive at net long-term gains and net short-term gains. These losses can be carried back against gains for three years and carried forward for five years but cannot be offset against ordinary income.

Of the dividends received by a corporation owning stock in another firm, 85 percent are excluded from the receiving firm's taxable income, but the firm must pay full taxes on the remaining 15 percent. Dividends paid are not treated as a tax-deductible expense. Regardless of the size of its earnings, a corporation does not have to pay dividends if it needs funds for expansion. If, however, the funds are not used for a legitimate purpose—if earnings are retained merely to enable stockholders to avoid paying personal income taxes on dividends received—the firm is subject to an improper accumulations tax. Interest received is taxable as ordinary income; interest paid is a deductible expense.

Unincorporated business income is taxed at the personal tax rates of the owners. Personal income tax rates for both individuals and married persons filing jointly are progressive—the higher the income, the higher the tax rate. The rates start at 14 percent of taxable income and rise to either 50 percent or 70 percent, depending on whether the income is considered earned income.

The holding period for long-term capital gains and losses is twelve months, which is similar to that for corporations. Short-term gains are taxed as ordinary income, and 40 percent of long-term gains are taxed at the regular tax rate.

The information presented here on the tax system is not designed to make a tax expert of the reader. It merely provides a few essentials for recognizing the tax aspects of business financial problems and for developing an awareness of the kinds of situations that should be dealt with by tax specialists. These basics are, however, referred to frequently throughout the text, because income taxes are often an important factor in business financial decisions.

Sole proprietorships and partnerships are easily formed. All earnings are taxed at the rate of the owner or partner as regular income. Owners and partners are also personally liable for the debts of the business.

The corporation has the advantage of limiting the liability of the participants, but it is generally more expensive to organize. Once organized it is easy to transfer ownership to others. Corporate earnings paid as dividends are subject to double taxation. The other tax differences between corporations and proprietorships or partnerships depend on the facts of individual cases.

Questions

3.1 Compare the marginal and the average tax rates of corporations for taxable incomes of $5,000, $50,000, $500,000, and $50,000,000. Can you make such a comparison for sole proprietorships or for partnerships?

3.2 Which is the more relevant tax rate—the marginal or the average—in determining the form of organization for a new firm? Have recent changes in the tax laws made the form of organization more or less important than formerly? Explain.

3.3 For tax purposes, how does the treatment of interest expense compare with the treatment of common stock dividends from each of the following standpoints: a firm paying the interest or dividends, an individual recipient, and a corporate recipient?

3.4 What is the purpose of the Internal Revenue Code provision dealing with improper accumulation of corporate surplus revenue?

3.5 Why is personal income tax information important for a study of business finance?

3.6 How do the tax rates for capital gains and losses affect an individual's investment policies and opportunities for financing a small business?

Problems

3.1 A corporation had net income of $40,000.
   a. How much income tax must the corporation pay?
   b. What is the marginal tax rate?
   c. What is the average tax rate?

3.2 The J. K. Lassit Corporation had net income from operations of $30,000. It also had $10,000 of interest expense and $25,000 of interest revenue during the year.

a. How much income tax must the corporation pay?

b. What is the marginal tax rate?

c. What is the average tax rate?

3.3 The Sunrise Corporation had net income of $100,000 in 1979, including $20,000 in dividend income on stocks of various major publicly held corporations.

a. How much tax must the corporation pay?

b. What is the average tax rate on net income?

3.4 Determine the effective marginal and average income tax rates for a corporation earning (a) $10,000; (b) $100,000; (c) $1,000,000, and (d) $100,000,000.

3.5 The taxable income of the Robbins Corporation, formed in 1974, is indicated below. (Losses are shown as minuses.)

Year	Taxable Income
1974	−$80,000
1975	60,000
1976	50,000
1977	70,000
1978	−120,000

What is the corporate tax liability for each year?

3.6 John Alexander has operated his small machine shop as a sole proprietorship for several years, but recent changes in the corporate tax structure have led him to consider incorporating.

Alexander is married and has two children. His only income, an annual salary of $40,000, is from operating the business. He reinvests any additional earnings in the business. His itemized deductions in excess of the applicable standard deduction are $6,100. Alexander estimates that his proprietorship earnings before salary and taxes for the period of 1979 to 1981 will be:

Year	Income before Salary and Taxes
1979	$50,000
1980	70,000
1981	90,000

a. What will his total taxes be under:

1. a proprietorship?

2. a corporate form of organization?

b. Should Alexander incorporate? Discuss.

Appendix 3A
Depreciation
Methods

The four principal methods of depreciation—straight line, sum-of-years'-digits, double declining balance, and units of production—and their effects on a firm's taxes are illustrated in this appendix. Assume at the start that a machine is purchased for $1,100 and has an estimated useful life of ten years or ten thousand hours. It will have a scrap value of $100 after ten years of use or after ten thousand hours, whichever comes first. Table 3A.1 illustrates each of the four depreciation methods and compares the depreciation charges of each method over the ten-year period.

**Table 3A.1
Comparison of Depreciation
Methods for a 10-Year, $1,100
Asset with a $100 Salvage Value**

		Depreciation Methods		
Year	Straight Line	Double Declining Balance	Sum-of-Years'-Digits	Units of Production
1	$ 100	$220	$ 182	$ 200
2	100	176	164	180
3	100	141	145	150
4	100	113	127	130
5	100	90	109	100
6	100	72	91	80
7	100	58	73	60
8	100	46	55	50
9	100	37	36	30
10	100	29	18	20
Total	$1,000	$982	$1,000	$1,000

The assumption is made that the machine is used the following number of hours: first year, 2,000; second year, 1,800; third year, 1,500; fourth year, 1,300; fifth year, 1,000; sixth year, 800; seventh year, 600; eighth year, 500; ninth year, 300; tenth year, 200.

Straight Line

With the straight line method, a uniform annual depreciation charge of $100 a year is provided. This figure is arrived at by simply dividing the economic life into the total cost of the machine minus the estimated salvage value:

$$\frac{(\$1,100 \text{ cost} - \$100 \text{ salvage value})}{10 \text{ years}} = \frac{\$100 \text{ a year}}{\text{depreciation charge.}}$$

If the estimated salvage value is not in excess of 10 percent of the original cost, it can be ignored, but we are leaving it for illustrative purposes.

Double Declining Balance

The double declining balance (DDB) method of accelerated depreciation requires the application of a constant rate of depreciation each year to the undepreciated value of the asset at the close of the previous year. In this case, since the annual straight line rate is 10 percent a year ($100 ÷ $1,000), the double declining rate is 20 percent (2 × 10 percent). This rate is applied to the full purchase price of the machine, not to the cost less salvage value.

Therefore, depreciation under the DDB method is $220 during the first year
(0.2 × $1,100). Depreciation amounts to $176 in the second year and is calculated by applying the 20 percent rate to the remaining undepreciated
value of the asset:

$$20\% \times (\$1,100 - \$220) = \$176$$

and so on, as the undepreciated balance declines. Notice that under DDB
the asset is not fully depreciated at the end of the tenth year. In our example
the remaining depreciation will be taken in the tenth year.[1]

Sum-of-Years'-Digits

Under the sum-of-years'-digits method, the yearly depreciation allowance is
determined as follows:

1. Calculate the sum of the years' digits; in our example, there is a total of
   55 digits: $1 + 2 + 3 + 4 + 5 + 6 + 7 + 8 + 9 + 10 = 55$. This figure can
   also be arrived at by means of an algebraic progression equation where
   N is the life of the asset:

$$\text{Sum} = N \left(\frac{N + 1}{2}\right)$$

$$= 10 \left(\frac{10 + 1}{2}\right) = 55.$$

2. Divide the number of remaining years by the sum of the years' digits and
   multiply this fraction by the depreciable cost (total cost minus salvage
   value) of the asset:

$$\text{Year 1: } \frac{10}{55} (\$1,000) = \$182 \text{ depreciation.}$$

$$\text{Year 2: } \frac{9}{55} (\$1,000) = \$164 \text{ depreciation.}$$

$$\vdots$$

$$\text{Year 10: } \frac{1}{55} (\$1,000) = \$18 \text{ depreciation.}$$

Units of Production

Under the units of production method, the expected useful life of ten thousand hours is divided into the depreciable cost (purchase price minus sal-

1. Actually, the company will switch from DDB to straight line whenever straight line depreciation on the
   remaining book value of the asset exceeds the DDB amount. Thus, in the ninth year the book value is
   $184, leaving $84 to be depreciated, so straight line depreciation would be $42 versus $37 if the
   change were not made.

vage value) to arrive at an hourly depreciation rate of ten cents. Since, in our example, the machine is run for two thousand hours in the first year, the depreciation in that year is $200; in the second year, $180; and so on. With this method, depreciation charges cannot be estimated precisely ahead of time; the firm must wait until the end of the year to determine what usage has been made of the machine and hence its depreciation.

Effect of Depreciation on Taxes Paid

The effect of the accelerated methods on a firm's income tax payment is easily demonstrated. In the first year, should the firm choose to use the straight line method, only $100 can be deducted from its earnings to arrive at earnings before taxes (the amount of earnings to which the tax rate applies). However, using any of the other three methods, the firm would have a much greater deduction and, therefore, a lower tax liability.

Changing the Depreciable Life of an Asset

Depreciation charges can actually be accelerated without resorting to changing the depreciation method simply by shortening the estimated life of an asset. The federal government establishes certain guidelines that set legal limits on the minimum life of classes of assets; by lowering these limits, the government can accomplish ends similar to permitting accelerated methods. Halving the minimum depreciable life of an asset, for example, effectively doubles the annual rate of depreciation.

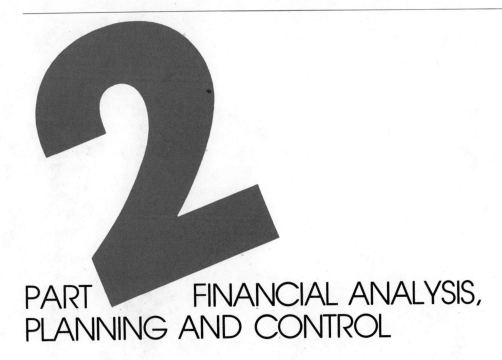

PART 2 FINANCIAL ANALYSIS, PLANNING AND CONTROL

Part 2 encompasses four chapters on financial planning, and control systems in firms. They provide the framework for planning the firm's growth and the development of financial controls for efficiency. While these areas of finance do not have the sophistication of the formal models that will be used in later chapters, they are vital to the firm's healthy profitability. Chapter 4 examines the construction and use of the basic ratios of financial analysis; through this ratio analysis, the firm's strengths and weaknesses can be pinpointed. Chapter 5 explains two key tools used in finan-

cial planning: breakeven analysis and the sources and uses of funds statement. Chapter 6 takes up financial forecasting: Given a projected increase in sales, how much money must the financial manager raise to support this level of sales? Finally, Chapter 7 considers the budget system and decentralized operations through which management controls and coordinates the firm and its divisions.

Finance deals, in the main, with very specific questions: Should we lease or buy the new machine? Should we expand capacity at the Hartford plant? Should we raise cap-

ital this year by long-term or short-term debt or by selling stock? Should we go along with the marketing department, which wants to expand inventories, or with the production department, which wants to reduce them? Such specific questions, typical of those facing the financial manager, are considered in the remainder of the book. But Part 2 takes an *overview* of the firm. Because all specific decisions are made within the context of the firm's overall position, this overview is critical to an understanding of any specific proposal.

CHAPTER **4** RATIO ANALYSIS

Planning is the key to the financial manager's success. Financial plans may take many forms, but any good plan must be related to the firm's existing strengths and weaknesses. The strengths must be understood if they are to be used to proper advantage, and the weaknesses must be recognized if corrective action is to be taken. For example, are inventories adequate to support the projected level of sales? Does the firm have too heavy an investment in accounts receivable, and does this condition reflect a lax collection policy? The financial manager can plan future financial requirements in accordance with the forecasting and budgeting procedures we will present in succeeding chapters, but the plan must begin with the type of financial analysis developed in this chapter.

Basic Financial Statements

Because ratio analysis employs financial data taken from the firm's balance sheet and income statement, it is useful to begin with a review of these accounting reports. For illustrative purposes, we shall use data taken from the Walker-Wilson Manufacturing Company, a manufacturer of specialized machinery used in the automobile repair business. Formed in 1961, when Charles Walker and Ben Wilson set up a small plant to produce certain tools they had developed while in the army, Walker-Wilson grew steadily and earned the reputation of being one of the best small firms in its line of business. In December 1976, both Walker and Wilson were killed in a crash of their private plane, and for the next two years the firm was managed by Walker-Wilson's accountant.

In 1978 the widows, who are the principal stockholders in Walker-Wilson, acting on the advice of the firm's bankers and attorneys, engaged David Thompson as president and general manager. Although Thompson is experienced in the machinery business, especially in production and sales, he does not have a detailed knowledge of his new company, so he has decided to conduct a careful appraisal of the firm's position and, on the basis of this position, to draw up a plan for future operations.

Balance Sheet

Walker-Wilson's balance sheet, given in Table 4.1, shows the value of the firm's assets, and of the claims on these assets, at two particular points in time, December 31, 1977, and December 31, 1978. The assets are arranged from top to bottom in order of decreasing liquidity; that is, assets toward the top of the column will be converted to cash sooner than those toward the bottom of the column. The top group of assets—cash, marketable securities, accounts receivable, and inventories, which are expected to be converted into cash within one year—is defined as *current assets*. Assets in the lower part of the statement—plant and equipment, which are not expected to be converted to cash within one year—are defined as *fixed assets*.

Table 4.1
Walker-Wilson Company
Illustrative Balance Sheet
(Thousands of Dollars)

Assets	Dec. 31, 1977		Dec. 31, 1978	
Cash		$ 52		$ 50
Marketable securities		175		150
Receivables		250		200
Inventories		355		300
Total current assets		$ 832		$ 700
Gross plant and equipment	$1,610		$1,800	
Less depreciation	−400		−500	
Net plant and equipment		1,210		1,300
Total assets		$2,042		$2,000

Claims on Assets	Dec. 31, 1977		Dec. 31, 1978	
Accounts payable		$ 87		$ 60
Notes payable (at 10%)		110		100
Accruals		10		10
Provision for federal income taxes		135		130
Total current liabilities		$ 342		$ 300
First mortgage bonds (at 8%)[a]		520		500
Debentures (at 10%)		200		200
Common stock (600,000 shares)	$600		$600	
Retained earnings	380		400	
Total net worth		980		1,000
Total claims on assets		$2,042		$2,000

[a]The sinking fund requirement for the mortgage bonds is $20,000 a year.

The right side of the balance sheet is arranged similarly. Those items toward the top of the claims column will mature and have to be paid off relatively soon; those further down the column will be due in the more distant future. Current liabilities must be paid within one year; because the firm never has to "pay off" common stockholders, common stock and retained earnings represent "permanent" capital.

**Income
Statement**

Walker-Wilson's income statement is shown in Table 4.2. Sales are at the top of the statement; various costs, including taxes, are deducted to arrive at the net income available to common stockholders. The figure on the last line represents earnings per share (EPS), calculated as net income divided by number of shares outstanding.

**Table 4.2
Walker-Wilson Company
Illustrative Income Statement
for Year Ended December 31, 1978**

Net sales		$3,000,000
Cost of goods sold		2,555,000
Gross profit		$ 445,000
Less operating expenses:		
Selling	$22,000	
General and administrative	40,000	
Lease payment on office building	28,000	90,000
Gross operating income		$ 355,000
Depreciation		100,000
Net operating income		$ 255,000
Plus other income:		
Royalties		15,000
Gross income		$ 270,000
Less other expenses:		
Interest on notes payable	$10,000	
Interest on first mortgage	40,000	
Interest on debentures	20,000	70,000
Net income before income tax		$ 200,000
Federal income tax (at 40%)		80,000
Net income, after income tax, available to common stockholders		$ 120,000
Earnings per share (EPS)		$ .20

**Statement of
Retained
Earnings**

Earnings can be paid out to stockholders as dividends or retained and reinvested in the business. Stockholders like to receive dividends, of course; but if earnings are plowed back into the business, the value of the stockholders' position in the company increases. Later in the book we shall consider the pros and cons of retaining earnings versus paying them out in dividends, but for now we are simply interested in the effects of dividends and retained earnings on the balance sheet. For this purpose, accountants use the statement of retained earnings, illustrated for Walker-Wilson in Table 4.3. Walker-Wilson earned $120,000 during the year, paid $100,000 in dividends to stockholders, and plowed $20,000 back into the business. Thus the retained earnings at the end of 1978, as shown both on the balance sheet and on the statement of retained earnings, is $400,000, which is $20,000 larger than the year-end 1977 figure.

Table 4.3
Walker-Wilson Company
Statement of Retained Earnings
for Year Ended December 31, 1978

Balance of retained earnings, December 31, 1977	$380,000
Plus net income, 1978	120,000
	$500,000
Less dividends to stockholders	−100,000
Balance of retained earnings, December 31, 1978	$400,000

Relationships among the Three Statements

It is important to recognize that the balance sheet is a statement of the firm's financial position *at a point in time,* whereas the income statement shows the results of operations *during an interval of time.* Thus, the balance sheet represents a snapshot of the firm's position on a given date, while the income statement is based on a flow concept, showing what occurred between two points in time.

The statement of retained earnings indicates how the retained earnings account on the balance sheet is adjusted between balance sheet dates. Since its inception, Walker-Wilson had retained a total of $380,000 by December 31, 1977. In 1978 it earned $120,000 and retained $20,000 of this amount. Thus, the retained earnings shown on the balance sheet for December 31, 1978, is $400,000.

A firm that retains earnings generally does so to expand the business— that is, to finance the purchase of assets such as plant, equipment, and inventories. As a result of operations in 1978, Walker-Wilson has $20,000 available for that purpose. Sometimes retained earnings are used to build up the cash account, but, as shown on the balance sheet, they are *not* cash. Through the years they have been invested in bricks and mortar and other assets, so they are not "available" for anything. The earnings *for the current year* may be available for investment, but the *past retained earnings* have already been employed.

Stated another way, the balance sheet item "retained earnings" simply shows how much of their earnings the stockholders, through the years, have elected to retain in the business. Thus, the retained earnings account shows the additional investment the stockholders as a group have made in the business over and above their initial investment at the inception of the company and through any subsequent issues of stock.

Basic Types of Financial Ratios

Each type of analysis has a purpose or use that determines the different relationships emphasized. The analyst may, for example, be a banker considering whether to grant a short-term loan to a firm. Bankers are primarily interested in the firm's near-term, or liquidity, position, so they stress ratios that measure liquidity. In contrast, long-term creditors place far more emphasis on earning power and operating efficiency. They know that unprofitable operations erode asset values and that a strong current position is no guarantee that funds will be available to repay a twenty-year bond issue. Equity investors are similarly interested in long-term profitability and efficiency. Management is, of course, concerned with all these aspects of financial analysis; it must be able to repay its debts to long- and short-term creditors as well as earn profits for stockholders.

It is useful to classify ratios into four fundamental types:

1. *Liquidity ratios,* which measure the firm's ability to meet its maturing short-term obligations.
2. *Leverage ratios,* which measure the extent to which the firm has been financed by debt.
3. *Activity ratios,* which measure how effectively the firm is using its resources.
4. *Profitability ratios,* which measure management's overall effectiveness as shown by the returns generated on sales and investment.

Specific examples of each ratio are given in the following sections, where the Walker-Wilson case history illustrates their calculation and use.

Liquidity Ratios

Generally, the first concern of the financial analyst is liquidity: Is the firm able to meet its maturing obligations? Walker-Wilson has debts totaling $300,000 that must be paid within the coming year. Can these obligations be satisfied? Although a full liquidity analysis requires the use of cash budgets (described in Chapter 7), ratio analysis, by relating the amount of cash and other current assets to the current obligations, provides a quick and easy-to-use measure of liquidity. Two commonly used liquidity ratios are presented here.

Current Ratio The current ratio is computed by dividing current assets by current liabilities. Current assets normally include cash, marketable securities, accounts receivable, and inventories; current liabilities consist of accounts payable, short-term notes payable, current maturities of long-term debt, accrued income taxes, and other accrued expenses (principally wages). The current ratio is the most commonly used measure of short-term solvency, since it indicates the extent to which the claims of short-term creditors are covered by assets that are expected to be converted to cash in a period roughly corresponding to the maturity of the claims.

The calculation of the current ratio for Walker-Wilson at year-end 1978 is shown below.

$$\text{Current ratio} = \frac{\text{Current assets}}{\text{Current liabilities}} = \frac{\$700,000}{\$300,000} = 2.3 \text{ times.}$$

$$\text{Industry average} = 2.5 \text{ times.}$$

The current ratio is slightly below the average for the industry, 2.5, but not low enough to cause concern. It appears that Walker-Wilson is about in line with most other firms in this particular line of business. Since current assets are near maturity, it is highly probable that they could be liquidated at close to book value. With a current ratio of 2.3, Walker-Wilson could liquidate current assets at only 43 percent of book value and still pay off current creditors in full.[1]

Although industry average figures are discussed later in the chapter, it should be stated at this point that the industry average is not a magic number that all firms should strive to maintain. In fact, some well-managed firms are above it, and other good firms are below it. However, if a firm's ratios are very far removed from the average for its industry, the analyst must be concerned about why this variance occurs; that is, a deviation from the industry average should signal the analyst to check further.

Quick Ratio or Acid Test The quick ratio is calculated by deducting inventories from current assets and dividing the remainder by current liabilities. Inventories are typically the least liquid of a firm's current assets and the assets on which losses are most likely to occur in the event of liquidation. Therefore, this measure of the firm's ability to pay off short-term obligations without relying on the sale of inventories is important.

$$\text{Quick ratio or acid test} = \frac{\text{Current assets} - \text{Inventory}}{\text{Current liabilities}} = \frac{\$400,000}{\$300,000}$$

$$= 1.3 \text{ times.}$$

$$\text{Industry average} = 1.0 \text{ times.}$$

The industry average quick ratio is 1, so Walker-Wilson's 1.3 ratio compares favorably with other firms in the industry. Thompson knows that if the mar-

1. $(1/2.3) = .43$, or 43 percent. Note that $(.43)(\$700,000) \approx \$300,000$, the amount of current liabilities.

ketable securities can be sold at par and if he can collect the accounts receivable, he can pay off his current liabilities without selling any inventory.

Leverage Ratios   Leverage ratios, which measure the funds supplied by owners as compared with the financing provided by the firm's creditors, have a number of implications. First, creditors look to the equity, or owner-supplied funds, to provide a margin of safety. If owners have provided only a small proportion of total financing, the risks of the enterprise are borne mainly by the creditors. Second, by raising funds through debt, the owners gain the benefits of maintaining control of the firm with a limited investment. Third, if the firm earns more on the borrowed funds than it pays in interest, the return to the owners is magnified. For example, if assets earn 10 percent and debt costs only 8 percent, there is a 2 percent differential accruing to the stockholders. Leverage cuts both ways, however; if the return on assets falls to 3 percent, the differential between that figure and the cost of debt must be made up from equity's share of total profits. In the first instance, where assets earn more than the cost of debt, leverage is favorable; in the second, it is unfavorable.

Firms with low leverage ratios have less risk of loss when the economy is in a downturn, but they also have lower expected returns when the economy booms. Conversely, firms with high leverage ratios run the risk of large losses but also have a chance of gaining high profits. The prospects of high returns are desirable, but investors are averse to risk. Decisions about the use of leverage, then, must balance higher expected returns against increased risk.[2]

In practice, leverage is approached in two ways. One approach examines balance sheet ratios and determines the extent to which borrowed funds have been used to finance the firm. The other approach measures the risks of debt by income statement ratios designed to determine the number of times fixed charges are covered by operating profits. These sets of ratios are complementary, and most analysts examine both.

Total Debt to Total Assets   The ratio of total debt to total assets, generally called the *debt ratio,* measures the percentage of total funds provided by creditors. Debt includes current liabilities and all bonds. Creditors prefer moderate debt ratios, since the lower the ratio, the greater the cushion against creditors' losses in the event of liquidation. In contrast to the creditors' preference for a low debt ratio, the owners may seek high leverage to magnify earnings or because raising new equity means giving up some degree of control. If the debt ratio is too high, there is a danger of encouraging

2. The problem of determining optimum leverage for a firm with given risk characteristics is examined extensively in Chapters 15 and 16.

irresponsibility on the part of the owners. The owners' stake can become so small that speculative activity, if it is successful, will yield them a substantial percentage return. If the venture is unsuccessful, however, they will incur only a moderate loss because their investment is small.

$$\text{Debt ratio} = \frac{\text{Total debt}}{\text{Total assets}} = \frac{\$1,000,000}{\$2,000,000} = 50\%.$$

$$\text{Industry average} = 33\%.$$

Walker-Wilson's debt ratio is 50 percent; this means that creditors have supplied half the firm's total financing. Since the average debt ratio for this industry—and for manufacturing generally—is about 33 percent, Walker-Wilson would find it difficult to borrow additional funds without first raising more equity capital. Creditors would be reluctant to lend the firm more money, and Thompson would probably be subjecting the stockholders to undue danger if he sought to increase the debt ratio even more by borrowing.[3]

Times Interest Earned The times-interest-earned ratio is determined by dividing earnings before interest and taxes (gross income in Table 4.2) by the interest charges. The ratio measures the extent to which earnings can decline without resultant financial embarrassment to the firm because of inability to meet annual interest costs. Failure to meet this obligation can bring legal action by the creditors, possibly resulting in bankruptcy. Note that the before-tax profit figure is used in the numerator. Because income taxes are computed after interest expense is deducted, the ability to pay current interest is not affected by income taxes.

$$\text{Times interest earned} = \frac{\text{Gross income}}{\text{Interest charges}}$$

$$= \frac{\text{Profit before taxes} + \text{Interest charges}}{\text{Interest charges}}$$

$$= \frac{\$270,000}{\$70,000} = 3.9 \text{ times}.$$

$$\text{Industry average} = 8.0 \text{ times}.$$

3. The ratio of debt to equity is also used in financial analysis. The debt to assets (B/A) and debt to equity (B/S) ratios are simply transformations of one another:

$$B/S = \frac{B/A}{1 - B/A} \quad \text{and} \quad B/A = \frac{B/S}{1 + B/S}.$$

Both ratios increase as a firm of a given size (total assets) uses a greater proportion of debt, but B/A rises linearly and approaches a limit of 100 percent while B/S rises exponentially and approaches infinity.

Walker-Wilson's interest charges consist of three payments totaling $70,000 (see Table 4.2). The firm's gross income available for servicing these charges is $270,000, so the interest is covered 3.9 times. Since the industry average is 8 times, the company is covering its interest charges by a minimum margin of safety and deserves only a poor rating. This ratio reinforces the conclusion based on the debt ratio that the company is likely to face some difficulties if it attempts to borrow additional funds.

Fixed Charge Coverage The fixed charge coverage ratio is similar to the times-interest-earned ratio, but it is somewhat more inclusive in that it recognizes that many firms lease assets and incur long-term obligations under lease contracts.[4] As we show in Chapter 21, leasing has become widespread in recent years, making this ratio preferable to the times-interest-earned ratio for most financial analyses. Fixed charges are defined as interest plus annual long-term lease obligations, and the fixed charge coverage ratio is defined as follows:

$$\text{Fixed charge coverage} = \frac{\begin{array}{c}\text{Profit}\\\text{before taxes}\end{array} + \begin{array}{c}\text{Interest}\\\text{charges}\end{array} + \begin{array}{c}\text{Lease}\\\text{obligations}\end{array}}{\text{Interest charges} + \text{Lease obligations}}$$

$$= \frac{\$200,000 + \$70,000 + \$28,000}{\$70,000 + \$28,000} = \frac{\$298,000}{\$98,000}$$

$$= 3.04 \text{ times.}$$

$$\text{Industry average} = 5.5 \text{ times.}$$

Walker-Wilson's fixed charges are covered 3.04 times, as opposed to an industry average of 5.5 times. Again, this indicates that the firm is somewhat weaker than creditors would prefer it to be, and it points up the difficulties Thompson would likely encounter if he attempted additional borrowing.[5]

Activity Ratios

Activity ratios measure how effectively the firm employs the resources at its command. These ratios all involve comparisons between the level of sales and the investment in various asset accounts. They presume that a "proper" balance should exist between sales and the various asset accounts—

4. Generally, a long-term lease is defined as one extending at least three years into the future. Thus, rent incurred under a one-year lease would not be included in the fixed charge coverage ratio, but rental payments under a three-year or longer lease would be defined as fixed charges.
5. A still more complete coverage ratio is the *debt service coverage ratio,* defined similarly to the fixed charge coverage except that mandatory annual payments to retire long-term debt (amortization payments, discussed in Chapter 20) are also included in the denominator. This ratio is not widely used, primarily because sinking fund obligations are not generally known to outside analysts. Moreover, it is difficult to develop industry averages for the ratio because of the absence of data. The information on lease obligations, in contrast, is almost always available in footnotes to financial statements.

inventories, accounts receivable, fixed assets, and others. As we shall see in the following chapters, this is generally a good assumption.

Inventory Turnover The inventory turnover defined as sales divided by inventory, is shown as follows:

$$\text{Inventory turnover} = \frac{\text{Sales}}{\text{Inventory}} = \frac{\$3,000,000}{\$300,000} = 10 \text{ times.}$$

Industry average = 9 times.

Walker-Wilson's turnover of 10 times compares favorably with an industry average of 9 times. This suggests that the company does not hold excessive stocks of inventory; excess stocks are, of course, unproductive and represent an investment with a low or zero rate of return. The company's high inventory turnover also reinforces Thompson's faith in the current ratio. If the turnover was low—say 3 or 4 times—Thompson would wonder whether the firm was holding damaged or obsolete materials not actually worth their stated value.

Two problems arise in calculating and analyzing the inventory turnover ratio. First, sales are at market prices; if inventories are carried at cost, as they generally are, it is more appropriate to use cost of goods sold in place of sales in the numerator of the formula. However, established compilers of financial ratio statistics, such as Dun & Bradstreet, use the ratio of sales to inventories carried at cost. Therefore, to develop a figure that can be compared with those developed by Dun & Bradstreet it is necessary to measure inventory turnover with sales in the numerator, as we do here.

Second, sales occur over the entire year, whereas the inventory figure is for one point in time. This makes it better to use an average inventory, computed by adding beginning and ending inventories and dividing by 2. If it is determined that the firm's business is highly seasonal, or if there has been a strong upward or downward sales trend during the year, it is essential to make some such adjustment. Neither of these conditions holds for Walker-Wilson; to maintain comparability with industry averages, Thompson did not use the average inventory figure.

Average Collection Period The average collection period, which is a measure of the accounts receivable turnover, is computed in two steps: (1) annual sales are divided by 360 to get the average daily sales,[6] and (2) daily sales are divided into accounts receivable to find the number of days' sales

---

6. Because information on credit sales is generally unavailable, total sales must be used. Since firms do not all have the same percentage of credit sales, there is a good chance that the average collection period will be somewhat in error. Also, note for convenience that the financial community generally uses 360 rather than 365 as the number of days in the year for purposes such as these.

tied up in receivables. This is defined as the average collection period, because it represents the average length of time the firm must wait after making a sale before receiving cash. The calculations for Walker-Wilson show an average collection period of 24 days, slightly above the 20-day industry average.

$$\text{Sales per day} = \frac{\$3,000,000}{360} = \$8,333.$$

$$\text{Average collection period} = \frac{\text{Receivables}}{\text{Sales per day}} = \frac{\$200,000}{\$8,333} = 24 \text{ days.}$$

$$\text{Industry average} = 20 \text{ days.}$$

This ratio can also be evaluated by comparison with the terms on which the firm sells its goods. For example, Walker-Wilson's sales terms call for payment within 20 days, so the 24-day collection period indicates that customers, on the average, are not paying their bills on time. If the collection period over the past few years had been lengthening while the credit policy had not changed, this would have been even stronger evidence that steps should be taken to expedite the collection of accounts receivable.

One additional financial tool should be mentioned in connection with accounts receivable analysis—the *aging schedule,* which breaks down accounts receivable according to how long they have been outstanding. The aging schedule for Walker-Wilson is given below.

Age of Account (Days)	Percent of Total Value of Accounts Receivable
0–20	50
21–30	20
31–45	15
46–60	3
Over 60	12
Total	100

The 24-day collection period looks bad by comparison with the 20-day sales term, and the aging schedule shows that the firm is having especially serious collection problems with some of its accounts: 50 percent are overdue, many for over a month; others pay quite promptly, bringing the average down to only 24 days. But the aging schedule shows this average to be somewhat misleading.

Fixed Assets Turnover The ratio of sales to fixed assets measures the turnover of plant and equipment.

$$\text{Fixed assets turnover} = \frac{\text{Sales}}{\text{Net fixed assets}} = \frac{\$3,000,000}{\$1,300,000} = 2.3 \text{ times.}$$

$$\text{Industry average} = 5.0 \text{ times.}$$

Walker-Wilson's turnover of 2.3 times compares poorly with the industry average of 5 times, indicating that the firm is not using its fixed assets to as high a percentage of capacity as are the other firms in the industry. Thompson should bear this in mind when his production people request funds for new capital investments.

Total Assets Turnover The final activity ratio, which measures the turnover of all the firm's assets, is calculated by dividing sales by total assets.

$$\text{Total assets turnover} = \frac{\text{Sales}}{\text{Total assets}} = \frac{\$3,000,000}{\$2,000,000} = 1.5 \text{ times.}$$

$$\text{Industry average} = 2.0 \text{ times.}$$

Walker-Wilson's turnover of total assets is well below the industry average. The company is simply not generating a sufficient volume of business for the size of its asset investment. Sales should be increased, or some assets should be disposed of, or both.

Profitability Ratios

Profitability is the net result of a large number of policies and decisions. The ratios examined thus far reveal some interesting things about the way the firm is operating, but the profitability ratios give final answers about how effectively the firm is being managed.

Profit Margin on Sales The profit margin on sales, computed by dividing net income after taxes by sales, gives the profit per dollar of sales.

$$\text{Profit margin} = \frac{\text{Net profit after taxes}}{\text{Sales}} = \frac{\$120,000}{\$3,000,000} = 4\%.$$

$$\text{Industry average} = 5\%.$$

Walker-Wilson's profit margin is somewhat below the industry average of 5 percent, indicating that the firm's prices are relatively low or that its costs are relatively high or both.

Return on Total Assets The ratio of net profit to total assets measures the return on total investment in the firm, or the ROI (as it is frequently called).[7]

---

7. In calculating the return on total assets, it is sometimes desirable to add interest to net profits after taxes to form the numerator of the ratios. The theory is that since assets are financed by both stockholders and creditors, the ratio should measure the productivity of assets in providing returns to both classes of investors. We have not done so at this point because the published averages we use for comparative purposes exclude interest. Later in the book, however, when we deal with leverage decisions, we will add back interest. This addition has a material bearing on the value of the ratio for utilities (which have large amounts of fixed assets financed by debt), and the revised ratio is the one normally used for them.

$$\text{Return on total assets} = \frac{\text{Net profit after taxes}}{\text{Total assets}} = \frac{\$120,000}{\$2,000,000} = 6\%.$$

Industry average $= 10\%$.

Walker-Wilson's 6 percent return is well below the 10 percent average for the industry. This low rate results from the low profit margin on sales and from the low turnover of total assets.

Return on Net Worth The ratio of net profit after taxes to net worth measures the rate of return on the stockholders' investment.

$$\text{Return on net worth} = \frac{\text{Net profit after taxes}}{\text{Net worth}} = \frac{\$120,000}{\$1,000,000} = 12\%.$$

Industry average $= 15\%$.

Walker-Wilson's 12 percent return is below the 15 percent industry average but not as far below as the return on total assets. In a later section of this chapter, where the du Pont method of analysis is applied to the Walker-Wilson case, we will see why this is so.

Summary of the Ratios

The individual ratios, which are summarized in Table 4.4, give Thompson a reasonably good idea of Walker-Wilson's main strengths and weaknesses. First, the company's liquidity position is reasonably good; its current and quick ratios appear to be satisfactory by comparison with the industry averages. Second, the leverage ratios suggest that the company is rather heavily indebted. With a debt ratio substantially higher than the industry average, and with coverage ratios well below the industry averages, it is doubtful that Walker-Wilson could do much additional debt financing except on relatively unfavorable terms. Even if Thompson could borrow more, to do so would be subjecting the company to the danger of default and bankruptcy in the event of a business downturn.

Turning to the activity ratios, the inventory turnover and average collection period both indicate that the company's current assets are pretty well in balance, but the low fixed asset turnover suggests that there has been too heavy an investment in fixed assets. This low turnover means, in effect, that the company probably could have operated with a smaller investment in fixed assets. Had the excessive fixed asset investment not been made, the company could have avoided some of its debt financing and would now have lower interest payments. This in turn would have led to improved leverage and coverage ratios.

The profit margin on sales is low, indicating that costs are too high or prices too low or both. In this particular case, the sales prices are in line with those of other firms; high costs are, in fact, the cause of the low mar-

**Table 4.4
Summary of Financial
Ratio Analyses**

Ratio	Formula for Calculation	Calculation	Industry Average	Evaluation
Liquidity				
Current	$\dfrac{\text{Current assets}}{\text{Current liabilities}}$	$\dfrac{\$700,000}{\$300,000} = 2.3$ times	2.5 times	Satisfactory
Quick ratio or acid test	$\dfrac{\text{Current assets} - \text{Inventory}}{\text{Current liabilities}}$	$\dfrac{\$400,000}{\$300,000} = 1.3$ times	1 time	Good
Leverage				
Debt to total assets	$\dfrac{\text{Total debt}}{\text{Total assets}}$	$\dfrac{\$1,000,000}{\$2,000,000} = 50$ percent	33 percent	Poor
Times interest earned	$\dfrac{\text{Profit before taxes plus interest charges}}{\text{Interest charges}}$	$\dfrac{\$270,000}{\$70,000} = 3.9$ times	8 times	Poor
Fixed charge coverage	$\dfrac{\text{Income available for meeting fixed charges}}{\text{Fixed charges}}$	$\dfrac{\$298,000}{\$98,000} = 3.04$ times	5.5 times	Poor
Activity				
Inventory turnover	$\dfrac{\text{Sales}}{\text{Inventory}}$	$\dfrac{\$3,000,000}{\$300,000} = 10$ times	9 times	Satisfactory
Average collection period	$\dfrac{\text{Receivables}}{\text{Sales per day}}$	$\dfrac{\$200,000}{\$8,333} = 24$ days	20 days	Satisfactory
Fixed assets turnover	$\dfrac{\text{Sales}}{\text{Fixed assets}}$	$\dfrac{\$3,000,000}{\$1,300,000} = 2.3$ times	5 times	Poor
Total assets turnover	$\dfrac{\text{Sales}}{\text{Total assets}}$	$\dfrac{\$3,000,000}{\$2,000,000} = 1.5$ times	2 times	Poor
Profitability				
Profit margin on sales	$\dfrac{\text{Net profit after taxes}}{\text{Sales}}$	$\dfrac{\$120,000}{\$3,000,000} = 4$ percent	5 percent	Fair
Return on total assets	$\dfrac{\text{Net profit after taxes}}{\text{Total assets}}$	$\dfrac{\$120,000}{\$2,000,000} = 6$ percent	10 percent	Poor
Return on net worth	$\dfrac{\text{Net profit after taxes}}{\text{Net worth}}$	$\dfrac{\$120,000}{\$1,000,000} = 12$ percent	15 percent	Fair

gin. Further, the high costs can be traced to high depreciation charges and high interest expenses, both of which are in turn attributable to the excessive investment in fixed assets.

Returns on total investment and net worth are also below the industry averages. These relatively poor results are directly attributable to the low profit margin on sales, which lowers the numerators of the ratios, and to the excessive investment, which raises the denominators.

Trend Analysis

While the preceding ratio analysis gives a reasonably good picture of Walker-Wilson's operation, it is incomplete in one important respect—it ignores the time dimension. The ratios are snapshots of the picture at one point in time, but there may be trends in motion that are in the process of rapidly eroding a relatively good present position. Conversely, an analysis of the ratios over the past few years may suggest that a relatively weak position is being improved at a rapid rate.

The method of trend analysis is illustrated in Figure 4.1, which shows graphs of Walker-Wilson's sales, current ratio, debt ratio, fixed assets turnover, and return on net worth. The figures are compared with industry averages. Industry sales have been rising steadily over the entire period, and the industry average ratios have been relatively stable throughout. Thus, any trends in the company's ratios are due to its own internal conditions, not to environmental influences on all firms. In addition, Walker-Wilson's deterioration since the death of the two principal officers is quite apparent. Prior to 1973, the company was growing more rapidly than the average firm in the industry; during the following two years, however, sales actually declined.

Walker-Wilson's liquidity position as measured by its current ratio has also gone downhill in the past two years. Although the ratio is only slightly below the industry average at the present time, the trend suggests that a real liquidity crisis may develop during the next year or two unless corrective action is taken immediately.

The debt ratio trend line shows that Walker-Wilson followed industry practices closely until 1976, when the ratio jumped to a full 10 percentage points above the industry average. Similarly, the fixed assets turnover declined during 1976, even though sales were still rising. The records reveal that the company borrowed heavily during 1976 to finance a major expansion of plant and equipment. Walker and Wilson had intended to use this additional capacity to generate a still higher volume of sales and to retire the debt out of expected high profits. Their untimely death, however, led to a decrease rather than an increase in sales, and the expected high profits that were to be used to retire the debt did not materialize. The analysis suggests that the

Figure 4.1
Illustration of Trend Analysis

Sales as a percent of 1967 sales

Walker-Wilson

Industry average

100

1967   1970   1973   1976   1979

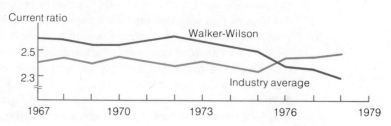

Current ratio

Walker-Wilson

2.5

2.3

Industry average

1967   1970   1973   1976   1979

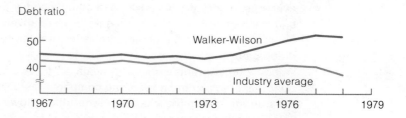

Debt ratio

Walker-Wilson

50

40

Industry average

1967   1970   1973   1976   1979

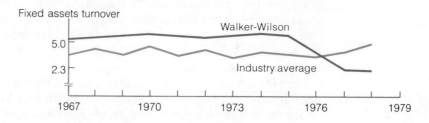

Fixed assets turnover

Walker-Wilson

5.0

2.3

Industry average

1967   1970   1973   1976   1979

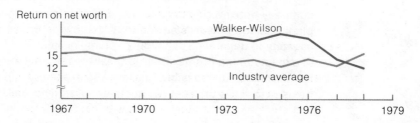

Return on net worth

Walker-Wilson

15

12

Industry average

1967   1970   1973   1976   1979

bankers were correct when they advised Mrs. Walker and Mrs. Wilson of the need for a change in management.

du Pont System of Financial Analysis

The du Pont system of financial analysis has achieved wide recognition in American industry, and properly so. It brings together the activity ratios and profit margin on sales and shows how these ratios interact to determine the profitability of assets. The nature of the system, modified somewhat, is set forth in Figure 4.2.

The right side of the figure develops the turnover ratio. It shows how current assets (cash, marketable securities, accounts receivable, and inventories) added to fixed assets give total investment. Total investment divided into sales gives the turnover of investment.

The left side of the figure develops the profit margin on sales. The individual expense items plus income taxes are subtracted from sales to produce net profits after taxes. Net profits divided by sales give the profit margin on sales. When the asset turnover ratio on the right side of Figure 4.2 is multiplied by the profit margin on sales developed on the left side of the figure, the product is the return on total investment (ROI) in the firm. This can be seen from the following formula:

$$\frac{\text{Profit}}{\text{Sales}} \times \frac{\text{Sales}}{\text{Investment}} = \text{ROI}.$$

Walker-Wilson's turnover was 1.5 times, as compared to an industry average of 2 times; its margin on sales was 4 percent, as compared to 5 percent for the industry. Multiplied together, turnover and profit margin produced a return on assets equal to 6 percent, a rate well below the 10 percent industry average. If Thompson is to bring Walker-Wilson back to the level of the rest of the industry, he should strive to boost both his profit margin and his total asset turnover. Tracing back through the du Pont system should help him in this task.

Extending the du Pont System to Include Leverage

Although Walker-Wilson's return on total assets is well below the 10 percent industry average, the firm's 12 percent return on net worth is only slightly below the 15 percent industry average. How can the return on net worth end up so close to the industry average when the return on total assets is so far below it? The answer is that Walker-Wilson uses more debt than the average firm in the industry.

Only half of Walker-Wilson's assets are financed with net worth; the other half are financed with debt. This means that the entire 6 percent return on assets (which is computed after interest charges on debt) goes to the common stockholders, so their return is boosted substantially. The precise for-

**Figure 4.2
Modified du Pont System of
Financial Control Applied to
Walker-Wilson**

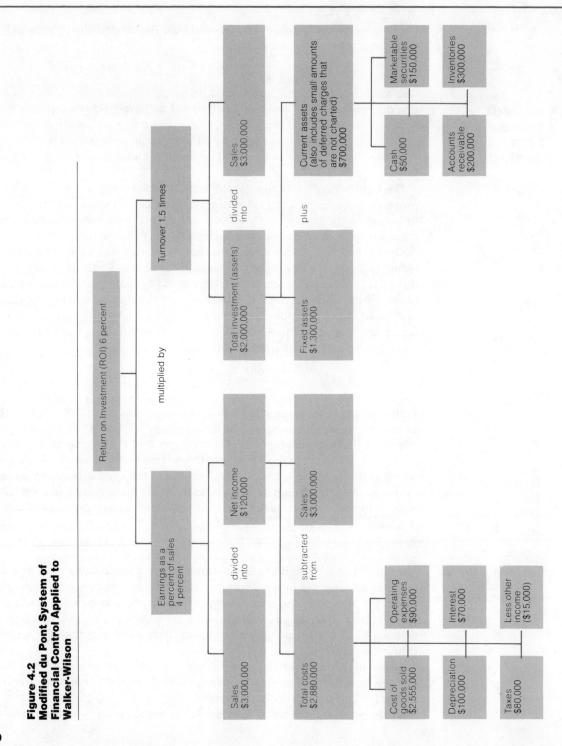

mula for measuring the effect of financial leverage on stockholder returns is shown below.

$$\text{Rate of return on net worth} = \frac{\text{Return on assets (ROI)}}{\text{Percent of assets financed by net worth}}$$

$$= \frac{\text{Return on assets (ROI)}}{1.0 - \text{Debt ratio}}.$$

Calculation for Walker-Wilson:

$$\text{Return on net worth} = \frac{6\%}{1.0 - 0.50} = \frac{6\%}{0.5} = 12\%.$$

Calculation for the industry average:

$$\text{Return on net worth} = \frac{10\%}{1.0 - 0.33} = \frac{10\%}{0.67} = 15\%.$$

This formula is useful for showing how financial leverage can be used to increase the rate of return on net worth.[8] But increasing returns on net worth by using more and more leverage causes the leverage ratios to rise higher and higher above the industry norms. Creditors resist this tendency, so there are limitations to the practice. Moreover, greater leverage increases the risk of bankruptcy and thus endangers the firm's stockholders. Since widows Walker and Wilson are entirely dependent on income from the firm for their support, they will be in a particularly bad position if the firm goes into default. Consequently, Thompson would be ill-advised to attempt to use leverage to boost the return on net worth much further.

Rates of Return in Different Industries

Would it be better to have a 5 percent margin on sales and a total asset turnover of 2 times or a 2 percent sales margin and a turnover of 5 times? It makes no difference; in either case the firm has a 10 percent return on investment. Actually, most firms are not free to make the kind of choice posed in this question. Depending on the nature of its industry, the firm *must* operate with more or fewer assets, and its turnover will depend on the characteristics of its particular line of business. In the case of a dealer in fresh fruits and vegetables, fish, or other perishable items, the turnover should be high—every day or two is most desirable. In contrast, some lines of business require heavy fixed investment or long production periods. A hydroelectric utility company, with its heavy investment in dams and transmis-

8. There are limitations on this statement; specifically, the return on net worth increases with leverage only if the return on assets exceeds the rate of interest on debt, after considering the tax deductibility of interest payments. This whole concept is explored in detail in Chapter 15, which is devoted entirely to financial leverage.

sion lines, requires heavy fixed investment; a shipbuilder or an aircraft producer needs a long production period. Such companies necessarily have a low asset turnover rate but a correspondingly higher profit margin on sales.

If a grocery chain has a high turnover and a chemical producer, with its heavy investment in fixed assets, a low turnover, should there be differences in their profit margins on sales? In general, yes. The chemical producer should have a considerably higher profit margin to offset its lower turnover. Otherwise, the grocery industry would be much more profitable than the chemical, investment would flow into the grocery industry, and profits in this industry would be eroded to the point where the rate of return was about equal to that in the chemical industry.

We know, however, that leverage must be taken into account when considering the rate of return on net worth. If the firms in one industry have a somewhat lower return on total assets but use slightly more financial leverage than do those in another industry, both sets of firms may end up with approximately the same rate of return on net worth.[9]

These points, which are all necessary for a complete understanding of ratio analysis, are illustrated in Table 4.5. There we see how turnover and profit margins interact with each other to produce varying returns on assets and how financial leverage affects the returns on net worth. Crown-Zellerbach, Kroger, and the average of all manufacturing firms are compared. Crown-Zellerbach, with its very heavy fixed asset investment, is seen to have a relatively low turnover; Kroger, a typical chain food store, has a very high sales-to-assets ratio. Crown-Zellerbach, however, ends up with

**Table 4.5
Turnover, Profit Margins, and
Returns on Net Worth**

	Sales to Total Assets (Times)	× Profit to Sales (Percent)	= Profit to Total Assets (Percent)	Debt to Total Assets (Percent)	Profit to Net Worth (Percent)[a]
All manufacturing firms	1.42	5.3	7.5	46	13.9
Crown-Zellerbach (forest products)	1.30	4.59	5.97	48.8	11.7
Kroger (food retailer)	8.43	0.65	5.48	32.8	8.1

[a] The figures in this column can be found as:

$$\text{Profit to net worth} = \frac{\text{Profit to total assets}}{1 - \text{Debt to total assets}}$$

Sources: FTC quarterly financial reports and company annual reports for 1976.

9. The factors that make it possible for firms to use more leverage are taken up in Chapters 15 and 20. It can be stated now, however, that the primary factors favoring leverage are sales and profit stability.

about the same rate of return on assets because its high profit margin on sales compensates for its low turnover. Both Kroger and Crown-Zellerbach use financial leverage to increase their return on net worth.

Sources of Comparative Ratios

In our analysis of the Walker-Wilson Company, we frequently used industry average ratios. Where are such averages obtained? Some important sources are listed below.

Dun & Bradstreet

Probably the most widely known and used of the industry average ratios are those compiled by Dun & Bradstreet. D&B provides fourteen ratios calculated for a large number of industries, samples and explanations of which are shown in Table 4.6. The complete data give the fourteen ratios, with the interquartile ranges, for 125 types of business activity based on their financial statements.[10] The 125 are comprised of 71 manufacturing and construction categories, 30 categories of wholesalers, and 24 categories of retailers.

Robert Morris Associates

Another group of useful ratios can be found in the annual *Statement Studies* compiled and published by Robert Morris Associates, the national association of bank loan officers. These are representative averages based on financial statements received by banks in connection with loans made. Eleven ratios are computed for 156 lines of business.

Quarterly Financial Report for Manufacturing Corporations

The Federal Trade Commission (FTC) publishes quarterly financial data on manufacturing companies. Both balance sheet and income statement data are developed from a systematic sample of corporations. The reports are published perhaps six months after the financial data have been made available by the companies. They include an analysis by industry groups and by asset size and financial statements in ratio form (or common-size analysis) as well. The FTC reports are a rich source of information and are frequently used for comparative purposes.

10. The median and quartile ratios can be illustrated by an example. The median ratio of current assets to current debt of manufacturers of airplane parts and accessories, as shown in Table 4.6, is 2.68. To obtain this figure, the ratios of current assets to current debt for each of the 63 concerns were arranged in a graduated series, with the largest ratio at the top and the smallest at the bottom. The median ratio of 2.68 is the ratio halfway between the top and the bottom. The ratio of 3.94, representing the upper quartile, is one-quarter of the way down from the top (or halfway between the top and the median). The ratio 1.85, representing the lower quartile, is one-quarter of the way up from the bottom (or halfway between the median and the bottom).

Table 4.6
Dun & Bradstreet Ratios
for Selected Industries

Line of Business (and Number of Concerns Reporting)[a]	Current Assets to Current Debt (Times)	Net Profits on Net Sales (Percent)	Net Profits on Tangible Net Worth (Percent)	Net Profits on Net Working Capital (Percent)	Net Sales to Tangible Net Worth (Times)	Net Sales to Net Working Capital (Times)	Collection Period (Days)
2873-74-75-79	3.73	5.97	18.79	31.32	5.44	8.66	23
Agricultural chemicals (51)	2.50	3.53	13.07	20.29	3.52	5.43	45
	1.75	1.78	5.92	10.59	2.08	3.12	65
3724-28	3.94	6.51	19.17	23.76	4.50	5.11	30
Airplane parts	2.68	5.13	13.77	16.27	2.63	3.58	47
and accessories (63)	1.85	2.38	6.00	7.25	1.84	3.02	60
2051-52	3.48	4.13	17.01	38.87	9.56	19.29	21
Bakery products (68)	2.01	1.86	9.63	24.79	5.55	12.41	24
	1.26	0.92	4.06	7.83	4.15	7.55	30
3312-13-15-16-17	3.01	5.70	15.08	31.08	3.50	6.96	34
Blast furnaces, steel	2.25	4.05	9.13	17.53	2.51	5.33	40
works, and rolling mills (52)	1.80	2.15	6.22	11.27	2.10	3.53	47
2331	2.68	4.00	21.52	25.52	13.20	15.06	27
Blouses and waists,	1.71	2.11	11.86	16.01	7.43	9.10	33
women's and misses' (49)	1.47	0.77	7.77	9.57	4.60	5.20	51
2731-32	4.02	8.53	16.13	19.65	3.56	4.23	41
Books, publishing,	2.65	5.03	9.60	13.54	2.17	2.94	57
publishing and printing (48)	1.86	1.56	4.48	5.97	1.52	2.16	72
2211	3.65	4.48	12.66	21.01	3.28	6.06	42
Broad woven	2.97	2.85	8.09	13.67	3.05	4.55	57
fabrics, cotton (42)	2.24	1.90	4.60	6.99	2.21	3.56	66
2032-33-34-35-37-38	2.61	3.93	14.85	19.50	5.33	13.54	15
Canned and preserved	1.82	2.00	7.51	11.15	3.83	6.65	23
fruits and vegetables (76)	1.24	0.50	0.70	0.80	2.79	4.25	31

[a] Standard Industrial Classification (SIC) categories.

Source: "The Ratios of Manufacturing," *Dun's Review,* December 1977, p. 93. Reprinted with the special permission of *Dun's Review,* December 1977. Copyright, 1977, Dun & Bradstreet Publications Corporation.

Individual Firms Credit departments of individual firms compile financial ratios and averages on their customers in order to judge their ability to meet obligations and on their suppliers in order to evaluate their financial ability to fulfill contracts. The First National Bank of Chicago, for instance, compiles semiannual re-

Table 4.6 Continued

Line of Business (and Number of Concerns Reporting)[a]	Net Sales to Inventory (Times)	Fixed Assets to Tangible Net Worth (Percent)	Current Debt to Tangible Net Worth (Percent)	Total Debt to Tangible Net Worth (Percent)	Inventory to Net Working Capital (Percent)	Current Debt to Inventory (Percent)	Funded Debts to Net Working Capital (Percent)
2873-74-75-79	16.6	22.9	25.6	44.1	33.5	96.9	8.9
Agricultural chemicals (51)	9.7	35.3	40.3	56.5	70.6	119.2	17.4
	5.6	60.7	79.9	128.5	100.1	183.8	60.5
3724-28	10.3	28.7	25.7	41.3	50.2	62.9	13.9
Airplane parts	5.4	48.7	43.3	62.8	72.0	98.5	38.3
and accessories (63)	3.9	61.6	71.3	120.6	100.7	147.2	70.4
2051-52	40.2	50.4	18.4	52.6	27.1	105.3	21.4
Bakery products (68)	25.8	76.3	46.5	84.9	59.5	171.6	69.4
	17.6	117.5	81.7	151.9	118.8	328.4	154.6
3312-13-15-16-17	6.8	52.2	28.0	59.8	72.0	56.6	46.7
Blast furnaces, steel	5.2	82.9	36.1	83.0	91.4	80.7	76.0
works, and rolling mills (52)	4.1	104.6	64.3	125.1	111.3	107.4	110.3
2331	16.2	3.6	46.6	62.3	54.8	95.8	7.1
Blouses and waists,	11.6	9.8	100.0	105.1	92.1	140.2	19.6
women's and misses' (49)	6.8	25.4	205.3	241.0	124.8	232.0	37.1
2731-32	8.1	9.8	21.5	45.0	53.2	53.7	12.4
Books, publishing,	5.0	27.8	41.0	60.7	67.8	92.7	23.6
publishing and printing (48)	3.1	49.9	73.7	124.1	97.2	234.6	80.3
2211	10.0	38.4	21.5	42.2	54.1	55.1	21.0
Broad woven	7.6	54.2	31.2	72.6	70.0	80.4	41.4
fabrics, cotton (42)	5.9	66.7	48.1	114.7	88.7	106.2	78.0
2032-33-34-35-37-38	8.7	38.9	40.5	70.2	87.5	65.0	18.3
Canned and preserved	4.4	62.6	66.9	120.4	129.3	91.0	46.1
fruits and vegetables (76)	3.5	94.0	123.9	188.2	257.9	130.4	108.5

ports on the financial data for finance companies. NCR gathers data for a large number of business lines.

Trade Associations and Public Accountants

Financial ratios for many industries are compiled by trade associations and constitute an important source to be checked by a financial manager seeking comparative data. These averages are usually the best obtainable. In addition to balance sheet data, they provide detailed information on operating expenses, which makes possible an informed analysis of the firms' efficiency.

Use of Financial Ratios in Credit Analysis

We have analyzed a rather long list of ratios, determining what each ratio is designed to measure. Sometimes it is unnecessary to go beyond a few of these calculations to determine that a firm is in very good or very bad condition, but often what one ratio will not indicate, another may. Also, a relationship vaguely suggested by one ratio may be corroborated by another. For these reasons, it is generally useful to calculate a number of different ratios.

In numerous situations, however, a few ratios tell the story. For example, a credit manager who has a great many invoices flowing across her desk each day may limit herself to three ratios as evidence of whether the prospective buyer of goods will pay promptly. She may use (1) either the current or the quick ratio to determine how burdened the prospective buyer is with current liabilities, (2) the debt to total assets ratio to determine how much of the prospective buyer's own funds are invested in the business, and (3) any of the profitability ratios to determine whether the firm has favorable prospects. If the profit margin is high enough, it may justify the risk of dealing with a slow-paying customer (profitable companies are likely to grow and thus to become better customers in the future). However, if the profit margin is low in relation to other firms in the industry, if the current ratio is low, and if the debt ratio is high, a credit manager probably will not approve a sale involving an extension of credit.[11]

Of necessity, the credit manager is more than a calculator and a reader of financial ratios. Qualitative factors may override quantitative analysis. For instance, in selling to truckers, oil companies often find that the financial ratios are adverse and that if they based their decisions solely on financial ratios, they would not make sales. Or, to take another example, profits may have been low for a period, but if the customer understands why and can remove the cause of the difficulty, a credit manager may be willing to approve a sale to that customer. This decision is also influenced by the profit margin of the selling firm. If it is making a large profit on sales, it is in a better position to take credit risks than if its own margin is low. Ultimately, the

11. Statistical techniques have been developed to improve the use of ratios in credit analysis. One such development is the discriminant analysis model reported by Edward I. Altman in "Financial Ratios, Discriminant Analysis, and the Prediction of Corporate Bankruptcy," *Journal of Finance* 23 (September 1968). In his model, Altman combines a number of liquidity, leverage, activity, and profitability ratios to form an index of a firm's probability of going bankrupt. His model has predicted bankruptcy quite well one or two years before it occurs. See also Edward I. Altman, Robert G. Haldeman, and P. Narayanan, "ZETA Analysis: A New Model to Identify Bankruptcy Risk of Corporations," *Journal of Banking and Finance* 1 (June 1977).

credit manager must judge each customer on character and management ability, and intelligent credit decisions must be based on careful consideration of conditions in the selling firm as well as in the buying firm.

Use of Financial Ratios in Security Analysis

We have emphasized the use of financial analysis by the financial manager and by outside credit analysts. However, this type of analysis is also useful in security analysis—the analysis of the investment merits of stocks and bonds. When the emphasis is on security analysis, the principal focus is on judging the long-run profit potential of the firm. Profitability is dependent in large part on the efficiency with which the firm is run; because financial analysis provides insights into this factor, it is useful to the security analyst.

Some Limitations of Ratio Analysis

Although ratios are exceptionally useful tools, they do have limitations and must be used with caution. Ratios are constructed from accounting data, and these data are subject to different interpretations and even to manipulation. For example, two firms may use different depreciation methods or inventory valuation methods; depending on the procedures followed, reported profits can be raised or lowered. Similar differences can be encountered in the treatment of research and development expenditures, pension plan costs, mergers, product warranties, and bad-debt reserves. Further, if firms use different fiscal years, and if seasonal factors are important, this can influence the comparative ratios. Thus, if the ratios of two firms are to be compared, it is important to analyze the basic accounting data upon which the ratios were based and to reconcile any major differences.

A financial manager must also be cautious in judging whether a particular ratio is "good" or "bad" and in forming a composite judgment about a firm on the basis of a set of ratios. For example, a high inventory turnover ratio could indicate efficient inventory management, but it could also indicate a serious shortage of inventories and suggest the likelihood of stock-outs. When financial ratio analysis indicates that the patterns of a firm depart from industry norms, this is not an absolutely certain indication that something is wrong with the firm. Such departures provide a basis for questions and further investigation and analysis. Additional information and discussions may establish sound explanations for the differences between the pattern for the individual firm and industry composite ratios. Or the differences may reveal forms of mismanagement calling for correction.

Conversely, conformance to industry composite ratios does not establish with certainty that the firm is performing normally and is managed well. In the short run many tricks can be used to make a firm look good in relation to industry standards. The analyst must develop first-hand knowledge of the operations and management of the firm to provide a check on the financial ratios. In addition, the analyst must develop a sixth sense—a touch, a smell, a feel—for what is going on in the firm. Sometimes it is this kind of business judgment that uncovers weaknesses in the firm. The analyst should not be anesthetized by financial ratios that appear to conform with normality.

Ratios, then, are extremely useful tools. But as with other analytical methods, they must be used with judgment and caution, not in an unthinking, mechanical manner. Financial ratio analysis is a useful part of an investigation process. But financial ratios alone are not the complete answer to questions about the performance of firms.

Summary

Ratio analysis, which relates balance sheet and income statement items to one another, permits the charting of a firm's history and the evaluation of its present position. It also allows the financial manager to anticipate reactions of investors and creditors and thus to gain insight into how attempts to acquire funds are likely to be received.

Ratios are classified into four basic types: liquidity, leverage, activity, and profitability. Data from the Walker-Wilson Manufacturing Company are used to compute each type of ratio and to show how a financial analysis is made in practice. An almost unlimited number of ratios can be calculated, but in practice a limited number of each type is sufficient.

A ratio is not a meaningful number in and of itself; it must be compared with something before it becomes useful. The two basic kinds of comparative analysis are (1) trend analysis, which involves computing the ratio of a particular firm for several years and comparing the ratios over time to see if the firm is improving or deteriorating, and (2) comparisons with other firms in the same industry. These two comparisons are often combined in the graphic analysis illustrated in Figure 4.1.

The du Pont system shows how the return on investment is dependent on the profit margin and asset turnover. The system is generally expressed in the form of the following equation:

$$\frac{Profit}{Sales} \times \frac{Sales}{Investment} = ROI.$$

The first term, the profit margin, times investment turnover equals the rate of return on investment. The kinds of actions discussed in this chapter can be used to effect needed changes in turnover and the profit margin and thus improve the return on investment.

The du Pont system can be extended to encompass financial leverage and to examine the manner in which turnover, sales margins, and leverage all combine to determine the rate of return on net worth. The following equation is used to show this relationship:

$$\text{Rate of return on net worth} = \frac{\text{Return on assets (ROI)}}{1.0 - \text{Debt ratio}}$$

The extended du Pont system shows why firms in different industries—even though they have widely different turnovers, profit margins, and debt ratios—may end up with very similar rates of return on net worth. In general, firms dealing with relatively perishable commodities are expected to have high turnovers but low profit margins; firms whose production processes require heavy investments in fixed assets are expected to have low turnover ratios but high profit margins.

Questions

4.1 "A uniform system of accounts, including identical forms for balance sheets and income statements, would be a most reasonable requirement for the SEC to impose on all publicly owned firms." Discuss.

4.2 We have divided financial ratios into four groups: liquidity, leverage, activity, and profitability. We could also consider financial analysis as being conducted by four groups of analysts: management, equity investors, long-term creditors, and short-term creditors.
a. Explain the nature of each type of ratio.
b. Explain the emphasis of each type of analyst.

4.3 Why can norms with relatively well-defined limits be stated in advance for some financial ratios but not for others?

4.4 How does trend analysis supplement the basic financial ratio calculations and their interpretation?

4.5 Why should the inventory turnover figure be more important to a grocery store than to a shoe repair store?

4.6 How can a firm have a high current ratio and still be unable to pay its bills?

4.7 "The higher the rate of return on investment (ROI), the better the firm's management." Is this statement true for all firms? Explain. If you disagree with the statement, give examples of instances in which it might not be true.

4.8 What factors would you, as a financial manager, want to examine if a firm's rate of return (a) on assets or (b) on net worth was too low?

4.9 Profit margins and turnover rates vary from industry to industry. What industry characteristics account for these variations? Give some contrasting examples to illustrate your answer.

4.10 Which relation would you, as a financial manager, prefer: (a) a profit margin of 10 percent and a capital turnover of 2, or (b) a profit margin of 20 percent and a capital turnover of 1? Can you think of any firm with a relation similar to b?

Problems

4.1 The Metler Company has $1,200,000 in current assets and $800,000 in current liabilities. How much can its short-term debt (notes payable) increase without violating a current ratio of 2 to 1? (The funds from the additional notes payable will be used to increase inventory.)

4.2 Complete the balance sheet and sales information (fill in the blanks) for the Fiske Company using the following financial data:

Debt/net worth: 40 percent
Acid test ratio: 1.2
Total asset turnover: 2.0 times
Days' sales outstanding in accounts receivable: 30
Gross profit margin: 30 percent
Sales to inventory turnover: 4 times

Balance Sheet

Cash	_____	Accounts payable	_____
Accounts receivable	_____	Common stock	$15,000
Inventories	_____	Retained earnings	$33,000
Plant and equipment	_____	Total liabilities	
Total assets	_____	and capital	_____
Sales	_____	Cost of goods sold	_____

4.3 The following data were taken from the financial statements of the Michigan Furniture Company for the calendar year 1975. The norms given below are based on industry averages for the Dun & Bradstreet category "wood household furniture and upholstered" taken from *Dun's Review*, December 1976.
   a. Fill in the ratios for the Michigan Furniture Company.
   b. Indicate by comparison with industry norms the possible errors in management policies reflected in these financial statements.

Michigan Furniture Company
Balance Sheet as of
December 31, 1975

Assets		Liabilities	
Cash	$ 11,000	Accounts payable	$ 45,000
Receivables	104,000	Notes payable (at 8%)	21,000
Inventory	250,000	Other current liabilities	39,000
Total current assets	$365,000	Total current liabilities	$105,000
Net fixed assets	110,000	Long-term debt (at 9%)	115,000
		Net worth	255,000
Total assets	$475,000	Total claims on assets	$475,000

**Michigan Furniture Company
Income Statement for Year Ended
December 31, 1975**

Sales		$760,000
Cost of goods sold:		
Material	$240,000	
Labor	210,000	
Heat, light, and power	25,600	
Indirect labor	30,000	
Depreciation	22,000	527,600
Gross profit		$232,400
Selling expense	$ 80,000	
General and administrative expense	110,000	190,000
Operating profit (EBIT)		$ 42,400
Less interest expense		−12,000
Net profit before tax		30,400
Less federal income tax (at 50%)		−15,200
Net profit		$ 15,200

Michigan Furniture Company

Ratio	Ratio	Industry Norm
$\dfrac{\text{Current assets}}{\text{Current liabilities}}$		3.1 times
$\dfrac{\text{Debt}}{\text{Total assets}}$		45%
Times interest earned		4.8 times
$\dfrac{\text{Sales}}{\text{Inventory}}$		5.2 times
Average collection period		46 days
$\dfrac{\text{Sales}}{\text{Total assets}}$		2.0 times
$\dfrac{\text{Net profit}}{\text{Sales}}$		2.8%
$\dfrac{\text{Net profit}}{\text{Total assets}}$		5.6%
$\dfrac{\text{Net profit}}{\text{Net worth}}$		10.2%

4.4 The following data were taken from the financial statements of Midland Drug and Proprietary Company, a wholesaler of drugs, drug proprietaries, and sundries, for the calendar year 1975. The norms given below are the industry averages for wholesale drugs, drug proprietaries, and sundries.

a. Fill in the ratios for Midland Drug and Proprietary Company.

b. Indicate by comparison with the industry norms the possible errors in management policies reflected in these financial statements.

**Midland Drug
and Proprietary Company
Balance Sheet as of
December 31, 1975
(Thousands of Dollars)**

Assets		Liabilities	
Cash	$ 193	Accounts payable	$ 316
Receivables	820	Notes payable (at 6%)	206
Inventory	592	Other current liabilities	283
Total current assets	$1,605	Total current liabilities	$ 805
Net fixed assets	715	Long-term debt (at 5%)	633
		Net worth	882
Total assets	$2,320	Total claims on assets	$2,320

**Midland Drug
and Proprietary Company
Income Statement for Year Ended
December 31, 1975 (Thousands
of Dollars)**

Sales	$3,936	
Cost of goods sold	3,411	
Gross profit		$525
Operating expenses	282	
Depreciation expense	79	
Interest expense	44	
Total expenses		405
Net income before tax		$120
Taxes (at 50%)		60
Net income		$ 60

**Midland Drug
and Proprietary Company**

Ratio	Ratio	Industry Norm
Current assets / Current liabilities		1.97 times
Debt / Total assets		60%
Times interest earned		3.79 times
Sales / Inventory		6.7 times
Average collection period		36 days
Sales / Total assets		2.94 times
Net profit / Sales		1.14%
Net profit / Total assets		3.35%
Net profit / Net worth		8.29%

4.5 Silicon Valley Electronic Supply Company, a closely held family manufacturer of electronic components, has, since the death of its founder/president
Marilyn Hickley two years ago, been managed by her nephew Ron, formerly
a company salesman. Ed Smith, the account manager at the firm's bank,
has received numerous complaints about Ron's actions from the family and
has asked you to evaluate his performance. The company's most recent
financial statements are reproduced below.
a. Calculate the relevant financial ratios for this analysis.
b. Apply a du Pont chart analysis to Silicon Valley.
c. Evaluate Ron's performance, and list specific areas that need improvement.

Industry Average Ratios

Current ratio: 2.2
Quick ratio: 1.0
Debt to total assets: 50%
Times interest earned: 5.2 times
Inventory turnover: 5.1 times
Average collection period: 52 days
Fixed assets turnover: 9.25 times
Total assets turnover: 1.85 times
Net profit on sales: 3.19%
Return on total assets: 5.90%
Return on net worth: 10.8%

**Common-Size Balance Sheets
for Electronic Components
Industry, 1975**

Assets	Norm (Percent)	Liabilities	Norm (Percent)
Cash	6.8	Due to banks—short term	7.6
Marketable securities	3.5	Due to trade	11.3
Receivables net	24.9	Income taxes	2.3
Inventory net	33.8	Current maturities—long-term debt	2.3
All other current	2.5	All other current	8.6
Total current	71.5	Total current debt	32.1
Fixed assets net	25.0	Noncurrent debt, unsubordinated	13.9
All other noncurrent	3.5	Subordinated debt	1.7
		Tangible net worth	52.3
Total assets	100.0	Total claim on assets	100.0

Note: The balance sheet is for 101 firms of asset size greater than $1 million and less than $10 million.

Based on data appearing in the 1976 Annual Statement Studies, copyrighted by Robert Morris Associates, 1976, p. 71, manufacturers of electronic components and accessories.

**Common-Size Income
Statements for Electronic
Components Industry, 1975**

Net sales	100.0%	
Cost of sales	77.9	
Gross profit		22.1%
Selling and delivery expenses	4.2%	
Officers' salaries	2.5	
Other general administrative expenses	8.5	
All other expenses net	1.1	
Operating expenses		16.3
Net income before tax		5.8%
Taxes at 45% (assumed)		2.61
Net income		3.19%

Note: The income statement is for 13 firms of asset size greater than $1 million and less than $10 million.

Based on data appearing in the 1976 Annual Statement Studies, copyrighted by Robert Morris Associates, 1976, p. 216, manufacturers of electronic components and accessories.

**Silicon Valley
Electronic Supply Company
Balance Sheet as of
December 31, 1975
(Thousands of Dollars)**

Assets			Liabilities		
Cash	$	90	Accounts payable	$450	
Marketable securities	$	40	Notes payable (at 11%)	380	
Receivables		1,550	Other current liabilities	280	
Inventory		1,190	Total current liabilities		$1,110
Total current assets		$2,870	Long-term debt (at 9%)		880
Net fixed assets		1,130	Total liabilities		$1.990
			Net worth		2,010
Total assets		$4,000	Total claims on assets		$4.000

**Silicon Valley
Electronic Supply Company
Income Statement for Year
Ended December 31, 1975
(Thousands of Dollars)**

Sales		$6,200
Cost of goods sold:		
Materials	$2,440	
Labor	1,540	
Heat, light, and power	230	
Indirect labor	370	
Depreciation	140	4,720
Gross profit		$1,480
Selling expenses	490	
General and administrative expenses	530	1,020
Operating profit		$ 460
Less interest expense		−121
Net profit before taxes		$ 339
Less federal income taxes (assumed 45% rate)		−152
Net profit		$ 187

Appendix 4A Impact of Inflation on Financial Ratios

Immediately after World War II, with the removal of price controls that had held prices to arbitrary levels, there was a burst of inflation. Annual price increases thereafter stayed mostly within 3 to 5 percent per annum until the escalation of hostilities in Southeast Asia in 1966, when inflation again erupted in the United States. In 1971, the U.S. departed from the convertibility of the dollar into gold, and the major nations adopted floating exchange rates in place of nominally fixed exchange rates. Double digit inflation as measured by the wholesale price index or consumer price index has been an actuality or a threat in the United States for more than a decade.

Inflation and the Measurement of Profitability

In an economy experiencing a high rate of price increases, the measurement of profitability becomes complicated. The times at which assets are purchased have a great impact on accounting profitability measures and on taxation. For example, Firm A purchased its assets in year 1, when their cost was $20,000,000, while Firm B purchased virtually identical assets five years later at a cost of $40,000,000. Let us assume that the assets will have an average twenty-year life, that both firms use straight-line depreciation, that the income before taxes for both firms is $5,000,000 per year over the life of the assets, and that their tax rate is 50 percent. Let us compare the financial profiles of the two companies:

	Firm A	Firm B
Income before taxes and depreciation	$5,000,000	$5,000,000
Less depreciation expense	−1,000,000	−2,000,000
Income before taxes	$4,000,000	$3,000,000
Taxes (at 50%)	2,000,000	1,500,000
Net income after taxes	$2,000,000	$1,500,000
Average return on investment	20%	7.5%

Since the cost of the assets will be depreciated down to zero over their twenty-year lives, their average value is half the original cost. The net income after taxes is assumed to be constant for each year so that the average annual returns are 20 percent for Firm A and 7.5 percent for Firm B. But does Firm A really have a return almost three times greater than Firm B's? The replacement value of Firm A's assets is $40,000,000, and the current depreciation expense is $2,000,000 per year, not $1,000,000. Is it correct for an investor to project Firm A's earning power into the future at 20 percent, or should the higher replacement cost of Firm A's assets that are being used up be taken into account? Should the tax-deductible depreciation expense for Firm A be $2,000,000 per year rather than $1,000,000?

There are no easy answers to these questions, which arise because of the changing values of assets. Some people feel that Firm A is gaining windfall profits because it is using assets that it was able to purchase at lower than current costs. Others argue that Firm A is paying excessive taxes because the real depreciation expense should be doubled. The lesson for management is that it should not necessarily buy assets early to avoid inflation, because the assets may become obsolete if purchased too early and if better equipment becomes available before the excess assets are put into use.

There are a number of possible reasons for the rising costs of later investments. An overriding influence in recent years, of course, has been the high rate of general inflation. Thus, during a period of general inflation, the return on investment of two different businesses may vary greatly simply due to the timing of their asset acquisitions. Even during periods when the rates of general price changes have been more moderate than those experienced in recent years, the timing of asset purchases can still affect profitability. There may, for example, be wide differences between the historical accounting costs and the current replacement costs of assets. Current replacement costs may be lower if a high rate of obsolescence in those assets has occurred. Or the current replacement value of assets may greatly increase, in the absence of general inflation, because of productivity increases achieved by improvements at modest cost in the utilization of equipment. In general, the net income earned by the firm should reflect the underlying replacement value of its assets. If this value is not adjusted, the resulting measures of return on investment may reflect a substantial distortion of true profitability levels.

Inflation and Inventory Valuation Methods

The divergence between economic and accounting measures of profitability results from the valuation of both fixed assets and inventories. During periods of inflation the method of inventory valuation for income statements and balance sheets has a major impact on profitability measurement.

By comparing FIFO (first-in-first-out) and LIFO (last-in-first-out) inventory costing and valuation methods, Table 4A.1 illustrates the difficulty of obtaining a meaningful economic measure of profitability during a period of unstable prices. During such a period, Firms C and D each have two batches of inventory. The first batch of 100 units was acquired at a cost of $1 per unit; the second was acquired later at $1.50 per unit. Firm C uses the FIFO method, and Firm D uses the LIFO method. The income statement for Firm C shows that it sold 100 units at $5 apiece. Since Firm C uses the FIFO method, it has figured the cost of goods sold (inventories used) as $100 (the cost of batch 1). Since Firm D uses the LIFO method, it has figured the cost of goods sold as $150 (the cost of batch 2). As a consequence, Firm C reports a net income of $100 and Firm D a net income of only $50.

However, the effects are reversed on the balance sheet, where Firm C carries batch 1 at $150 and Firm D at $100. On this basis, Firm C reports total assets of $1,000 and Firm D $950. The return on assets is thus 10 percent for Firm C and 5.3 percent for Firm D.

During a period of rising price levels, the use of LIFO results in an expense item on the income statement that is closer to the current replacement cost of items used from inventories. However, using LIFO also means that the balance sheet amount of inventory investment is carried at historical costs rather than current costs. Thus, although LIFO comes closer to a correct measure of *expenses* for the income statement, it results in an understatement of *investment* on the balance sheet and hence, an overstatement of the measured profitability ratio. Conversely, if FIFO is used, the expense item on the income statement is understated and the balance sheet valuation of inventories is closer to current costs. The consequences

**Table 4A.1
Effects of FIFO and LIFO Inventory
Costing and Valuation**

Firm C (FIFO)			Firm D (LIFO)		
Income Statement			Income Statement		
Sales 100 (at $5)		$500	Sales 100 (at $5)		$500
Inventories used	$100		Inventories used	$150	
Other costs	300		Other costs	300	
Total costs		400	Total costs		450
Net income		$100	Net income		$ 50
Balance Sheet			Balance Sheet		
Inventories on hand		$ 150	Inventories on hand		$100
Other assets		850	Other assets		850
Total assets		$1,000	Total assets		$950
Return on assets		10%	Return on assets		5.3%

Note: Inventories for both companies are batch 1: 100 units at $1 per unit, for a total of $100; batch 2: 100 units at $1.50 per unit, for a total of $150.

are similar to those for depreciation based on historical acquisition costs versus current replacement costs.

These simple examples illustrate the impact inflation has on reported financial results and, therefore, on financial ratios. Because of the lack of comparability among financial statements as a consequence of rising price levels, proposals have been made to modify accounting procedures so as to recognize that the traditional postulate of a stable measuring unit is no longer valid. In December 1974 the Financial Accounting Standards Board (FASB) issued an exposure draft of a proposed statement entitled "Financial Reporting in Units of General Purchasing Power." On March 23, 1976, the Securities and Exchange Commission (SEC) issued Accounting Series Release No. 190. This release requires disclosure of replacement costs for inventory items and depreciable plant from registrants with $100 million or more (at historical cost) of gross plant assets and with inventories constituting 10 percent or more of their total assets. (Starting in 1977, the SEC now requires additional details on the replacement costs of plant assets and inventories.)

In its Status Report No. 37, issued June 4, 1976, the FASB announced that action was being deferred on the issuance of its "Statement on Financial Reporting in Units of General Purchasing Power." The board stated that its action did not imply anything about the merits of the proposal; it said: "General purchasing power information is not now sufficiently well understood by preparers and users and the need for it is not now sufficiently well demonstrated to justify imposing the cost of implementation upon all preparers of financial statements at this time." An April 1978 announcement by the FASB recommended that the impact of inflation be disclosed as a supplement to financial statements without alterations in traditional financial statements.

It has been pointed out that, in a period of inflation, distortions result from the use of the historical cost postulate. Assets are recorded at cost, but revenue and other expense flows are in dollars of different purchasing power. The amortization of fixed costs does not reflect the current cost of these assets.[1] Furthermore, net income during periods when assets are held does not reflect the effects of management's decision to hold the assets rather than sell them. Since assets are not stated on the balance sheet at their current values, the firm's financial position cannot be accurately evaluated. And when assets are sold, gains or losses are reported during that period even though these results reflect prior decisions to hold the assets.[2]

Procedures in Replacement Cost Accounting

In replacement cost accounting, two major categories of problems must be solved: (1) how to measure the current value of assets, and (2) how to measure income and financial position. Three methods of measuring the current value of assets have been identified: (1) current replacement cost, (2) net realizable value, and (3) present value of future cash flow (discounted cash flow).

Current replacement cost has been referred to as an entry value. It can be defined as the current cost of an identical asset or of an asset equivalent in capacity and service. The SEC requirement mentioned earlier is not for current values in general but for one specific measure of current values—replacement costs. Other measures of current value can be disclosed in addition to, but not as a substitute for, replacement costs.

However, for a company that liquidates by selling off its assets, the relevant measure of value is the net realizable value of the individual assets. In applying this approach, the only assets for which current market values are quoted are those continuously traded, such as marketable securities. Consequently, net realizable values are hardly relevant for a going concern for which liquidation is not contemplated.

The present value of future cash flow, or the discounted cash flow, method is considered by many to represent economic value. Its practical implementation requires dependable forecasts and selection of the applicable discount rates. Most companies continue to make new investments, seeking to add to the earning power of existing assets. Hence it is difficult to segregate the future cash flows of the firm from existing assets and new

1. R.C. Thompson and Robert Koons, "Accounting for Changes in General Price Levels and Current Values," *Modern Accountant's Handbook,* ed. James D. Edwards and Homer A. Black (Homewood, Ill.: Dow Jones–Irwin, 1976), pp. 560–561.
2. Sidney Davidson et al., *Financial Accounting* (Hinsdale, Ill.: Dryden Press, 1975), p. 441.

investments. Thus the discounted cash flow method, while widely and effectively used in evaluating individual investment projects, is more difficult to apply in valuing the physical assets of the firm as a whole.

It has been stated that in judging the ability of a business to do the same kinds of things in the future as in the past and to pay dividends or to finance expansion without requiring new external financing, "replacement costs are perhaps the most useful measure of current value."[3] It might also be argued that the discounted cash flow method, soundly applied, yields results consistent with the current replacement value method.

Once a measure of replacement costs has been achieved, the task of measuring income and financial position is considered. A number of concepts of income are involved. A simplified illustration presented by Falkenstein and Weil is reproduced in Table 4A.2, along with three concepts of income.

Pretax distributable income is defined as revenues less expenses based on replacement costs. It is a measure of income that can be distributed as taxes and returns to owners without impairing the firm's physical capacity to remain in business at current levels.

Realized income is distributable income plus holding gains that have been realized during the period. The realized holding gain is the replacement value of goods sold less their historical cost. The sum of the distributable income and the realized holding gain is the realized income. This is the same as the conventional measure of income based on the realization principle. Replacement cost data make it possible to separate distributable income and realized holding gains.

The sum of realized income plus unrealized holding gains has been called economic income. This view holds that an increase in the value of assets is economic income whether or not the asset has been sold. The economic measure of income has been defined as the income that can be consumed during the period while leaving the person or firm as well off at the end of the period as at the beginning. This leads to an emphasis on the physical capacity of the firm. Thus a company is said to be as well off at the end of the period as at the beginning only if it has sufficient physical assets to carry on the same level of business activity. Under this view, holding gains, whether or not realized, are tied up in the net assets required to conduct the operations of the firm at the current physical levels of activity. Thus it might be more appropriate to label the third measure of income "realized plus unrealized income unadjusted for general purchasing power changes."

Taking distributable income as the most relevant measure of income, Falkenstein and Weil compare it with income as conventionally reported for the

3. A. Falkenstein and R. L. Weil, "Replacement Cost Accounting," *Financial Analysts' Journal* 33 (January–February 1977), pp. 47–48.

**Table 4A.2
Simple Illustration of
Replacement Cost Income
Statement**

Assumed Data		Acquisition Cost (Historical)	Replacement Cost
Inventory, 1/1/76		$ 900	$1,100
Inventory, 12/31/76		1,200	1,550
Cost of goods sold for 1976		4,000	4,500
Sales for 1976	$5,200		

Income Statement for 1976

Sales	$5,200
Cost of goods sold, replacement cost basis	4,500
1. Distributable income	$ 700
Realized holding gains	500[a]
2. Realized income	$1,200
Unrealized holding gains	150[b]
3. Economic income	$1,350

[a] Realized holding gain during a period is replacement cost of goods sold less historical cost of goods sold; for 1976 the realized holding gain was $500 = $4,500 − $4,000.
[b] The total unrealized holding gain at any time is replacement cost of inventory on hand at that time less historical cost of that inventory. The unrealized holding gain during a period is the unrealized holding gain at the end of the period less the unrealized holding gain at the beginning of the period. The unrealized holding gain prior to 1976 was $200 = $1,100 − $900. The unrealized holding gain during 1976 was ($1,550 − $1,200) − ($1,100 − $900) = $350 − $200 = $150.

Source: A. Falkenstein and R. L. Weil, "Replacement Cost Accounting," *Financial Analysts' Journal* 33 (January–February 1977), p. 49. Reprinted by permission.

Dow-Jones Industrials for 1975. As conventionally reported, income approximated $14.5 billion. Using replacement costs, the cost of goods sold increased by $2.2 billion, and depreciation increased by $6.5 billion. Distributable income dropped to somewhat under $6 billion, representing 40 percent of the conventionally measured income.

While dividends were about 50 percent of conventional income, they were 127 percent of distributable income. Income taxes currently payable were 63 percent of pretax conventional income but almost 81 percent of distributable income. A wide variation among the individual companies reflected variations in the economic characteristics of their industries, the extent of their use of LIFO accounting methods, and other individual circumstances. Thus the impact of inflation was different on individual companies.

The use of current replacement costs in calculating a distributable income measure can result in substantial changes in income as well as financial position. When economic changes are so large that current values of assets differ greatly from their historical values, major distortions may result if these changes are not taken into account in accounting procedures and practices.

General Purchasing Power Reporting (GPPR)

Because both the realized and unrealized holding gains in the use of replacement accounting may simply reflect a declining value of the unit of account, more general adjustments are needed. These adjustments, which recognize that the assumption of a stable unit of account is no longer valid in most parts of the world, have resulted in proposals for General Purchasing Power Reporting (GPPR) along the lines of the FASB draft proposal of December 1974.

The GPPR seeks to adjust the current value of nonmonetary items by using a general price index. It retains the historical cost basis of accounting but adjusts it also by a price index. That is, it adjusts original cost data to compensate for changes in the purchasing power of the dollar and in capital consumption expenses and then adjusts the value of goods sold from inventory. A new entry is introduced to financial reports: net holding gains on monetary items. Operationally, monetary and nonmonetary items must be separated in financial statements, and a price index must be selected. Cash, claims to cash, and claims on cash fixed in terms of dollars are designated as monetary items.

While the adjustments can be quite detailed, some simplifications can be made. When income and expenses are spread in a relatively uniform way throughout the year, a roughly accurate measure of monetary gain or loss can be calculated on the basis of the average balance of monetary items rather than on the transactions that created them. Consider the following balance sheets, for which the general price level rose 10 percent between the two balance sheet dates.

GPPR Company
Balance Sheets for 19X1 and 19X2

	19X1	19X2
Monetary Assets		
Cash	$ 8,000	$ 10,000
Receivables	12,000	20,000
Nonmonetary Assets		
Inventories	30,000	40,000
Net fixed assets	50,000	60,000
Total assets	$100,000	$130,000

	19X1	19X2
Monetary Liabilities		
Current liabilities	$ 10,000	$ 15,000
Deferred income taxes	2,000	3,000
Long-term debt	28,000	36,000
Net holding gains on monetary items		2,000
Nonmonetary Liabilities		
Net worth	60,000	74,000
Total claims	$100,000	$130,000

The net balance of monetary items was ($20,000) in 19X1 and ($24,000) in 19X2. The average net monetary liability was $22,000. The rate of inflation during the year was 10 percent. Hence the value of the net monetary liability at the end of the year price index was $22,000 divided by 1.10, or $20,000; the constant dollar value of the net monetary liabilities decreased by $2,000; and the net holding gains on monetary items were $2,000.[4]

The broad significance of the two major forms of adjustments can be indicated by some aggregate measures that have been made. We have already seen the major impact of current replacement accounting on financial measures for the Dow-Jones Industrial Averages. We will illustrate further from some other aggregate measures.

Table 4A.3 shows the effects on selected financial ratios for U.S. nonfinancial corporations over the last eleven years of utilizing current value reporting versus conventional reporting. Note that debt to equity ratios of over 130 percent under conventional reporting fell to below 100 percent under current value reporting.

However, the operating income coverage of interest liability dropped from somewhat less than 2 to approximately 1. This is because the operating income to equity ratio dropped from about 12 percent to 6 percent in recent years. The ratio of taxes to operating income, which had been in the region of 42 percent under conventional reporting, rose to 60 percent or more under current value reporting.

This illustrates how the use of current value reporting can have a substantial impact on ratios involving the operating performance and financial position of business firms. Given the substantial changes that have taken place in the economy during the past decade, and given that the inflation rate has been in the two-digit range, supplemental accounting information is necessary. Without taking into account changes in the purchasing power of the monetary unit, changes in the relative value of assets held by different busi-

4. See a similar illustration in Thompson and Koons, "Accounting for Changes," pp. 580–581.

Table 4A.3
Selected Financial Ratios for
U.S. Nonfinancial Corporations

	Conventional Reporting				Current Value Reporting			
	Debt/ Equity (1)	Operating Income/ Interest Liability (2)	Operating Income/ Equity (3)	Taxes/ Operating Income (4)	Debt/ Equity (5)	Operating Income/ Interest Liability (6)	Operating Income/ Equity (7)	Taxes/ Operating Income (8)
1965	0.97	5.3	0.15	0.42	0.91	5.4	0.15	0.41
1966	1.02	4.8	0.15	0.42	0.92	4.4	0.14	0.42
1967	1.08	3.9	0.13	0.43	1.02	3.4	0.13	0.43
1968	1.14	3.7	0.14	0.47	0.96	3.0	0.12	0.49
1969	1.21	2.7	0.12	0.50	0.94	2.1	0.09	0.53
1970	1.28	1.8	0.09	0.49	1.01	1.4	0.07	0.57
1971	1.30	2.0	0.10	0.47	1.06	1.6	0.08	0.54
1972	1.29	2.2	0.11	0.44	1.07	1.9	0.09	0.48
1973	1.32	2.1	0.13	0.43	1.00	1.7	0.08	0.52
1974	1.36	1.8	0.13	0.42	0.95	0.9	0.05	0.77
1975	1.34	1.7	0.12	0.42	0.92	1.1	0.06	0.60

Source: R. W. Kopcke, "Current Accounting Practices and Proposals for Reform," *New England Economic Review,* Federal Reserve Bank of Boston (September/October 1976), p. 23. By permission of R. W. Kopcke, Federal Reserve Bank of Boston.

ness firms in the same industry, and the differential impact of changes on different industries, conventional accounting reporting based on historical cost postulates can be seriously misleading. A reworking of financial ratio analysis based on current values therefore becomes a highly desirable check on financial ratio analysis that utilizes conventional accounting reports.

CHAPTER 5 PROFIT PLANNING

The preceding chapter described how ratios are used in financial analysis and showed how the basic ratios are related to one another. A major area of financial management involves a continuous review of these ratios to ensure that no aspects of the firm's existing operations get out of control. Still other tools are available to aid the financial manager in the planning and control process. Two of them are discussed in this chapter: (1) breakeven analysis, which is especially useful in considering plant expansion and new product decisions; and (2) the sources and uses of funds statement, which is an important aid in seeing how the firm has obtained funds and how these funds have been used.

Breakeven Analysis

Breakeven analysis is an analytical technique for studying the relationships among fixed costs, variable costs, and profits. If a firm's costs were all variable, the problem of breakeven volume would seldom arise; but by having some variable and some fixed costs, the firm suffers losses until a given volume has been reached.

Breakeven analysis is a formal profit-planning approach based on established relationships between costs and revenues. It is a device for determining the point at which sales will just cover total costs. If the firm is to avoid losses, its sales must cover all costs—those that vary directly with production and those that do not change as production levels change. Costs that fall into each of those categories are outlined in Table 5.1.

The nature of breakeven analysis is depicted in Figure 5.1, the basic breakeven chart. The chart is on a unit basis, with units produced shown on the horizontal axis and income and costs measured on the vertical axis. Fixed costs of $40,000 are represented by a horizontal line; they are the same (fixed) regardless of the number of units produced. Variable costs are assumed to be $1.20 a unit. Total costs rise by $1.20, the amount of the vari-

Table 5.1
Fixed and Variable Costs

Fixed Costs[a]	Direct or Variable Costs
Depreciation on plant and equipment	Factory labor
Rentals	Materials
Interest charges on debt	Sales commissions
Salaries of research staff	
Salaries of executive staff	
General office expenses	

[a] Some of these costs—for example, salaries and office expenses—can be varied to some degree; however, firms are reluctant to reduce these expenditures in response to temporary fluctuations in sales. Such costs are often called *semivariable* costs.

Figure 5.1
Breakeven Chart

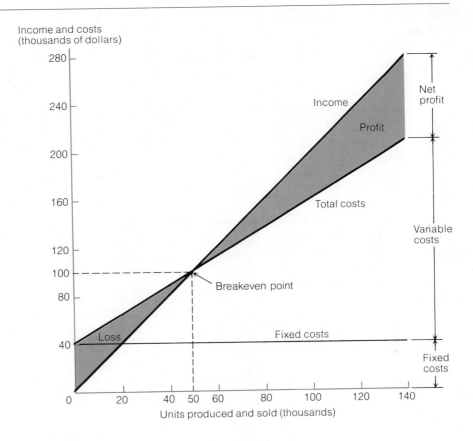

able costs, for each additional unit produced. Units are assumed to be sold at $2 apiece, so the total income is pictured as a straight line, which must also increase with production. The slope (or rate of ascent) of the total income line is steeper than that of the total cost line. This must be true, because the firm is gaining $2 of revenue for every $1.20 paid out for labor and materials—the variable costs.

Up to the breakeven point, found at the intersection of the total income and total cost lines, the firm suffers losses. After that point, it begins to make profits. Figure 5.1 indicates a breakeven point at a sales and cost level of $100,000 and a production level of 50,000 units.

More exact calculations of the breakeven point can be carried out algebraically or by trial and error. In Section A of Table 5.2, profit and loss relations are shown for various levels of sales; in Section B the algebraic calculations are carried out.

Table 5.2
Relations among Units Sold, Variable Costs, Fixed Costs, Total Costs, Sales, and Net Profit or Loss

A. Trial-and-Error Calculations

Units Sold	Variable Costs	Fixed Costs	Total Costs	Sales	Net Profit (Loss)
20,000	$ 24,000	$40,000	$ 64,000	$ 40,000	− $24,000
40,000	48,000	40,000	88,000	80,000	−8,000
50,000	60,000	40,000	100,000	100,000	—
60,000	72,000	40,000	112,000	120,000	8,000
80,000	96,000	40,000	136,000	160,000	24,000
100,000	120,000	40,000	160,000	200,000	40,000
120,000	144,000	40,000	184,000	240,000	56,000
140,000	168,000	40,000	208,000	280,000	72,000

B. Algebraic Solution to Breakeven Point

1. The breakeven quantity is defined as that volume of output at which revenue is just equal to total costs (fixed costs plus variable costs).

2. Let:

    P = sales price per unit.
    Q = quantity produced and sold.
    FC = fixed costs.
    vc = variable costs per unit.

3. Then:

$$P \cdot Q = FC + (vc \cdot Q)$$
$$(P \cdot Q) - (vc \cdot Q) = FC$$
$$Q(P - vc) = FC$$
$$Q = \frac{FC}{P - vc} \text{ at breakeven } Q.$$

4. Illustration:

$$Q = \frac{\$40,000}{\$2.00 - \$1.20}$$
$$= 50,000 \text{ units.}$$

Nonlinear Breakeven Analysis

In breakeven analysis, linear (straight line) relationships are generally assumed. Although introducing nonlinear relationships complicates matters slightly, it is easy enough to extend the analysis in this manner. For example, it is reasonable to think that increased sales can be obtained only if prices are reduced. Similarly, empirical studies suggest that the average variable cost per unit falls over some range of output and then begins to rise. These assumptions are illustrated in Figure 5.2, where we see a loss region when sales are low, then a profit region (and a maximum profit), and finally another loss region at very high output levels.

Figure 5.2
Nonlinear Breakeven Chart

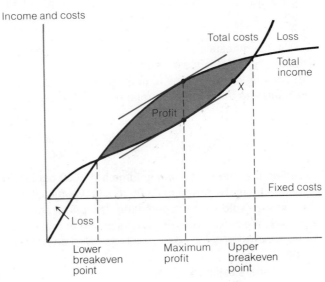

Income and costs

Total costs / Loss

Total income

X

Profit

Fixed costs

Loss

Lower
breakeven
point

Maximum
profit

Upper
breakeven
point

Units produced and sold

Note: The angle of a line from the origin to a point on the total income line measures price (that is, total income/units sold), and a line from the origin to the total costs curve measures cost per unit. We can see that the angle of the line to the income curve declines as we move toward higher sales, which means that price reductions are necessary to obtain higher unit sales volume. Unit costs (total costs/units produced) declines to point *X*, the tangency point of a line from the origin to the total costs curve, then begins to rise.

The slopes of the total costs and total income lines measure marginal cost (MC) and marginal revenue (MR), respectively. At the point where the slopes of the two total curves are equal, MR = MC, and profits are at a maximum.

An Example of Breakeven Analysis: New Product Decision

Breakeven analysis can be used in three separate but related ways:

1. In new product decisions, to determine how large sales volume on a new product must be if the firm is to break even on the proposed project. (This topic is illustrated below.)
2. To study the effects of a general expansion in the level of operations. (This topic is covered later in the chapter in the section on the breakeven point based on dollar sales.)
3. To analyze a program to modernize and automate, where the firm would be operating in a more mechanized, automated manner and substituting fixed costs for variable costs. (This topic is covered later in the chapter in the section on operating leverage.)

The textbook publishing business provides a good example of the effective use of breakeven analysis for new product decisions. To illustrate, consider the analysis of production costs for a hypothetical college textbook of 600 pages, described in Table 5.3. The costs and revenues are graphed in Figure 5.3.

The fixed costs can be estimated; the variable costs are set mostly by contracts. The sales price is variable, but competition keeps prices within a sufficiently narrow range to make a linear total revenue curve reasonable. Formulating the breakeven relationship, we have:

$$\$60,000 + 9X = 15X$$
$$6X = \$60,000$$
$$X = 10,000$$

We find that the breakeven volume is 10,000 copies. The breakeven volume used to be in the range of 6,000 to 8,000 copies, but increased fixed costs of editorial development, typesetting, sampling, and other gratis items have increased the breakeven. For books aimed at markets that involve less sampling and other fixed costs, the breakeven point may fall as low as 4,000 to 5,000 copies.

Publishers estimate the size of the total market for a given book, the competition, and so on. With these data as a base, they evaluate the possibility that sales of a given book will reach or exceed the breakeven point. If the estimate is that they will not, the publisher may consider cutting production

Table 5.3
Cost and Revenue Figures
for a Textbook

Fixed Costs

Editorial development (reviewing, copy editing, and so on)	$20,000
Art work	5,000
Typesetting	20,000
Instructor's manuals and other gratis items	3,000
Sampling of copies to instructors	6,000
General and administrative expenses	6,000
Total fixed costs	$60,000

Variable Costs per Copy

Paper, printing, and binding (PPB)	$ 2.20
Bookstore discount (at 20% of sales price)	3.00
Sales and advertising expenses	2.00
Author's royalties (at 15% of the selling price less the bookstore discount)	1.80
Total variable costs per copy	$ 9.00
Sales price per copy	$15.00

**Figure 5.3
Breakeven Chart for a
Hypothetical Textbook**

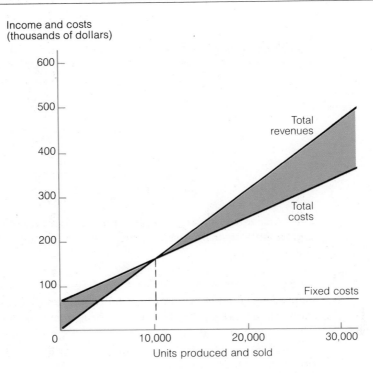

Income and costs
(thousands of dollars)

600 —

500 —
                                                    Total
                                                    revenues

400 —

300 —
                                                    Total
                                                    costs

200 —

100 —
                                                    Fixed costs

0   10,000   20,000   30,000
           Units produced and sold

costs by, say, spending less on art work and editing, using a lower grade of paper, and negotiating lower royalty rates. In this business—and for new product decisions in many others—linear breakeven analysis has proved a useful tool.

**Breakeven Point
Based on Dollar
Sales**

Calculating breakeven points on the basis of dollar sales rather than units of output is frequently useful. The main advantage of this method, which is illustrated in Table 5.4, is that it enables one to determine a general break-even point for a firm that sells many products at varying prices. Furthermore, the procedure requires a minimum of data. Only three values are needed: sales, fixed costs, and variable costs. Sales and total cost data are readily available from corporate annual reports and from investment manuals. Total costs are segregated into fixed and variable components. The major fixed charges (rent, interest, depreciation, and general and administrative expenses) are taken from the income statement. Finally, variable costs are calculated by deducting fixed costs from total costs.

Breakeven Point Based on Units of Output

It is also possible to calculate the breakeven point on the basis of units of output. This can be done by rewriting the equation derived in Table 5.4:

$$P \cdot Q^* = \frac{FC}{1 - \dfrac{VC}{P \cdot Q}} = \frac{FC}{\dfrac{P \cdot Q - VC}{P \cdot Q}}$$

$$P \cdot Q^* = \frac{FC}{\dfrac{Q(P - vc)}{P \cdot Q}}$$

$$Q^* = \frac{FC}{P - vc}.$$

From this equation, it is clear that the breakeven quantity increases as fixed and variable costs increase and decreases as prices rise.

Operating Leverage

To a physicist, *leverage* implies the use of a lever to raise a heavy object with a small force. In business terminology, a high degree of leverage implies that a relatively small change in sales results in a large change in profits. We can divide leverage into two categories: financial leverage (discussed briefly in Chapter 4 and much more extensively in Chapter 15), and operating leverage, the subject of this section.

The significance of the degree of operating leverage is clearly illustrated by Figure 5.4. Three firms—A, B, and C—with differing degrees of leverage, are contrasted. Firm A has a relatively small amount of fixed charges; it does not have much automated equipment, so its depreciation cost is low. However, its variable cost line has a relatively steep slope, denoting that its variable costs per unit are higher than those of the other firms.

Firm B is considered to have a normal amount of fixed costs in its operations. It uses automated equipment (with which one operator can turn out a few or many units at the same labor cost) to about the same extent as the average firm in the industry. Firm B breaks even at a higher level of operations than does Firm A. At a production level of 40,000 units, B loses $8,000 but A breaks even.

Firm C has the highest fixed costs. It is highly automated, using expensive, high-speed machines that require very little labor per unit produced. With such an operation, its variable costs rise slowly. Because of the high overhead resulting from charges associated with the expensive machinery, Firm C's breakeven point is higher than that for either Firm A or Firm B.

**Table 5.4
Calculation of Breakeven Point
Based on Dollar Sales**

$$\text{Breakeven point} \atop \text{(sales volume)} = \frac{\text{Total fixed costs}}{1 - \dfrac{\text{Total variable costs}}{\text{Total sales volume}}} = \frac{FC}{1 - \dfrac{VC}{P \cdot Q}} = Q^*.$$

Procedure

Take any sales level and use the related data to determine the breakeven point. For example, assume that 20,000 units were actually produced and sold, and use the data related to that output in Table 5.2:

$$\text{Breakeven point} = \frac{\$40,000}{1 - \dfrac{\$24,000}{\$40,000}} = \frac{\$40,000}{0.4} = \$100,000.$$

Rationale

1. At the breakeven point, sales $(P \cdot Q^*)$ are equal to fixed costs (FC) plus total variable costs (VC):

   $$P \cdot Q^* = FC + VC.$$

2. Because both the sale price and the variable costs per unit are assumed to be constant in breakeven analysis, the ratio $VC/P \cdot Q$ for *any* level of sales is also constant and can be found from the annual income statement.

3. Since variable costs are a constant percentage of sales, Equation 5.1 can be rewritten as:

   $$P \cdot Q^* = FC + \frac{VC}{P \cdot Q}(P \cdot Q^*)$$

   $$P \cdot Q^* \left(1 - \frac{VC}{P \cdot Q}\right) = FC$$

   $$P \cdot Q^* = \frac{FC}{1 - \dfrac{VC}{P \cdot Q}}.$$

Once Firm C reaches its breakeven point, however, its profits rise faster than do those of the other firms.

Alternative leverage decisions can have a great impact on the unit cost positions of the individual firms. Consider the relationships when 200,000 units are sold. We can calculate the average per unit costs of production for each firm, dividing total costs by the 200,000 units sold, to obtain:

Costs per Unit

Firm A	$1.60
Firm B	$1.40
Firm C	$1.30

**Figure 5.4
Operating Leverage**

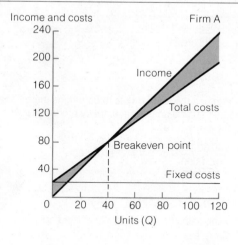

Income and costs
Firm A

Selling price = $2
Fixed costs   = $20,000
Variable costs = $1.50 Q

Units Sold (Q)	Sales	Costs	Profit
20,000	$ 40,000	$ 50,000	−$10,000
40,000	80,000	80,000	0
60,000	120,000	110,000	10,000
80,000	160,000	140,000	20,000
100,000	200,000	170,000	30,000
120,000	240,000	200,000	40,000
200,000	400,000	320,000	80,000

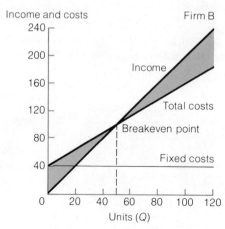

Income and costs
Firm B

Selling price = $2
Fixed costs   = $40,000
Variable costs = $1.20 Q

Units Sold (Q)	Sales	Costs	Profit
20,000	$ 40,000	$ 64,000	−$24,000
40,000	80,000	88,000	− 8,000
60,000	120,000	112,000	8,000
80,000	160,000	136,000	24,000
100,000	200,000	160,000	40,000
120,000	240,000	184,000	56,000
200,000	400,000	280,000	120,000

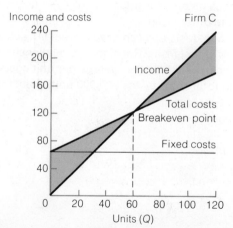

Income and costs
Firm C

Selling price = $2
Fixed costs   = $60,000
Variable costs = $1 Q

Units Sold (Q)	Sales	Costs	Profit
20,000	$ 40,000	$ 80,000	−$40,000
40,000	80,000	100,000	−20,000
60,000	120,000	120,000	0
80,000	160,000	140,000	20,000
100,000	200,000	160,000	40,000
120,000	240,000	180,000	60,000
200,000	400,000	260,000	140,000

These results have important implications. At a high volume of operations of 200,000 units per period, Firm C has a substantial cost superiority over the other two firms and particularly over Firm A. Firm C could cut the price of its product to $1.50 per unit, which represents a level that would be unprofitable for Firm A, and still have more than a 13 percent ($.20/$1.50) return on sales. (The average pretax margin on sales for manufacturing firms is about 9 to 10 percent.) Another illustration of this idea is the difference in unit costs for Japanese versus U.S. steel companies. Most Japanese steel companies can produce 10 million tons or more per year, while only one or two U.S. steel companies can produce as much as 5 million tons per year. Operating at such a high capacity (in part due to the benefit of growth through export sales) the Japanese companies have been able to sell steel in the United States at prices below the costs of the U.S. steel companies. While the total story is complex, the firms' operating leverage factor is an important influence on their relative costs per unit.

Degree of Operating Leverage Operating leverage can be defined more precisely in terms of the way a given change in volume affects profits. For this purpose we use the following definition: The degree of operating leverage is the percentage change in operating income that results from a percentage change in units sold. Algebraically:

$$\text{Degree of operating leverage} = \frac{\text{Percentage change in operating income}}{\text{Percentage change in units sold}}$$

For Firm B in Figure 5.4, the degree of operating leverage (OL_B) for a change in units of output from 100,000 to 120,000 is:

$$OL_B = \frac{\dfrac{\Delta \text{ Income}}{\text{Income}}}{\dfrac{\Delta Q}{Q}}$$

$$= \frac{\dfrac{\$56,000 - \$40,000}{\$40,000}}{\dfrac{120,000 - 100,000}{100,000}} = \frac{\dfrac{\$16,000}{\$40,000}}{\dfrac{20,000}{100,000}}$$

$$= \frac{40\%}{20\%} = \boxed{2.0}$$

Here Δ income is the increase in income, Q is the quantity of output in units, and ΔQ is the increase in output. For this calculation we assume an increase in volume from 100,000 to 120,000 units, but the calculated OL would have been the same for any other increase from 100,000 units.

For linear breakeven, a formula has been developed to aid in calculating the degree of operating leverage at any level of output, Q:

$$\text{Degree of operating leverage at Point } Q = \frac{Q(P - vc)}{Q(P - vc) - FC} \qquad (5.2)^1$$

$$= \frac{P \cdot Q - VC}{P \cdot Q - VC - FC} \qquad (5.2a)$$

Here again P is the price per unit, vc is the variable cost per unit, FC is fixed costs, $P \cdot Q$ is total sales, and VC is total variable costs. Equation 5.2 expresses the relationship in terms of units, while Equation 5.2a expresses it in terms of total dollar figures. Using the equations, we find Firm B's degree of operating leverage at 100,000 units of output to be

$$\text{OL}_B \text{ at 100,000 units} = \frac{100,000\,(\$2.00 - \$1.20)}{100,000\,(\$2.00 - \$1.20) - \$40,000}$$

$$= \frac{\$200,000 - \$120,000}{\$200,000 - \$120,000 - \$40,000}$$

$$= \frac{\$80,000}{\$40,000} = \boxed{2.0}$$

The two methods must, of course, give consistent answers.

Equation 5.2 can also be applied to Firms A and C. When this is done, we find the degree of operating leverage at 100,000 units to be 1.67 for A and 2.5 for C. Thus, for a 100 percent increase in volume, Firm C, the company with the most operating leverage, will experience a profit increase of 250 percent; for the same 100 percent volume gain, Firm A, the one with the least leverage, will have only a 167 percent profit gain.

In summary, the calculation of the degree of operating leverage shows algebraically the same pattern that Figure 5.4 shows graphically—that the profits of Firm C, the company with the most operating leverage, are most sensitive to changes in sales volume, while those of Firm A, which has only a small amount of operating leverage, are relatively insensitive to volume

1. Equation 5.2 is developed as follows: The change in output is defined as ΔQ. Fixed costs are constant, so the change in profits is $\Delta Q(P - vc)$, where P = price per unit and vc = variable cost per unit. The initial profit is $Q(P - vc) - FC$, so the percentage change in profit is

$$\frac{\Delta Q(P - vc)}{Q(P - vc) - FC}.$$

The percentage change in output is $\Delta Q/Q$, so the ratio of the change in profits to the change in output is

$$\frac{\dfrac{\Delta Q(P - vc)}{Q(P - vc) - FC}}{\dfrac{\Delta Q}{Q}} = \frac{\Delta Q(P - vc)}{Q(P - vc) - FC} \cdot \frac{Q}{\Delta Q} = \frac{P \cdot Q - VC}{P \cdot Q - VC - FC}.$$

changes. Firm B, with an intermediate degree of leverage, lies between the two extremes.[2]

The degree of operating leverage measures the effect on profitability of a change in either direction in the volume of output sold—that is, an increase or decrease in quantity sold. The measure has important implications for a number of areas of business and financial policy. Firm C's high degree of operating leverage suggests gains from increasing volume. Suppose Firm C could increase its quantity sold from 100,000 units to 120,000 units by cutting the price per unit to $1.90. The equation for profit is

$$\text{Profit} = PQ - vc - F$$
$$= \$1.90(120,000) - 120,000(\$1) - \$60,000$$
$$= \$228,000 - \$120,000 - \$60,000$$
$$= \$48,000.$$

The equation shows that Firm C could increase its profits from $40,000 at a volume of 100,000 to $48,000 at a volume of 120,000. Thus a high degree of operating leverage suggests that an aggressive price policy may increase profits, particularly if the market is responsive to small price cuts.

On the other hand, Firm C's high degree of operating leverage tells us that the company is subject to large swings in profits as its volume fluctuates. Thus, if Firm C's industry is one whose sales are greatly affected by changes in the overall level of economic activity (as are, for example, the durable goods industries, such as machine tools, steel, and autos), its profits are subject to large fluctuations. Hence, the degree of financial leverage appropriate for Firm C to take on is lower than that for a firm with a lower degree of operating leverage and for industries whose sales are less sensitive to fluctuations in the level of the economy. (Financial leverage is discussed further in Chapter 15.)

Cash Breakeven Analysis

Some of the firm's fixed costs are noncash outlays, and, for a period, some of its revenues may be in receivables. The cash breakeven chart for Firm B, constructed on the assumption that $30,000 of the fixed costs from the previous illustration are depreciation charges and, therefore, a noncash outlay, is shown in Figure 5.5. The nature of depreciation as a noncash charge is explained later in the chapter. Because fixed cash outlays are only $10,000,

2. The degree of operating leverage is a form of *elasticity concept* and thus is akin to the familiar price elasticity developed in economics. Since operating leverage is an elasticity, it varies depending on the particular part of the breakeven graph that is being considered. For example, in terms of our illustrative firms, the degree of operating leverage is greatest close to the breakeven point, where a very small change in volume can produce a very large percentage increase in profits simply because the base profits are close to zero near the breakeven point.

Figure 5.5
Cash Breakeven Analysis

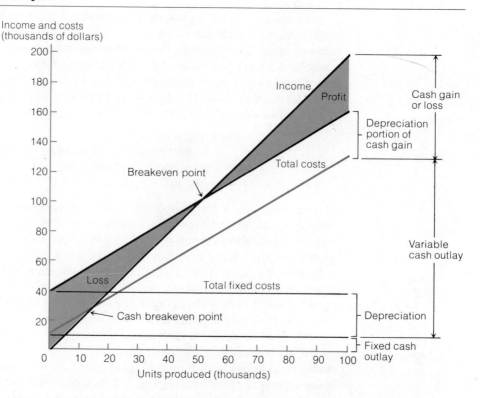

the cash breakeven point is at 12,500 units rather than 50,000 units, which is the profit breakeven point.

An equation for the cash breakeven point based on sales dollars can be derived from the equation for the profit breakeven point (see Table 5.4). The only change is to reduce fixed costs by the amount of noncash outlays:

$$P \cdot Q^* = \frac{FC - \text{Noncash outlays}}{1 - \dfrac{VC}{P \cdot Q}}$$

If noncash outlays are very close to total fixed costs, the cash breakeven point approaches zero. The cash breakeven point based on units of output is comparable to the profit breakeven quantity, except that fixed costs must be adjusted for noncash outlays:

$$Q^* = \frac{FC - \text{Noncash outlays}}{P - vc}$$

Here again, if noncash outlays are very large, the cash breakeven point may be low, despite a large amount of fixed charges.

Cash breakeven analysis does not fully represent cash flows; for this a cash budget is required. But it is useful because it provides a picture of the flow of funds from operations. A firm may incur a level of fixed costs that will result in losses during business downswings but large profits during upswings. If cash outlays are small, even during periods of loss the firm may be able to operate above the cash breakeven point. Thus, the risk of insolvency (in the sense of inability to meet cash obligations) is small. This allows a firm to reach out for higher profits through automation and operating leverage.

Limitations of Breakeven Analysis

Breakeven analysis is useful in studying the relations among volume, prices, and costs; it is thus helpful in pricing, cost control, and decisions about expansion programs. It has limitations, however, as a guide to managerial actions.

Linear breakeven analysis is especially weak in what it implies about the sales possibilities for the firm. Any linear breakeven chart is based on a constant sales price. Therefore, in order to study profit possibilities under different prices, a whole series of charts is necessary—one for each price. Alternatively, nonlinear breakeven analysis can be used.

Breakeven analysis is also deficient with regard to costs; the relations indicated by the chart do not hold at all outputs. As sales increase, the existing plant and equipment are worked to capacity, additional workers are hired, and overtime pay increases; all this causes variable costs to rise sharply. Additional equipment and plant are required, thereby increasing fixed costs. Finally, over a period, the products sold by the firm change in quality and quantity. Such changes in product mix influence the level and slope of the cost function. Linear breakeven analysis is useful as a first step in developing the basic data required for pricing and for financial decisions. But more detailed analysis is required before final judgments can be made.

Sources and Uses of Funds Statement

If a firm requests a loan, the bank's loan officer will doubtless pose these three questions: What has the firm done with the money it has? What will it do with the new funds? How will it repay the loan? The sources and uses statement helps provide answers to these questions as well as to questions that other interested parties may have about the firm. This information can indicate whether the firm is making progress or whether problems are arising.

Depreciation as a Source of Funds

Before constructing a sources and uses of funds statement, we shall discuss why, in financial analysis, we consider depreciation a source of funds. But first, what is depreciation? *Depreciation* is an annual charge against income that reflects the cost of the capital equipment used in the production process. For example, suppose a machine with an expected useful life of ten years and no expected salvage value was purchased in 1970 for $100,000. This cost must be charged against production during the machine's ten-year life; otherwise, profits will be overstated. If the machine is depreciated by the straight-line method, the annual charge is $10,000. This amount is deducted from sales revenues, along with such other costs as labor and raw materials, to determine income. *However, depreciation is not a cash outlay. Funds were expended back in 1970, so the depreciation charged against income each year is not a cash outlay, as are labor or raw materials payments.*

To illustrate the significance of depreciation in cash flow analysis, consider the Dallas Fertilizer and Chemical Company, which has the following income statement for 1978:

Sales	$300,000,000
Costs excluding depreciation	$270,000,000
Depreciation	10,000,000
Profit before taxes	$ 20,000,000
Taxes	8,000,000
Profit after taxes	$ 12,000,000

Assuming that sales are for cash and that all costs except depreciation are paid during 1978, how much cash is available from operations to pay dividends, retire debt, or make investments in fixed or current assets (or both)? The answer is $22 million, the sum of profit after taxes plus depreciation. The sales are all for cash, so the firm took in $300 million in cash money. Its costs other than depreciation were $270 million, and these were paid in cash, leaving $30 million. Depreciation *is not* a cash charge—the firm does not pay out the $10 million of depreciation expenses—so $30 million of cash money is still left after depreciation. Taxes, on the other hand, are paid in cash, so $8 million for taxes must be deducted from the $30 million gross operating cash flow, leaving a net cash flow from operations of $22 million. This $22 million is, of course, exactly equal to profit after taxes plus depreciation: $12 million plus $10 million equals $22 million.

This example shows the rationale behind the statement that depreciation is a source of funds. However, we should note that without sales revenues, depreciation will *not* be a source of funds. If a strike idles the plant, the $300 million of sales revenues will vanish, and cash flows from depreciation will evaporate.[3] Nevertheless, most firms do not suffer shutdowns for long periods, so normally a firm's depreciation does indeed constitute a source of funds, as we use the term.

Sources and Uses Analysis

Several steps are involved in constructing a sources and uses of funds statement. First, the changes in balance sheet items from one year to the next must be tabulated and then classified as either sources or uses of funds, according to the following pattern:

1. *Source of funds* means either a decrease in asset items or an increase in liability items.
2. *Use of funds* means either an increase in asset items or a decrease in liability items.

Table 5.5 gives Dallas Chemical's comparative balance sheets for 1977 and 1978 along with net changes in each item, classified as to source or use.

The next step in constructing a sources and uses statement involves (1) making adjustments to reflect net income and dividends and (2) isolating changes in working capital (current assets and current liabilities). These changes are reflected in the sources and uses statement shown in Table 5.6. Net income in 1978 amounted to $12 million, and dividends of $2 million were paid. The $12 million is treated as a source, the $2 million as a use. The $10 million in retained earnings shown in Table 5.5 is deleted from Table 5.6 to avoid double counting. This statement of sources and uses of funds tells the financial manager that plant size was expanded, that fixed assets amounting to $25 million were acquired, that inventories and net receivables increased as sales increased, and that the firm needed funds to meet working capital and fixed assets demands.

Previously, Dallas had been financing its growth through bank credit (notes payable). In the present period of growth, management decided to obtain some financing from permanent sources—long-term debt. It obtained enough long-term debt not only to finance some of the asset growth but also to pay back some of its bank credit and to reduce accounts payable. In addition to the long-term debt, it obtained funds from earnings and from depreciation charges. Moreover, the firm had been accumulating mar-

---

3. This potential problem was brought to the authors' attention in connection with a project involving a financial plan for Communications Satellite Corporation. Comsat has very healthy projected cash flows that seem capable of supporting a substantial amount of debt. However, Comsat's revenues are derived almost entirely from three satellites (over the North Atlantic, Pacific, and Indian oceans); and if these satellites fail, it will take months to replace them. Thus, when we recognized the degree of uncertainty about these cash flows, we adjusted downward our estimates of how much debt Comsat could safely carry.

**Table 5.5
Dallas Fertilizer and Chemical
Company
Comparative Balance Sheets and
Sources and Uses of Funds
(Millions of Dollars)**

Assets	Dec. 31, 1977	Dec. 31, 1978	Source	Use
Cash	$ 10	$ 5	$ 5	
Marketable securities	25	15	10	
Net receivables	15	20		$ 5
Inventories	25	35		10
Gross fixed assets	150	175		25
Less accumulated depreciation[a]	−40	−50	10	
Net fixed assets	110	125		
Total assets	$185	$200		
Liabilities				
Accounts payable	$ 10	$ 6		$ 4
Notes payable	15	10		5
Other current liabilities	10	14	4	
Long-term debt	60	70	10	
Preferred stock	10	10	—	—
Common stock	50	50	—	—
Retained earnings	30	40	10	
Total claims on assets	$185	$200		

[a] The accumulated depreciation is actually a "liability" account (a contra-asset) that appears on the left side of the balance sheet. Note that it is deducted, not added, when totaling the column.

ketable securities in anticipation of this expansion program, and some were sold to pay for new buildings and equipment. Finally, cash that had been accumulated in excess of the firm's needs was also worked down. In summary, this example illustrates how the sources and uses of funds statement can provide both a fairly complete picture of recent operations and a good perspective on the flow of funds within the company.

**Pro Forma
Sources and
Uses of Funds**

A pro forma, or projected, sources and uses of funds statement can also be constructed to show how a firm plans to acquire and employ funds during some future period. In the next chapter we will discuss financial forecasting, which involves the determination of future sales, the level of assets necessary to generate these sales (the left side of the projected balance sheet), and the manner in which the assets will be financed (the right side of the projected balance sheet). Given the projected balance sheet and supplemen-

**Table 5.6
Dallas Fertilizer and Chemical
Company
Statement of Sources and Uses
of Funds, 1978
(Millions of Dollars)**

Sources		Amount		Percent	
Net Income		$12		23.5	
Depreciation		10		19.6	
Decreases in working capital:					43.1
Reduction in cash	$ 5			9.8	
Sale of marketable securities	10			19.6	
Increase in other liabilities	4			7.9	
Total decrease in working capital		19		37.3	
Increase in long-term debt		10		19.6	
Total sources of funds		$51		100.0	

Uses		Amount		Percent	
Increases in working capital:					
Inventory investment	$10			19.6	
Increase in receivables	5			9.8	
Reduction in notes payable	5			9.8	
Reduction in accounts payable	4			7.9	
Total increase in working capital		$24		47.1	
Gross fixed assets expansion		25		49.0	
Dividends to stockholders		2		3.9	52.9
Total uses of funds		$51		100.0	

tary projected data on earnings, dividends, and depreciation, the financial manager can construct a pro forma sources and uses of funds statement to summarize the firm's projected operations over the planning horizon. Such a statement is obviously of much interest to lenders as well as to the firm's own management.

Summary

This chapter analyzes two important financial tools—breakeven analysis and the sources and uses of funds statement—and the key concept of operating leverage.

Breakeven analysis is a method of relating fixed costs, variable costs, and total revenues to show the level of sales that must be attained if the firm is to operate at a profit. The analysis can be based on the number of units produced or on total dollar sales. It can be used for the entire company or for a particular product or division. With minor modifications, it can be put on a cash basis instead of a profit basis. Ordinarily, breakeven analysis is conducted on a linear, or straight-line, basis. However, this is not necessary; nonlinear breakeven analysis is feasible and at times desirable.

Operating leverage is defined as the extent to which fixed costs are used in operations. The degree of operating leverage, defined as the percentage change in operating income that results from a specific percentage change in units sold, provides a precise measure of how much operating leverage a particular firm is employing. Breakeven analysis presents a graphic view of the effects on profits of changes in sales; the degree of operating leverage presents the same picture in algebraic terms.

The sources and uses of funds statement indicates where cash came from and how it was used. When a firm wishes to borrow funds, one of the first questions posed by the bank's loan officer is: "What has the firm done with the money it has?" This question is answered by the sources and uses of funds statement. The information it provides may indicate that the firm is making progress or that problems are arising. Sources and uses data may also be analyzed on a pro forma, or projected, basis to show how a firm plans to acquire and employ funds during some future period.

Questions

5.1 What benefits can be derived from breakeven analysis?

5.2 What is operating leverage? Explain how profits or losses can be magnified in a firm with high operating leverage as opposed to a firm without this characteristic.

5.3 What data are necessary to construct a breakeven chart?

5.4 What is the general effect of each of the following changes on a firm's breakeven point?
   a. An increase in selling price with no change in units sold.
   b. A change from the leasing of a machine for $5,000 a year to the purchase of the machine for $100,000. The useful life of this machine will be twenty years, with no salvage value. Assume straight-line depreciation.
   c. A reduction in variable labor costs.

5.5 In what sense can depreciation be considered a source of funds?

Problems

5.1 The Bodwin Corporation produces toasters, which it sells for $18. Fixed costs are $110,000 for up to 30,000 units of output. Variable costs are $10 per unit.
   a. What is the firm's gain or loss at sales of 12,000 units? of 18,000 units?
   b. What is the breakeven point? Illustrate by means of a chart.
   c. What is Bodwin's degree of operating leverage at sales of 14,000 units? 18,000 units? of 24,000 units?

5.2 For Reeder Industries the following relationships exist. Each unit of output is sold for $75; the fixed costs are $240,000; variable costs are $35 a unit.
   a. What is the firm's gain or loss at sales of 5,000 units? of 8,000 units?
   b. What is the breakeven point? Illustrate by means of a chart.

c. What is Reeder's degree of operating leverage at sales of 5,000 units? of 8,000 units?

d. What happens to the breakeven point if the selling price rises to $85? What is the significance of the change to financial management? Illustrate by means of a chart.

e. What happens to the breakeven point if the selling price rises to $85 but variable costs rise to $45 a unit? Illustrate by means of a chart.

5.3 For Grady Industries the following relations exist. Each unit of output is sold for $40; the fixed costs are $125,000, of which $100,000 are annual depreciation charges; variable costs are $15 a unit.

a. What is the firm's gain or loss at sales of 4,000 units? of 7,000 units?

b. What is the profit breakeven point? Illustrate by means of a chart.

c. What is the cash breakeven point? Illustrate by means of a chart.

d. Assume Grady is operating at a level of 3,500 units. Are creditors likely to seek the liquidation of the company if it is slow in paying its bills?

5.4 The consolidated balance sheets for the Norton Corporation at the beginning and end of 1978 are shown below. The company bought $225 million worth of fixed assets. The charge for current depreciation was $45 million. Earnings after taxes were $114 million, and the company paid out $30 million on dividends.

a. Fill in the amount of source or use in the appropriate column.

b. Prepare a percentage statement of sources and uses of funds.

c. Briefly summarize your findings.

Norton Corporation
Balance Sheet for Beginning and
End of 1978 (Millions of Dollars)

	Jan. 1	Dec. 31	Source	Use
Cash	$ 45	$ 21	____	____
Marketable securities	33	0	____	____
Net receivables	66	90	____	____
Inventories	159	225	____	____
Total current assets	$303	$336	____	____
Gross fixed assets	$225	$450	____	____
Less reserve for depreciation	−78	−123	____	____
Net fixed assets	147	327	____	____
Total assets	$450	$663	____	____
Accounts payable	$ 45	$ 54	____	____
Notes payable	45	9	____	____
Other current liabilities	21	45	____	____
Long-term debt	24	78	____	____
Common stock	114	192	____	____
Retained earnings	201	285	____	____
Total claims on assets	$450	$663	____	____

5.5 Transistor Electronics is considering development of a new miniature calculator. The quantity (Q) sold is a function of the price (P) where

$$Q = 2,000 - 10P$$

Fixed costs are $24,000, and variable costs per unit are $60.
   a. Graphically determine the breakeven point for the calculator in units and
      in dollars.
   b. What is the company's price at an output of 700 units?
   c. What is its profit at that output?
   d. What happens to the price and profit if the company sells 1,000 units?

CHAPTER
FORECASTING

6

FINANCIAL

The planning process is an integral part of the financial manager's job. As we will see in subsequent chapters, long-term debt and equity funds are raised infrequently and in large amounts, primarily because the cost per dollar raised by selling such securities decreases as the size of the issue increases. Because of these considerations, it is important that the firm have a working estimate of its total needs for funds for the next few years. It is therefore useful to examine methods of forecasting these needs, and this is the subject of the chapter.

Cash Flow Cycle

Firms need assets to make sales; that is, if sales are to be increased, assets must also be expanded. Growing firms require new investments—immediate investment in current assets and, as full capacity is reached, investment in fixed assets as well. New investments must be financed, and new financing carries with it commitments and obligations to service the capital obtained.[1] A growing, profitable firm is likely to require additional cash for investments in receivables, inventories, and fixed assets. Such a firm can, therefore, have a cash flow problem. The nature of this problem, as well as the cause and effect relationship between assets and sales, is illustrated in the following discussion, which traces the consequences of a series of transactions.

Effects on the Balance Sheet

1. Two partners invest a total of $50,000 to create the Glamour Galore Dress Company. The firm rents a plant; equipment and other fixed assets cost $30,000. The resulting financial situation is shown by Balance Sheet 1.

Balance Sheet 1

Assets		Liabilities	
Current assets:		Capital stock	$50,000
Cash	$20,000		
Fixed assets:			
Plant and equipment	30,000		
Total assets	$50,000	Total liabilities and net worth	$50,000

2. Glamour Galore receives an order to manufacture 10,000 dresses. The order itself has no effect on the balance sheet, but in preparation for the manufacturing activity the firm buys $20,000 worth of cotton cloth on

1. "Servicing" capital refers to the payment of interest and principal on debt and to dividends on common stocks.

terms of net 30 days. Without additional investment by the owners, total assets increase by $20,000, financed by the trade accounts payable to the supplier of the cotton cloth.

After the purchase, the firm spends $20,000 on labor for cutting the cloth to the required pattern. Of the $20,000 total labor cost, $10,000 is paid in cash and $10,000 is owed in the form of accrued wages. These two transactions are reflected in Balance Sheet 2, which shows that total assets increase to $80,000. Current assets are increased; net working capital—total current assets minus total current liabilities—remains constant. The current ratio declines to 1.67, and the debt ratio rises to 38 percent. The financial position of the firm is weakening. If it should seek to borrow at this point, Glamour Galore could not use the work-in-process inventories as collateral, because a lender would find little use for partially manufactured dresses.

Balance Sheet 2

Assets			Liabilities	
Current assets:			Accounts payable	$20,000
Cash		$10,000	Accrued wages payable	10,000
Inventories—work in process:			Total current liabilities	$30,000
Materials		20,000	Capital stock	$50,000
Labor		20,000		
Total current assets		$50,000		
Fixed assets:				
Plant and equipment		30,000		
Total assets		$80,000	Total liabilities and net worth	$80,000

3. In order to complete the dresses, Glamour Galore incurs additional labor costs of $20,000, which it pays in cash. The firm desires to maintain a minimum cash balance of $5,000. Since the initial cash balance is $10,000, it must borrow an additional $15,000 from its bank to meet the wage bill. The borrowing is reflected in notes payable in Balance Sheet 3.

Balance Sheet 3

Assets			Liabilities	
Current assets:			Accounts payable	$20,000
Cash		$ 5,000	Notes payable	15,000
Inventory—finished goods		60,000	Accrued wages payable	10,000
Total current assets		$65,000	Total current liabilities	$45,000
Fixed assets:			Capital stock	50,000
Plant and equipment		30,000		
Total assets		$95,000	Total liabilities and net worth	$95,000

Total assets rise to $95,000, with a finished goods inventory of $60,000. The current ratio drops to 1.4, and the debt ratio rises to 47 percent. These ratios show a further weakening of the firm's financial position.

4. Glamour Galore ships the dresses on the basis of the original order, invoicing the purchaser for $100,000 within 30 days. Accrued wages and accounts payable have to be paid now, so Glamour Galore must borrow an additional $30,000 in order to maintain the $5,000 minimum cash balance. These transactions are shown in Balance Sheet 4. In this balance sheet, finished goods inventory is replaced by receivables, with the markup reflected as retained earnings. This causes the debt ratio to drop to 33 percent. Since the receivables are carried at the sales price, current assets increase to $105,000 and the current ratio rises to 2.3. Compared with the conditions reflected in Balance Sheet 3, most of the financial ratios show improvement. However, the absolute amount of debt is large.

Balance Sheet 4

Assets			Liabilities	
Current assets:			Notes payable	$ 45,000
Cash		$ 5,000	Total current liabilities	$ 45,000
Accounts receivable		100,000	Capital stock	50,000
Total current assets		$105,000	Retained earnings	40,000
			Total net worth	$ 90,000
Fixed assets:				
Plant and equipment		30,000		
Total assets		$135,000	Total liabilities and net worth	$135,000

Whether the firm's financial position is really improved depends on the creditworthiness of the purchaser of the dresses. If the purchaser is a good credit risk, Glamour Galore may be able to borrow further on the basis of the accounts receivable.

5. The firm receives payment for the accounts receivable, pays off the bank loan, and is in the highly liquid position shown by Balance Sheet 5. If a new

Balance Sheet 5

Assets			Liabilities	
Current assets:			Capital stock	$50,000
Cash		$60,000	Retained earnings	40,000
Fixed assets:				
Plant and equipment		30,000		
Total assets		$90,000	Total liabilities and net worth	$90,000

order for 10,000 dresses is received, it will have no effect on the balance sheet, but a cycle similar to the one described will begin.

6. The idea of the cash flow cycle can now be generalized. An order that requires the purchase of raw materials is placed with a firm. The purchase in turn generates an accounts payable. As labor is applied, work-in-process inventories build up. To the extent that wages are not fully paid at the time labor is used, accrued wages will appear on the liability side of the balance sheet. As goods are completed, they move into finished good inventories. The cash needed to pay for the labor to complete the goods may make it necessary for the firm to borrow.

Finished goods inventories are usually sold on credit, which gives rise to accounts receivable. Since the firm has not received cash, this point in the cycle represents the peak in financing requirements. If the firm did not borrow at the time finished goods inventories were at their maximum, it may do so as inventories are converted into receivables by credit sales. Income taxes (which were not considered in the example) can add to the problem. As accounts receivable become cash, short-term obligations can be paid off.

Financing Patterns

The influence of sales on current asset levels has been illustrated. Over the course of several cycles, the fluctuations in sales are accompanied in most industries by a rising long-term trend. Figure 6.1 shows the consequences of such a pattern. Total permanent assets increase steadily in the form of current and fixed assets. Increases of this nature should be financed by long-term debt, by equity, or by "spontaneous" increases in liabilities (such as accrued taxes and wages and accounts payable), which naturally accompany increasing sales. However, temporary increases in assets can be covered by short-term liabilities. The distinction between temporary and permanent asset levels may be difficult to make in practice, but it is neither illusory nor unimportant. Short-term financing of long-term needs is dangerous. A profitable firm may be unable to meet its cash obligations if funds borrowed on a short-term basis become tied up in permanent asset needs.

Percent-of-Sales Method

It is apparent from the preceding discussion that *the most important variable influencing a firm's financing requirements is its projected dollar volume of sales.* Thus a good sales forecast is an essential foundation for forecasting financial requirements. In spite of its importance, we do not go into sales forecasting here. Instead we assume that a sales forecast has been made; then we estimate financial requirements on the basis of this fore-

Figure 6.1
**Fluctuating versus Permanent
Assets**

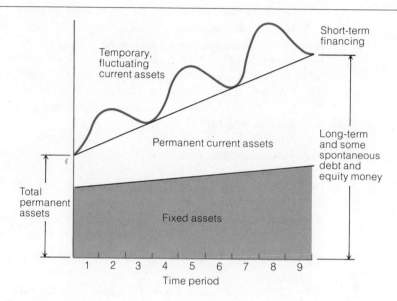

cast.[2] We describe the principal methods of forecasting financial requirements in this and the following sections.

The simplest approach to forecasting financial requirements expresses
the firm's needs in terms of the percentage of annual sales invested in each
balance sheet item. As an example, consider the Moore Company, whose
balance sheet as of December 31, 1978, is shown in Table 6.1. The company's sales are running at about $500,000 a year, which is its capacity limit;

Table 6.1
**The Moore Company
Balance Sheet as of
December 31, 1978**

Assets		Liabilities	
Cash	$ 10,000	Accounts payable	$ 50,000
Receivables	85,000	Accrued taxes and wages	25,000
Inventories	100,000	Mortgage bonds	70,000
Fixed assets (net)	150,000	Common stocks	100,000
		Retained earnings	100,000
Total assets	$345,000	Total liabilities and net worth	$345,000

2. For a discussion of demand forecasting, see E. F. Brigham and J. L. Pappas, *Managerial Economics*,
3rd ed. (Hinsdale, Ill.: Dryden Press, 1979).

the profit margin after tax on sales is 4 percent. During 1978, the company earned $20,000 after taxes and paid out $10,000 in dividends, and it plans to continue paying out half of net profits as dividends. How much additional financing will be needed if sales expand to $800,000 during 1979? The per-cent-of-sales method of calculating this figure is explained below.[3]

First, isolate those balance sheet items that can be expected to vary di-rectly with sales. In the case of the Moore Company, this step applies to each category of assets; a higher level of sales necessitates more cash for transactions, more receivables, higher inventory levels, and additional fixed plant capacity. On the liability side, accounts payable as well as accruals can be expected to increase with increases in sales. Retained earnings will go up as long as the company is profitable and does not pay out 100 per-cent of earnings, but the percentage increase is not constant. However, neither common stock nor mortgage bonds will increase spontaneously with an increase in sales.

The items that can be expected to vary directly with sales are tabulated as a percentage of sales in Table 6.2. For every $1 increase in sales, assets must increase by $.69; this $.69 must be financed in some manner. Ac-counts payable will increase spontaneously with sales, as will accruals; these two items will supply $.15 of new funds for each $1 increase in sales. Subtracting the 15 percent for spontaneously generated funds from the 69

**Table 6.2
The Moore Company
Balance Sheet Items Expressed
as a Percent of Sales, as of
December 31, 1978**

Assets		Liabilities	
Cash	2.0	Accounts payable	10.0
Receivables	17.0	Accrued taxes and wages	5.0
Inventories	20.0	Mortgage bonds	a
Fixed assets (net)	30.0	Common stock	a
		Retained earnings	a
Total assets	69.0	Total liabilities and net worth	15.0
Assets as percent of sales			69.0
Less spontaneous increase in liabilities			−15.0
Percent of each additional dollar of sales that must be financed			54.0

[a] Not applicable.

3. We recognize, of course, that as a practical matter, business firms plan their needs in terms of specific items of equipment, square feet of floor space, and other factors, and not as a percentage of sales. However, the outside analyst does not have access to this information, and even the manager who has the information on specific items needs to check forecasts in aggregate terms. The percent-of-sales method serves both these needs surprisingly well.

percent funds requirement leaves 54 percent. Thus, for each $1 increase in sales, the Moore Company must obtain $.54 of financing either from internally generated funds or from external sources.

In the case at hand, sales are scheduled to increase by $300,000 from $500,000 to $800,000. Applying the 54 percent developed in the table to the expected increase in sales leads to the conclusion that $162,000 will be needed. Some of that need will be met by retained earnings. Total revenues during 1979 will be $800,000; if the company earns 4 percent after taxes on this volume, profits will amount to $32,000. Assuming that the 50 percent dividend payout ratio is maintained, $16,000 will be paid out in dividends, and $16,000 will be retained. Subtracting the retained earnings from the $162,000 that was needed leaves a figure of $146,000—the amount of funds that must be obtained through borrowing or by selling new common stock.

This process can be expressed in equation form:

$$\text{External funds needed} = \frac{A}{TR}(\Delta TR) - \frac{B}{TR}(\Delta TR) - bm(TR_2), \qquad \textbf{(6.1)}$$

where:

$\dfrac{A}{TR}$ = assets that increase spontaneously with total revenues or sales as a percent of total revenues or sales.

$\dfrac{B}{TR}$ = liabilities that increase spontaneously with total revenues or sales as a percent of total revenues or sales.

ΔTR = change in total revenues or sales.

m = profit margin on sales.

TR_2 = total revenues projected for the year.

b = earnings retention ratio.

For the Moore Company, then:

$$\begin{aligned}
\text{External funds needed} &= 0.69(\$300,000) - 0.15(\$300,000) \\
&\quad - 0.04(\$800,000)(0.5) \\
&= 0.54(\$300,000) - 0.02(\$800,000) \\
&= \$146,000.
\end{aligned}$$

The $146,000 found by the formula method must, of course, equal the amount derived previously.

Notice what would have occurred if the Moore Company's sales forecast for 1979 had been only $515,000, or a 3 percent increase. Under the formula, the external funds requirements would have been as follows:

$$\begin{aligned}
\text{External funds needed} &- 0.54(\$15,000) - 0.02(\$515,000) \\
&= \$8,100 - \$10,300 \\
&= (\$2,200).
\end{aligned}$$

In this case, no external funds would have been required. In fact, the company would have had $2,200 in excess of its requirements and could have planned to increase dividends, retire debt, or seek additional investment opportunities.

The example shows not only that higher levels of sales bring about a need for funds but also that while small percentage increases can be financed through internally generated funds, larger increases cause the firm to go into the market for outside capital. In other words, a certain level of growth can be financed from internal sources, but higher levels of growth require external financing.[4]

Note that the increase in sales equals $(1 + g)TR_1$ where g equals the growth rate in sales. The increase in sales can therefore be written:

$$\Delta TR = (1 + g)TR_1 - TR_1 = TR_1(1 + g - 1) = gTR_1.$$

Next, the expression for external funds needed, equation 6.1, can be used to derive the percentage of the increase in sales that will have to be financed externally (PEFR) as a function of the critical variables involved. In equation 6.1 let

$$\left(\frac{A}{TR} - \frac{B}{TR}\right) = I,$$

substitute for ΔTR and TR_2, and divide both sides by $\Delta TR + gTR_1$:

$$PEFR = I - \frac{m}{g}(1 + g)b. \tag{6.2}$$

Using equation 6.2, we can now investigate the influence of factors such as an increased rate of inflation on the percentage of sales growth that must be financed externally. Based on the relationships for all manufacturing industries, some representative values of the terms on the right-hand side of the equation are: $I = 0.5$, $m = 0.05$, and $b = 0.60$.

During the period before the onset of inflation in the United States after 1966, the economy was growing at about 6 to 7 percent per annum. A firm that was in an industry growing at the same rate as the economy and that maintained its market share position in its industry would also be growing at 6 to 7 percent per annum. What are the implications for external financing requirements of such a firm? With a growth rate of 6 or 7 percent the per-

---

4. At this point, one might ask two questions: "Shouldn't depreciation be considered a source of funds?" and "Won't this reduce the amount of external funds needed?" The answer to both questions is no. In the percent-of-sales method, the implicit assumption is that funds generated through depreciation (in the sources and uses of funds sense) must be used to replace the assets to which the depreciation is applicable. Accordingly, depreciation does not enter the calculations in this forecasting technique; it is netted out.

centage of sales increase that would have to be financed externally would be:

$$PEFR = 0.5 - \frac{0.05}{0.06}(1.06)(0.6)$$

$$= 0.50 - 0.53 = -0.03 = -3\%$$

$$PEFR = 0.5 - \frac{0.05}{0.07}(1.07)(0.6)$$

$$= 0.50 - 0.46 = 0.04 = 4\%$$

Thus at a growth rate of 6 percent the percentage of external financing to sales growth would be -3 percent. In other words, the firm would have excess funds with which it could increase either dividends or its investment in marketable securities. With a growth rate of 7 percent the firm would have a moderate 4 percent requirement of external financing as a percentage of sales increase.

Following 1966 the inflation rate in some years was in the two digit range—10 percent or more. If we were to add to the previous 6 to 7 percent growth rate sufficient percentage points per annum of an inflation rate to obtain a growth rate of 15 or 20 percent for a firm, the external financing requirements would be:

$$PEFR = 0.5 - \frac{0.05}{0.15}(1.15)(0.6)$$

$$= 0.50 - 0.23 = 0.27 = 27\%.$$

$$PEFR = 0.5 - \frac{0.05}{0.20}(1.20)(0.6)$$

$$= 0.50 - 0.18 = 0.32 = 32\%.$$

With a growth rate in sales of 15 percent, external financing would rise to 27 percent of the firm's sales growth. If inflation caused the firm's growth rate to rise to 20 percent, then the external financing percentage would rise to 32 percent.

The substantial increase in companies' growth rate of sales, measured in inflated dollars in recent years, points up why external financing has become more important for firms. It underscores also why the finance function has taken on increased importance. There is simply a much bigger job to be done, particularly in requirements for using external financing sources to maintain a firm's sales growth. Even if a firm were not growing at all in real terms, an inflation rate of, say, 10 percent would make it necessary for the firm to raise external financing of 17 percent of its growth in sales in inflated dollars. This again underscores why financing has come to the fore as an important function of the firm.

The percent-of-sales method of forecasting financial requirements is neither simple nor mechanical, although the explanation of its ideas requires only simple illustrations. Practical experience in applying the technique suggests the importance of understanding (1) the basic technology of the firm and (2) the logic of the relationship between its sales and assets. A great deal of experience and judgment is required to apply the technique.

The percent-of-sales method is most appropriately used for forecasting relatively short-term changes in financing needs. It is less useful for longer-term forecasting for reasons that are described in connection with the analysis of the regression method of financial forecasting discussed in the next section.

Scatter Diagram, or Simple Regression Method

An alternative method of forecasting financial requirements is the scatter diagram, or simple regression method. A scatter diagram is a graphic portrayal of joint relations. Proper use of this method requires practical but not necessarily statistical sophistication.

Table 6.3 and Figure 6.2 illustrate the use of the scatter diagram method and demonstrate its superiority over the percent-of-sales method for long-range forecasting. As in all financial forecasting, the sales forecast is the starting point. The financial manager either is given the sales forecast or participates in formulating it. Suppose the manager has data through 1979 and is making a forecast of inventories for 1984, as indicated in Table 6.3. Under the simple regression method, in Figure 6.2 a line is drawn through the points from 1974 to 1979. The line that fits the scatter of points—in this example a straight line—is called the *line of best fit,* or the *regression line.* Of course, it seldom happens that all points fall exactly on the regression line, and the line itself may be curved instead of linear.[5]

If the percent-of-sales method had been used, some difficulties would have arisen immediately. Table 6.3 gives percent of sales for 1974 through 1979. What relationship should be used? The 44 percent for 1974? The 11 percent for 1979? Or some average of them? If the relationship for 1979 had been used, a forecast of $55,000 for inventories in 1984 would have been made (compared with $42,000 by the scatter diagram method). That forecast represents a large error.

The regression method is thus seen to be superior for forecasting financial requirements, particularly longer-term forecasts. When a firm is likely to

5. In these illustrations, inventories are used as the item to be forecast. Much theory suggests that inventories increase as a square root of sales. This characteristic would tend to turn the regression line between inventories and sales slightly downward, as would improvements in inventory control techniques. However, the increased diversity of types, models, and styles would tend to increase inventories. Applications (by the authors' students) of the regression method to hundreds of companies indicate that the linear straight-line relationships frequently represent the line of best fit or, at worst, involve only a small error. If the line were in fact curved over, a curved line could be fitted to the data and used for forecasting purposes.

Table 6.3
Illustrative Relationship
between Sales and
Inventories

Year	Sales	Inventory	Inventory as a Percent of Sales
1974	$ 50,000	$22,000	44
1975	100,000	24,000	24
1976	150,000	26,000	17
1977	200,000	28,000	14
1978	250,000	30,000	12
1979	300,000	32,000	11
.	.	.	.
.	.	.	.
.	.	.	.
1984 (estimated)	500,000	40,000	8

have a base stock of inventory or fixed assets, the ratio of the item to sales declines as sales increase. In such cases, the percent-of-sales method results in large errors.[6]

Multiple Regression Method

A more sophisticated approach to forecasting a firm's assets calls for the use of multiple regression analysis. In simple regression, sales are assumed to be a function of only one variable; in multiple regression, they are recognized to depend on a number of variables. For example, in simple regression, sales can be seen strictly as a function of GNP. With multiple regression, sales can be seen as dependent on both GNP and a set of additional variables. For example, sales of ski equipment depend on—among other things—(1) the general level of prosperity as measured by GNP, personal disposable income, or other indicators of aggregate economic activity; (2) population increases; (3) number of lifts operating; (4) weather conditions; and (5) advertising.

We shall not go into detail on the use of multiple regression analysis at this time. However, most computer installations have "canned" regression programs incorporated into their systems, making the method extremely easy to use. Multiple regression is widely used by at least the larger corporations.

---

6. The widespread use of the percentage method makes for lax control. It would be easy to reduce inventories below the $55,000 percent-of-sales forecast level and still be inefficient because the correct target amount is closer to $40,000.

Figure 6.2
Illustrative Relationship between
Sales and Inventories

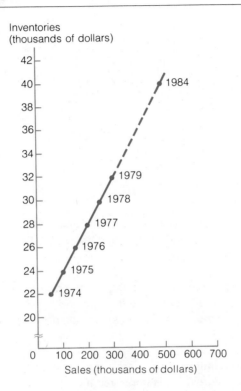

Comparison of Forecasting Methods

Thus far we have considered three methods used in financial forecasting: (1) percent of sales, (2) scatter diagram, or simple linear regression, and (3) multiple regression. In this section we will summarize and compare those methods.

Percent of Sales

The percent-of-sales method of financial forecasting assumes that certain balance sheet items vary directly with sales—that is, the ratio of a given balance sheet item to sales remains constant. This postulated relationship is shown in Figure 6.3. *Notice that the percent-of-sales method implicitly assumes a linear relationship that passes through the origin.* That is, the slope of the line representing the relationship may vary, but the line always passes through the origin. The relationship is implicitly established by finding one point, or ratio, such as that designated as *X* in Figure 6.3, and connecting

Figure 6.3
Percent of Sales

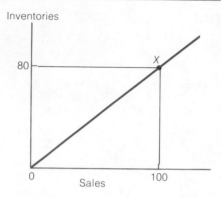

this point with the origin. Then, for any projected level of sales, the
forecasted level of the particular balance sheet item can be determined.

Scatter Diagram,
or Simple Linear
Regression

The scatter diagram method differs from the percent-of-sales method principally in that it does not assume that the line of relationship passes through
the origin. In its simplest form, the scatter diagram method calls for calculating the ratio between sales and the relevant balance sheet item at two
points in time, extending a line through these two points, and using the line
to describe the relationship between sales and the balance sheet item. The
accuracy of the regression is improved if more points are plotted, and the
regression line can be fitted mathematically (by a technique known as the
method of least squares) as well as drawn in by eye.

The scatter diagram method is illustrated in Figure 6.4, where the percent-
of-sales relationship is also shown for comparison. The error induced by
the use of the percent-of-sales method is represented by the gap between
the two lines. At a sales level of 125, the percent-of-sales method would
call for an inventory of 100 versus an inventory of only 90 for the scatter
diagram forecast. The error is very small if sales continue to run at approximately the current level, but the gap widens and the error increases as sales
deviate in either direction from current levels, as they probably would if
a long-run forecast were being made.

Multiple
Regression

In our illustrations to this point, we have been assuming that the observations fall exactly on the relationship line. This implies perfect correlation—
something that seldom occurs in reality. The actual observations are instead
scattered about the regression line. What causes the deviations from the

**Figure 6.4
Scatter Diagram, or Simple
Linear Regression**

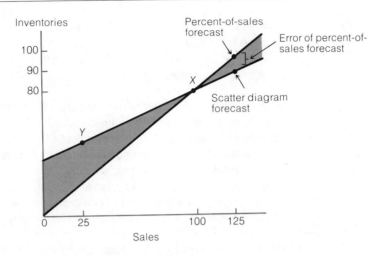

regression line? One answer is that inventories are determined by factors in addition to sales. Inventory levels are certainly influenced by work stoppages at suppliers' plants. A steel fabricator who anticipates a strike in the steel industry will stock up on steel products. Such hedge buying causes actual inventories to rise above the level forecast on the basis of sales projections. Then, assuming the strike does occur and continues for many months, inventories are drawn down and may end up well below the predicted level. Multiple regression techniques, which introduce additional variables (such as work stoppages) into the analysis, are employed to further improve financial forecasting.

The need for more complicated forecasting techniques varies from situation to situation. For example, the percent-of-sales method may be perfectly adequate for making short-run forecasts where conditions are relatively stable, while multiple regression may be deemed essential for longer-run forecasts in more dynamic industries. As in all other applications of financial analysis, the cost of using more refined techniques must be balanced against the benefits of increased accuracy.

Summary

Firms need assets to make sales; if sales are to be increased, assets must also be expanded. The illustration of the relationship between sales and assets shows how even a growing, profitable firm can have a cash flow problem.

The most important causal variable in determining a firm's financial requirements is its projected dollar volume of sales, and a good sales forecast is an essential foundation for forecasting financial requirements. The two principal methods used for making financial forecasts are (1) the percent-of-sales method and (2) the regression method. The first has the virtue of simplicity; the forecaster computes past relationships between asset and liability items and sales, assumes these relationships will continue, and then applies the new sales forecast to get an estimate of the financial requirements.

However, since the percent-of-sales method assumes that the balance-sheet-to-sales relationships will remain constant, it is useful only for relatively short-run forecasting. When longer-range forecasts are needed, the regression method is preferable because it allows for changing balance-sheet-to-sales relationships. Further, linear regression can be expanded to curvilinear regression and simple regression to multiple regression. These more complex methods are useful in certain circumstances, but their increased accuracy must be balanced against the increased costs of using them.

The tools and techniques of financial forecasting are generally used in the following manner. As a first step, one of the long-range forecasting techniques is used to make a long-run forecast of the firm's financial requirements over a three- to five-year period. This forecast is then used to make the strategic financing plans during the planning period. Long lead times are necessary when companies sell bonds or stocks; otherwise financial managers might be forced to go into the market for funds during unfavorable periods.

In addition to long-run strategic forecasting, the financial manager must also make accurate short-run forecasts to be sure that bank funds will be available to meet seasonal and other short-run requirements. This topic is considered in the following chapter.

Questions

6.1 What should be the approximate point of intersection between the sales-to-asset regression line and the vertical axis (Y-axis intercept) for the following: inventory, accounts receivable, fixed assets? State your answer in terms of positive, zero, or negative intercept. Can you think of any accounts that might have a negative intercept?

6.2 How does forecasting financial requirements in advance of needs help financial managers perform their responsibilities more effectively?

6.3 Explain how a downturn in the business cycle could either cause a cash shortage for a firm or generate excess cash.

6.4 Explain this statement: To a considerable extent, current assets represent permanent assets.

6.5 What advantages might a multiple regression technique have over a simple regression technique in forecasting sales? What might be some drawbacks in the actual use of this technique?

Problems

6.1 In 1978, the Brock Company's total assets were $1.9 million. Sales, which were $3.8 million, will increase by 20 percent in 1979. The 1978 ratio of assets to sales will be maintained throughout 1979. Common stock amounted to $545,000 in 1978, and retained earnings were $500,000. Debt will increase by 10 percent in 1979, but common stock will remain unchanged; net profit after taxes will be 5 percent of sales, and no dividends will be declared or paid. What amount of new financing will be needed in 1979?

6.2 The Kaplan Company's 1978 balance sheet is shown below. Sales in 1978 totaled $1 million. The ratio of net profit to sales was 3 percent, with a dividend payout ratio of 60 percent of net income. Sales are expected to increase by 25 percent during 1979. No long-term debt will be retired. Using the percentage of sales method, determine how much outside financing is required.

**Kaplan Company
Balance Sheet as of
December 31, 1978**

Assets		**Liabilities**	
Cash	$ 15,000	Accounts payable	$ 10,000
Accounts receivable	35,000	Accruals	5,000
Inventory	75,000	Notes payable	35,000
Current assets	$125,000	Total current liabilities	$ 50,000
Fixed assets	375,000	Long-term debt	150,000
		Total debt	$200,000
		Capital stock	175,000
		Retained earnings	125,000
Total assets	$500,000	Total liabilities and net worth	$500,000

6.3 Given the following data on the Solari Corporation, predict next year's balance sheet:

This year's sales: $50,000,000
Next year's sales: $60,000,000
After-tax profits: 5% of sales
Dividend payout: 40%
This year's retained earnings: $10,200,000
Cash as percent of sales: 5%
Receivables as percent of sales: 15%
Inventory as percent of sales: 20%

Net fixed assets as percent of sales: 35%

Accounts payable as percent of sales: 10%

Accruals as percent of sales: 15%

Next year's common stock: $13,000,000

**Solari Corporation
Balance Sheet as of
December 31, 19XX**

Assets		Liabilities	
Cash	_____	Accounts payable	_____
Accounts receivable	_____	Notes payable	_____
Inventory	_____	Accruals	_____
Total current assets	_____	Total current liabilities	_____
Fixed assets	_____	Common stock	_____
		Retained earnings	_____
Total assets	_____	Total liabilities	_____

6.4 The Universal Supply Company is a wholesale steel distributor. It purchases steel in carload lots from more than twenty producing mills and sells to several thousand steel users. The items carried include sheets, plates, wire products, bolts, windows, pipe, and tubing.

The company owns two warehouses of 15,000 square feet each and is contemplating the erection of another warehouse of 20,000 square feet. The nature of the steel supply business requires that the company maintain large inventories to take care of customer requirements in the event of mill strikes or other delays.

In examining patterns from 1972 through 1977, the company found consistent relationships among the following accounts as a percent of sales.

Current assets: 60%

Net fixed assets: 30%

Accounts payable: 5%

Other current liabilities, including accruals and provision for income
  taxes but not bank loans: 5%

Net profit after taxes: 3%

The company's sales for 1978 were $3 million, and its balance sheet on December 31, 1978, is shown below. The company expects its sales to increase by $400,000 each year. If this level is achieved, what will the company's financial requirements be at the end of the five-year period? Assume that accounts not tied directly to sales (for example, notes payable) remain constant and that the company pays no dividends.

a. Construct a pro forma balance sheet for the end of 1983, using "additional financing needed" as the balancing item.

b. What are the crucial assumptions you made in your projection method?

Universal Supply Company
Balance Sheet as of
December 31, 1978

Assets		Liabilities	
Current assets	$1,800,000	Accounts payable	$ 150,000
Fixed assets	900,000	Notes payable	400,000
		Other current liabilities	150,000
		Total current liabilities	$ 700,000
		Mortgage loan	300,000
		Common stock	550,000
		Retained earnings	1,150,000
Total assets	$2,700,000	Total liabilities and net worth	$2,700,000

6.5 One useful method of evaluating a firm's financial structure in relation to its industry is comparing it with financial ratio composites for the industry. A new firm, or one contemplating entering a new industry, may use such composites as a guide to its likely approximate financial position after the initial settling-down period.

The following data represent ratios for the publishing and printing industry for 1979.

Sales to net worth: 2.3 times
Current debt to net worth: 42%
Total debt to net worth: 75%
Current ratio: 2.9 times
Net sales to inventory: 4.7 times
Average collection period: 64 days
Fixed assets to net worth: 53.2%

a. Complete the pro forma balance sheet (round to nearest thousand) for Creative Printers whose 1979 sales are $3 million.
b. What does the use of the financial ratio composites accomplish?
c. What other factors will influence the financial structure of the firm?

Creative Printers, Inc.
Pro Forma Balance Sheet as of
December 31, 1979

Cash	_____	Current debt	_____
Accounts receivable	_____	Long-term debt	_____
Inventory	_____	Total debt	_____
Current assets	_____	Net worth	_____
Fixed assets	_____		
Total assets	_____	Total liabilities and net worth	_____

6.6 The 1978 sales of Electrosonics, Inc., were $12 million. Common stock and notes payable are constant. The dividend payout ratio is 50 percent. Retained earnings as shown on the December 31, 1977, balance sheet were

$60,000. The percent of sales in each balance sheet item that varies directly with sales is expected to be:

	Percent
Cash	4
Receivables	10
Inventories	20
Net fixed assets	35
Accounts payable	12
Accruals	6
Profit rate (after taxes) on sales	3

a. Complete the balance sheet given below.
b. Suppose that in 1979 sales will increase by 10 percent over 1978 sales. How much additional (external) capital will be required?
c. Construct the year-end 1979 balance sheet. Set up an account for "financing needed" or "funds available."
d. What would happen to capital requirements under each of the following conditions?
   1. The profit margin went from 3 percent to 6 percent? from 3 percent to 1 percent? Set up an equation to illustrate your answers.
   2. The dividend payout rate was raised from 50 percent to 80 percent? was lowered from 50 percent to 30 percent? Set up an equation to illustrate your answers.
   3. Slower collections caused receivables to rise to 45 days of sales.

Electrosonics, Inc.
Balance Sheet as of
December 31, 1978

Cash	_____	Accounts payable	_____
Receivables	_____	Notes payable	630,000
Inventory	_____	Accruals	_____
Total current assets	_____	Total current liabilities	_____
Fixed assets	_____	Common stock	5,250,000
		Retained earnings	_____
Total assets	_____	Total liabilities and net worth	_____

6.7 Jones Klein, a large drug manufacturer, had the following balance sheet and income statement for 1975. (Also shown is the industry norm for each item based on RMA Statement Studies of the drug industry.) The industry norm for sales to assets is 1.5 times.
a. Given only the total sales figure of $606,300, project a balance sheet and income statement using the same format. Show liabilities below assets (round to hundreds).
b. For each item, compute the percent difference between actual and pro forma in the form (actual/pro forma) − 1.
c. Comment on the difference between the actual and pro forma account based on the industry norms.

Jones Klein, Inc.
Balance Sheet as of
December 31, 1975

Assets	Firm	Norm	Liabilities	Firm	Norm
Cash and securities	$186,700	12.5%	Accounts payable	$ 33,400	10.0%
Receivables	125,100	22.8	Notes payable	77,700	8.0
Inventories	105,700	28.0	Other current liabilities	52,600	8.3
Other current assets	9,900	1.2	Total current liabilities	$163,700	26.3%
Total current assets	$427,400	64.5%			
Net fixed assets	143,300	31.5	Long-term debt	111,000	22.6
Other tangible assets	16,200	4.0	Net worth	312,200	51.1
Total assets	$586,900	100.0%	Total claims on assets	$586,900	100.0%

Jones Klein, Inc.
Income Statement for Year
Ended December 31, 1975

	Firm	Norm
Sales	$606,300	100.0%
Cost of goods sold	228,000	60.2
Gross profit	$378,300	39.8%
Selling and administrative expense	269,800	21.6
Operating Income	$108,500	18.2%
Less interest expense	−14,200	−1.4
Net income before tax	$ 94,300	16.8%
Less federal income tax	−30,600	−8.4
Net income	$ 63,700	8.4%

6.8 A firm has the following relationships. The ratio of assets to sales is 60 percent. Liabilities that increase spontaneously with sales are 15 percent. The profit margin on sales after taxes is 5 percent. The firm's dividend payout ratio is 40 percent.

    a. If the firm's growth rate on sales is 10 percent per annum, what percentage of the sales increase in any year must be financed externally?

    b. If the firm's growth rate on sales increases to 20 percent per annum, what percentage of the sales increase in any year must be financed externally?

    c. How will your answer to Part a change if the profit margin increases to 6 percent?

    d. How will your answer to Part b change if the firm's dividend payout is reduced to 10 percent.

    e. If the profit margin increases from 5 percent to 6 percent and the dividend payout ratio is 20 percent, at what growth rate in sales will the external financing requirement percentage be exactly zero?

CHAPTER 7 FINANCIAL PLANNING AND CONTROL BUDGETING

In the preceding chapter we first examined the relationship between assets and sales, then considered several procedures the financial manager can use to forecast requirements. In addition to long-range forecasts, the financial manager is concerned with short-term needs for funds. It is embarrassing for a corporate treasurer to "run out of money." Even though a bank loan can probably be negotiated on short notice, this plight may cause the banker to question the soundness of the firm's management and, accordingly, to reduce the company's line of credit or raise the interest rate. Therefore, attention must be given to short-term budgeting, with special emphasis on cash forecasting, or cash budgeting, as it is commonly called.

The cash budget is, however, only one part of the firm's overall budget system. The nature of the budget system, especially the way it can be used for both planning and control purposes, is also discussed in this chapter.

Budgeting

A budget is simply a financial plan. A household budget itemizes the family's sources of income and describes how this income will be spent—so much for food, housing, transportation, entertainment, education, savings, and so on. Similarly, the federal budget indicates the government's income sources and allocates funds to defense, welfare, agriculture, education, and the like. By the same token, a firm's budget is a plan detailing how funds will be spent on labor, raw materials, capital goods, and so on, and how the funds for these expenditures will be obtained. Just as the federal budget can be used as a device to ensure that the Department of Defense, Department of Agriculture, and others limit their expenditures to specific amounts, the corporate budget can also be used as a device for formulating the firm's plans and for exercising control over the various departments.

Budgeting is thus a management tool used for both planning and control. Depending on the nature of the business, detailed plans may be formulated for the next few months, the next year, the next five years, or even longer. A company engaged in, say, heavy construction is constantly extending bids that may or may not be accepted; it cannot, and indeed need not, plan as far ahead as an electric utility company. The electric utility can base its projections on population growth, which is predictable for five- to ten-year periods, and it *must* plan asset acquisitions years ahead because of the long lead times involved in constructing dams, nuclear power plants, and the like.

Nature of the Budgeting Process

Fundamentally, the budgeting process is a method to improve operations—a continuous effort to specify what should be done to get the job completed in the best possible way. Corporate budgeting should not be thought of as a device for limiting expenditures; instead it should be seen as a tool for obtaining the most productive and profitable use of the company's resources. The budget requires a set of performance standards, or targets, that can be compared to actual results. This process, called "controlling to plan," is a continuous monitoring procedure that reviews and evaluates performance with reference to previously established standards.

Establishing standards requires a realistic understanding of the activities carried on by the firm. Arbitrary standards, set without a basic understanding of the minimum costs as determined by the nature of the firm's operations, can do more harm than good. Budgets imposed in an arbitrary fashion may represent impossible targets at the one extreme or standards that are too lax at the other. If standards are unrealistically high, frustrations and resentment will develop. If they are unduly low, costs will swing out of control, profits will suffer, and morale will deteriorate. However, a set of budgets based on a clear understanding and careful analysis of operations can play an important positive role for the firm.[1]

Budgets can provide valuable guides to both high-level executives and middle-management personnel. Well-formulated and effectively developed budgets make subordinates aware that top management has a realistic understanding of the nature of the business's operations. Such budgets can be an important communication link between top management and the divisional personnel whom they guide.

Budgets also represent planning and control devices that enable management to anticipate change and adapt to it. Business operations in today's economic environment are complex and subject to heavy competitive pressures and many kinds of changes. The rate of growth of the economy as a whole fluctuates, and these fluctuations affect different industries in a number of different ways. If a firm plans ahead, the budget and control process can provide management with a good basis for understanding the firm's operations in relation to the general environment. This understanding can enable the firm to react quickly to developing events, thereby increasing its ability to perform effectively.

In summary, the budgeting process improves internal coordination. Decisions for each product at each stage and level—research, engineering, production, marketing, personnel, and finance—have an impact on the firm's profits. Planning and control are the essence of profit planning, and

---

1. The authors are familiar with one case where an unrealistic budget ruined a major national corporation. Top management set impossible performance and growth goals for the various divisions. The divisions, in an effort to meet the sales and profit projections, expanded into high-risk product lines (especially real estate development ventures), employed questionable accounting practices that tended to overstate profits, and the like. Debt financing was emphasized in order to leverage earnings. Things looked good for several years, but eventually the true situation became apparent. Top management brought in a team of consultants in an attempt to correct the problems, but it was too late; the firm was beyond help. To us, the most interesting point is that the consultants traced the firm's difficulties *directly* back to the unrealistic targets established by top management without adequate consultation with the division managers.

the budget system provides an integrated picture of the firm's operations as a whole. It thus enables division managers to see the relationship of their part of the enterprise to the totality of the firm. For example, a production decision to alter the level of work-in-process inventories or a marketing decision to change the terms under which a particular product is sold can be traced through the entire budget system to show its effects on the firm's overall profitability. The budgeting system is thus a most important financial tool.

Budget System

The nature of the budget process is outlined in Figure 7.1. Budgeting is part of the total planning activity in the firm, so we must begin with a statement of corporate goals or objectives. The statement of goals (shown in the box at the top of the figure) determines the second section of the figure, the corporate long-range plan. Moving down the figure, a segment of the corporate long-range plan includes a long-range sales forecast. This forecast requires a determination of the number and types of products that will be manufactured both at present and in the future years encompassed by the long-range plan—the product mix strategy.

Short-term forecasts and budgets are formulated within the framework of the long-range plan. For example, one might begin with a sales forecast covering six months or one year. This forecast provides a basis for (and is dependent on) the broad range of policies indicated in the lower portion of Figure 7.1. First, the manufacturing policies that cover the choice of types of equipment, plant layout, and production-line arrangements must be chosen. In addition, the kind of durability built into the products and their associated costs must be considered. Second, a broad set of marketing policies must be formulated. These policies relate to the development of the firm's own sales organization versus the use of outside sales organizations; the number of salespeople, and the method by which they will be compensated; the forms of, types of, and amounts spent on advertising; and other factors. Third, the research and general management policies must be determined. Research policies deal with the relative emphasis on basic versus applied research and the product areas emphasized by both types of research. Fourth, the financial policies (the subject of this chapter) must be set. The four major policies must be established simultaneously, since each affects the others. We shall concentrate on financial control policies, but it is important to realize the interdependence of financial and other policies.

**Financial
Control
Policies**

Financial control policies encompass the organization and content of various kinds of financial control budgets, including budgets for individual products and for every significant activity of the firm. Additional budgets, for-

**Figure 7.1
Overall View of the Total
Budgeting Process and Relations**

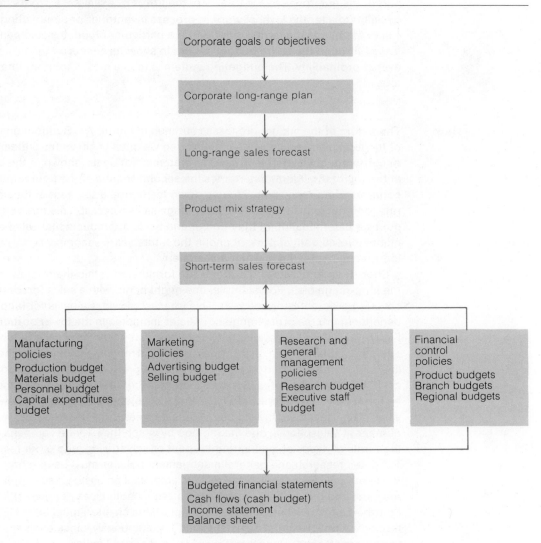

mulated to control operations at individual branch offices, are grouped and
modified to control regional operations as well.

In a similar manner, policies established at the manufacturing, marketing,
research, and general management levels give rise to another series of
budgets. For example, the production budget reflects the use of materials,

parts, labor, and facilities; and each of its major elements is likely to have its own budget program. There is usually a materials budget, a labor or personnel requirements budget, and a facilities or long-run capital expenditures budget. After the product is produced, the next step in the process is the creation of a marketing budget. Related to the overall process are the general office and executive requirements, which are reflected in the general and administrative budget system.

The results of projecting all these elements of cost are reflected in the budgeted (also called "pro forma" or "projected") income statement. Anticipated sales give rise to contemplation of the various types of investments needed to produce the products; these investments, plus the beginning balance sheet, provide the necessary data for developing the assets side of the balance sheet.

Assets must be financed, but first a cash flow analysis (the cash budget) is needed. The cash budget indicates the combined effects of the budgeted operations on the firm's cash flows. A positive net cash flow indicates that the firm has ample financing. However, if an increase in the volume of operations leads to a negative cash flow, additional financing is required. This leads directly to choices of financing, which is the subject of a considerable portion of the remainder of the book.

Since the structures of the income statement and the balance sheet have already been covered in Chapter 4, the rest of this section will deal with the two remaining aspects of the budgeting process—the cash budget and the concept of variable, or flexible, budgets.

Cash Budgeting

The cash budget indicates not only the total amount of financing required but its timing as well. It shows the amount of funds needed month by month, week by week, or even day by day; and it is one of the financial manager's most important tools. Because a clear understanding of the nature of cash budgeting is important, the process is described by means of an example that makes the elements of the cash budget explicit.

Marvel Toy is a medium-sized toy manufacturer. Sales are highly seasonal, the peak occuring in September, when retailers stock up for the Christmas season. All sales are on terms that allow a cash discount for payments made within thirty days; if the discount is not taken, the full amount must be paid in sixty days. However, Marvel, like most other companies, finds that some of its customers delay payment up to ninety days. Experience has shown that on 20 percent of the sales, payment is made within thirty days; on 70 percent it is made within sixty days, and on 10 percent it is made within ninety days.

Marvel's production is geared to future sales. Purchased materials and parts, which amount to 70 percent of sales, are bought the month before the company expects to sell the finished product. Its own purchase terms permit Marvel to delay payment on its purchase for one month. Thus, if August sales are forecast at $30,000, Marvel's purchases during July will amount to $21,000, which it will pay in August.

Wages and salaries, rent, and other cash expenses for Marvel are given in Table 7.1. The company also has a tax payment of $8,000 coming due in August. Its capital budgeting plans call for the purchase in July of a new machine tool costing $10,000, payment to be made in September. Assuming the company needs to keep a $5,000 cash balance at all times and has $6,000 on July 1, what are Marvel's financial requirements for the period July through December?

The cash requirements are worked out in the cash budget shown in Table 7.1. The top half of the table provides a worksheet for calculating collections on sales and payments on purchases. The first line in the worksheet gives the sales forecast for the period May through January (May and June sales are necessary to determine collections for July and August). The second line shows cash collections. The first line under this heading shows that 20 percent of the sales during any given month are collected that month. The second line shows the collections on the prior month's sales—70 percent of sales in the preceding month. The third line gives collections from sales two months earlier—10 percent of sales in that month. The collections are summed to find the total cash receipts from sales during each month under consideration.

With the worksheet completed, the cash budget itself can be considered. Receipts from collections are given on the top line. Next, payments during each month are summarized. The difference between cash receipts and cash payments is the net cash gain or loss during the month; for July, there is a net cash loss of $4,200. The initial cash on hand at the beginning of the month is added to the net cash gain or loss during the month to yield the cumulative cash that will be on hand if no financing is done; at the end of July, Marvel Toy will have cumulative cash equal to $1,800. The desired cash balance, $5,000, is subtracted from the cumulative cash balance to determine the amount of financing the firm needs if it is to maintain the desired level of cash. At the end of July, Marvel will need $3,200; thus loans outstanding will total $3,200 at that time.

The same procedure is used in the following months. Sales will expand seasonally in August; with increased sales will come increased payments for purchases, wages, and other items. Moreover, the $8,000 tax bill is due in August. Receipts from sales will go up too, but the firm will still be left with a $10,800 cash deficit during the month. The total financial requirements at the end of August will be $14,000—the $3,200 needed at the end of July plus the $10,800 cash deficit for August. Thus loans outstanding will total $14,000 at the end of August.

Table 7.1
Marvel Toy Company
Worksheet and Cash Budget

Worksheet	May	June	July	Aug.	Sept.	Oct.	Nov.	Dec.	Jan.
Sales (net of cash discounts)	$10,000	$10,000	$20,000	$30,000	$40,000	$20,000	$20,000	$10,000	$10,000
Collections:									
First month (at 20%)	2,000	2,000	4,000	6,000	8,000	4,000	4,000	2,000	2,000
Second month (at 70%)		7,000	7,000	14,000	21,000	28,000	14,000	14,000	7,000
Third month (at 10%)			1,000	1,000	2,000	3,000	4,000	2,000	2,000
Total	$ 2,000	$ 9,000	$12,000	$21,000	$31,000	$35,000	$22,000	$18,000	$11,000
Purchases (70% of next month's sales)	$ 7,000	$14,000	$21,000	$28,000	$14,000	$14,000	$ 7,000	$ 7,000	
Payments (one month lag)		$ 7,000	$14,000	$21,000	$28,000	$14,000	$14,000	$ 7,000	$ 7,000

Cash Budget

Cash Budget	May	June	July	Aug.	Sept.	Oct.	Nov.	Dec.	Jan.
Receipts:									
Collections			$12,000	$21,000	$31,000	$35,000	$22,000	$18,000	$11,000
Payments:									
Purchases			$14,000	$21,000	$28,000	$14,000	$14,000	$ 7,000	
Wages and salaries			1,500	2,000	2,500	1,500	1,500	1,000	
Rent			500	500	500	500	500	500	
Other expenses			200	300	400	200	200	100	
Taxes			—	—	—	—	—	—	
Payment on machine			—	8,000	10,000	—	—	—	
Total payments			$16,200	$31,800	$41,400	$16,200	$16,200	$ 8,600	
Net cash gain (loss) during month			–$4,200	–$10,800	–$10,400	$18,800	$ 5,800	$ 9,400	
Cash at start of month if no borrowing is done			6,000	1,800	–9,000	–19,400	–600	5,200	
Cumulative cash (cash at start plus gains or minus losses)			$ 1,800	–$ 9,000	–$19,400	–$ 600	$ 5,200	$14,600	
Less: Desired level of cash			–5,000	–5,000	–5,000	–5,000	–5,000	–5,000	
Total loans outstanding to maintain $5,000 cash balance			$ 3,200	$14,000	$24,400	$ 5,600	—	—	
Surplus cash			—	—	—	—	$ 200	$ 9,600	

Sales peak in September, and the cash deficit during this month will amount to another $10,400. The total need for funds through September will increase to $24,400. Sales, purchases, and payments for past purchases will fall markedly in October; collections will be the highest of any month because they will reflect the high September sales. As a result, Marvel Toy will enjoy a healthy $18,800 cash surplus during October. This surplus can be used to pay off borrowings, so the need for financing will decline by $18,800 to $5,600.

Marvel will have another cash surplus in November, and this extra cash will permit the company to eliminate completely the need for financing. In fact, the company is expected to have $200 in surplus cash by the month's end, while another cash surplus in December will swell the amount of extra cash to $9,600. With such a large amount of unneeded funds, Marvel's treasurer will doubtless want to make investments in some interest-bearing securities or put the funds to use in some other way. (Types of investments for excess funds are discussed in Chapter 9.)

Variable, or Flexible, Budgets

Budgets are planned allocations of a firm's resources, based on forecasts for the future. Two important elements influence actual performance. One is the impact of external influences over which the firm has little or no control—developments in the economy as a whole and competitive developments in the firm's own industry. The other is the firm's level of efficiency at a given volume of sales, which is controllable. It is necessary to separate these two elements in evaluating individual performances.

The essence of the variable budget system is its introduction of flexibility into budgets by its recognition that certain types of expenditures vary at different levels of output. Thus a firm may have alternative levels of outlay budgeted for different volumes of operations—high, low, medium. One of management's responsibilities is to determine which of the alternative budgets should be in effect for the planning period under consideration.

The regression method, described in the preceding chapter in connection with financial forecasting, can also be used to establish the basis for flexible budgeting. To illustrate: Suppose that a retail store, the Hubler Department Store, has had the experience indicated by the historical data set forth in Table 7.2. It is apparent from the data that the number of employees the firm needs is dependent on the dollar volume of sales in each month. This is seen more easily from the scatter diagram of Figure 7.2. The freehand regression line is sloped positively because the number of employees increases as the volume of sales increases. The independent variable, dollar volume of sales, is called the control variable. Variations in the control variable cause changes in total expenses. The volume of sales can be forecast and the need for employees read from the regression chart. The relations are expressed in tabular form in Table 7.3. Given the forecast of sales, standards can be provided for the expected number of employees and the weekly payroll.[2]

**Table 7.2
Hubler Department Store
Relationship between Sales and
Employees**

Month	Sales (in Millions of Dollars)	Number of Employees
January	$ 4	42
February	5	51
March	6	60
April	7	75
May	10	102
June	8	83
July	5	55
August	9	92

**Figure 7.2
Scatter Diagram and Regression
Line: Hubler Department Store**

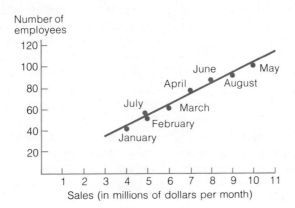

2. Regression analysis provides even more flexibility in budgeting than do the high, medium, and low levels mentioned earlier. Also, it is possible to include confidence levels when using the regression method. For example, Table 7.3 shows that when volume is at $8 million, Hubler expects to have 82 employees and a weekly payroll of $8,200. Although this relationship probably will not hold *exactly*, actual observations should be between 78 and 86 employees at this sales volume 95 percent of the time. Thus, 95 percent confidence levels encompass the range 78 to 86. Similar ranges can be determined for other volumes. As a matter of control policy, management may investigate whenever actual performances are outside this expected range.

Table 7.3
Hubler Department Store
Budget Allowance

Sales (in Millions of Dollars)	Number of Employees	Weekly Payroll Estimate (Average Wage $100)
$ 6	62	$ 6,200
7	72	7,200
8	82	8,200
9	92	9,200
10	102	10,200
11	112	11,200

Problems of Budgeting

Four major problems are encountered when using budget systems. First, budgetary programs can grow to be so complete and so detailed that they become cumbersome, meaningless, and unduly expensive. Overbudgeting is dangerous.

Second, budgetary goals may come to supersede enterprise goals. A budget is a tool, not an end in itself. Enterprise goals by definition supersede subsidiary plans, of which budgets are a part. Moreover, budgets are based on future expectations that may not be realized. There is no acceptable reason for neglecting to alter budgets as circumstances change. This reasoning is the core of the argument in favor of more flexible budgets.

Third, budgets can hide inefficiencies by continuing initial expenditures in succeeding periods without proper evaluation. Budgets growing from precedent usually contain undesirable expenditures. They should not be used as umbrellas under which slovenly, inefficient management can hide. Consequently, the budgetary process must contain a provision for reexamination of standards and other bases of planning by which policies are translated into numerical terms.

Finally, budgets used as pressure devices can defeat their basic objectives. Budgets that are instruments of tyranny cause resentment and frustration, which in turn lead to inefficiency. In order to counteract this effect, top management should increase the participation of subordinates in preparing budgets.

Use of Financial Plans and Budgets

Forecasts, or long-range plans, are necessary in all the firm's operations. The personnel department must have a good idea of the scale of future operations if it is to plan its hiring and training activities properly. The production department must be sure that productive capacity is available to meet the projected product demand. The finance department must be sure that funds are on hand to meet the firm's financial requirements.

The tools and techniques discussed in this and preceding chapters are used in several separate but related ways. First, the percent-of-sales method or, preferably, the regression method is used to make a long-range forecast of financial requirements over a projected three- to five-year period. This forecast is used to draw up the strategic financing plans during the planning period. The company might, for example, plan to meet its financial requirements with retained earnings and short-term bank debt during, say, 1980 and 1981, float a bond issue in 1982, use retained earnings in 1983, and finally sell an issue of common stock in 1984. Fairly long lead times are necessary when companies sell bonds or stocks; otherwise, they might be forced to go into the market during unfavorable periods.

In addition to long-run strategic planning, financial managers must also make accurate short-run forecasts to be sure that funds will be available to meet seasonal and other short-run requirements. They may, for example, meet with a bank loan officer to discuss their company's need for funds during the coming year. Prior to the meeting, the firm's accountants may prepare a detailed cash budget showing the maximum amount of money needed during the year, how much will be needed each month, and how cash surpluses will be generated at some point to enable the firm to repay the bank loan.

Financial managers will also have their firm's pro forma and most recent balance sheets and income statements, from which they will calculate the key financial ratios to show both actual and projected financial positions to the banker. If the firm's financial position is sound and its cash budget reasonable, the bank will commit itself to make the required funds available. Even if the bank decides that the request is unreasonable and denies the loan request, the firm's financial managers will have time to seek other sources of funds. While it might not be pleasant to have to look elsewhere for money, it is much better to know ahead of time if a loan request will be refused.

Divisional Control in a Decentralized Firm

In our discussion of the du Pont system of financial control in Chapter 4, we considered its use for the firm as a whole. However, the du Pont system is mainly used to control the various parts of a multidivisional firm.

For organizational reasons, large firms are generally set up on a decentralized basis. For example, General Electric establishes separate divisions for heavy appliances, light appliances, power transformers, fossil fuel generating equipment, nuclear generating equipment, and so on. Each division is defined as a *profit center,* and each has its own investments—fixed and current assets, together with a share of such general corporate assets as research labs and headquarters buildings—and is expected to earn an appropriate return on them.

The corporate headquarters, or central staff, typically controls the various divisions by a form of the du Pont system. When it is used for divisional control, the procedure is frequently referred to as ROI (return on investment) control. Here "profits" are measured by operating earnings—income before taxes—as shown in Figure 7.3. Sometimes the earnings figure is calculated before depreciation, and total gross assets are measured before deduction of the depreciation reserve. Measurement on gross assets has the advantage of avoiding differences in ROI due to differences in the average age of the fixed assets. Older assets are more fully depreciable and have a higher depreciation reserve and lower net fixed asset amount. This causes the ROI on net total assets to be higher when fixed assets are older.

If a particular division's ROI falls below a target figure, then the centralized corporate staff helps the division's own financial staff trace back through the du Pont system to determine the cause of the substandard ROI. Each division manager is judged by the division's ROI and rewarded or penalized accordingly. Division managers are thus motivated to keep their ROI up to the target level. Their individual actions should in turn maintain the firm's ROI at an appropriate level.

In addition to its use in managerial control, ROI can be used to allocate funds to the various divisions. The firm as a whole has financial resources—retained earnings, cash flow from depreciation, and the ability to obtain additional debt and equity funds from capital markets. These funds can be allocated on the basis of the divisional ROIs, with divisions having high ROIs receiving more funds than those with low ones.[3]

A number of problems can arise if ROI control is used without proper safeguards. Since the divisional managers are rewarded on the basis of their ROI performance, it is absolutely essential for their morale that they feel their divisional ROI does indeed provide an accurate measure of relative performance. But ROI is dependent on a number of factors in addition to managerial competence, some of which are listed below.

1. *Depreciation.* ROI is very sensitive to depreciation policy. If one division is writing off assets at a relatively rapid rate, its annual profits—and hence its ROI—will be reduced.
2. *Book value of assets.* If an older division is using assets that have been largely written off, both its current depreciation charges and its investment base will be low. This will make its ROI high in relation to newer divisions.
3. *Transfer pricing.* In most corporations some divisions sell to other divisions. At General Motors, for example, the Fisher Body Division sells to the Chevrolet Division. In such cases the price at which goods are trans-

3. The point of this procedure is to increase the firm's ROI. To maximize the overall ROI, marginal ROI among divisions should be equalized.

Figure 7.3
du Pont Chart for Divisional
Control

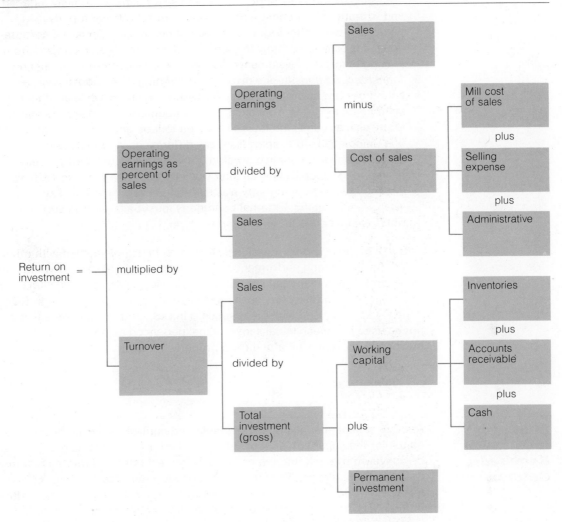

ferred between divisions has a fundamental effect on divisional profits. If
the transfer price of auto bodies is set relatively high, then Fisher Body
will have a relatively high ROI and Chevrolet a relatively low one.

4. *Time periods.* Many projects have long gestation periods, during which
expenditures must be made for research and development, plant con-

struction, market development, and the like. Such expenditures add to the investment base without a commensurate increase in profits for several years. During this period, a division's ROI can be seriously reduced; and without proper constraints, its manager may be improperly penalized. Given the frequency of personnel transfers in larger corporations, it is easy to see how the timing problem can keep managers from making long-term investments that are in the best interests of the firm.

5. *Industry conditions.* If one division is operating in an industry where conditions are favorable and rates of return are high, while another is in an industry suffering from excessive competition, the environmental differences may cause the favored division to look good and the unfavored one to look bad, quite apart from any differences in their managers. Signal Companies' aerospace division, for example, could hardly be expected to show up as well as their truck division in a year like 1973, when the entire aerospace industry was suffering severe problems and truck sales were booming. External conditions must be taken into account when appraising ROI performance.

Because of these factors, divisions' ROIs must be supplemented with other criteria for evaluating performance. For example, a division's growth rate in sales, profits, and market share (as well as its ROI) in comparison with other firms in its own industry has been used in such evaluations. Although ROI control has been used with great success in U.S. industry, the system cannot be used in a mechanical sense by inexperienced personnel. As with most other tools, it is helpful if used properly but destructive if misused.

Effects of Inflation on Required Returns

Another aspect of applying any planning and control system is the need to adjust for the impact of inflation. The nature of the corrections required can be conveyed by analyzing the patterns of interest rates and returns before the impact of inflation. Three major influences determine the levels of interest rates and returns: the real productivity rate in the economy, a positive differential for greater risk, and a positive differential for longer maturities. Here we will abstract from short-term demand and supply conditions, which sometimes push short-term interest rates above long-term interest rates. The real productivity rate is the basic rate of growth in the economy; it provides the source of payment to savers for postponing their consumption from the present to the future. The basic real interest rate reflecting the productivity rate in the economy is 2.5 to 3 percent per annum. This is also the rate of interest on short-term government securities free of the risk of nonpayment at maturity. For longer-term government securities, the rate rises with the length of maturity, reflecting the greater risk of interest rate fluctuations. This adds another 1.5 to 2 percent to the basic 2.5 to 3 percent interest rate.

For prime short-term business debt such as commercial paper, we add 1 to 1.5 percent to the government short-term debt rates. For longer-term corporate debt, we add about the same 1 to 1.5 percent differential to rates on longer-term government securities. Since common stocks of corporations carry still greater risk, we risk adjustment premiums of 2 to 3 percentage points to the corporate bond rates.

To each of the interest rates and common stock returns we must also add a factor based on the expected rate of inflation, so that real returns are maintained after adjusting for inflation. Taking inflation into account, the pattern of rates appears something like this:

	Price Level Rise per Year		
	Basic Rates	2%	5%
Short-term government bills	2.5–3%	4.5–5%	7.5–8%
Long-term government bonds	4–5	6–7	9–10
Short-term business debt	3.5–4	5.5–6	8.5–9
Long-term corporate bonds	5.5–7	7.5–9	10.5–12
Common stocks of corporations	7.5–10	9.5–13	12.5–15

Technically, we adjust nominal yields or returns for inflation by the procedures indicated in Table 7.4. Column 1 shows data on the rates of interest on short-term business debt for a period of years. Column 2 gives a measure of the price level for each year. Column 3 calculates the purchasing power of the currency as compared to the previous year. Column 4 multiplies Columns 1 and 3 (and subtracts 1) to obtain the real interest rate. Note that the real interest rate on short-term business loans has remained constant, al-

**Table 7.4
Calculation of Real Interest
Rates on Short-Term
Business Debt**

Year	One Plus Nominal Returns (1)	Price Index (P_t) (2)	$\dfrac{P_{t-1}}{P_t}$ (3)	One Plus Real Rate of Return [(1) × (3)] (4)
19X1		100		
19X2	1.10	106	0.94	1.03
19X3	1.11	114	0.93	1.03
19X4	1.12	124	0.92	1.03
19X5	1.13	136	0.91	1.03
19X6	1.14	151	0.90	1.03

though nominal interest rates have risen from 10 percent to 14 percent over the period of years.

The impact of inflation in recent years has been unfavorable to U.S. business firms. In fact, it is doubtful whether their level of real returns has been maintained. The situation is indicated in Table 7.5; following the same methodology as in Table 7.4, we see that while nominal returns have risen from 10 to 14 percent, real returns have declined from 8 percent to 0. The impact of inflation at different industries has varied, but it tends to be unfavorable for the following reasons. Firms in a given industry with fixed assets and inventories acquired at lower historical costs are able to offer severe price competition because they are operating from a lower historical cost basis. Since accounting is predominantly based on the expiration of historical costs, the higher current replacement costs of fixed assets and inventories may not be reflected in the prices charged by firms in industries such as paper, cement, and steel. As a consequence, reported profits for some individual companies may be severely depressed.

Table 7.5
Calculation of Real Returns on Common Stocks

Year	One Plus Nominal Returns (1)	Price Index (P_t) (2)	$\dfrac{P_{t-1}}{P_t}$ (3)	One Plus Real Rate of Return [(1) × (3)] (4)
19X1		100		
19X2	1.10	102	0.98	1.08
19X3	1.11	106	0.96	1.07
19X4	1.12	116	0.91	1.02
19X5	1.13	130	0.89	1.01
19X6	1.14	148	0.88	1.00

Business people have recognized a need to earn higher nominal rates of return to offset the influence of inflation on real returns. This is illustrated in the following quotation:

The necessity of a higher rate of return on investment was also mentioned by R. F. Mettler, president of TRW Inc., in a recent interview.

"There is really a need for a higher rate of return in an inflationary economy," he said. "Until three years ago, when inflation became so strong, we had been going along making our investments on the basis of approximately a 10 percent after-tax return on assets employed. We had a 40 percent debt-equity ratio, and that produced a 14 to 15 percent return on equity."

"In this inflationary economy, however, we have to get a 15 percent return on assets, a 20 percent return on equity and want to get our debt-equity ratio to 30 percent. That would produce the resources and the profit to permit growth when inflation runs in the 6 to 7 percent range that it is now."[4]

The presence of inflation means that the value of the currency unit in which results are expressed may no longer be valid. This greatly complicates the measurement of financing requirements and the formulation of standards for performance.

External Uses of Financial Forecasts and Budgets

We have stressed the use of planning and budgeting for internal purposes—that is, to increase the efficiency of a firm's operations. With relatively minor modifications, the same tools and techniques can be used in both credit and security analysis. For example, outside security analysts can forecast a given firm's sales and, through the income statement and balance sheet relationships, can prepare pro forma (projected) balance sheets and income statements. Credit analysts can make similar projections to help estimate their customers' needs for funds and the likelihood that borrowers can make prompt repayment.

These kinds of analysis have actually been conducted on a large scale in recent years. Very complete financial data going back some twenty years on several thousand large, publicly owned corporations are now available on magnetic tapes (Standard & Poor's Compustat tapes). These tapes are being used by security analysts in highly sophisticated ways. From what we have seen, analyses conducted in such a manner offer large potential benefits. The same tapes, frequently supplemented with additional data, are being used by the major lending institutions—banks and insurance companies—to forecast their customers' needs for funds and to plan their own financial requirements.

Summary

A budget is a plan stated in terms of specific expenditures for specific purposes; it is used for both planning and control. Its overall purpose is to improve internal operations, thereby reducing costs and raising profitability. A budgeting system starts with a set of performance standards, or targets. The targets constitute, in effect, the firm's financial plan. The budgeted figures are compared with actual results; this is the control phase of the budget system, and it is a critical step in well-operated companies.

Although the entire budget system is vital to corporate management, one aspect of the system is especially important to the financial manager—the cash budget. The cash budget is, in fact, the principal tool for making short-run financial forecasts. If used properly, it is highly accurate and can

4. Thomas E. Mullaney, "The G.N.P. Gap," *New York Times,* July 10, 1977.

pinpoint the funds that will be needed, when they will be needed, and when cash flows will be sufficient to retire any loans that might be necessary.

A good budget system recognizes that some factors lie outside the firm's control. Especially important here is the state of the economy and its effects on sales. Flexible budgets are set up as targets for the different departments, assuming different levels of sales. A good system also ensures that those responsible for carrying out a plan are involved in its preparation; this procedure helps guard against the establishment of unrealistic targets and unattainable goals.

As a firm becomes larger, it is necessary for it to decentralize operations to some extent. But decentralized operations still require some centralized control. The principal tool used for such control is the return on investment (ROI) method. There are problems with ROI control; but if care is taken in its use, the method can be quite valuable to a decentralized firm.

Questions

7.1 What use might a confidence interval scheme have in variable budgeting?

7.2 Why is a cash budget important even when there is plenty of cash in the bank?

7.3 What is the difference between the long-range financial forecasting concept (for example, the percent-of-sales method) and the budgeting concept? How might they be used together?

7.4 Assume that a firm is making up its long-run financial budget. What period should this budget cover—one month, six months, one year, three years, five years, or some other period? Justify your answer.

7.5 Is a detailed budget more important to a large, multidivisional firm than to a small, single-product firm?

7.6 Assume that your uncle is a major stockholder in a multidivisional firm that uses a naive ROI criterion for evaluating divisional managers and that bases managers' salaries in large part on this evaluation. You can have the job of division manager in any division you choose. If you are a salary maximizer, what divisional characteristics will you seek? If, because of your good performance, you become president of the firm, what changes will you make?

Problems

7.1 The Emory Company has been studying its own and industry income statement and balance sheet relationships for a number of years. It has established the following relationships:

Number of days' sales in cash: 20
Number of days' sales in receivables: 36
Number of days' sales in inventories: 54
Total costs: $5,000,000 + $6,000
Corporate income tax rate: 40%

Emory has sufficient capacity to handle a 30 percent increase in the quantity of products sold.

a. Emory expects to sell 11,000 units in the forthcoming year for total sales of $12,060,000. What are the appropriate amounts to budget for each of the current asset items and for net income after taxes?

b. Emory actually sells 13,200 units, at the same selling price, for total sales of $14,472,000. The increase in sales results from a one-time extra promotion and selling effort that costs $1,000,000. By how much have total current assets increased over the amount initially budgeted, and to what extent does the increase in net income finance the increase in the required investment in current assets?

7.2 You are presented with the following data on the fixed asset accounts of two companies in relation to all manufacturing companies as of the end of 1977:

	Denby Corporation	Korman Company	All Manufacturing Companies
Gross depreciable fixed assets	$83,627,410	$90,861,000	$586,039,000
Reserve for depreciation	14,680,000	76,320,000	286,474,000
Net fixed assets	68,947,410	14,541,000	341,078,000

a. How do the ratios of net to gross fixed assets compare for the three?

b. What percent of gross fixed assets have been charged off by depreciation in each case?

c. Give some reasons for the Denby Corporation and Korman Company departing so greatly from the average relationship between net and fixed assets indicated by all manufacturing corporations.

d. If the extent to which gross fixed assets in all manufacturing companies are depreciated is rising over time, what does this indicate?

7.3 The yields on Aaa corporate bonds and the consumer price index are presented in the following table:

Year	Moody's Aaa Corporate Bond Yields	Consumer Price Index (1967 = 100)
1964	4.40	92.9
1965	4.49	94.5
1966	5.13	97.2
1967	5.51	100.0
1968	6.18	104.2
1969	7.03	109.8
1970	8.04	116.3
1971	7.39	121.3
1972	7.21	125.3
1973	7.44	133.1
1974	8.57	147.7
1975	8.83	161.2
1976	8.43	170.5
1977	8.02	181.5

a. Calculate the "real" yield to investors after taking into account the yearly decline in purchasing power of the U.S. dollar.

b. Discuss the trends in the "real" yields.

7.4 The Blanton Company is preparing its cash budget for the first six months of 1979. The sales data for 1978 and sales forecasts for January through July are:

Actual Sales

1978

November	$200
December	200

Sales Forecast

1979

January	$200
February	250
March	400
April	500
May	300
June	200
July	200

All sales are made on credit, with 70 percent collected in the first month following the sale and 30 percent in the second month. Purchases are 60 percent of the following month's sales and are paid in the following month. Monthly expenses equal to 30 percent of the current month's sales are paid currently each month. Beginning cash is $100 and should not be permitted to fall below $100 in any of the following months. Bank borrowing is used to bring cash back to the $100 level. Whenever cash exceeds $100, the excess is used to pay off any bank loans outstanding. Formulate the cash budget for January through June 1979.

7.5 The Simmons Company is planning to request a line of credit from its bank. The following sales forecasts have been made for parts of 1979 and 1980:

May 1979	$150,000
June	150,000
July	300,000
August	450,000
September	600,000
October	300,000
November	300,000
December	75,000
January 1980	150,000

Collection estimates obtained from the credit and collection department are as follows: collected within the month of sale, 5 percent; collected the month following the sale, 80 percent; collected the second month following the sale, 15 percent. Payments for labor and raw materials are typically made during the month following the month in which these costs are incurred. Total labor and raw materials costs are estimated for each month as follows:

May 1979	$ 75,000
June	75,000
July	105,000
August	735,000
September	255,000
October	195,000
November	135,000
December	75,000

General and administrative salaries will amount to approximately $22,500 a month; lease payments under long-term lease contracts will be $7,500 a month; depreciation charges will be $30,000 a month; miscellaneous expenses will be $2,250 a month; income tax payments of $52,500 will be due in both September and December; and a progress payment of $150,000 on a new research laboratory must be paid in October. Cash on hand on July 1 will amount to $110,000, and a minimum cash balance of $75,000 will be maintained throughout the cash budget period.

a. Prepare a monthly cash budget for the last six months of 1979.

b. Prepare an estimate of required financing (or excess funds)—that is, the amount of money the Simmons Company will need to borrow (or will have available to invest)—for each month during the period.

c. Assume that receipts from sales come in uniformly during the month (that is, cash payments come in at the rate of 1/30th each day), but all outflows are paid on the fifth of the month. Will this have an effect on the cash budget (that is, will the cash budget you have prepared be valid under these assumptions)? If not, what can be done to make a valid estimate of financing requirements?

7.6 Gulf and Eastern, Inc., is a diversified multinational corporation that produces a wide variety of goods and services, including chemicals, soaps, tobacco products, toys, plastics, pollution control equipment, canned food, sugar, motion pictures, and computer software. The corporations's major divisions were brought together in the early 1960s under a decentralized form of management; each division was evaluated in terms of its profitability, efficiency, and return on investments. This decentralized organization persisted through most of the decade, during which Gulf and Eastern experienced a high average growth rate in total assets, earnings, and stock prices.

Toward the end of 1975, however, those trends were reversed. The organization was faced with declining earnings, unstable stock prices, and a generally uncertain future. This situation persisted into 1976, but during that year a new president, Lynn Thompson, was appointed by the board of directors. Thompson, who had served for a time on the financial staff of I. E. du Pont, used the du Pont system to evaluate the various divisions. All showed definite weaknesses.

Thompson reported to the board that a principal reason for the poor overall performance was a lack of control by central management over each division's activities. She was particularly disturbed by the consistently poor results of the corporation's budgeting procedures. Under that system, each division manager drew up a projected budget for the next quarter, along with estimated sales, revenue, and profit; funds were then allocated to the divisions, basically in proportion to their budget requests. However, actual budgets seldom matched the projections; wide discrepancies occurred; and this, of course, resulted in a highly inefficient use of capital.

In an attempt to correct the situation, Thompson asked the firm's chief financial officer to draw up a plan to improve the budgeting, planning, and control processes. When the plan was submitted, its basic provisions included the following:

1. To improve the quality of the divisional budgets, the division managers should be informed that the continuance of wide variation between their projected and actual budgets would result in dismissal.

2. A system should be instituted under which funds would be allocated to divisions on the basis of their average return on investment (ROI) during the last four quarters. Since funds were short, divisions with high ROIs would get most of the available money.

3. Only about half of each division manager's present compensation should be received as salary; the rest should be in the form of a bonus related to the division's average ROI for the quarter.

4. Each division should submit to the central office for approval all capital expenditure requests, production schedules, and price changes. Thus the company would be recentralized.

a. 1. Is it reasonable to expect the new procedures to improve the accuracy of budget forecasts?

   2. Should all divisions be expected to maintain the same degree of accuracy?

   3. In what other ways might the budgets be made?

b. 1. What problems would be associated with the use of the ROI criterion in allocating funds among the divisions?

   2. What effect would the period used in computing ROI (that is, four quarters, one quarter, two years, and so on) have on the effectiveness of this method?

   3. What problems might occur in evaluating the ROI in the crude rubber and auto tires divisions? between the sugar products and pollution control equipment divisions?

c. What problems would be associated with rewarding each manager on the basis of the division's ROI?

d. How well would Thompson's policy of recentralization work in this highly diversified corporation, particularly in light of the financial officer's three other proposals?

PART 3
MANAGEMENT
WORKING CAPITAL

Part 1 viewed the firm in its broad environmental setting. Part 2 examined a number of aspects of the financial planning and control systems in firms, analyzing operations in an aggregate manner. Part 3 looks at these financial pictures in more detail, focusing on the top half of the balance sheet—current assets, current liabilities, and the interrelationship between the two. This type of analysis is commonly called *working capital management*.

Chapter 8 examines some general principles of working capital management. Chapter 9 considers the determinants of current assets: cash, marketable securities, accounts receivable, and inventories. Finally, Chapter 10 discusses current liabilities, considering in some detail the principal sources and forms of short-term funds.

CHAPTER **8**
CAPITAL POLICY

WORKING

Working capital is a firm's investments in short-term assets—cash, short-term securities, accounts receivable, and inventories. *Gross working capital* is the firm's total current assets. *Net working capital* is current assets minus current liabilities. *Working capital management,* which encompasses all aspects of the administration of both current assets and current liabilities, has two main functions:

1. To adjust to changes in the firm's level of sales activity caused by seasonal, cyclical, and random factors. This function is important because a firm with favorable long-run prospects may experience severe difficulties and losses due to adverse short-run developments.
2. To apply valuation concepts (which are developed throughout the text). Current asset holdings, for example, should be expanded to the point where marginal returns on increases in such assets are just equal to the cost of capital required to finance the increases. Current liabilities should be used in place of long-term debt whenever their use lowers the average cost of capital.

Importance of Working Capital Management

Working capital management includes a number of aspects that make it an important topic for study:

1. Surveys indicate that the largest portion of a financial manager's time is devoted to the day-by-day internal operations of the firm, which can appropriately be subsumed under the heading of working capital management.
2. Characteristically, current assets represent more than half the total assets of a business firm. Because they represent such a large investment and because this investment tends to be relatively volatile, current assets are worthy of the financial manager's careful attention.
3. Working capital management is particularly important for small firms. Although such firms can minimize their investment in fixed assets by renting or leasing plant and equipment, they cannot avoid investment in cash, receivables, and inventories. Therefore, current assets are particularly significant for the financial manager of a small firm. Further, because a small firm has relatively limited access to the long-term capital markets, it must necessarily rely heavily on trade credit and short-term bank loans, both of which affect net working capital by increasing current liabilities.
4. The relationship between sales growth and the need to finance current assets is close and direct. For example, if the firm's average collection period is forty days and its credit sales are $1,000 a day, it has an investment of $40,000 in accounts receivable. If sales rise to $2,000 a day, the investment in accounts receivable rises to $80,000. Sales increases pro-

duce similar immediate needs for additional inventories and, perhaps, for cash balances. All such needs must be financed; and since they arise so quickly, it is imperative that the financial manager keep aware of developments in the working capital segment of the firm. Of course, continued sales increases require additional long-term assets, which must also be financed. However, fixed asset investments, while critically important to the firm in a strategic, long-run sense, do not generally have the same urgency as do current asset investments.

Original Concept of Working Capital

The term *working capital* originated at a time when most industries were closely related to agriculture. Processors would buy crops in the fall, process them, sell the finished product, and end up just before the next harvest with relatively low inventories. Bank loans with maximum maturities of one year were used to finance both the purchase and the processing costs, and these loans were retired with the proceeds from the sale of the finished products.

This situation is depicted in Figure 8.1, where fixed assets are shown to be growing steadily over time, while current assets jump at harvest season, then decline during the year, ending at zero just before the next crop is harvested. Current assets are financed with short-term credit, and fixed assets are financed with long-term funds. Thus, the top segment of the graph deals with working capital.

The figure represents, of course, an idealized situation. Current assets build up gradually as crops are purchased and processed, inventories are drawn down less regularly, and ending inventory balances do not decline to zero. Nevertheless, the example does illustrate the general nature of the production and financing process. Working capital management consists of decisions relating to the top section of the graph—managing current assets and arranging the short-term credit used to finance them.

Extending the Working Capital Concept

As the economy became less oriented toward agriculture, the production and financing cycles of "typical" businesses changed. Although seasonal patterns still existed and business cycles caused asset requirements to fluctuate, it became apparent that current assets rarely, if ever, dropped to zero. This realization led to the development of the idea of permanent current assets, diagrammed in Figure 8.2. As the figure is drawn, it maintains the traditional notion that permanent assets should be financed with long-term capital and temporary assets with short-term credit.

**Figure 8.1
Fixed and Current Assets and
Their Financing**

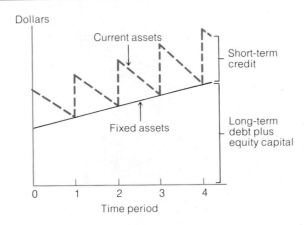

The pattern shown in Figures 8.1 and 8.2 was considered desirable because it minimized the risk of the firm being unable to pay off its maturing obligations. To illustrate: Suppose a firm borrows on a one-year basis and uses the funds obtained to build and equip a plant. Cash flows from the plant (profits plus depreciation) are not sufficient to pay off the loan at the end of the year, so the loan has to be renewed. If the lender refuses to renew the loan, the firm has problems. If the plant had been financed with long-term debt, however, cash flows would have been sufficient to retire the loan, and the problem of renewal would not have arisen. Thus, if a firm finances permanent assets with long-term capital and temporary assets with short-term capital, its financial risk is lower than if permanent assets are financed with short-term debt.

At the limit, a firm can attempt to match the maturity structure of its assets and liabilities exactly. A machine expected to last for five years could be financed by a five-year loan, a twenty-year building could be financed by a twenty-year mortgage bond, inventory expected to be sold in twenty days could be financed by a twenty-day bank loan, and so on. Actually, of course, uncertainty about the lives of assets prevents this exact maturity matching—a point that will be examined in the following sections.

Figure 8.2 shows the situation for a firm that attempts to match asset and liability maturities exactly. Although this policy can be followed, firms can choose other maturity-matching policies if they so desire. Figure 8.3, for example, illustrates the situation for a firm that finances all its fixed assets

**Figure 8.2
Matching Financing to Asset
Permanence**

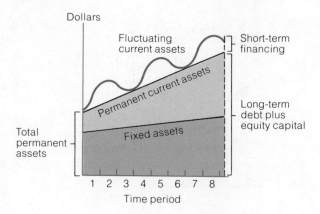

**Figure 8.3
Short-Term Financing of Some
Permanent Assets**

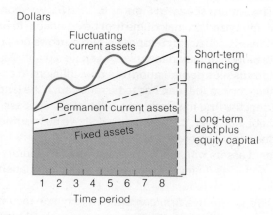

with long-term capital but part of its permanent current assets with short-term credit.[1]

The dashed line could even have been drawn *below* the line designating fixed assets, indicating that all the current assets and part of the fixed assets are financed with short-term credit; this would be a highly aggressive,

1. Firms generally have some short-term credit in the form of "spontaneous" funds—accounts payable and accruals (see Chapter 6). Used within limits, these constitute "free" capital, so virtually all firms employ at least some short-term credit at all times. We could modify the graphs to take this into account, but nothing is lost by simply abstracting from spontaneous funds, as we do.

Figure 8.4
Fluctuating versus Permanent
Assets and Liabilities

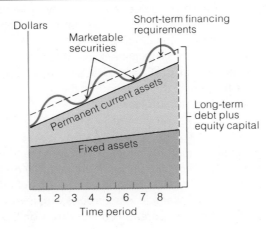

nonconservative position, and the firm would certainly be subject to loan renewal problems and high risk.

Alternatively, as in Figure 8.4, the dashed line could be drawn *above* the line designating permanent current assets, indicating that long-term capital is being used to meet seasonal demands. In this case, the firm uses a small amount of short-term credit to meet its peak seasonal requirements, but it also meets part of its seasonal needs by "storing liquidity" in the form of marketable securities during the off-season. The humps above the dashed line represent short-term financing; the troughs below it represent short-term security holdings.

Long-Term versus Short-Term Debt	The larger the percentage of funds obtained from long-term sources, the more conservative the firm's working capital policy. The reason for this, of course, is that during times of stress the firm may not be able to renew its short-term debt. This being so, why would firms ever use short-term credit (other than spontaneous credit)? Why not just use long-term funds? There are three primary answers to this question: flexibility, cost, and risk.
Flexibility of Short-Term Debt	If the need for funds is seasonal or cyclical, the firm may not want to commit itself to long-term debt. Such debt can be refunded, provided the loan agreement includes a call or prepayment provision; but even so, prepayment penalties can be expensive. Accordingly, if a firm expects its needs

for funds to diminish in the near future, or if it thinks there is a good chance that such a reduction will occur, it may choose short-term debt for flexibility.

A cash budget is used to analyze the flexibility aspect of the maturity structure of debt. To illustrate: Suppose Communications Satellite Corporation (Comsat) is planning to launch a series of satellites in 1980 with an estimated life of seven years. This generation of satellites will provide cash flows—depreciation plus profit—over its seven-year life. If Comsat uses debt to finance the series, it may schedule the debt's retirement to the expected cash flows from the project.

Cost of Long-Term versus Short-Term Debt

The cost aspect of the maturity decision involves the term structure of interest rates, or the relationship between the maturity of debt and its interest rate. Interest rates are usually lower on short-term debt than on long-term debt. In March 1978, for example, discussions with investment bankers indicated that the Universal Corporation could borrow on the following terms:

Loan Maturity	Interest Rate (Percent)
90 days	6$^1/_2$
6 months	7
1 year	7$^1/_2$
3 years	8
5 years	8$^1/_4$
10 years	8$^1/_2$
20 years	9

These points are graphed in Figure 8.5, a chart commonly called a yield curve, or a term to maturity curve. While the yield curve presented in Figure 8.5 is a fairly typical one, with short-term rates lower than long-term rates, there are times when the yield curve is downward sloping. At such times, which almost always occur when both long-term and short-term rates are relatively high, short-term debt costs more than long-term debt. Nevertheless, since short-term rates have *generally* been lower than long-term rates, a firm's capital will probably be less costly if it borrows for the short term rather than the long term.

Figure 8.6 shows the pattern of long-term and short-term interest rates during the 1960s and 1970s. The long-term rate is represented by the Aaa bond rate—the rate on high-grade, long-term (twenty-five years or more) corporate bonds; the short-term rate is represented by the rate on prime commercial paper—the four-to-six-month debt of top-quality firms.

Three points should be made about the graph: (1) both long-term and short-term rates generally rose over the period; (2) short-term rates were more volatile than long-term rates; and (3) only during 1966 and parts of

**Figure 8.5
Hypothetical Term Structure of
Interest Rates for Universal,
March 1978**

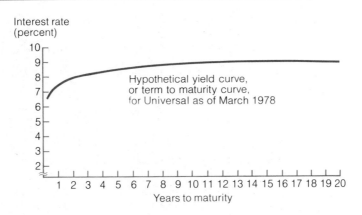

1969, 1970, and 1973 were long-term rates below short-term rates. Except for a period of a few months in the mid-1950s, the long-term rate was consistently above the short-term rate in all years from 1929 to 1966. This confirms an earlier statement about the yield curve generally sloping upward. Whenever the long-term rate in Figure 8.6 is above the short-term rate, the yield curve in Figure 8.5 must be upward sloping.

**Relationship
between
Long-Term and
Short-Term
Interest Rates**

Expectations theory states that long-term interest rates can generally be regarded as an average of expected future short-term interest rates. Thus the relationship between long- and short-term rates depends on what is expected to happen in the future to short-term interest rates, as illustrated in Table 8.1.

In Section A it is assumed that short-term interest rates will rise 1 percent each year, beginning at 2 percent in Year 1. The corresponding long-term interest rate in Year 1 for a five-year period is approximately 4 percent—the average of the five short-term rates. Thus, in Year 1, the long-term rate is double the short-term rate.

Consider, however, the situation in Section B. In a tight-money situation in Year 1, short-term rates are 6 percent, but they are expected to decline by 1 percent each year. The average of these rates is the same as in Section A, because the numbers are identical; their order is simply reversed. Now, however, the long-term rate of 4 percent lies below the initial short-term rate of 6 percent.

These examples do not prove the relationship between short- and long-

**Figure 8.6
Long- and Short-Term
Interest Rates**

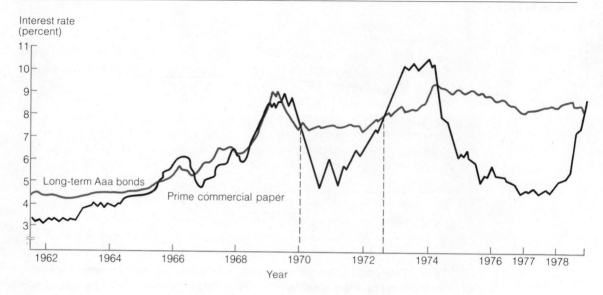

Source: *Federal Reserve Bulletin,* various issues.

term rates. They do, however, illustrate the pattern that would exist if the only factor operating was expected changes in interest rate movements, which themselves reflect a broad group of supply and demand factors. However, many other factors operate in the market. Some of them are differences in the risks of loss and failure among individual business firms, in the economic outlook for different industries, in the degree to which price-level changes affect different products and industries, and in the impact that changes in government legislation have on different firms in an industry.

**Table 8.1
Relationship between Short-Term
and Long-Term Interest Rates**

Year	Section A 5-Year Note	Section A Short-Term Rates	Section B 5-Year Note	Section B Short-Term Rates
1	4%	2%	4%	6%
2		3		5
3		4		4
4		5		3
5		6		2

**Risk of
Long-Term
versus
Short-Term Debt**

Even though short-term debt is generally less expensive than long-term debt, its use subjects the firm to more risk than does long-term debt. This risk effect occurs for two reasons:

1. If a firm borrows on a long-term basis, its interest costs will be relatively stable over time; but if it borrows on a short-term basis, its interest expenses will fluctuate widely, at times going quite high. For example, from January to June 1974, the short-term rate for large corporations almost doubled—going from $6^1/_2$ percent to 12 percent.
2. If a firm borrows heavily on a short-term basis, it may find itself unable to repay the debt, or it may be in such a shaky financial position that the lender will not extend the loan; thus, the firm can be forced into bankruptcy. These risk factors will be discussed in detail in the following sections.

Impact of a Rise in Rates on Interest Expenses During the period up to 1970 the yield curve was flat, indicating that long-term and short-term rates were about the same. This can be seen in Figure 8.6, which shows that the long-term and short-term rates were both about 7 percent. Suppose that in 1970 we were considering two firms, each with $100 million of debt. Firm S has only short-term debt, Firm L only long-term debt. Both are stable, mature companies. The total assets of each remain relatively constant from year to year, and the debt of each stays at the $100 million level.

Firm S must "turn over" its debt every year, borrowing at the prevailing short-term interest rate. For simplicity, we assume that Firm L's debt will not mature for twenty years, so its interest rate is fixed at 7 percent for the next twenty years regardless of what happens to either long-term or short-term rates during that time.

Now let's consider the interest expense of the two firms one year later, in 1971. Firm L still has $100 million of 7 percent debt, so its interest expense is $7 million annually. Firm S, on the other hand, has $100 million of debt that now costs 5 percent, so its interest expense has fallen to $5 million. If other costs and revenues have remained constant between 1970 and 1971, Firm L's profits after interest will have remained constant, but those of Firm S will have risen sharply. Of course, if we had used as a starting point that date in 1972 when long-term and short-term rates were equal, then things would have worked out better (at least through 1974) for Firm L. Of course, Firm S would have benefited from the decline in interest rates from 1974 to the end of 1976. The significant point is that while firm L *knows* what its future interest expenses will be, Firm S does not, and this very absence of precise knowledge makes Firm S the more risky one.

Another consideration reinforces the conclusion that the short-term borrowing policy is, in general, more risky. The comparison was made between short-term debt and long-term debt one year later to keep the analysis simple. But it would be more appropriate from both a conceptual and a practical standpoint to consider a longer period of time. For an extended time period, longer-term borrowing can be no worse than a succession of short-term borrowings. Recall that long-term rates reflect an average of future short-term rates. Thus the use of long-term borrowing already reflects the short-term rates that are expected to be experienced in the future.

Some might argue that short-term borrowing rates may actually be lower in the future than the rates reflected in current long-term borrowings. This is possible, of course; but if it happens, it will be an unexpected, essentially random occurrence. As such, the unanticipated changes could go in either direction with equal probability, so no average gain or loss from unexpected changes in short-term rates can reasonably be argued.

Danger of Being Unable to Refund In addition to the risk of fluctuating interest charges, Firm S faces another risk vis-à-vis Firm L. It may run into temporary difficulties that prevent it from being able to refund its debt. Remember that when Firm S's debt matures each year, the firm must negotiate new loans with its creditors, paying the going short-term rate. But suppose the loan comes up for renewal at a time when the firm is facing labor problems, a recession in demand for its products, extreme competitive pressures, or some other set of difficulties that has reduced its earnings.

The creditors will look at Firm S's ratios, especially the times-interest-earned and current ratios, to judge its creditworthiness. Firm S's current ratio is, of course, always lower than that of Firm L, but in good times this is overlooked. If earnings are high, the interest will be well covered and lenders will tolerate a low current ratio. If, however, earnings decline, pulling down the interest coverage ratio, creditors will certainly reevaluate Firm S's creditworthiness. At the very least, because of the perceived increased riskiness of the company, creditors will raise the interest rate charged; at the extreme, they will refuse to renew the loan. In the latter event, the firm will be forced to raise the funds needed to pay off the loan by selling assets at bargain basement prices, borrowing from other sources at exorbitant interest rates, or, in the extreme, going bankrupt.

Example of the Risk-Return Tradeoff

We have seen that short-term debt is typically less costly than long-term debt but that its use entails greater risk. Thus, we are faced with a tradeoff between risk and rate of return. Although we are not prepared to resolve the conflict at this point in the book, another example will help clarify the issues involved in risk and rate of return.

Table 8.2 illustrates the nature of the tradeoff. Here, we assume that the firm has $100 million of assets, half held as fixed assets and half as current assets, and that it will earn 15 percent before interest and taxes on these as-

**Table 8.2
Effect of Maturity Structure of
Debt on Return on Equity
(Millions of Dollars)**

	Conservative	Average	Aggressive
Current assets	$ 50.00	$ 50.00	$ 50.00
Fixed assets	50.00	50.00	50.00
Total assets	$100.00	$100.00	$100.00
Short-term credit (at 6%)	—	$ 25.00	$ 50.00
Long-term debt (at 8%)	50.00	25.00	—
Total debt (debt/assets = 50%)	50.00	50.00	50.00
Equity	50.00	50.00	50.00
Total liabilities and net worth	$100.00	$100.00	$100.00
Earnings before interest and taxes (EBIT)	15.00	15.00	15.00
Less interest	−4.00	−3.50	−3.00
Taxable income	$ 11.00	$ 11.50	$ 12.00
Less taxes (at 50%)	−5.50	−5.75	−6.00
Earnings on common stock	$ 5.50	$ 5.75	$ 6.00
Rate of return on equity	11.0%	11.5%	12.0%
Current ratio	∞	2:1	1:1

sets. The debt ratio has been set at 50 percent, but the policy issue of whether to use short-term debt, costing 6 percent, or long-term debt, costing 8 percent, has not been determined. Working through the relationships, we see that a conservative policy of using no short-term credit results in a rate of return on equity of 11 percent, while a more aggressive policy of using only short-term credit boosts the rate of return to 12 percent.

What occurs when uncertainty is introduced into this example? We noted earlier that a firm that makes extensive use of short-term credit may find its earnings fluctuating widely. Suppose, for example, that interest rates rise significantly, say from 6 percent to 10 percent, which is not at all unrealistic. This rise will not affect the firm using the conservative policy, but it will increase the interest expense under the average policy to $4.5 million and under the aggressive policy to $5 million. The rates of return on equity for the three policies will consequently be 11 percent, 10.5 percent, and 10 percent, respectively—a reversal in relative ranking by rate of return. Of course, a decline in interest rates will have the opposite effect on the rates of return, but it should be clear that the variability of the return under an aggressive policy is more than that under a conservative policy.

Fluctuations in earnings before interest and taxes (EBIT) can pose even more problems. If EBIT declines, lenders may simply refuse to renew short-term debt or may agree to renew it only at very high rates of interest. To illustrate: Suppose the EBIT of $15 million in Table 8.2 declines to only $5 million. Since the firm's ability to repay has diminished, creditors will certainly be reluctant to lend to it. They will thus require a higher return on their investment, thereby raising the interest expense. This will, of course, jeopardize the firm's future even more and, at the same time, compound the effects of the declining EBIT on stockholder returns.

It is possible for the general level of interest rates to rise at the same time a firm's EBIT is falling, and the compound effects can cause the situation to deteriorate so much that the aggressive firm may be unable to renew its credit at any interest rate. The result is bankruptcy.

Notice that if the firm follows a conservative policy of using all long-term debt, it need not worry about short-term temporary changes either in the term structure of interest rates or in its own EBIT. Its only concern is with its long-run performance, and its conservative financial structure may permit it to survive in the short run to enjoy better times in the long run.

Extending the Example

These concepts can be incorporated into our earlier example.[2] A firm has assets of $100 million and is considering the three financial structures, or policies, shown in Table 8.2. Management makes estimates of the future level of riskless interest rates (the Treasury bill rate) and the level of EBIT for the coming year. It knows that the firm's earnings for next year will be the prime determinant of the risk premium that will be added to the riskless rate.[3]

Probability distributions for riskless rates and EBIT are given in Table 8.3. Assuming that the two probability distributions are independent of each other, we can determine the expected interest rate for the next year by the technique shown in Table 8.4. Column 1 gives the possible riskless rates of interest. Column 2 shows the possible risk premiums. Column 3 combines the riskless rates of interest with the risk premiums to give the possible rates of interest the firm may face. Column 4 indicates the joint probabilities—the probability of the simultaneous occurrence of each possible riskless rate and risk premium. Column 5 gives the products of each joint probability multiplied by its associated interest rate; the sum of Column 5 is the expected interest rate—10.8 percent.

Since the expected value of the firm's short-term rate exceeds that of the long-term rate (8 percent), the firm should probably use long-term rather

2. This illustration uses the concept of a probability distribution, a topic discussed at some length in Chapter 13. A *probability* is the chance of an event occurring, or the odds on the occurrence of the event. The sum of the probabilities must equal 1, or 100 percent. The statistical aspects of this section can be omitted without loss of continuity if the statistical concepts are totally new.
3. As we see in detail later in the book, the higher the risk associated with a given loan, the higher the interest rate required by lenders. The difference between the United States government bond rate and the rate the firm must pay is defined as the *risk premium*. Obviously, the risk premium for AT&T or General Motors is lower than that for a smaller, less seasoned borrower.

**Table 8.3
Probability Distributions for
Riskless Rates and EBIT**

Treasury Bill Rate One Year Hence

i (Percent)	Probability
3	0.2
5	0.3
7	0.3
9	0.2

**EBIT for Next Year and Associated Risk
Premiums Expected on Next Year's
Renewal of Short-Term Credit**

EBIT (in Millions)	Risk Premium (Percent)	Probability
−$ 5	25.0	0.15
5	5.0	0.20
15	2.0	0.30
25	1.2	0.20
35	1.0	0.15

than short-term financing. More importantly, however, there is a 15 percent probability that the interest rate will be 28 percent or higher. Because total debt is $50 million, a 28 percent rate of interest will require an EBIT of $14 million to break even. But when this high rate is applied, EBIT will be *minus* $5 million, so the firm will run a loss before taxes of $19 million. This loss will reduce equity and increase the debt ratio, making the situation even more tense the next time the loan comes up for renewal. Good times may be just around the corner; but if the aggressive firm's EBIT is subject to wide swings, the company may not survive until then.

Our example is unrealistic in that few firms will be able to actually generate the data needed to construct a table like Table 8.4. However, the events described are realistic, and the example does illustrate that the maturity structure of a firm's debt affects its overall risk. It also shows that the risk tolerance of the firm with respect to the maturity composition of its liabilities depends to a large extent on the amount of risk already present in the firm owing to industry business risk, operating leverage, and overall financial leverage. It is important to keep the overall risk level of the firm within reasonable limits. Thus a firm with high business risk should probably not use a very aggressive policy in its financial structure (and especially not in its maturity structure), but a firm in a stable industry might use such a policy to advantage. Of course, the firm's asset maturity structure has a bearing on its ability to employ short-term debt (covered in the next section).

Table 8.4
Firm's Expected Interest Rate
One Year Hence

i (1)	Risk Premium (Percent) (2)	Interest Rate to Firm (Percent) [(1) + (2)] (3)	Joint Probability[a] (4)	Product (Percent) [(3) × (4)] (5)
3%	1.0	4.0	0.030	0.120
	1.2	4.2	0.040	0.168
	2.0	5.0	0.060	0.300
	5.0	8.0	0.040	0.320
	25.0	28.0	0.030	0.840
5%	1.0	6.0	0.045	0.270
	1.2	6.2	0.060	0.372
	2.0	7.0	0.090	0.630
	5.0	10.0	0.060	0.600
	25.0	30.0	0.045	1.350
7%	1.0	8.0	0.045	0.360
	1.2	8.2	0.060	0.492
	2.0	9.0	0.090	0.810
	5.0	12.0	0.060	0.720
	25.0	32.0	0.045	1.440
9%	1.0	10.0	0.030	0.300
	1.2	10.2	0.040	0.408
	2.0	11.0	0.060	0.660
	5.0	14.0	0.040	0.560
	25.0	34.0	0.030	0.102
			1.000	10.822

Expected interest rate = 10.822%

[a] Joint probabilities are developed by multiplying the probabilities contained in Table 8.3 by each other. For example, the joint probability at the top of column 4 is the product 0.2 × 0.15 = 0.03, the second is the product 0.2 × 0.20 = 0.04, and so on. The expected value, or most likely interest rate, is found by multiplying the possible interest rates shown in column 3 by the joint probabilities given in column 4, then adding these products.

Relationship of Current Assets to Fixed Assets

In the chapters that deal with capital budgeting, we will see that capital budgeting decisions involve estimating the stream of benefits expected from a given project and then discounting the expected cash flows back to the present to find the present value of the project. Although current asset investment analysis is similar to fixed asset analysis in the sense that it also requires estimates of the effects of such investments on profits, it is different in two key respects:

1. Increasing the firm's current assets—especially cash and marketable securities—while holding constant expected production and sales re-

duces the riskiness of the firm, but it also reduces the overall return on assets.

2. Although both fixed and current asset holdings are functions of *expected* sales, only current assets can be adjusted to *actual* sales in the short run; hence, adjustments to short-run fluctuations in demand lie in the domain of working capital management.

Some of these ideas are illustrated in Figure 8.7, which shows the short-run relationship between the firm's current assets and output. The firm's fixed assets, assumed to be $50 million, cannot be altered in response to short-run fluctuations in output. Three possible current asset policies are depicted. CA_1 represents a conservative policy; relatively large balances of cash and marketable securities are maintained, large "safety stocks" of inventories are kept on hand, and sales are maximized by adoption of a credit policy that causes a high level of accounts receivable. CA_2 is somewhat less conservative than CA_1, and CA_3 represents a risky, aggressive policy.

Current asset holdings are highest at any output level under policy CA_1 and lowest under CA_3. For example, at an output of 100,000 units, CA_1 calls for $33 million of current assets versus only $23 million for CA_3. If demand strengthens and short-run plans call for production to increase from 100,000 to 200,000 units, current asset holdings will likewise increase. Under CA_1 current assets rise to $61 million, but under CA_3 they rise to only $38 million. As we shall see in the following section, the more aggressive policy leads to a higher expected rate of return; it also entails greater risk.

Risk-Return Tradeoff for Current Asset Holdings

If it could forecast perfectly, a firm would hold exactly enough cash to make disbursements as required, exactly enough inventories to meet production and sales requirements, exactly the accounts receivable called for by an optimal credit policy, and no marketable securities unless the interest returns on such assets exceeded the cost of capital (an unlikely occurrence). The current asset holdings under the perfect foresight case would be the theoretical minimum for a profit-maximizing firm. Any larger holdings would, in the sense of the du Pont chart we described earlier, increase the firm's assets without a proportionate increase in its returns, thus lowering its rate of return on investment. Any smaller holdings would mean the inability to pay bills on time, lost sales and production stoppages because of inventory shortages, and lost sales because of an overly restrictive credit policy.

When uncertainty is introduced into the picture, current asset management involves (1) determination of the minimum required balances of each type of asset and (2) addition of a safety stock to account for the fact that forecasters are imperfect. If a firm follows policy CA_1 in Figure 8.7, it is adding relatively large safety stocks; if it follows CA_3, its safety stocks are mini-

Figure 8.7
Relationship between Current
Assets and Output

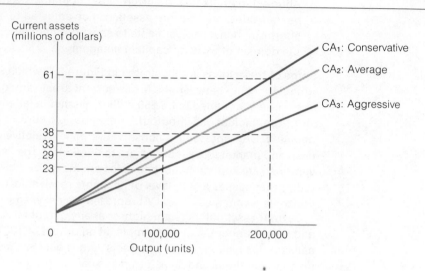

mal. In general, CA_3 produces the highest expected returns on investment, but it also involves the greatest risk; that is, following this policy may actually result in the *lowest* rate of return.

The effects of the three alternative policies on expected profitability is illustrated in Table 8.5. Under the conservative policy, CA_1, the rate of return on assets before interest and taxes is 13.5 percent; the return rises to 15 percent for the average policy and to 17 percent for the risky, aggressive policy, CA_3. However, we know that CA_3 is the most risky policy, since lost sales, lost customer goodwill, and bad credit ratings caused by poor liquidity ratios can combine to bring the actual realized rate of return well below the anticipated 17 percent.

In the real world, things are considerably more complex than this simple example suggests. For one thing, different types of current assets affect both risk and returns differently. Increased holdings of cash do more to improve the firm's risk posture than a similar dollar increase in receivables or inventories; idle cash penalizes earnings more severely than does the same investment in marketable securities. Generalizations are difficult when we consider accounts receivable and inventories, because it is difficult to measure either the earnings penalty or the risk reduction that results from increasing the balances of these items beyond their theoretical minimums.

In subsequent chapters, we will consider the optimal balances of each

Table 8.5
Effects of Alternative Current
Asset Policies on Rates of
Return and Asset Turnover

	Conservative (CA$_1$)	Average (CA$_2$)	Risky (CA$_3$)
Sales:			
Units	200,000	200,000	200,000
Dollars	$100,000,000	$100,000,000	$100,000,000
EBIT	15,000,000	15,000,000	15,000,000
Current assets	61,000,000	50,000,000	38,000,000
Fixed assets	50,000,000	50,000,000	50,000,000
Total assets	$111,000,000	$100,000,000	$ 88,000,000
Rate of return on assets (EBIT/assets)	13.5%	15.0%	17.0%

type of current asset (with *optimal* including the theoretical minimum as well as an optimal safety stock). First, however, we must complete our generalized discussion of working capital policy by combining current asset and current liability management.

Combining Current Asset and Current Liability Management

Table 8.6 illustrates the effect of working capital policy on expected returns and on risk as measured by the current ratio. A conservative policy calling for no short-term debt and large holdings of current assets results in a 9.6 percent expected after-tax return on equity and a very high current ratio. The actual return probably is quite close to 9.6 percent. An aggressive policy, with minimal holdings of current assets and short-term rather than long-term debt, raises the expected return to 14 percent. But the current ratio under this policy is only .86, a dangerously low level for most industries. Simultaneously, the increasing risks associated with the aggressive policy may adversely affect stock market opinion about the company; therefore, even if working capital policy pushes rates of return up, the net effect still may be a lowering of stock prices.

Can we resolve this risk-return tradeoff to determine *precisely* the firm's optimal working capital policy—the policy that will maximize the value of existing common stock? In theory the answer is yes, but in practice it is no. Determining the optimal policy would require detailed information on a complex set of variables—information that is unobtainable today. Progress is being made in the development of computer simulation models designed to help determine the effects of alternative financial policy choices, including working capital decisions; but no one using such models suggests that

Table 8.6
Effects of Working Capital Policy
on the Rate of Return on
Common Equity

	Conservative— Long-Term Debt Large Investment in Current Assets (CA_1)	Average— Average Use of Short-Term Debt; Average Investment in Current Assets (CA_2)	Aggressive— All Short-Term Debt; Minimal Investment in Current Assets (CA_3)
Current assets	$ 61,000,000	$ 50,000,000	$ 38,000,000
Fixed assets	50,000,000	50,000,000	50,000,000
Total assets	$111,000,000	$100,000,000	$ 88,000,000
Current liabilities (at 6%)	—	$ 25,000,000	$ 44,000,000
Long-term debt (at 8%)	55,500,000	25,000,000	—
Total debt (debt/assets = 50%)	$ 55,500,000	$ 50,000,000	$ 44,000,000
Equity	55,500,000	50,000,000	44,000,000
Total liabilities and net worth	$111,000,000	$100,000,000	$ 88,000,000
Sales in dollars	$100,000,000	$100,000,000	$100,000,000
EBIT	15,000,000	15,000,000	15,000,000
Less interest	−4,400,000	−3,500,000	−2,640,000
Taxable income	$ 10,600,000	$ 11,500,000	$ 12,360,000
Less taxes (at 50%)	−5,300,000	−5,750,000	−6,180,000
Earnings on equity	$ 5,300,000	$ 5,750,000	$ 6,180,000
Rate of return on equity	9.6%	11.5%	14.0%
Current ratio	a	2.1	0.86

[a] Under policy CA_1, the current ratio is shown to be infinitely high. Actually, the firm would doubtless have some spontaneous credit, but the current ratio would still be quite high.

they can actually reach *optimal* solutions. We can, however, establish guidelines, or ranges of values, for each type of current asset; and we do have ways of examining the various types of short-term financing and their effects on the cost of capital. Because such information, used with good judgment, can be helpful to the financial manager, we will consider this topic in the remaining chapters of Part 3.

Summary

Working capital is a firm's investments in short-term assets. *Gross working capital* is the firm's total current assets, and *net working capital* is current assets minus current liabilities. *Working capital management* involves all aspects of the administration of current assets and current liabilities.

Working capital policy is concerned with two sets of relationships among balance sheet items. First is the policy question of the level of total current assets to be held. Current assets vary with sales, but the ratio of current assets to sales is a policy matter. A firm that elects to operate aggressively will hold relatively small stocks of current assets, which will reduce the required level of investment and increase the expected rate of return on investment. However, an aggressive policy also increases the likelihood of running out of cash or inventories or of losing sales because of an excessively tough credit policy.

The second policy question concerns the relationships among types of assets and the way these assets are financed. One policy calls for matching asset and liability maturities and financing short-term assets with short-term debt and long-term assets with long-term debt or equity. This policy is unsound, because current assets are permanent investments as sales grow. If the policy is followed, the maturity structure of the debt is determined by the level of fixed versus current assets. Since short-term debt is frequently less expensive than long-term debt, the expected rate of return may be higher if short-term debt is used. However, large amounts of short-term credit increase the risks of having to renew this debt at higher interest rates and of being unable to renew the debt at all if the firm experiences difficulties.

Both aspects of working capital policy involve risk-return tradeoffs. In the following chapter, we will examine methods used to determine the optimal levels of each type of current asset. Then, in Chapter 10, we will explore alternative sources and forms of short-term credit.

Questions

8.1 How does the seasonal nature of a firm's sales influence the decision about the amount of short-term credit in the financial structure?

8.2 What is your reaction to this statement: Merely increasing the level of current asset holdings does not necessarily reduce the riskiness of the firm. Rather, the composition of the current assets, whether highly liquid or highly illiquid, is the important factor to consider.

8.3 What is the advantage of matching the maturities of assets and liabilities? What are the disadvantages?

8.4 There have been times when the term structure of interest rates has been such that short-term rates were higher than long-term rates. Does this necessarily imply that the best financial policy for a firm is to use all long-term debt and no short-term debt? Explain.

8.5 Assuming a firm's volume of business remained constant, would you expect it to have higher cash balances (demand deposits) during a tight-money period or an easy-money period? Does this situation have any ramifications for federal monetary policy?

Problems

8.1 Suppose that expected future short-term interest rates have the following alternative patterns:

Year	A	B	C	D
1	4%	8%	4%	8%
2	5	7	6	7
3	6	6	15	5
4	7	5	6	7
5	8	4	4	8

a. Using a simple arithmetic average, what is the current rate on a five-year note for each of the four patterns?

b. Using a geometric average, answer the same question as for Part a. (Hint: Multiply the five numbers, then take their fifth root. On a hand calculator use the y^x or x^x button with 0.2, which equals $1/5$. For example, for Interest Rate A the product is 6,720, and the fifth root is 5.827 percent.)

c. Optional:
   1. Calculate the current two-, three-, and four-year note yields using both the arithmetic and geometric averages, and graph the resulting yield curves in four graphs of two curves each.
   2. Is the height of the yield curve based on the arithmetic averages higher or lower than that based on the geometric averages?

8.2 From the group of yield curves presented at the top of page 193, what generalizations can be made on the behavior of financial markets between August 30, 1974, and November 26, 1976?

8.3 From a recent issue of the *Federal Reserve Bulletin* or from another convenient source:

a. Construct a yield curve for the most complete 1978 data for U.S. government securities, using market yields for maturities of one year or less and the capital market rates for constant maturities for the maturities from two to twenty years.

b. Construct yield curves for the 1976 and 1977 average rates. Comment on any shifts you observe.

c. Next, add to the graph you developed in Part b the yield curve for the latest week available in the source you are using. Comment on any shifts in relation to 1977.

d. Why does the yield curve show only U.S. government security yields instead of including yields on commercial paper and corporate bonds?

8.4 The Morgan Tile Corporation is attempting to determine the optimal level of current assets for the coming year. Management expects sales to increase to approximately $1.2 million as a result of asset expansion presently being undertaken. Fixed assets total $500,000, and the firm wishes to maintain a 60 percent debt ratio. Morgan's interest cost is currently 8 percent on both short-term debt and longer-term debt (which the firm uses in its permanent structure). Three alternatives regarding the projected current asset level are available to the firm: (1) an aggressive policy requiring current assets of

**Yields on U.S. Government
Securities**

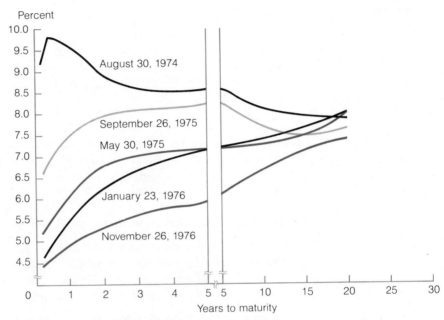

Source: Federal Reserve Bank of St. Louis, December 10, 1976.

only 45 percent of projected sales; (2) an average policy of 50 percent of sales as current assets; and (3) a conservative policy requiring current assets of 60 percent of sales. The firm expects to generate earnings before interest and taxes at a rate of 12 percent on total sales.

a. What is the expected return on equity under each current asset level? (Assume a 50 percent tax rate.)

b. In this problem, we have assumed that interest rates and level of expected sales are independent of current asset policy. Is this a valid assumption?

c. How would the overall riskiness of the firm vary under each policy? Discuss specifically the effect of current asset management on demand, expenses, fixed charge coverage, risk of insolvency, and so on.

8.5 Three companies—Aggressive, Between, and Conservative—have different working capital management policies as implied by their names. For example, Aggressive employs only minimal current assets and finances almost entirely with current liabilities and equity. This tight ship approach has a dual effect. It keeps total assets low, and this tends to increase return on assets. But for reasons such as stock-outs total sales are reduced; and since inventory is ordered more frequently and in smaller quantities, variable costs are increased. Condensed balance sheets for the three companies are presented below.

Balance Sheets

	Aggressive	Between	Conservative
Current assets	$150,000	$200,000	$300,000
Fixed assets	200,000	200,000	200,000
Total assets	$350,000	$400,000	$500,000
Current liabilities (at 8%)	$200,000	$100,000	50,000
Long-term debt (at 10%)	0	100,000	200,000
Total debt	$200,000	$200,000	$250,000
Equity	150,000	200,000	250,000
Total claims on assets	$350,000	$400,000	$500,000
Current ratio	0.75:1	2:1	6:1

The cost of goods sold functions for the three firms are as follows:

$$\text{Cost of goods sold} = \text{Fixed costs} + \text{Variable costs}$$
Aggressive: Cost of goods sold = $200,000 + 0.7(sales)
Between: Cost of goods sold = $250,000 + 0.6(sales)
Conservative: Cost of goods sold = $300,000 + 0.6(sales)

A company with normal net working capital, such as Between, will sell $1 million in a year when economic growth is average. If the economy is weak, sales for Between will be reduced by $100,000; if strong, sales will increase $100,000. In any given economic condition, Aggressive will sell $100,000 less than Between, and Conservative will sell $100,000 more. This is because of the working capital differences.

a. Make out income statements for each company for strong, average, and weak economies using the following pattern:

Sales
Less cost of goods sold
Earnings before interest and taxes (EBIT)
Less interest expense
Taxable income
Less taxes (at 50%)
Net income

b. Compare the rates of return (EBIT/Assets and return on equity). Which company is best in a strong economy? in an average economy? In a weak economy?

c. What considerations for management of working capital are indicated by this problem?

8.6 Indicate the effects of the transactions listed below on each of the following: total current assets, working capital, current ratio, and net profit. Use +

to indicate an increase, − to indicate a decrease, and 0 to indicate no effect. State necessary assumptions and assume an initial current ratio of more than 1 to 1.

	Total Current Assets	Net Working Capital[a]	Current Ratio	Net Profit
1. Cash is acquired through issuance of additional common stock.	____	____	____	____
2. Merchandise is sold for cash.	____	____	____	____
3. Federal income tax due for the previous year is paid.	____	____	____	____
4. A fixed asset is sold for less than book value.	____	____	____	____
5. A fixed asset is sold for more than book value.	____	____	____	____
6. Merchandise is sold on credit.	____	____	____	____
7. Payment is made to trade creditors for previous purchases.	____	____	____	____
8. A cash dividend is declared and paid.	____	____	____	____
9. Cash is obtained through short-term bank loans.	____	____	____	____
10. Short-term notes receivable are sold at a discount.	____	____	____	____
11. A profitable firm increases its fixed assets depreciation allowance account.	____	____	____	____
12. Marketable securities are sold below cost.	____	____	____	____
13. Uncollectable accounts are written off against the allowance account.	____	____	____	____
14. Advances are made to employees.	____	____	____	____
15. Current operating expenses are paid.	____	____	____	____
16. Short-term promissory notes are issued to trade creditors for prior purchases.	____	____	____	____
17. Ten-year notes are issued to pay off accounts payable.	____	____	____	____
18. A wholly depreciated asset is retired.	____	____	____	____
19. Accounts receivable are collected.	____	____	____	____
20. A stock dividend is declared and paid.	____	____	____	____
21. Equipment is purchased with short-term notes.	____	____	____	____
22. The allowance for doubtful accounts is increased.	____	____	____	____
23. Merchandise is purchased on credit.	____	____	____	____
24. The estimated taxes payable are increased.	____	____	____	____

[a] *Net working capital* is defined as current assets minus current liabilities.

9 CHAPTER

CURRENT ASSET MANAGEMENT

In Chapter 8 we viewed working capital management in a general sense. Now we will focus our attention on the firm's investment in specific current assets, examining cash, marketable securities, accounts receivable, and inventories. According to Federal Trade Commission reports, at the beginning of 1978, current assets represented almost 50 percent of manufacturing companies' assets, so current asset management is clearly an important subject.

Cash Management

Controlling the investment in current assets begins with cash management. Cash consists of the firm's holdings of currency and demand deposits—the latter being by far the more important for most firms.

Why Hold Cash?

Businesses (and individuals) have three primary motives for holding cash: (1) the transactions motive, (2) the precautionary motive, and (3) the speculative motive.

Transactions Motive The transactions motive for holding cash is to enable the firm to conduct its ordinary business—making purchases and sales. In lines of business where billings can be cycled throughout the month (such as the utilities) cash inflows can be scheduled and synchronized with the need for the cash outflows. We expect the cash-to-revenues ratio and cash-to-total-assets ratio for such firms to be relatively low. In retail trade, by contrast, sales are more random, and a number of transactions may actually be conducted with physical currency. As a consequence, retail trade requires a higher ratio of cash to sales and of cash to total assets.

The seasonality of a business may give rise to a need for cash to purchase inventories. For example, raw materials may be available only during a harvest season and may be perishable, as in the food-canning business. Or sales may be seasonal, as they are in department stores (with the peaks around the Christmas and Easter holidays), giving rise to an increase in cash needs.

Precautionary Motive The precautionary motive for holding cash relates primarily to the predictability of cash inflows and outflows. If the predictability is high, less cash need be held against an emergency or any other contingency. Another factor that strongly influences the precautionary motive is the ability to borrow additional cash on short notice. Borrowing flexibility is primarily a matter of the strength of the firm's relationships with banking institutions and other credit sources. The need for holding cash is satisfied in large part by having near-money assets such as short-term government securities.

Speculative Motive The speculative motive for holding cash is to enable the firm to accept profit-making opportunities that may arise. By and large, business accumulation of cash for speculative purposes is not widely found. Such accumulation is more common among individual investors. However, the firm's cash and marketable securities account may rise to rather sizable levels on a temporary basis as funds are accumulated to meet specific future needs. For example, at the end of 1977, IBM held $252 million in cash and $5.2 billion in marketable securities. Combined, these items represented 28.5 percent of IBM's year-end total assets of $14.0 billion. Whenever IBM introduces a new computer development, the cash requirements are quite substantial, since the total investment and production costs will be recovered over several years in monthly rental receipts.

Specific Advantages of Adequate Cash

In addition to these general motives, sound working capital management requires maintenance of an ample amount of cash for several specific reasons:

1. It is essential that the firm have sufficient cash to take trade discounts. The payment schedule for purchases is referred to as the "term of the sale." A commonly encountered billing procedure, or "term of trade," is that of a 2 percent discount on a bill paid within ten days, with full payment required in thirty days regardless of whether the discount is taken. (This is usually stated as 2/10, net 30.) Since the net amount is due in thirty days, failure to take the discount means paying the extra 2 percent for using the money an additional twenty days. A company paying 2 percent for every twenty-day period over the year (considered to be 360 days) would pay the extra for eighteen such periods:

$$\frac{360 \text{ days}}{20 \text{ days}} = 18.$$

This represents an annual interest rate of 37 percent.[1] Most firms' cost of capital is substantially lower than 37 percent.

---

1. The following equation can be used for calculating the cost, on an annual basis, of not taking discounts:

$$\text{Cost} = \frac{\text{Discount percent}}{(100 - \text{Discount percent})} \times \frac{360}{(\text{Final due date} - \text{Discount period})}.$$

The denominator in the first term (100 − Discount percent) equals the funds made available by not taking the discount. To illustrate, the cost of not taking a discount when the terms are 2/10, net 30 is computed:

$$\text{Cost} = \frac{2}{98} \times \frac{360}{20} = 0.0204 \times 18 = 36.72\%.$$

Continued

2. Since the current and acid test ratios are key items in credit analysis, it is essential that the firm, in order to maintain its credit standing, meet the standards of the line of business in which it is engaged. A strong credit standing enables the firm to purchase goods from trade suppliers on favorable terms and to maintain its line of credit with banks and other sources of credit.
3. Ample cash is useful for taking advantage of favorable business opportunities that may come along from time to time.
4. The firm should have sufficient liquidity to meet emergencies, such as strikes, fires, or marketing campaigns of competitors.

Using the knowledge about the general nature of cash flows presented in Chapter 6, financial managers may be able to improve the inflow-outflow pattern of cash. They can do so by better synchronization of flows and by reduction of float, explained in the following sections.

Synchronization of Cash Flows

An example of synchronization demonstrates how cash flows can be improved through more frequent requisitioning of funds by divisional offices from the firm's central office. Some Gulf Oil Corporation divisional field offices, for instance, formerly requisitioned funds once a week; now the treasurer's office insists on daily requisitions, thus keeping cash on tap as many as four days longer. On the basis of twenty offices, each requiring $1 million a week, the staggered requisitions free the equivalent of $40 million for one day each week. At 6 percent interest, this earns better than $336,000 a year.

Moreover, effective forecasting can reduce the firm's investment in cash. The cash flow forecasting at CIT Credit Corporation illustrates this idea. An assistant treasurer forecasts planned purchases of automobiles by the dealers. He estimates daily the number of cars shipped to the 10,000 dealers who finance their purchases through CIT. He then estimates how much money should be deposited in Detroit banks that day to pay automobile manufacturers. On one day he estimated a required deposit of $6.4 million; the actual bill for the day was $6.397 million, a difference of 0.5 percent. Although such close forecasting cannot be achieved by every firm, the system enables CIT to economize on the amount of money it must borrow and thereby keeps interest expense to a minimum.

Notice that the calculated cost can be reduced by paying late. Thus, if the firm pays in sixty days rather than the specified thirty, the credit period becomes $60 - 10 = 50$, and the calculated cost becomes:

$$\text{Cost} = \frac{2}{98} \times \frac{360}{50} = 0.0204 \times 7.2 = 14.7\%.$$

In periods of excess capacity, some firms may be able to get away with late payments, but such firms may suffer a variety of problems associated with being "slow-payer" accounts.

Expediting Collections and Check Clearing

One of the easiest ways to improve cash flow is to expedite the preparation of bills. A firm can control this process easily, and the cash free-up can be substantial. AT&T, for example, uses the computer to transmit billing information over telephone lines. Prompt mailing of bills also improves cash flow. Getting the bills out is one of the most efficient, yet most easily overlooked, methods of increasing receivables turnover and thereby improving cash flow.

Another important method of economizing on the amount of cash required is to hasten the process of clearing checks. Checks sent from customers in distant cities are subject to delays because of the time required for the check to travel in the mail and to be cleared through the banking system.

Even after a check has been received by a firm and deposited in its account, the funds cannot be spent until the check has been cleared. The bank in which the check is deposited presents the check to the bank on which it was drawn. Only when the latter bank transfers funds to the bank of deposit are they available for use by the depositor. Checks are generally cleared through the Federal Reserve System or through a clearinghouse set up by the banks in a particular city. Of course, if the check is drawn on the bank of deposit, that bank merely transfers funds from one depositor to another with bookkeeping entries. The length of time required for checks to clear is a function of the distance between the payer's and the payee's banks; in the case of clearinghouses, it can range from one day to three or four days. The maximum time for checks cleared through the Federal Reserve System is two days.

To reduce this delay, a *lockbox plan* can be used. If a firm makes a number of sales in distant cities, it can establish a lockbox in a post office located near its customers. It can then arrange for customers to send payments to that box and for a bank to pick up the checks and deposit them in a special checking account. The bank has the checks cleared in the local area and remits the money by wire to the firm's bank of deposit. If the distant customers are scattered, the firm can establish the lockbox in its own city and have the checks picked up by its own bank. The bank begins the clearing process and notifies the firm that a check has been received. In this way the clearing process starts before the firm processes the check. Using these methods reduces collection time by one to five days. Some firms have reported freeing funds in the amount of $5 million or more by these methods.

Slowing Disbursements

Just as expediting the collection process conserves cash, slowing disbursements accomplishes the same thing by keeping cash on hand for longer periods. An obvious way to do this is simply to delay payments, but this involves equally obvious difficulties. Firms have, in the past, devised rather ingenious methods for "legitimately" lengthening the collection period on their own checks, ranging from maintaining deposits in distant banks to using slow, awkward payment procedures. Since such practices are usually recognized for what they are, their use is severely limited.

The most widely publicized procedure in recent years has been the use of drafts. While a check is payable on demand, a draft must be transmitted to the issuer, who approves it and deposits funds to cover it, after which it can be collected. AT&T has used drafts in the following way:

In handling its payrolls, for instance, AT&T can pay an employee by draft on Friday. The employee cashes the draft at his local bank, which sends it on to AT&T's New York bank. It may be Wednesday or Thursday before the draft arrives. The bank then sends it to the company's accounting department, which has until 3 P.M. that day to inspect and approve it. Not until then does AT&T deposit funds in its bank to pay the draft.[2]

Insurance companies also use drafts to pay claims.

Both banks and those who receive drafts dislike them. They represent an awkward, clumsy, costly anachronism in an age when computer transfer mechanisms are reducing the time and expense involved in transfers of funds.

Using Float

Checks that firms (or individuals) write are not deducted from bank records until they are actually received by the bank, which may take several days. The lag between the time the check is written until the time the bank receives it is known as *float*.

Some firms are able to exploit float to create what is effectively an interest-free loan. For example, a firm with only a moderate balance in its checking account and $100,000 in its savings account may write a check for $100,000, knowing that it will not clear for six or seven days. After six days it can move the $100,000 from the savings account to the checking account so the check will be covered. In the meantime, six days of interest ($100 at 6 percent) will have been earned on the savings account. This is the gain from float.

In reality, the problem is more complex. The check-writing firm in the illustration also receives checks, which it deposits in its savings account. Historically, banks have considered these deposits to be available to the company when they are deposited. If the firm is slow to deposit such checks, float is reduced.

Suppose a firm writes checks totaling about $5,000 each day. It takes about six or seven days for these checks to clear and to be deducted from the firm's bank account. Thus the firm's own checking records show a balance $30,000 less than that shown by the bank's records. If the firm re-

2. "More Firms Substitute Drafts for Checks to Pay, Collect Bills," *Wall Street Journal,* August 29, 1971.

201

ceives checks in the amount of $5,000 daily and loses only four days while these checks are being deposited, its own books show a balance that is $20,000 larger than the bank's balance. Thus the firm's float—the difference between the $30,000 and the $20,000—is $10,000.

Clearly there are gains to be had from the skillful use of float. These gains are maximized by covering checks written at the last possible date and depositing checks received as quickly as possible. As previously noted, the effect is similar to an interest-free loan from the bank.

In the past, banks have compensated for loss of funds due to float by raising prices of other services, which are paid for by all customers. They may, for example, offset float costs by higher interest rates on loans or higher service charges. Thus other customers of the bank bear part of the cost if one firm uses float successfully. Clearly, this is not desirable for either the bank or the other customers, and efforts to reduce the gains from using float have intensified in recent years.

One method banks would like to employ to reduce these gains is the electronic funds transfer system. EFTS, as it is called, would create a nationwide computer network that would substantially reduce float time. It presently takes several days to clear checks across the country. Under EFTS the time could be reduced to hours or even minutes. As yet no nationwide system exists, but developments in that direction are moving rapidly.

In addition to reducing the actual time it takes to clear a check, banks are attempting to more accurately match costs and revenues on individual accounts. One effect of this matching is a further reduction in the gains from using float. Table 9.1 depicts a typical commercial checking account service charge analysis. In the earnings credit section, the customer is credited for the average collected balance at the interest rate of 5 percent. The collected balance is determined as the daily balance adjusted for the typical time it takes for the bank to collect on checks deposited. Thus, the estimated days of float will be low for a business dealing mostly with local customers and high for a business that receives payments from out-of-state customers. In this way the individual firm bears the cost of float directly. The expense part of the analysis is straightforward. In reality there are many more expense classifications than the few itemized here—among them lockbox charges, computer service billings, required compensating balances.

In the illustration, the service charge to the firm is $10.98 after allowing for the earnings credit. In the event that the earnings credit exceeds the expenses, current regulations do not permit paying it to the depositor. But this regulation is under scrutiny and is likely to be changed in the near future.

The key point to remember is that the potential gains from using float are relative. Even though banks have taken steps to reduce the gains, the company that deposits checks from customers promptly and delays bank clearing of checks it writes for as long as possible will still have a relative advantage from float.

**Table 9.1
State National Bank
Commercial Service Charge Analysis
Mail Order Supply Company
September 1978**

Earnings credit

1	Days in month	31	
2	Less average days float	6	
3	Basis for earnings credit	25	
4	Average daily balance	$21,300.00	
5	Daily rate factor (at 5%)	0.000139	
6	Earnings credit ($3 \times 4 \times 5$)		$74.02

Service debits

7	20 deposits (at $.25 each)	$ 5.00	
8	3,200 checks deposited (at $.02 each)	64.00	
9	200 checks written (at $.08 each)	16.00	
10	Total service debits ($7 + 8 + 9$)		85.00
	Service charge ($10 - 6$)		$10.98

If a firm's own collection and clearing process is more efficient than that of the recipients of its checks—and this is often true of large, efficient firms—then the firm could show a negative balance on its own records and a positive balance on its bank's books. Some firms indicate that they *never* have true positive cash balances. One large manufacturer of construction equipment stated that, while its account according to its bank's records shows an average cash balance of about $2 million, its actual cash balance is *minus* $2 million; thus it has $4 million of float. Obviously, the firm must be able to forecast its positive and negative clearings accurately in order to make such heavy use of float.

**Cost of Cash
Management[3]**

We have just described a number of procedures that can be used to hold down cash balance requirements. Implementing these procedures, however, is not a costless operation. How far should a firm go in making its cash operations more efficient? As a general rule, a firm should incur these expenses so long as its marginal returns exceed its marginal expenses.

For example, suppose that by establishing a lockbox system and increasing the accuracy of cash inflow and outflow forecasts, a firm can reduce its investment in cash by $1.2 million. Further suppose that the firm borrows at

---

3. We are abstracting from the security aspects of cash management—the prevention of fraud and embezzlement. These topics are better covered in accounting than in finance courses.

an effective rate of 10 percent.[4] The steps taken release $1.2 million, and the cost of capital required to carry this $1.2 million investment in cash is $120,000. If the costs of the procedures necessary to release the $1.2 million are less than $120,000, the move is a good one; if the costs exceed $120,000, the greater efficiency is not worth the cost. It is clear that larger firms, with larger cash balances, can better afford to hire the personnel necessary to maintain tight control over their cash positions. Cash management is one element of business operations in which economies of scale are clearly present. In sum, the value of careful cash management depends on the cost of funds invested in cash, which in turn depends on the current rate of interest. In the 1970s, with interest rates at historic highs, firms are devoting more care than ever to cash management.

Determining the Minimum Cash Balance

Thus far we have seen that cash is held primarily for transactions purposes; the other traditional motives for holding cash—the speculative and precautionary motives—are today met largely by reserve borrowing and by holding short-term marketable securities. Some minimum cash balance (which can actually be negative if float is used effectively) is required for transactions, and an additional amount over and above this figure may be held as a safety stock. For many firms the total of transactions balances plus safety stock constitutes the minimum cash balance—the point at which the firm either borrows additional cash or sells part of its portfolio of marketable securities. For many other firms, however, banking relationships require still larger balances.

Compensating Balances

We have seen that banks provide services to firms. They clear checks, operate lockbox plans, supply credit information, and the like. These services cost the bank money, so the bank must be compensated for rendering them.

Banks earn most of their income by lending money at interest, and most of the funds they lend are obtained in the form of deposits. If a firm maintains a deposit account with an average balance of $100,000 and if the bank can lend these funds at a return of $8,000, then the account is, in a sense, worth $8,000 to the bank. Thus it is to the bank's advantage to provide services worth up to $8,000 to attract and hold the account.

Banks first determine the costs of the services rendered to their larger customers and then decide on the average account balances necessary to

---

4. The borrowing rate, 10 percent, is used rather than the firm's average cost of capital, because cash is a less risky investment than the firm's average assets. Notice also that before-tax figures are used here; the analysis can employ either before-tax or after-tax figures so long as consistency is maintained.

provide enough income to compensate for the costs. Firms often maintain these balances, called *compensating balances,* instead of paying cash service charges to the bank.[5]

Compensating balances are also required by some bank loan agreements. During periods when the supply of credit is restricted and interest rates are high, banks frequently insist that borrowers maintain accounts that average some percentage of the loan amount (15 percent is typical) as a condition for granting the loan. If the balance is larger than what the firm would otherwise maintain, then the effective cost of the loan is increased; the excess balance presumably compensates the bank for making the loan at a rate below what it could earn on the funds if they were invested elsewhere.[6]

Compensating balances can be established (1) as an absolute minimum, say $100,000, below which the actual balance must never fall, or (2) as a minimum average balance, perhaps $100,000 over a certain period, generally a month. The absolute minimum is a much more restrictive requirement, because the average amount of cash held during the month must be above $100,000 by the amount of transactions balances. The $100,000 in this case is "dead money" from the firm's standpoint. Under the minimum average, however, the balance can fall to zero one day provided it is $200,000 some other day, with the average working out to $100,000. Thus the $100,000 in this case is available for transactions.

Statistics on compensating balance requirements are not available, but average balances are typical and absolute minimums are rare for business accounts. Discussions with bankers, however, indicate that absolute balance requirements are less rare during times of extremely tight money, such as the late 1960s and early 1970s.

The firm's minimum cash balance is set as the larger of (1) its transactions balances plus precautionary balances (that is, safety stocks) or (2) its required compensating balances. Statistics are not available on which factor is generally controlling, but in our experience compensating balance requirements generally dominate, except for firms subject to absolute minimum balances.[7]

---

5. Banks are compensated for services rendered either by compensating balances or by direct fees.
6. The interest rate effect of compensating balances is discussed further in Chapter 10.
7. This point is underscored by an incident that occurred at a professional finance meeting. A professor presented a scholarly paper that used operations research techniques to determine optimal cash balances for a sample of firms. He reported that actual cash balances of the firm greatly exceeded optimal balances, suggesting inefficiency and the need for more refined techniques. The discussant of the paper reported that she had written to the sample firms, asking why they were holding so much cash. The firms uniformly replied that their cash holdings were set by compensating balance requirements. The model thus was useful to determine the optimal cash balance in the absence of compensating balance requirements, but it was precisely those requirements that determined actual balances. Since the model did not include compensating balances as a determinant of cash balances, its usefulness is questionable.

Overdraft System   Most countries outside the United States use *overdraft systems.* In such systems a depositor can write checks in excess of the bank balance, and the bank automatically extends a loan to cover the shortage. The maximum amount of such loans must, of course, be established ahead of time. Statistics are not available on the usage of overdrafts in the United States, but a number of firms have worked out informal, and in some cases formal, overdraft arrangements; and the use of overdrafts has been increasing in recent years.

**Cash
Management**   Several types of mathematical models have been developed to help determine optimal cash balances.[8] These models are interesting, and they are beginning to become practical. A wide range of methods to control the investment in cash has also been developed.

Recently, cash management has begun receiving increased emphasis, primarily in response to the high inflation rates that threaten to devalue any idle or unaccounted for cash. Corporations are tightening their cash controls to ensure that cash will not be forgotten in a dormant bank account or a distant subdivision. For example, Foremost-McKesson tightened internal controls and introduced an electronic funds transfer system, thereby gleaning an extra $30 million from operations. In order to protect its cash during an inflationary period, a firm must know exactly how much cash it has, and where it is. This explains the appearance of complicated cash management systems.

Interest in cash management is also being generated by the large number of firms expanding overseas. Floating exchange rates compel firms to develop worldwide cash control systems. A centralized cash management system is necessary to prevent large currency exchange losses. Even if a firm wishes to avoid currency speculation, it still must carefully monitor exposure to rate changes and develop an appropriate system of hedges and other means for reducing risk. In many firms, the cash manager takes full responsibility for covering exposure, determining daily or weekly exchange rates for use by all divisions and subsidiaries.

**Marketable
Securities**   Firms sometimes report sizable amounts of short-term marketable securities such as Treasury bills or bank certificates of deposit among their current assets. Why are marketable securities held? The two primary reasons—the need for a substitute for cash and the need for a temporary investment—are considered in this section.

---

8. Examples of cash management models are presented in J. Fred Weston and Eugene F. Brigham, *Managerial Finance,* 6th ed. (Hinsdale, Ill.: Dryden Press, 1978), pp. 212–221.

Substitute for Cash

Some firms hold portfolios of marketable securities in lieu of large cash balances, liquidating part of the portfolio to increase the cash account when cash outflows exceed inflows. Data are not available to indicate the extent of this practice, but our impression is that it is not common. Most firms prefer to let their banks maintain such liquid reserves, and they borrow to meet temporary cash shortages.

Temporary Investment

In addition to using marketable securities as a buffer against cash shortages, firms also hold them on a strictly temporary basis. Firms engaged in seasonal operations, for example, frequently have surplus cash flows during part of the year and deficit cash flows the rest of the time. (See Table 7.1 for an example.) Such firms may purchase marketable securities during their surplus periods, then liquidate them when cash deficits occur. Other firms, particularly those in capital goods industries, where fluctuations are violent, attempt to accumulate cash or near-cash securities during a downturn in volume in order to be ready to finance an upturn.

Firms also accumulate liquid assets to meet predictable financial requirements. For example, if a major modernization program is planned for the near future, or if a bond issue is about to mature, the marketable securities portfolio may be increased to provide the required funds. Marketable securities holdings are also frequently increased immediately before quarterly corporate tax payments are due.

Some firms accumulate resources as a protection against a number of contingencies. When they make uninsurable product warranties, for example, companies must be ready to meet any claims that may arise. Firms in highly competitive industries must have resources to carry them through substantial shifts in the market structure. And firms in an industry in which new markets are emerging—for example, foreign markets—need to have resources to meet developments. These funds may be on hand for fairly long periods.

Criteria for Selecting Securities Portfolios

Different types of securities, varying in risk of default, marketability, and length of maturity, are available. We will discuss some of the characteristics of these securities and the criteria that are applied in choosing among them.

Risk of Default The firm's liquidity portfolio is generally held for a specific, known need; if it depreciates in value, the firm will be financially embarrassed. Most nonfinancial corporations do not have investment departments specializing in appraising securities and determining the probability of their going into default. Accordingly, the marketable securities portfolio is generally confined to securities with a minimal risk of default. However, the lowest risk securities also provide the lowest returns, so safety is bought at the expense of yield.

Marketability The securities portfolio is usually held to provide liquid reserves or to meet known needs at a specific time. In either case, the firm must be able to sell its holdings and realize cash on short notice. Accordingly, the securities held in the portfolio must be readily marketable.

Maturity We shall see in Chapter 14 that at interest rate levels below 8 percent, the price of a long-term bond fluctuates much more with changes in interest rates than does the price of a similar short-term security. Further, as we saw in the last chapter, interest rates fluctuate widely over time. These two factors combine to make long-term bonds riskier than short-term securities for a firm's marketable securities portfolio. However, partly because of this risk differential, higher yields are more frequently available on long-term than on short-term securities; so again risk-return tradeoffs must be recognized.

Given the motives most firms have for holding marketable securities portfolios, it is generally not feasible for them to be exposed to a high degree of risk from interest rate fluctuations. Accordingly, firms generally confine their portfolios to securities with short maturities. Only if the securities are expected to be held for a long period and not be subject to forced liquidation on short notice will long-term securities be chosen.

Investment Alternatives

The main investment alternatives open to business firms are given in Table 9.2. Returns are lower on the lower-risk government securities and on shorter maturities. Average rate levels vary with the general level of interest rates. Late 1974 was a period of relatively high interest rate levels. After dropping to substantially lower levels by mid-1977, interest rates began to firm up in 1978. By mid-1978, long-term rates had exceeded their high levels of 1974. However, short-term rates were still somewhat below the 1974 peaks.

The financial manager decides on a suitable maturity pattern for the holdings on the basis of how long the funds are to be held. The numerous alternatives can be selected and balanced in such a way that maturities and risks appropriate to the financial situation of the firm are obtained. Commercial bankers, investment bankers, and brokers provide the financial manager with detailed information on each of the listed forms of investment. Because the characteristics of investment outlets change with shifts in financial market conditions, it would be misleading to attempt to give detailed descriptions of them here. The financial manager should keep up to date on these characteristics and follow the principle of making investment selections that offer maturities, yields, and risks appropriate to the firm.

Table 9.2
Alternative Marketable
Securities for Investment

	Approximate Maturities[a]	Approximate Yields[b]	
		April 1977	May 1978
U.S. Treasury bills	91–182 days	4.81%	6.52%
U.S. Treasury certificates	9–12 months	5.20	7.78
U.S. Treasury notes	1–5 years	6.41	8.03
U.S. Treasury bonds	Over 5 years	7.45	8.33
Negotiable certificates of deposit with U.S. banks	Varies, up to 3 years	5.35	8.00
Prime commercial paper	Varies, up to 270 days	4.70	7.00
Eurodollar bank time deposits	Varies, up to 1 year	5.18	7.82
Bonds of other corporations (AAA)	Varies, up to 30 years	8.53	9.02

[a] The maturities are those at issue date. For outstanding securities, maturities varying almost by day or week are available.
[b] Estimated yields for median maturities in the class.

Effects of Inflation

Inflation devalues money very rapidly, making the careful investment of cash essential to the health of the firm. An improved cash management system keeps track of idle cash; but once this cash has been found, it can act as a hedge against inflation only if it is invested appropriately. During periods of tight money, neither small nor large firms can be confident of receiving bank loans to meet cash shortages. Therefore, it is imperative for them to keep cash reserves for future contingencies.

To protect these cash reserves against inflation, companies have begun to invest the funds aggressively, seeking higher yields. Idle cash is no longer merely kept in the bank or invested exclusively in Treasury bills. Certificates of deposit, municipal securities, and commercial paper offer higher rates of return and are therefore gaining in popularity. Firms are even using foreign instruments. For example, NCR invests in commercial paper, the Euromarket, and both domestic and Japanese certificates of deposit to increase pretax earnings by about $1 million per year. Litton Industries invests part of its portfolio in Swiss franc and German mark denominated time deposits and in foreign certificates of deposit. Even AT&T is liberalizing its liquid asset investment policies. It trades Treasury bills, looking for the best yield, rather than holding them to maturity. Its other investments include commercial paper, bankers' acceptances, certificates of deposit, and overnight repurchase agreements. (Overnight repurchase agreements—repos—have a very short maturity, frequently no longer than one day. Therefore, they are especially appropriate for investing money that will be needed immediately.)

Management of Accounts Receivable: Credit Policy

The level of accounts receivable is determined by the volume of credit sales and the average period between sales and collections. The average collection period is dependent partly on economic conditions (during a recession or a period of extremely tight money, for example, customers may be forced to delay payment) and partly on a set of controllable factors—*credit policy variables.* The major policy variables include (1) credit standards—the maximum riskiness of acceptable credit accounts; (2) credit period—the length of time for which credit is granted; (3) discounts given for early payment; and (4) the firm's collection policy. We will discuss each policy variable separately and in qualitative rather than quantitative terms; then we will illustrate the interaction of these elements and discuss the actual establishment of a firm's credit policy.

Credit Standards

If a firm makes credit sales to only the strongest of customers, it will never have bad debt losses, and it will incur few credit department expenses. On the other hand, it will probably lose sales, and the profit it foregoes on these lost sales may be far greater than the costs it avoids. Determining the optimal credit standard involves relating the marginal costs of credit to the marginal profits on the increased sales.

Marginal costs include production and selling costs, but abstracting from them at this point we will consider only those costs associated with the "quality" of the marginal accounts, or *credit quality costs.* These costs include (1) default, or bad debt losses; (2) higher investigation and collection costs; and (3) if less creditworthy customers delay payment longer than stronger customers, higher costs of capital tied up in receivables.

Since credit costs and credit quality are correlated, it is important to be able to judge the quality of an account, and perhaps the best way to do this is in terms of the probability of default. Probability estimates are for the most part subjective; but credit rating is a well-established practice, and a good credit manager can make reasonably accurate judgments of the probability of default by different classes of customers.

To evaluate the credit risk, credit managers consider the five Cs of credit: character, capacity, capital, collateral, and conditions. *Character* refers to the probability that a customer will try to honor obligations. This factor is of considerable importance, because every credit transaction implies a promise to pay. Will the creditor make an honest effort to pay the debts, or is he or she likely to try to get away with something? Experienced credit managers frequently insist that the moral factor is the most important issue in a credit evaluation.

Capacity is a subjective judgment of the customer's ability to pay. It is gauged by the person's past record, supplemented by physical observation of the plant or store and business methods.

Capital is measured by the general financial position of the firm as indicated by a financial ratio analysis, with special emphasis on the tangible net worth of the enterprise.

Collateral is represented by assets offered by the customer as a pledge for security of the credit extended.

Finally, *conditions* refers to the impact of general economic trends on the firm or to special developments in certain areas of the economy that may affect the customer's ability to meet the obligation.

The five Cs of credit represent the factors by which the credit risk is judged. Information on these items is obtained from the firm's previous experience with the customer, supplemented by a well-developed system of information-gathering. Two major sources of external information are available. The first is the credit associations. By periodic meetings of local groups and by correspondence, information on experience with creditors is exchanged. More formally, Credit Interchange, a system developed by the National Association of Credit Management for assembling and distributing information of debtors' past performance, is provided. The interchange reports show the paying record of the debtor, the industries from which he or she is buying, and the trading areas in which the purchases are being made.[9]

The second source of external information is the credit-reporting agencies, the best known of which is Dun & Bradstreet. Agencies that specialize in coverage of a limited number of industries also provide information. Representative of these are the National Credit Office and Lyon Furniture Mercantile Agency. These agencies provide data that can be used by the credit manager in the credit analysis; they also provide ratings similar to those available on corporate bonds.

An individual firm can translate its credit information into risk classes, grouped according to the probability of loss associated with sales to a customer. The combination of rating and supplementary information might lead to the following groupings of loss experience:

Risk Class Number	Loss Ratio (in Percentages)
1	None
2	0–$\frac{1}{2}$
3	Over $\frac{1}{2}$–1
4	Over 1–2
5	Over 2–5
6	Over 5–10
7	Over 10–20
8	Over 20

9. For additional information, see a publication of the National Association of Credit Management, *Credit Management Handbook,* 2d ed. (Homewood, Ill.: Richard D. Irwin, 1965).

If the selling firm has a 20 percent margin over the sum of direct operating costs and all delivery and selling costs, and if it is producing at less than full capacity, it may adopt the following credit policies: selling on customary credit terms to groups 1 to 5; selling to groups 6 and 7 under more stringent credit terms, such as cash on delivery; and requiring advance payment from group 8. As long as the bad debt loss ratios are less than 20 percent, the additional sales are contributing something to overhead. However, the opportunity costs of the increased investment in receivables also must be taken into account in the analysis, as will be shown in the case example later in the chapter.

Statistical techniques, especially regression analysis and discriminant analysis, have been used with some success in judging creditworthiness.[10] These methods work best when individual credits are relatively small and a large number of borrowers are involved, as in retail credit, consumer loans, mortgage lending, and the like. As the increase in credit card use and similar procedures builds up, as computers are used more frequently, and as credit records on individuals and small firms are developed, statistical techniques promise to become much more important than they are today.[11]

Terms of Credit

The terms of credit specify the period for which credit is extended and the discount, if any, for early payment. For example, as we saw earlier, if a firm's credit terms to all approved customers are stated as "2/10, net 30," then a 2 percent discount from the stated sales price is granted if payment is made within ten days, and the entire amount is due thirty days from the invoice date if the discount is not taken. If the terms are stated "net 60," this indicates that no discount is offered and that the bill is due and payable sixty days after the invoice date.

If sales are seasonal, a firm may use seasonal dating. Jensen, Inc., a bathing suit manufacturer, sells on terms of "2/10, net 30, May 1 dating." This means that the effective invoice date is May 1, so the discount can be taken until May 10, or the full amount must be paid on May 30, regardless of when the sale was made. Jensen produces output throughout the year, but retail sales of bathing suits are concentrated in the spring and early summer. Because of its practice of offering seasonal datings, Jensen induces some cus-

10. Discriminant analysis is similar to multiple regression analysis, except that it partitions a sample into two or more components on the basis of a set of characteristics. The sample, for example, might be loan applicants at a consumer loan company. The components into which they are classified might be those likely to make prompt repayment and those likely to default. The characteristics might be whether the applicant owns his or her home, how long the person has been with the current employer, and so on.

11. It has been said that the biggest single deterrent to the increased automation of credit processes is George Orwell's classic book, *1984,* in which he described the social dangers of centralized files of information on individuals. Orwell's omnipresent watcher, Big Brother, is mentioned frequently in congressional sessions discussing mass storage of information relevant to credit analysis.

tomers to stock up early, saving Jensen storage costs and also "nailing down sales."

Credit Period Lengthening the credit period stimulates sales, but there is a cost to tying up funds in receivables. For example, if a firm changes its terms from net 30 to net 60, the average receivables for the year may rise from $100,000 to $300,000—the increase caused partly by the longer credit terms and partly by the larger volume of sales. If the cost of capital needed to finance the investment in receivables is 8 percent, then the marginal cost of lengthening the credit period is $16,000 ($200,000 × 8 percent). If the incremental profit—sales price minus all direct production, selling, and credit costs associated with the additional sales—exceeds $16,000, then the change in credit policy is profitable. Determining the optimal credit period involves locating the point where marginal profits on increased sales are exactly offset by the costs of carrying the higher amount of accounts receivable.

Cash Discounts The effect of granting cash discounts can be analyzed similarly to the credit period. For example, if a firm changes its terms from "net 30" to "2/10, net 30," it may well attract customers who want to take discounts, thereby increasing gross sales. Also, the average collection period will be shortened, as some old customers pay more promptly to take advantage of the discount. Offsetting these benefits is the cost of the discounts taken. The optimal discount is established at the point where costs and benefits are exactly offsetting.

Collection Policy

Collection policy refers to the procedures the firm follows to obtain payment of past-due accounts. For example, it may send a letter to such accounts when they are ten days past due; it may use a severer letter, followed by a telephone call, if payment is not received within thirty days; and it may turn the account over to a collection agency after ninety days.

The collection process can be expensive in terms of both out-of-pocket expenditures and lost goodwill, but at least some firmness is needed to prevent an undue lengthening in the collection period and to minimize outright losses. Again, a balance must be struck between the costs and benefits of different collection policies.

Accounts Receivable versus Accounts Payable

Whenever goods are sold on credit, two accounts are created. An asset item called an *account receivable* appears on the books of the selling firm, and a liability item called an *account payable* appears on the books of the purchaser. At this point we are analyzing the transaction from the viewpoint of the seller, so we have concentrated on the type of variables under the seller's control. (In Chapter 10 we will examine the transaction from the viewpoint of the purchaser, discussing accounts payable as a source of funds and considering the cost of these funds vis-à-vis funds obtained from other sources.)

Establishing a Credit Policy: An Illustration

Some profitability aspects of establishing a credit policy are illustrated in the following case example. The Wales Company is considering changes in its credit policies. A proposal has been made to relax these policies in order to increase sales and to expand the allowable discount terms in order to keep the investment in receivables unchanged.[12] The company has annual sales of $2.4 million under the present credit policy. Under a liberalized credit policy, sales will increase to $3 million; but the average collection period will increase from one to two months. The unit selling price is $10 and the unit variable cost $7. The firm's required return on investment is 20 percent. The change in discount policy will bring the collection period back to one month. Should the firm make the changes proposed?

In developing a solution, one issue that has to be faced is whether the investment in the additional receivables should be carried at the cost of investment as measured by variable costs or at the sales value of the goods on which collections have not been made. There are two grounds for using the sales value. The first is that the alternative to having receivables is to have made the sales. If the sales are made, they will necessarily be at sales value. While the actual costs are less than the sales value, the opportunity cost must include the sales value that has been lost by having the receivables. The second ground is that on a change in credit policy that results in collections instead of funds tied up in receivables, the increase in cash flow that otherwise would not occur is the actual cash sales receipts. Thus, in solving the problem, the lack of symmetry if sales value is not used will result in different answers depending on whether the problem is solved in two steps or combined so that only the net change in receivables is considered. Under the correct procedure, the answer will be the same whether solved in two steps or one. The correct procedure with two steps is shown in Table 9.3.

Each of the two changes in policy results in a gain to the firm. The liberalized credit policy adds $120,000 to net profits, and the change in discount policy adds $20,000 to net profits. The total benefit from the two policy changes is $140,000. Table 9.4 shows the calculations needed when the two policy changes are made simultaneously.

The effect of changing directly from the existing credit policy to an easier

12. This example is based on Tirlochan S. Walia, "Explicit and Implicit Cost of Changes in the Level of Accounts Receivable," *Financial Management,* Winter 1977, pp. 75–78. Other points not directly related to this discussion are found in two other papers in the same issue by Edward Dyl and by Joseph Atkins and Yong Kim.

Table 9.3
Two Analyses of Credit
Policy Changes

	Existing Policy	Liberalized Policy
Annual sales	$2,400,000	$3,000,000
Additional sales	—	$600,000
Additional profits	—	$180,000 (0.3 × $600,000)
Level of receivables	$200,000	$500,000
Additional receivables	—	$300,000
Opportunity cost of additional receivables	—	$60,000 (0.2 × $300,000)
Net profit	—	$120,000

	Liberalized Policy	Discount Policy
Annual sales	$3,000,000	$3,000,000
Level of receivables	$500,000	$250,000
Reduction in receivables	—	$250,000
Return on funds released	—	$50,000 (0.2 × $250,000)
Cost of discount	—	$30,000 (0.02 × 0.5 × $3,000,000)
Net profit	—	$20,000

Table 9.4
One-Step Analysis of Credit
Policy Changes

	Existing Policy	Discount Policy
Annual sales	$2,400,000	$3,000,000
Additional sales	—	$600,000
Additional profits	—	$180,000 (0.3 × $600,000)
Level of receivables	$200,000	$250,000
Additional receivables	—	$50,000
Opportunity cost of additional receivables	—	$10,000 (0.2 × $50,000)
Cost of discount	—	$30,000 (0.02 × 0.5 × $3,000,000)
Net profit	—	$140,000

credit policy with a new discount policy is to increase annual net profits by $140,000. This is the same as when the two credit policy changes were considered in sequence. Thus, when a firm formulates a policy that shifts cash collections to receivables, the opportunity cost involved is the cash sales that otherwise would have increased cash inflows; and the relevant cost requires a consideration of the opportunity cost, not just the explicit cost of the additional investment in increased receivables.

This kind of analysis requires that some very difficult judgments be made. Estimating the changes in sales and costs associated with changes in credit policies is, to say the least, a highly uncertain business. Also, even if the sales and cost estimates are reasonably accurate, there is no assurance that some other credit policy would not be even better. For instance, an easy

215

credit policy that involved a different mix of the four policy variables might be superior to the one examined in Tables 9.3 and 9.4.

For both these reasons, firms usually move slowly toward optimal credit policies. One or two credit variables are changed slightly, the effect of the changes is observed, and a decision is made to change these variables even more or to retract them. Further, different credit policies are appropriate at different times, depending on economic conditions. Thus, credit policy is not a static, once-for-all-time decision. Rather, it is fluid, dynamic, and ever changing in its effort to reach a continually moving optimal target.

Inventory

Manufacturing firms generally have three kinds of inventories: (1) raw materials, (2) work in process, and (3) finished goods. The level of *raw materials inventories* is influenced by anticipated production, seasonality of production, reliability of sources of supply, and efficiency of scheduling purchases and production operations. *Work-in-process inventory* is strongly influenced by the length of the production period, which is the time between placing raw material in production and completing the finished product. Inventory turnover can be increased by decreasing the production period. One means of accomplishing this is to perfect engineering techniques, thereby speeding up the manufacturing process. Another means is to buy items rather than make them.

The level of *finished goods inventories* is a matter of coordinating production and sales. The financial manager can stimulate sales by changing credit terms or by granting credit to marginal risks. Whether the goods remain on the books as inventories or as receivables, the financial manager has to finance them. Many times, firms find it desirable to make the sale, so they are one step nearer to realizing cash. The potential profits can outweigh the additional collection risk.

Our primary focus in this section is control of investment in inventories. Inventory models, developed as an aid in this task, have proved extremely useful in minimizing inventory requirements. As our examination of the du Pont system in Chapter 4 showed, any procedure that can reduce the investment required to generate a given sales volume may have a beneficial effect on the firm's rate of return and hence on the value of the firm.

Determinants of the Size of Inventories

Although wide variations occur, inventory to sales ratios are generally concentrated in the 12 to 20 percent range, and inventory to total assets ratios are concentrated in the 16 to 30 percent range.

The major determinants of investment in inventory are (1) level of sales, (2) length and technical nature of the production processes, and (3) durability versus perishability (the style factors) in the end product. Inventories in the tobacco industry, for example, are large because of the long curing process. Similarly, in the machinery manufacturing industries, inventories are large because of the long work-in-process period. However, inventories are low in coal mining and in oil and gas production because no raw materials are used and the goods in process are small in relation to sales. In the canning industry, average inventories are large because of the seasonality of the raw materials.

With respect to durability and style factors, large inventories are found in the hardware and the precious metals industries because durability is great and the style factor is small. Inventories are small in baking because of the perishability of the final product and in printing because the items are manufactured to order.

Within limits set by the economics of a firm's industry, there exists a potential for improvement in inventory control from the use of computers and operations research. Although the techniques are far too diverse and complicated for a complete treatment in this text, the financial manager should be prepared to use the contributions of specialists who have developed effective procedures for minimizing the investment in inventory.

An illustration of the techniques at the practical level is Harris Electronic's inventory system, which works like this: Tabulator cards are inserted in each package of five electronic tubes leaving Harris's warehouse. They are identified by account number, type of merchandise, and price of the units ordered. As the merchandise is sold, the distributor collects the cards and files the replacement order, without any paperwork, by simply sending in the cards.

Western Union Telegraph Co. equipment accepts the punched cards and transmits information on them to the warehouse, where it is duplicated on other punched cards. A typical order of 5,000 tubes of varying types can be received in about seventeen minutes, assembled in about ninety minutes, and delivered to Boston's Logan Airport in an additional forty-five minutes. Orders from 3,000 miles away can be delivered within twenty-four hours, a saving of thirteen days in some cases.

Information on the order also goes into a computer, which keeps track of stock-on-hand data for each item. When an order draws the stock down below the *order point,* this triggers action in the production department, where additional units of the item are then manufactured for stock. In the next section, we will examine both the optimal order point and the number of units that should be manufactured—called the *economic ordering quantity (EOQ).*

**Generality of
Inventory
Analysis**

Managing assets of all kinds is basically an inventory problem; the same method of analysis applies to cash and fixed assets as to inventories themselves. First, a basic stock must be on hand to balance inflows and outflows of the items, the size of the stock depending on the patterns of flows, whether regular or irregular. Second, because the unexpected may always occur, it is necessary to have safety stocks on hand, representing the little extra to avoid the costs of not having enough to meet current needs. Third, additional amounts may be required to meet future growth needs; these are called anticipation stocks. Related to anticipation stocks is the recognition that there are optimum purchase sizes, defined as *economic ordering quantities.* In borrowing money, in buying raw materials for production, or in purchasing plants and equipment, it is cheaper to buy more than just enough to meet immediate needs.

With the foregoing as a basic foundation, we can develop the theoretical basis for determining the optimal investment in inventory, which is illustrated in Figure 9.1. Some costs rise with larger inventories; among these are warehousing costs, interest on funds tied up in inventories, insurance, and obsolescence. Other costs decline with larger inventories; these include the loss of profits resulting from sales lost because of lack of stock, costs of production interruptions caused by inadequate inventories, and possible purchase discounts.

The costs that decline with higher inventories are designated by the declining curve in Figure 9.1; those that rise with larger inventories are designated by the rising curve. The total costs curve is the total of the rising and declining curves, and it represents the total cost of ordering and holding inventories. At the point where the absolute value of the slope of the rising curve is equal to the absolute value of the slope of the declining curve (that is, where marginal rising costs are equal to marginal declining costs), the total costs curve is at a minimum. This represents the optimum size of investment in inventory.

Inventory Decision Models

The generalized statements in the preceding section can be made much more specific. In fact, it is usually possible to specify the curves shown in Figure 9.1, at least to a reasonable approximation, and actually to find the minimum point on the total costs curve. Since entire courses (in operations research programs) are devoted to inventory control techniques, and since a number of books have been written on the subject, we obviously cannot deal with inventory decision models in a very complete fashion. The model we illustrate, however, is probably the most widely used, even by quite sophisticated firms, and it can be readily expanded to encompass any desired refinements.

The cost of holding inventories—the cost of capital tied up, storage costs, insurance, depreciation, and so on—rises as the size of inventory holdings increases. Conversely, the cost of ordering inventories—the costs of placing orders, of shipping and handling, of quantity discounts lost, and so on—falls as the average inventory increases. The total cost of inventories is

**Figure 9.1
Determination of Optimum
Investment in Inventory**

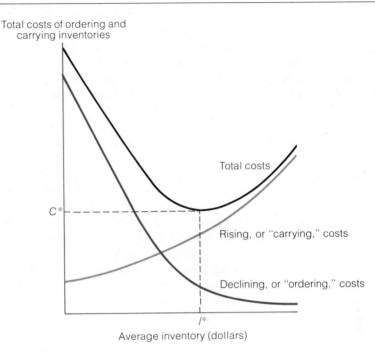

Average inventory (dollars)

the sum of these rising and declining costs, or the total costs curve in Figure 9.1. It has been shown that, under reasonable assumptions, the minimum point on the total costs curve can be found by an equation called the EOQ formula:

$$EOQ = \sqrt{\frac{2FU}{CP}},$$

where:

EOQ = the economic ordering quantity, or the optimum quantity to be ordered each time an order is placed.

F = fixed costs of placing and receiving an order.

U = annual usage in units.

C = carrying cost expressed as a percentage of inventory value.

P = purchase price per unit of inventory.

For any level of usage, dividing U by EOQ indicates the number of orders that must be placed each year. The average inventory on hand (the average balance sheet inventory figure) will be:

$$\text{Average inventory} = \frac{EOQ}{2}.$$

The derivation of the EOQ model assumes (1) that usage is at a constant rate and (2) that delivery lead times are constant. In fact, usage is likely to vary considerably for most firms. Demand, for example, may be unexpectedly strong for any number of reasons; if it is, the firm may run out of stock and suffer sales losses or production stoppages. Similarly, delivery lead times will vary depending on weather, strikes, demand in the suppliers' industries, and so on. Because of these factors, firms add safety stocks to their inventory holdings; thus:

$$\text{Average inventory} = \frac{EOQ}{2} + \text{safety stock}.$$

The size of the safety stock will be relatively large if uncertainties about usage rates and delivery times are great and relatively low if these factors do not vary greatly. Similarly, the safety stock will be larger if the costs of running out of stock are great. For example, if customer ill will may cause a permanent loss of business or if an elaborate production process may have to stop if an item is out of stock, then large safety stocks will be carried.[13]

Use of EOQ Model: An Illustration

Let us assume that the following values are determined to be appropriate for a particular firm:

U = usage = 100 units.
C = carrying cost = 20 percent of inventory value.
P = purchase price = \$1 per unit.
F = fixed cost of ordering = \$10.

Substituting these values into the formula, we obtain:

$$EOQ = \sqrt{\frac{2FU}{CP}}$$

$$= \sqrt{\frac{2 \times 10 \times 100}{0.2 \times 1}} = \sqrt{\frac{2,000}{0.2}} = \sqrt{10,000}$$

$$= 100 \text{ units.}$$

---

13. Formal methods have been developed to assist in striking a balance between the cost of carrying larger safety stocks and the cost of stock-outs (inventory shortages). A discussion of these models, which goes beyond the scope of this book, can be found in most production textbooks.

If the desired safety stock is 10 units, then the average inventory (A) will be:

$$A = \frac{EOQ}{2} + \text{safety stock}$$

$$= \frac{100}{2} + 10$$

$$= 60 \text{ units.}$$

Since the cost of purchasing or manufacturing inventory is $1 a unit, the average inventory in dollars will be $60 for this item.

Effects of Inflation on EOQ

During inflation, formal models such as the EOQ may lose applicability. As freight costs rise, the cost of placing an order may increase rapidly. Purchase prices may also rise abruptly and repeatedly. Therefore, the values used in the EOQ equation may not remain constant for any appreciable length of time. If so, the optimal order quantity will not remain fixed. Some companies will need greater flexibility in the timing of their orders than that afforded by the "automatic order point." This is because they may be able to buy marginal production at reduced prices. Also, certain companies may stockpile inventories. This takes advantage of the opportunity to purchase supplies before major price increases and provides protection against shortages. Therefore, during periods of inflation and tight money, a firm may need more flexible inventory management as it attempts to take advantage of bargains and provide for future contingencies. The basic logic of the inventory model remains intact: Some costs will rise with larger inventories, and others will fall. Although an optimum is still there to be found, it may change and require repeated findings.

Cash Management as an Inventory Problem

In our cash budgeting discussion in Chapter 7, we indicated that firms generally have minimum desired cash balances. Then, in discussing cash management, we considered the various factors that influence cash holdings. We did not, however, attempt to specify optimum cash balances, which can be found by the use of inventory type models such as those discussed above. Cash management, together with inventory controls, is the area of financial management where mathematical tools have proved most useful.

Sophisticated cash management models recognize the uncertainty inherent in forecasting both cash inflows and cash outflows. Inflows are represented, in effect, by the orders in our inventory model; they come principally from receipts, borrowing, and sales of securities. The primary carrying cost of cash is the opportunity cost of having funds tied up in nonearning assets (or in low-yielding near-cash items); the principal ordering costs are brokerage costs associated with borrowing funds or converting marketable securities into cash.

Recent Restructuring of Current Asset Management

During recent years, inflation has exerted serious pressure on most firms' liquidity positions, leading to extensive restructuring of current asset accounts. The bankruptcy of cash-poor Penn Central Transportation Co. in 1970 helped to trigger a growing concern about liquidity. When money becomes tight, banks become more selective in granting loans and cannot be relied upon to rescue a firm experiencing a sudden shortage of cash. Therefore, many firms have attempted to improve their liquidity positions through tightening inventory control, increasing receivables turnover, and reducing the dividend payout ratio. Inventories are sometimes stockpiled as a hedge against inflation and shortages. This is an obvious tradeoff between liquidity and inventory level. In the early 1970s, Texas Instruments quadrupled its cash to assets ratio by liquidating inventory, decreasing receivables, and "hoarding" profits. The growing tendency is for firms to retain earnings to build large cash balances.

International Business Machines Corporation is an example of a highly liquid company, with cash reaching $5.4 billion in early 1978. IBM's high level of liquidity is not completely a matter of design. Management is afraid of diminishing returns if a higher percentage of profits are plowed back into the business, and acquisitions may lead to antitrust litigation. Therefore, management is in search of an outlet for excess cash. IBM repurchased $721 million worth of shares in 1977 and may increase future dividends. But whether the high degree of liquidity is contrived or inevitable, IBM's situation is similar to that of many firms. Cash assets are growing faster than noncash assets, indicating a possible tradeoff between liquidity and future growth. Current asset management is therefore gaining new urgency and importance.

Summary

This chapter focused attention on four types of current assets—cash, marketable securities, accounts receivable, and inventories. It examined the motives for holding cash and ways of minimizing the investment in cash. Then the minimum cash balance a firm is likely to hold was considered. This minimum is the higher (1) of compensating balance requirements or (2) of transactions balances plus a safety stock.

Marketable securities are held as a substitute for cash safety stocks and as temporary investments while the firm is awaiting permanent investment of funds. Safety stocks are almost always held in low-risk, short-maturity securities; temporary investments are held in securities whose maturity depends on the length of time before the funds are permanently employed.

The investment in accounts receivable is dependent on sales and on the firm's credit policy. The credit policy, in turn, involves four controllable variables: credit standards, the length of the credit period; cash discounts, and the collection policy. The significant aspect of credit policy is its effect on sales. An easy credit policy stimulates sales but involves costs of capital tied up in receivables, bad debts, discounts, and higher collection costs. The optimal credit policy is one in which these costs are just offset by the profits on sales generated by the credit policy change.

Inventories—raw materials, work in process, and finished goods—are necessary in most businesses. Rather elaborate systems for controlling the level of inventories have been designed. These systems frequently use computers for keeping records of all the items in stock. An inventory control model that considers anticipated sales, ordering costs, and carrying costs can be used to determine EOQs for each item.

The basic inventory model recognizes that certain costs (carrying costs) rise as average inventory holdings increase but that certain other costs (ordering costs and stock-out costs) fall as these holdings increase. The two sets of costs make up the total cost of ordering and carrying inventories, and the EOQ model is designed to locate an optimal order size that will minimize total inventory costs.

Questions

9.1 How can better methods of communication reduce the necessity for firms to hold large cash balances?

9.2 Discuss this statement: The highly developed financial system of the United States, with its myriad of different near-cash assets, has greatly reduced cash balance requirements by reducing the need for transactions balances.

9.3 Would you expect a firm with a high growth rate to hold more or fewer precautionary and speculative cash balances than a firm with a low growth rate? Explain.

9.4 Many firms that find themselves with temporary surplus cash invest these funds in Treasury bills. Since Treasury bills frequently have the lowest yield of any investment security, why are they chosen as investments?

9.5 Assume that a firm sells on terms of net 30 and that its accounts are, on the average, thirty days overdue. What will its investment in receivables be if its annual credit sales are approximately $720,000?

9.6 Evaluate this statement: It is difficult to judge the performance of many of our employees but not that of the credit manager. If the credit manager is performing perfectly, credit losses are zero; the higher our losses (as a percent of sales), the worse the performance.

9.7 Explain how a firm can reduce its investment in inventory by having its supplier hold raw materials inventories and its customers hold finished goods inventories. What are the limitations of such a policy?

9.8 What factors are likely to reduce the holdings of inventory in relation to sales in the future? What factors will tend to increase the ratio? What, in your judgment, is the net effect?

9.9 What are the probable effects of the following on inventory holdings?
   a. Manufacture of a part formerly purchased from an outside supplier.
   b. Greater use of air freight.
   c. Increase, from 7 to 17, in the number of styles produced.
   d. Large price reductions to your firm from a manufacturer of bathing suits if the suits are purchased in December and January.

9.10 Inventory decision models are designed to help minimize the cost of obtaining and carrying inventory. Describe the basic nature of the fundamental inventory control model, discussing specifically the nature of increasing costs, decreasing costs, and total costs. Illustrate your discussion with a graph.

Problems

9.1 Hayes Associates is short on cash and is attempting to determine if it would be advantageous for them to forego the discount on this month's purchases or to borrow funds to take advantage of the discount. The discount terms are 2/10, net 45.
   a. What is the maximum annual interest rate that Hayes Associates should pay on borrowed funds? Why?
   b. What are some of the intangible disadvantages associated with foregoing the discount?

9.2 Scott, Inc., currently has a centralized billing system located in New York City. However, over the years its customers gradually have become less concentrated on the East Coast and now cover the entire United States. On average, it requires five days from the time customers mail payments until Scott is able to receive, process, and deposit their payments. To shorten this time, Scott is considering the installation of a lockbox collection system. It estimates that the system will reduce the time lag from customer mailing to deposit by three and one-half days. Scott has a daily average collection of $700,000.
   a. What reduction in cash balances can Scott achieve by initiating the lockbox system?
   b. If Scott has an opportunity cost of 8 percent, how much is the lockbox system worth on an annual basis?
   c. What is the maximum monthly charge Scott can pay for the lockbox system?

9.3 Gulf Distributors makes all sales on a credit basis; once each year it routinely evaluates the creditworthiness of all its customers. The evaluation proce-

dure ranks customers from 1 to 5, in order of increasing risk. Results of
the ranking are as follows:

Category	Percentage Bad Debts	Average Collection Period (Days)	Credit Decision	Annual Sales Lost Due to Credit Restrictions
1	None	10	Unlimited credit	None
2	1.0	12	Unlimited credit	None
3	3.0	20	Limited credit	$360,000
4	9.0	60	Limited credit	$180,000
5	16.0	90	No credit	$720,000

a. Using this credit procedure, gross profit has averaged 10 percent of
sales during the past five years. The opportunity cost of investment in
receivables is 12 percent. What do you estimate to be the effect on net
profits of extending full credit to each of categories 3, 4, and 5?

b. The implicit assumption in Part a is that all costs leading to gross profit
are variable. Recalculate your answers assuming that variable costs
equal 85 percent of sales (excluding bad debts and cost of receivables).

9.4 A firm issues checks in the amount of $1 million each day and deducts
them from its own records at the close of business on the day they are written. On average, the bank receives and clears the checks (deducts them
from the firm's bank balance) the evening of the fourth day after they are
written; for example, a check written on Monday will be cleared on Friday
afternoon. The firm's loan agreement with the bank requires it to maintain a
$750,000 minimum average compensating balance; this is $250,000 greater
than the cash safety stock the firm would otherwise have on deposit.

a. Assuming that the firm makes its deposit in the late afternoon (and the
bank includes the deposit in the day's transactions), how much must the
firm deposit each day to maintain a sufficient balance once it reaches a
steady state?

b. How many days of float does the firm carry?

c. What ending daily balance should the firm try to maintain at the bank
and on its own records?

d. Explain how float can help increase the value of the firm's common
stock. Use a partial balance sheet and the du Pont system concept in
your answer.

9.5 Callaway Electronics Company is considering changing its credit terms
from 2/15, net 30, to 3/10, net 45. All its sales are "credit sales," but 75 percent of the customers presently take the 2 percent cash discount. Under the
new terms this percentage is expected to decline to 65 percent. The average collection period is also expected to change under the new policy,
from seventeen days at present to twenty days under the new plan. (Note
that these averages are heavily weighted with customers who pay within ten
days.) Expected sales, before discounts are deducted, are $600,000 with the
present terms but $675,000 if the new terms are used. Assume that (1) Cal-
laway achieves a 12 percent profit margin after all costs, including credit
costs, on present sales after a change in credit policy; (2) sales will have a

12 percent margin *before* incremental credit-associated costs; and (3) a 10 percent opportunity cost applies to the investment in receivables. Calculate the following:

a. the increase in gross profits
b. the increase in discount costs
c. the increased cost of carrying receivables
d. the net change in pretax profits

9.6 The following relationships for inventory purchase and storage costs have been established for the Lomer Fabricating Corporation.

1. Orders must be placed in multiples of 100 units.
2. Requirements for the year are 300,000 units. (Use fifty weeks in a year for calculations.)
3. The purchase price per unit is $3.
4. The carrying cost is 25 percent of the purchase price of goods.
5. The cost per order placed is $20.
6. Desired safety stock is 10,000 units (on hand initially).
7. Two weeks are required for delivery.

   a. What is the most economical order quantity?
   b. What is the optimal number of orders to be placed?
   c. At what inventory level should a reorder be made? (Hint: The inventory level should be sufficient to cover the amount used during delivery, plus the safety stock.)

9.7 The following relationships for inventory purchase and storage costs have been established for the Milton Processing Corporation.

1. Orders must be placed in multiples of 100 units.
2. Requirements for the year are 400,000 units. (Use fifty weeks in a year for calculations.)
3. The purchase price per unit is $5.
4. The carrying cost is 20 percent of the purchase price of goods.
5. The cost per order placed is $25.
6. Desired safety stock is 10,000 units (on hand initially).
7. Two weeks are required for delivery.

   a. What is the most economical order quantity? (Round to the 100s.)
   b. What is the optimal number of orders to be placed?
   c. At what inventory level should a reorder be made?
   d. If annual unit sales double, what is the percent increase in the EOQ? What is the elasticity of EOQ with respect to sales (percent change in EOQ/percent change in sales)?
   e. If the cost per order placed doubles, what is the percent increase in EOQ? What is the elasticity of EOQ with respect to cost per order?
   f. If the carrying cost declines by 50 percent, what is the elasticity of EOQ with respect to the change in carrying cost?
   g. If purchase price declines 50 percent, what is the elasticity of EOQ with respect to the change in purchase price?

CHAPTER 10 MAJOR SOURCES AND
FORMS OF SHORT-TERM FINANCING

In Chapter 8 we discussed the maturity structure of the firm's debt and showed how this structure can affect both risk and expected returns. However, a variety of short-term credits are available to the firm, and the financial manager must know the advantages and disadvantages of each. Accordingly, in the present chapter we take up the main forms of short-term credit, considering both the characteristics and the sources of this credit.

Short-term credit is defined as debt originally scheduled for repayment within one year. The three major sources of funds with short maturities, ranked in descending order by volume of credit supplied, are (1) trade credit among firms, (2) loans from commercial banks, and (3) commercial paper.

Trade Credit

In the ordinary course of events, a firm buys its supplies and materials on credit from other firms, recording the debt as an *account payable.* Accounts payable, or *trade credit,* is the largest single category of short-term credit, representing about 40 percent of the current liabilities of nonfinancial corporations.[1] This percentage is somewhat larger for small firms; because small companies may not qualify for financing from other sources, they rely rather heavily on trade credit.

Trade credit is a spontaneous source of financing in that it arises from ordinary business transactions. For example, suppose a firm makes average purchases of $2,000 a day on terms of net 30. On the average it will owe 30 times $2,000, or $60,000, to its suppliers. If its sales and, consequently, its purchases double, accounts payable will also double—to $120,000. The firm will have spontaneously generated an additional $60,000 of financing. Similarly, if the terms of credit are extended from 30 to 40 days, accounts payable will expand from $60,000 to $80,000; thus lengthening the credit period, as well as expanding sales and purchases, generates additional financing.

Credit Terms

The terms of sales, or *credit terms,* describe the payment obligation of the buyer. The following discussion outlines the four main factors that influence the length of credit terms: the economic nature of the product, the seller's circumstances, the buyer's circumstances, and cash discounts.

Economic Nature of the Product Commodities with high sales turnover are sold on relatively short credit terms; buyers resell the products rapidly, generating cash that enables them to pay the suppliers. Groceries have a high turnover, but perishability also plays a role. The credit extended for

---

1. In Chapter 9, we discussed trade credit from the viewpoint of minimizing investment in current assets. In the present chapter we look at the other side of the coin—trade credit as a source of rather than a use of financing. In Chapter 9, the use of trade credit by customers resulted in an asset investment called *accounts receivable.* In the present chapter, the use of trade credit gives rise to short-term obligations, generally called *accounts payable.*

fresh fruits and vegetables might run from five to ten days, whereas the credit extended on canned fruits and vegetables would more likely be fifteen to thirty days. Terms for items that have a slow retail turnover, such as jewelry, may run six months or longer.

Seller Circumstances Financially weak sellers must require cash or exceptionally short credit terms. For example, farmers sell livestock to meatpacking companies on a cash basis. In many industries, variations in credit terms can be used as a sales promotion device. Although the use of credit as a selling device could endanger sound credit management, the practice does occur, especially when the seller's industry has excess capacity. Also, large sellers can use their position to impose relatively short credit terms. However, the reverse appears more often in practice; that is, financially strong sellers are suppliers of funds to small firms.

Buyer Circumstances In general, financially sound retailers who sell on credit may, in turn, receive slightly longer terms. Some classes of retailers regarded as selling in particularly risky areas (such as clothing) receive extended credit terms but are offered large discounts to encourage early payment.

Cash Discounts A cash discount is a reduction in price based on payment within a specified period. The costs of not taking cash discounts often exceed the rate of interest at which the buyer can borrow, so it is important that a firm be cautious in its use of trade credit as a source of financing; it could be quite expensive. If the firm borrows and takes the cash discount, the period during which accounts payable remain on the books is reduced. The effective length of credit is thus influenced by the size of discounts offered. Credit terms typically express the amount of the cash discount and the date of its expiration, as well as the final due date. Earlier we noted that one of the most frequently encountered terms is 2/10, net 30. (If payment is made within ten days of the invoice date, a 2 percent cash discount is allowed. If the cash discount is not taken, payment is due thirty days after the date of invoicing.) The cost of not taking cash discounts can be substantial, as shown here.[2]

Credit Terms	Cost of Credit If Cash Discount Not Taken (Percent)
1/10, net 20	36.36
1/10, net 30	18.18
2/10, net 20	73.47
2/10, net 30	36.73

2. The method of calculating the effective interest rate on accounts payable was described in Chapter 9.

Concept of Net Credit

Trade credit has double-edged significance for the firm. It is a source of credit for financing purchases, and it is a use of funds to the extent that the firm finances credit sales to customers. For example, if, on the average, a firm sells $3,000 worth of goods a day and has an average collection period of forty days, at any balance sheet date it will have accounts receivable of approximately $120,000.

If the same firm buys $2,000 worth of materials a day and the balance is outstanding for twenty days, accounts payable will average $40,000. The firm is thus extending net credit of $80,000—the difference between accounts receivable and accounts payable.

Large firms and well-financed firms of all sizes tend to be net suppliers of trade credit; small firms and undercapitalized firms of all sizes tend to be net users of trade credit. It is impossible to generalize about whether it is better to be a net supplier or a net user; the choice depends on the firm's circumstances and on the various costs and benefits of receiving and using trade credit.

Advantages of Trade Credit as a Source of Financing

Trade credit, a customary part of doing business in most industries, is convenient and informal. A firm that does not qualify for credit from a financial institution may receive trade credit because previous experience has familiarized the seller with the creditworthiness of the customer. The seller knows the merchandising practices of the industry and is usually in a good position to judge the capacity of the customer and the risk of selling on credit. The amount of trade credit fluctuates with the buyer's purchases, subject to any credit limits that may be operative.

Whether trade credit costs more or less than other forms of financing is a moot question. The buyer often does not have any alternative form of financing available, and the costs may be commensurate with the risks to the seller. But in some instances trade credit is used simply because the buyer does not realize how expensive it is. In such circumstances, careful financial analysis may lead to the substitution of alternative forms of financing.

At the other extreme, trade credit may represent a virtual subsidy or sales promotion device offered by the seller. The authors know, for example, of cases where manufacturers quite literally supplied *all* the financing for new firms by selling on credit terms substantially longer than those of the new company. In one instance a manufacturer, eager to obtain a dealership in a particular area, made a loan to the new company to cover operating expenses during the initial phases and geared the payment of accounts payable to cash receipts. Even in such instances, however, the buying firm must be careful that it is not really paying a hidden financing cost in the form of higher product prices than could be obtained elsewhere. Extending credit involves a cost to the selling firm, and this firm may well be raising its own prices to offset the "free" credit it extends.

Importance of Good Supplier Relations during Inflation

During the recent period of inflation and tight money, firms have raised their standards for extending trade credit to their customers. Since "cleaning up" accounts receivable is one way to obtain a more favorable liquidity position, suppliers are becoming more selective when extending trade credit. Therefore, it is important for a firm to earn the confidence of its suppliers. This can be achieved by showing good financial ratios and by paying promptly. But even if these indicators are unfavorable, a firm may be able to obtain trade credit by offering realistic plans for improving its situation. The experience of W. T. Grant Company is illustrative. For the fiscal year ended January 31, 1975, W. T. Grant showed an operating loss of $177 million. Top management announced policy changes, replaced key personnel, and offered security through an inventory lien. Grant's suppliers continued to extend trade credit, some in amounts greater than $1 million. W. T. Grant lost another $111 million in the next six months and went bankrupt. But its experience shows that it is possible to achieve continuity in the supply of trade credit even in adversity when the credit relationship is well managed.

Short-Term Financing by Commercial Banks

Commercial bank lending, which appears on the balance sheet as *notes payable,* is second in importance to trade credit as a source of short-term financing. Banks occupy a pivotal position in the short-term and intermediate-term money markets. Their influence is greater than it appears to be from the dollar amounts they lend because the banks provide nonspontaneous funds. As a firm's financing needs increase, it requests additional funds from banks. If the request is denied, often the alternative is to slow down the rate of growth or to cut back operations.

Characteristics of Loans from Commercial Banks

In the following sections, the main characteristics of lending patterns of commercial banks are briefly described.

Forms of Loans A single loan obtained from a bank by a business firm is not different in principle from a loan obtained by an individual. In fact, it is often difficult to distinguish a bank loan to a small business from a personal loan. The loan is obtained by signing a conventional promissory note. Repayment is made in a lump sum at maturity (when the note is due) or in installments throughout the life of the loan.

A *line of credit* is a formal or informal understanding between the bank and the borrower concerning the maximum loan balance the bank will allow the borrower. For example, a bank loan officer may indicate to a financial manager that the bank regards the firm as "good" for up to $80,000 for the forthcoming year. Subsequently, the manager signs a promissory note for $15,000 for 90 days—thereby "taking down" $15,000 of the total line of credit. This amount is credited to the firm's checking account at the bank. At maturity, the checking account is charged for the amount of the loan. Interest may be deducted in advance or may be paid at maturity. Before repayment of the $15,000, the firm may borrow additional amounts up to the total of $80,000.

A more formal procedure may be followed if the firm is quite large. To illustrate, Chrysler Corporation arranged a line of credit for over $100 million with a group of banks. The banks were formally committed to lend Chrysler the funds if they were needed. Chrysler in turn paid a commitment fee of approximately 0.25 percent of the unused balance of the commitment to compensate the banks for making the funds available.

Size of Customers Banks make loans to firms of all sizes. By dollar amount, the bulk of loans from commercial banks is obtained by firms with total assets of $5 million and more. But by number of loans, firms with total assets of $50,000 and less account for about 40 percent of bank loans.

Maturity Commercial banks concentrate on the short-term lending market. Short-term loans make up about two-thirds of bank loans by dollar amount, whereas "term loans" (loans with maturities longer than one year) make up only one-third.

Security If a potential borrower is a questionable credit risk, or if the firm's financing needs exceed the amount that the loan officer of the bank considers to be prudent on an unsecured basis, some form of security is required. More than half the dollar value of bank loans is secured. (The forms of security are described later in this chapter.) In terms of the number of bank loans, two-thirds are secured or endorsed by a third party who guarantees payment of the loan in the event the borrower defaults.

Compensating Balances Banks typically require that a regular borrower maintain an average checking account balance equal to 15 or 20 percent of the outstanding loan. These balances, commonly called *compensating balances*, are a method of raising the effective interest rate. For example, if a firm needs $80,000 to pay off outstanding obligations but must maintain a 20 percent compensating balance, it must borrow $100,000 in order to obtain the required $80,000. If the stated interest rate is 5 percent, the effective cost is actually 6¹/₄ percent ($5,000 divided by $80,000).[3] These *loan* compensating balances are, of course, added to any *service* compensating balances (discussed in Chapter 9) that the firm's bank may require.

Repayment of Bank Loans Because most bank deposits are subject to withdrawal on demand, commercial banks seek to prevent firms from using bank credit for permanent financing. A bank may therefore require its borrowers to "clean up" their short-term bank loans for at least one month each year. If a firm is unable to become free of bank debt at least part of each year, it is using bank financing for permanent needs and should develop additional sources of long-term or permanent financing.

Cost of Commercial Bank Loans Most loans from commercial banks have recently cost from 6 to 12 percent, with the effective rate depending on the characteristics of the firm and the level of interest rates in the economy. If the firm can qualify as a prime risk because of its size and financial strength, the rate of interest will be one-half to three-quarters of a percent above the rediscount rate charged by federal reserve banks to commercial banks. On the other hand, a small firm with below-average financial ratios may be required to provide collateral security and to pay an effective rate of interest of more than 12 percent.

"Regular" Interest Determination of the effective, or true, rate of interest on a loan depends on the stated rate of interest and the lender's method of charging interest. If the interest is paid at the maturity of the loan, the stated rate of interest is the effective rate of interest. For example, on a $10,000 loan for one year at 7 percent, the interest is $700.

$$\text{"Regular" loan, interest paid at maturity} =$$

$$\frac{\text{Interest}}{\text{Borrowed amount}} = \frac{\$700}{\$10,000} = 7\%.$$

Discounted Interest If the bank deducts the interest in advance (discounts the loan), the effective rate of interest is increased. On the $10,000 loan for one year at 7 percent, the discount is $700, and the borrower obtains the use of only $9,300. The effective rate of interest is 7.5 percent (versus 7 percent on a "regular" loan):

$$\text{Discounted loan} = \frac{\text{Interest}}{\text{Borrowed amount} - \text{Interest}} = \frac{\$700}{\$9,300} = 7.5\%.$$

---

3. Note, however, that the compensating balance is generally set as a minimum monthly average; if the firm maintains this average anyway, the compensating balance requirement does not entail higher effective rates.

Installment Loan If the loan is repaid in twelve monthly installments but the interest is calculated on the original balance, then the effective rate of interest is even higher. The borrower has the full amount of the money only during the first month and by the last month has already paid eleven-twelfths of the loan. Thus the borrower of $10,000 pays $700 for the use of about half the amount received ($10,000 or $9,300, depending on the method of charging interest), since the *average* amount outstanding during the year is only $5,000 or $4,650. If interest is paid at maturity, the approximate effective rate on an installment loan is calculated as follows:

$$\text{Interest rate on original amount of installment loan} = \frac{\$700}{\$5,000} = 14\%.$$

Under the discounting method, the effective cost of the installment loan is approximately 15 percent:

$$\text{Interest rate on discounted installment loan} = \frac{\$700}{\$4,650} = 15.05\%.$$

Here we see that interest is paid on the *original* amount of the loan, not on the amount actually outstanding (the declining balance), and this causes the effective interest rate to be approximately double the stated rate. Interest is calculated by the installment method on most consumer loans (for example, automobile loans), but it is not often used for business loans larger than about $5,000.

Choice of Banks

Banks have direct relationships with their borrowers. There is much personal association over the years, and the business problems of the borrower are frequently discussed. Thus banks often provide informal management counseling services. A potential borrower seeking such a relationship should recognize the important differences among banks, which are considered in the following discussion.

1. Banks have different basic policies toward risk. Some are inclined to follow relatively conservative lending practices; others engage in what are properly termed creative banking practices. The policies reflect partly the personalities of the bank officers and partly the characteristics of the bank's deposit liabilities. Thus a bank with fluctuating deposit liabilities in a static community tends to be a conservative lender. A bank whose deposits are growing with little interruption may follow liberal credit policies. A large bank with diversification over broad geographical regions or among several industries can obtain the benefit of combining and averaging risks. Thus marginal credit risks that may be unacceptable to a small bank or to a specialized unit bank can be pooled by a branch

banking system to reduce the overall risks of a group of marginal accounts.

2. Some bank loan officers are active in providing counsel and in stimulating development loans with firms that are in their early and formative years. Certain banks even have specialized departments to make loans to firms expected to become growth firms. The personnel of these departments can provide much counseling to customers.

3. Banks differ in the extent to which they support a borrower's activities in bad times. This characteristic is referred to as the bank's degree of loyalty. Some banks put great pressure on a business to liquidate its loans when the firm's outlook becomes clouded, whereas others stand by the firm and work diligently to help it attain a more favorable condition.

4. Another characteristic by which banks differ is the degree of deposit stability. Instability arises not only from fluctuations in the level of deposits but also from the composition of deposits. Deposits can take the form of *demand deposits* (checking accounts) or *time deposits* (savings accounts, certificates of deposit, Christmas clubs). Total deposits tend to be more stable when time deposits are substantial. Differences in deposit stability go a long way toward explaining differences in the extent to which banks are willing or able to help borrowers work their way out of difficulties or even crises.

5. Banks differ greatly in the degree of loan specialization. Larger banks have separate departments specializing in different kinds of loans, such as real estate, installment, and commercial loans. Within these broad categories they may specialize by line of business, such as steel, machinery, or textiles. Smaller banks are likely to reflect the nature of the business and economic environment in which they operate. They tend to become specialists in specfic lines, such as oil, construction, or agriculture. The borrower can obtain more creative cooperation and more active support at the bank that has the greatest experience and familiarity with the borrower's particular type of business. The financial manager should therefore choose a bank with care. The bank that is excellent for one firm may be unsatisfactory for another.

6. The size of a bank can be an important characteristic. Since the maximum loan a bank can make to any customer is generally limited to 10 percent of the bank's capital accounts (capital stock plus retained earnings), it generally is not appropriate for large firms to develop borrowing relationships with small banks.

7. With the heightened competition among commercial banks and other financial institutions, the aggressiveness of banks has increased. Modern commercial banks now offer a wide range of financial and business services. Most large banks have business development departments that provide counseling to firms and serve as intermediaries on a wide variety of their requirements.

Commercial Paper

Commercial paper, which consists of promissory notes of large firms, is sold primarily to other business firms, insurance companies, pension funds, and banks. Although the amounts of commercial paper outstanding are much smaller than bank loans outstanding, this form of financing has grown rapidly in recent years.

Maturity and Cost

Maturities of commercial paper generally vary from two to six months, with an average of about five months. The rates on prime commercial paper vary, but they are generally about half a percent below those on prime business loans. And since compensating balances are not required for commercial paper, the *effective* cost differential is still wider.[4]

Use

The use of the open market for commercial paper is restricted to a comparatively small number of concerns that are exceptionally good credit risks. Dealers prefer to handle the paper of concerns whose net worth is $10 million or more and whose annual borrowing exceeds $1 million.

Advantages and Disadvantages

The commercial paper market has some significant advantages:

1. It permits the broadest and the most advantageous distribution of paper.
2. It provides more funds at lower rates than do other methods.
3. The borrower avoids the inconvenience and expense of financing arrangements with a number of institutions, each of which requires a compensating balance.
4. Publicity and prestige accrue to the borrower as its product and paper become more widely known.
5. The commercial paper dealer frequently offers valuable advice to clients.

A basic limitation of the commercial paper market is that the size of the funds available is limited to the excess liquidity that corporations (the main suppliers of funds) have at any particular time. Another disadvantage is that a debtor who is in temporary financial difficulty receives little help because commercial paper dealings are impersonal. Banks are much more

4. However, this factor is offset to some extent by the fact that firms issuing commercial paper are sometimes required by commercial paper dealers to have unused bank lines of credit to back up their outstanding commercial paper, and fees must be paid on these lines.

personal and much more likely to help a good customer weather a temporary storm.[5]

Effects of Inflation

During periods of inflation and tight money, many commercial paper sellers are pushed out of the market. Ryder System, a Florida trucking company, was forced to turn to bank loans for $10 million of financing during 1974, after they were able to find buyers for only $15 million of their commercial paper. Thus, during inflationary periods, firms may be forced to seek the more expensive bank loans since they can no longer sell the cheaper commercial paper.

Banker's Acceptances during Inflation

Banker's acceptances gain popularity during inflationary periods. A banker's acceptance is a draft drawn by an individual and accepted by a bank; it orders the bank to pay a specific sum to a third party at a particular time. Banker's acceptances are an effective method of short-term financing since the drawer gains time before funds are due. The appeal of banker's acceptances, which are traded in an active secondary market, results from two basic characteristics. First, they are safe. Since they usually finance the shipment and storage of goods, the inventory can be pledged as collateral. Return to investors is usually comparable to the return on a good certificate of deposit. During periods of inflation, when investors become increasingly selective, a banker's acceptance may look safer than commercial paper or even the certificates of deposit of some banks. Second, when an acceptance is backed by readily marketable goods and a warehouse receipt has been issued, the acceptance is eligible for rediscount with the Federal Reserve.

Use of Security in Short-Term Financing

Given a choice, it is ordinarily better to borrow on an unsecured basis, since the bookkeeping costs of secured loans are often high. However, it frequently happens that a potential borrower's credit rating is not sufficiently strong to justify the loan. If the loan can be secured by some form of collat-

5. This point was emphasized dramatically in the aftermath of the Penn Central bankruptcy. Penn Central had a large amount of commercial paper that went into default and embarrassed corporate treasurers who had been holding the paper as part of their liquidity reserves. Immediately after the bankruptcy, the commercial paper market dried up to a large extent, and some companies that had relied heavily on this market found themselves under severe liquidity pressure as their commercial paper matured and could not be refunded. Chrysler, for example, had to seek bank loans of over $500 million because it could not sell commercial paper for a time. Without adequate bank lines, Chrysler might well have been forced into bankruptcy itself, even though it was basically sound, because of the Penn Central panic. Incidentally, the Federal Reserve Board recognized that many other firms would be in the same position as Chrysler, so the Fed expanded bank reserves in order to enable the banking system to take up the slack caused by the withdrawal of funds from the commercial paper market.

eral to be claimed by the lender in the event of default, then the lender may extend credit to an otherwise unacceptable firm. Similarly, a firm that can borrow on an unsecured basis may elect to use security if it finds that this will induce lenders to quote a lower interest rate.

Several different kinds of collateral can be employed—marketable stocks or bonds, land or buildings, equipment, inventory, and accounts receivable. Marketable securities make excellent collateral, but few firms hold portfolios of stocks and bonds. Similarly, real property (land and buildings) and equipment are good forms of collateral, but they are generally used as security for long-term loans. The bulk of secured short-term business borrowing involves the pledge of short-term assets—accounts receivable or inventories.

In the past, state laws varied greatly with regard to the use of security in financing. By the late 1960s, however, most states had adopted the *Uniform Commercial Code,* which standardized and simplified the procedure for establishing loan security.

The heart of the UCC is the *security agreement,* a standardized document, or form, on which are stated the specific pledged assets. The assets can be items of equipment, accounts receivable, or inventories. Procedures for financing under the UCC are described in the following sections.

Financing Accounts Receivable

Accounts receivable financing involves either the assigning of receivables or the selling of receivables (factoring). Pledging of accounts receivable is characterized by the fact that the lender not only has a lien on the receivables but also has recourse to the borrower (seller); if the person or firm that bought the goods does not pay, the selling firm must take the loss. In other words, the risk of default on the accounts receivable pledged remains with the borrower. Also, the buyer of the goods is not ordinarily notified about the pledging of the receivables. The financial institution that lends on the security of accounts receivable is generally either a commercial bank or one of the large industrial finance companies.

Factoring, or selling accounts receivable, involves the purchase of accounts receivable by the lender without recourse to the borrower (seller). The buyer of the goods is notified of the transfer and makes payment directly to the lender. Since the factoring firm assumes the risk of default on bad accounts, it must do the credit checking. Accordingly, factors provide not only money but also a credit department for the borrower. Incidentally, the same financial institutions that make loans against pledged receivables also serve as factors. Thus, depending on the circumstances and the wishes of the borrower, a financial institution will provide either form of receivables financing.

**Procedure for
Pledging
Accounts
Receivable**

The financing of accounts receivable is initiated by a legally binding agreement between the seller of the goods and the financing institution. The
agreement sets forth in detail the procedure to be followed and the legal
obligations of both parties. Once the working relationship has been established, the seller periodically takes a batch of invoices to the financing institution. The lender reviews the invoices and makes an appraisal of the
buyers. Invoices of companies that do not meet the lender's credit standards
are not accepted for pledging. The financial institution seeks to protect itself
at every phase of the operation. Selection of sound invoices is the essential
first step. If the buyer of the goods does not pay the invoice, the lender still
has recourse against the seller of the goods. However, if many buyers default, the seller may be unable to meet the obligation to the financial institution.

Additional protection afforded the lender is that the loan is generally for
less than 100 percent of the pledged receivables; for example, the lender
may advance the selling firm 75 percent of the amount of the pledged receivables.

**Procedure for
Factoring
Accounts
Receivable**

The procedure for factoring is somewhat different from that for pledging.
Again, an agreement between the seller and the factor is made to specify
legal obligations and procedural arrangements. When the seller receives an
order from a buyer, a credit approval slip is written and immediately sent to
the factoring company for a credit check. If the factor does not approve the
sale, the seller generally refuses to fill the order. This procedure informs the
seller, prior to the sale, about the buyer's creditworthiness and acceptability
to the factor. If the sale is approved, shipment is made and the invoice is
stamped to notify the buyer to make payment directly to the factoring company.

The factor performs three functions in carrying out the procedure outlined above: (1) credit checking, (2) lending, and (3) risk bearing. The seller
can select various combinations of these functions by changing provisions
in the factoring agreement. For example, a small- or medium-sized firm can
avoid establishing a credit department. The factor's service may well be less
costly than a department that has a capacity in excess of the firm's credit
volume. Also, if the firm uses a part-time noncredit specialist to perform
credit checking, the person's lack of education, training, and experience
may result in excessive losses.

The seller may, for example, have the factor perform the credit checking
and risk taking functions but not the lending function. In this situation, the
following procedure is carried out on receipt of a $10,000 order. The factor
checks and approves the invoices, and the goods are shipped on terms of
net 30. Payment is made to the factor, who remits to the seller. But the fac-

tor who has received only $5,000 by the end of the credit period must still remit $10,000 to the seller (less the factor's fee, of course). If the remaining $5,000 is never paid, the factor sustains a $5,000 loss.

Now consider the more typical situation, where the factor performs a lending function by making payment in advance of collection. The goods are shipped, and even though payment is not due for thirty days, the factor immediately makes funds available to the seller. Suppose $10,000 worth of goods are shipped; the factoring commission for credit checking is $2^1/_2$ percent of the invoice price, or $250; and the interest expense is computed at a 9 percent annual rate on the invoice balance, or $75.[6] The seller's accounting entry is as follows:

Cash	$9,175	
Interest expense	75	
Factoring commission	250	
Reserve: Due from factor on collection of account	500	
Accounts receivable		$10,000

The $500 due from the factor on collection of the account is a reserve established by the factor to cover disputes between sellers and buyers on damaged goods, goods returned by the buyer to the seller, and failure to make an outright sale of the goods. The amount is paid to the seller firm when the factor collects on the account.

Factoring is normally a continuous process rather than the single cycle described above. The seller of the goods receives orders and transmits the purchase orders to the factor for approval; on approval, the goods are shipped; the factor advances the money to the seller; the buyers pay the factor when payment is due; and the factor periodically remits any excess reserve to the seller of the goods. Once a routine is established, a continuous circular flow of goods and funds takes place among the seller, the buyers, and the factor. Thus, once the factoring agreement is in force, funds from this source are *spontaneous*.

Cost of Receivables Financing

Accounts receivable pledging and factoring services are convenient and advantageous, but they can be costly. The credit checking commission is 1 to 3 percent of the amount of invoices accepted by the factor, and the cost of

---

6. Since the interest is for only one month, we take one-twelfth of the stated rate, 9 percent, and multiply this by the $10,000 invoice price:

$$^1/_{12} \times 0.09 \times \$10,000 = \$75.$$

Note that the effective rate of interest is really more than 9 percent, because a discounting procedure is used and the borrower does not get the full $10,000. In many instances, however, the factoring contract calls for interest to be computed on the invoice price *less* the factoring commission and the reserve account.

money is reflected in the interest rate of 8 to 12 percent charged on the unpaid balance of the funds advanced by the factor. Where the risk to the factor is excessive, the factor purchases the invoices (with or without recourse) at discounts from face value.

Evaluation of Receivables Financing

It cannot be said categorically that accounts receivable financing is always either a good or a bad method of raising funds for an individual business. Among the advantages is, first, the flexibility of this source of financing. As the firm's sales expand and more financing is needed, a larger volume of invoices is generated automatically. Because the dollar amounts of invoices vary directly with sales, the amount of readily available financing increases. Second, receivables or invoices provide security for a loan that a firm might otherwise be unable to obtain. Third, factoring provides the services of a credit department that might otherwise be available to the firm only under much more expensive conditions.

Accounts receivable financing also has disadvantages. First, when invoices are numerous and relatively small in dollar amount, the administrative costs involved may render this method of financing inconvenient and expensive. Second, the firm is using a highly liquid asset as security. For a long time, accounts receivable financing was frowned on by most trade creditors; it was regarded as confession of a firm's unsound financial position. It is no longer regarded in this light, however, and many sound firms engage in receivables pledging or factoring. Still, the traditional attitude causes some trade creditors to refuse to sell on credit to a firm that is factoring or pledging its receivables, on the ground that this practice removes one of the most liquid of the firm's assets and, accordingly, weakens the position of other creditors.

Future Use of Receivables Financing

We will make a prediction at this point. In the future, accounts receivable financing will increase in relative importance. Computer technology is rapidly advancing toward the point where credit records of individuals and firms can be kept in computer memory units. Systems already have been devised whereby a retailer can insert an individual's magnetic credit card into a box and receive a signal showing if the person's credit is "good" and if a bank is willing to "buy" the receivable created when the store completes the sale. The cost of handling invoices will be greatly reduced over present-day costs because the new systems will be so highly automated. This will make it possible to use accounts receivable financing for very small sales, and it will reduce the cost of all receivables financing. The net result will be a marked expansion of accounts receivable financing.

Inventory Financing

A rather large volume of credit is secured by business inventories. If a firm is a relatively good credit risk, the mere existence of the inventory may be a sufficient basis for receiving an unsecured loan. If the firm is a relatively poor risk, the lending institution may insist on security, which often takes the form of a blanket lien against the inventory. Alternatively, trust receipts, field warehouse financing, or collateral certificates can be used to secure the loan. These methods of using inventories as security are discussed below.

Blanket Inventory Lien

The blanket inventory lien gives the lending institution a lien against all inventories of the borrower. However, the borrower is free to sell the inventories; thus the value of the collateral can be reduced.

Trust Receipts

Because of the weaknesses of the blanket lien for inventory financing, another kind of security is often used—the trust receipt. A trust receipt is an instrument acknowledging that the borrower holds the goods in trust for the lender. On receiving funds from the lender, the borrowing firm conveys a trust receipt for the goods. The goods can be stored in a public warehouse or held on the borrower's premises. The trust receipt provides that the goods are held in trust for the lender or are segregated on the borrower's premises on behalf of the lender, and proceeds from the sale of such goods are transmitted to the lender at the end of each day. Automobile dealer financing is the best example of trust receipt financing.

One defect of this form of financing is the requirement that a trust receipt must be issued for specific goods. For example, if the security is bags of coffee beans, the trust receipts must indicate the bags by number. In order to validate its trust receipts, the lending institution must send someone to the borrower's premises to see that the bag numbers are correctly listed. Furthermore, complex legal requirements for trust receipts require the attention of a bank officer. Problems are compounded if borrowers are widely separated geographically from the lender. To offset these inconveniences, warehousing is coming into wide use as a method of securing loans with inventory.

Field Warehouse Financing

Like trust receipts, field warehouse financing uses inventory as security. A public warehouse represents an independent third party engaged in the business of storing goods. Sometimes the warehouse is not practical because of the bulkiness of goods and the expense of transporting them to and from the borrower's premises. Field warehouse financing represents an economical method of inventory financing in which the "warehouse" is established on the borrower's premises. To provide inventory supervision, the lending institution employs a third party in the arrangement, the field warehousing company. This company acts as the control (or supervisory) agent for the lending institution.

Field warehousing is illustrated by a simple example. Suppose a potential borrower has stacked iron in an open yard on his premises. A field warehouse can be established if, say, a field warehousing concern places a temporary fence around the iron and erects a sign stating: ''This is a field warehouse supervised and conducted by the Smith Field Warehousing Corporation.''

The example illustrates the two elements in the establishment of a warehouse: (1) public notification of the field warehouse arrangement and (2) supervision of the warehouse by a custodian of the field warehouse concern. When the field warehousing operation is relatively small, the second condition is sometimes violated by hiring an employee of the borrower to supervise the inventory. This practice is viewed as undesirable by the lending institution because there is no control over the collateral by a person independent of the borrowing concern.[7]

The field warehouse financing operation is described best by a specific illustration. Assume that a tomato canner is interested in financing operations by bank borrowing. The canner has funds sufficient to finance 15 to 20 percent of operations during the canning season. These funds are adequate to purchase and process an initial batch of tomatoes. As the cans are put into boxes and rolled into the storerooms, the canner needs additional funds for both raw materials and labor.

Because of the canner's poor credit rating, the bank decides that a field warehousing operation is necessary to secure its loans. The field warehouse is established, and the custodian notifies the lending institution of the description, by number, of the boxes of canned tomatoes in storage and under his control. Thereupon the lending institution establishes for the canner a deposit on which it can draw. From this point on, the bank finances the operations. The canner needs only enough cash to initiate the cycle. The farmers bring more tomatoes; the canner processes them; the cans are boxed and the boxes put into the field warehouse; field warehouse receipts are drawn up and sent to the bank; the bank establishes further deposits for the canner on the basis of the receipts; and the canner can draw on the deposits to continue the cycle.

---

7. This absence of independent control was the main cause of the breakdown that resulted in the huge losses connected with loans to the Allied Crude Vegetable Oil Company headed by Anthony (Tino) DeAngelis. American Express Field Warehousing Company hired men from Allied's staff as custodians. Their dishonesty was not discovered because of another breakdown—the fact that the American Express touring inspector did not actually take a physical inventory of the warehouses. As a consequence, the swindle was not discovered until losses running into the hundreds of millions of dollars had been suffered. See Norman C. Miller, *The Great Salad Oil Swindle* (Baltimore, Md.: Penguin Books, 1965). pp. 72–77.

Of course, the canner's ultimate objective is to sell the canned tomatoes. As the canner receives purchase orders, it transmits them to the bank, and the bank directs the custodian to release the inventories. It is agreed that, as remittances are received by the canner, they will be turned over to the bank. These remittances pay off the loans made by the bank.

Typically, a seasonal pattern exists. At the beginning of the tomato harvesting and canning season, the canner's cash needs and loan requirements begin to rise, and they reach a maximum by the end of the canning season. It is hoped that, just before the new canning season begins, the canner has sold a sufficient volume to have paid off the loan completely. If for some reason the canner has had a bad year, the bank may carry the company over another year to enable it to sell off its inventory.

Acceptable Products In addition to canned foods, which account for about 17 percent of all field warehouse loans, many other product inventories provide a basis for field warehouse financing. Some of these are miscellaneous groceries, which represent about 13 percent; lumber products, about 10 percent; and coal and coke, about 6 percent.

These products are relatively nonperishable and are sold in well-developed, organized markets. Nonperishability protects the lender who has to take over the security. For this reason a bank will not make a field warehousing loan on perishables such as fresh fish. However, frozen fish, which can be stored for a long time, can be field warehoused. An organized market also aids the lender in disposing of inventory that it takes over. Banks are not interested in going into the canning or the fish business. They want to be able to dispose of an inventory quickly and with the expenditure of a minimum amount of their own time.

Cost of Financing The fixed costs of a field warehousing arrangement are relatively high; such financing is therefore not suitable for a very small firm. If a field warehouse company sets up the warehouse itself, it typically sets a minimum charge of about $350 to $600 a year, plus about 1 or 2 percent of the amount of credit extended to the borrower. Furthermore, the financing institution charges from 8 to 12 percent interest. The minimum size of an efficient warehousing operation requires an inventory of about $100,000.

Appraisal The use of field warehouse financing as a source of funds for business firms has many advantages. First, the amount of funds available is flexible because the financing is tied to the growth of inventories, which in turn is related directly to financing needs. Second, the arrangement increases the acceptability of inventories as loan collateral. Some inventories are not accepted by a bank as security without a field warehousing arrangement. Third, the necessity for inventory control, safekeeping, and the use of specialists in warehousing has resulted in improved warehouse practices.

The services of the field warehouse companies have often saved money for the firm in spite of the financing costs mentioned above. The field warehouse company may suggest inventory practices that reduce both the number of people the firm has to employ and inventory damage and loss as well.

The major disadvantage of a field warehousing operation is the fixed cost element, which reduces the feasibility of this form of financing for small firms.

Collateral Certificates

A collateral certificate guarantees the existence of the amount of inventory pledged as loan collateral. It is a statement issued periodically to the lender by a third party, who certifies that the inventory exists and that it will be available if needed.

This method of bank financing is becoming increasingly popular, primarily due to its flexibility. First, there is no need for physical segregation or possession of inventories. Therefore, collateral certificates can even be used to cover work-in-process inventories, which allows considerable freedom in the movement of goods. Second, the collateral certificate can provide for a receivables financing plan, allowing financing to continue smoothly as inventories are converted into receivables. Third, the certificate issuer usually provides a number of services to simplify loan administration for both the borrower and the lender.

Summary

Short-term credit is debt originally scheduled for repayment within one year. The three major sources of short-term credit are trade credit among firms, loans from commercial banks, and commercial paper.

Trade credit (represented by accounts payable) is the largest single category of short-term credit; it is especially important for smaller firms. Trade credit is a *spontaneous source of financing* in that it arises from ordinary business transactions; as sales increase, so does the supply of financing from accounts payable.

Bank credit occupies a pivotal position in the short-term money market. Banks provide the marginal credit that allows firms to expand more rapidly than is possible through retained earnings and trade credit. A denial of bank credit often means that a firm must slow its rate of growth.

Bank interest rates are quoted in three ways—regular compound interest, discount interest, and installment interest. Regular interest needs no adjustment; it is correct as stated. Discount interest requires a small upward adjustment to make it comparable to regular compound interest rates. Installment interest rates require a large adjustment, and frequently the true interest rate is double the quoted rate for an installment loan.

Bank loans are personal in the sense that the financial manager meets with the banker, discusses the terms of the loan, and reaches an agreement that requires direct and personal negotiation. Commercial paper, however, although it is physically similar to a bank loan, is sold in a broad, impersonal market. A California firm might, for example, sell commercial paper to a manufacturer in the Midwest.

Only the very strongest firms are able to use the commercial paper markets. The nature of these markets is such that the firm selling the paper must have a reputation so good that buyers of the paper are willing to buy it without any sort of credit check. Interest rates in the commercial paper market are the lowest available to business borrowers.

The most common forms of collateral used for short-term credit are inventories and accounts receivable. Accounts receivable financing can be done either by pledging the receivables or by selling them outright (often called factoring). When the receivables are pledged, the borrower retains the risk that the person or firm owing the receivables will not pay; in factoring, this risk is typically passed on to the lender. Because factors take the risk of default, they investigate the purchaser's credit; therefore, factors can perform three functions: lending, risk bearing, and credit checking. When receivables are pledged, the lender typically performs only the first of these functions.

Loans secured by inventories are not satisfactory under many circumstances. For certain kinds of inventory, however, the technique known as field warehousing is used to provide adequate security to the lender. Under a field warehousing arrangement, the inventory is physically controlled by a warehouse company, which releases the inventory only on order from the lending institution. Canned goods, lumber, steel, coal, and other standardized products are goods usually covered in field warehouse arrangements.

Questions

10.1 It is inevitable that firms will obtain a certain amount of their financing in the form of trade credit, which is (to some extent) a free source of funds. What are some other reasons for firms to use trade credit?

10.2 Discuss the statement: Commercial paper interest rates are always lower than bank loan rates to a given borrower. Nevertheless, many firms perfectly capable of selling commercial paper employ higher-cost bank credit. Indicate (a) why commercial paper rates are lower than bank rates and (b) why firms might use bank credit in spite of its higher cost.

10.3 Discuss the statement: Trade credit has an explicit interest rate cost if discounts are available but not taken. There are also some intangible costs associated with the failure to take discounts.

10.4 A large manufacturing firm that had been selling its products on a 3/10, net 30 basis changed its credit terms to 1/20, net 90. What changes might be anticipated on the balance sheets of the manufacturer and of its customers?

10.5 The availability of bank credit is more important to small firms than to large ones. Why?

10.6 What factors should a firm consider in selecting its primary bank? Would it be feasible for a firm to have a primary deposit bank (the bank where most of its funds are deposited) and a different primary loan bank (the bank where it does most of its borrowing)?

10.7 Indicate whether each of the following changes will raise or lower the cost of a firm's accounts receivable financing, and explain why this occurs:
a. The firm eases up on its credit standards in order to increase sales.
b. The firm institutes a policy of refusing to make credit sales if the amount of the purchase (invoice) is below $100. Previously, about 40 percent of all invoices were below $100.
c. The firm agrees to give recourse to the finance company for all defaults.
d. A firm that already has a recourse arrangement is merged into a larger, stronger company.
e. A firm without a recourse arrangement changes its terms of trade from net 30 to net 90.

10.8 Would a firm that manufactures specialized machinery for a few large customers be more likely to use a form of inventory financing or a form of accounts receivable financing? Why?

10.9 Discuss the statement: A firm that factors its accounts receivable will look better in a ratio analysis than one that discounts its receivables.

10.10 Why would it not be practical for a typical retailer to use field warehouse financing?

10.11 Describe an industry that might be expected to use each of the following forms of credit, and explain your reasons for choosing each one:
a. field warehouse financing
b. factoring
c. accounts receivable discounting
d. trust receipts
e. none of these

Problems

10.1 What is the equivalent annual interest rate that would be lost if a firm failed to take the cash discount under each of the following terms?
a. 1/15, net 30
b. 2/10, net 60
c. 3/10, net 60
d. 2/10, net 40
e. 1/10, net 40

10.2 Dixon Associates is negotiating with Commerce Bank for a $100,000, one-year loan. Commerce has offered Dixon the following three alternatives:

1. A 12 percent interest rate, no compensating balance, and interest due at the end of the year.
2. A 10 percent interest rate, a 20 percent compensating balance, and interest due at the end of the year.

3. A 9 percent interest rate, a 15 percent compensating balance, and the loan discounted.

If Dixon wishes to minimize the effective interest rate, which alternative will it choose?

10.3 Wagner Industries is having difficulty paying its bills and is considering foregoing its trade discounts on $100,000 of accounts payable. As an alternative, Wagner can obtain a sixty-day note with a 12 percent annual interest rate. The note will be discounted, and the trade credit terms are 2/10, net 70.
a. Which alternative has the lower effective cost?
b. If Wagner does not take its trade discounts, what conclusions may outsiders draw?

10.4 Supreme Catsup Company is considering the following two alternatives for financing next year's canning operations:

1. Establishing a $1 million line of credit with a 12 percent annual interest rate on the used portion and a 1 percent commitment fee rate on the unused portion. A $150,000 compensating balance will be required at all times on the entire $1 million line.
2. Using field warehousing to finance $850,000 of inventory. Financing charges will be a flat fee of $500, plus 2 percent of the maximum amount of credit extended, plus a 10 percent annual interest rate on all outstanding credit.

Supreme has $150,000 of funds available for inventory financing, so financing requirements will be equal to the expected inventory level minus $150,000. All financing is done on the first of the month and is sufficient to cover the value of the inventory at the end of the month. Expected inventory levels are as follows:

Month	Amount	Month	Amount
July 1979	$ 150,000	January 1980	$600,000
August	400,000	February	450,000
September	600,000	March	350,000
October	800,000	April	225,000
November	1,000,000	May	100,000
December	750,000	June	0

Which financing plan has the lowest cost? (Hints: Under the bank loan plan, borrowings in July are $150,000 and in December $750,000; under the field warehousing plan, July borrowings are zero and December borrowings are $600,000.)

10.5 The balance sheet of the Atlantic Credit Corporation is shown here.
a. Calculate commercial paper as a percentage of short-term financing, as a percentage of total-debt financing, and as a percentage of all financing.
b. Why do finance companies such as Atlantic Credit use commercial paper to such a great extent?
c. Why do they use both bank loans and commercial paper?

Atlantic Credit Corporation
Balance Sheet
(Millions of Dollars)

Assets		Liabilities	
Cash	$ 75	Bank loans	$ 250
Net receivables	2,400	Commercial paper	825
Marketable securities	150	Others	375
Repossessions	5	Total due within a year	$1,450
Total current assets	$2,630	Long-term debt	1,000
Other assets	170	Total shareholders' equity	350
Total assets	$2,800	Total claims	$2,800

10.6 The Shelby Saw Corporation had sales of $4 million last year and earned a 3 percent after-tax return on total assets. Although its terms of purchase are thirty days, accounts payable represent sixty days' purchases. The company is seeking to increase bank borrowings in order to become current in meeting its trade obligations (that is, reduce them to thirty days). The company's balance sheet is shown below.

  a. How much bank financing is needed to eliminate past-due accounts payable?

  b. As a bank loan officer, would you make the loan? Explain.

Shelby Saw Corporation
Balance Sheet

Assets		Liabilities	
Cash	$ 100,000	Accounts payable	$ 600,000
Accounts receivable	300,000	Bank loans	500,000
Inventory	1,400,000	Accruals	400,000
Current assets	$1,800,000	Current liabilities	$1,500,000
Land and buildings	700,000	Mortgage or real estate	600,000
Equipment	500,000	Net worth	900,000
Total assets	$3,000,000	Claims on assets	$3,000,000

10.7 Collins Manufacturing needs an additional $100,000. The financial manager is considering two methods of obtaining this money: a loan from a commercial bank or a factoring arrangement. The bank charges 8 percent per annum interest, discount basis. It also requires a 12 percent compensating balance. The factor is willing to purchase Collins's accounts receivable and to advance the amount purchased, less a 3 percent factoring commission on the invoices purchased each month. (All sales are on thirty-day terms.) An 8 percent annual interest rate will be charged on the total invoice price and deducted in advance. Also, under the factoring agreement, Collins can eliminate its credit department and reduce credit expenses by

$2,000 per month. Bad debt losses of 1 percent on the factored amount can also be avoided.

a. How much should the bank loan be in order to net $100,000? How much accounts receivable should be factored to net $100,000?

b. What are the effective interest rates and the annual total dollar costs, including credit department expenses and bad debt losses, associated with each financing arrangement?

c. Discuss some considerations other than cost that may influence management's choice between factoring and a commercial bank loan.

10.8 Fair Deal Co. estimates that due to the seasonal nature of its business it will require an additional $200,000 of cash for the month of November. Fair Deal has three options available to provide the needed funds. It can:

1. Establish a one-year line of credit for $200,000 with a commercial bank. The commitment fee will be 0.5 percent, and the interest charge on the used funds will be 10 percent per annum. The minimum time the funds can be used is thirty days.

2. Forego the November trade discount of 2/10, net 40 on $200,000 of accounts payable.

3. Issue $200,000 of sixty-day commercial paper at an 8 percent per annum interest rate. Since the funds are required for only thirty days, the excess funds ($200,000) can be invested in 7 percent per annum marketable securities for the month of December. The total transaction fee on purchasing and selling the marketable securities is 0.5 percent of the fair value.

Which financing arrangement results in the lowest cost?

10.9 Susan Smith plans to open the simplest of retail trade establishments, a grocery store with an emphasis on health foods. She has received an allowance from her parents for some years and has been able to save a little over $1,000. After making some inquiries, she has recognized that she must consider such things as location, potential flow of customer traffic, and present and potential competition. Also, she has realized that she must analyze the alternatives of buying or renting a store and buying or renting the equipment and fixtures she will need—counters, shelving, cash register, and the like. The store space she has in mind has not been occupied by a grocery before, so it lacks shelves and counters.

a. Should she buy or rent the store facilities?

b. How should she acquire the equipment and fixtures?

c. What kinds of questions is she likely to face with regard to choice of product line?

d. For planning purposes, assume a profit ratio of net income before taxes to sales of 4 percent and sales per day first of $100, then of $300, and finally of $500. In each situation, what are her earnings per hour before taxes, assuming that she works ten hours per day, seven days a week, for fifty weeks per year?

e. With a sales to net worth ratio of 15 times, what investment on her part is indicated at each level of sales? Comment on how she can raise the funds if several years are required to reach an alternative level of sales. Comment also on the implications of her withdrawing funds from the business.

f. What additional questions must she face if she sells on credit?

g. What critical problems are likely to occur if sales start at $500 per day?

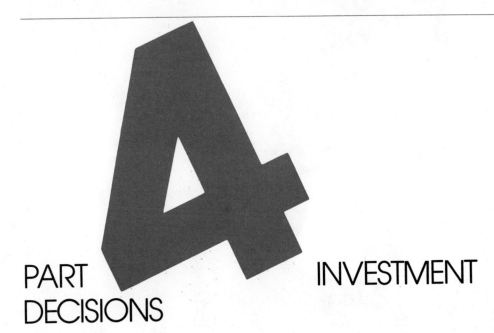

PART 4

DECISIONS

INVESTMENT

Part 3 dealt with the top portion of the firm's balance sheet—the current assets and liabilities. Part 4 considers investment decisions with respect to the entire asset side of the balance sheet, emphasizing the decisions involved in fixed asset acquisitions.

Chapter 11 discusses the concepts of compound interest and the time value of money, important subjects in all long-term financial decisions. Chapter 12 covers capital budgeting—the planning of expenditures whose returns will extend beyond one year. Chapter 13 introduces uncertainty about both the costs and the returns associated with a project. Since projects differ in riskiness, that chapter develops methods of analysis that can be used to incorporate risk into the decision-making process.

11

CHAPTER   THE INTEREST FACTOR IN FINANCIAL DECISIONS

We have not yet considered the theory of compound interest, although we could have brought up the subject in previous chapters. Our aim has been to increase the complexity of the balance sheet analysis gradually. But we have reached the point where this subject must be dealt with.

The time value of money is essential to an understanding of capital budgeting (the topic of the following chapter), and interest rate theory is an integral part of several topics taken up later in the text. Financial structure decisions, lease versus purchase decisions, bond refunding operations, security valuation techniques, and the whole question of the cost of capital are subjects that cannot be understood without a knowledge of compound interest.

Many people are afraid of the subject and simply avoid it. It is certainly true that many successful business persons—even some bankers—know essentially nothing about it. However, as technology advances, as more engineers become involved in general management, and as modern business administration programs turn out more highly qualified graduates, this "success in spite of yourself" pattern will become more difficult to achieve. Furthermore, a fear of compound interest relationships is quite unfounded; the subject matter is not inherently difficult. Almost all problems involving compound interest can be handled with only a few basic formulas.

Compound Value

A person deposits $1,000 in a savings and loan association that pays 5 percent interest compounded annually. How much will he have at the end of one year? To treat the matter systematically, let us define the following terms:

P_0 = principal, or beginning amount, at time 0.
i = interest rate.
$P_0 i$ = total dollar amount of interest earned.
V_t = value at the end of t periods.

When t equals 1, V_t can be calculated as follows:

$$V_1 = P_0 + P_0 i$$
$$= P_0 (1 + i). \qquad (11.1)$$

Equation 11.1 shows that the ending amount (V_1) is equal to the beginning amount (P_0) times the factor $(1 + i)$. In the example, where P_0 is $1,000, i is 5 percent, and t is one year, V_t is determined as follows:

$$V_1 = \$1,000 \,(1.0 + 0.05) = \$1,000 \,(1.05) = \$1,050.$$

Multiple Periods If the person leaves the $1,000 on deposit for five years, to what amount will it have grown at the end of that period? Equation 11.1 can be used to construct Table 11.1, which indicates the answer. Note that V_2, the balance at the end of the second year, is found as follows:

$$V_2 = V_1 (1 + i) = P_0 (1 + i) (1 + i) = P_0 (1 + i)^2.$$

Similarly, V_3, the balance after three years, is found as:

$$V_3 = V_2 (1 + i) = P_0 (1 + i)^3.$$

Table 11.1
Compound Interest Calculations

Period	Beginning Amount	$\times (1 + i) =$	Ending Amount (V_t)
1	$1,000	1.05	$1,050
2	1,050	1.05	1,102
3	1,102	1.05	1,158
4	1,158	1.05	1,216
5	1,216	1.05	1,276

In general, V_t, the compound amount at the end of any year t, is found as:

$$V_t = P_0 (1 + i)^t. \tag{11.2}$$

Equation 11.2 is the fundamental equation of compound interest. Equation 11.1 is simply a special case of Equation 11.2, where $t = 1$.

While an understanding of the derivation of Equation 11.2 will facilitate the understanding of much of the remaining material in this chapter (and in subsequent chapters), the concept can be applied quite readily in a mechanical sense. Tables have been constructed for values of $(1 + i)^t$ for wide ranges of i and t. Table 11.2 is illustrative, although Table A.1 (in Appendix A at the end of the book) is more complete.

Letting CVIF (compound value interest factor) $= (1 + i)^t$, Equation 11.2 can be written as $V_t = P_0$ (CVIF). It is necessary only to go to an appropriate interest table to find the proper interest factor. For example, the correct interest factor for the illustration given in Table 11.1 can be found in Table 11.2. Look down the period column to 5, then across this row to the appropriate number in the 5 percent column to find the interest factor, 1.276. Then, using this interest factor, the compound value of the $1,000 after five years is:

$$V_5 = P_0 \text{(CVIF)} = \$1,000 (1.276) = \$1,276.$$

This is precisely the same figure that was obtained by the long method in Table 11.1.

Table 11.2
Compound Value of $1 (CVIF)

Period	1%	2%	3%	4%	5%	6%	7%	8%	9%	10%
1	1.010	1.020	1.030	1.040	1.050	1.060	1.070	1.080	1.090	1.100
2	1.020	1.040	1.061	1.082	1.102	1.124	1.145	1.166	1.188	1.210
3	1.030	1.061	1.093	1.125	1.158	1.191	1.225	1.260	1.295	1.331
4	1.041	1.082	1.126	1.170	1.216	1.262	1.311	1.360	1.412	1.464
5	1.051	1.104	1.159	1.217	1.276	1.338	1.403	1.469	1.539	1.611
6	1.062	1.126	1.194	1.265	1.340	1.419	1.501	1.587	1.677	1.772
7	1.072	1.149	1.230	1.316	1.407	1.504	1.606	1.714	1.828	1.949
8	1.083	1.172	1.267	1.369	1.477	1.594	1.718	1.851	1.993	2.144
9	1.094	1.195	1.305	1.423	1.551	1.689	1.838	1.999	2.172	2.358
10	1.105	1.219	1.344	1.480	1.629	1.791	1.967	2.159	2.367	2.594
11	1.116	1.243	1.384	1.539	1.710	1.898	2.105	2.332	2.580	2.853
12	1.127	1.268	1.426	1.601	1.796	2.012	2.252	2.518	2.813	3.138
13	1.138	1.294	1.469	1.665	1.886	2.133	2.410	2.720	3.066	3.452
14	1.149	1.319	1.513	1.732	1.980	2.261	2.579	2.937	3.342	3.797
15	1.161	1.346	1.558	1.801	2.079	2.397	2.759	3.172	3.642	4.177

Graphic View of the Compounding Process: Growth

Figure 11.1 shows how the interest factors for compounding grow as the compounding period increases. Curves can be drawn for any interest rate, including fractional rates; we have plotted curves for 0 percent, 5 percent, and 10 percent from data in Table 11.2.

Figure 11.1 shows how $1 (or any other sum) grows over time at various rates of interest. The higher the rate of interest, the faster the rate of growth. The interest rate is, in fact, the growth rate; if a deposited sum earns 5 percent, then the funds on deposit grow at the rate of 5 percent per year.

Present Value

Suppose you are offered the alternative of either $1,276 at the end of five years or X dollars today. There is no question that the $1,276 will be paid in full (perhaps the payer is the United States government). Having no current need for the money, you deposit it in a savings association paying a 5 percent dividend; the 5 percent is your "opportunity cost." How small must X be to induce you to accept the promise of $1,276 five years hence?

Table 11.1 shows that the initial amount of $1,000 growing at 5 percent a year yields $1,276 at the end of five years. Thus, you should be indifferent about the choice between $1,000 today and $1,276 at the end of five years. The $1,000 is the present value of $1,276 due in five years when the applicable interest rate is 5 percent. The subscript zero in the term P_0 indicates the present. Hence present value quantities can be identified by either P_0 or PV.

Finding present values (*discounting,* as it is commonly called) is simply

Figure 11.1
Relationships among Compound
Value Interest Factors, Interest
Rates, and Time

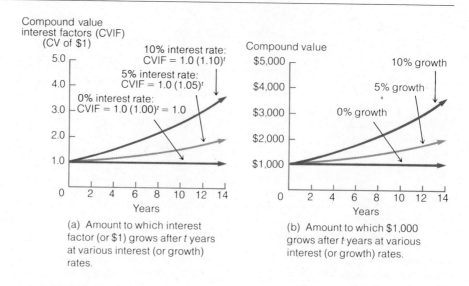

(a) Amount to which interest factor (or $1) grows after *t* years at various interest (or growth) rates.

(b) Amount to which $1,000 grows after *t* years at various interest (or growth) rates.

the reverse of compounding, and Equation 11.2 can readily be transformed into a present value formula.

$$\text{Present value} = P_0 = \frac{V_t}{(1 + i)^t} = V_t \left[\frac{1}{(1 + i)^t} \right]. \tag{11.3}$$

Tables have been constructed for the bracketed term for various values of *i* and *t*. Table 11.3 is an example, but Table A.2 (in Appendix A at the end of

Table 11.3
Present Values of $1 (PVIF)

Period	1%	2%	3%	4%	5%	6%	7%	8%	9%	10%	12%	14%	15%
1	0.990	0.980	0.971	0.962	0.952	0.943	0.935	0.926	0.917	0.909	0.893	0.877	0.870
2	0.980	0.961	0.943	0.925	0.907	0.890	0.873	0.857	0.842	0.826	0.797	0.769	0.756
3	0.971	0.942	0.915	0.889	0.864	0.840	0.816	0.794	0.772	0.751	0.712	0.675	0.658
4	0.961	0.924	0.889	0.855	0.823	0.792	0.763	0.735	0.708	0.683	0.636	0.592	0.572
5	0.951	0.906	0.863	0.822	0.784	0.747	0.713	0.681	0.650	0.621	0.567	0.519	0.497
6	0.942	0.888	0.838	0.790	0.746	0.705	0.666	0.630	0.596	0.564	0.507	0.456	0.432
7	0.933	0.871	0.813	0.760	0.711	0.665	0.623	0.583	0.547	0.513	0.452	0.400	0.376
8	0.923	0.853	0.789	0.731	0.677	0.627	0.582	0.540	0.502	0.467	0.404	0.351	0.327
9	0.914	0.837	0.766	0.703	0.645	0.592	0.544	0.500	0.460	0.424	0.361	0.308	0.284
10	0.905	0.820	0.744	0.676	0.614	0.558	0.508	0.463	0.422	0.386	0.322	0.270	0.247

the book) is more complete. For the case being considered, look down the 5 percent column in Table 11.3 to the fifth row. The figure shown there, 0.784, is the present value interest factor (PVIF) used to determine the present value of $1,276 payable in five years, discounted at 5 percent.

$$P_0 = V_5 \text{ (PVIF)}$$
$$= \$1,276 \text{ (0.784)}$$
$$= \$1,000.$$

Graphic View of the Discounting Process

Figure 11.2 shows how the interest factors for discounting decrease as the discounting period increases. The curves in the figure, plotted from data in Table 11.3, show that the present value of a sum to be received at some future date decreases (1) as the payment date is extended further into the future and (2) as the discount rate increases. If relatively high discount rates apply, funds due in the future are worth very little today; even at relatively low discount rates, funds due in the distant future are not worth much today. For example, $1,000 due in ten years is worth $247 today if the discount rate is 15 percent, but it is worth $614 today at a 5 percent discount rate. Similarly, $1,000 due in ten years at 10 percent is worth $386 today, but the same amount at the same discount rate due in five years is worth $621 today.[1]

Compound Value versus Present Value

Because a thorough understanding of compound value concepts is vital to understanding the remainder of this book and because the subject gives many students trouble, it will be useful to examine in more detail the relationship between compounding and discounting.

Notice that Equation 11.2, the basic equation for compounding, is developed from the logical sequence set forth in Table 11.1; the equation merely presents in mathematical form the steps outlined in the table. The present value interest factor ($PVIF_{i,t}$) in Equation 11.3 (the basic equation for discounting or finding present values) is the reciprocal of the compound value interest factor ($CVIF_{i,t}$) for the same i,t combination:

$$PVIF_{i,t} = \frac{1}{CVIF_{i,t}}.$$

For example, the *compound value* interest factor for 5 percent over five years is seen in Table 11.2 to be 1.276. The *present value* interest factor for 5 percent over five years must therefore be the reciprocal of 1.276:

---

1. Note that Figure 11.2 is not a mirror image of Figure 11.1. The curves in Figure 11.1 approach ∞ as t increases; in Figure 11.2, the curves approach zero, not $-∞$, as t increases.

**Figure 11.2
Relationships among Present
Value Interest Factors, Interest
Rates, and Time**

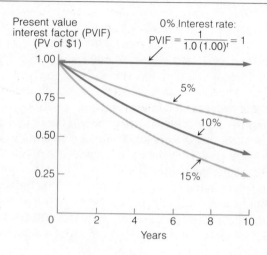

$$PVIF_{5\%,\ 5\ years} = \frac{1}{1.276} = 0.784.$$

The PVIF found in this manner must, of course, correspond with the PVIF shown in Table 11.3.

The reciprocal nature of the relationship between present value and compound value permits us to find present values in two ways—by multiplying or by dividing. Thus the present value of $1,000 due in five years and discounted at 5 percent can be found as:

$$P_0 = PV = V_t\ (PVIF_{i,\ t}) = V_t \left(\frac{1}{1+i}\right)^t = \$1,000\ (0.784) = \$784,$$

or

$$P_0 = PV = \frac{V_t}{CVIF_{i,\ t}} = \frac{V_t}{(1+i)^t} = \frac{\$1,000}{1.276} = \$784.$$

In the second form, it is easy to see why the present value of a given future amount (V_t) declines as the discount rate increases.

To conclude this comparison of present and compound values, compare Figures 11.1 and 11.2. Notice that the vertical intercept is at 1.0 in each case, but compound value interest factors rise while present value interest factors decline. The reason for this divergence is, of course, that present value factors are reciprocals of compound factors.

Compound Value of an Annuity

An *annuity* is defined as a series of payments of a fixed amount for a specified number of years. Each payment occurs at the end of the year:[2] For example, a promise to pay $1,000 a year for three years is a three-year annuity. If you were to receive such an annuity and were to deposit each annual payment in a savings account paying 5 percent interest, how much would you have at the end of three years? The answer is shown graphically in Figure 11.3. The first payment is made at the end of year 1, the second at the end of year 2, and the third at the end of year 3. The last payment is not compounded at all; the next to the last is compounded for one year; the second from the last for two years, and so on back to the first, which is compounded for $t - 1$ years. When the compound values of each of the payments are added, their total is the sum of the annuity. In the example, this total is $3,152.

Figure 11.3
Graphic Illustration of an Annuity:
Compound Sum

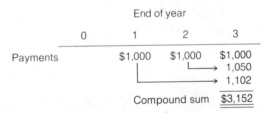

Expressed algebraically, with S_t defined as the compound sum, a as the periodic receipt, t as the length of the annuity, and $CVIF_a$ as the compound value interest factor for an annuity, the formula for S_t is:

$$S_t = a(1 + i)^{t-1} + a(1 + i)^{t-2} + \cdots + a(1 + i)^1 + a(1 + i)^0$$

$$= a[(1 + i)^{t-1} + (1 + i)^{t-2} + \cdots + (1 + i)^1 + (1 + i)^0]$$

$$= a[CVIF_a]. \tag{11.4}$$

The expression in brackets, $CVIF_a$, has been given values for various combinations of t and i. An illustrative set of these annuity interest factors is given in Table 11.4; a more complete set appears in Table A.3 in Appendix A. To find the answer to the three-year, $1,000 annuity problem, simply refer to Table 11.4, look down the 5 percent column to the row for the third year,

2. Had the payment been made at the beginning of the period, each receipt would simply have been shifted back one year. The annuity would have been called an *annuity due;* the one in the present discussion, where payments are made at the end of each period, is called a *regular annuity* or, sometimes, a *deferred annuity.*

and multiply the factor 3.152 by $1,000. The answer is the same as the one derived by the long method illustrated in Figure 11.3:

$$S_t = a \times \text{CVIF}_a$$
$$S_3 = \$1{,}000 \times 3.152 = \$3{,}152.$$

Notice that CVIF_a for the sum of an annuity is always *larger* than the number of years the annuity runs.

Present Value of an Annuity

Suppose you were offered the following alternatives: a three-year annuity of $1,000 a year or a lump-sum payment today. You have no need for the money during the next three years, so if you accept the annuity you will simply deposit the money in a savings account paying 5 percent interest. How large must the lump-sum payment be to make it equivalent to the annuity? Figure 11.4 helps explain the problem.

The present value of the first receipt is $a[1/(1 + i)]$, that of the second is $a[1/(1 + i)]^2$, and so on. Defining the present value of an annuity of t years as PV_{at} and the present value interest factor for an annuity as PVIF_a, we can write the following equation:

$$\text{PV}_{at} = a\left[\frac{1}{1+i}\right] + a\left[\frac{1}{1+i}\right]^2 + \cdots + a\left[\frac{1}{1+i}\right]^t$$

$$= a\left[\frac{1}{(1+i)} + \frac{1}{(1+i)^2} + \cdots + \frac{1}{(1+i)^t}\right]$$

$$= a[\text{PVIF}_a]. \tag{11.5}$$

Again, tables have been worked out for the PVIF_a, the term in the brackets. Table 11.5 is illustrative; a more complete table is found in Table A.4 in Ap-

**Table 11.4
Sum of an Annuity of $1 for t
Years (CVIF$_a$)**

Period	1%	2%	3%	4%	5%	6%	7%	8%
1	1.000	1.000	1.000	1.000	1.000	1.000	1.000	1.000
2	2.010	2.020	2.030	2.040	2.050	2.060	2.070	2.080
3	3.030	3.060	3.091	3.122	3.152	3.184	3.215	3.246
4	4.060	4.122	4.184	4.246	4.310	4.375	4.440	4.506
5	5.101	5.204	5.309	5.416	5.526	5.637	5.751	5.867
6	6.152	6.308	6.468	6.633	6.802	6.975	7.153	7.336
7	7.214	7.434	7.662	7.898	8.142	8.394	8.654	8.923
8	8.286	8.583	8.892	9.214	9.549	9.897	10.260	10.637
9	9.369	9.755	10.159	10.583	11.027	11.491	11.978	12.488
10	10.462	10.950	11.464	12.006	12.578	13.181	13.816	14.487

Figure 11.4
Graphic Illustration of an Annuity:
Present Value

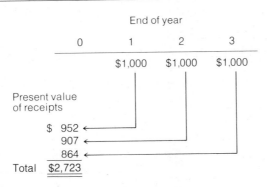

pendix A. From Table 11.5, the PVIF$_a$ for a three-year, 5 percent annuity is found to be 2.723. Multiplying this factor by the $1,000 annual receipt gives $2,723, the present value of the annuity:

$$PV_{at} = a \times PVIF_a \qquad (11.6)$$
$$PV_{a3} = \$1,000 \times 2.723$$
$$= \$2,723.$$

Notice that PVIF$_a$ for the present value of an annuity is always less than the number of years the annuity runs, whereas CVIF$_a$ for the sum of an annuity is larger than the number of years.

Table 11.5
Present Value of an Annuity of $1

Period	1%	2%	3%	4%	5%	6%	7%	8%	9%	10%
1	0.990	0.980	0.971	0.962	0.952	0.943	0.935	0.926	0.917	0.909
2	1.970	1.942	1.913	1.886	1.859	1.833	1.808	1.783	1.759	1.736
3	2.941	2.884	2.829	2.775	2.723	2.673	2.624	2.577	2.531	2.487
4	3.902	3.808	3.717	3.630	3.546	3.465	3.387	3.312	3.240	3.170
5	4.853	4.713	4.580	4.452	4.329	4.212	4.100	3.993	3.890	3.791
6	5.795	5.601	5.417	5.242	5.076	4.917	4.766	4.623	4.486	4.355
7	6.728	6.472	6.230	6.002	5.786	5.582	5.389	5.206	5.033	4.868
8	7.652	7.325	7.020	6.733	6.463	6.210	6.971	5.747	5.535	5.335
9	8.566	8.162	7.786	7.435	7.108	6.802	6.515	6.247	5.985	5.759
10	9.471	8.983	8.530	8.111	7.722	7.360	7.024	6.710	6.418	6.145

Annual Payments for Accumulation of a Future Sum

Thus far in the chapter all the equations have been based on Equation 11.2. The present value equation merely involves a transposition of Equation 11.2, and the annuity equations merely take the sum of the basic compound interest equation for different values of t. We now examine some additional modifications of the equations.

Suppose we want to know the amount of money that must be deposited at 5 percent for each of the next five years in order to have $10,000 available to pay off a debt at the end of the fifth year. Dividing both sides of Equation 11.4 by $CVIF_a$, we obtain:

$$a = \frac{S_t}{CVIF_a}.$$

Looking up the sum of an annuity interest factor for five years at 5 percent in Table 11.4 and dividing that figure into $10,000 we find:

$$a = \frac{\$10,000}{5.526} = \$1,810.$$

Thus, if $1,810 is deposited each year in an account paying 5 percent interest, at the end of five years the account will have accumulated $10,000. We will employ this procedure in later chapters when we discuss sinking funds set up to provide for bond retirements.

Annual Receipts from an Annuity

Suppose that on September 1, 1979, you receive an inheritance of $7,000. The money is to be used for your education and is to be spent during the academic years beginning September 1980, 1981, and 1982. If you place the money in a bank account paying 5 percent annual interest and make three equal withdrawals at each of the specified dates, how large can each withdrawal be to leave you with exactly a zero balance after the last one has been made?

The solution requires application of the present value of an annuity formula, Equation 11.6. Here, however, we know that the present value of the annuity is $7,000, and the problem is to find the three equal annual payments when the interest rate is 5 percent. This calls for dividing both sides of Equation 11.6 by $PVIF_a$ to make Equation 11.7.

$$PV_{at} = a \times PVIF_a \qquad (11.6)$$

$$a = \frac{PV_{at}}{PVIF_a}. \qquad (11.7)$$

The interest factor ($PVIF_a$) is found in Table 11.5 to be 2.723; substituting this value in Equation 11.7, we find the three equal annual withdrawals to be $2,571 a year:

$$a = \frac{\$7,000}{2.723} = \$2,570.69.$$

This particular kind of calculation frequently is used in setting up insurance and pension plan benefit schedules; it is also used to find the periodic payments necessary to retire a loan within a specified period. For example, if you want to retire a $7,000 bank loan, bearing interest at 5 percent on the unpaid balance, in three equal annual installments, the amount of each payment is $2,570.69. In this case, you are the borrower, and the bank is "buying" an annuity with a present value of $7,000.

Determining Interest Rates

In many instances the present values and cash flows associated with a payment stream are known, but the interest rate is not known. Suppose a bank offers to lend you $1,000 today if you sign a note agreeing to pay the bank $1,469 at the end of five years. What rate of interest would you be paying on the loan? To answer the question, we use Equation 11.2:

$$V_t = P_0 (1 + i)^t = P_0 (\text{CVIF}). \tag{11.2}$$

We simply solve for CVIF, then look up this value of CVIF in Table 11.2 (or A.1) under the row for the fifth year:

$$\text{CVIF} = \frac{V_5}{P_0} = \frac{\$1,469}{\$1,000} = 1.469.$$

Looking across the row for the fifth year, we find the value 1.469 in the 8 percent column; therefore, the interest rate on the loan is 8 percent.

Precisely the same approach is taken to determine the interest rate implicit in an annuity. For example, suppose a bank will lend you $2,577 if you sign a note in which you agree to pay the bank $1,000 at the end of the next three years. What interest rate is the bank charging you? To answer the question, we solve Equation 11.6 for PVIF$_a$, then look up PVIF$_a$ in Table 11.5 (or A.4):

$$\text{PV}_{at} = a \times \text{PVIF}_a \tag{11.6}$$

$$\text{PVIF}_a = \frac{\text{PV}_{a3}}{a} = \frac{\$2,577}{\$1,000} = 2.577.$$

Looking across the third-year row, we find the factor 2.577 under the 8 percent column; therefore, the bank is lending you money at 8 percent interest.

Linear Interpolation

The tables give values for even interest rates (such as 8 percent or 9 percent). Suppose you need to find the present value of $1,000 due in ten years and discounted at 8¼ percent. The appropriate PVIF is not in the tables, but a very close approximation to the correct factor can be estimated by the method of *linear interpolation*. The PVIF for 8 percent, ten years, is 0.463; that for 9 percent is 0.422. The difference is 0.041. Since $8^1/4$ is 25 percent of the way between 8 and 9, we can subtract 25 percent of 0.041 from 0.463 and obtain 0.453 as the PVIF for $8^1/4$ percent due in ten years. Thus, if the appropriate discount rate is $8^1/4$ percent, $1,000 due in ten years is worth $453 today.

In general, the formula used for interpolation is as follows:

$$\text{IF for intermediate interest rate} = \left(\frac{i - i_L}{i_H - i_L}\right)(IF_H - IF_L) + IF_L. \quad \textbf{(11.7)}$$

Here i is the interest rate in question, i_L is the interest rate in the table just lower than i, i_H is the interest rate in the table just higher than i, and IF_H and IF_L are the interest factors for i_H and i_L, respectively. Using the equation with the preceding example, we have:

$$\text{PVIF for } 8^1/4\% \text{ due in 10 years} = \left(\frac{8.25 - 8}{9 - 8}\right)(.422 - .463) + .463$$

$$= \left(\frac{.25}{1}\right)(-.041) + .463 = .453,$$

which is the PVIF found above. The equation can be used for each type of factor expression, PVIF, CVIF, $PVIF_a$, or $CVIF_a$.

Interpolation can also be used to determine interest rates, given interest factors. For example, suppose an investment that costs $163,500 promises to yield $50,000 per year for four years, and we want to know the rate of return on the investment. We use Equation 11.6 to find the $PVIF_a$:

$$PVIF_a = \frac{\$163,500}{\$50,000} = 3.27.$$

Looking this value up in Table 11.5, period 4, we see that it lies between 8 and 9 percent. Applying the interpolation formula, but solving for i, we have:

$$PVIF_a \text{ for } i\% = 3.27 = \left(\frac{i - 8}{9 - 8}\right)(3.240 - 3.312) + 3.312$$

$$3.27 = (i - 8)(-.072) + 3.312$$

$$-.042 = -.072i + .576$$

$$.072i = .618$$

$$i = 8.58\%.$$

Present Value of an Uneven Series of Receipts	The definition of an annuity includes the words *fixed amount;* in other words, annuities deal with constant, or level, payments or receipts. Although many financial decisions do involve constant payments, many others (especially those dealt with in the next chapter) are concerned with uneven flows

of cash. Consequently it is necessary to expand our analysis to deal with varying payment streams. Since most of the applications call for present values, not compound sums or other figures, this section is restricted to the present value (PV).

To illustrate the calculating procedure, suppose someone offers to sell you a series of payments consisting of $300 after one year, $100 after two years, and $200 after three years. How much will you be willing to pay for the series, assuming the appropriate discount rate (interest rate) is 6 percent? To determine the purchase price, we simply compute the present value of the series; the calculations are worked out in Table 11.6. The receipts for each year are shown in the second column; the discount factors (from Table 11.3) are given in the third column; and the product of these two columns, the present value of each individual receipt, is given in the last column. When the individual present values in the last column are added together, the sum is the present value of the investment—$539.90. Under the assumptions of the example, you should be willing to pay this amount for the investment.

Table 11.6
Calculating the Present Value of an Uneven Series of Payments

Period	Receipt	× Interest Factor (PVIF)	= Present Value (PV or P_0)
1	$300	0.943	$282.90
2	100	0.890	89.00
3	200	0.840	168.00
		PV of investment	$539.90

6%

If the series of payments are somewhat different—say $300 at the end of the first year, $200 at the end of the second year, then eight annual payments of $100 each—we will probably want to use a different procedure for finding the investment's present value. We can, of course, set up a calculating table such as Table 11.6, but because most of the payments are part of an annuity, we can use a short cut. The calculating procedure is shown in Table 11.7, and the logic of the table is diagramed in Figure 11.5.

Table 11.7
Calculating Procedure for an Uneven Series of Payments That Includes an Annuity

1. PV of $300 due in one year = $300 (0.943) = $ 282.90
   PV of $200 due in two years = $200 (0.890) =   178.00
2. PV of eight-year annuity with $100 receipts
   a. PV at beginning of year 3: $100 (6.210) = $621.00
   b. PV of $673.30 = $621.00 (0.890) =   552.69
3. PV of total series = $1,013.59

Figure 11.5
Graphic Illustration of Present
Value Calculations for an Uneven
Series of Payments That Includes
an Annuity

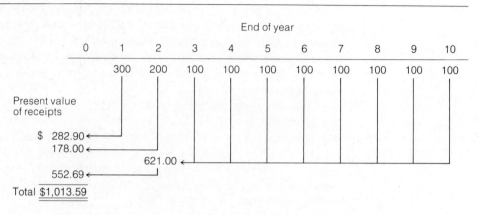

Section 1 of Table 11.7 deals with the $300 and the $200 received at the end of the first and second years, respectively; their present values are found to be $282.90 and $178. Section 2 deals with the eight $100 payments. In Part a, the value of a $100, eight-year, 6 percent annuity is found to be $621.00. However, the first receipt under the annuity comes at the end of the third year, so it is worth less than $621.00 today. Specifically, it is worth the present value of $621.00, discounted back two years at 6 percent, or $552.69; this calculation is shown in Part b of Section 2.[3] When the present values of the first two payments are added to the present value of the annuity component, the sum is the present value of the entire investment, or $1,013.59.

Semiannual and Other Compounding Periods[4]

In all the examples used thus far, it has been assumed that returns were received annually. For example, in the section dealing with compound values, it was assumed that funds were placed on deposit in a savings and loan association and grew by 6 percent a year. However, suppose the advertised rate had been 6 percent compounded semiannually. What would this have meant? Consider the following example.

You deposit $1,000 in a bank savings account and receive a return of 6

3. The present value of the annuity portion, $552.69, could also have been found by subtracting the PVIF$_a$ for a two-year annuity from the PVIF$_a$ for a ten-year annuity, then multiplying the result by $100.
4. This section can be omitted without loss of continuity.

percent compounded semiannually. How much will you have at the end of one year? Semiannual compounding means that interest is actually paid each six months, a fact taken into account in the tabular calculations in Table 11.8. Here, the annual interest rate is divided by two, but twice as many compounding periods are used because interest is paid twice a year. Comparing the amount on hand at the end of the second six-month period, $1,060.90, with what would have been on hand under annual compounding, $1,060, shows that semiannual compounding is better for the saver. This result occurs, of course, because the saver earns interest on interest more frequently.

Table 11.8
Compound Interest Calculations
with Semiannual Compounding

Period	Beginning Amount (P_0)	$\times$	$(1 + i)$	=	Ending Amount (P_t)
1	$1,000.00		(1.03)		$1,030.00
2	1,030.00		(1.03)		1,060.90

General formulas can be developed for use when compounding periods are more frequent than once a year. To demonstrate this, Equation 11.2 is modified as follows:

$$V_t = P_0 (1 + i)^t. \tag{11.2}$$

$$V_t = P_0 \left(1 + \frac{i}{q}\right)^{qt}. \tag{11.8}$$

Here, q is the number of times per year compounding occurs. When banks compute daily interest, the value of q is set at 365, and Equation 11.8 is applied.

The interest tables can be used when compounding occurs more than once a year. Simply divide the nominal, or stated, interest rate by the number of times compounding occurs, and multiply the years by the number of compounding periods per year. For example, to find the amount to which $1,000 will grow after five years if semiannual compounding is applied to a stated 6 percent interest rate, divide 6 percent by two and multiply the five years by two. Then look in Table 11.2 (or Table A.1) under the 3 percent column and in the row for the tenth period, where you will find an interest factor of 1.344. Multiplying this by the initial $1,000 gives a value of $1,344, the amount to which $1,000 will grow in five years at 6 percent compounded semiannually. This compares with $1,338 for annual compounding.

The same procedure is applied in all the cases covered—compounding, discounting, single payments, and annuities. To illustrate semiannual compounding in finding the present value of an annuity, for example, consider the case described in the section on present value of an annuity; $1,000 a year for three years, discounted at 6 percent. With annual discounting or compounding the interest factor is 2.673, and the present value of the annuity is $2,673. For semiannual compounding look under the 3 percent column and in the year 6 row of Table 11.5 to find an interest factor of 5.417. Then multiply by half of $1,000, or the $500 received each six months, to get the present value of the annuity, $2,708.50. The payments come a little more rapidly (the first $500 is paid after only six months) so the annuity is a little more valuable if payments are received semiannually rather than annually.

By letting q approach infinity, Equation 11.8 can be modified to the special case of *continuous compounding*. Continuous compounding is extremely useful in theoretical finance, and it also has practical applications. For example, some banks and savings and loan associations pay interest on a continuous basis.

A Special Case of Semiannual Compounding: Bond Values[5]

Most bonds pay interest semiannually, so semiannual compounding procedures are appropriate for determining bond values. To illustrate: Suppose a particular bond pays interest in the amount of $30 each six months, or $60 a year. The bond will mature in ten years, paying $1,000 (the "principal") at that time. Thus, if you buy the bond you will receive an annuity of $30 each six months, or twenty payments in total, plus $1,000 at the end of ten years (or twenty six-month periods). What is the bond worth, assuming that the appropriate market discount (or interest) rate is (a) 6 percent; (b) higher than 6 percent, say 8 percent; and (c) lower than 6 percent, say 4 percent?

At 6 Percent Interest
Step 1. You are buying an annuity plus a lump sum of $1,000. Find the PV of the interest payments:

1. Use $i/q = 6\%/2 = 3\%$ as the "interest rate."
2. Look up the $PVIF_a$ in Table A.4 for 20 periods at 3 percent, which is 14.877.
3. Find the PV of the stream of interest payments:

$$\text{PV of the interest} = \$30\ (PVIF_a)$$

$$= \$30\ (14.877) = \$446.$$

Step 2. Find the PV of the $1,000 maturity value:

1. Use $i/q = 6\%/2 = 3\%$ as the "interest rate."

---

5. This section can be omitted without loss of continuity. The topic is also covered in Chapter 15.

2. Look up the PVIF in Table A.2 for 20 periods at 3 percent, which is .554.
3. Find the PV of that value at maturity:

PV of the maturity value = $1,000 (PVIF)

$$= \$1,000\ (.554) = \$554.$$

Step 3. Combine the two component PVs to determine the value of the bond:

Bond value = $446 + $554 = $1,000.

At 8 Percent Interest Repeating the process, we have:

Step 1. 8%/2 = 4% = the "interest rate."

$PVIF_a$ from Table A.4 = 13.59.

PVIF from Table A.2 = .456.

Step 2. Bond value = $30 (13.59) + $1,000 (.456)

$$= \$408 + \$456$$

$$= \$864.$$

Notice that the bond is worth less when the going rate of interest for investments of similar risk is 8 percent than when it is 6 percent. At a price of $864, this bond provides an annual rate of return of 8 percent; at a price of $1,000, it provides an annual return of 6 percent. If 6 percent is the coupon rate on a bond of a given degree of risk, then whenever interest rates in the economy rise to the point where bonds of this degree of risk have an 8 percent return, the price of our bond will decline to $864, at which price it will yield the competitive rate of return, 8 percent.

At 4 Percent Interest Using the same process produces the following results:

Step 1. 4%/2 = 2% = the "interest rate."

$PVIF_a$ from Table A.4 = 16.351.

PVIF from Table A.2 = .673.

Step 2. Bond value = $30 (16.351) + $1,000 (.673)

$$= \$491 + \$673 = \$1,164.$$

The bond is worth *more* than $1,000 when the going rate of interest is less than 6 percent, because then it offers a yield higher than the going rate. Its price rises to $1,164, where it provides a 4 percent annual rate of return. This calculation illustrates the fact that when interest rates in the economy decline, the prices of outstanding bonds rise.

Appropriate Compounding or Discounting Rates

Throughout the chapter, assumed compounding or discounting rates have been used in the examples. Although we provided some background in Chapter 2, it is useful at this point to summarize what the appropriate interest rate for a particular investment might be.[6]

The starting point is, of course, the general level of interest rates (for each type of investment) in the economy as a whole, which is set by the interaction of supply and demand forces.

There is no single rate of interest in the economy; at any given time, there is an array of different rates. The lowest rates are set on the safest investments and the highest rates on the most risky ones. Usually, there is less risk on investments that mature in the near future than on longer-term investments, so higher rates are usually associated with long-term investments.

People who have money to invest can buy short-term United States government securities and incur no risk whatever. However, they generally must accept a relatively low yield on investment. Those willing to assume a little more risk can invest in high-grade corporate bonds and get a higher fixed rate of return. And people willing to accept still more risk can move into common stocks to obtain variable (and, they hope, higher) returns (dividends plus capital gains) on investment. Still other alternatives are bank and savings and loan deposits, long-term government bonds, mortgages, apartment houses, land held for speculation, and various forms of international securities and investments.

Risk Premiums

With only a limited amount of money to invest, one must pick and choose among investments, the final selection involving a tradeoff between risk and return. Suppose, for example, that you are indifferent about the choice of a five-year government bond yielding 7 percent a year, a five-year corporate bond yielding 9 percent, and a share of stock on which you can expect a 12 percent return. Given this situation, the government bond is assumed to be a riskless security, a 2 percent risk premium is attached to the corporate bond, and a 5 percent risk premium is attached to the share of stock. Risk premiums, then, are the added returns that risky investments must command over less risky ones if there is to be a demand for them. (The concept of the risk premium is discussed in more detail in Chapters 13, 14, and 16.)

Opportunity Costs

Although there are many potential investments available in the economy at any given time, individual investors actively consider only a limited number

6. For convenience, in this chapter we speak of *interest rates,* which implies that only debt is involved. In later chapters the concept is broadened considerably, and the term *rate of return* is used in lieu of *interest rate.*

of them. After making adjustments for risk differentials, they rank the various alternatives from most attractive to least attractive. Then, presumably, they put their available funds into the most attractive investment. If they are offered a new investment, they must compare it with the best of the existing alternatives. If they take the new investment, they must give up the opportunity of investing in the best of the old alternatives. *The yield on the best of the alternatives is defined as the opportunity cost of investing in the new alternative.* For example, suppose you have funds invested in a bank time deposit that pays 6 percent. Now someone offers you another investment of equal risk. To make the new investment, you must withdraw funds from the bank deposit; therefore, 6 percent is the opportunity cost of the new investment.

The interest rates used in the examples throughout this chapter were all determined as opportunity costs available to the person in the example. This concept is also used in the following chapter, where we consider business decisions on investments in projects or assets—the *capital budgeting decision.*

Summary

A knowledge of compound interest and present value techniques is essential to an understanding of many important aspects of finance: capital budgeting, financial structure, security valuation, and many other topics.

Compound value *(V$_t$)*, or compound amount, is defined as the sum to which a beginning amount of principal (P$_0$) will grow over *t* years when interest is earned at the rate of *i* percent a year. The equation for finding compound value is:

$$V_t = P_0 (1 + i)^t.$$

Tables giving the compound value of $1 for a large number of different years and interest rates have been prepared. The compound value of $1 is called the compound value interest factor (CVIF); illustrative values are given in Table 11.2, and a more complete set of interest factors is given in Appendix Table A.1.

The present value of a future payment (PV) is the amount that, if we had it now and if we invested it at the specified interest rate *(i)*, would equal the future payment (V$_t$) on the date the future payment is due. For example, if you were to receive $1,276 after five years and if you decide that 5 percent is the appropriate interest rate (called the *discount rate* when computing present values), then you could find the present value of the $1,276 by applying the following equation:

$$PV = V_t \left[\frac{1}{(1+i)^t} \right] = \$1,276 \,[\,0.784\,] = \$1,000.$$

The term in brackets is called the present value interest factor (PVIF), and values for it have been worked out in Table 11.3 and Appendix Table A.2.

An *annuity* is defined as a series of payments of a fixed amount *(a)* for a specified number of years. The compound value of an annuity is the total amount one will have at the end of the annuity period if each payment is invested at a certain interest rate and is held to the end of the annuity period. For example, suppose we have a three-year, $1,000 annuity invested at 5 percent. There are formulas for annuities, but tables are available for the relevant interest factors. The $CVIF_a$ for the compound value of a three-year annuity at 5 percent is 3.152, and it can be used to find the present value of the illustrative annuity:

$$\text{Compound value} = CVIF_a \times \text{Annual receipt} = 3.152 \times \$1,000 = \$3,152.$$

Thus, $3,152 is the compound value of the annuity.

The present value of an annuity is the lump sum one would need to have on hand today in order to be able to withdraw equal amounts *(a)* each year and end up with a balance exactly equal to zero at the end of the annuity period. For example, if you wish to withdraw $1,000 a year for three years, you could deposit $2,723 today in a bank account paying 5 percent interest, withdraw the $1,000 in each of the next three years, and end up with a zero balance. Thus, $2,723 is the present value of an annuity of $1,000 a year for three years when the appropriate discount rate is 5 percent. Again, tables are available for finding the present value of annuities. To use them, we simply look up the interest factor ($PVIF_a$) for the appropriate number of years and interest rate, then multiply the $PVIF_a$ by the annual receipt:

$$\text{PV of annuity} = PVIF_a \times \text{Annual receipt} = 2.723 \times \$1,000 = \$2,723.$$

All interest factors given in the tables are for $1; for example, 2.723 is the $PVIF_a$ for finding the present value of a three-year annuity. It must be multiplied by the annual receipt ($1,000 in the example) to find the actual value of the annuity. Students—and even financial managers—sometimes make careless mistakes when looking up interest factors, using the wrong table for the purpose. This can be avoided by recognizing the following sets of relations:

1. *Compound value, single payment.* The CVIF for the compound value of a single payment, with normal interest rates and holding periods, is *always* more than 1.0 but seldom more than about 3.0.
2. *Present value, single payment.* The PVIF for the present value of a single payment is *always* less than 1.0 (for example, 0.784 is the PVIF for 5 percent held for five years). CVIF is, of course, more than 1.0.
3. *Compound value of an annuity.* The $CVIF_a$ for the compound value of an annuity is *always* greater than the number of years the annuity has to run. (For example, the $CVIF_a$ for a three-year annuity is greater than 3.0,

while the CVIF$_a$ for a ten-year annuity is greater than 10.0.) Just how much greater depends on the interest rate. At low rates the interest factor is slightly greater than the number of years; at high rates it is very much greater.

4. *Present value of an annuity.* The PVIF$_a$ for the present value of an annuity is always less than the number of years it has to run. (For example, the PVIF$_a$ for the present value of a three-year annuity is less than 3.0; at high rates it is very much less than 3.0.)

The four basic interest formulas can be used in combination to find such things as the present value of an uneven series of receipts. The formulas can also be transformed to find (1) the annual payments necessary to accumulate a future sum, (2) the annual receipts from a specified annuity, (3) the periodic payments necessary to amortize a loan, and (4) the interest rate implicit in a loan contract.

The appropriate interest rate to be used is critical when working with compound interest problems. The true nature of the interest rates to be used when working with business problems can be understood only after examining the chapters dealing with the cost of capital. Risk premiums and opportunity costs are important considerations in determining the most attractive investments.

Questions

11.1 What kinds of financial decisions require explicit consideration of the interest factor?

11.2 Compound interest relationships are important for decisions other than financial ones. Why are they important to marketing managers?

11.3 Would you rather have a savings account that pays 5 percent interest compounded semiannually or one that pays 5 percent interest compounded daily? Why?

11.4 For a given interest rate and a given number of years, is the interest factor for the sum of an annuity greater or smaller than the interest factor for the present value of the annuity?

11.5 Suppose you are examining two investments, A and B. Both have the same maturity, but A pays a 6 percent return and B yields 5 percent. Which investment is probably riskier? How do you know?

Problems

11.1 Which amount is worth more at 9 percent: $1,000 today or $2,000 after eight years?

11.2 The current production target for the five-year plan of the Logo Co. is to increase output by 4 percent a year. If the 1974 production is 3.81 million tons, what is the target production for 1979?

11.3 At a growth rate of 9 percent, how long does it take a sum to double?

11.4 a. What amount will be paid for a $1,000 ten-year bond that pays $40 interest semiannually ($80 a year) and that yields 10 percent, compounded semiannually?

b. What will be paid if the bond is sold to yield 8 percent?

c. What will be paid if semiannual interest payments are $50 and the bond yields 6 percent?

11.5 On December 31, Diane Baker buys a building for $80,000, paying 20 percent down and agreeing to pay the balance in fifteen equal annual installments that are to include principal plus 8 percent compound interest on the declining balance. What are the equal installments?

11.6 The Evans Company has established a sinking fund to retire a $900,000 mortgage that matures on December 31, 1988. The company plans to put a fixed amount into the fund each year for ten years. The first payment was made on December 31, 1978; the last will be made on December 31, 1988. The company anticipates that the fund will earn 9 percent a year. What annual contributions must be made to accumulate the $900,000 as of December 31, 1988?

11.7 You have just purchased a newly issued $1,000 five-year Kelly Company bond at par. This bond (Bond A) pays $60 in interest semiannually ($120 a year). You are also negotiating the purchase of a $1,000 six-year Kelly Company bond that returns $30 in semiannual interest payments and has six years remaining before it matures (Bond B).

a What is the going rate of return on bonds of the risk and maturity of Kelly Company's bonds?

b. What should you be willing to pay for Bond B?

c. How will your answer to Part b change if Bond A pays $40 in semiannual interest instead of $60 but still sells for $1,000? (Bond B still pays $30 semiannually and $1,000 at the end of six years.)

11.8 An investment of $1,000 earns 8 percent interest per year for three years. A second investment earns 1 percent for the first and second years and 22 percent the third year.

a. What is the average (arithmetic) return on the two investments over the three years?

b. Compute the terminal value of each investment. Which is larger?

c. What is the compound rate of interest at which the initial $1,000 rises to the terminal value of each investment?

d. What is the geometric mean of the return on each project?

e. How do your results in Part d compare with your results in Part c? Comment on the implications.

11.9 You need $129,200 at the end of seventeen years. You know that the best you can do is to make equal payments into a bank account on which you can earn 5 percent interest compounded annually. Your first payment is to be made at the end of the first year.

a. What amount must you plan to pay annually to achieve your objective?

b. Instead of making annual payments, you decide to make one lump-sum payment today. To achieve your objective of $129,200 at the end of the seventeen-year period, what should this sum be? (You can still earn 5 percent interest compounded annually on your account.)

11.10 You can buy a note for $13,420. If you buy it, you will receive ten annual payments of $2,000, the first payment to be made one year from today. What rate of return, or yield, does the note offer?

11.11 You can buy a bond for $1,000 that will pay no interest during its eight-year life but will have a value of $1,851 when it matures. What rate of interest will you earn if you buy the bond and hold it to maturity?

11.12 A bank agrees to lend you $1,000 today in return for your promise to pay back $1,838 nine years from today. What rate of interest is the bank charging you?

11.13 If earnings in 1979 are $2.66 a share, while seven years earlier (in 1972) they were $1, what has been the rate of growth in earnings?

11.14 The Randolf Company's sales last year were $1 million.
   a. Assuming that sales grow 18 percent a year, calculate sales for each of the next six years.
   b. Plot the sales projections.
   c. If your graph is correct, your projected sales curve is nonlinear. If it had been linear, would this have indicated a constant, increasing, or decreasing percentage growth rate? Explain.

11.15 You are considering two investment opportunities, A and B. A is expected to pay $400 a year for the first ten years, $600 a year for the next fifteen years, and nothing thereafter. B is expected to pay $1,000 a year for ten years and nothing thereafter. You find that other investments of similar risk to A and B yield 8 percent and 14 percent, respectively.
   a. Find the present value of each investment. Show your calculations.
   b. Which is the more risky investment? Why?
   c. Assume that your rich uncle will give you a choice of A or B without cost to you and that you (1) must hold the investment for its entire life (cannot sell it), or (2) are free to sell it at its going market price. Which investment would you prefer under each of the two conditions?

11.16 The Bronson Company's common stock paid a dividend of $1 last year. Dividends are expected to grow at a rate of 18 percent for each of the next six years.
   a. Calculate the expected dividend for each of the next six years.
   b. Assuming that the first of these six dividends will be paid one year from now, what is the present value of the six dividends? (Given the riskiness of the dividend stream, 18 percent is the appropriate discount rate.)
   c. Assume that the price of the stock will be $27 six years from now. What is the present value of this "terminal value"? Use an 18 percent discount rate.
   d. Assume that you will buy the stock, receive the six dividends, then sell the stock. How much should you be willing to pay for it?
   e. Do not do any calculations for this question, but explain in words what

would happen to the price of this stock (1) if the discount rate declined because the riskiness of the stock declined, and (2) if the growth rate of the dividend stream increased.

11.17 The Programmatics Consulting Company is considering the purchase of a new computer that will provide the following net cash flow (or profit) stream:

Year

1	$10,000
2	20,000
3	30,000
4	40,000
5	50.000

a. What is the present value of the profit stream, using a 12 percent discount rate?

b. If the computer costs $100,000, should Programmatics purchase it?

11.18 The Martan Company pays $480,000 for a machine that provides savings of $50,000 per year for twenty years. What is the return on the investment in the machine?

11.19 The Gorton Company invests $60,000 in a new item of equipment. The savings from the equipment during the five years of its economic life are:

Year

1	$10,000
2	10,000
3	10,000
4	24,150
5	24,150

a. At what discount rate is it profitable for the company to make the purchase?

b. What changes would simplify the analysis?

11.20 The Brinkner Company has a cost of capital of 12 percent. It invests in a machine that provides savings of $18,000 per year for six years. What is the maximum that can be paid for the machine if it is to earn the required 12 percent cost of capital?

11.21 You are considering the economic value of an MBA. Assuming that you can and do enroll in a business school immediately, expenses are $4,000 per year and foregone income $6,000 per year for the required two years. Your expected yearly income for the following eighteen years is increased by $3,713.

a. What is the return on investment earned? (Hint: It is more than 10 percent.)

b. What are some of the major complicating factors ignored in the information presented?

11.22 The Walton Welding Company is considering the purchase of a new welding unit that will provide the following net cash flow (or profit) stream:

Year

1	$10,000
2	20,000
3	30,000
4	40,000
5	50,000
6	60,000

a. Using a 10 percent discount rate, calculate the present value of the profit stream.
b. If the unit costs $100,000, should Walton purchase it?

CHAPTER 12

CAPITAL BUDGETING TECHNIQUES

Capital budgeting involves the entire process of planning expenditures whose returns are expected to extend beyond one year. The choice of one year is arbitrary, of course, but it is a convenient cutoff point for distinguishing among kinds of expenditures. Obvious examples of capital outlays are expenditures for land, buildings, equipment, and permanent additions to working capital associated with plant expansion. Advertising or promotion campaigns and programs of research and development are also likely to have an impact beyond one year, so they too can be classified as capital budgeting expenditures.

Capital budgeting is important for the future well-being of the firm. It is also a complex, conceptually difficult topic. As we shall see later in this chapter, the optimum capital budget—the level of investment that maximizes the present value of the firm—is determined by the interaction of supply and demand forces under conditions of uncertainty. *Supply forces* refers to the supply of capital to the firm, or its *cost of capital schedule. Demand forces* relates to the investment opportunities open to the firm, as measured by the *stream of revenues* resulting from an investment decision. *Uncertainty* enters the decision because it is impossible to know exactly either the cost of capital or the stream of revenues that will be derived from a project.

To facilitate an exposition of the investment decision process, we have broken the topic down into its major components. In this chapter, we consider the capital budgeting process and the techniques generally employed by reasonably sophisticated business firms. Our focus is the time factor, and we use extensively the compound interest concepts covered in the preceding chapter. In Chapter 13 we explicitly and formally consider uncertainty, and in Chapters 14 and 16 we develop and relate the cost of capital concept to capital budgeting.

Significance of Capital Budgeting

A number of factors combine to make capital budgeting perhaps the most important decision with which financial management is involved. All departments of a firm are vitally affected by capital budgeting decisions, so all executives, no matter what their primary responsibility, must be aware of how such decisions are made.

Long-Term Effects

First and foremost, the fact that the results continue over an extended period means that the decision maker, who must make a commitment into the future, loses some flexibility. For example, the purchase of an asset with an economic life of ten years requires a long period of waiting before the final results of the action can be known. The decision maker must commit funds for this period and thus becomes a hostage of future events.

Asset expansion is fundamentally related to expected future sales. A decision to buy or to construct a fixed asset that is expected to last five years involves an implicit five-year sales forecast. Indeed, the economic life of a purchased asset represents an implicit forecast for the duration of the asset's economic life. Hence, failure to forecast accurately results in overinvestment or underinvestment in fixed assets.

An erroneous forecast of asset requirements can have serious consequences. If the firm has invested too much in fixed assets, it will incur unnecessarily heavy expenses. If it has not spent enough, two serious problems may arise: (1) the firm's equipment may not be sufficiently modern to enable it to produce competitively; and (2) if it has inadequate capacity, it may lose a portion of its share of the market to rival firms. To regain lost customers typically requires heavy selling expenses, price reductions, product improvements, and so on.

Timing the Availability of Capital Assets

Another problem is to phase the availability of capital assets so they come "on stream" at the correct time. For example, the executive vice-president of a decorative tile company gave the authors an illustration of the importance of capital budgeting. His firm tried to operate near capacity most of the time. For about four years there had been intermittent spurts in the demand for its product; when these spurts occurred, the firm had to turn away orders. After a sharp increase in demand, the firm would add capacity by renting an additional building, then purchasing and installing the appropriate equipment. It would take six to eight months to have the additional capacity ready. At this point the company frequently would find no demand for its increased output. Other firms had already expanded operations and had taken an increased share of the market, with the result that demand for this firm's products had leveled off. If the firm had properly forecast demand and had planned its increase in capacity six months or one year in advance, it would have been able to maintain its market; indeed, it might have obtained a larger share of the market.

Quality of Capital Assets

Good capital budgeting improves the timing of asset acquisitions and the quality of assets purchased; this follows from the nature of capital goods and their producers. Capital goods are not ordered by firms until they see that sales are beginning to press on capacity—an occasion that occurs simultaneously for many firms. When the heavy orders come in, the producers of capital goods go from a situation of idle capacity to one where they cannot meet all the orders placed. Consequently, large backlogs accumulate. Since the production of capital goods involves a relatively long work-in-process period, a year or more of waiting may be involved before the additional capital goods are available. This factor has obvious implications for purchasing agents and plant managers.

Raising Funds

Another important aspect of capital budgeting is that asset expansion typically involves substantial expenditures. Before a firm spends a large amount of money, it must make the proper plans, since large amounts of funds are not available automatically. A firm contemplating a major capital expenditure program may need to arrange its financing several years in advance to be sure of having the required funds.

Ability to Compete

Finally, many firms fail not because they have too much capital equipment but because they have too little. While the conservative approach of having a small amount of capital equipment may be appropriate at times, it also may be fatal if a firm's competitors install modern, automated equipment that permits them to produce a better product and sell it at a lower price. The same thing holds true for nations. If United States firms fail to modernize but those of other nations do, then the United States will be unable to compete in world markets. Thus an understanding of business investment behavior and of factors that motivate firms to undertake investment programs is vital for congressional leaders and others involved in government policy making.

A Simplified View of Capital Budgeting

Capital budgeting is, in essence, an application of a classic proposition from the economic theory of the firm—that a firm should operate at the point where its marginal revenue is just equal to its marginal cost. When this rule is applied to the capital budgeting decision, marginal revenue is taken to be the percentage rate of return on investments, while marginal cost is the firm's marginal cost of capital.

A simplified version of the concept is depicted in Figure 12.1(a). Here the horizontal axis measures the dollars of investment during a year, while the vertical axis shows both the percentage cost of capital and the rate of return on projects. The projects are denoted by boxes. Project A, for example, calls for an outlay of $3 million and promises a 17 percent rate of return; Project B requires $1 million and yields about 16 percent. The last investment, Project G, simply involves buying 4 percent government bonds, which can be purchased in unlimited quantities. In Figure 12.1(b) the concept is generalized to show smoothed investment opportunity schedules (IRR), and three alternative schedules are presented.[1]

The curve MCC designates the marginal cost of capital, or the cost of each additional dollar acquired for purposes of making capital expendi-

---

1. The investment opportunity schedules measure the rate of return on each project, which is generally called the *internal rate of return (IRR)*. This is why we label the investment opportunity schedules *IRR*. The process of calculating the IRR is explained later in the chapter.

Figure 12.1
Illustrative Capital Budgeting
Decision Process

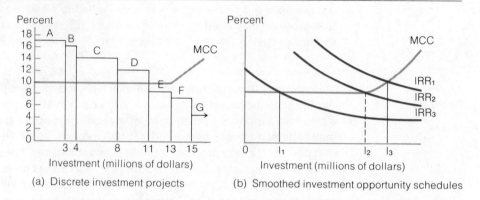

(a) Discrete investment projects

(b) Smoothed investment opportunity schedules

tures. As it is drawn in Figure 12.1(a), the marginal cost of capital is constant at 10 percent until the firm has raised $13 million, after which the curve turns up.[2] To maximize profits, the firm should accept Projects A through D, obtaining and investing $11 million, and reject E, F, and G.

Notice that three alternative investment opportunity schedules are shown in Figure 12.1(b). IRR_1 designates relatively few good projects. The three different curves could be interpreted as applying either to three different firms or to one firm at three different times. As long as the IRR curve cuts the MCC curve to the left of I_2—for example, at I_1—the marginal cost of capital is constant. To the right of I_2—for example, at I_3—the cost of capital is rising. Therefore, if investment opportunities are such that the IRR curve cuts the MCC curve to the right of I_2, the *actual* marginal cost of capital (a single point) varies depending on the IRR curve. In this chapter we generally assume that the IRR curve cuts the MCC curve to the left of I_2; this permits us to assume that the cost of capital is constant. Our assumption is relaxed in Chapter 16, where we show how the MCC varies with the amount of funds raised during a given year.

Application of the Concept

At the applied level, the capital budgeting process is much more complex than the preceding example suggests. Projects do not just appear; a continuing stream of good investment opportunities results from hard thinking, careful planning, and, often, large outlays for research and development.

2. The reasons for assuming this particular shape for the marginal cost of capital curve are explained in Chapter 16.

Moreover, some very difficult measurement problems are involved. The sales and costs associated with particular projects must be estimated, frequently for many years into the future, in the face of great uncertainty. Finally, some difficult conceptual and empirical problems arise over the methods of calculating rates of return and the cost of capital.

Businesses are required to take action, however, even in the face of the kinds of problems described; this requirement has led to the development of procedures to assist in making optimal investment decisions. One such procedure, forecasting, was discussed in Chapter 6; another, uncertainty, is discussed in formal terms in the next chapter; and still another, the cost of capital, is deferred to Chapter 16. The essentials of the other elements of capital budgeting are taken up in the remainder of this chapter.

Investment Proposals

Aside from the actual generation of ideas, the first step in the capital budgeting process is to assemble a list of the proposed new investments together with the data necessary to appraise them. Although practices vary from firm to firm, proposals dealing with asset acquisitions are frequently grouped according to the following four categories: (1) replacements, (2) expansion—additional capacity in existing product lines, (3) expansion—new product lines, and (4) other (for example, pollution control equipment). These groupings are somewhat arbitrary, and it is frequently difficult to decide the appropriate category for a particular investment. In spite of such problems, the scheme is widely used—with good reason (as we shall see).

Ordinarily, replacement decisions are the simplest to make. Assets wear out or become obsolete, and they must be replaced if production efficiency is to be maintained. The firm has a good idea of the cost savings to be obtained by replacing an old asset, and it knows the consequences of nonreplacement. All in all, the outcomes of most replacement decisions can be predicted with a high degree of confidence.

An example of the expansion of capacity is a proposal for adding more machines of a type already in use or opening another branch of a citywide chain of food stores. Expansion investments are frequently incorporated in replacement decisions. For example, an old, inefficient machine may be replaced by a larger, more efficient one.

A degree of uncertainty—sometimes extremely high—is clearly involved in expansion, but the firm at least has the advantage of examining past production and sales experience with similar machines or stores. When it considers an investment of the third kind, expansion into new product lines, little, if any, data are available on which to base decisions. To illustrate: When Union Carbide decided to develop the laser for commercial application, it had very little idea of either the development costs or the specific applications to which lasers could be put. Under such circumstances, any estimates must at best be treated as crude approximations.

The "other" category is a catchall and includes intangibles (such as a proposal to boost employee morale and productivity by installing a music system). Mandatory pollution control devices, which must be installed even though they produce no revenues, are another example of the "other" category. Major strategic decisions, such as plans for overseas expansion or mergers, can also be included here, but they are often treated separately from the regular capital budget.

Administrative Details

The remaining aspects of capital budgeting involve administrative matters. Approval is typically required at higher levels within the organization as we move away from replacement decisions and as the sums involved increase. One of the most important functions of the board of directors is to approve the major outlays in a capital budgeting program. Such decisions are crucial for the future well-being of the firm.

The planning horizon for capital budgeting programs varies with the nature of the industry. When the industry is such that sales can be forecast with a high degree of reliability for ten to twenty years, the planning period is likely to be correspondingly long. (Electric utilities are an example of this kind of industry.) Also, when the product technology developments in the industry require eight to ten years before the introduction of a new major product, as in certain segments of the aerospace industry, a correspondingly long planning period is necessary.

After a capital budget has been adopted, payments must be scheduled. Characteristically, the finance department is responsible for scheduling payments and for acquiring funds to meet payment schedule requirements. This department is also primarily responsible for cooperating with the members of operating divisions to compile systematic records on the uses of funds and of equipment purchased in capital budgeting programs. Effective programs require such information as the basis for periodic review and evaluation of capital expenditure decisions—the feedback and control phase of capital budgeting (often called the "post audit").

The foregoing represents a brief overview of the administrative aspects of capital budgeting. The analytical problems are considered next.

Analysis: Choosing among Alternative Proposals

In most firms there are more proposals for projects than the firm is either able or willing to finance. Some proposals are good; others are bad; and methods must be developed for distinguishing between them. The end product is a ranking of the proposals and a cutoff point for determining how far down the ranked list to go.

Proposals are eliminated in part because they are mutually exclusive.

Mutually exclusive proposals are alternative methods of doing the same job. If one piece of equipment is chosen to do the job, the others will not be required. Thus, if there is a need to improve the materials handling system in a chemical plant, the job may be done either by conveyer belts or by forklift trucks. The selection of one method of doing the job makes it unnecessary to use the other. They are mutually exclusive items.

Independent items are pieces of capital equipment being considered for different kinds of projects or tasks that need to be accomplished. For example, in addition to the materials handling system, the chemical firm may need equipment to package the end product—a packaging machine—and the purchase of equipment for this purpose is independent of the purchase of equipment for materials handling.

To distinguish among the many items that compete for the allocation of the firm's capital funds, a ranking procedure must be developed. This procedure requires calculating the estimated benefits from the use of equipment and then translating these benefits into a measure of the advantage of purchasing the equipment. Thus an estimate of benefits is required, and a method for converting the benefits into a ranking measure must be developed.

Importance of Good Data

Probably nothing in the entire capital budgeting procedure is of greater importance than a reliable estimate of the cost savings or revenue increases that will be achieved from the prospective outlay of capital funds. The increased output and sales revenue resulting from expansion programs are obvious benefits. Cost reduction benefits include changes in quality and quantity of direct labor; in amount and cost of scrap and rework time; in fuel costs; and in maintenance expenses, downtime, safety, flexibility, and so on. So many variables are involved that it is impossible to make neat generalizations. However, this should not minimize the crucial importance of the required analysis of benefits derived from capital expenditures. Each capital equipment expenditure must be examined in detail for possible additional costs and savings.

All the subsequent procedures for ranking projects are not better than the data input—the old saying "garbage in, garbage out" is certainly applicable to capital budgeting analysis. Thus the data assembly process is not a routine clerical task to be performed on a mechanical basis. It requires continuous monitoring and evaluation of estimates by those competent to make such evaluations—engineers, accountants, economists, cost analysts, and other qualified persons.

After costs and benefits have been estimated, they are used to rank alternative investment proposals. How this ranking is accomplished is our next topic.

Ranking Investment Proposals

The point of capital budgeting—indeed, the point of all financial analysis—is to make decisions that maximize the value of the firm's common stock. The capital budgeting process is designed to answer two questions: (1) Which of several mutually exclusive investments should be selected? (2) How many projects, in total, should be accepted?

Among the many methods used for ranking investment proposals, three are discussed here:

1. *Payback method* (or *payback period*): number of years required to return the original investment.
2. *Net present value (NPV) method:* present value of future returns discounted at the appropriate cost of capital, minus the cost of the investment.
3. *Internal rate of return (IRR) method:* interest rate that equates the present value of future returns to the investment outlay.[3]

Future returns are defined as the net income after taxes, plus depreciation, that result from a project; they are also equal to net operating income before deduction of payments to the financing sources but after deduction of applicable taxes. Thus net operating income after taxes is before deduction of financial payments such as interest on debt and dividends to shareholders. The net operating income after taxes is divided by the value of the firm to obtain the after-tax cost of capital for the firm as a whole:

$$\text{Cost of capital} = \text{Net income plus depreciation} / \text{Value of the firm}$$

$$= [(\text{Net operating income plus depreciation})\,(1 - T) + T(\text{depreciation})]/V(\text{value of the firm})$$

Since interest costs are included in the net operating income, they are reflected in the measurement of the cost of capital for the firm. In other words, *returns* are synonymous with *net operating cash flows from investments*.

Next, the nature and characteristics of the three methods are illustrated and explained. To make the explanations more meaningful, the same data are used to illustrate each procedure.

Payback Method

Assume that two projects are being considered by a firm. Each requires an investment of $1,000. The firm's marginal cost of capital is 10 percent.[4] The

---

3. A number of "average rate of return" methods have been discussed in the literature and used in practice. These methods are generally unsound and, with the widespread use of computers, completely unnecessary. We discussed them in earlier editions, but they are deleted from this edition. We also note that a "benefit/cost," or "profitability index," method is sometimes used; this is the ratio of the present value of inflows to the present value of outflows.

4. A discussion of how the cost of capital is calculated is presented in Chapter 16. For now, it should be considered as the firm's opportunity cost of making a particular investment. That is, if the firm does not make a particular investment, it "saves" the cost of this investment; and if it can invest the funds in another project that provides a return of 10 percent, then its "opportunity cost" of making the first investment is 10 percent.

net cash flows (net operating income after taxes plus depreciation) from Investments A and B are shown in Table 12.1. The *payback period* is the number of years it takes a firm to recover its original investment from net cash flows. Since the cost is $1,000, the payback period is $2^1/_3$ years for Investment A and 4 years for Investment B. If the firm were employing a 3-year payback period, Investment A would be accepted, but Investment B would be rejected.

Table 12.1
Net Cash Flows

$1000

Year	A	B
1	$500	$100
2	400	200
3	300	300
4	100	400
5	10	500
6	10	600

PB $2^1/_3$ 4

Although the payback period is very easy to calculate, it can lead to the wrong decisions. As the illustration demonstrates, it ignores income beyond the payback period. If the project is one maturing in later years, the use of the payback period can lead to the selection of less desirable investments. Investments with longer payback periods are characteristically those involved in long-range planning—developing a new product or tapping a new market. They are the strategic decisions that determine a firm's fundamental position, but they also involve investments that do not yield their highest returns for a number of years. This means that the payback method may be biased against the very investments that are most important to a firm's long-run success.

Recognition of the longer period over which an investment is likely to yield savings points up another weakness in the use of the payback method for ranking investment proposals—its failure to take into account the time value of money. Consider two assets, X and Y, each costing $300 and each having the following cash flows:

Year	X	Y
1	$200	$100
2	100	200
3	100	100

Each asset has a two-year payback; hence, each appears equally desirable. However, we know that a dollar today is worth more than a dollar next year, so Asset X, with its faster cash flow, is certainly more desirable.

The use of the payback method is sometimes defended on the ground that returns beyond three or four years are fraught with such great uncertainty that it is best to disregard them altogether in a planning decision. However, this is clearly an unsound procedure. Some investments with the highest returns may not come to fruition for many years. For example, the new product cycle in industries involving advanced technologies may not have a payoff for eight or nine years. Furthermore, even though returns that occur after three, four, or five years may be highly uncertain, it is important to make a judgment about the likelihood of their occurrence. To ignore them is to assign a zero probability to these distant receipts, which can hardly produce the best results.

Another defense of the payback method is that a firm short of cash must necessarily give great emphasis to a quick return of its funds so they can be put to use in other places or in meeting other needs. However, this does not relieve the payback method of its many shortcomings, and there are better methods for handling the cash shortage situation.[5]

A third defense of the payback method is that, typically, projects with faster paybacks have more favorable short-run effects on earnings per share. However, firms that use payback for this reason are sacrificing future growth for current accounting income, and in general this practice does not maximize the value of the firm. If used properly, the discounted cash flow techniques discussed in the next section automatically give consideration to the present earnings versus future growth tradeoff and strike the balance that maximizes the firm's value.

Fourth, the payback method is sometimes used simply because it is so easy to apply. If a firm is making many small capital expenditure decisions, the costs of using more complex methods may outweigh the benefits of possibly "better" choices among competing projects. Thus many electric utility companies with very sophisticated capital budgeting procedures use discounted cash flow techniques for larger projects but the payback method for certain small, routine replacement decisions. When sophisticated companies do use the payback method, however, they generally do so only after special studies have indicated that it will provide sufficiently accurate answers for the decisions at hand.

Finally, many firms use the payback method in combination with one of the discounted cash flow procedures described below. The NPV or IRR method is used to appraise a project's profitability, while the payback method is used to show how long the initial investment will be at risk; that is, payback is used as a risk indicator. Recent surveys have shown that when larger firms use payback in connection with major projects, it is almost always handled in this manner.

---

5. We interpret a cash shortage as a firm's high opportunity cost for funds and its high cost of capital. We consider this high cost of capital in the internal rate of return method or the net present value method, thus taking account of the cash shortage.

Net Present Value Method

As the flaws in the payback method were observed, people began to search for methods of evaluating projects that would recognize that a dollar received immediately is preferable to a dollar received at some future date. This search led to the development of *discounted cash flow (DCF) techniques* to take account of the time value of money. One such technique is the *net present value method* (sometimes referred to simply as the *present value method*). To implement this approach, find the present value of the expected net cash flows of an investment, discounted at the cost of capital, and subtract from it the initial cost outlay of the project.[6] If the net present value is positive, the project should be accepted; if negative, it should be rejected. If the two projects are mutually exclusive, the one with the higher net present value should be chosen.

The equation for the net present value (NPV) is:

$$NPV = \left[\frac{F_1}{(1+k)^1} + \frac{F_2}{(1+k)^2} + \cdots + \frac{F_N}{(1+k)^N} \right] - I$$

$$= \sum_{t=1}^{N} \frac{F_t}{(1+k)^t} - I.^{[7]}$$

(12.1)

Here F_1, F_2, and so on represent the net cash flows; k is the marginal cost of capital; I is the initial cost of the project; and N is the project's expected life.

The net present values of Projects A and B are calculated in Table 12.2. Project A has an NPV of $92, while B's NPV is $400. On this basis, both should be accepted if they are independent, but B should be chosen if they are mutually exclusive.

When a firm takes on a project with a positive NPV, the value of the firm increases by the amount of the NPV. In our example, the value of the firm increases by $400 if it takes on Project B but by only $92 if it takes on Project A. Viewing the alternatives in this manner, it is easy to see why B is preferred to A; it is also easy to see the logic of the NPV approach.

6. If costs are spread over several years, this must be taken into account. Suppose, for example, that a firm bought land in 1975, erected a building in 1976, installed equipment in 1977, and started production in 1978. One could treat 1975 as the base year, comparing the present value of the costs as of 1975 to the present value of the benefit stream as of that same date.

7. The second equation is simply a shorthand expression in which sigma (Σ) signifies "sum up" or add the present values of N profit terms. If $t = 1$, then $F_t = F_1$ and $1/(1+k)^t = 1/(1+k)^1$; if $t = 2$, then $F_t = F_2$ and $1/(1+k)^t = 1/(1+k)^2$; and so on until $t = N$, the last year the project provides any profits. The symbol $\sum_{t=1}^{N}$ simply says: Go through the following process. Let $t = 1$ and find the PV of F_1; then let $t = 2$ and find the PV of F_2. Continue until the PV of each individual profit has been found; then add the PVs of these individual profits to find the PV of the asset.

**Table 12.2
Calculating the Net Present
Value (NPV) of Projects with a
$1,000 Cost**

	Project A			Project B		
Year	Net Cash Flow	PVIF (10%)	PV of Cash Flow	Net Cash Flow	PVIF (10%)	PV of Cash Flow
1	$500	0.91	$ 455	$100	0.91	$ 91
2	400	0.83	332	200	0.83	166
3	300	0.75	225	300	0.75	225
4	100	0.68	68	400	0.68	272
5	10	0.62	6	500	0.62	310
6	10	0.56	6	600	0.56	336
		PV of inflows	$1,092		PV of inflows	$1,400
		Less cost	−1,000		Less cost	−1,000
		NPV	$ 92		NPV	$ 400

**Internal Rate of
Return Method**

The *internal rate of return (IRR)* is defined as the interest rate that equates the present value of the expected future cash flows, or receipts, to the initial cost outlay. The equation for calculating the internal rate of return is:

$$\frac{F_1}{(1+r)^1} + \frac{F_2}{(1+r)^2} + \cdots + \frac{F_N}{(1+r)^N} - I = 0.$$

$$\sum_{t=1}^{N} \frac{F_t}{(1+r)^t} - I = 0. \qquad (12.2)$$

Here we know the value of I and the values of $F_1, F_2, \ldots, F_N$, but we do not know the value of r. Thus we have an equation with one unknown, and we can solve for the value of r. Some value of r will cause the sum of the discounted receipts to equal the initial cost of the project, making the equation equal to zero; and that value of r is defined as the internal rate of return. That is, the solution value of r is the IRR.

The internal rate of return formula, Equation 12.2, is simply the NPV formula, Equation 12.1, solved for the particular value of k that causes the NPV to equal zero. In other words, the same basic equation is used for both methods, but in the NPV method the discount rate (k) is specified and the NPV is found, while in the IRR method the NPV is specified to equal zero and the value of r that forces the NPV to equal zero is found.

The internal rate of return can be found by trial and error. First, compute the present value of the cash flows from an investment, using an arbitrarily selected interest rate. (Since the cost of capital for most firms is in the range of 10 to 15 percent, projects should promise a return of at least 10 percent. Therefore, 10 percent is a good starting point for most problems.) Then, compare the present value so obtained with the investment's cost. If the present value is higher than the cost figure, try a higher interest rate and go through the procedure again. If the present value is lower than the cost, lower the interest rate and repeat the process. Continue until the present value of the flows from the investment is approximately equal to its cost. The interest rate that brings about this equality is defined as the internal rate of return.[8]

This calculation is illustrated in Table 12.3 for Projects A and B. First, the 10 percent interest factors are obtained from Table A.2 at the end of the

in the appropriate columns. For example, the PVIF of 0.91 is multiplied by $500, and the product, $455, is placed in the first row of Column A.

The present values of the yearly cash flows are then summed to get the investment's total present value, and the cost of the project is subtracted

Table 12.3
Finding the Internal Rate of Return

		Cash Flows (F_t Values)		
		Year	F_A	F_B
I = Investment = $1,000		1: $F_1 =$	$500	$100
		2: $F_2 =$	400	200
		3: $F_3 =$	300	300
		4: $F_4 =$	100	400
		5: $F_5 =$		500
		6: $F_6 =$		600

		10 Percent			15 Percent			20 Percent		
			Present Value			Present Value			Present Value	
Year	PVIF	A	B	PVIF	A	B	PVIF	A	B
1	0.91	$ 455	$ 91	0.87	$ 435	$ 87	0.83	$415	$ 83
2	0.83	332	166	0.76	304	152	0.69	276	138
3	0.75	225	225	0.66	198	198	0.58	174	174
4	0.68	68	272	0.57	57	228	0.48	48	192
5	0.62	6	310	0.50	5	250	0.40	4	200
6	0.56	6	336	0.43	4	258	0.33	3	198
Total present value		$1,092	$1,400		$1,003	$1,173		$920	$985
Net present value = PV − I		$92	$400		$3	$173		−$80	−$15

8. In order to reduce the number of trials required to find the internal rate of return, it is important to minimize the error at each point. One reasonable approach is to make as good a first approximation as possible, then to "straddle" the internal rate of return by making fairly large changes in the interest rate early in the process. In practice, if many projects are to be evaluated or if many years are involved, relatively inexpensive hand calculators can be used to solve for the internal rate of return.

from this figure to get the net present value. Since the net present values of both investments are positive at the 10 percent rate, increase the rate to 15 percent and try again. At this point the net present value of investment A is approximately zero, which indicates that its internal rate of return is approximately 15 percent. Continuing, B is found to have an internal rate of return of approximately 20 percent.[9]

What is so special about the particular discount rate that equates the cost of a project with the present value of its future cash flows? Suppose that the weighted cost of all of the funds obtained by the firm is 10 percent. If the internal rate of return on a particular project is 10 percent, the same as the cost of capital, the firm will be able to use the cash flow generated by the investment to repay the funds obtained, including the costs of the funds. If the internal rate of return exceeds 10 percent, the value of the firm increases. If it is less than 10 percent, the value of the firm declines. It is this "breakeven" characteristic increasing or decreasing the value of the firm that makes the internal rate of return particularly significant.

Assuming that the firm uses a cost of capital of 10 percent, the internal rate of return criterion states that if the two projects are independent, both should be accepted; they both do better than break even. If they are mutually exclusive, B ranks higher and should be accepted, while A should be rejected.

A more complete illustration of how the internal rate of return is used in

Table 12.4
The Prospective Projects Schedule

Nature of Proposal	Amount of Funds Required	Cumulative Total	IRR
1. Purchase of leased space	$2,000,000	$ 2,000,000	23%
2. Mechanization of accounting system	1,200,000	3,200,000	19
3. Modernization of office building	1,500,000	4,700,000	17
4. Addition of power facilities	900,000	5,600,000	16
5. Purchase of affiliate	3,600,000	9,200,000	13
6. Purchase of loading docks	300,000	9,500,000	12
7. Purchase of tank trucks	500,000	10,000,000	11
			10% cutoff
8. Installation of conveyor system	200,000	10,200,000	9
9. Construction of new plant	2,300,000	12,500,000	8
10. Purchase of executive aircraft	200,000	12,700,000	7

9. The IRR can also be estimated graphically. First, calculate the NPV at two or three discount rates as in Table 12.3. Next, plot these NPVs against the discount rates (see Figure 12.2 in the next section for an example). The horizontal axis intercept is the IRR; with graph paper and a sharp pencil the IRR can be estimated to three decimal places.

practice is given in Table 12.4. Assuming a 10 percent cost of capital, the firm should accept Projects 1 through 7, reject Projects 8 through 10, and have a total capital budget of $10 million.

IRR for Level Cash Flows

If the cash flows from a project are level, or equal in each year, then the project's internal rate of return can be found by a relatively simple process. In essence, such a project is an annuity; the firm makes an outlay, I, and receives a stream of cash flow benefits, F, for a given number of years. The IRR for the project is found by applying Equation 11.6, discussed in Chapter 11.

To illustrate: Suppose a project has a cost of $10,000 and is expected to produce cash flows of $1,627 a year for ten years. The $10,000 is the present value of an annuity of $1,627 a year for ten years, so applying Equation 11.6 we obtain:

$$\frac{I}{F} = \frac{\$10,000}{\$1,627} = 6.146 = \text{PVIF}_a.$$

Looking up PVIF_a in Table A.4, across the ten-year row, we find it (approximately) under the 10 percent column. Accordingly, 10 percent is the IRR on the project. In other words, 10 percent is the value of r that would force Equation 12.2 to zero when F is constant at $1,627 for ten years and I is $10,000. This procedure works only if the project has constant annual cash flows; if it does not, the IRR must be found by trial and error or by using a calculator.

Basic Differences between the NPV and IRR Methods[10]

As noted above, the NPV method accepts all independent projects whose NPV is greater than zero and ranks mutually exclusive projects by their NPVs. It selects the project with the higher NPV according to Equation 12.1:

$$\text{NPV} = \sum_{t=1}^{N} \frac{F_t}{(1+k)^t} - I. \tag{12.1}$$

The IRR method, on the other hand, finds the value of r that makes Equation 12.2 equal zero:

$$\text{NPV} = \sum_{t=1}^{N} \frac{F_t}{(1+r)^t} - I = 0. \tag{12.2}$$

The IRR method calls for accepting independent projects where r, the internal rate of return, is greater than k, the cost of capital, and for selecting

10. This section is relatively technical and can be omitted on a first reading without loss of continuity.

among mutually exclusive projects depending on which has the higher IRR.

It is apparent that the only structural difference between the NPV and the IRR methods lies in the discount rates used in the two equations; all the values in the equations are identical, except for r and k. Further, we can see that if $r > k$, then NPV > 0.[11] Accordingly, the two methods give the same accept-reject decisions for specific projects; a project that is acceptable under the NPV criterion is also acceptable if the IRR method is used.

However, under certain conditions the NPV and IRR methods can *rank* projects differently, and if mutually exclusive projects are involved or if capital is limited, then rankings can be important. The conditions under which different rankings can occur are as follows:

1. The cost of one project is larger than that of the other.
2. The timing of the projects' cash flows differs. For example, the cash flows of one project may increase over time, while those of the other may decrease; or the projects may have different expected lives.

The first point can be seen by considering two mutually exclusive projects, L and S, of greatly differing sizes. Project S calls for the investment of $1 and yields $1.50 at the end of one year. Its IRR is 50 percent, and at a 10 percent cost of capital its NPV is $.36. Project L costs $1 million and yields $1.25 million at the end of the year. Its IRR is only 25 percent, but its NPV at 10 percent is $113,625. The two methods rank the projects differently: $IRR_S > IRR_L$, but $NPV_L > NPV_S$. This is, of course, an extreme case, but whenever projects differ in size, the NPV and the IRR can give different rankings.[12]

The effect of differential cash flows is somewhat more difficult to understand, but it can be illustrated by an example. Consider two projects, A and B, whose cash flows over their three-year lives are given below:

Cash Flow from Project

Year	A	B
1	$1,000	$ 100
2	500	600
3	100	1,100

Project A's cash flows are higher in the early years, but B's cash flows in-

---

11. This can be seen by noting that NPV = 0 only when $r = k$:

$$NPV = \sum_{t=1}^{N} \frac{F_t}{(1+k)^t} - I = \sum_{t=1}^{N} \frac{F_t}{(1+r)^t} - I = 0,$$

if and only if $r = k$. If $r > k$, then NPV > 0, and if $r < k$, then NPV < 0. We should also note that under certain conditions there may be more than one root to Equation 12.2; hence multiple IRRs are found.

12. Projects of different sizes can be ranked the same by the NPV and IRR methods; that is, different sizes do not necessarily mean different rankings.

crease over time and exceed those of A in later years. Each project costs $1,200. The NPVs, discounted at the specified rates, are shown below:

Discount Rate	NPV A	B
0%	$400	$600
5	300	400
10	200	200
15	100	50
20	50	−85
25	−25	−175
30	−100	−250

At a zero discount rate, the NPV of each project is simply the sum of its receipts less its cost. Thus the NPV of Project A at 0 percent is $1,000 + $500 + $100 − $1,200 = $400; that of Project B is $100 + $600 + $1,100 − $1,200 = $600. As the discount rate rises from zero, the NPVs of the two projects fall from these values.

The NPVs are plotted against the appropriate discount rates in Figure 12.2, a graph defined as a *present value profile*. Notice that the vertical axis intercepts are the NPVs when the discount rate is zero, while the horizontal axis intercepts show each project's IRR. The internal rate of return is de-

Figure 12.2
Present Value Profile

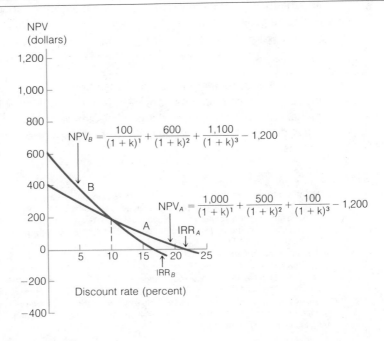

$$NPV_B = \frac{100}{(1+k)^1} + \frac{600}{(1+k)^2} + \frac{1,100}{(1+k)^3} - 1,200$$

$$NPV_A = \frac{1,000}{(1+k)^1} + \frac{500}{(1+k)^2} + \frac{100}{(1+k)^3} - 1,200$$

fined as that point where NPV is zero; therefore, A's IRR is 22 percent, while B's is 17 percent. Because its largest cash flows come late in the project's life, when the discounting effects of time are most significant, B's NPV falls rapidly as the discount rate rises. However, since A's cash flows come early, when the impact of higher discount rates is not so severe, its NPV falls less rapidly as interest rates increase.

Notice that at a cost of capital below 10 percent, B has the higher NPV but the lower IRR, while at a cost of capital above 10 percent, A has both the higher NPV and the higher IRR. We can generalize these results: Whenever the NPV profiles of two projects cross one another, a conflict will exist if the cost of capital is below the crossover rate. For our illustrative projects, no conflict would exist if the firm's cost of capital exceeded 10 percent, but the two methods would rank A and B differently if k were less than 10 percent.

How should such conflicts be resolved? For example, when the NPV and IRR methods yield conflicting ranking, which of two mutually exclusive projects should be selected? Assuming that management is seeking to maximize the value of the firm, the correct decision is to select the project with the higher NPV. After all, the NPVs measure the projects' contributions to the value of the firm, so the one with the higher NPV must be contributing more to the firm's value. This line of reasoning leads to the conclusion that firms should, in general, use the NPV method for evaluating capital investment proposals.[13] Recognizing this point, sophisticated firms generally rely on the NPV method. These firms often calculate (by computer) both the NPV and the IRR, but they rely on the NPV when conflicts arise among mutually exclusive projects.

Capital Budgeting Project Evaluation

Thus far the problem of measuring cash flows—the benefits used in the present value calculations above—has not been dealt with directly. This matter will now be discussed and a few simple examples given. The procedures developed here can be used for both expansion and replacement decisions.

13. The question of why the conflict arises is an interesting one. Basically, it has to do with the reinvestment of cash flows. The NPV method implicitly assumes reinvestment at the marginal cost of capital (MCC), while the IRR method implicitly assumes reinvestment at the internal rate of return. For a value-maximizing firm, reinvestment at the MCC is the better assumption. The rationale is as follows: A value-maximizing firm will expand to the point where it accepts all projects yielding more than the MCC (projects with NPV > 0). How the projects are financed is irrelevant; the point is that they will be financed and accepted. Now, consider the question of the cash flows from a particular project. If these cash flows are reinvested, at what rate will reinvestment occur? All projects that yield more than the cost of capital have already been accepted; thus these cash flows can be invested only in physical assets yielding less than the MCC, or else they can be used in lieu of other capital with a cost of MCC. A rational firm will take the second alternative, so reinvested cash flows will save the firm the cost of capital. This means that cash flows are reinvested to yield the cost of capital, which is the assumption implicit in the NPV method.

Simplified Model for Determining Cash Flows[14]

One way of considering the cash flows attributable to a particular investment is to think of them in terms of comparative income statements. This is illustrated in the following example.

The widget division of the Culver Company, a profitable, diversified manufacturing firm, purchased a machine five years ago at a cost of $7,500. The machine had an expected life of fifteen years at time of purchase and a zero estimated salvage value at the end of the fifteen years. It is being depreciated on a straight line basis and has a book value of $5,000 at present. The division manager reports that he can buy a new machine for $12,000 (including installation), which, over its ten-year life, will expand sales from $10,000 to $11,000 a year. Furthermore, it will reduce labor and raw materials usage sufficiently to cut operating costs from $7,000 to $5,000. The new machine has an estimated salvage value of $2,000 at the end of ten years. The old machine's current market value is $1,000. Taxes are at the 40 percent rate and are paid quarterly, and the firm's cost of capital is 10 percent. Should Culver buy the new machine?

The decision calls for five steps: (1) estimating the actual cash outlay attributable to the new investment, (2) determining the incremental cash flows, (3) finding the present value of the incremental cash flows, (4) adding the present value of the expected salvage value to the present value of the total cash flows, and (5) seeing whether the NPV is positive or whether the IRR exceeds the cost of capital.

Estimating Cash Outlay The net initial cash outlay consists of these items: (1) payment to the manufacturer, (2) tax effects, and (3) proceeds from the sale of the old machine. Culver must make a $12,000 payment to the manufacturer of the machine, but its next quarterly tax bill will be reduced because of the loss it will incur when it sells the old machine:

$$\text{Tax saving} = \text{Loss} \times \text{Tax rate} = \$4,000 \times 0.4 = \$1,600.$$

The tax reduction will occur because the old machine, which is carried at $5,000, will be written off by $4,000 ($5,000 less $1,000 salvage value) immediately if the new one is purchased.

To illustrate: Suppose the Culver Company's taxable income in the quarter in which the new machine is to be purchased will be $100,000 without the purchase of the new machine and the consequent write-off of the old machine. With a 40 percent tax rate, Culver will have to write a check for $40,000 to pay its tax bill. However, if it buys the new machine and sells the old one, it will take an operating loss of $4,000—the $5,000 book value on

---

14. The procedure described in this section facilitates an understanding of the capital investment analysis process, but for repeated calculations the alternative worksheet illustrated in the next section is preferred. Note also that we use straight line depreciation in the chapter but accelerated depreciation in its appendix illustration.

the old machine less the salvage value. (The loss is an operating loss, not a capital loss, because it is simply a recognition that depreciation charges—an operating cost—were too low during the old machine's five-year life.)[15] With this $4,000 additional operating cost, next quarter's taxable income will be reduced from $100,000 to $96,000 and the tax bill from $40,000 to $38,400. This means, of course, that the firm's cash outflow for taxes will be $1,600 less *because* it has purchased the new machine.

In addition, there is to be a cash inflow of $1,000 from the sale of the old machine. The net result is that the purchase of the new machine involves an immediate net cash outlay of $9,400; this is its cost for capital budgeting purposes:

Invoice price of new machine	$12,000
Less: Tax savings	−1,600
Salvage of old machine	−1,000
Net cash outflow (cost)	$ 9,400

If additional working capital is required as a result of a capital budgeting decision (which generally is true for expansion-type investments as opposed to cost-reducing replacement investments), this factor must be taken into account. The amount of net working capital (additional current assets required as a result of the expansion minus any spontaneous funds generated by the expansion) is estimated and added to the initial cash outlay. We assume that Culver will not need any additional working capital; hence the factor is ignored in this example.

Determining Incremental Cash Flows Column 1 in Table 12.5 shows the widget division's estimated income statement as it will look without the new machine; Column 2 shows the statement as it will look if the new machine is bought. (It is assumed that these figures are applicable for each of the next ten years; if this is not the case, then cash flow estimates must be made for each year.) Column 3 shows the differences between the first two columns.

For capital budgeting analysis the cash flows that are discounted are the net after-tax operating cash flows. The data in Table 12.5 represent accounting income and must be adjusted in order to be on a cash rather than accrual basis and to exclude all payments to the sources of financing. In Table 12.5 depreciation is a noncash charge; interest charges and dividends paid are cash flows to the financing sources. While depreciation is a noncash charge, it is deductible for computing income tax, and income tax payments are cash flows. The cash flows must include the depreciation tax benefits.

Table 12.6 shows the operating cash flows without the new investment and with the new investment and the difference or incremental flows.

---

15. If Culver trades in the old machine as partial payment for the new one, the loss will be added to the depreciable cost of the new machine, and there will be no immediate tax saving.

**Table 12.5
Comparative Accounting Income
Statement Framework for
Considering Cash Flows**

	Without New Investment (1)	With New Investment (2)	Difference (2)−(1) (3)
Sales	$10,000	$11,000	$1,000
Operating costs	$7,000	$5,000	−$2,000
Depreciation	500	1,000	500
Interest charges	500	1,000	500
Income before taxes	$ 2,000	$ 4,000	$2,000
Taxes (at 40%)	−800	−1,600	−800
Income after taxes	$ 1,200	$ 2,400	$1,200
Dividends paid	−600	−1,200	−600
Additions to retained earnings	$ 600	$ 1,200	$ 600

**Table 12.6
Net Operating Cash Flow
Statement**

	Without New Investment (1)	With New Investment (2)	Difference of Incremental Flows (2)−(1) (3)
Sales $(P \cdot Q)$	$10,000	$11,000	$1,000
Operating cash costs (O)[a]	7,000	5,000	−2,000
Net operating cash income (NOI)[a]	$ 3,000	$ 6,000	$3,000
Taxes (at 40%) (T)	1,200	2,400	1,200
After-tax operating (NOI$[1 − T]$)	$ 1,800	$ 3,600	$1,800
Depreciation tax benefit $(T \times \text{Dep})$	200	400	200
Net cash flows (F)	$ 2,000	$ 4,000	$2,000

[a]Does not include depreciation as a cash cost since this is a cash flow statement.

The incremental cash flows can also be calculated using the following equation. Let ΔSales be the change in sales, ΔO the change in operating costs, ΔNOI the change in operating cash income, ΔDep the change in depreciation, and T the marginal corporate income tax rate. Then:

$$\Delta\text{Cash flow} = \text{Change in after-tax operating cash income}$$
$$+ \text{Change in depreciation tax benefit.}$$
$$\Delta F = \Delta\text{NOI}(1 − T) + T\Delta\text{Dep}$$
$$= (\Delta\text{Sales} − \Delta O)(1 − T) + T\Delta\text{Dep}$$
$$= ([\text{Sales}_2 − \text{Sales}_1] − [O_2 − O_1])(1 − T)$$
$$+ T(\text{Dep}_2 − \text{Dep}_1). \tag{12.3}$$

For the widget division analysis:

$$\Delta F = ([\$11{,}000 - \$10{,}000] - [\$5{,}000 - \$7{,}000])(1 - .4)$$
$$+ (.4)(\$1{,}000 - \$500)$$
$$= (\$1{,}000 - [-\$2{,}000])(.6) + (.4)(\$500)$$
$$= \$1{,}800 + \$200$$
$$= \$2{,}000.$$

This $2,000 result checks out with the bottom line figure in the last column of Table 12.6. What happens, however, if there is no change in sales? The equation is still valid, but $\Delta Sales = 0$. In this case, the problem is a simple replacement decision, with a new machine replacing an old one to reduce costs. The sales levels are the same with and without the investment and do not show up in the incremental flows column.

Finding the PV of the Incremental Cash Flows We have explained in detail how to measure the annual benefits. The next step is to determine the present value of the benefit stream. The interest factor for a ten-year, 10 percent annuity is found to be 6.145 from Appendix Table A.4. This factor multiplied by the $2,000 incremental cash flow results in a present value of $12,290.

Adding the PV of the Salvage Value to the PV of the Cash Flows The new machine has an estimated salvage value of $2,000; that is, Culver expects to be able to sell the machine for $2,000 in ten years. The present value of an inflow of $2,000 due in ten years is $772, found as $2,000 × 0.386. If additional working capital were required and included in the initial cash outlay, this amount would be added to the salvage value of the machine because the working capital would be recovered if and when the project was abandoned.

Notice that the salvage value is a return of capital, not taxable income, so it is *not* subject to income taxes. Of course, when the new machine is actually retired ten years hence, it may be sold for more or less than the expected $2,000, so either taxable income or a deductible operating loss may arise; but $2,000 is the best present estimate of the new machine's salvage value.

Determining Whether the NPV Is Positive The project's net present value is the sum of the present values of the inflows, or benefits, less the outflows, or costs:

Inflows: PV of annual benefits	$12,290
PV of salvage value, new machine	772
Less net cash outflow, or cost	−9,400
Net present value (NPV)	$ 3,662

Since the NPV is positive, the project should be accepted.

**Worksheet for
Determining
Cash Flows**

Table 12.7 summarizes the five-step capital budgeting decision process described above. Using the Culver Company investment problem as an example, we first calculate the total outflows for the proposed project by subtracting from the cost of the new machine the sum of the funds received from the sale of the old machine plus the tax savings resulting from that

**Table 12.7
Worksheet for Capital Budgeting
Project Evaluation**

1. **Project Cost, or Initial Outflows Required to Undertake the Project[a]**

Investment in new equipment	$12,000
Receipt from sale of old machine	−1,000
Add (or subtract) the taxes (or tax savings) resulting from the gain (or loss) on the old machine: tax rate (T) times gain or loss	−1,600
Total project cost	$ 9,400

2. **Calculation of Annual Benefits[b]**

ΔSales	$ 1,000
Less: ΔO	−2,000[c]
ΔDep	500
ΔTaxable income	$ 2,500
Less Δtax (at 40%)	1,000
ΔAfter-tax profits	$ 1,500
Plus ΔDep	500
ΔCash flow	$ 2,000

3. **Present Value of Benefits**

$\Delta F \times$ Interest factor	
$2,000 \times 6.145 =$	$12,290

4. **Present Value of Expected Salvage**

Expected salvage value $\times$ Interest factor	
$2,000 \times 0.386 =$	$ 772

5. **Net Present Value**

PV of inflows: Annual benefits	$12,290
Salvage	772
	$13,062
Less: Project cost	9,400
NPV	$ 3,662

[a] If project costs are incurred over a number of years, then their present value must be calculated.
[b] If the annual cash flows are not level, the annuity format cannot be used. Also, if accelerated depreciation is used, the annuity format can almost never be used; in this case, cash flows are unlikely to be uniform from year to year. These restrictions might appear to present serious problems to practical applications in capital budgeting, but they really do not. Most corporations have either their own computer facilities or time-sharing arrangements with computer service facilities that handle these nonannuity cases without difficulty.
[c] Refer to Equation 12.4. We are subtracting the change in cost from the change in sales: $\Delta C =$ $5,000 − $7,000 = −$2,000. Therefore, ΔSales − $\Delta C = $1,000 − (−$2,000) = $3,000.

sale. Recall that a $4,000 operating loss will occur if the old machine with a book value of $5,000 is sold for $1,000. Since the old machine is sold at a loss, the $1,000 received from the sale is not taxed. (Only the *gain* on the sale of any asset is taxed.) Furthermore the $4,000 loss is a tax deduction for next quarter's tax payment, and it results in a tax savings of $1,600.

Next, we calculate the net annual benefits. Then, we find the present value of this benefit stream, which is $12,290.

Now, we find the present value of the expected salvage value of the new machine, $772. Since salvage value is a *return of capital,* not taxable income, no taxes are deducted from it. Finally, we sum up the PV of the inflows and deduct the project cost to determine the NPV—$3,662 in this example. Since the NPV is positive, the project should be accepted.[16]

Alternative Capital Budgeting Worksheet

Table 12.8 presents an alternative worksheet for evaluating capital projects. The top section shows net cash flows at the time of investment; since all these flows occur immediately, no discounting is required and the interest factor is 1.0. The lower section of the table shows future cash flows—benefits from increased sales and/or reduced costs, depreciation, and salvage value. These flows do occur over time, so it is necessary to convert them to present values. The NPV as determined in the alternative format—$3,662—agrees with the figure as calculated in Table 12.7.

Capital Rationing

Ordinarily, firms operate as illustrated in Figure 12.1; that is, they take on investments to the point where the marginal returns from investment are just equal to their estimated marginal cost of capital. For firms operating in this

16. Alternatively, the internal rate of return on the project could have been computed and found to be 18 percent. Because this is substantially in excess of the 10 percent cost of capital, the IRR method also indicates that the investment should be undertaken. In this case, the r is found as follows:

$$\text{PV of benefit stream} + \text{PV of salvage} - \text{Cost} = 0.$$

$$\sum_{t=1}^{10} \frac{\$2,000}{(1+r)^t} + \frac{\$2,000}{(1+r)^{10}} - \$9,400 = 0.$$

$$\$2,000 \text{ (IF for PV of 10-year annuity)} + \$2,000 \text{ (PV of \$1 in 10 years)} - \$9,400 = 0.$$

Try PVIFs for 18%:

$$\$2,000(4.94) + \$2,000(0.191) - \$9,400 = \$8,988 + \$382 - \$9,400 = -\$30.$$

which is very close to zero, indicating that the internal rate of return is approximately equal to 18 percent.

**Table 12.8
Alternative Worksheet for Capital
Budgeting Project Evaluation**

	Amount before Tax	Amount after Tax[a]	Year Event Occurs	PV Factor at 10%	PV
Outflows at Time Investment Is Made					
Investment in new equipment	$12,000	$12,000	0	1.0	$12,000
Salvage value of old equipment	−1,000	−1,000	0	1.0	−1,000
Tax effect of the sale[b]	−4,000	−1,600	0	1.0	−1,600
Increased working capital (if necessary)	[c]	—	0	1.0	—
Total initial ouflows (PV of costs)					$ 9,400
Inflows, or Annual Returns					
Benefits[d]	$ 3,000	$ 1,800	1–10	6.145	$11,061
Depreciation on new equipment (annual)[b]	1,000	400	1–10	6.145	2,458
Depreciation on old equipment (annual)[b]	−500	−200	1–10	6.145	−1,229
Salvage value of new equipment	2,000	2,000	10	0.386	772
Return of working capital (if necessary)	[c]	—	10	0.386	—
Total periodic inflows (PV of benefits)					$13,062

NPV = PV of benefits less PV of cost = $13,062 − $9,400 = $3,662.

[a] Amount after tax equals amount before tax times T or $(1 - T)$, where T = tax rate.
[b] Deductions (tax loss and depreciation) are multiplied by T.
[c] Not applicable.
[d] Benefits are multiplied by $(1 - T)$.

way, the decision process is as described above. They make those investments having positive net present values, reject those whose net present values are negative, and choose among mutually exclusive investments on the basis of the higher net present value. However, firms occasionally set an absolute limit on the size of their capital budget for a particular year that is less than the level of investment they would undertake on the basis of the criteria described above.

The principal reason for such action is that some firms are reluctant to engage in external financing (borrowing or selling stock). One company's management may recall the plight of firms with substantial amounts of debt in the 1930s and simply refuse to use debt. Another company's management, which has no objection to using debt, may not want to sell equity capital for fear of losing some measure of voting control. Still another may refuse to use any form of outside financing, considering safety and control to be more important than additional profits. These are all cases of capital rationing, and they result in limiting the rate of expansion to a slower pace than would be dictated by purely "rational" profit-maximizing behavior.[17]

Project Selection under Capital Rationing

How should projects be selected under conditions of capital rationing? First, note that under conditions of true capital rationing, the firm's value is not being maximized; if management were maximizing, then it would move to the point where the marginal project's NPV was zero, and capital rationing as defined would not exist. So if a firm uses capital rationing, it has ruled out value maximization. The firm may, however, want to maximize value subject to the constraint that the capital ceiling not be exceeded. Constrained maximization behavior will, in general, result in a lower value than unconstrained maximization behavior, but some type of constrained maximization may produce reasonably satisfactory results. Linear programming is one method of constrained maximization that has been applied to capital rationing.

If a financial manager faces capital rationing and cannot get the constraint lifted, what should be done? The objective should be to select projects, subject to the capital rationing constraint, such that the sum of the projects' NPVs is maximized. Linear programming can be used, but there is really no practical alternative that will approximate the true maximum. Reasonably satisfactory results can be obtained by ranking projects by their internal rates of return and then, starting at the top of this list of projects, taking investments of successively lower rank until the available funds have been exhausted. However, no investment with a negative NPV (or an internal rate of return below the cost of capital) should be undertaken.

A firm might, for example, have the investment opportunities shown in Table 12.9 and only $6 million available for investment. In this situation, the

17. We should make three points here. First, we do not necessarily consider a decision to hold back on expansion irrational. If the owners of a firm have what they consider to be plenty of income and wealth, then it might be quite rational for them to "trim their sails," relax, and concentrate on enjoying what they have already earned rather than on earning still more. Such behavior is not, however, appropriate for a publicly owned firm.

Second, it is incorrect to interpret as capital rationing a situation where the firm is willing to sell additional securities at the going market price but finds that it cannot because the market will simply not absorb more of its issues. Rather, such a situation indicates that the cost-of-capital curve is rising. If more acceptable investments are indicated than can be financed, then the cost of capital being used is too low and should be raised.

Third, firms sometimes set a limit on capital expenditures not because of a shortage of funds but because of limitations on other resources, especially managerial talent. A firm might, for example, feel that its personnel development program is sufficient to handle an expansion of no more than 10 percent a year, then set a limit on the capital budget to ensure that expansion is held to that rate. This is not *capital* rationing; rather, it involves a downward reevaluation of project returns if growth exceeds some limit. That is, expected rates of return are, after some point, a decreasing function of the level of expenditures. See H. M. Weingartner, "Capital Rationing: n Authors in Search of a Plot," *Journal of Finance* 32 (December 1977).

**Table 12.9
The Prospective Projects
Schedule**

Nature of Proposal	Project's Cost	Cumulative Total of Costs	Internal Rate of Return	PV of Benefits	Project's NPV
1. Purchase of leased space	$2,000,000	$ 2,000,000	23%	$3,200,000	$1,200,000
2. Mechanization of accounting system	1,200,000	3,200,000	19	1,740,000	540,000
3. Modernization of office building	1,500,000	4,700,000	17	2,070,000	570,000
4. Addition of power facilities	900,000	5,600,000	16	1,125,000	225,000
5. Purchase of affiliate	3,600,000	9,200,000	13	4,248,000	648,000
6. Purchase of loading docks	300,000	9,500,000	12	342,000	42,000
7. Purchase of tank trucks	500,000	10,000,000	11	540,000	40,000 cutoff
8. Installation of conveyor system	200,000	10,200,000	9	186,000	−14,000
9. Construction of new plant	2,300,000	12,500,000	8	2,093,000	−207,000
10. Purchase of executive aircraft	200,000	12,700,000	7	128,000	−72,000

firm should probably accept Projects 1 through 4 and Project 6, ending with a capital budget of $5.9 million and a cumulative NPV of $2.6 million. Under no circumstances should it accept Projects 8, 9, or 10, since they all have internal rates of return of less than 10 percent (and NPVs less than zero).

Public Expenditure Decisions

Capital budgeting decisions must also be made by government agencies. A series of hearings before Congress on methods and procedures of capital budgeting at the federal level revealed (1) that congressional leaders and the heads of the major government agencies agreed that government capital budgeting should be conducted under a method equivalent to our risk-adjusted discount rate procedure, but (2) that federal agencies are having a difficult time determining appropriate discount rates.[18] In other words, the federal government tends to follow the same capital budgeting procedures

18. U.S. Congress, Subcommittee on Economy in Government of the Joint Economic Committee, *Economic Analysis of Public Investment Decisions: Interest Rate Policy and Discounting Analysis* (Washington, D.C.: Government Printing Office, 1968).

as do the more sophisticated business firms, and the procedures described in this book are applicable to both.

Summary

Capital budgeting, which involves commitments for large outlays whose benefits (or drawbacks) extend well into the future, is of great significance to a firm. Decisions in this area have a major impact on the firm's future well-being. Capital budgeting decisions can more effectively contribute to the health and growth of a firm if systematic procedures and rules are developed for preparing a list of investment proposals, for evaluating them, and for selecting a cutoff point.

One of the most crucial phases in the process of evaluating capital budget proposals is obtaining a dependable estimate of the benefits of undertaking a project. The firm must allocate the making of these judgments to competent and experienced personnel.

The cash inflow from an investment is the incremental change in after-tax net operating cash income plus the incremental depreciation tax benefit; the cash outflow is the cost of the investment less the salvage value received on an old machine plus any tax loss (or less any tax savings) when the machine is sold.

Three commonly used procedures for ranking investment proposals are the payback method, the net present value method, and the internal rate of return method.

Payback is defined as the number of years required to return the original investment. Although the payback method is used frequently, it has serious conceptual weaknesses. Essentially, it ignores the facts that some receipts come in beyond the payback period and that a dollar received today is more valuable than a dollar received in the future.

Net present value is defined as the present value of future returns, discounted at the cost of capital, minus the cost of the investment. The NPV method overcomes the conceptual flaws noted in the use of the payback method.

Internal rate of return is defined as the interest rate that equates the present value of future returns to the investment outlay. The IRR method, like the NPV method, meets the objections to the payback approach.

In most cases, the two discounted cash flow methods give identical answers to these questions: Which of two mutually exclusive projects should be selected? How large should the total capital budget be? However, under certain circumstances, conflicts may arise. Such conflicts are caused by the fact that the NPV and IRR methods make different assumptions about the rate at which cash flows may be reinvested or the opportunity cost of cash flows. In general, the assumption of the NPV method—that the opportunity cost is the cost of capital—is the correct one. Accordingly, we prefer to use the NPV method to make capital budgeting decisions.

Questions

12.1 A firm has $100 million available for capital expenditures. Suppose project A involves purchasing $100 million of grain, shipping it overseas, and selling it within a year at a profit of $20 million. The project has an IRR of 20 percent and an NPV of $20 million, and it will cause earnings per share (EPS) to rise within one year. Project B calls for the use of the $100 million to develop a new process, acquire land, build a plant, and begin processing. Project B, which is not postponable, has an NPV of $50 million and an IRR of 30 percent. But the fact that some of the plant costs will be written off immediately, combined with the fact that no revenues will be generated for several years, means that accepting project B will reduce short-run EPS.
   a. Should the short-run effects on EPS influence the choice between the two projects?
   b. How might situations such as the one described here influence a firm's decision to use payback as a screening criterion?

12.2 Are there conditions under which a firm might be better off if it chose a machine with a rapid payback rather than one with the largest rate of return?

12.3 Company X uses the payback method in evaluating investment proposals and is considering new equipment whose additional net after-tax earnings will be $150 a year. The equipment costs $500, and its expected life is ten years (straight-line depreciation). The company uses a three-year payback as its criterion. Should the equipment be purchased under the above assumptions?

12.4 What are the most critical problems that arise in calculating a rate of return for a prospective investment?

12.5 What other factors in addition to rate of return analysis should be considered in determining capital expenditures?

12.6 Would it be beneficial for a firm to review its past capital expenditures and capital budgeting procedures? Explain.

12.7 Fiscal and monetary policies are tools used by the government to stimulate the economy. Using the analytical devices developed in this chapter, explain how each of the following might be expected to stimulate the economy by encouraging investment:
   a. A speedup of tax-allowable depreciation (for example, the accelerated methods permitted in 1954 or the guideline depreciable life revisions of 1962 discussed in Appendix 3A).
   b. An easing of interest rates.
   c. Passage of a new federal program giving more aid to the poor.
   d. An investment tax credit.

Problems

12.1 Two pieces of equipment, a truck and an overhead pulley, are being considered in this year's capital budget. The projects are not mutually exclusive. The outlay for the truck is $9,869, and the outlay for the pulley is
$17,845. The firm's cost of capital is 12 percent. Cash flows are shown
below:

Year	Truck	Pulley
1	$3,300	$6,500
2	3,300	6,500
3	3,300	6,500
4	3,300	6,500
5	3,300	6,500

Calculate the IRR and NPV on each project, and indicate the correct adopt-
reject decision for each.

12.2 You are choosing between a gas-powered and an electric-powered forklift
truck for moving materials in the factory. Since they both perform the same
function, you will choose only one. (They are mutually exclusive investments.) The electric-powered truck will cost more but be less expensive to
operate. It will cost $16,628, while the gas-powered truck will cost $13,302.
The cost of capital that applies to both investments is 10 percent. The life
for both types of trucks is estimated to be six years, during which the net
cash flows for the electric-powered truck will be $5,000 per year and the net
cash flows for the gas-powered truck will be $4,000 per year. Calculate the
NPV and IRR on each type of truck and decide which to recommend for
purchase.

12.3 The Gilbert Company has cash inflows (CIF) of $140,000 per year and cash
outflows (COF) of $100,000 per year on Project A. The investment outlay (I)
on the project is $100,000; its life (N) is ten years; the tax rate (T) is 40 per-
cent. The applicable cost of capital (k) is 12 percent.
   a. Present two formulations of the net cash flows adjusted for depreciation
      tax shelter (F).
   b. Calculate the net present value for Project A, using straight-line depre-
      ciation for tax purposes.

12.4 The Madison Company is considering the replacement of a riveting machine
with a new one that will increase the earnings before depreciation from
$20,000 per year to $51,000 per year. The new machine will cost $100,000
and have an estimated life of eight years with no salvage value. The applicable corporate tax rate is 40 percent, and the firm's cost of capital is 12
percent. The old machine has been fully depreciated and has no salvage
value. Should it be replaced by the new one?

12.5 Assume that the Madison Company will be able to realize an investment tax
credit of 10 percent on the purchase of the new machine (which will have a
salvage value of $12,000). Assume further that the old machine has a book
value of $40,000 and a remaining life of eight years. If replaced, the old
machine can be sold now for $15,000. Should the machine replacement be
made?

12.6 Sparkling Beverages is contemplating the replacement of one of its bottling machines with a newer and more efficient one. The old machine has a book value of $500,000 and a remaining useful life of five years. The firm does not expect to realize any return from scrapping the old machine in five years, but it can sell the machine now to another firm in the industry for $300,000.

Answers

The new machine has a purchase price of $1.1 million, an estimated useful life of five years, and an estimated salvage value of $100,000. It is expected to economize on electric power usage, labor, and repair costs and to reduce the number of defective bottles. In total, an annual saving of $200,000 will be realized if the new machine is installed. The company is in the 40 percent tax bracket, has a 10 percent cost of capital, and uses straight-line depreciation. (Note: To calculate depreciation, assume that the salvage value is deducted from initial cost to get the depreciable cost.)

720,000   a. What is the initial cash outlay required for the new machine?

160,000   b. What are the cash flows in Years 1 to 5?

100,000   c. What is the cash flow from the salvage value in Year 5?

NPV −51340   d. Should Sparkling Beverages purchase the new machine? Support your answer.

e. In general, how would each of the following factors affect the investment decision, and how should each be treated?
1. The expected life of the existing machine decreases.
2. Capital rationing is imposed on the firm.
3. The cost of capital is not constant but is rising.
4. Improvements in the equipment to be purchased are expected to occur each year, and the result will be to increase the returns or expected savings from the new machine over the savings expected with this year's model for every year in the foreseeable future.

12.7 The Gilmore Company is using a machine whose original cost was $72,000. The machine is two years old and has a current market value of $16,000. The asset is being depreciated over a twelve-year original life toward a zero estimated final salvage value. Depreciation is on a straight-line basis, and the tax rate is 50 percent.

Management is contemplating the purchase of a replacement that costs $75,000 and has an estimated salvage value of $10,000. The new machine will have a greater capacity, enabling annual sales to increase by $10,000 from $1 million to $1.01 million. Operating efficiencies with the new machine will also produce expected savings of $10,000 a year. Depreciation will be on a straight-line basis over a ten-year life, the cost of capital will be 8 percent, and a 50 percent tax rate will apply. The company's total depreciation costs are currently $120,000, and the total annual operating costs are $800,000.

36407   a. Should the firm replace the asset? Use Equation 12.5 (showing the cash flow difference) to solve the problem.

44815   b. How will your decision be affected if a second new machine is available that costs $140,000, has a $20,000 estimated salvage value, increases sales by $10,000 a year, and is expected to provide $25,000 in annual savings over its ten-year life? (There are now three alternatives: keep the old machine, replace it with a $75,000 machine, or replace it with a $140,000 machine.) Depreciation is still on a straight-line basis. For purposes of answering this question use both the NPV (which you must calculate) and the IRR (which you can assume to be 25 percent for the $75,000 project and 17 percent for the $140,000 project).

c. Disregarding the changes in Part b (that is, under the original assumption that one $75,000 replacement machine is available), how will your decision be affected if a new generation of equipment that will provide increased annual savings and have the same cost, asset life, and salvage value is expected to be on the market in about two years?

d. What factors in addition to the quantitative ones listed above are likely to require consideration in a practical situation?

e. How will your decision be affected if the asset lives of the various alternatives are not the same?

12.8 The Stanton Company is considering the purchase of a new machine tool to replace an obsolete one. The machine being used for the operation has both a tax book value and a market value of zero; it is in good working order and will last, physically, for at least an additional fifteen years. The proposed machine will perform the operation so much more efficiently that Stanton engineers estimate that labor, material, and other direct costs of the operation will be reduced $4,500 a year if it is installed. The proposed machine costs $24,000 delivered and installed, and its economic life is estimated to be fifteen years with zero salvage value. The company expects to earn 12 percent on its investment after taxes (12 percent is the firm's cost of capital). The tax rate is 50 percent, and the firm uses straight-line depreciation.

a. Should Stanton buy the new machine?

-3266

-1588

b. Assume that the tax book value of the old machine is $6,000, that the annual depreciation charge is $400, and that the machine has no market value. How do these assumptions affect your answer?

411.35

c. Answer Part b, assuming that the old machine has a market value of $4,000.

3519.60

d. Answer Part b, assuming that the annual saving will be $6,000.

e. Answer Part a, assuming that the relevant cost of capital is now 6 percent. What is the significance of this change? What can be said about Parts b, c, and d under this assumption?

f. In general, how would each of the following factors affect the investment decision, and how should each be treated?
1. The expected life of the existing machine decreases.
2. Capital rationing is imposed on the firm.
3. The cost of capital is not constant but is rising.
4. Improvements in the equipment to be purchased are expected to occur each year, and the result will be to increase the returns or expected savings from the new machine over the savings expected with this year's model for every year in the foreseeable future.

12.9 Each of two mutually exclusive projects involves an investment of $120,000. Cash flows (after-tax profits plus depreciation) for the two projects have a different time pattern, although the totals are approximately the same. Project M will yield high returns early and lower returns in later years. (It is a mining type of investment, and the expense of removing the ore is lower at the entrance to the mine, where there is easier access.) Project O yields low returns in the early years and higher returns in the later years. (It is an orchard type of investment, and it takes a number of years for trees to mature and be fully bearing.) The cash flows from the two investments are as follows:

Year	Project M	Project O
1	$70,000	$10,000
2	40,000	20,000
3	30,000	30,000
4	10,000	50,000
5	10,000	80,000

a. Compute the present value of each project when the firm's cost of capital is 0 percent, 6 percent, 10 percent, and 20 percent.

12.86%

15.78

b. Compute the internal rate of return (IRR) for each project.

c. Graph the present value of the two projects, putting net present value (NPV) on the Y-axis and the cost of capital on the X-axis.

d. Can you determine the IRR of the projects from your graph? Explain.

e. Which project would you select, assuming no capital rationing and a constant cost of capital of 8 percent? of 10 percent? of 12 percent? Explain.

f. If capital was severely rationed, which project would you select?

Appendix 12A
Accelerated
Depreciation

In the illustrations of capital budgeting given in Chapter 12, it was assumed that straight-line depreciation was used. This enabled us to derive uniform cash flows over the life of the investment. Realistically, however, firms usually employ accelerated depreciation methods. Such methods call for the modification of procedures outlined thus far.[1] In terms of the framework given in Table 12.5, accelerated depreciation makes it necessary to recompute the differential cash flow for each year during the life of the investment.

Table A12.1 contains present value factors for accelerated depreciation. The table is constructed as follows:

1. Depreciation is a deductible item for tax purposes, and the taxes saved are equal to $T \times Dep$. At a 40 percent tax rate, $1 of depreciation saves $.40; that is, tax saving = 0.4 ($1) = $.40.

2. Depreciation is taken over the life of the asset; accordingly, the tax savings occur over this life. For capital budgeting purposes, we want to

---

1. For a discussion of accelerated depreciation methods, see Appendix 3A.

**Table A12.1
Tables for Present Value of
Depreciation for Sum-of-Years'-
Digits and Double Declining
Balance Methods at Different
Costs of Capital**

Sum-of-Years'-Digits (SYD)

Period	6%	8%	10%	12%	14%	15%	16%
1	—	—	—	—	—	—	—
2	—	—	—	—	—	—	—
3	0.908	0.881	0.855	0.831	0.808	0.796	0.786
4	0.891	0.860	0.830	0.802	0.776	0.763	0.751
5	0.875	0.839	0.806	0.775	0.746	0.732	0.719
6	0.859	0.820	0.783	0.749	0.718	0.703	0.689
7	0.844	0.801	0.761	0.725	0.692	0.676	0.661
8	0.829	0.782	0.740	0.702	0.667	0.650	0.635
9	0.814	0.765	0.720	0.680	0.643	0.626	0.610
10	0.800	0.748	0.701	0.659	0.621	0.604	0.587
11	0.786	0.731	0.683	0.639	0.600	0.582	0.565
12	0.773	0.715	0.665	0.620	0.581	0.562	0.545
13	0.760	0.700	0.648	0.602	0.562	0.543	0.526
14	0.747	0.685	0.632	0.585	0.544	0.525	0.508
15	0.734	0.671	0.616	0.569	0.527	0.508	0.491
16	0.722	0.657	0.601	0.553	0.511	0.492	0.475
17	0.711	0.644	0.587	0.538	0.496	0.477	0.460
18	0.699	0.631	0.573	0.524	0.482	0.463	0.445
19	0.688	0.618	0.560	0.510	0.468	0.449	0.432
20	0.677	0.606	0.547	0.497	0.455	0.436	0.419

Double Declining Balance (DDB)

Period	6%	8%	10%	12%	14%	15%	16%
1	—	—	—	—	—	—	—
2	—	—	—	—	—	—	—
3	0.920	0.896	0.873	0.851	0.831	0.821	0.811
4	0.898	0.868	0.840	0.814	0.789	0.777	0.766
5	0.878	0.843	0.811	0.781	0.753	0.739	0.727
6	0.858	0.819	0.783	0.749	0.718	0.704	0.689
7	0.840	0.796	0.756	0.720	0.687	0.671	0.656
8	0.821	0.774	0.731	0.692	0.657	0.641	0.625
9	0.804	0.753	0.708	0.667	0.630	0.614	0.597
10	0.787	0.733	0.685	0.643	0.605	0.588	0.571
11	0.771	0.714	0.664	0.620	0.582	0.564	0.547
12	0.755	0.696	0.644	0.599	0.559	0.541	0.524
13	0.740	0.678	0.625	0.579	0.539	0.521	0.504
14	0.725	0.661	0.607	0.560	0.520	0.501	0.484
15	0.711	0.645	0.590	0.542	0.502	0.483	0.466
16	0.697	0.630	0.573	0.526	0.485	0.466	0.450
17	0.684	0.615	0.558	0.510	0.469	0.451	0.434
18	0.671	0.601	0.543	0.495	0.454	0.436	0.419
19	0.659	0.587	0.529	0.480	0.440	0.422	0.405
20	0.647	0.574	0.515	0.467	0.427	0.409	0.392

know the *present value* of the tax savings. To illustrate the calculation of this PV, assume that an asset with a $2 cost, a five-year depreciable life, and zero salvage value is to be depreciated by the sum-of-years'-digits method (see Appendix 3A for an explanation of the method). The firm is taxed at a 40 percent rate, and its cost of capital is 10 percent. Thus the firm will save taxes of $T \times Dep = 0.4\ (\$2) = \$.80$, but these savings will occur over a five-year period.

3. We first find a new "interest factor," the PV of $1 received in accordance with the sum-of-years'-digits over a five-year period, discounted at 10 percent:

Year	Depreciation Fraction Applied to Asset Cost	Amount of Depreciation	10% Discount Factor	Product
1	5/15	$0.33333	0.909	$0.303
2	4/15	0.26667	0.826	0.220
3	3/15	0.20000	0.751	0.150
4	2/15	0.13333	0.683	0.091
5	1/15	0.06667	0.621	0.042
Totals	1.00	$1.00000	Factor =	$0.806

4. We now find the PV of the depreciation tax savings (DTS) as follows:

$$PV_{DTS} = T \times \text{Depreciable cost} \times \text{Factor}$$
$$= 0.4 \times \$2 \times 0.806 = \$.6448.$$

Thus the present value of the depreciation tax savings resulting from an investment of $2 is $.6448.

5. Table A12.1 gives factors for both the sum-of-years'-digits and double declining depreciation methods, for various asset lives and for different discount rates. The factor calculated above, 0.806, can also be found in the upper half of Table A12.1 in the 10 percent column at period 5.

We can utilize these accelerated depreciation factors to recalculate the Culver example given in Chapter 12, using the alternative, and somewhat streamlined, decision format shown in Table A12.2. The top section of the table presents the cash outflows at the time the investment is made. All these flows occur immediately, so no discounting is required, and the present value factor is 1.0. No tax adjustment is necessary on the invoice price of the new machine, but, as we saw above, the $4,000 loss on the old machine gives rise to a $1,600 tax reduction, which is deducted from the price of the new machine. Also, the $1,000 salvage value on the old machine is treated as a reduction in cash outflows necessary to acquire the new machine. Notice that since the $1,000 is a recovery of capital investment, it is not considered taxable income; hence, no tax adjustment is made for the salvage value.

In the lower section of the table we see that revenues increase by $3,000 a year—a sales increase of $1,000 plus a cost reduction of $2,000. However, this amount is taxable, so with a 40 percent tax, the after-tax benefits are reduced to $1,800. This $1,800 is received each year for ten years, so it is an annuity. The present value of the annuity, discounted at the 10 percent cost of capital, is $11,061.

Cash inflows also come from the depreciation on the new machine. This depreciation totals $10,000, and the tax saving totals $4,000. In Table A12.2 we assume that the new investment is depreciated by the double declining balance (DDB) method over a ten-year period; hence, a factor taken from Table A12.1—0.685—is applied to the after-tax depreciation figure of $4,000 to obtain a present value of $2,740 for the depreciation "tax shelter."[2]

**Table A12.2
Calculations for
Replacement Decision:
Accelerated Depreciation**

	Amount before Tax	Amount after Tax[a]	Year Event Occurs	Present Value Factor at 10%	Present Value
Outflows at Time Investment Is Made:					
Investment in new equipment	$12,000	$12,000	—	1.00	$12,000
Salvage value of old equipment[b]	−1,000	−1,000	0	1.00	−1,000
Tax loss on sale	−4,000	−1,600	0	1.00	−1,600
Total outflows (present value of costs)					$ 9,400
Inflows, or Annual Returns:					
Benefits	3,000	1,800	1–10	6.145	$11,061
Depreciation on new equipment (total)	10,000	4,000	1–10	0.685	2,740
Depreciation on old equipment (annual)	−500	−200	1–10	6.145	−1,229
Salvage value of new equipment[b]	2,000	2,000	10	0.386	772
Total inflows (present value of benefits)					$13,344

Present value of inflows less present value of outflows = $3,944.

[a] The "tax loss on sale" and depreciation figures are multiplied by T, the tax rate, to obtain the "after-tax" figures, while the benefits are multiplied by $(1 − T)$.
[b] Salvage value is not an issue in this example. However, the table is structured to show how this value would be handled in cases where it is applicable.

The old machine was being depreciated by the straight-line method; hence, it provides a cash flow of $500 before taxes and $200 after taxes for ten years. Observe that the depreciation on the old machine is *subtracted* from

2. The term *tax shelter,* or *tax shield,* is frequently used to denote the value of depreciation and other items that "shelter" or "shield" income from taxes.

the inflows section. The logic here is that, had the replacement *not* been made, the company would have had the benefit of the $500 depreciation each year for the next ten years. With the replacement, however, all this depreciation is taken immediately as an operating loss and is shown as the tax loss on sale in the upper section of the table.

When the present values of the inflows and outflows are summed, we obtain the project's NPV. In this example, the NPV is $3,944, versus $3,662 for the straight-line text example. In general, NPVs are higher when accelerated depreciation is used, since the PV of the depreciation benefit is higher than it would be under the straight-line method.

CHAPTER 13 INVESTMENT DECISIONS
UNDER UNCERTAINTY

In order to set forth systematically the concepts and procedures of capital budgeting, the preceding chapter did not consider the riskiness of alternative projects. Therefore, this chapter will add the missing dimension to capital budgeting analysis.[1] The basic idea is that greater risk requires a higher return. Hence, the discount rate used in the analysis of projects with uncertain outcomes must include a risk adjustment factor, which requires that the applicable discount rate be increased. But a higher discount factor applied to a given cash flow stream results in a reduced present value. Thus it is also necessary to determine whether the new present value still exceeds the cost of the investment and thereby adds to the value of the firm. This depends on how much the discount rate is increased by the addition of a risk adjustment factor, and the amount of the risk adjustment factor depends on how risk is measured and how the risk adjustment factor is related to the risk measure.

Risk in Financial Analysis

The riskiness of an asset is defined in terms of the likely variability of future returns from the asset. For example, if one buys a $1 million short-term government bond expected to yield 5 percent, then the return on the investment, 5 percent, can be estimated quite precisely, and the investment is defined as relatively risk-free. However, if the $1 million is invested in the stock of a company being organized to prospect for uranium in Central Africa, then the probable return cannot be estimated precisely. The rate of return on the $1 million investment could range from minus 100 percent to some extremely large figure; because of this high variability, the project is defined as relatively risky. Similarly, sales forecasts for different products of a single firm might exhibit differing degrees of riskiness. For example, Union Carbide might be quite sure that sales of its Eveready batteries will range between 50 and 60 million for the coming year but be highly uncertain about how many units of a new laser measuring device will be sold during the year. Risk, then, is associated with project variability. The more variable the expected future returns, the riskier the investment. However, risk can be defined more precisely, and it is useful to do so. The definition requires a step-by-step development, and this constitutes the remainder of the section.

Probability Distributions

Any investment decision—or, for that matter, almost *any* kind of business decision—implies a forecast of future events that is either explicit or implicit. Ordinarily, the forecast of annual cash flow is a single figure, or *point estimate,* frequently called the "most likely" or "best" estimate. For exam-

---

1. This chapter is long and introduces some important new concepts that will be applied in subsequent chapters as well.

ple, one might forecast that the cash flows from a particular project will be $500 a year for three years.

How good is this point estimate? That is, how confident is the forecaster of the predicted return—very certain, very uncertain, or somewhere in between? This degree of uncertainty can be defined and measured in terms of the forecaster's *probability distribution*—the probability estimates associated with each possible outcome. In its simplest form, a probability distribution could consist of just a few potential outcomes. For example, in forecasting cash flows, we could make an optimistic estimate, a pessimistic estimate, and a most likely estimate; or we could make high, low, and "best guess" estimates. We might expect our high, or optimistic, estimate to be realized if the national economy booms, our pessimistic estimate to hold if the economy is depressed, and our best guess to occur if the economy runs at a normal level. These ranges are illustrated in Table 13.1. The figures in the table represent some improvement over our earlier best guess estimate of $500, since additional information has been provided. However, some critical information is still missing: How likely is it that we will have a boom, a recession, or normal economic conditions? If we have estimates of the probabilities of these events, we can develop a weighted average cash flow estimate and a measure of our degree of confidence in this estimate. This point is explored in the next section.

Table 13.1
Expected Cash Flows under
Different Economic Conditions

State of the Economy	Cash Flows
Recession	$400
Normal	500
Boom	600

Risk Comparisons

To illustrate how the probability distribution concept can be used to compare the riskiness of alternative investment projects, suppose we are considering two investment decisions, each calling for an outlay of $1,000 and each expected to produce a cash flow of $500 a year for three years. (The best estimate cash flow is $500 a year for each project.) If the discount rate is 10 percent, we can use the methods developed in the preceding chapter to estimate each project's net present value:

$$\text{NPV} = \$500 \times 2.487 - \$1,000$$
$$= \$1,243.50 - \$1,000$$
$$= \$243.50$$

for each project. The projects have the same expected returns. Does this mean that they are equally desirable? To answer the question, we need to know whether the projects are also equally risky, since "desirability" depends on both returns and risk.

Suppose that Project A calls for the replacement of an old machine used in normal operations by a more efficient one and the benefits are savings in labor and raw materials. Suppose also that Project B calls for the purchase of an entirely new machine to produce a new product, the demand for which is highly uncertain. The replacement machine (Project A) will be used more; hence savings will be greater if demand for the product is high (a booming economy). Expected demand for the new product (Project B) is also greatest when the economy is booming.

We stated above that the expected annual returns from each project are $500. These figures are developed in the following manner:

1. First, we estimate project returns under different states of the economy, as in Table 13.2. Tables of this kind are typically referred to as *payoff matrices.*

Table 13.2
Payoff Matrix for Projects A and B

State of the Economy	Annual Cash Flows	
	Project A	Project B
Recession	$400	$ 0
Normal	500	500
Boom	600	1,000

2. Next, we estimate the likelihood of different states of the economy. Assume our economic forecasts indicate that, given current trends in economic indicators, the chances are two out of ten that recession will occur, six out of ten that the economy will be normal, and two out of ten that there will be a boom.

3. Redefining the word *chance* as "probability," we find that the probability of a recession is $2/10 = 0.2$, or 20 percent; the probability of normal times is $6/10 = 0.6$, or 60 percent; and the probability of a boom is $2/10 = 0.2$, or 20 percent. Notice that the probabilities add up to 1.0, or 100 percent: $0.2 + 0.6 + 0.2 = 1.0$, or 100 percent.

4. Finally, in Table 13.3 we calculate weighted averages of the possible returns by multiplying each dollar return by its probability of occurrence. When Column 4 of the table is summed, we obtain a weighted average of the outcomes for each alternative under various states of the economy, defined as the *expected value* of the cash flows from the project. It need not, of course, be equal to the project's outcome for a normal state of the economy (although this is the case for Project A but not for Project B).

We can graph the results indicated in Table 13.3 to obtain a picture of the

Table 13.3
Calculation of Expected Values

State of the Economy (1)	Probability of State Occurring (2)	Outcome If State Occurs (3)	Expected Value (2) × (3) (4)
Project A			
Recession	0.2	$400	$ 80
Normal	0.6	500	300
Boom	0.2	600	120
	1.0	Expected value =	$500
Project B			
Recession	0.2	$ 0	$ 0
Normal	0.6	500	300
Boom	0.2	1,000	200
	1.0	Expected value =	$500

variability of actual outcomes—shown in the bar charts in Figure 13.1. The height of each bar signifies the probability that a given outcome will occur. The range of probable outcomes for Project A is $400 to $600, with an average or *expected value* of $500. The expected value for Project B is also $500, but the range of possible outcomes is from $0 to $1,000.

Continuous Distributions Thus far we have assumed that only three states of the economy can exist: recession, normal, and boom. Actually, of course, the state of the economy can range from a deep depression, as in the early 1930s, to a fantastic boom; and there are an unlimited number of possibilities in between. Suppose we had the time and patience to assign a probability to each possible state of the economy (with the sum of the probabilities still equaling 1.0) and a monetary outcome to each project for each possible state. We would have a table similar to Table 13.3 except that it would have many more entries for "probability" and "outcome." This table could be used to calculate expected values, as shown above; and the probabilities and outcomes could be graphed as the continuous curves presented in Figure 13.2. Here we have changed the assumptions so there is zero probability that Project A will yield less than $400 or more than $600 and zero probability that Project B will yield less than $0 or more than $1,000.

Figure 13.2 is a graph of the *probability distributions* of returns on Projects A and B. In general, the tighter the probability distribution (or the more peaked the distribution), the more likely it is that the actual outcome will be close to the expected value. Since Project A has a relatively tight probability distribution, its *actual* profits are likely to be closer to the *expected* $500 than are those of Project B.

**Figure 13.1
Relationship between the State of
the Economy and Project Returns**

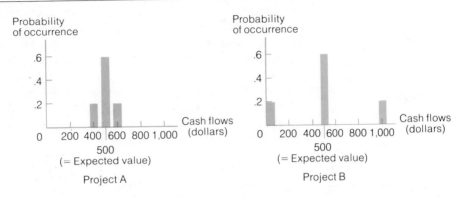

Project A

Project B

**Risk versus
Uncertainty**

Sometimes a distinction is made between *risk* and *uncertainty:* Risk is associated with situations in which a probability distribution of the returns on a given project can be estimated, and uncertainty is associated with situations in which insufficient evidence is available even to estimate a probability distribution. We do not make this distinction, however; risk and uncertainty are used synonymously in this chapter.

We do, however, recognize that probability distributions of expected re-

**Figure 13.2
Probability Distribution Showing
Relationship between State of the
Economy and Project Returns**

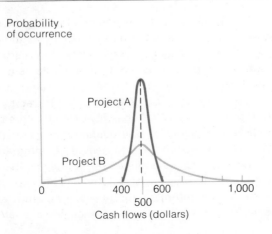

turns can themselves be estimated with greater or lesser precision. In some instances, the probability distribution can be estimated *objectively* with statistical techniques. For example, a large oil company may be able to estimate from past recovery data the probability distribution of recoverable oil reserves in a given field. When statistical procedures can be used, risk is said to be measured by *objective probability distributions.* There are, however, many situations in which statistical data cannot be used. For example, a company considering the introduction of a totally new product will have some idea about the required investment outlay, the demand for the product, the production costs, and so on. These estimates are not, however, determined by statistics; they are determined subjectively and are defined as *subjective probability distributions.*

Traditional Measures of Risk of Individual Projects

Risk is difficult to measure unambiguously. The traditional measures of risk have been applied to individual projects in isolation. Newer approaches have recognized that these projects can be combined with other projects into groups of projects, or portfolios. Viewing an individual project in its broader portfolio context changes the appropriate measure of risk to be applied. We will start with a discussion of the traditional measures of risk applied to individual projects so the relationships between the different approaches can be seen later.

The traditional measure of risk applied to individual projects is stated in terms of probability distributions such as those presented in Figure 13.2. The tighter the probability distribution of expected future returns, the smaller the risk of a given project. According to this view, Project A is less risky than Project B because each of the possible returns for A is closer to the expected return than is true for B.

Measuring Risk: Standard Deviation

The traditional approach uses a measure of the tightness of the probability distribution of project returns—the standard deviation (the symbol for which is σ—"sigma"). The tighter the probability distribution, the smaller the standard deviation. We can confirm this statement by the actual calculation of the standard deviation as presented in Table 13.4.

Column 1 lists the states of the world as portrayed by the states of the economy. Column 2 lists the probability of each of the states occurring. Column 3 lists the outcome if a particular state occurs (the outcomes are the possible returns from a given project under alternative states). Column 4 shows the expected values obtained by multiplying the probability with its associated outcome. The sum of Column 4 is the expected value for the distribution of probable returns; it represents a weighted average of the various possible outcomes. Column 5 subtracts the expected value from each

**Table 13.4
Calculation of Standard
Deviations**

State of the Economy (1)	Probability of State Occurring (2)	Outcome If State Occurs (3)	Expected Value (2) × (3) (4)	Deviation (5)	Squared Deviation (6)	Variance (2) × (6) (7)
Project A						
Boom	0.2	$600	$120	$100	$10,000	$2,000
Normal	0.6	500	300	0	0	0
Recession	0.2	400	80	−100	10,000	2,000
		Expected value =	$500		Variance =	$4,000
					Standard deviation (σ) =	$63.25
Project B						
Boom	0.2	$1,000	$200	$500	$250,000	$ 50,000
Normal	0.6	500	300	0	0	0
Recession	0.2	0	0	−500	250,000	50,000
		Expected value =	$500		Variance =	$100,000
					Standard deviation (σ) =	$316.23

possible outcome to obtain a set of deviations about the expected value. Column 6 squares each deviation. Column 7 multiplies the squared deviation by the probability of occurrence for its related outcome and sums these products to obtain the variance of the probability distribution. The standard deviation is then obtained by taking the square root of the variance.

Using these procedures, we observe in Table 13.4 that the standard deviation of Project A is $63.25 and that of Project B is $316.23. By the standard deviation criterion, Project B is riskier because its standard deviation is much larger than that for Project A. Since the expected values of the net present values for returns from the two projects are equal at $500, Project A is preferred. It has the same expected value but a smaller variance and smaller standard deviation.

**Measuring Risk:
The Coefficient
of Variation**

Certain problems can arise when the standard deviation is used as a measure of risk. To illustrate: Consider Figure 13.3, which shows the probability distributions for Investments C and D. Investment C has an expected return of $1,000 and a standard deviation of $300. Investment D also has a standard deviation of $300, but its expected return is $4,000. The likely percentage deviation from the mean of Investment C is considerably higher than that from the mean of Investment D; put another way, C has more risk *per dollar of return* than D. On this basis, it is reasonable to assign a higher degree of risk to Investment C than to Investment D even though they have identical standard deviations.

The usual procedure for handling this problem is to divide the standard

**Figure 13.3
Probability Distributions of Two
Investments with Different
Expected Returns**

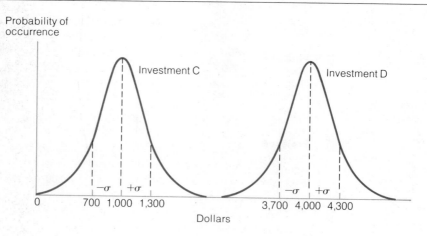

deviation (σ_j) by the mean, or expected value of net cash flows (F_j), to obtain the *coefficient of variation (CV)*:

$$CV_j = \frac{\sigma_j}{\overline{F}_j}$$

For Investment C we divide the $300 standard deviation by the $1,000 expected value or mean, obtaining 0.30 as the coefficient of variation. Similarly, for Investment D we divide the standard deviation of $300 by the mean value $4,000 to obtain 0.075. This is a much lower coefficient of variation than for Investment C. Since Investment D has a lower coefficient of variation, it has less risk per unit of return than Investment C. For the higher expected return and lower standardized measure of risk, Investment D is unambiguously preferred. Thus, if the standard deviation is to be used as a measure of risk for investments viewed in isolation, the normalization obtained by dividing through by the respective means to obtain the coefficient of variation should be used.

**Riskiness over
Time**

We can also use Figure 13.2 to consider the riskiness of a stream of receipts over time. Visualize, for example, Investment A as being the expected cash flow from a particular project during Year 1 and Investment B as being the expected cash flow from the *same* project in the tenth year. The expected return is the same for each of the two years, but the subjectively estimated standard deviation (hence the coefficient of variation) is larger for the more distant return. In this case, riskiness is *increasing over time.*

Figure 13.4 may help clarify the concept of increasing riskiness over time. Figure 13.4a simply shows the probability distribution of expected cash flows in two years—Years 1 and 10. The distribution is flatter in Year 10, indicating that there is more uncertainty about expected cash flows in distant years. Figure 13.4b represents a three-dimensional plot of the expected cash flows over time and their probability distributions. These distributions should be visualized as extending out from the page. The dashed lines show the standard deviations attached to the cash flows of each year; the fact that these lines diverge from the expected cash flow line indicates that riskiness is increasing over time. If risk were thought of as being constant over time— that is, if the cash flow in a distant year could be estimated equally as well as the cash flow in a close year—then the standard deviation would be constant, and the boundary lines would not diverge from the expected cash flow line. The fact that the standard deviation is increasing over time while the expected return is constant causes the coefficient of variation to increase similarly.

Sensitivity Analysis

In the final analysis, the NPV of a project will depend on such factors as quantity of sales, sales prices, input costs, and the like. If these values turn out to be favorable—if output and sales prices are high and costs are low— then profits, the realized rate of return, and the actual NPV will be high. Conversely, if poor results are experienced, then these three items will be low. Recognizing the causal relationships, business persons often calculate projects' NPVs under alternative assumptions, then see just how sensitive NPV is to changing conditions. To illustrate: A fertilizer company was comparing two types of phosphate plants. Fuel represents a major cost to the company. One plant used coal, which can be obtained under a long-term fixed cost contract; the other plant used oil, which must be purchased at current market prices. Considering present and projected future prices, the oil-fired plant looked better; it had a considerably higher NPV. However, oil prices are volatile; and if prices were to rise by more than the expected rate, this plant would be unprofitable. The coal-fired plant, on the other hand, had a lower NPV under the expected conditions; but this NPV was not sensitive to changing conditions in the energy market. The company finally selected the coal plant because the sensitivity analysis indicated it to be less risky.

Decision Trees

Important decisions are generally not made at one point in time; rather, they are made in stages. For example, a petroleum firm considering the possibil-

Figure 13.4
Risk as a Function of Time

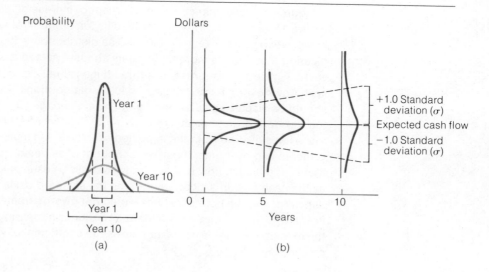

(a)   (b)

ity of expanding into agricultural chemicals may take the following steps: (1) spend $100,000 for a survey of supply-demand conditions in the agricultural chemical industry; (2) if the survey results are favorable, spend $500,000 on a pilot plant to investigate production methods; and (3) depending on the costs estimated from the pilot study and the demand potential from the market study, either abandon the project, build a large plant, or build a small one. Thus the final decision actually is made in stages, with subsequent decisions depending on the results of previous ones.

The sequence of events can be shown as branches of a tree—hence the name *decision tree.* As an example, consider Figure 13.5. There it is assumed that the petroleum company has completed its industry supply-demand analysis and pilot plant study and has determined that it should proceed to develop a full-scale production facility. The firm must now decide whether to build a large plant or a small one. Demand expectations for the plant's products are 50 percent for high demand, 30 percent for medium demand, and 20 percent for low demand. Depending on demand, net cash flows (sales revenues minus operating costs, all discounted to the present) will range from $1.4 million to $8.8 million if a large plant is built, and from $1.4 million to $2.6 million if a small plant is built.

The initial costs of the large and small plants are shown in Column 5; when these investment outlays are subtracted from the PV of cash flows, the result is the set of possible NPVs shown in Column 6. One (and only one) of these NPVs will actually occur. Finally, we multiply Column 6 by Column 3

Figure 13.5
Illustrative Decision Tree

Action (1)	Demand Conditions (2)	Probability (3)	Present Value of Cash Flows (4)	Less Initial Cost (5)	Possible NPV (4) − (5) (6)	Probable NPV (3) × (6) (7)
Build big plant: Invest $5 million	High	0.5	$8,800,000	$5,000,000	$3,800,000	$1,900,000
	Medium	0.3	$3,500,000	$5,000,000	($1,500,000)	($450,000)
	Low	0.2	$1,400,000	$5,000,000	($3,600,000)	($720,000)
					Expected NPV	$730,000
Build small plant: Invest $2 million	High	0.5	$2,600,000	$2,000,000	$600,000	$300,000
	Medium	0.3	$2,400,000	$2,000,000	$400,000	$120,000
	Low	0.2	$1,400,000	$2,000,000	($600,000)	($120,000)
					Expected NPV	$300,000

Decision point

to obtain Column 7, and the sums in Column 7 give the expected NPVs of the large and small plants.

Because the expected NPV of the large plant ($730,000) is larger than that of the small plant ($300,000), should the decision be to build the large plant? Perhaps, but not necessarily. Notice that the range of outcomes is greater if the large plant is built, with the possible NPVs (Column 4 in Figure 13.5 minus the investment cost) varying from $3.8 million to minus $3.6 million. However, a range of only $600,000 to minus $600,000 exists for the small plant. Since the required investments for the two plants are not the same, we must examine the coefficients of variation of the net present value possibilities in order to determine which alternative actually entails the greater risk. The coefficient of variation for the large plant's present value is 4.3, while that for the small plant is only 1.5.[2] Thus risk is greater if the decision is to build the large plant.

2. Using Equation 13.3 and the data on possible returns in Figure 13.5, the standard deviation of returns for the larger plant is found to be $3.155 million and for the smaller one $458,260. Dividing each of these standard deviations by the expected returns for their respective plant size gives the coefficients of variation.

Computer Simulation

The concepts embodied in decision tree analysis can be extended to computer simulation. To illustrate the technique, let us consider a proposal to build a new textile plant. The cost of the plant is not known for certain, although it is expected to run about $150 million. If no problems are encountered, the cost can be as low as $125 million, while an unfortunate series of events—such as strikes, unprojected increases in materials costs, and technical problems—could result in a cost as high as $225 million.

Revenues from the new facility, which will operate for many years, will depend on population growth and income in the region, competition, developments in synthetic fabrics research, and textile import quotas. Operating costs will depend on production efficiency, materials and labor cost trends, and the like. Since both sales revenues and operating costs are uncertain, annual profits are also uncertain.

Assuming that probability distributions can be assigned to each of the major cost and revenue determinants, a computer program can be constructed to simulate what is likely to happen. In effect, the computer selects one value at random from each of the relevant distributions, combines it with other values selected from the other distributions, and produces an estimated profit and net present value, or rate of return on investment.[3] The particular profit and rate of return occur, of course, only for the particular combination of values selected during this trial. The computer goes on to select other sets of values and to compute other profits and rates of return repeatedly, for perhaps several hundred trials. A count is kept of the number of times each rate of return is computed; and when the computer runs are completed, the frequency with which the various rates of return occurred can be plotted as a frequency distribution.

The procedure is illustrated in Figures 13.6 and 13.7.[4] Figure 13.6 is a flowchart outlining the simulation procedure described above, while Figure 13.7 illustrates the frequency distribution of rates of return generated by such a simulation for two investments—X and Y—each with an expected cost of $20 million. The expected rate of return on Investment X is 15 percent and that on Investment Y is 20 percent. However, these are only the *average* rates of return generated by the computer; simulated rates range from 5 to 25 percent for Investment X and from −10 percent to +45 percent for Investment Y. The standard deviation generated for X is only 4 percentage points—68 percent of the computer runs had rates of return between

---

3. If the variables are not independent, then conditional probabilities must be employed. For example, if demand is weak, then both sales in units and sales prices are likely to be low; and these interrelationships must be taken into account in the simulation.

4. The methodology illustrated in Figure 13.6 was developed in an article by David B. Hertz, "Risk Analysis in Capital Investment," *Harvard Business Review* (January–February 1964).

**Figure 13.6
Simulation for Investment
Planning**

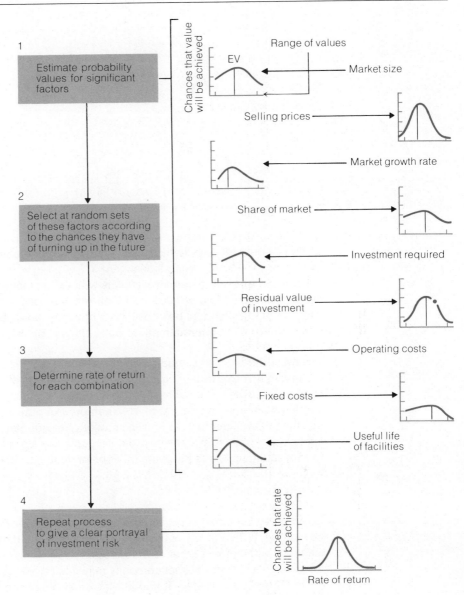

Figure 13.7
Expected Rates of Return on
Investments X and Y

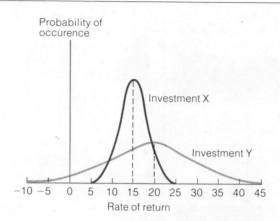

11 and 19 percent—while that for Y is 12 percentage points. Clearly, then, Investment Y is riskier than Investment X.

The computer simulation provides us with an estimate of both the expected returns on two projects and their relative risks. A decision about which alternative should be chosen can now be made, perhaps by using the risk-adjusted discount rate method or perhaps in an informal manner by the decision maker.

However, computer simulation is not always feasible for risk analysis. The technique involves obtaining probability distributions about a number of variables—investment outlays, unit sales, product prices, input prices, asset lives, and so on—and paying for a fair amount of programming and machine time. Therefore, full-scale simulation is not generally worthwhile except for large and expensive projects, such as major plant expansions or new-product decisions involving millions of dollars.

Risk Analysis in a Portfolio Context

In recent years, a new approach that views risk in a portfolio framework has been developed. It involves a consideration of the relationship between a single investment and other existing assets or potential investment opportunities. To illustrate: A steel company may decide to diversify into residential construction materials. It knows that when the economy is booming, the demand for steel is high and the returns from the steel mill are large. It also knows that residential construction tends to be countercyclical; that is, when the economy as a whole is in a recession, the demand for construction materials is high.[5] Because of these cyclical patterns, a diversified firm with investments in both steel and construction could expect to have a more stable pattern of revenues than could a firm engaged exclusively in either steel or residential construction. In other words, the deviations in the returns on the *portfolio of assets, σ,* may be less than the sum of the deviations in the returns from the individual assets.[6]

The point is illustrated in Figure 13.8. Figure 13.8(a) shows the rate of return variations for the steel plant; Figure 13.8(b) shows the fluctuations for the residential construction material division; and Figure 13.8(c) shows the rate of return for the combined company. When the returns from steel are large, those from residential construction are small, and vice versa. As a consequence, the combined rate of return is relatively stable.

If we calculate the correlation between rates of return on the steel and construction divisions, we find the correlation coefficient to be negative; whenever rates of return on the steel plant are high, those on the construction material plants are low. If any two projects, A and B, have a high degree of *negative correlation,* then taking on the two investments reduces the firm's overall risk. This risk reduction is defined as a *portfolio effect.*

On the other hand, if there is a high *positive correlation* between Projects A and B—that is, if returns on A are high, at the same time those on B are high—overall risk is not reduced significantly by diversification. If the correlation between A and B is +1.0, the risk reduction is zero, so no portfolio effect is obtained. If the returns from the two projects are completely uncorrelated—the correlation coefficient between them is zero—then diversification will benefit the firm to at least some extent. The larger the number of uncorrelated, or independent, projects the firm takes on, the smaller the variation in its overall rate of return.[7] Uncorrelated projects are not as useful for reducing risk as are negatively correlated ones, but they are better than positively correlated ones.

Correlation coefficients range from +1.0, indicating perfect positive correlation, to −1.0, indicating perfect negative correlation. If the correlation coefficient is zero, then the projects are independent, or uncorrelated.

5. The countercyclical behavior of the residential construction industry has to do with the availability of credit. When the economy is booming, interest rates are high. High interest rates seem to discourage potential home buyers more than they do other demanders of credit. As a result, the residential construction industry has historically shown marked countercyclical tendencies.
6. These conclusions obviously hold also for portfolios of financial assets—stocks and bonds. In fact the basic concepts of portfolio theory were developed specifically for common stocks by Harry Markowitz and were first presented in his article, "Portfolio Selection," *Journal of Finance* 7 (March 1952). The logical extension of portfolio theory to capital budgeting calls for considering firms as having "portfolios of tangible assets."
7. The principle involved here is the so-called law of large numbers. As the number of independent projects is increased, the standard deviation of the returns on the portfolio of projects decreases with the square root of the number of projects taken on.

**Figure 13.8
Relationship of Returns on Two
Hypothetical Investments**

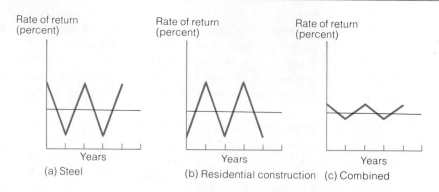

(a) Steel (b) Residential construction (c) Combined

We can summarize the arguments on portfolio risk that have been presented thus far:

1. If *perfectly negatively correlated* projects are available in sufficient
   number, then diversification can completely eliminate risk. Perfect negative correlation is, however, almost never found in the real world.
2. If *uncorrelated* projects are available in sufficient number, then diversification can reduce risk significantly—to zero at the limit.
3. If all alternative projects are *perfectly positively correlated,* then diversification cannot reduce risk at all.

In fact, most projects are *positively* correlated but not *perfectly* correlated.
The degree of intercorrelation depends on economic factors, and these factors are usually amenable to analysis. Returns on investment in projects
closely related to the firm's basic products and markets are ordinarily highly
correlated with returns on the remainder of the firm's assets, and such investments do not generally reduce the firm's risk. However, investments in
other product lines and in other geographic markets may have a low degree
of correlation with other components of the firm and may, therefore, reduce
overall risk. Accordingly, if an asset's returns are not too closely related to
the firm's other major assets (or, better still, are negatively correlated with
them), this asset is more valuable to a risk-averting firm than is a similar
asset whose returns are positively correlated with the bulk of the firm's assets.

**Portfolio
Opportunities**

A *portfolio* is defined as a combination of assets, and portfolio theory deals
with the selection of optimal portfolios—portfolios that provide the highest
possible return for any specified degree of risk or the lowest possible risk

for any specified rate of return. Portfolio theory has been developed most thoroughly for financial assets—stocks and bonds.[8] However, extension of the theory to physical assets is readily made, and certainly the concepts are relevant in capital budgeting.

Suppose we are considering N assets, with N being any number greater than 1. These assets can be combined into an almost limitless number of portfolios, and each possible portfolio will have an expected rate of return, $E(k_p)$, and risk, σ_p. The hypothetical set of all possible portfolios—defined as the *attainable set*—is graphed as the shaded area in Figure 13.9.

Given the full set of potential portfolios that can be constructed from the available assets, which portfolio should be chosen? The choice involves two separate decisions: (1) determining the efficient set of portfolios and (2) choosing from the efficient set the single portfolio that is best for the individual investor. The remainder of this section discusses the concept of the efficient set of portfolios; the next section considers choices among efficient portfolios.

An *efficient portfolio* is a portfolio that provides the highest possible expected return for any degree of risk or the lowest possible degree of risk for any expected return. In Figure 13.9 the boundary BCDE defines the efficient set of portfolios.[9] Portfolios to the left of the efficient set are not possible, because they lie outside the attainable set; that is, there is no set of k_i values that will yield a portfolio with an expected rate of return $E(k_p)$ and risk σ_p represented by a point to the left of BCDE. Portfolios to the right of the efficient set are inefficient, because some other portfolio could provide either a higher return with the same degree of risk or a lower risk for the same rate of return. To illustrate: Consider Point X. Portfolio C provides the same rate of return as Portfolio X, but C is less risky. At the same time, Portfolio D is as risky as Portfolio X, but D provides a higher expected rate of return. Points C and D (and other points on the boundary of the efficient set between C and D) are said to dominate Point X.

Risk-Return Indifference Curves

Given the efficient set of portfolio combinations, which specific portfolio should an investor choose? To determine this, we must know the investor's attitude toward risk, or the risk-return tradeoff function.

An investor's risk-return tradeoff function is based on the standard economic concept of indifference curves, as illustrated in Figure 13.10. The curves labelled I_A and I_B represent the indifference curves of Individuals A

8. Financial assets are highly divisible and available in large numbers, and a great deal of data are available on them. Capital assets such as plant and equipment, on the other hand, are "lumpy," and the data needed to apply portfolio theory to such assets are not readily available.
9. A computational procedure for determining the efficient set of portfolios was developed by Harry Markowitz and first reported in his article "Portfolio Selection."

Figure 13.9
The Efficient Set of Investments

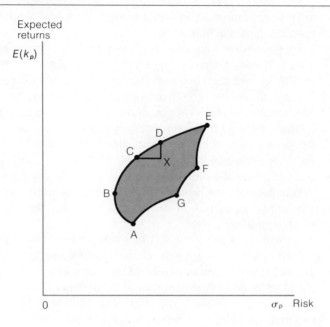

and B. A is equally well satisfied with a riskless 4 percent return, an expected 6 percent return with risk of $\sigma_p = 4$ percent, and so on. B is indifferent in regard to the riskless 4 percent portfolio, a portfolio with an expected return of 6 percent but with a risk of $\sigma_p = 2$ percent, and so on.

Notice that B requires a higher expected rate of return as compensation for a given increase in risk than does A; thus B is more risk averse than A. For example, if $\sigma_p = 4$ percent, B requires a return of 10 percent, while A requires a return of only 6 percent. In other words, B requires a *risk premium*—the difference between the riskless return (4 percent) and the required return—of 6 percentage points to compensate for the risk $\sigma_p = 4$ percent, while A's risk premium for this degree of risk is only 2 percentage points.

An infinite number of utility curves representing the risk-return tradeoff for different levels of satisfaction could be drawn for each individual, as shown in Figure 13.11. For a given level of σ_p, a greater $E(k_p)$ is received as the curves move farther out to the left. Each point on Curve I_{A2} represents a higher level of satisfaction, or greater utility, than any point on I_{A1}; and I_{A3} represents more utility than I_{A2}. Also, different individuals are likely to have different sets of curves or different risk-return tradeoffs. Since the curves of B start from the same point and have a greater slope in the risk-return plane than the curves of A, this indicates that Investor B requires a higher return

**Figure 13.10
Indifference Curves for Risk and
Expected Rate of Return**

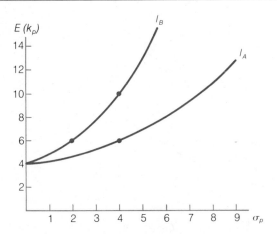

for the same amount of risk. Then, similarly for Investor B, as the curves
move to the left, this represents high levels of satisfaction.

**The Optimal
Portfolio for an
Investor**

We can now combine the efficient set of portfolios with indifference curves
to determine an individual investor's optimal portfolio. In Figure 13.12 we
see that the optimal portfolio is found at the tangency point between the efficient set of portfolios and an indifference curve. This tangency point marks
the highest level of satisfaction the investor can attain. A picks a combination of securities (a portfolio) that provides an expected return of about 13
percent and has a risk of about $\sigma_p = 5$ percent. B, who is more risk averse
than A, picks a portfolio with a lower expected return (about 11 percent) but
a riskiness of only $\sigma_p = 3.7$ percent.

Figure 13.12 presents a framework for analyzing risky investments in a
portfolio context. We cannot in general say that Point A for Individual A is
better than Point B for Individual B or vice versa. All the points on the portfolio boundary segment MN are efficient in the sense that they achieve
the highest return for a given amount of risk or for a given return minimizing
the amount of risk. The choice of portfolios that carry different combinations of risk and return reflects the attitude of the individual decision maker
toward the tradeoffs between risk and return. An individual who has a high
degree of risk aversion (as illustrated by Individual B in Figure 13.12) is willing to bear only a small amount of risk and earns a relatively smaller amount
of return. An individual who is less risk averse is compensated for bearing
more risk by a higher expected return.

**Figure 13.11
Family of Indifference Curves
for Individuals A and B**

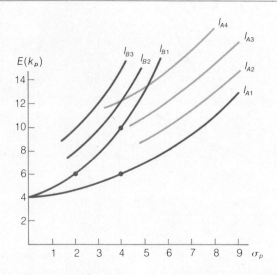

The coefficient of variation (0.05/0.13) for Individual A is 0.38; this is higher than the coefficient of variation (0.37/0.11) for Individual B, which is 0.24. Under this measure, Individual B is incurring less risk than Individual A, but this does not mean that Individual B's investment is "better" in any sense. The decisions of Individual A and Individual B represent a point at which their utility function is tangent to an efficient boundary of portfolio choices.

The Capital Asset Pricing Model

From the portfolio approach to the measurement of risk, the capital asset pricing model (CAPM) sets forth a theory of the relationship between the risk of an asset and the required risk adjustment factor.[10] This relationship is expressed in the security market line (SML) as:

$$E(k_j) = R_F + [E(k_M) - R_F]\beta_j, \qquad (13.1)$$

where:

$E(k_j)$ = the expected return on an investment or security.
R_F = a risk-free return.
$E(k_m)$ = the expected return on the market.

10. See J. Fred Weston and Eugene F. Brigham, *Managerial Finance*, 6th ed. (Hinsdale, Ill.: Dryden Press, 1978), app. D to chap. 11, for a formal development of the CAPM from the theory of portfolio choices.

Figure 13.12
Optimal Portfolio Selection

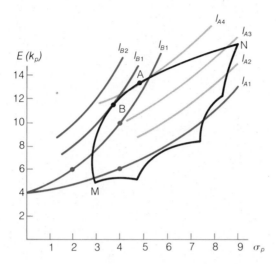

β_i(beta) = a measure of the volatility of the individual investment's returns relative to the market returns.

The logic of the security market line equation is that the required return on an investment is a risk-free return plus a risk adjustment factor. The risk adjustment factor is obtained by multiplying the risk premium required for the market return by the riskiness of the individual investment. If the returns on the individual investment fluctuate by exactly the same degree as the returns on the market as a whole, the beta for the security is 1. In this situation the required return on the individual investment is the same as the required return on the total market. If the variation in the returns of an individual investment is greater than the variation in the market returns, the beta of the individual investment is greater than 1, and its risk adjustment factor is greater than the risk adjustment factor for the market as a whole.

The relationship between the riskiness of an individual investment as measured by its beta and the risk adjustment factor is illustrated in Figure 13.13. The risk-free return is given as 6 percent. If we use 11 percent as the long-term average return on the market, the market risk premium is 11 percent minus 6 percent, which is 5 percent, the slope of the SML. If the risk-free return is 6 percent, the required return on the market is 6 percent plus a risk adjustment factor of 5 percent, totaling 11 percent.

The required return on an individual investment depends on the size of its beta, which measures the variations in its returns in relation to the returns on the market. If the beta of an individual investment is 1.2, its risk adjustment factor is 1.2 times the market risk adjustment factor of 5 percent. The

**Figure 13.13
Graph of the Security
Market Line**

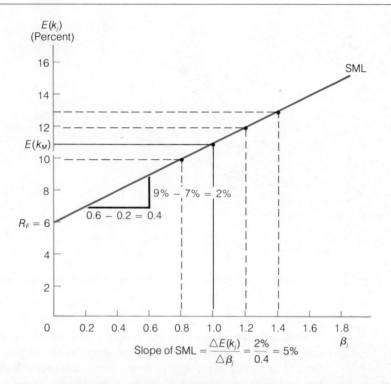

Slope of SML $= \dfrac{\triangle E(k_j)}{\triangle \beta_j} = \dfrac{2\%}{0.4} = 5\%$

risk adjustment factor for the individual investment is therefore 6 percent, and its required return is 12 percent. If the beta measure of an investment is 1.4, its risk adjustment factor is 7 percent, and its required return is 13 percent. An investment with a beta of 0.8 has a risk adjustment factor of 4 percent and a required return of 10 percent.

The advantages of the security market line approach to measuring the risk adjustment factor and the required return on an investment are that the relationships can be quantified and that they have been subjected to considerable statistical testing. But it would be premature to discard the earlier approach that analyzes the risk of an individual investment by its standard deviation and coefficient of variation. There are a number of reasons for keeping both approaches:

1. Some studies have found that the standard deviation does in fact have an influence on the required return of a security.
2. Empirical studies of the SML confirm a positive relationship between risk and return, but the observed SML appears to be tilted clockwise from the theoretical line, as shown in Figure 13.14. Low beta assets earn more

Figure 13.14
Theoretical versus Statistical
Estimates of the SML

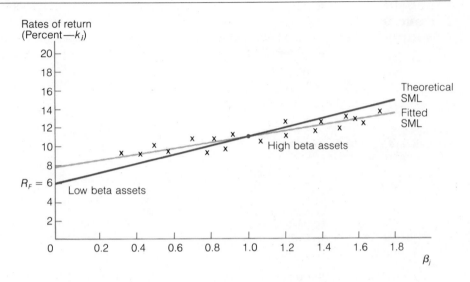

than the CAPM would predict, and high beta assets earn less than the CAPM would predict.

3. The CAPM utilizes historical data, and all the terms in the SML can be different, depending on the time period selected for measurement. Thus, for some time periods, the average return on the market may be as low as 5 to 6 percent (or even negative). The risk-free rate may rise or fall depending on the expected rate of inflation. Note, however, that if the rate of inflation causes the risk-free rate and market return to rise by the same number of percentage points, the market risk adjustment factor is unchanged. For example, suppose that with an expected rate of inflation of 3 percent per year, the risk-free rate is 5 percent and the market rate of return 10 percent. With an expected rate of inflation of 4 percent, the risk-free rate may rise to 6 percent and the market rate of return to 11 percent. In both cases, the market risk adjustment factor remains at 5 percent.

4. The β for an individual security reflects industry characteristics and management policies that determine how returns fluctuate in relation to variations in overall market returns. If the general economic environment is stable, if industry characteristics remain unchanged, and if management policies have continuity, the measure of β will be relatively stable when calculated for different time periods. However, if these conditions do not exist, the value of β will vary as the characteristics of investments or securities change in their relationship to the total market.

The Use of Risk-Adjusted Discount Rates: An Example

The CV and SML methods both aid in the analysis of investment decisions under uncertainty. In addition, the use of these two alternative approaches to measuring the risk adjustment factor does not necessarily give conflicting results. This is the case even when the coefficient of variation is greater for one investment while its beta is smaller. Assume that the risk-free rate is 6 percent and the expected market return is 11 percent. Consider two investments, I and J, for which the measures in Table 13.5 have been calculated.

Table 13.5
Return and Risk Estimates for Two Investment Projects

	Investment I	Investment J
Expected return (k)	0.20	0.14
Standard deviation (σ)	0.80	0.42
Coefficient of variation (CV)	4.00	3.00
Beta (β)	1.50	2.00

If the financial manager uses the SML, the required returns for the two investments are:

$$k_I^* = 0.06 + (0.11 - 0.06)\ 1.5 = 0.12.$$
$$k_J^* = 0.06 + (0.11 - 0.06)\ 2.0 = 0.16.$$

Using the CAPM, Investment I has a required return of 12 percent but an expected return of 20 percent; Investment J has a required return of 16 percent but an expected return of 14 percent. For Investment I the expected return exceeds the required return by 8 percentage points; for Investment J the expected return falls short of the required return by 2 percentage points.

But the coefficient of variation of Investment I is greater than the coefficient of variation of Investment J. Suppose the decision maker formulates a risk adjustment relationship based on the coefficient of variation, such as:

$$k^* = \text{Risk-free return} + 0.03\ \text{CV}$$

The required return for Investment I is 18 percent, while the required return for Investment J is 15 percent. Now the decision is closer, because the expected return on Investment I is only 2 percentage points above its required return, while the expected return for Investment J is only 1 percentage point below its required return. Investment I still exceeds its required return, but Investment J falls somewhat short of its required return.

If the investments are mutually exclusive (for example, a gas-powered versus an electric-powered forklift truck for handling materials in a factory), Investment I will probably be preferred to Investment J. But with the results so close, the financial manager may request that estimates of revenues, investment costs, maintenance costs, and all other factors that might affect the measures in Table 13.5 be reexamined and reworked. A sensitivity analysis of the critical factors affecting the level and variability of returns would be useful to estimate their influence on the measures in Table 13.5. Thus the use of both the CV and β approaches might result in better insights and decisions by the financial manager.

Summary

Two facts of life in finance are (1) that investors are averse to risk and (2) that at least some risk is inherent in most business decisions. Given investor aversion to risk and differing degrees of risk in different financial alternatives, it is necessary to consider the subject of risk in financial analysis.

The first task is to define what is meant by *risk;* the second task is to measure it. The concept of *probability* is a fundamental element in both the definition and the measurement of risk. A probability distribution shows the probability of occurrence of each possible outcome, assuming a given investment is undertaken. The mean, or weighted average, of the distribution is defined as the *expected value* of the investment. The coefficient of variation of the distribution or sometimes the standard deviation (both of which measure the extent to which actual outcomes are likely to vary from the expected value) are useful measures of risk.

Under most circumstances, distant returns are considered to be riskier than near-term returns. Thus the standard deviation and coefficient of variation for distant cash flows are likely to be higher than those for cash flows expected relatively soon, even when the cash flows are from the same project.

In appraising the riskiness of an individual capital investment, both the variability of the expected returns of the project itself and the correlation between expected returns on this project and the remainder of the firm's assets must be taken into account. This relationship is called the *portfolio effect* of the particular project. Favorable portfolio effects are strongest when a project is negatively correlated with the firm's other assets and weakest when it is positively correlated. Portfolio effects lie at the heart of the firm's efforts to diversify into product lines not closely related to the main line of business.

The use of the portfolio approach to analyzing investments resulted in the development of the capital asset pricing model (CAPM), which measures the tradeoff between risk and return with the use of the security market line (SML). The SML estimates the required return on investment by adding a risk adjustment factor, or premium, to the risk-free return. The risk adjustment factor is the risk premium in the market return (the expected return on the market minus the risk-free return) multiplied by a measure of the riskiness of the individual investment or security—its beta measure. The beta measure is the ratio of the variability of returns on an individual investment to the variability of returns on the market as a whole.

The SML is useful in quantifying the relationship between return and risk. However, its estimates are subject to change over time and have not been measured with precision. SML measures must be combined with judgmental estimates to arrive at financial decisions. In formulating judgments, the earlier measures of risk—the standard deviation and the coefficient of variation—will also aid in the analysis.

Thus we have two useful formal approaches to investment decisions under uncertainty. In addition, the formal approaches should be supplemented by techniques such as decision tree formulations, sensitivity analysis, and simulation of the consequences of alternative estimates of critical variables in the calculations. Simulation of possible outcomes enables us to determine the variations in the measures used in the formal approaches resulting from alternative estimates of critical input variables. Formal approaches, simulation with sensitivity analysis, and judgmental methods are all required in the effort to make sound investment decisions in a world in which outcomes are uncertain.

Questions

13.1 Define the following terms, using graphs to illustrate your answers wherever feasible:
a. risk
b. uncertainty
c. probability distribution
d. expected value
e. standard deviation
f. coefficient of variation
g. portfolio effects

13.2 The probability distribution of a less risky expected return is more peaked than that of a risky return. What shape would the probability distribution have for
a. completely certain returns?
b. completely uncertain returns?

13.3 Project A has an expected return of $500 and a standard deviation of $100. Project B also has a standard deviation of $100, but it has an expected return of $300. Which project is riskier? Why?

13.4 Assume that residential construction and industries related to it are countercyclical to the economy in general and to steel in particular. Does this negative correlation between steel and construction-related industries necessarily mean that a savings and loan association, whose profitability tends to vary with construction levels, would be less risky if it diversified by acquiring a steel distributor?

13.5 What is the value of decision trees in managerial decision making?

13.6 In computer simulation, the computer makes a large number of "trials" to show what the various outcomes of a particular decision might be if the decision could be made many times under the same conditions. In practice, the decision will be made only once, so how can simulation results be useful to the decision maker?

13.7 Suppose that inflation causes the nominal risk-free return and the market return to rise by an equal amount. Will the market risk premium be affected?

Problems

13.1 An investment proposal has been analyzed, and the following information has been established:

Cash Flow	
Probability	Amount
0.3	$15,000
0.5	20,000
0.2	25,000

The outlay is $100,000, the expected life is ten years, and the cost of capital is 12 percent. Assume zero salvage.
a. Calculate the expected NPV and expected IRR.
b. Calculate the probability that the investment will be a good one (that is, have NPV > 0).

13.2 The Rowan Company is faced with two mutually exclusive investment projects. Each project costs $4,500, and each has an expected life of three years. Annual net cash flows from each project begin one year after the initial investment is made and have the following probability distributions:

Project A		Project B	
Probability	Cash Flow	Probability	Cash Flow
0.2	$4,000	0.2	$ 0
0.6	4,500	0.6	4,500
0.2	5,000	0.2	12,000

Rowan has decided to evaluate the riskier project at a 12 percent rate and the less risky project at a 10 percent rate.
a. What is the expected value of the annual net cash flows from each project?
b. What is the risk-adjusted NPV of each project?
c. If it were known that Project B was negatively correlated with other cash flows of the firm, while Project A was positively correlated, how should this knowledge affect the decision?

13.3 Your firm is considering the purchase of a tractor. It has been established that this tractor will cost $32,000, will produce revenues in the neighborhood of $10,000 (before tax), and will be depreciated via straight line to zero in eight years. The board of directors, however, is having a heated debate as to whether the tractor can be expected to last eight years. Specifically, Wayne Brown insists that he knows of some that have lasted only five years. Tom Miller agrees with Wayne but argues that it is more likely that the tractor will give eight years of service. Wayne agrees. Finally, Ralph Evans says he has seen some last as long as ten years. Given this discussion, the board asks you to prepare a sensitivity analysis to ascertain how important the uncertainty about the life of the tractor is. Assume a 40 percent tax rate on both income and capital loss, zero salvage value, and a cost of capital of 10 percent.

13.4 You have an investment opportunity for which the outlay and cash flows are uncertain. Analysis has produced the following subjective probability assessments:

Outlay		Annual Cash Flow	
Probability	Amount	Probability	Amount
0.4	$ 80,000	0.2	$14,000
0.3	100,000	0.5	16,000
0.2	120,000	0.3	18,000
0.1	140,000		

Let the cost of capital be 12 percent, life expectancy be ten years, and salvage value be zero.
   a. Construct a decision tree for this investment to show probabilities, payoffs, and expected NPV.
   b. Calculate the expected NPV, again using expected cash flow and expected outlay.
   c. What is the probability of and the NPV of the worst possible outcome?
   d. What is the probability of and the NPV of the best possible outcome?
   e. Compute the probability that this will be a good investment.

13.5 Your firm is considering two mutually exclusive investment projects—Project A at a cost of $110,000 and Project B at a cost of $140,000. The planning division of your firm has estimated the following probability distribution of cash flows to be generated by each project in each of the next five years:

Project A		Project B	
Probability	Cash Flow	Probability	Cash Flow
0.2	$15,000	0.2	$10,000
0.6	30,000	0.6	40,000
0.2	35,000	0.2	60,000

   a. Which of the projects is the riskier if the coefficient of variation is used as a measure of risk?
   b. Each project's risk is different from that of the firm as a whole. The firm's management adjusts for risk by means of the formula:

$$k_j = R_F + 10CV$$

   where:

   k_j = the required rate of return on the jth project.
   R_F = the risk-free rate and is equal to 6 percent.
   CV = coefficient of variation of the project's cash flows.

   What are the required rates of return on Projects A and B?

c. Which of the projects, if either, should be accepted by the firm? Explain and support your answer. In calculating the NPVs, round the cost of capital figures calculated in Part b to the nearest whole number.

13.6 The risk-free rate is 4 percent, and the market risk premium is 5 percent. Under consideration for investment outlays are Projects A, B, and C, with estimated betas of 0.8, 1.2, and 2, respectively. What will be the required rates of return on these projects based on the security market line approach?

13.7 The risk-free rate of return is 6 percent, and the market risk premium is 5 percent. The beta of the project under analysis is 1.8, with expected net cash flows after taxes estimated at $600 for five years. The required investment outlay on the project is $1,800.
   a. What is the required risk-adjusted return on the project?
   b. Should the project be accepted?

13.8 The McWilliams Company is considering two investment projects, A and B, for which the following measures have been calculated:

	Investment A	Investment B
Investment outlay required (I)	$20,000	$20,000
Expected return (k)	0.20	0.20
Standard deviation of returns (σ)	0.40	0.60
Coefficient of variation of returns (CV)	2.0	3.0
Beta of returns (β)	1.8	1.2

The vice-president of finance has formulated a risk adjustment relationship based on the coefficient of variation:

   Required return on a project = Risk-free return + 0.04CV.

He also takes into consideration the security market line relationship, using 6 percent as the estimate of the risk-free return and 5 percent as the market risk premium.
   a. What is the required return on each project using alternative methods of calculating the risk adjustment factor?
   b. If the two projects are independent, should they both be accepted?
   c. If the projects are mutually exclusive, which one should be accepted?
   d. Why might the two investments have different risks, depending upon the approach to risk measurement used?
   e. What additional analysis might be performed before a final decision is made?

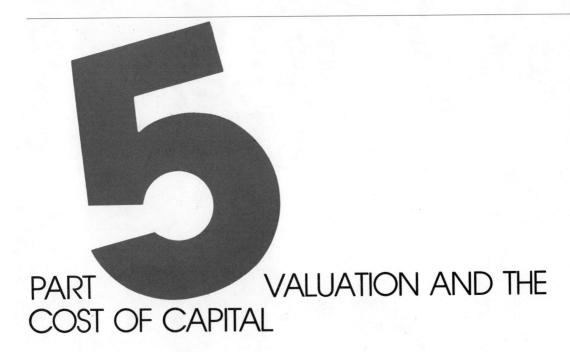

PART 5

VALUATION AND THE COST OF CAPITAL

Part 4 developed the concepts needed for making investment decisions; in a number of places it made use of cost of capital. Part 5 provides the basis for determining the relevant cost of capital and how it is influenced by financial decisions. It also examines financing decisions in their broad categories of debt versus equity. It attempts to determine the optimal financial structure—the financial structure that simultaneously minimizes the firm's cost of capital and maximizes the market value of its common stock. Financing decisions and in-vestment decisions are interdependent—the optimal financing plan and the optimal level of investment must be determined simultaneously—so Part 5 also serves the important function of integrating the theory of capital budgeting with the theory of capital structure.

Part 5 contains four chapters. Chapter 14 examines the way risk and return interact to determine value. Chapter 15 highlights the manner in which debt generally increases both expected earnings and the firm's risk position. Chapter 16 draws on the two preceding chapters to establish the firm's optimal capital structure and cost of capital. Finally, Chapter 17 analyzes the decision of whether to pay out earnings in the form of dividends or to retain earnings for reinvestment in the business. It also shows the relationship between capital budgeting and the cost of capital.

CHAPTER

OF RETURN

VALUATION AND RATES

One of the financial manager's principal goals is to maximize the value of the firm's stock; accordingly, this chapter explains how the market values securities and why this knowledge is essential to sound financial management. Also, the rate of return concepts developed in the chapter are used extensively in Chapters 15 and 16, which analyze the optimal capital structure and show how to calculate a marginal cost of capital for use in capital budgeting.

Definitions of Value

While it may be difficult to ascribe monetary returns to certain kinds of assets—works of art, for instance—the fundamental characteristic of business assets is that they give rise to income flows. Sometimes these flows are easy to determine and measure; the interest return on a bond is an example. At other times, the cash flows attributable to the asset must be estimated, as was done in Chapters 12 and 13 in the evaluation of projects. Regardless of the difficulties of measuring income flows, it is the prospective income from business assets that gives them value.

Liquidating Value versus Going-Concern Value

Several different definitions of *value* exist in the literature and in practice; different definitions are appropriate at different times. The first distinction that must be made is that between liquidating value and going-concern value. *Liquidating value* is the amount that can be realized if an asset or a group of assets (the entire assets of a firm, for example) is sold separately from the organization that has been using them. If the owner of a machine shop decides to retire, he may auction off his inventory and equipment, collect his accounts receivable, and sell his land and buildings to a grocery wholesaler for use as a warehouse. The sum of the proceeds from each category of assets is the liquidating value of the assets. If the owner's debts are subtracted from this amount, the difference represents the liquidating value of his ownership in the business.

The *going-concern value* of a company is its worth as an operating business to another firm or individual. If this value exceeds the liquidating value, the difference represents the value of the organization as distinct from the value of the assets.[1]

Book Value versus Market Value

Book value, the accounting value at which an asset is carried, must also be distinguished from *market value,* the price at which the asset can be sold. If the asset in question is a firm, it actually has two market values—a liquidat-

---

1. Accountants have termed this difference "goodwill," but "organization value" would be a more appropriate description.

ing value and a going-concern value. Only the higher of the two is generally referred to as the market value.

For stocks, book value per share is the firm's total common equity—common stock, capital or paid-in surplus, and accumulated retained earnings—divided by shares outstanding. Market value, what people will actually pay for a share of the stock, can be above or below book value. Nuclear Research, for example, has a book value of $8.27 per share and a market value of $25.50; West Virginia Railroad, on the other hand, has a book value of $112.80 and a market value of only $6.75. Nuclear Research's assets produce a high and rapidly growing earnings stream; West Virginia Railroad's assets are far less productive. Since market value depends on earnings, while book value reflects historical cost, it is not surprising to find deviations between book and market values in a dynamic, uncertain world.

Market Value versus Fair or Reasonable Value

The concept of fair or reasonable value (sometimes called intrinsic value) is widespread in the literature on stock market investments. Although the market value of a security is known at any given time, the security's fair value as viewed by different investors can differ. Graham, Dodd, and Cottle, authors of a leading investments text, define *fair value* as "that value which is justified by the facts; e.g., assets, earnings, dividends. . . . The computed [fair] value is likely to change at least from year to year, as the factors governing that value are modified."[2]

Although Graham, Dodd, and Cottle have developed this concept for security (that is, stock and bond) valuation, the idea applies to all business assets. It basically involves estimating the future net cash flows attributable to an asset; determining an appropriate capitalization, or discount, rate; and then finding the present value of the cash flows. This, of course, is exactly what was done in Chapters 11, 12, and 13, where the concept of reasonable value was developed to help find the present value of investment opportunities.

The procedure for determining an asset's value is known as the *capitalization-of-income method of valuation*—a fancy name for the present value of a stream of earnings, discussed at length in Chapter 11. In going through the present chapter, keep in mind that *value, or the price of securities, is exactly analogous to the present value of assets* as determined in Chapters 12 and 13. From this point on, whenever the word value is used, it means the present value found by capitalizing expected future cash flows.

2. B. Graham, D. L. Dodd, and S. Cottle, *Security Analysis* (New York: McGraw-Hill, 1961), p. 28.

**The Required
Rate of
Return**

The first step in using the capitalization of income procedure is to establish the proper capitalization, or discount, rate for the security. This rate, defined as the required rate of return, is the minimum rate of return necessary to induce investors to buy or hold the security. For any given risky security, j, the expected rate of return, $\bar{k}_j$, is equal to the riskless rate of interest, R_F, plus a risk premium, ρ_j ("rho" of security):[3]

$$\bar{k}_j = R_F + \rho_j = R_F + (\bar{k}_M - R_F)\beta_j. \tag{14.1}$$

Equation 14.1 is the security market line (SML), which specifies the relationship between risk and the expected rate of return. One advantage of using the SML is that the components of risk can be identified and estimated from readily available published data. The risk premium is composed of two parts—the risk premium on the market as a whole and a risk measure for the individual security. The risk premium for the market as a whole is the amount by which the return on a broad market index, such as the Standard & Poor's 500 stock index, exceeds a risk-free return measured by the current yield on U.S. government securities, which are free of default risk. The return on the market can be referred to as $\bar{k}_M$; thus:

$$\text{Market risk premium} = \bar{k}_M - R_F. \tag{14.1a}$$

It can be demonstrated that the securities market pays a premium only for the part of the security's risk that cannot be eliminated by diversification (systematic risk); this risk is measured by the covariance of the returns on the individual security with the returns on the market portfolio. When normalized by the variance of the market returns, the systematic risk of a security is referred to as the "beta" of the security. Thus:

$$\beta_j = \frac{\text{Cov}(k_j, k_M)}{\text{Var}(k_M)},$$

where:

β_j = the risk of an individual security j.
$\text{Cov}(k_j, k_M)$ = the covariance of the returns on the individual security with the returns on the market.
$\text{Var}(k_M)$ = the variance of the returns on the market.

To illustrate the application of these concepts, we shall use some realistic magnitudes for each of the terms involved. The return on the market, $\bar{k}_M$, has ranged from 9 percent to 13 percent; the variance of the returns on the market, $\text{Var}(k_M)$, is about 1 percent; the risk-free rate, R_F, has ranged from about 5

3. In Chapter 13 the application of the capital asset pricing model to analyzing investment decisions under uncertainty was set forth. Here the application of the CAPM to the determination of the required rate of return on different types of securities and therefore to valuation questions is developed.

percent to 7 percent. Using the midpoint of the ranges of values for the risk-free rate and market returns, we have:

$$\overline{k}_M - R_F = .11 - .06 = .05 = 5\%. \tag{14.1b}$$

The risk premium, ρ_j, is the product of the market risk premium times the risk of the individual security, β_j, which varies somewhat above and below 1.[4] Hence, for a β_j of 1.2, the value of the risk premium, ρ_j, on the individual security j is:

$$\rho_j = \beta_j(\overline{k}_M - R_F) = 1.2(.11 - .06) = .06 = 6\%.$$

This indicates that 6 percent is added to the risk-free return, R_F, to obtain a required return of 12 percent on the individual security j.[5] Note that the two measures, the risk-free return, R_F, and the market risk premium, $\overline{k}_M - R_F$, are economy-wide parameters. Thus they can be used with the beta of any security to obtain its expected return. This is demonstrated by Figure 14.1, which presents a graph of the SML. The expected rate of return is shown on the vertical axis, and risk (measured here as the beta of the security) is shown on the horizontal axis. According to the capital asset pricing model (CAPM), the capital markets price all risky securities according to the security market line equation. Since the SML prices all securities, it can be applied not only to the securities of different firms but also to each class of security of a single firm.

Short-term securities of the U.S. government are free of default risk, so they carry a risk-free return. The debt securities of individual firms probably carry a risk premium.[6] Since a riskless asset by definition has no risk, R_F lies on the vertical axis. As risk increases, the expected rate of return also increases. A relatively low-risk security, such as a bond, might have a risk index of $\beta_b = 0.4$ and an expected rate of return of $k_b = 8$ percent. A more risky security, such as common stock equity, might have a risk index of $\beta_s = 1.4$ and an expected rate of return of $k_s = 13$ percent.

In Figure 14.1 the slope of the SML is 0.05, indicating that the expected rate of return rises by 1 percent for each 0.2 increase in the security's beta. The beta is 0.4 for the firm's bonds, so their risk premium is 2 percent (0.05 × 0.4); the beta on the firm's stocks is 1.4, making their risk premium 7 per-

---

4. The covariance of the market returns with the market returns is its variance, so the beta of the market is $Var(k_M)/Var(k_M)$, which equals 1. Normal values of the betas of individual securities are from about 0.5 to 1.5.

5. Since the SML is a marketwide relationship, the expected return on a security is required for market equilibrium relationships. In a later section on common stock valuation, the return on stock equity *required* by equilibrium relationships will be designated as k_s^* in contrast to $\overline{k}_s$, a return *expected* from individual security earnings and price relationships.

6. However, for large firms with small amounts of debt, the risk premium may not change with moderate increases in leverage; thus, over a narrow range of leverage, the cost of the debt may not rise.

**Figure 14.1
The Relationship between Risk
and the Expected Rate of Return:
The Security Market Line (SML)**

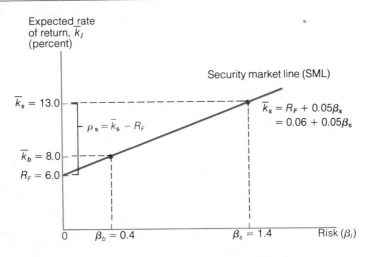

cent (0.05×1.4). When these two risk premiums are added to the riskless rate, R_F, we obtain the expected rates of return:

$$\overline{k}_b = 6\% + 2\% = 8\%.$$
$$\overline{k}_s = 6\% + 7\% = 13\%.$$

Notice that the graph can be used to analyze each class of a firm's securities. Since a firm's bonds have a smaller beta than its common stock, $\overline{k}_b$ might be the expected rate of return on the bonds, while $\overline{k}_s$ might refer to its common stock. The company's preferred stock and convertibles would lie on the SML between $\overline{k}_b$ and $\overline{k}_s$. Thus one approach to understanding the levels of returns required for different classes of securities is to look at the different levels of risk and to price out this risk by the SML. There is no need for absolute precision in viewing the relationships; we can think simply of a positive relationship between increased risk and the associated required higher return.

**Bond
Valuation**

The rate of return concepts developed here can now be used to explain the process of security valuation. This section examines bond values; the two following sections explain preferred and common stocks.

Bond values are relatively easy to determine. The expected cash flows are the annual interest payments plus the principal due when the bond matures. Depending on differences in the risk of default on interest or principal, the appropriate capitalization (or discount) rate applied to different bonds varies. A U.S. Treasury security, for example, has less risk than a security issued by a corporation; consequently, a lower discount (or capitalization) rate is applied to its interest payments. The actual calculating procedures employed in bond valuation are illustrated by the following examples.

Perpetual Bond

After the Napoleonic Wars (1814), England sold a huge bond issue, which it used to pay off many smaller issues that had been floated in prior years to pay for the war. Since the purpose of the new issue was to consolidate past debts, the individual bonds were called Consols. Suppose the bonds paid $50 interest annually to perpetuity. (Actually, interest was stated in pounds.) What would the bonds be worth under current market conditions?

First, note that the value v_b of any perpetuity is computed as follows:

$$v_b = \frac{c}{(1+k_b)^1} + \frac{c}{(1+k_b)^2} + \cdots$$

$$= \frac{c}{k_b}. \quad [7]$$

(14.2)

Here c is the constant annual interest in dollars and k_b the appropriate interest rate (or required rate of return) for the bond issue. In this chapter, we use k_b, k_{ps}, and k_s to designate the required rates of return on debt, preferred stock, and common stock, respectively. Equation 14.2 is an infinite series of $1 a year, and the value of the bond is the discounted sum of the infinite series.

7. A perpetuity is a bond that never matures, that pays interest indefinitely. Equation 14.2 is simply the present value of an infinite series; its proof is demonstrated below. Rewrite Equation 14.2 as follows:

$$v_b = c\left[\frac{1}{(1+k_b)^1} + \frac{1}{(1+k_b)^2} + \cdots + \frac{1}{(1+k_b)^N}\right].$$

(1)

Multiply both sides of Equation 1 by $(1+k_b)$:

$$v_b(1+k_b) = c\left[1 + \frac{1}{(1+k_b)^1} + \frac{1}{(1+k_b)^2} + \cdots + \frac{1}{(1+k_b)^{N-1}}\right].$$

(2)

Subtract Equation 1 from Equation 2, obtaining:

$$v_b(1+k_b-1) = c\left[1 - \frac{1}{(1+k_b)^N}\right].$$

(3)

As $N \to \infty$, $\frac{1}{(1+k_b)^N} \to 0$, so Equation 3 approaches

$$v_b k_b = c,$$

and

$$v_b = \frac{c}{k_b}.$$

(14.2)

We know that the Consol's annual interest payment is $50; therefore, the only other thing we need in order to find its value is the appropriate interest rate. This is commonly taken as the going interest rate, or yield, on bonds of similar risk. Suppose we find such bonds to be paying 4 percent under current market conditions. Then the Consol's value is determined as follows:

$$V_b = \frac{c}{k_b} = \frac{\$50}{0.04} = \$1{,}250.$$

If the going rate of interest rises to 5 percent, the value of the bond falls to $1,000 ($50/0.05). If interest rates continue rising, when the rate goes as high as 6 percent, the value of the Consol will be only $833.33. Values of this perpetual bond for a range of interest rates are given in the following table:

Current Market Interest Rate	Current Market Value
2%	$2,500.00
3	1,666.67
4	1,250.00
5	1,000.00
6	833.33
7	714.29
8	625.00

Short-Term Bond

Suppose the British government issues bonds with the same risk of default as the Consols but with a three-year maturity. The new bonds also pay $50 interest and have a $1,000 maturity value. What will the value of these new bonds be at the time of issue if the going rate of interest is 4 percent? To find this value, we must solve Equation 14.3:

$$V_b = \frac{c_1}{(1 + k_b)^1} + \frac{c_2}{(1 + k_b)^2} + \frac{c_3 + M}{(1 + k_b)^3}. \qquad \textbf{(14.3)}$$

Here M is the maturity value of the bond. The solution is given in the following tabulation.[8]

Year	Receipt	4 Percent Discount Factors	Present Value
1	$50	0.962	$ 48.10
2	$50	0.925	46.25
3	$50 + $1,000	0.889	933.45
		Bond value =	$1,027.80

8. If the bond has a long maturity, twenty years for example, we would certainly want to calculate its present value by finding the present value of a twenty-year annuity and adding to it the present value of the $1,000 principal received at maturity. Special bond tables have been devised to simplify the calculation procedure. Note also that k_b frequently differs for the long- and short-term bonds; as we saw in Chapter 8, unless the yield to maturity curve is flat, long- and short-term rates differ.

At the various rates of interest used in the perpetuity example, this three-year bond will have the following values:

Current Market Interest Rate	Current Market Value
2%	$1,086.15
3	1,056.45
4	1.027.80
5	1,000.00
6	973.65
7	947.20
8	922.85

Interest-Rate Risk

Figure 14.2 shows how the values of the long-term bond (the Consol) and the short-term bond change in response to changes in the going market rate of interest. Note how much less sensitive the short-term bond is to changes in interest rates. At a 5 percent interest rate, both the perpetuity and the short-term bonds are valued at $1,000. When rates rise to 8 percent, the long-term bond falls to $625, while the short-term bond falls only to $923. A similar situation occurs when rates fall below 5 percent. *This differential responsiveness to changes in interest rates depends on the required yield levels.* At the lower yields depicted in Figure 14.2, the longer the maturity of a security, the greater its price change in response to a given change in interest rates. This helps explain why corporate treasurers are reluctant to hold their near-cash reserves in the form of long-term debt instruments. These reserves are held at moderate interest levels for precautionary purposes, and treasurers are unwilling to sacrifice safety for a little higher yield on a long-term bond. However, for deep discount bonds at yields of 10 percent or more, the further decline in price with higher required yields is at a lesser rate for longer-term bonds than for shorter-term bonds. This is depicted in Figure 14.3, where the value of the thirty-year bond falls less rapidly than the value of a twenty-year bond as required yields rise from 10 to 25 percent.[9]

Yield to Maturity

The rate of return expected if a bond is held to its maturity date is defined as the *yield to maturity.* Suppose a perpetuity has a stated par value of $1,000 and a 5 percent coupon rate (that is, it pays 5 percent, or $50 annually, on

---

9. We are indebted to Professor Charles Higgins of the University of Redlands for pointing out this switchover.

Figure 14.2
Values of Long-Term and
Short-Term Bonds, 5 Percent
Coupon Rate, at Different Market
Interest Rates

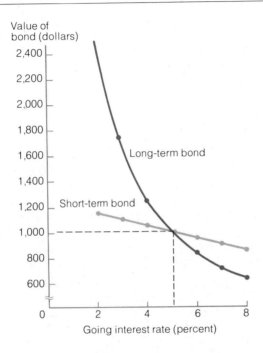

this stated value) and that it is currently selling for $625. We can solve Equation 14.2 for k_b to find the yield on the bond:

$$\text{Yield on a perpetuity} = k_b = \frac{c}{v_b} = \frac{\$50}{\$625} = 8\%.$$

If the bond sells for $1,250, the formula shows that the yield is 4 percent.

For the three-year bond paying $50 interest a year, if the price of the bond is $922.85, the yield to maturity is found by solving Equation 14.3. The solution PVIF is the one for 8 percent:

$$\$922.85 = \$50\,(\text{PVIF}) + \$50\,(\text{PVIF}) + \$1,050\,(\text{PVIF})$$
$$= \$50\,(0.926) + \$50\,(0.857) + \$1,050\,(0.794)$$
$$= \$46.30 + \$42.85 + \$833.70 = \$922.85.$$

The interest factors are taken from the 8 percent column of Table A.2. The solution procedure is exactly like that for finding the internal rate of return

**Figure 14.3
Values of 20-Year and 30-Year
Bonds at Required Yields of 10
to 25 Percent**

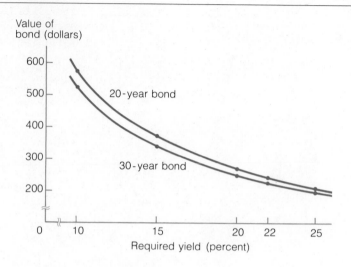

in capital budgeting, and the trial-and-error method is required unless special tables are available.[10]

Preferred Stock Valuation

Most preferred stocks entitle their owners to regular, fixed dividend payments similar to bond interest. Although some preferred issues are eventually retired, most are perpetuities whose value is found as follows:

$$V_{ps} = \frac{d_{ps}}{k_{ps}}.$$ (14.4)

In this case, d_{ps} is the dividend on the preferred stock, and k_{ps} is the appropriate capitalization rate for investments of this degree of risk. For example, General Motors has a preferred stock outstanding that pays a $3.75

---

10. We first tried the PVIFs for 6 percent, found that the equation did not "work," then raised the PVIF to 8 percent, where the equation did "work." This indicated that 8 percent was the yield to maturity on the bond. In practice, specialized interest tables (called *bond tables*) generated by a computer are available to facilitate determination of the yield to maturity on bonds with different stated interest rates, and on bonds selling for various discounts below or premiums above their maturity values. The results can also be obtained directly on a programmable hand calculator.

annual dividend. The average annual yield on preferred stocks in late 1946, when the stock was issued, was 3.79 percent. The GM preferred stock was a no par stock that sold at 100 to yield 3.75 percent at the issue date. Preferred stock yields during March 1977 averaged 7.14 percent. On April 21, 1977, the $3.75 preferred stock of General Motors closed at $52. The yield on a preferred stock is similar to that on a perpetual bond and is found by solving Equation 14.4 for k_{ps}. For the GM issue, the current price of the stock is observed in newspaper market quotations to be $52, and its annual dividend is seen to be $3.75. Thus the yield is 7.21 percent, calculated as follows:

$$k_{ps} = \frac{d_{ps}}{v_{ps}} = \frac{\$3.75}{\$52} = 7.21\%.$$

The valuation relationship expressed by Equation 14.4 is also implied. If we know the promised dividend payment on the preferred stock and its current yield, we can determine its value:

$$v_{ps} = \frac{\$3.75}{0.0721} = \$52.$$

Common Stock Valuation and Rates of Return

While the same principles apply to the valuation of common stocks as to bonds or preferred stocks, two features make their analysis much more difficult. First is the degree of certainty with which receipts can be forecast. For bonds and preferred stocks, this forecast presents little difficulty, since the interest payments or preferred dividends are known with relative certainty. However, in the case of common stocks, forecasting future earnings, dividends, and stock prices is exceedingly difficult. The second complicating feature is that, unlike interest and preferred dividends, common stock earnings and dividends are generally expected to grow, not remain constant. Hence, while standard annuity formulas can be applied, more difficult conceptual schemes must also be used.

Estimating the Value of a Stock: The Single-Period Case

The price today of a share of common stock, p_0, depends on the cash flows investors expect to receive if they buy the stock and the riskiness of these expected cash flows. The expected cash flows consist of two elements: (1) the dividend expected in each year t, defined as d_t, and (2) the price investors expect to receive when they sell the stock at the end of year n, defined as p_n. The price includes the return of the original investment plus a capital gain (or minus a capital loss). If investors expect to hold the stock for one year, and if the stock price is expected to grow at the rate g, the valuation equation is:

$$p_0 = \frac{\text{expected dividend} + \text{expected price (both at end of year 1)}}{1.0 + \text{required rate of return}}$$

$$= \frac{d_1 + p_1}{(1 + k_s)} = \frac{d_1 + p_0(1 + g)}{(1 + k_s)}, \tag{14.5}$$

which can be simplified to yield Equation 14.6.

$$p_0 = \frac{d_1}{k_s - g}.^{11} \tag{14.6}$$

Equations 14.5 and 14.6 represent the present value of the expected dividends and the year-end stock price, discounted at the required rate of return. Solving Equation 14.6 gives the expected or intrinsic price for the stock. To illustrate: Suppose you are thinking of buying a share of Universal Rubber common stock and holding it for one year. You note that Universal Rubber earned $3.43 per share last year and paid a dividend of $1.90. Earnings and dividends have been rising at about 5 percent a year, on the average, over the last ten to fifteen years, and you expect this growth to continue. Further, if earnings and dividends grow at the expected rate, you think the stock price will likewise grow by 5 percent a year.

The next step is to determine the required rate of return on Universal Rubber stock. The current rate of interest on U.S. Treasury securities, R_F, is 6 percent, but Universal Rubber is clearly more risky than government securities. Competitors can erode the company's market; labor problems can disrupt operations; an economic recession can cause sales to fall below the breakeven point; auto sales can decline, pulling down Universal Rubber's own sales and profits; and so on. Further, even if sales, earnings, and dividends meet projections, the stock price can still fall as a result of a generally weak market.

Given all these risk factors, you conclude that a 6 percent risk premium is justified, so you calculate your required rate of return on Universal Rubber's stock, k_s^*, as follows:

11.
$$p_0 = \frac{d_1 + p_0(1 + g)}{(1 + k_s)} \tag{14.5}$$
$$p_0(1 + k_s) = d_1 + p_0(1 + g)$$
$$p_0(1 + k_s - 1 - g) = d_1$$
$$p_0(k_s - g) = d_1$$
$$p_0 = \frac{d_1}{k_s - g}. \tag{14.6}$$

Notice that this equation is developed for a one-year holding period. In a later section, we will show that it is also valid for longer periods, provided the expected growth rate is constant.

$$k_s^* = R_F + \rho = 6\% + 6\% = 12\%.$$

Next, you estimate the dividend for the coming year, d_1, as follows:

$$d_1 = d_0 (1 + g) = \$1.90 \, (1.05) = \$2.$$

Now you have the necessary information to estimate the fair value of the stock by the use of Equation 14.6:

$$p_0 = \frac{d_1}{k_s^* - g} \qquad \qquad (14.6)$$

$$= \frac{\$2}{0.12 - 0.05} = \$28.57.$$

To you, $28.57 represents a reasonable price for Universal Rubber's stock. If the actual market price is less, you will buy it; if the actual price is higher, you will not buy it, or you will sell if you own it.[12]

Estimating the Rate of Return on a Stock

In the preceding section we calculated the expected price of Universal Rubber's stock to a given investor. Let us now change the procedure somewhat and calculate the rate of return you can expect if you purchase the stock at the current market price per share. The expected rate of return, defined as $\overline{k}_s$, is analogous to the internal rate of return on a capital project: $\overline{k}_s$ is the discount rate that equates the present value of the expected dividends, d_1, and the final stock price, p_1, to the present stock price, p_0:

$$p_0 = \frac{d_1 + p_1}{(1 + \overline{k}_s)} = \frac{d_1 + p_0 (1 + g)}{(1 + \overline{k}_s)}.$$

If Universal Rubber is selling for $40 per share, you can calculate $\overline{k}_s$ as follows:

$$\$40 = \frac{\$2 + \$40 \, (1.05)}{(1 + \overline{k}_s)} = \frac{\$2 + \$42}{(1 + \overline{k}_s)}$$

$$\$40 (1 + \overline{k}_s) = \$44$$
$$1 + \overline{k}_s = 1.10$$
$$\overline{k}_s = 0.10 \text{ or } 10\%.$$

12. Notice the similarity between this process and the NPV method of capital budgeting described in Chapter 12. In the earlier chapter, we (1) estimated a cost of capital for the firm, which compares with estimating k_s^*, our required rate of return; (2) discounted expected future cash flows, which are analogous to dividends plus the future stock price; (3) found the present value of future cash flows, which corresponds to the fair value of the stock; (4) determined the initial outlay for the project, which compares with finding the actual price of the stock; and (5) accepted the project if the PV of future cash flows exceeded the initial cost of the project, which is similar to comparing the fair value of the stock to its market price.

Thus, if you expect to receive a $2 dividend and a year-end price of $42, your expected rate of return on the investment is 10 percent.

Notice that the expected rate of return, $\bar{k}_s$, consists of two components, an expected dividend yield and an expected capital gains yield:

$$\bar{k}_s = \frac{\text{expected dividend}}{\text{present price}} + \frac{\text{expected increase in price}}{\text{present price}}$$

$$= \frac{d_1}{p_0} + g. \tag{14.7}$$

For Universal Rubber bought at a price of $40:

$$\bar{k}_s = \frac{\$2}{\$40} + \frac{\$2}{\$40} = 5\% + 5\% = 10\%.$$

Given an expected rate of return of 10 percent, should you make the purchase? This depends on how the expected return compares with the required return. If $\bar{k}_s$ exceeds k_s^*, buy; if $\bar{k}_s$ is less than k_s^*, sell; and if $\bar{k}_s$ equals k_s^*, the stock price is in equilibrium and you should be indifferent. In this case, your 12 percent required rate of return for Universal Rubber exceeds the 10 percent expected return, so you should not buy the stock.[13]

Market Equilibrium: Required versus Expected Returns

In the two preceding sections we calculated expected and required rates of return and expected stock prices. We saw that buy–no-buy decisions can be based on a comparison of either k_s^* versus $\bar{k}_s$ or expected stock value versus actual market price. In this section, we will show that the two decision rules are entirely consistent and then illustrate the process by which stock market equilibrium is maintained.

Consider again the Universal Rubber example, with the following data applicable:

Expected dividend at year end $= \bar{d}_1 = \$2.$
Expected growth rate in stock price $= \bar{g} = 5\%.$
Required rate of return $= k_s^* = 12\%.$

First we calculate an expected stock price of $28.57. Next we find that the actual market price, as read from a newspaper or obtained from a stockbroker, is $40. On the basis of that price we calculate a 10 percent expected rate of return. By either the rate of return or the calculated price criteria, Universal Rubber's stock is overvalued:

Actual price $= \$40 >$ expected price $= \$28.57;$

---

13. Notice the similarity between this process and the IRR method of capital budgeting. The expected rate of return, $\bar{k}_s$ corresponds to the IRR on a project, and the required rate of return, k_s^*, corresponds to the cost-of-capital cutoff rate used in capital budgeting.

and

Required rate of return, $k_s^* = 12\% >$ expected rate of return, $\bar{k}_s = 10\%$.

You should not buy this stock at the $40 price; and if you own it, you should sell.

Now assume that you are a typical or representative investor and that your expectations and actions actually determine stock market prices. You and others start selling Universal Rubber stock, and this selling pressure causes the price to decline. The decline continues until the price reaches $28.57, which you (the typical investor) feel is its intrinsic value. At this price, the expected rate of return also equals the required rate of return:

$$\bar{k}_s = \frac{d_1}{p_0} + g = \frac{\$2}{\$28.57} + 5\% = 7\% + 5\% = 12\%;$$

and

$$k_s^* = R_F + \rho = 6\% + 6\% = 12\%.$$

This situation always holds. Whenever the actual market price is equal to the fair price as calculated by a typical investor, required and expected returns also are equal, and the market is in equilibrium; that is, there is no tendency for the stock price to go up or down.

Factors Leading to Changes in Market Prices

Assume that Universal Rubber's stock is in equilibrium, selling at a price of $28.57 per share. If all expectations are exactly met, over the next year the price will gradually rise to $30 (5 percent). However, many different events can occur to cause a change in the equilibrium price of the stock. To illustrate the forces at work, consider again the stock price model, the set of inputs used to develop the price of $28.57, and a new set of assumed input variables:

	Variable Value	
	Original	New
Riskless rate (R_F)	6%	5%
Market risk premium $\bar{k}_m - R_F$)	0.04	0.05
Index of stock's risk (β)	1.5	1.2
Expected growth rate (g)	5%	6%

The first three variables influence k_s^*, which declines as a result of the new set of variables from 12 to 11 percent:

Original: $k_s^* = 6\% + (0.04)(1.5) = 12\%$.
New: $\quad k_s^* = 5\% + (0.05)(1.2) = 11\%$.

Using these values, together with the new d and g values, we find that p_0 rises from $28.57 to $40.20:

$$\text{Original: } p_0 = \frac{\$1.90(1.05)}{0.12 - 0.05} = \frac{\$2}{0.07} = \$28.57.$$

$$\text{New: } \quad p_0 = \frac{\$1.90(1.06)}{0.11 - 0.06} = \frac{\$2.01}{0.05} = \$40.20.$$

At the new price, the expected and required rates of return are equal:

$$\overline{k}_s = \frac{\$2.01}{\$40.20} + 6\% = 11\% = k_s^*,$$

as found above.

Evidence suggests that securities adjust quite rapidly to disequilibrium situations. Consequently, equilibrium ordinarily exists for any given stock, and in general the required and expected returns are equal. Stock prices certainly change, sometimes violently and rapidly; but this simply reflects changing conditions and expectations. There are, of course, times when a stock continues to react for several months to a favorable or unfavorable development, but this does not signify a long adjustment period; it merely shows that as more information about the situation becomes available, the market adjusts to the new information. Throughout the remainder of this book, we will assume that security markets are in equilibrium, with $k^* = \overline{k}$. Hence we shall generally use k (with the appropriate subscript) for the required return or applicable discount rate unless we are directly contrasting the required return, k^*, with the expected return, $\overline{k}$.

Marketability and Rates of Return

So far, whenever we have discussed the required rate of return on securities, we have concentrated on two factors—the riskless rate of interest and the risk inherent in the security in question. However, we should note that investors also value flexibility, or maneuverability. An investor who becomes disenchanted with a particular investment or who needs funds for consumption or other investments finds it highly desirable to be able to liquidate the holdings. Other things being equal, the higher the liquidity, or marketability, the lower the investment's required rate of return. Accordingly, we expect to find listed stocks selling on a lower yield basis than over-the-counter stocks and widely traded stocks selling at lower yields than stocks with no established market. Since investments in small firms are generally less liquid than those in large companies, we have another reason for expecting to find higher required returns among smaller companies.

Summary

In the discussion of the capital budgeting process in Chapter 12, the discount rate used in the calculations was seen to be of vital importance. At that time, we simply assumed that the cost of capital—the discount rate used in the present value process—was known, and we used this assumed rate in the calculations. In this chapter, however, we began to lay the foundations for actually calculating the cost of capital.

Since the cost of capital is integrally related to investors' returns on capital, it is necessary to understand the basic principles underlying valuation theory and the definitions of value. The different types of value defined are: (1) liquidating value versus going-concern value, (2) book value versus market value, and (3) fair value versus current market price. Market value is fundamentally dependent on discounted cash flow concepts and procedures; it involves estimating future cash flows and discounting them back to the present at an appropriate rate of interest.

Rates of return on bonds and preferred stocks are simple to understand and to calculate, but those on common stock returns are more difficult. First, common stock returns consist of both dividends and capital gains rather than a single type of payment (as in the case of bonds and preferred stocks). This fact necessitates the development of a rate of return formula that considers both types of payment. The rate of return formula for common stock is, therefore, a two-part equation:

Rate of return = Dividend yield + Capital gains yield.

The second complicating feature of common stock is the degree of uncertainty involved. Bond and preferred stock payments are relatively predictable, but forecasting common stock dividends and, even more, capital gains, is a highly uncertain business.

The expected rate of return for common stocks can be expressed as $\overline{k}_s = d_1/p_0 + g$ if the growth rate is a constant; p_0 is the price, d_1 is the dividend expected this year, and g refers to expected *future* growth.

Stock values are determined as the present value of a stream of cash flows. Therefore, the time pattern of these expected cash flows is very important in valuation of stock. The earnings and dividends of most companies have been increasing at a rate of 3 to 5 percent a year; this is considered a normal growth rate. Some companies may have prospects for no growth at all; others may anticipate a period of supernormal growth before settling down to a normal growth rate; still others may grow in a random fashion.

The required rate of return on any security, k_j^*, is the minimum rate of return necessary to induce investors to buy or to hold the security; it is a function of the riskless rate of interest and the investment's risk characteristics:

$$\overline{k}_j = R_F + \rho_j = R_F + (\overline{k}_M - R_F)\beta_j.$$

When graphed, this equation is called the security market line (SML), from which the required return, k_j^*, is specified. Because investors generally dislike risk, the required rate of return is higher on riskier securities. As a class, bonds are less risky than preferred stocks; and preferred stocks, in turn, are less risky than common stocks. As a result, the required rate of return is lowest for bonds, higher for preferred stocks, and highest for common stocks. Within each of these security classes, there are variations among the issuing firms' risks; hence, required rates of return vary among firms.

In equilibrium, the expected rate of return, $\overline{k}$ and the required rate of return, k^*, for a firm, j, are equal. If, however, some disturbance causes them to be different, the market price of the stock (and thus its dividend yield) quickly changes to establish a new equilibrium where k_j^*, and $\overline{k}_j$ are again equal.

The required rate of return also depends on the marketability of a given security issue. The stocks and bonds of larger, better-known firms are more marketable; hence the required rates of return on such securities are lower than those on smaller, less well-known firms. As we shall see in Chapter 16, the required rate of return is in essence a firm's cost of capital; so if small firms have relatively high required rates of return, they also have relatively high costs of capital.

Questions

14.1 Explain what is meant by the term *yield to maturity* in reference to (a) bonds and (b) preferred stocks. Is it appropriate to talk of a yield to maturity on a preferred stock that has no specific maturity date?

14.2 Explain why bonds with longer maturities experience wider price movements from a given change in interest rates than do shorter maturity bonds. Answer first in words (intuitively) and then mathematically.

14.3 Explain why a share of no-growth common stock is similar to a share of preferred stock. Use one of the equations developed in the chapter as part of your explanation.

14.4 Explain the importance in common stock valuation of:
a. current dividends
b. current market price
c. the expected future growth rate
d. the market capitalization rate

14.5 Suppose a firm's charter explicitly precludes it from ever paying a dividend. Investors know that this restriction will never be removed. Earnings for 1979 were $1 a share, and they are expected to grow at the rate of 4 percent forever. If the required rate of return is 10 percent, what is the firm's theoretical P/E ratio?

14.6 Describe the factors that determine the market rate of return on a particular stock at a given point in time.

14.7 Explain how the following influence stock and bond prices:
a. interest rates
b. investors' aversion to risk

14.8 Most inheritance tax laws state that for estate tax purposes, property shall be valued on the basis of "fair market value." Describe how an inheritance tax appraiser might use the valuation principles discussed in this chapter to establish the value of:

a. shares of a stock listed on the New York Stock Exhange

b. shares representing 20 percent of a stock that is not publicly traded

Problems

14.1 The Camden Company has two issues of bonds outstanding. Both bear coupons of 7 percent, and the effective yield required on each is 5 percent. Bond A has a maturity of ten years and Bond B a maturity of twenty years. Both pay interest annually.

a. What is the price of each bond?

b. If the effective yield on each bond rises to 6 percent, what is the price of each bond?

c. Explain why the price of one bond falls more than the price of the other when the effective yield rises.

14.2 The Lytes Company has two issues of bonds outstanding. Both bear coupons of 10 percent, and the effective yield required on each is 18 percent because of the uncertain future of the company. Bond C has a maturity of twenty years and Bond D a maturity of thirty years. Both pay interest annually.

a. What is the price of each bond?

b. If the effective yield on each bond rises to 24 percent, what is the price of each bond?

c. Explain why the price of one bond falls more than the price of the other when the effective yield rises.

d. Compare the results in this problem with the results in the previous problem.

14.3 What will be the yield to maturity of a perpetual bond with a $1,000 par value, an 8 percent coupon rate, and a current market price of $800? of $1,000? of $1,200? Assume interest is paid annually.

14.4 Assuming that a bond has four years remaining to maturity and that interest is paid annually, what will be the yield to maturity on the bond with a $1,000 maturity value, an 8 percent coupon interest rate, and a current market price of $825? of $1,107?

a. Would you pay $825 for the bond if your required rate of return for securities in the same risk class was 10 percent (k_b = 10%)? Explain.

14.5 a. The bonds of the Stanroy Corporation are perpetuities bearing a 9 percent coupon. Bonds of this type yield 8 percent. The par value of the bonds is $1,000. What is the price of the Stanroy bonds?

b. Interest rate levels rise to the point where such bonds now yield 12 percent. What is the price of the Stanroy bonds now?

c. Interest rate levels drop to 9 percent. At what price do the Stanroy bonds sell?

d. How would your answers to parts a, b, and c change if the bonds had a definite maturity date of nineteen years?

14.6 a. Trans-Atlantic Aviation is currently earning $8 million a year after taxes;

369

4.5 million shares are authorized, and 4 million shares are outstanding. What are the company's earnings per share?

b. Investors require a 16 percent rate of return on stocks in the same risk class as Trans-Atlantic (k_s = 16%). At what price will the stock sell if the previous dividend was $1 ($d_0$ = $1) and investors expect dividends to grow at a constant compound annual rate of −6 percent? 0 percent? 6 percent? 12 percent? (Hint: Use $d_1 = d_0 (1 + g)$, not d_0, in the formula.)

c. In Part b, what is the formula price if the required rate of return is 16 percent and the expected growth rate is 16 percent? 21 percent? Are these reasonable results? Explain.

d. At what price/earnings (P/E) ratio will the stock sell, assuming each of the growth expectations given in Part b?

14.7 Kathy Kobb plans to invest in common stocks for a period of twelve years, after which she will sell out, buy a lifetime room-and-board membership in a retirement home, and retire. She feels that Ogden Mines is currently, but temporarily, undervalued by the market; and she expects their current earnings and dividend to double in the next twelve years. Ogden Mines' last dividend was $2, and its stock currently sells for $45 a share.

a. If Kobb requires a 10 percent return on her investment, will Ogden Mines be a good buy for her?

b. What is the maximum that Kobb can pay for Ogden Mines and still earn her required 10 percent?

c. What might be the cause of Ogden Mines' market undervaluation?

d. Given Kobb's assumption, what market capitalization rate for Ogden Mines does the current price imply?

14.8 In a 1972 study prepared for the Federal Recreation Commission, it was determined that the following equation can be used to estimate the required rates of return on various types of long-term capital market securities (stocks and bonds of various companies): $k_j^* = R_F + .04\beta_j$. Here k_j^* is the required rate of return on the jth security; R_F is the riskless rate of interest as measured by the yield on long-term United States government bonds; and β_j is the beta of the jth security's rate of return during the past five years.

a. What is the required rate of return, k_j^*, if the riskless rate of return is 6 percent and the security in question has a beta of 0.2? 0.5? 1.0? 1.5? Graph the results.

b. What is the required rate of return, k_j^*, using the betas given in Part a but assuming the riskless rate rises to 8 percent? falls to 4 percent? Graph the results.

c. Suppose the required rate of return equation changes from $k_j^* = 6\% + 0.04\beta_j$ to $k_j^* = 6\% + 0.05\beta_j$. What does this imply about investor's risk aversion? Illustrate with a graph.

d. Suppose the equation $k_j^* = 6\% + 0.04\beta_j$ is the appropriate one; that is, this is the equation for the security market line (SML). Further suppose that a particular stock sells for $20 a share, is expected to pay a $1 dividend at the end of the current year, and has a beta of expected returns of 0.8; that is, $\beta_j = 0.8$. Information reaches investors that causes them to expect a future growth rate of 3 percent, which is different from the former expected growth rate. β_j does not change.

1. What was the former growth rate, assuming the stock was in equilibrium before the changed expectations as to growth?
2. What will happen to the price of the stock? That is, calculate the new equilibrium price, and explain the process by which it will be reached. (The expected dividend for the current year is still $1.)

14.9 Because of ill health and old age, John Ashby contemplates the sale of his shoe store. His corporation has the following balance sheet:

Assets		Liabilities and Net Worth	
Cash	$ 6,000	Notes payable—bank	$ 2,000
Receivables, net	2,000	Accounts payable	4,000
Inventories	13,000	Accruals	1,000
Fixtures and equipment less $10,000 reserve for depreciation	14,000	Common stock plus surplus	28,000
Total assets	$35,000	Total liabilities and net worth	$35,000

Annual before-tax earnings (after rent, interest, and salaries) for the preceding three years have averaged $8,000.

Ashby has set a price of $40,000, which includes all the assets of the business except cash; the buyer is to assume all debts. The assets include a five-year lease on the building in which the store is located and the goodwill associated with the name of Ashby Shoes. Assume that both Ashby and the potential purchaser are in the 50 percent tax bracket.

a. Is the price of $40,000 a reasonable one? Explain.
b. What other factors should be taken into account in arriving at a selling price?
c. What is the significance, if any, of the five-year lease?

14.10 The Ellis Company is a small jewelry manufacturer. The company has been successful and has grown. Now, Ellis is planning to sell an issue of common stock to the public for the first time, and it faces the problem of setting an appropriate price on its common stock. The company feels that the proper procedure is to select firms similar to it, with publicly traded common stock, and to make relevant comparisons.

The company finds several jewelry manufacturers similar to it with respect to product mix, size, asset composition, and debt/equity proportions. Of these, Bonden and Seeger are most similar.

Relationships	Bonden	Seeger	(Ellis Totals)
Earnings per share, 1978	$ 5.00	$ 8.00	$ 1,500,000
Average, 1972–1978	4.00	5.00	1,000,000
Price per share, 1978	48.00	65.00	—
Dividends per share, 1978	3.00	4.00	700,000
Average, 1972–1978	2.50	3.25	500,000
Book value per share	45.00	70.00	12,000,000
Market-book ratio	107%	93%	—

a. How can these relationships be used to help Ellis arrive at a market value for its stock?

b. What price do you recommend if Ellis sells 500,000 shares?

Appendix 14A Multi-Period Stock Valuation Models

The discussion of stock values and rates of return in Chapter 14 focused on a single-period model, which expects investors to hold the stock for one year, receive one dividend, and then sell the stock at the end of the year. This appendix expands the analysis to deal with more realistic—and more complicated—multi-period models.

Expected Dividends as the Basis for Stock Values

According to generally accepted theory, stock prices are determined as the present value of a stream of cash flows. In other words, the capitalization of income procedure applies to stocks as well as to bonds and other assets. What are the cash flows that corporations provide to their stockholders? What flows do the markets in fact capitalize? A number of different models have been formulated, and at least four different categories of flows have been capitalized in alternative formulations: (1) the stream of dividends, (2) the stream of earnings, (3) the current earnings plus flows resulting from future investment opportunities, and (4) the discounting of cash flows as in capital budgeting models. Miller and Modigliani have demonstrated that these different approaches are equivalent and yield the same valuations.[1]

Since multi-period valuation models are inherently complicated, we shall illustrate the methodology involved by using the least complicated one—the stream of dividends approach. In this formulation, a share of common stock is regarded as similar to a perpetual bond or a share of perpetual preferred stock, and its value is established as the present value of its stream of dividends:

$$\text{Value of stock} = p_0 = \text{PV of expected future dividends}$$

$$= \frac{d_1}{(1 + k_s)^1} + \frac{d_2}{(1 + k_s)^2} + \cdots$$

$$= \sum_{t=1}^{\infty} \frac{d_t}{(1 + k_s)^t}. \tag{A14.1}$$

Unlike bond interest and preferred dividends, common stock dividends are not generally expected to remain constant in the future; hence the conve-

1. See their "Dividend Policy, Growth, and the Valuation of Shares," *Journal of Business* 34 (October 1961).

nient annuity formulas cannot be used. This fact, combined with the much greater uncertainty about common stock dividends than about bond interest or preferred dividends, makes common stock valuation a more complex task than bond or preferred stock valuation.

Equation A14.1 is a general stock valuation model in the sense that the time pattern of d_t can be anything; that is, d_t can rise, fall, remain constant, or even fluctuate randomly, and Equation A14.1 will still hold. For many purposes, however, it is useful to estimate a particular time pattern for d_t and then develop a simplified (easier to evaluate) version of the stock valuation model expressed in Equation A14.1. The following sections consider the special cases of zero growth, constant growth, and supernormal growth.

Stock Values with Zero Growth

Suppose the rate of growth is measured by the rate at which dividends are expected to increase. If future growth is expected to be zero, the value of the stock reduces to the same formula as that developed for a perpetual bond:

$$\text{Price} = \frac{\text{Dividend}}{\text{Capitalization rate}}$$

$$p_0 = \frac{d_1}{k_s}. \tag{14.2}$$

Solving for k_s, we obtain:

$$k_s = \frac{d_1}{p_0}, \tag{A14.2a}$$

which states that the required rate of return on a share of stock that has no growth prospects is simply the dividend yield.

Normal, or Constant, Growth

Year after year, the earnings and dividends of most companies have been increasing. In general, this growth is expected to continue in the foreseeable future at about the same rate as GNP. On this basis, it is expected that an average, or normal, company will grow at a rate of from 3 to 5 percent a year. Thus, if such a company's previously paid dividend was d_0, its dividend in any future year t will be $d_t = d_0 (1 + g)^t$, where g = the expected rate of growth. For example, if Universal Rubber just paid a dividend of $1.90 ($d_0$ = $1.90) and its investors expect a 5 percent growth rate, the estimated dividend one year hence is $d_1 = (\$1.90)(1.05) = \$2$; two years hence is $2.10; and five years hence is:

$$d_t = d_0(1+g)^t$$
$$= \$1.90(1.05)^5$$
$$= \$2.42.$$

Using this method of estimating future dividends, the current price, p_0, is determined as follows:

$$p_0 = \frac{d_1}{(1+k_s)^1} + \frac{d_2}{(1+k_s)^2} + \frac{d_3}{(1+k_s)^3} + \cdots$$
$$= \frac{d_0(1+g)^1}{(1+k_s)^1} + \frac{d_0(1+g)^2}{(1+k_s)^2} + \frac{d_0(1+g)^3}{(1+k_s)^3} + \cdots$$
$$= \sum_{t=1}^{\infty} \frac{d_0(1+g)^t}{(1+k_s)^t}. \tag{A14.3}$$

If g is constant, Equation A14.3 can be simplified as follows:

$$p_0 = \frac{d_1}{k_s - g}. \quad ^2 \tag{A14.4}$$

2. The proof of Equation A14.4 is as follows. Rewrite Equation A14.3 as:

$$p_0 = d_0 \left[\frac{(1+g)}{(1+k_s)} + \frac{(1+g)^2}{(1+k_s)^2} + \frac{(1+g)^3}{(1+k_s)^3} + \cdots + \frac{(1+g)^N}{(1+k_s)^N} \right] \tag{1}$$

Multiply both sides of Equation 1 by $(1+k_s)/(1+g)$:

$$p_0 \left[\frac{(1+k_s)}{(1+g)} \right] = d_0 \left[1 + \frac{(1+g)}{(1+k_s)} + \frac{(1+g)^2}{(1+k_s)^2} + \cdots + \frac{(1+g)^{N-1}}{(1+k_s)^{N-1}} \right] \tag{2}$$

Subtract Equation 1 from Equation 2 to obtain:

$$p_0 \left[\frac{(1+k_s)}{(1+g)} - 1 \right] = d_0 \left[1 - \frac{(1+g)^N}{(1+k_s)^N} \right]$$
$$p_0 \left[\frac{(1+k_s) - (1+g)}{(1+g)} \right] = d_0 \left[1 - \frac{(1+g)^N}{(1+k_s)^N} \right].$$

Assuming $k_s > g$, as $N \to \infty$, the term in brackets on the right side of the equation $\to 1.0$, leaving:

$$p_0 \left[\frac{(1+k_s) - (1+g)}{(1+g)} \right] = d_0.$$

which simplifies to:

$$p_0(k_s - g) = d_0(1+g) = d_1$$

$$p_0 = \frac{d_1}{k_s - g}. \tag{A14.4}$$

Notice that the constant growth model expressed in Equation A14.4 is identical to the single-period model, Equation 14.6, developed in an earlier section.

A necessary condition for the constant growth model is that k_s be greater than g; otherwise, Equation A14.4 gives nonsense answers. If k_s equals g, the equation blows up, yielding an infinite price; if k_s is less than g, a negative price results. Since neither infinite nor negative stock prices make sense, it is clear that in equilibrium k_s must be greater than g.

Note that Equation A14.4 is sufficiently general to encompass the no-growth case described above. If growth is zero, this is simply a special case, and Equation A14.4 is equal to Equation A14.2.[3]

Supernormal Growth

Firms typically go through life cycles; during part of these cycles their growth is much faster than that of the economy as a whole. Automobile manufacturers in the 1920s and computer and office equipment manufacturers in the 1960s are examples. Figure A14.1 illustrates such supernormal growth and compares it with normal growth, zero growth, and negative growth.[4]

A hypothetical supernormal growth firm is expected to grow at a 20 percent rate for ten years, then to have its growth rate fall to 4 percent, the norm for the economy. The value of the firm with this growth pattern is determined by the following equation:

Present price = PV of dividends during supernormal growth period + Value of stock price at end of supernormal growth period discounted back to present

$$p_0 = \sum_{t=1}^{N} \frac{d_0(1+g_s)^t}{(1+k_s)^t} + \left(\frac{d_{N+1}}{k_s - g_n}\right)\left(\frac{1}{(1+k_s)^N}\right), \tag{A14.5}$$

where:

g_s = the supernormal growth rate.
g_n = the normal growth rate.
N = the period of supernormal growth.

Working through an example will help make this clear. Consider a supernormal growth firm whose previous dividend was $1.92 ($d_0 = \$1.92$), with the dividend expected to increase by 20 percent a year for ten years and thereafter at 4 percent a year indefinitely. If stockholders' required rate of return is 9 percent on an investment with this degree of risk, what is the

---

3. One technical point should at least be mentioned here. The logic underlying the analysis implicitly assumes that investors are indifferent to dividend yield or capital gains. Empirical work has not conclusively established whether this is true, but the question is discussed in Chapter 17.
4. A negative growth rate represents a declining company. A mining company whose profits are falling because of a declining ore body is an example.

**Figure A14.1
A Comparison of Four Companies'
Dividend Growth Rates**

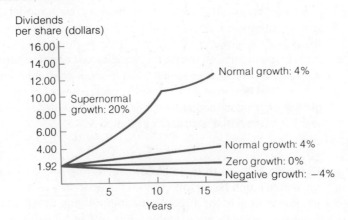

value of the stock? On the basis of the calculations in Table A14.1, the value is $138.19, the present value of the dividends during the first ten years plus the present value of the stock at the end of the tenth year.

Comparing Companies with Different Expected Growth Rates

A comparison of four companies' illustrative dividend growth rates graphed in Figure A14.1 will help summarize this section. Using the valuation equations developed in this chapter, the conditions assumed in the preceding examples, and the additional assumptions that each firm had earnings per share of $3.60 ($EPS_0 = \$3.60$) during the preceding reporting period and paid out 53.3 percent of its reported earnings (therefore, that dividends per share last year, d_0, were $1.92 for each company), we show prices, dividend yields, and price/earnings (P/E) ratios in Table A14.2.

Investors require and expect a return of 9 percent on each of the stocks. For the declining firm, this return consists of a relatively high current dividend yield combined with a capital loss amounting to 4 percent a year. For the no-growth firm, there is neither a capital gain nor a capital loss expectation, so the 9 percent return must be obtained entirely from the dividend yield. The normal growth firm provides a relatively low current dividend yield but a 4 percent per year capital gain expectation. Finally, the supernormal growth firm has the lowest current dividend yield but the highest capital gain expectation.

What is expected to happen to the prices of the four firms' stocks over time? Three of the four cases are straightforward. The zero growth firm's

Table A14.1
Method of Calculating the Value
of a Stock with Supernormal
Growth

Assumptions:

a. Stockholders' capitalization rate is 9 percent ($k_s = 9\%$).
b. Growth rate is 20 percent for ten years, 4 percent thereafter ($g_s = 20\%$, $g_n = 4\%$, and $N = 10$).
c. Last year's dividend was $1.92 ($d_0 = \$1.92$).

Step 1. Find present value of dividends during rapid growth period.

End of Year	Dividend $1.92 $(1.20)^t$	PVIF $= 1/(1.09)^t$	PV
1	$ 2.30	0.917	$2.11
2	2.76	0.842	2.32
3	3.32	0.772	2.56
4	3.98	0.708	2.82
5	4.78	0.650	3.11
6	5.73	0.596	3.42
7	6.88	0.547	3.76
8	8.26	0.502	4.15
9	9.91	0.460	4.56
10	11.89	0.422	5.02

$$\text{PV of first ten years' dividends} = \sum_{t=1}^{10} \frac{d_0(1+g_s)^t}{(1+k_s)^t} = \$33.83$$

Step 2. Find present value of year 10 stock price.
a. Find value of stock at end of year 10:

$$p_{10} = \frac{d_{11}}{k_s - g_n} = \frac{\$11.89\,(1.04)}{0.05} = \$247.31.$$

b. Discount p_{10} back to present:

$$PV = p_{10}\left(\frac{1}{1+k_s}\right)^{10} = \$247.31\,(0.422) = \$104.36.$$

Step 3. Sum to find total value of stock today:

$$p_0 = \$33.83 + \$104.36 = \$138.19.$$

price is expected to be constant ($p_t = p_{t+1}$); the declining firm is expected to have a falling stock price; and the normal growth firm's stock is expected to grow at a constant rate, 4 percent. The supernormal growth case is more complex, but what is expected can be seen from the data in Table A14.1.

It can readily be shown that:

$$\sum_{t=1}^{N} \frac{(1+g_s)^t}{(1+k_s)^t} = \frac{(1+g_s)[(1+h)^{10}-1]}{g_s - k_s} = \frac{(1+g_s)h}{(g_s - k_s)}\left[\frac{(1+h)^{10}-1}{h}\right]$$

where $\dfrac{(1+g_s)}{(1+k_s)}=(1+h)$ for ease of expression.[5]

The third term is expressed in the sum of an annuity form by multiplying the second term by h/h, as shown above.

For the example in Table A14.1, we have:

$$1+h=\frac{(1+g_s)}{(1+k_s)}=\frac{1.20}{1.09}=1.1009 \qquad \frac{(1+g_s)}{(g_s-k_s)}=\frac{1.2}{0.11}=10.909$$

$$(1+h)^{10}=(1.1009)^{10}=2.615$$

$$(1+h)^{10}-1=1.615$$

$$\frac{(1+g_s)[(1+h)^{10}-1]}{(g_s-k_s)}=10.909 \times 1.615=17.623$$

$$d_0(17.623)=1.92(17.623)=33.836.$$

5. The numerical calculation procedure for a summation expression is:

$$\sum_{t=1}^{10}\frac{d_0(1+g_s)^t}{(1+k_s)^t}=d_0\sum_{t=1}^{10}\frac{(1+g_s)^t}{(1+k_s)^t}.$$

Write out the summation expression:

$$\sum_{t=1}^{10}\left(\frac{1+g_s}{1+k_s}\right)^t=\left(\frac{1+g_s}{1+k_s}\right)+\left(\frac{1+g_s}{1+k_s}\right)^2+\cdots+\left(\frac{1+g_s}{1+k_s}\right)^{10}.$$

Factor $\left(\dfrac{1+g_s}{1+k_s}\right)$ from all terms:

$$=\left(\frac{1+g_s}{1+k_s}\right)\left[1+\left(\frac{1+g_s}{1+k_s}\right)+\cdots+\left(\frac{1+g_s}{1+k_s}\right)^9\right].$$

Use the formula for the summation of a geometric progression over N periods and simplify:

$$S_N=\frac{r^N-1}{r-1}=\frac{1+g_s}{1+k_s}\frac{\left[\left(\frac{1+g_s}{1+k_s}\right)^{10}-1\right]}{\left(\frac{1+g_s}{1+k_s}\right)-1}=\frac{(1+g_s)\left[\left(\frac{1+g_s}{1+k_s}\right)^{10}-1\right]}{(1+k_s)\frac{1+g_s-1-k_s}{(1+k_s)}}=\frac{(1+g_s)}{(g_s-k_s)}\left[\left(\frac{1+g_s}{1+k_s}\right)^{10}-1\right].$$

Let $\left(\dfrac{1+g_s}{1+k_s}\right)=(1+h)$. Then:

$$S_N=\frac{(1+g_s)}{(g_s-k_s)}[(1+h)^{10}-1].$$

Multiply by $\dfrac{h}{h}$:

$$S_N=\left[\frac{(1+g_s)(h)}{(g_s-k_s)}\right]\left[\frac{[(1+h)^{10}-1]}{h}\right].$$

The second term is the sum of an annuity. Thus:

$$\sum_{t=1}^{N}\frac{d_0(1+g_s)^t}{(1+k_s)^t}=d_0\left(\frac{1+g_s}{g_s-k_s}\right)[(1+h)^N-1]=d_0\frac{(1+g_s)(h)}{(g_s-k_s)}\left[\frac{(1+h)^{10}-1}{h}\right].$$

**Table A14.2
Prices, Dividend Yields, and
Price/Earnings Ratios for 9
Percent Returns under Different
Growth Assumptions**

		Price	Current Dividend Yield	P/E Ratio[a]
Declining firm:	$p_0 = \dfrac{d_1}{k_s - g} = \dfrac{\$1.84}{0.09 - (-0.04)}$	\$ 14.15	13%	3.9
No-growth firm:	$p_0 = \dfrac{d_1}{k_s} = \dfrac{\$1.92}{0.09}$	21.33	9	5.9
Normal growth firm:	$p_0 = \dfrac{d_1}{k_s - g} = \dfrac{\$2.00}{0.09 - 0.04}$	40.00	5	11.1
Supernormal growth firm:	$p_0 =$ (See Table A 14–1)	138.19	1.7	38.4

[a] The beginning of this example assumed that each company is earning \$3.60 initially. Divided into the various prices, this \$3.60 gives the indicated P/E ratios.

Also, as the supernormal growth rate declines toward the normal rate (or as the time when this decline will occur becomes more imminent), the high P/E ratio must approach the normal P/E ratio; that is, the P/E of 38.4 will decline year by year and equal 11.1, that of the normal growth company, in the tenth year. See A. A. Robichek and M. C. Bogue, "A Note on the Behavior of Expected Price/Earnings Ratios over Time," *Journal of Finance*, June 1971.

The dividend, d_1, which differs for each firm, is calculated as follows:

$$d_1 = \text{EPS}_0\,(1 + g)\,(\text{payout}) = \$3.60\,(1 + g)\,(0.533).$$

The PV of the first ten years' dividends shown in Table A14.1 is \$33.83, which is approximately the same. Note that the present price, p_0, is \$138.19 and that the expected price in year 10, p_{10}, is \$247.31. This represents an average growth rate of 6 percent.[6] We do not show—although we could do so—that the expected growth rate of the stock's price is more than 6 percent in the early part of the ten-year supernormal growth period and less than 6 percent toward the end of the period, as investors perceive the approaching end of the supernormal period. From year 11 on, the company's stock price and dividend are expected to grow at the normal rate, 4 percent.

The relationships among the P/E ratios, shown in the last column of Table A14.2, are similar to what can be intuitively expected—the higher the expected growth (all other things being equal), the higher the P/E ratio.[7]

6. Found from Table A14.1; \$247.31/\$138.19 = 1.79, and this is approximately the CVIF for a 6 percent growth rate.
7. Differences in P/E ratios among firms can also arise from differences in the rates of return, k_s, that investors use in capitalizing the future dividend streams. If one company has a higher P/E ratio than another, this could be caused by a higher g, a lower k, or a combination of these two factors.

15

CHAPTER
AND RISK

FINANCIAL LEVERAGE

In the last chapter we saw that each security has a required rate of return, k^*, and an expected rate of return, $\bar{k}$. The required rate of return is determined in part by the level of interest rates (the risk-free rate) in the economy and in part by the riskiness of the individual security. The expected rate of return on a bond or a share of preferred stock is determined primarily by interest or preferred dividends, while the expected rate of return on common stock depends on earnings available for distribution as cash dividends and growth. Both risk and expected returns can be affected by financial leverage, as we will see in this chapter.

Basic Definitions

To avoid ambiguity in the use of key concepts, the meanings of frequently used expressions are given here. *Financial structure* refers to the way the firm's assets are financed; it is the entire right-hand side of the balance sheet. *Capital structure* is the permanent financing of the firm, represented primarily by long-term debt, preferred stock, and common equity, but excluding all short-term credit. Thus a firm's capital structure is only a part of its financial structure. *Common equity* includes common stock, capital surplus, and accumulated retained earnings.

The key concept for this chapter is *financial leverage,* or the *leverage factor,* defined as the ratio of total debt to total assets or total value of the firm. For example, a firm having a total value of $100 million and a total debt of $50 million would have a leverage factor of 50 percent.[1] Thus $B/V = 50$ percent. The B/V ratio implies a debt to common stock (B/S) ratio. B/S is equal to $B/V \div (1 - B/V)$. Thus, if $B/V = 0.5$, then $B/S = 1$.

Finally, we should distinguish at the outset between business risk and financial risk. *Business risk* is the inherent uncertainty or variability of expected pretax returns on the firm's portfolio of assets. This kind of risk was examined in Chapter 13, where it was defined in terms of the probability distribution of returns on the firm's assets. *Financial risk* is the additional risk induced by the use of financial leverage.

Theory of Financial Leverage

Perhaps the best way to understand the proper use of financial leverage is to analyze its impact on profitability and fluctuations in profitability under

---

1. The present discussion will consider variations in financial leverage in the context of a debt-equity tradeoff. No distinction will be made between long- and short-term debt. Also, V is the market value of the firm, while TA is the book value of total assets.

Table 15.1
Four Alternative Financial
Structures, Universal Machine
Company, Based on Book Values
(Thousands of Dollars)

Structure 1 $(B/S = 0\%;\ B/TA = 0\%)$

		Total debt	$ 0
		Common stock ($10 par)	10,000
Total assets	$10,000	Total claims	$10,000

Structure 2 $(B/S = 25\%;\ B/TA = 20\%)$

		Total debt (10%)	$ 2,000
		Common stock ($10 par)	8,000
Total assets	$10,000	Total claims	$10,000

Structure 3 $(B/S = 100\%;\ B/TA = 50\%)$

		Total debt (10%)	$ 5,000
		Common stock ($10 par)	5,000
Total assets	$10,000	Total claims	$10,000

Structure 4 $(B/S = 400\%;\ B/TA = 80\%)$

		Total debt (10%)	$ 8,000
		Common stock ($10 par)	2,000
Total assets	$10,000	Total claims	$10,000

various leverage conditions.[2] As an example, consider four alternative financial structures for the Universal Machine Company, a manufacturer of equipment used by industrial firms. The alternative balance sheets are displayed in Table 15.1.

Structure 1 uses no debt and consequently has a leverage factor of zero; structure 2 has a leverage factor of 20 percent; structure 3 has a leverage factor of 50 percent; and structure 4 has a leverage factor of 80 percent. How do these different financial patterns affect stockholder returns? As can be seen from Table 15.2, the answer depends partly on Universal's level of sales and partly on the probability assessments associated with its alternative potential sales levels. The probability distribution for future sales, constructed by Universal's marketing department in cooperation with representatives from the general staff group of top management, was based on their knowledge of present supply and demand conditions along with estimates for future economic conditions and sales. The probable conditions range

2. We shall initially hold the level of investment constant, considering only different financial structures for a firm of the same size. Since firms also face decisions that require a choice between debt and equity for financing an increase in investment, this second type of decision will next be analyzed with the benefit of the perspective provided by the more general analysis of the financial structure decision in its pure form.

**Table 15.2
Stockholders' Returns and
Earnings per Share under
Various Leverage and Economic
Conditions, Universal Machine
Company (Thousands of Dollars)**

Probability of indicated sales	0.1	0.3	0.4	0.2
Sales in dollars	$ 0	$6,000	$10,000	$20,000
Fixed costs	2,000	2,000	2,000	2,000
Variable costs (40% of sales)	—	2,400	4,000	8,000
Total costs (except interest)	$2,000	$4,400	$ 6,000	$10,000
Earnings before interest and taxes (EBIT)	−$2,000	$1,600	$ 4,000	$10,000
Capital Structure 1				
EBIT	−$2,000	$1,600	$ 4,000	$10,000
Less: Interest	0	0	0	0
Less: Income taxes (50%)[a]	−1,000	800	2,000	5,000
Net profit after taxes	−$1,000	$ 800	$2,000	$ 5,000
Earnings per share on 1,000 shares	−$1.00	$.80	$2.00	$5.00
Return on stockholders' equity	−10%	8%	20%	50%
Capital Structure 2				
EBIT	−$2,000	$1,600	$ 4,000	$10,000
Less: Interest (10% × $2,000)	$ 200	$ 200	$ 200	$ 200
Earnings before taxes	−2,200	1,400	3,800	9,800
Less: Income taxes (50%)[a]	−1,100	700	1,900	4,900
Net profit after taxes	−$1,100	$ 700	$1,900	$ 4,900
Earnings per share on 800 shares	−$1.38	$.88	$2.38	$6.13
Return on stockholders' equity	−13.8%	8.8%	23.8%	61.3%
Capital Structure 3				
EBIT	−$2,000	$1,600	$ 4,000	$10,000
Less: Interest (10% × $5,000)	$ 500	$ 500	$ 500	$ 500
Earnings before taxes	−2,500	1,100	3,500	9,500
Less: Income taxes (50%)[a]	−1,250	550	1,750	4,750
Net profit after taxes	−$1,250	$ 550	$1,750	$ 4,750
Earnings per share on 500 shares	−$2.50	$1.10	$3.50	$9.50
Return on stockholders' equity	−25%	11%	35%	95%
Capital Structure 4				
EBIT	−$2,000	$1,600	$ 4,000	$10,000
Less: Interest (10% × $8,000)	$ 800	$800	$ 800	$ 800
Earnings before taxes	−2,800	800	3,200	9,200
Less: Income taxes (50%)[a]	−1,400	400	1,600	4,600
Net profit after taxes	−$1,400	$400	$ 1,600	$ 4,600
Earnings per share on 200 shares	−$7.00	$2.00	$8.00	$23.00
Return on stockholders' equity	−70%	20%	80%	230%

[a] The tax calculation assumes that losses are carried back and result in tax credits.

from very poor (zero sales due to a labor strike resulting from some very difficult labor negotiations currently underway) to very good under an optimistic assessment of the future outlook. It is assumed that the firm has total assets of $10,000,000.[3] The rate of interest on debt is 10 percent, and the assumed tax rate is 50 percent. Variable costs are estimated to be 40 percent of sales, and fixed costs equal $2,000,000.

Table 15.2 lays out the pattern of the analysis. It begins by listing the probability of sales at levels indicated by the next line. The fixed costs as shown remain the same for each level of sales. The total amount of variable costs increases with the level of sales, since variable costs are 40 percent of sales. The fixed costs and variable costs are added to obtain total costs. Sales minus total costs equals earnings before interest and taxes (EBIT). Based on the indicated level of earnings before interest and taxes for the four sales levels associated with probabilities ranging from 0.1 to 0.4, the effects of the four alternative capital structures are analyzed.

Capital structure 1 is considered first. Since it employs no leverage, the interest expense is zero. EBIT divided by the 1 million shares of common stock gives earnings per share associated with each of the probability factors and with each of the alternative levels of sales. The rate of return on common stock is EBIT minus taxes divided by stockholders' equity.

When debt is introduced into the capital structure (starting with structure 2), interest on the debt is deducted from EBIT before the tax rate is applied and the net profit after taxes calculated. Then, earnings per share on the indicated number of shares and the return on stockholders' equity are calculated as before. Capital structure 1 (the one with no debt) is now compared with capital structure 3 (the one with the 50 percent leverage factor), since structure 3's leverage factor approximates that for all manufacturing industries in the United States in recent years. For capital structure 1, earnings per share range from a loss of $1 per share to a profit of $5 a share—a range of $6. Under capital structure 3, the range in earnings per share is from a loss of $2.50 to a profit of $9.50. This is a range of $12, double the range in earnings per share of structure 1. Similarly, the return on shareholders' equity for structure 1 has a range of 60 percentage points, while the return for structure 3 has a range of 120 percentage points.

Table 15.2 shows the two return relationships—earnings per share and return on stockholders' equity—associated with leverage. Under any given financial structure, earnings per share and the return on stockholders' equity increase with improved sales levels. Also, these earnings are magnified as leverage is increased. Thus increased leverage increases the degree of fluctuation in earnings per share and in returns on equity for any given degree of fluctuation in sales and its related return on total assets. If

---

3. The numbers are rounded for convenience; in most tables and calculations the analysis will be made in thousands of dollars, and the last three zeros will be explicitly omitted.

**Table 15.3
Return-Risk Analysis of the Four
Financial Structure Alternatives**

	s	p_s	EPS	p_sEPS	EPS − E(EPS)	[EPS − E(EPS)]²	p_s[EPS − E(EPS)]²
Structure 1	1	0.1	− $1.00	−0.10	−2.94	8.6436	0.8644
	2	0.3	$.80	0.24	−1.14	1.2996	0.3899
	3	0.4	$2.00	0.80	0.06	0.0036	0.0014
	4	0.2	$5.00	1.00	3.06	9.3636	1.8727
			E(EPS) =	$1.94		σ^2 =	3.1284
						σ =	1.7687

$$CV = \sigma/E(EPS) = .912$$

	s	p_s	EPS	p_sEPS	EPS − E(EPS)	[EPS − E(EPS)]²	p_s[EPS − E(EPS)]²
Structure 2	1	0.1	− $1.38	−0.138	−3.68	13.5424	1.3542
	2	0.3	$.88	0.264	−1.42	2.0164	0.6049
	3	0.4	$2.38	0.952	0.08	0.0064	0.0026
	4	0.2	$6.13	1.226	3.83	14.6689	2.9338
			E(EPS) =	$2.30		σ^2 =	4.8955
						σ =	2.2126

$$CV = .962$$

	s	p_s	EPS	p_sEPS	EPS − E(EPS)	[EPS − E(EPS)]²	p_s[EPS − E(EPS)]²
Structure 3	1	0.1	− $2.50	−0.25	−5.88	34.5744	3.4574
	2	0.3	$1.10	0.33	−2.28	5.1984	1.7155
	3	0.4	$3.50	1.40	0.12	0.0144	0.0058
	4	0.2	$9.50	1.90	6.12	37.4544	7.4909
			E(EPS) =	$3.38		σ^2 =	12.6696
						σ =	3.5594

$$CV = 1.05$$

	s	p_s	EPS	p_sEPS	EPS − E(EPS)	[EPS − E(EPS)]²	p_s[EPS − E(EPS)]²
Structure 4	1	0.1	− $7.00	−0.70	−14.70	216.09	21.6090
	2	0.3	$2.00	0.60	−5.70	32.49	9.7470
	3	0.4	$8.00	3.20	0.30	0.09	0.0360
	4	0.2	$23.00	4.60	15.30	234.09	46.8180
			E(EPS) =	$7.70		σ^2 =	78.2100
						σ =	8.8436

$$CV = 1.15$$

used successfully, leverage increases the returns to the owners of the firm; but if unsuccessful, it can result in inability to pay fixed charge obligations and, ultimately, in financial difficulties leading to financial reorganization or bankruptcy.[4]

Table 15.3 performs a return-risk analysis of the four financial structures. Applying the probability factors to each of the associated earnings per share results, the table calculates the expected earnings per share and the as-

---

4. See Chapter 25 for an explanation of the nature of financial reorganization and bankruptcy.

Figure 15.1
Relationship between Return
and Leverage

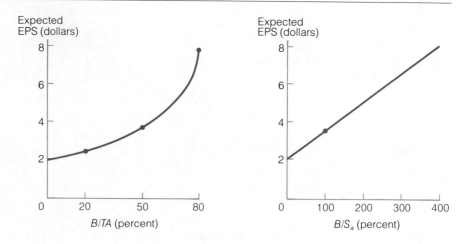

sociated variance and standard deviation for each financial structure. Then it divides the standard deviation by the expected earnings per share to obtain the coefficient of variation. Figure 15.1 provides a graph of the expected earnings per share as calculated in Table 15.3 in relation to the four alternative debt to equity and debt to total asset ratios. The figure shows that the expected earnings per share increase linearly with the debt to equity ratio and increase at an increasing rate when the leverage factor is measured by the debt to total asset ratio.

We now turn to a consideration of measures of the riskiness of the expected returns in relation to the alternative levels of sales and the alternative financial structures employed. We have noted how leverage increases the variability of earnings per share and the variability of returns to stockholders. For example, using no leverage, earnings per share range from a loss of $1 to a gain of $5. With a leverage of 80 percent the range is from a loss of $7 to a gain of $23.

There are three measures of this variability in earnings induced by leverage; each is, in some sense, a measure of risk. The three measures of risk are the standard deviation, the coefficient of variation, and the beta coefficient. The standard deviation and coefficient of variation of expected earnings per share are calculated in Table 15.3. In each case the coefficient of variation is calculated by dividing the standard deviation by the average earnings per share. The coefficient of variation rises from 0.912 in structure 1 to 1.15 in structure 4. Clearly, both these measures of risk rise with increased leverage.

Another measure of risk widely used in the financial community is beta, which was introduced in the preceding chapter. Beta measures the volatility of the returns on a security in response to changes in the returns on the market. Since the beta of a security is affected by financial leverage, the beta concept gives us another measure of the influence of financial leverage on the riskiness of a security.

It has been established that the relationship between a beta measure including the effects of leverage and a beta measure when a firm employs no financial leverage is given by the following expression:

$$\beta_j = \beta_u[1 + (B/S)(1 - T)].$$

With this expression we can calculate the influence of leverage on beta. Table 15.4 indicates how the beta with leverage is increased at various levels of leverage, measured by the ratio of debt to equity. Suppose that a firm employing no leverage has a beta of 1.2 and a tax rate of 40 percent. Its beta can be calculated for the levels of leverage indicated in the first column of Table 15.4.

We can better visualize the influence of leverage on beta by graphing the relationship between B/S and β_j in Figure 15.2, where the relationship between leverage and beta is a straight line. Thus the effect of increasing leverage in a firm is to increase its beta in a straight line relationship. Since beta is a measure of a security's risk, we therefore have another method of seeing how leverage increases the riskiness of a security.

What is common to the portrayals of the relationship between risk and leverage is that to obtain the higher expected earnings, whether measured by earnings per share or return on stockholders' equity that go with increased leverage, the firm must incur more risk. As previously indicated, there is a positive relationship between return and risk and a positive relationship between risk and the degree of leverage employed.

Another dimension of the return-leverage-risk relationship is exhibited by Figure 15.3, which sets forth a relationship between rates of return on assets and rates of return on net worth under different leverage conditions. For zero leverage, the line of relationship begins at the origin and has a slope that is less steep than the slope of the relationship when leverage is employed. With leverage, the intercept of the line is negative, indicating that

**Table 15.4
Influence of Leverage on the
Beta Measure**

B/S	(B/S)(1 − T)	[1 + (B/S)(1 − T)]	β_j
0.2	0.12	1.12	1.34
0.6	0.36	1.36	1.63
1.0	0.60	1.60	1.92
1.5	0.90	1.90	2.28
2.0	1.20	2.20	2.64

**Figure 15.2
Relationship between Leverage
and Risk Measured by β**

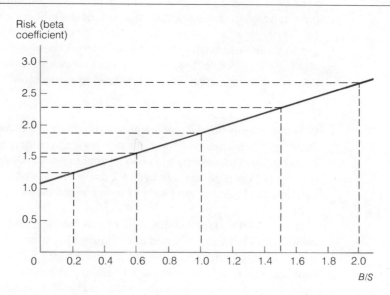

at low rates of return on total assets, the return on net worth is negative
(representing a loss). The intersection of the three lines is at the 10 percent
rate of return on total assets, which is equal to the before-tax interest cost
of debt. At this intersection point the return on net worth is 5 percent. The
50 percent tax rate reduces the 10 percent return on total assets to a return
of 5 percent on net worth regardless of the degree of leverage. When returns on assets are higher than 10 percent, debt-financed assets can cover
interest cost and still leave something over for the stockholders. But the reverse holds if assets earn less than 10 percent. Figure 15.3 illustrates a general proposition: Whenever the return on assets exceeds the cost of debt,
leverage is favorable, and the higher the leverage factor the higher the rate
of return on common equity.

Analysis of Alternative Methods of Financing

Thus far in the analysis we have simply varied leverage, holding constant
the total amount of investment by the firm. In real world decision making it
is often necessary to perform an analysis in which alternative leverage structures are considered along with financing that increases the firm's amount
of investment and size of total assets. This aspect of combining the financing and leverage decisions will be developed by a continuation of the Universal Machine Company example. Universal's latest balance sheet is set

**Figure 15.3
Relationship between Rates of
Return on Assets and Rates of
Return on Net Worth under
Different Leverage Conditions**

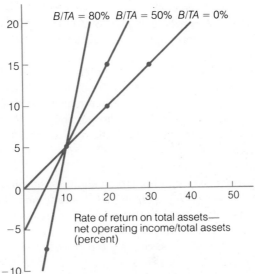

forth in Table 15.5. Universal manufactures equipment used in industrial manufacturing. Its major product is a lathe used to trim the rough edges off sheets of fabricated steel. The lathes sell for $100,000 each. As is typically the case for producers of durable capital assets, the company's sales fluctuate widely, far more than does the overall economy. For example, during nine of the preceding twenty-five years, the company's sales have been below the breakeven point, so losses have been relatively frequent.

**Table 15.5
Universal Machine Company
Balance Sheet for Year
Ended December 31, 1977
(Thousands of Dollars)**

Cash	$ 300	Total liabilities having	
Receivables (net)	1,200	an average cost of 10%	$ 5,000
Inventories	1,400		
Plant (net)	3,000	Common stock ($10 par)	5,000
Equipment (net)	4,100		
Total assets	$10,000	Total claims on assets	$10,000

Although future sales are uncertain, current demand is high and appears to be headed higher. Thus, if Universal is to continue its sales growth, it will have to increase capacity. A capacity increase involving $2 million of new capital is under consideration. James Watson, the financial vice-president, learns that he can raise the $2 million by selling bonds with a 10 percent coupon or by selling 100,000 shares of common stock at a market price of $20 per share. Fixed costs after the planned expansion will be $2 million a year. Variable costs excluding interest on the debt will be 40 percent of sales.[5] The probability distribution for future sales possibilities is the same as was set forth in the previous section analyzing the pure leverage decision for Universal.

Although Watson's recommendation will be given much weight, the final decision for the method of financing rests with the company's board of directors. Procedurally, the financial vice-president analyzes the situation, evaluates all reasonable alternatives, comes to a conclusion, and then presents the alternatives with his recommendations to the board. For his own analysis, as well as for presentation to the board, Watson prepares the materials shown in Table 15.6.

The top third of the table calculates earnings before interest and taxes (EBIT) for different levels of sales ranging from $0 to $20 million. The firm suffers an operating loss until sales are $3.3 million, but beyond that point it enjoys a rapid rise in gross profit.

The middle third of the table shows the financial results that will occur at the various sales levels if bonds are used. First, the $700,000 annual interest charges ($500,000 on existing debt plus $200,000 on the new bonds) are deducted from the earnings before interest and taxes. Next, taxes are taken out; and if the sales level is so low that losses are incurred, the firm receives a tax credit. Then, net profits after taxes are divided by the 500,000 shares outstanding to obtain earnings per share (EPS) of common stock.[6] The various EPS figures are multiplied by the corresponding probability estimates to obtain an expected EPS of $3.18.

The bottom third of the table calculates the financial results that will occur with stock financing. Net profit after interest and taxes is divided by 600,000—the original 500,000 plus the new 100,000 shares ($20 × 100,000 = $2 million)—to find earnings per share. Expected EPS is computed in the same way as for the bond financing.

Figure 15.4 shows the probability distribution of earnings per share. Stock financing has the tighter, more peaked distribution. We know from Table

5. The assumption that variable costs will be a constant percentage of sales over the entire range of output is not valid, but variable costs are relatively constant over the output range likely to occur.
6. The number of shares initially outstanding can be calculated by dividing the $5 million common stock figure given on the balance sheet by the $10 par value.

Table 15.6
Profit Calculations at Various
Sales Levels, Universal Machine
Company (Thousands of Dollars)

Probability of indicated sales	0.1	0.3	0.4	0.2
Sales in units	0	60	100	200
Sales in dollars	$ 0	$6,000	$10,000	$20,000
Fixed costs	2,000	2,000	2,000	2,000
Variable costs (40% of sales)	0	2,400	4,000	8,000
Total costs (except interest)	$2,000	$4,400	$ 6,000	$10,000
Earnings before interest and taxes (EBIT)	−$2,000	$1,600	$ 4,000	$10,000

Financing with Bonds ($B/A = 58.3\%$; $B/S = 140\%$)

Less: Interest (10% × $7,000)	$ 700	$ 700	$ 700	$ 700
Earnings before taxes	−2,700	900	3,300	9,300
Less: Income taxes (50%)	−1,350	450	1,650	4,650
Net profit after taxes	−$1,350	$ 450	$ 1,650	$ 4,650
EPS on 500 shares[a]	−$2.70	$.90	$3.30	$9.30
Expected EPS $3.18				

Financing with Stock ($B/A = 41.7\%$; $B/S_j = 71.4\%$)

Less: Interest (10% × $5,000)	$ 500	$ 500	$ 500	$ 500
Earnings before taxes	−2,500	1,100	3,500	9,500
Less: Income taxes (50%)	−1,250	550	1,750	4,750
Net profit after taxes	−$1,250	$ 550	$ 1,750	$ 4,750
EPS on 600 shares[a]	−$ 2.08	$.92	$2.92	$7.91
Expected EPS $2.82				

[a]The EPS figures can also be obtained using the following formula:

$$EPS = \frac{(\text{Sales} - \text{Fixed costs} - \text{Variable costs} - \text{Interest})(1 - \text{Tax rate})}{\text{Shares outstanding}}$$

For example, at sales = $10 million:

$$EPS_{bonds} = \frac{(10 - 2 - 4 - 0.7)(0.5)}{0.5} = \$3.30.$$

$$EPS_{stock} = \frac{(10 - 2 - 4 - 0.5)(0.5)}{0.6} = \$2.92.$$

15.3 that it will also have a smaller coefficient of variation than bond financing. Hence, stock financing is less risky than bond financing. However, the expected earnings per share are lower for stock than for bonds, so we are again faced with the kind of risk-return tradeoff that characterizes most financial decisions.

The nature of the tradeoff can be made more specific. In Table 15.7 we present two illustrative measures of the leverage return and risk relationships. In Part A of the table the leverage ratio, as measured by debt to total

Figure 15.4
Probability Curves for Stock and
Bond Financing

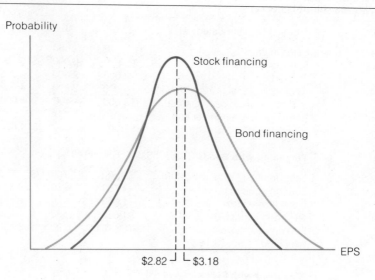

assets at book values, is related to expected earnings per share and the coefficient of variation. In Part B the leverage, as measured by debt to equity at market values, is related to the expected return on equity and the beta measure of risk.

The nature of these relationships is depicted graphically in Figure 15.5. There is an upward curvilinear relationship between the coefficient of varia-

Table 15.7
Leverage, Return, and Risk
Relationships

Part A	Leverage Ratio B/TA	Expected EPS	Coefficient of Variation
	0%	1.94	0.912
	20	2.30	0.962
	50	3.38	1.050
	80	7.70	1.150

Part B[a]	Leverage B/V	Return on Equity	Beta Coefficient
	0%	8.25	0.65
	8.16	8.40	0.68
	19.20	8.65	0.73
	29.10	8.95	0.79

[a]For calculations, see J. Fred Weston and Eugene F. Brigham, *Managerial Finance*, 6th ed. (Hinsdale, Ill. Dryden Press, 1978).

Figure 15.5
EPS and Coefficient of Variation
and Return on Equity and Beta

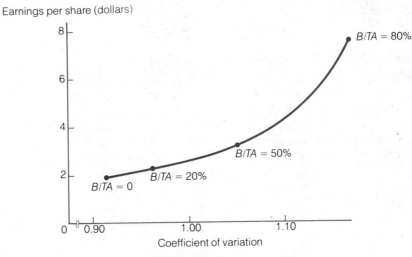

Earnings per share (dollars)

(a) EPS and coefficient of variation

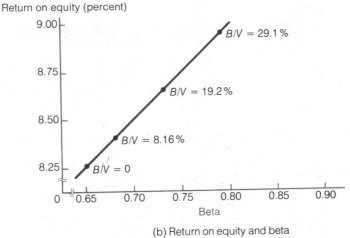

Return on equity (percent)

(b) Return on equity and beta

tion and earnings per share when the leverage ratio is measured by debt to total assets at book value. There is a linear relationship between beta and the return on equity when leverage is measured by the debt to equity ratio at market values. But regardless of whether the relationship is linear or non-linear, there is agreement that in order to obtain the higher expected earnings that go with increased leverage, the firm must accept more risk.

What choice should Watson recommend to the board? How much leverage should Universal Machine use? These questions cannot be answered at this point; the answers must be deferred until some additional concepts have been covered and the effects of leverage on the cost of both debt and equity capital have been examined.

Breakeven Analysis

Another way of presenting the data on Universal's two financing methods is shown in Figure 15.6, a breakeven chart similar to the charts used in Chapter 5. If sales are depressed to zero, the debt financing line cuts the y-axis at $-\$2.70$, below the $-\$2.08$ intercept of the common stock financing line. The debt line has a steeper slope and rises faster, however, showing that earnings per share will go up faster with increases in sales if debt is used. The two lines cross at sales of $6.2 million. Below that sales volume, the firm will be better off issuing common stock; above that level, debt financing will produce higher earnings per share.[7]

If Watson and his board of directors *know with certainty* that sales will never again fall below $6.2 million, bonds are the preferred method of financing the asset increase. But they cannot know this for certain. In fact, they know that in previous years, sales have fallen below this critical level. Further, if any detrimental long-run events occur, future sales may again fall well below $6.2 million. If sales continue to expand, however, there will be higher earnings per share from using bonds; and no officer or director will want to forego these substantial advantages.

Watson's recommendation and the directors' decision will depend on (1) each person's appraisal of the future and (2) each person's psychological attitude toward risk.[8] The pessimists, or risk averters, will prefer to employ common stock, while the optimists, or those less sensitive to risk, will favor bonds. This example, which is typical of many real world situations, suggests that the major disagreements over the choice of forms of financing

---

7. Since the equation in this case is linear, the breakeven or indifference level of sales $(P \cdot Q)$ can be found as follows:

$$EPS_s = \frac{(P \cdot Q - 2.0 - 0.4P \cdot Q - 0.5)(0.5)}{0.6} = \frac{(P \cdot Q - 2.0 - 0.4P \cdot Q - 0.7)(0.5)}{0.5} = EPS_B$$

$$P \cdot Q = \$6.2 \text{ million, and EPS} = \$1.02.$$

8. Theory suggests that the decision should be based on stockholders' utility preferences, or the market risk-return tradeoff function discussed in Chapter 13. In practice, it is difficult to obtain such information as *data*, so decisions of this sort are generally based on the subjective judgment of the decision maker. A knowledge of the theory, even if it cannot be applied directly, is extremely useful in making good judgmental decisions. Further, knowing the theory permits the firm to structure research programs and data-collecting systems that will make direct application of the theory increasingly feasible in future years.

**Figure 15.6
Earnings per Share for Stock and
Debt Financing**

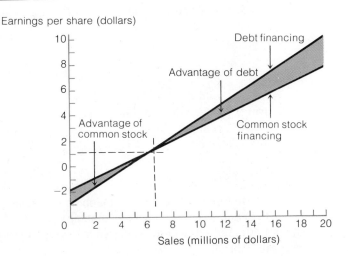

are likely to reflect uncertainty about the future levels of the firm's sales. The uncertainty in turn reflects the characteristics of the firm's environment—general business conditions, industry trends, and quality and aggressiveness of management.

Relationship of Financial Leverage to Operating Leverage[9]

Chapter 5 showed that a firm has some degree of control over its production processes; it can, within limits, use either a highly automated production process with high fixed costs but low variable costs or a less automated process with lower fixed costs but higher variable costs. If a firm uses a high degree of operating leverage, its breakeven point is at a relatively high sales level, and changes in the sales level have a magnified (or "leveraged") impact on profits. Notice that financial leverage has exactly the same kind of effect on profits; the higher the leverage factor, the higher the breakeven sales volume and the greater the impact on profits from a given change in sales volume.

In Chapter 5 the *degree of operating leverage* was defined as the percentage change in operating profits associated with a given percentage change

9. This section can be omitted without loss of continuity.

in sales volume, and Equation 5.2 was developed for calculating operating leverage:

$$\text{Degree of operating leverage at Point } Q = \frac{Q(P-vc)}{Q(P-vc)-FC} \quad \textbf{(5.2)}$$

$$= \frac{P \cdot Q - VC}{P \cdot Q - VC - FC}, \quad \textbf{(5.2a)}$$

where:

Q = units of output.
P = average sales price per unit of output.
vc = variable cost per unit.
FC = total fixed costs.
PQ = sales in dollars.
VC = total variable costs.

Applying the formula to Universal Machine at a sales level of $10,000 (see Table 15.2) and assuming that one machine sells for $100, operating leverage is 1.50; thus a 100 percent increase in volume produces a 150 percent increase in profit:

$$\text{Degree of operating leverage} = \frac{100(\$100-\$40)}{100(\$100-\$40)-\$2,000}$$

$$= \frac{\$10,000-\$4,000}{\$10,000-\$4,000-\$2,000}$$

$$= \frac{\$6,000}{\$4,000} = 1.50 \text{ or } 150\%.$$

Operating leverage affects earnings before interest and taxes (EBIT), while financial leverage affects earnings after interest and taxes, the earnings available to common stockholders. In terms of Table 15.6, operating leverage affects the top section of the table and financial leverage the lower sections. Thus, if Universal had more operating leverage, its fixed costs would be higher than $2,000, its variable cost ratio would be lower than 40 percent of sales, and earnings before interest and taxes would vary with sales to a greater extent. Financial leverage takes over where operating leverage leaves off, further magnifying the effect on earnings per share of a change in the level of sales. For this reason, operating leverage is sometimes referred to as first-stage leverage and financial leverage as second-stage leverage.

Degree of Financial Leverage

The *degree of financial leverage* is defined as the percentage change in earnings available to common stockholders that is associated with a given percentage change in earnings before interest and taxes (EBIT). An equation has been developed as an aid in calculating the degree of financial leverage for any given level of EBIT and interest charges *(iB)*.[10]

$$\text{Degree of financial leverage} = \frac{\text{EBIT}}{\text{EBIT} - iB}. \tag{15.1}$$

For Universal Machine at an output of 100 units and an EBIT of $4,000, the degree of financial leverage with bond financing is:

$$\text{Financial leverage for bonds} = \frac{\$4,000}{\$4,000 - \$700} = 1.21.$$

Therefore, a 100 percent increase in EBIT results in a 121 percent increase in earnings per share. If stock financing is used, the degree of financial leverage can be calculated and found to be 1.14; thus a 100 percent increase in EBIT produces a 114 percent increase in EPS.

Combining Operating and Financial Leverage

Operating leverage causes a change in sales volume to have a magnified effect on EBIT; and if financial leverage is superimposed on operating leverage, changes in EBIT have a magnified effect on earnings per share. Therefore, if a firm uses a considerable amount of both operating leverage and

---

10. The equation is developed as follows:

a. Notice that $\text{EBIT} = Q(P - vc) - FC$.

b. Earnings per share (EPS) $= \dfrac{(\text{EBIT} - iB)(1 - T)}{N}$,

where:
EBIT = earnings before interest and taxes.
iB = interest paid.
T = corporate tax rate.
N = number of shares outstanding.

c. iB is a constant, so ΔEPS, the change in EPS, is:

$$\Delta\text{EPS} = \frac{\Delta\text{EBIT}(1 - T)}{N}.$$

d. The percentage increase in EPS is the change in EPS over the original EPS, or

$$\frac{\dfrac{\Delta\text{EBIT}(1 - T)}{N}}{\dfrac{(\text{EBIT} - iB)(1 - T)}{N}} = \frac{\Delta\text{EBIT}}{\text{EBIT} - iB}.$$

e. The degree of financial leverage is the percentage change in EPS over the percentage change in EBIT, so:

$$\text{Financial leverage} = \frac{\dfrac{\Delta\text{EBIT}}{\text{EBIT} - iB}}{\dfrac{\Delta\text{EBIT}}{\text{EBIT}}} = \frac{\text{EBIT}}{\text{EBIT} - iB}.$$

financial leverage, even small changes in the level of sales will produce wide fluctuations in EPS.

Equation 5.2 for the degree of operating leverage can be combined with Equation 15.1 for financial leverage to show the total leveraging effect of a given change in sales on earnings per share.[11]

$$\text{Combined leverage effect} = \frac{Q(P-vc)}{Q(P-vc) - FC - iB}. \tag{15.2}$$

For Universal Machine at an output of 100 units (or $10 million of sales) the combined leverage effect, using debt financing, is:

$$\text{Combined leverage effect} = \frac{100(\$100 - \$40)}{100(\$100 - \$40) - \$2,000 - \$700}$$

$$= \frac{\$6,000}{\$6,000 - \$2,000 - \$700}$$

$$= 181.8 \text{ percent.}$$

A 100 percent increase in sales from 100 units to 200 units will cause EPS to increase by 181.8 percent, so the new EPS figure will be 1.818 times the original EPS:

$$\text{EPS}_{200 \text{ units}} = \text{EPS}_{100 \text{ units}} + (\text{EPS}_{100 \text{ units}}) \times 1.818$$

$$= \text{EPS}_{100 \text{ units}} \times (1 + 1.818)$$

$$= \$3.30 \times 2.818 = \$9.30.$$

These figures agree, of course, with those worked out in Table 15.6.

Financial and operating leverage can be employed in various combinations. In the Universal Machine example, the combined leverage factor of 1.818 was obtained by using degree of operating leverage of 1.50 and degree of financial leverage of 1.21, but many other combinations of financial and operating leverage would have produced the same combined leverage

---

11. Equation 15.2 is developed as follows:

a. Recognize that $EBIT = Q(P-vc) - FC$; then rewrite Equation 15.1 as:

$$\frac{EBIT}{EBIT - iB} = \frac{Q(P-vc) - FC}{Q(P-vc) - FC - iB}. \tag{15.1a}$$

b. The total leverage effect is equal to the degree of operating leverage times the degree of financial

$$\text{Combined leverage effect} = \text{Equation 5.2} \times \text{Equation 15.1a}$$

$$= \frac{Q(P-vc)}{Q(P-vc) - FC} \cdot \frac{Q(P-vc) - FC}{Q(P-vc) - FC - iB}$$

$$= \frac{Q(P-vc)}{Q(P-vc) - FC - iB} \tag{15.2}$$

factor. Within limits, firms can and do make tradeoffs between financial and operating leverage.

The usefulness of the degree of leverage concept lies in the facts that (1) it enables firms to specify the precise effect of a change in sales volume on earnings available to common stock, and (2) it permits firms to show the interrelationship between operating and financial leverage. The concept can, for example, be used to show a business person that a decision to automate and to finance new equipment with bonds will result in a situation where a 10 percent decline in sales will produce a 50 percent decline in earnings, whereas a different operating and financial leverage package will be such that a 10 percent sales decline will cause earnings to decline by only 20 percent. In our experience, having the alternatives stated in this manner gives decision makers a better idea of the ramifications of their actions.[12]

Variations in Financial Structure

As might be expected, wide variations in the use of financial leverage can be observed among industries and among the individual firms in each industry. Illustrative of these differences is the range of ratios of debt to total assets shown in Table 15.8. Service industries use the most leverage, reflecting (1) that services include financial institutions, which as a group have high liabilities; and (2) that there are many smaller firms in the service industries, and small firms as a group are heavy users of debt. Public utility use of debt stems from a heavy fixed asset investment coupled with extremely stable sales. Mining and manufacturing firms use less debt because of their exposure to fluctuating sales.

Within the broad category of manufacturing, wide variations occur among the individual industries. Table 15.9 presents an array of total debt to total assets ratios for selected manufacturing industries. The lowest ratios are found among soft drink companies and sawmills, in which cost pressures have been severe. Low debt ratios are also found among the durable goods industries. The highest debt ratios are found in consumer nondurable goods, where demand is relatively insensitive to fluctuations and general business activity.

Even within a given industry, there are wide variations in the use of financial leverage, as illustrated for the electric utility industry in Table 15.10. These variations reflect a number of different considerations, including the volatility of business in the companies' operating areas, the extent to which they use preferred stock, and their managements' willingness to assume risk.

12. The concept is also useful for investors. If firms in an industry are classified as to their degrees of total leverage, an investor who is optimistic about prospects for the industry may favor those firms with high leverage, and one who is pessimistic may favor those with low leverage.

**Table 15.8
Variations in Financial Leverage
in Selected Industries and
Industry Groups**

Category	Total Liabilities to Total Assets
Miscellaneous	
Farms	64
Metal mining, iron ores	44
Coal mining	50
Crude petroleum and natural gas	44
Contract construction	31
Manufacturing	
Grain mill products	47
Tobacco manufacturers	47
Textile mill products	41
Paper and allied products	50
Chemicals and allied products	41
Petroleum refining	38
Farm machinery	57
Electronic components	58
Utilities	
Railroad transportation	52
Air transportation	72
Telephone and telegraph	50
Electric utilities	60
Wholesale trade	
Motor vehicles	63
Petroleum	57
Retail trade	
Retail food stores	52
Retail drugstores	55
Retail furniture	58
Services, hotels	72

Source: From the book *Almanac of Business and Industrial Ratios 1974* by Leo Troy. © 1974 by Prentice-Hall, Inc. Published by Prentice-Hall, Inc., Englewood Cliffs, New Jersey. Based on *Statistics of Income Data* of the Internal Revenue Service.

Factors Influencing Financial Structure

Thus far the discussion has touched on the factors that are generally considered when a firm formulates basic policies relating to its financial structure. The more important of these financial structure determinants will now be briefly discussed. They are: (1) growth rate of future sales, (2) stability of future sales, (3) competitive structure of the industry, (4) asset structure of

**Table 15.9
Financial Leverage in Selected
Manufacturing Industries, 1975**

Category	Total Debt to Total Assets
Soft drinks	32%
Sawmills and planing mills	36
Industrial chemicals	41
Blast furnaces and steel works	44
Motor vehicles	46
Farm machinery and equipment	49
Electrical industrial apparatus	50
Toys and sporting goods	51
Textiles	55

Source: "The Ratios of Manufacturing, 1975," *Dun's Review,* December 1976.
Reprinted with the special permission of *Dun's Review.* Copyright, 1976 Dun &
Bradstreet Publications Corporation.

**Table 15.10
Debt-to-Total-Capitalization
Ratios (Selected Electric Utility
Companies, 1975)**

Category	Total Debt to Total Assets
Central Illinois Public Service	47%
Detroit Edison	49
Consolidated Edison of New York	50
Montana Power	51
Dayton Power & Light	51
Middle South Utilities	54
American Electric Power	56

Source: Debt-to-total capitalization ratios (selected electric utility companies,
1975), from *Moody's Handbook of Common Stocks,* Spring 1977. Moody's Investors
Service, Inc.

the firm, (5) control position and attitudes toward risk of owners and management, and (6) lenders' attitudes toward the firm and the industry.

**Growth Rate of
Sales**

The future growth rate of sales is a measure of the extent to which the earnings per share of a firm are likely to be magnified by leverage. If sales and earnings grow at a rate of 8 to 10 percent a year, for example, financing by debt with limited fixed charges should magnify the returns to owners of the stock.[13] This can be seen from Figure 15.6 earlier in the chapter.

13. Such a growth rate is also often associated with a high profit rate.

However, the common stock of a firm whose sales and earnings are growing at a favorable rate commands a high price; thus it sometimes appears that equity financing is desirable. The firm must weigh the benefits of using leverage against the opportunity of broadening its equity base when it chooses between future financing alternatives. Such firms are expected to have a moderate to high level of debt financing.

Sales Stability

Sales stability and debt ratios are directly related. With greater stability in sales and earnings, a firm can incur the fixed charges of debt with less risk than when its sales and earnings are subject to periodic declines; in the latter instance it will have difficulty meeting its obligations. The stability of the utility industry, combined with relatively favorable growth prospects, has resulted in high leverage ratios in that industry.

Competitive Structure

Debt-servicing ability is dependent on the profitability, as well as the volume, of sales. Hence, the stability of profit margins is as important as the stability of sales. The ease with which new firms can enter the industry and the ability of competing firms to expand capacity both influence profit margins. A growth industry promises higher profit margins, but such margins are likely to narrow if the industry is one in which the number of firms can be easily increased through additional entry. For example, the franchised fast-service food companies were a very profitable industry in the early 1960s, but it was relatively easy for new firms to enter this business and compete with the older firms. As the industry matured during the late 1960s and early 1970s, the capacity of the old and the new firms grew at an increased rate. As a consequence, profit margins declined.

Asset Structure

Asset structure influences the sources of financing in several ways. Firms with long-lived fixed assets, especially when demand for their output is relatively assured (for example, utilities), use long-term mortgage debt extensively. Firms that have their assets mostly in receivables and in inventory whose value is dependent on the continued profitability of the individual firm (for example, those in wholesale and retail trade) rely less on long-term debt financing and more on short-term financing.

Management Attitudes

The management attitudes that most directly influence the choice of financing are those concerning control of the enterprise and risk. Large corporations whose stock is widely owned may choose additional sales of common stock because the sales will have little influence on the control of the company. Also, because management represents a stewardship for the owners, it is often unwilling to take the risk of heavy fixed charges.[14]

In contrast, the owners of small firms may prefer to avoid issuing common stock in order to be assured of continued control. Because they generally have confidence in the prospects of their companies and because they can see the large potential gains to themselves resulting from leverage, managers of such firms are often willing to incur high debt ratios.

The converse can, of course, also hold; the owner-manager of a small firm may be *more* conservative than the manager of a large company. If the net worth of the small firm is, say, $1 million, and if it all belongs to the owner-manager, that individual may well decide that he or she is already prosperous enough and may elect not to risk using leverage in an effort to become still more wealthy.

Lender Attitudes   Regardless of managements' analyses of the proper leverage factors for their firms, there is no question but that lenders' attitudes are frequently important—sometimes the most important—determinants of financial structures. In the majority of cases, the corporation discusses its financial structure with lenders and gives much weight to their advice. But when management is so confident of the future that it seeks to use leverage beyond norms for the industry, lenders may be unwilling to accept such debt increases. They emphasize that excessive debt reduces the credit standing of the borrower and the credit rating of the securities previously issued. The lenders' point of view has been expressed by a borrower (a financial vice-president), who stated. "Our policy is to determine how much debt we can carry and still maintain an AA bond rating, then use that amount less a small margin for safety."

In the following chapter the concepts developed to this point in the book will be extended to the formal theory of the cost of capital. The way investors appraise the relative desirability of increased returns versus higher risks

14. It would be inappropriate to delve too far into motivational theory in a finance book, but it is interesting to note that the managers of many larger, publicly owned corporations have a relatively small ownership position and derive most of their income from salaries. Some writers assert that in such cases managements do not strive for profits, especially if this effort involves using leverage (with its inherent risk). Presumably, these managers feel that the risks of leverage for them—the ones who actually decide to use debt or equity—outweigh the potential gains from successful leverage. If sales are low, there is a chance of failure and the loss of their jobs, whereas if sales and profits are high, it is the stockholders, not management, who receive the benefits. Another way of looking at the situation is to say that most stockholders are more diversified than most managers; if the firm fails, stockholders lose only that percentage of their net worth invested in the firm, but managers lose 100 percent of their jobs. While there is undoubtedly some merit to this argument, it should be pointed out that companies are increasingly using profit-based compensation schemes—bonus systems and stock option plans—to motivate management to seek profitability, and low leverage companies are subject to take-over bids (see Chapter 24).

is a most important consideration—one that, in general, invalidates the theory that firms should strive for maximum earnings per share regardless of the risks involved.

Summary

Financial leverage, which means using debt to boost rates of return on net worth over the returns available on assets, is the primary topic covered in this chapter. Whenever the return on assets exceeds the cost of debt, leverage is favorable, and the return on equity is raised by using it. However, leverage is a two-edged sword, and if the returns on assets are less than the cost of debt, then leverage reduces the returns on equity. The more leverage a firm employs, the greater this reduction. As a net result, leverage may be used to boost stockholder returns, but it is used at the risk of increasing losses if the firm's economic fortunes decline.

Whenever available, probability data can be used to make the risk-return tradeoff involved in the use of financial leverage more precise. The expected earnings per share (EPS) and coefficient of variation (CV) of these earnings can be calculated under alternative financial plans, and these EPS versus CV comparisons aid in making choices among plans.

Financial leverage is similar to operating leverage—a concept discussed in Chapter 5. As is true for operating leverage, financial leverage can be defined rigorously and measured in terms of the *degree of financial leverage.* In addition, the effects of financial and operating leverage can be combined, with the combined leverage factor showing the percentage changes in earnings per share that will result from a given percentage change in sales.

Questions

15.1 How will each of the occurrences listed below affect a firm's financial structure, capital structure, and net worth?
   a. The firm retains earnings of $100 during the year.
   b. A preferred stock issue is refinanced with bonds.
   c. Bonds are sold for cash.
   d. The firm repurchases 10 percent of its outstanding common stock with excess cash.
   e. An issue of convertible bonds is converted.

15.2 From an economic and social standpoint, is the use of financial leverage justifiable? Explain by listing some advantages and disadvantages.

15.3 Financial leverage and operating leverage are similar in one very important respect. What is this similarity, and why is it important?

15.4 How does the use of financial leverage affect the breakeven point?

15.5 Would you expect risk to increase proportionately, more than proportionately, or less than proportionately with added financial leverage? Explain.

15.6 What are some reasons for variations of debt ratios among the firms in a given industry?

15.7 Why is the following statement true? "Other things being the same, firms with relatively stable sales are able to incur relatively high debt ratios."

15.8 Why do public utility companies usually pursue a different financial policy from that of trade firms?

15.9 The use of financial ratios and industry averages in the financial planning and analysis of a firm should be approached with caution. Why?

15.10 Some economists believe that swings in business cycles will not be as wide in the future as they have been in the past. Assuming that they are correct in their analysis, what effect might this added stability have on the types of financing used by firms in the United States? Is your answer true for all firms?

Problems

15.1 The Hollister Company has total assets of $10 million. Earnings before interest and taxes were $2 million in 1978, and the tax rate was 40 percent. Given the following leverage ratios and corresponding interest rates, calculate Hollister's rate of return on equity (net income/equity) for each amount of debt.

Leverage (Debt/Total Assets)	Interest Rate on Debt
0%	—
10	10%
30	10
50	12
60	15

15.2 The Bergman Company wishes to calculate next year's return on equity under different leverage ratios. Bergman's total assets are $10 million, and its tax rate is 40 percent. The company is able to estimate next year's earnings for three possible states of the world. It estimates that 1979 earnings before interest and taxes will be $3 million with a 0.2 probability, $2 million with a 0.5 probability, and $500,000 with a 0.3 probability. Calculate Bergman's expected return on equity, the standard deviation, and the coefficient of variation for each of the following leverage ratios:

Leverage (Debt/Total Assets)	Interest Rate
0%	—
10	10%
30	10
50	12
60	15

15.3 Olmstead Company has 1 million shares of common stock outstanding, with a $10 par value. The tax rate is 40 percent, and earnings before interest and taxes are $2 million. Calculate earnings per share, price per share, and the leverage ratio, using both book and market values of equity, for the information given below:

Debt (B)	Interest Rate (k_b)	Return on Equity (k_s)
$ 0	—	12%
1,000,000	10%	12
3,000,000	10	13
5,000,000	11	16
6,000,000	14	20

Calculate price per share by dividing EPS by k_s. Next, calculate the number of shares of equity retired by dividing each amount of increase in debt by the share price resulting from the previous level of debt. (The number of equity shares retired is subtracted from the previous number of equity shares to obtain the number of shares of stock remaining for each level of debt.)

15.4 The beta for the Rutledge Company is 0.8 if it employs no leverage, and its tax rate is 40 percent. The financial manager of Rutledge uses the following expression to calculate the influence of leverage on beta:

$$\beta_j = \beta_u [1 + (B/S)(1 - T)].$$

a. Several alternative target leverage ratios are being considered. What will be the beta on the common stock of Rutledge Company if the following alternative leverage ratios are employed—that is, B/S = 0.4? 0.8? 1.0? 1.2? 1.6?

b. If the financial manager of Rutledge uses the SML to estimate the required return on equity, what are the required rates of return on equity at each of the above leverage ratios? (The estimated risk-free return is 6 percent, and the market risk premium is 5 percent.)

15.5 The Peterson Company plans to raise a net amount of $240 million for new equipment financing and working capital. Two alternatives are being considered. Common stock may be sold at a market price of $42 a share to net $40, or debentures yielding 9 percent may be issued with a 2 percent flotation cost. The balance sheet and income statement of the Peterson Company prior to financing are given below:

**The Peterson Company
Balance Sheet as of
December 31, 1978
(Millions of Dollars)**

Current assets	$ 800	Accounts payable	$ 150
Net fixed assets	400	Notes payable to bank	250
		Other current liabilities	200
		Total current liabilities	$ 600
		Long-term debt	250
		Common stock, $2 par	50
		Retained earnings	300
Total assets	$1,200	Total claims	$1,200

**The Peterson Company
Income Statement for Year
Ended December 31, 1978
(Millions of Dollars)**

Sales	$2,200
Net income before taxes (10%)	$ 220
Interest on debt	40
Net income subject to tax	$ 180
Tax (50%)	90
Net income after tax	$ 90

Annual sales are expected to be distributed according to the following probabilities:

Annual Sales	Probability
$1,400	0.20
2,000	0.30
2,500	0.40
3,200	0.10

a. Assuming that net income before interest and taxes remains at 10 percent of sales, calculate earnings per share under both the stock financing and the debt financing alternatives at each possible level of sales.
b. Calculate expected earnings per share under both debt and stock financing.

15.6 American Battery Corporation produces one product, a long-life rechargeable battery for use in small calculators. Last year 50,000 batteries were sold at $20 each. American Battery's income statement is shown below:

**American Battery Corporation
Income Statement for Year
Ended December 31, 1978**

Sales		$1,000,000
Less: Variable costs	$400,000	
Fixed costs	200,000	600,000
EBIT		$ 400,000
Less: Interest		125,000
Net income before tax		$ 275,000
Less: Income tax ($T = 0.40$)		110,000
Net income		$ 165,000
EPS (100,000 shares)		$1.65

a. Calculate the following for American Battery's 1978 level of sales:
   1. the degree of operating leverage
   2. the degree of financial leverage
   3. the combined leverage effect
b. American Battery is considering changing to a new production process for manufacturing the batteries. Highly automated and capital inten-

sive, the new process will double fixed costs to $400,000 but will decrease variable costs to $4 a unit. If the new equipment is financed with bonds, interest will increase by $70,000; if it is financed by common stock, total stock outstanding will increase by 20,000 shares. Assuming that sales remain constant, calculate for each financing method:

1. earnings per share
2. the combined leverage

c. Under what conditions would you expect American Battery to want to change its operations to the more automated process?

d. If sales are expected to increase, which alternative will have the greatest impact on EPS? Illustrate with an example.

15.7 The Hunter Corporation plans to expand assets by 50 percent. To finance the expansion, it is choosing between a straight 7 percent debt issue and common stock. Its current balance sheet and income statement are shown below:

**Hunter Corporation
Balance Sheet as of
December 31, 1980**

		Debt (at 6%)	$140,000
		Common stock, $10 par	350,000
		Retained earnings	210,000
Total assets	$700,000	Total claims	$700,000

**Hunter Corporation
Income Statement for Year
Ended December 31, 1980**

Sales	$2,100,000	
Total costs (excluding interest)	1,881,600	
Net income before taxes	$ 218,400	
Debt interest	8,400	
Income before taxes	$ 210,000	
Taxes (at 50%)	105,000	
Net income	$ 105,000	

Earnings per share: $\dfrac{\$105,000}{35,000} = \$3$

Price/earnings ratio: 10×[a]

Market price: 10 × $3 = $30

[a] The price/earnings ratio is the market price per share divided by earnings per share. It represents the amount of money an investor is willing to pay for $1 of current earnings. The higher the riskiness of a stock, the lower its P/E ratio, other things held constant. The concept of price/earnings ratio is discussed at some length in Chapter 14.

If Hunter Corporation finances the $350,000 expansion with debt, the rate on the incremental debt will be 7 percent, and the price/earnings ratio of the common stock will be 8 times. If the expansion is financed by equity, the new stock can be sold at $25, the rate on debt will be 6 percent, and the price/earnings ratio of all the outstanding common stock will remain at 10 times.

a. Assuming that net income before interest and taxes (EBIT) is 10 percent of sales, what are the earnings per share at sales levels of $0, $700,000, $1,400,000, $2,100,000, $2,800,000, $3,500,000, and $4,200,000, when financing is with common stock? when financing is with debt? (Assume no fixed costs of production.)

b. Make a breakeven chart for EPS, and indicate the breakeven point in sales (where EPS using bonds = EPS using stock).

c. Using the price/earnings ratio, calculate the market value per share of common stock for each sales level for both the debt and the equity financing.

d. Using data from Part c, make a breakeven chart of market value per share for the company, and indicate the breakeven point.

e. Which form of financing should be used if the firm follows the policy of seeking to maximize
   1. EPS?
   2. market price per share?

f. Now assume that the following probability estimates of future sales have been made: 5 percent chance of $0, 7.5 percent chance of $700,000, 20 percent chance of $1,400,000, 35 percent chance of $2,100,000, 20 percent chance of $2,800,000, 7.5 percent chance of $3,500,000, and 5 percent chance of $4,200,000. Calculate expected values for EPS and market price per share under each financing alternative.

g. What other factors should be taken into account in choosing between the two forms of financing?

h. Would it matter if the presently outstanding stock was all owned by the final decision maker (the president) and that this represented his entire net worth? Would it matter if he was compensated entirely by a fixed salary? if he had a substantial number of stock options?

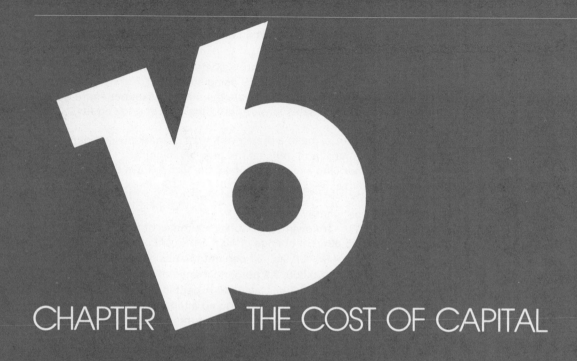

CHAPTER 16 THE COST OF CAPITAL

The cost of capital is a critically important topic for three reasons. First, as we saw in Chapter 12, capital budgeting decisions have a major impact on the firm, and proper capital budgeting requires an estimate of the cost of capital. Second, as we saw in Chapter 15, financial structure can affect both the size and the riskiness of the firm's earnings stream and hence the value of the firm. A knowledge of the cost of capital and how it is influenced by financial leverage is useful in making capital structure decisions. Finally, a number of other decisions—including those related to leasing, to bond refunding, and to working capital policy—require estimates of the cost of capital.[1]

This chapter first points out the necessity of using a weighted average cost of capital. Second, it considers the cost of the individual components of the capital structure—debt, preferred stock, and equity. Because investors perceive different classes of securities as having different degrees of risk, there are variations in cost of the different types of securities. Third, it brings the individual component costs together to form a weighted cost of capital. Fourth, it illustrates the concepts developed in the earlier sections with an example of the cost of capital calculation for an actual company. Finally, it develops the interrelationship between the cost of capital and the investment opportunity schedule and discusses the simultaneous determination of the marginal cost of capital and the marginal return on investment.

Composite, or Overall, Cost of Capital

Suppose a particular firm's cost of debt is estimated to be 8 percent, its cost of equity is estimated to be 12 percent, and the decision has been made to finance next year's projects by selling debt. The argument is sometimes advanced that the cost of these projects is 8 percent because debt is being used to finance them. However, this position contains a basic fallacy. To finance a particular set of projects with debt implies that the firm is also using up some of its potential for obtaining new low-cost debt. As expansion occurs in subsequent years, at some point the firm will find it necessary to use additional equity financing to keep the debt ratio from becoming too large.

To illustrate: Suppose a firm has an 8 percent cost of debt and a 12 percent cost of equity. In the first year it borrows heavily, using up its debt

---

1. The cost of capital is also vitally important in regulated industries, including electric, gas, telephone, and transportation. In essence, regulatory commissions seek to measure a utility's cost of capital, then set prices so the company will just earn this rate of return. If the estimate is too low, the company will not be able to attract sufficient capital to meet long-run demands for service, and the public will suffer. If the estimate is too high, customers will pay too much for service.

capacity in the process, to finance projects yielding 9 percent. In the second year it has projects available that yield 11 percent (well above the return on first-year projects), but it cannot accept them because they will have to be financed with 12 percent equity money. To avoid this problem, the firm should view itself as an ongoing concern, and its cost of capital should be calculated as a weighted average, or composite, of the various types of funds it uses: debt, preferred stock, and common equity.

Basic Definitions

Both students and financial managers are often confused about how to calculate and use the cost of capital. To a large extent, this confusion results from imprecise, ambiguous definitions; but a careful study of the following definitions will eliminate the confusion.

Capital (or financial) *components* are the items on the right-hand side of the balance sheet; they include various types of debt, preferred stock, and common equity. Any net increase in assets must be financed by an increase in one or more capital components.

Capital is a necessary factor of production; like any other factor, it has a cost. The cost of each component is defined as its *component cost*. For example, if a firm can borrow money at 8 percent, by definition, its component cost of debt is 8 percent.[2] This chapter will concentrate primarily on debt, preferred stock, retained earnings, and new issues of common stock. These are the capital structure components, and their component costs are identified by the following symbols:

k_b = interest rate on firm's new debt = component cost of debt, before tax.

$k_b(1-T)$ = component cost of debt, after tax, where T = marginal tax rate; $k_b(1-T)$ is the debt cost used to calculate the marginal cost of capital.

k_{ps} = component cost of preferred stock.

k_r = component cost of retained earnings (or internal equity).

k_e = component cost of new issues of common stock (or external equity). In Chapter 14, k_s was defined as the required rate of return on common equity. Here equity obtained from retained earnings is distinguished from equity obtained by selling new stock—hence the distinction between k_e and k_r.

---

2. We will see later that there is a before-tax cost of debt; for now it is sufficient to know that 8 percent is the before-tax component cost of debt. (The effects of debt on the cost of equity will also be considered later.)

$k =$ an average, or composite, cost of capital. If a firm raises $1 of new capital to finance asset expansion, and if it is to keep its capital structure in balance (that is, if it is to keep the same percentage of debt, preferred stock, and common equity funds), then it will raise part of the $1 as debt, part as preferred stock, and part as common equity (with equity coming either from retained earnings or from the sale of new common stock).[3] k is also a *marginal cost;* that is, a value of k exists for each dollar the firm raises during the year. In effect, k is the marginal cost of capital used in Chapter 12, and the relationship between k and the amount of funds raised during the year is expressed as the MCC schedule in Figure 12.1.[4]

These definitions and concepts are explained in detail in the remainder of the chapter, which seeks to accomplish two goals: (1) to develop a marginal cost of capital schedule (k = MCC) that can be used in capital budgeting, and (2) to determine the mix of types of capital that will minimize the MCC schedule. If the firm finances so as to minimize its MCC, uses this MCC to calculate NPVs, and makes capital budgeting decisions on the basis of the NPV method, this will lead to a maximization of stock prices.

Before-Tax Component Cost of Debt (k_b)

If a firm borrows $100,000 for one year at 6 percent interest, it must pay the investors who purchase the debt a total of $6,000 annual interest on their investment:

$$k_b = \text{Before-tax cost of debt} = \frac{\text{Interest}}{\text{Principal}} = \frac{\$6,000}{\$100,000} = 6\%. \quad \textbf{(16.1)}$$

For now, assume that the firm pays no corporate income tax (the effect of income taxes on the analysis of cost of capital is treated in a later section of the chapter). Under this assumption, the firm's dollar interest cost is $6,000, and its percentage cost of debt is 6 percent. As a first approximation, *the component cost of debt is equal to the rate of return earned by investors, or*

---

3. Firms do try to keep their debt, preferred stock, and common equity in balance; they do not try to maintain any proportional relationship between the common stock and retained earnings accounts as shown on the balance sheet.
4. As discussed in Chapter 13, k also reflects the riskiness of the firm's various assets. If a firm uses risk-adjusted discount rates for different capital projects, the average of these rates weighted by the sizes of the various investments should equal k.

the interest rate on debt.[5] If the firm borrows and invests the borrowed funds to earn a return just equal to the interest rate, then the earnings available to common stock remain unchanged.[6] This is demonstrated below.

The ABC Company has sales of $1 million, operating costs of $900,000, and no debt. Its income statement is shown in the "before" column of Table 16.1. The firm borrows $100,000 at 6 percent and invests the funds in assets whose use causes sales to rise by $7,000 and operating costs to rise by $1,000. Hence, profits before interest rise by $6,000. The new situation is shown in the "after" column. Earnings are unchanged, since the investment just earns its component cost of capital. Note that the cost of debt applies to *new* debt, not to the interest of any previously outstanding debt. In other words, we are interested in the cost of new debt, or the *marginal* cost of debt. The primary concern with the cost of capital is its use in a decision-making process—the decision whether to obtain capital to make new in-

5. The cost of convertible debt is slightly more complicated, but it can be calculated using the following formula:

$$M = \sum_{t=1}^{N} \frac{c}{(1 + k_c)^t} + \frac{tv}{(1 + k_c)^{N}},$$

where:

M = the price of the convertible bond.
c = the annual interest in dollars.
tv = the expected terminal value of the bond in Year N.
N = the expected number of years the bond will be outstanding.
k_c = the required rate of return on the convertible.

The risk to an investor holding a convertible is somewhat higher than that on a straight bond but somewhat less than that on common stock. Accordingly, the cost of convertibles is generally between that on bonds and that on stock. (This concept is discussed in detail in Chapter 22.) Note also that the after-tax cost of a convertible is found as k_c in the equation, but here c is multiplied by $(1 - T)$, where T is the marginal corporate tax rate.

6. Note that this definition is a *first approximation;* it is modified later to take account of the deductibility of interest payments for income tax purposes. Note also that here the cost of debt is considered in isolation. The impact of debt on the cost of equity, as well as on future increments of debt, is treated when the weighted cost of a combination of debt and equity is derived. Finally, flotation costs, or the costs of selling the debt, are ignored. Flotation costs for debt issues are generally quite low; in fact, most debt is placed directly with banks, insurance companies, pension funds, and the like and involves no flotation costs. If flotation costs are involved, the cost of debt can be approximated by the following equation:

$$k_b = \frac{c_t + \dfrac{M - p_b}{N}}{\dfrac{M + p_b}{2}},$$

where:

c_t = the periodic interest payment in dollars.
M = the par or maturity value of the bond.
p_b = the bond's issue price (hence $M - p_b$ is the premium or discount).
N = the life of the bond.

The equation is an approximation, as it does not consider compounding effects. However, the approximation is quite close; for example, with a 5 percent, twenty-five-year, $1,000 par value bond sold at $980, the formula gives $k_b = 5.13$ versus 5.15 as found from a bond table.

**Table 16.1
Income Statement for the
ABC Company**

	Before	After
Sales	$1,000,000	$1,007,000
Operating costs	900,000	901,000
Earnings before interest	$ 100,000	$ 106,000
Interest	—	6,000
Earnings	$ 100,000	$ 100,000

vestments. Whether the firm borrowed at high or low rates in the past is irrelevant.[7]

Preferred Stock

Preferred stock, described in detail in Chapter 20, is a hybrid between debt and common stock. Like debt, preferred stock carries a fixed commitment on the part of the corporation to make periodic payments; and in liquidation the claims of the preferred stockholders take precedence over those of the common stockholders. Failure to make the preferred dividend payments does not result in bankruptcy, however, as does nonpayment of interest on bonds. Thus, to the firm, preferred stock is somewhat more risky than common stock but less risky than bonds. Just the reverse holds for investors. To the investor, preferred is less risky than common but more risky than bonds. Thus an investor who is willing to buy the firm's bonds on the basis of a 6 percent interest return might, because of risk aversion, be unwilling to purchase the firm's preferred stock at a yield of less than 8 percent. Assuming the preferred issue is a perpetuity that sells for $100 a share and pays an $8 annual dividend, its yield is calculated as follows:

$$\text{Preferred yield} = \frac{\text{Preferred dividend}}{\text{Price of preferred stock}} = \frac{d_{ps}}{p_{ps}} = \frac{\$8}{\$100} = 8\%. \quad (16.2)$$

Assuming the firm can sell additional preferred stock at $100 a share, its cost of preferred is also 8 percent. In other words, as a first approximation, the component cost of preferred stock (k_{ps}) is equal to the return investors receive on the shares as calculated in Equation 16.2.

If the firm receives less than the market price of preferred stock when it sells new preferred, p_{ps} in the denominator of Equation 16.2 should be the net price received by the firm. Suppose, for example, the firm must incur a selling, or *flotation,* cost of $4 a share. In other words, buyers of the preferred issue pay $100 a share, but brokers charge a selling commission of $4

---

7. Whether the firm borrowed at high or low rates in the past is, of course, important in terms of the effect of the interest charges on current profits, but it is not relevant for current decisions. For current financial decisions, only current interest rates are relevant.

a share, so the firm nets $96 a share. The cost of new preferred to the firm is calculated in Equation 16.2a:

$$k_{ps} = \text{Cost of preferred} = \frac{d_{ps}}{p_{ps}} = \frac{\$8}{\$96} = 8.33\%. \qquad \textbf{(16.2a)}$$

Tax Adjustment

As they stand, the definitions of the *component costs of debt* and *of preferred stock* are incompatible when taxes are introduced into the analysis, because interest payments are a deductible expense whereas preferred dividends are not. The following example illustrates the point.

The ABC Company can borrow $100,000 at 8 percent, or it can sell 1,000 shares of $8 preferred stock to net $100 a share. Assuming a 46 percent tax rate, its before-investment situation is given in the "before" column of Table 16.2. At what rate of return must the company invest the proceeds from the new financing to keep the earnings available to common shareholders from changing?

As can be seen from the tabulations in Table 16.2, if the funds are invested to yield 8 percent before taxes, earnings available to common stockholders are constant if debt is used, but they decline if the financing is with preferred stock. To maintain the $54,000 net earnings requires that funds generated from the sale of preferred stock be invested to yield 14.815 percent before taxes or 8 percent after taxes.[8]

Table 16.2
Tax Adjustment for Cost of Debt

		Invest in Assets Yielding		
	Before	8% Debt	8% Preferred	14.815% Preferred
Earnings before interest and taxes (EBIT)	$100,000	$108,000	$108,000	$114,815
Interest	—	−8,000	—	—
Earnings before taxes (EBT)	$100,000	$100,000	$108,000	$114,815
Taxes (at 46%) (T)	−46,000	−46,000	49,680	−52,815
Preferred dividends	—	—	−8,000	−8,000
Available for common dividends	$ 54,000	$ 54,000	$ 50,320	$ 54,000

Since stockholders are concerned with after-tax rather than before-tax earnings, only the cost of capital *after* corporate taxes should be used. The cost of preferred stock is already on an after-tax basis as defined, but a simple adjustment is needed to arrive at the after-tax cost of debt. It is recognized that interest payments are tax deductible; the higher the firm's interest payments, the lower its tax bill. In effect, the federal government pays

---

8. The 14.815 percent is found as follows: 8%/(1 − Tax rate) = 8%/0.54.

part of a firm's interest charges. Therefore, the cost of debt capital is calculated as follows:

$$k_b(1 - T) = \text{After-tax cost of debt}$$
$$= \text{Before-tax cost} \times (1.0 - \text{Tax rate}). \qquad \textbf{(16.3)}$$

Whenever the weighted cost of capital (k) *is calculated,* $k_b(1 - T)$—*not* k_b—*is used.*

Example. Before-tax cost of debt = 8 percent; tax rate = 46 percent.
$k_b(1 - T)$ = after-tax cost = (0.08) (1 − 0.46) = (0.08) (0.54) = 4.32 percent.

Cost of Retained Earnings (k$_r$)[9]

The cost of preferred stock is based on the return that investors require if they are to purchase the preferred stock; the cost of debt is based on the interest rate investors require on debt issues, adjusted for taxes. The cost of equity obtained by retaining earnings can be defined similarly. It is k_r, the rate of return stockholders require on the firm's common stock (k_r is identical to k_s as developed in Chapter 14).

As we saw in Chapter 14, the value of a share of common stock depends ultimately on the dividends paid on the stock:

$$p_0 = \frac{d_1}{(1 + k_r)} + \frac{d_2}{(1 + k_r)^2} + \cdots \qquad \textbf{(16.4)}$$

where:

p_0 = the current price of the stock.
d_1 = the dividend expected to be paid at the end of Year 1.
d_2 = the dividend expected to be paid at the end of Year 2.
k_r = the required rate of return.

As we saw in Chapter 14, if dividends are expected to grow at a constant rate, Equation 16.4 reduces to:

$$p_0 = \frac{d_1}{k_r - g}. \qquad \textbf{(16.5)}$$

9. The term *retained earnings* can be interpreted to mean the balance sheet item "retained earnings," consisting of all the earnings retained in the business throughout its history; or it can mean the income statement item "additions to retained earnings." The latter definition is used in this chapter. *For our purpose, retained earnings* refers to that part of current earnings not paid out in dividends but retained and reinvested in the business.

Equity is defined in this chapter to *exclude* preferred stock. Equity is the sum of capital stock, capital surplus, and accumulated retained earnings. Note that our treatment of the cost of retained earnings abstracts from certain complications caused by personal income taxes on dividend income and by brokerage costs incurred in reinvesting dividend income. Similarly, we do not explicitly treat the cost of depreciation generated funds in the chapter. These topics are, however, discussed at length in J. Fred Weston and Eugene F. Brigham, *Managerial Finance,* 6th ed. (Hinsdale, Ill.: Dryden Press, 1978), app. A to chap. 19.

417

In equilibrium, the expected and required rates of return must be equal, so we can solve for k_r to obtain the required rate of return on common equity:

$$k_r = \frac{d_1}{p_0} + \text{Expected } g. \tag{16.6}$$

To illustrate this calculation, consider Aubey Rents, a firm expected to earn $2 a share and to pay a $1 dividend during the coming year. The company's earnings, dividends, and stock price have all been growing at about 5 percent a year, and this growth rate is expected to continue indefinitely. The stock is in equilibrium and currently sells for $20 a share. Using this information, the required rate of return on the stock in equilibrium can be computed using Equation 16.6:

$$k_r = \frac{\$1}{\$20} + 5\% = 10\%.$$

The expected growth rate for the price of the shares is 5 percent, which, on the $20 initial price, should lead to a $1 increase in the value of the stock, to $21. Barring changes in the general level of stock prices, this price increase will be attained if Aubey invests the $1 of retained earnings to yield 10 percent. However, if the $1 is invested to yield only 5 percent, then earnings will grow by only 5 cents a share during the year, not by the expected 10 cents a share. The new earnings will be $2.05, a growth of only 2.5 percent, rather than the expected $2.10, or 5 percent increase. If investors believe that the firm will earn only 5 percent on retained earnings in the future and attain only a 2.5 percent growth rate, they will reappraise the value of the stock downward according to Equation 16.5:

$$p_0 = \frac{d_1}{k_r - g} = \frac{\$1}{0.10 - 0.025} = \frac{\$1}{0.075} = \$13.33.$$

Note, however, that Aubey Rents will suffer this price decline only if it invests equity funds—retained earnings—at less than its component cost of capital.

If Aubey refrains from making new investments and pays all its earnings in dividends, it will cut its growth rate to zero. However, the price of the stock will not fall because investors will still get the required 10 percent rate of return on their shares:

$$k_r = \frac{d_1}{p_0} + g = \frac{\$2}{\$20} + 0 = 10\%,$$

or

$$p_0 = \frac{\$2}{0.10 - 0} = \$20.$$

All the return would come in the form of dividends, but the actual rate of return would match the required 10 percent.

This example demonstrates a fundamentally important fact. If a firm earns its required rate of return, k_r, then when it retains earnings and invests them in its operations, its current stock price will not change as a result of this financing and investment. However, if it earns less than k_r, the stock price will fall; and if it earns more, the stock price will rise.

Cost of New Common Stock, or External Equity Capital (k_e)

The cost of new common stock, or *external* equity capital, k_e, is higher than the cost of retained earnings, k_r, because of flotation costs involved in selling new common stock. What rate of return must be earned on funds raised by selling stock to make the action worthwhile? To put it another way, what is the cost of new common stock? The answer is found by applying the following formula:

$$k_e = \frac{d_1}{p_0(1-f)} + g = \frac{d_1}{p_n} + g$$

$$= \frac{\text{Dividend yield}}{1 - \text{Flotation percentage}} + \text{Growth.}[10] \qquad (16.7)$$

10. The equation is derived as follows:

Step 1. The old stockholders expect the firm to pay a stream of dividends, d_t; this income stream is derived from existing assets. New investors likewise expect to receive the same stream of dividends, d_t. For new investors to obtain this stream without impairing that of the old investors, the new funds obtained from the sale of stock must be invested at a return high enough to provide a dividend stream whose present value is equal to the price the firm receives:

$$p_n = \sum_{t=1}^{\infty} \frac{d_t}{(1+k_e)^t}. \qquad (16.8)$$

where:
p_n = the net price to the firm.
d_t = the dividend stream to new stockholders.
k_e = the cost of new outside equity.

Step 2. If flotation costs are expressed as a percentage, f, of the gross price of the stock, p_0, we can express p_n as follows:

$$p_n = p_0(1-f).$$

Step 3. When growth is a constant, Equation 16.8 reduces to

$$p_n = p_0(1-f) = \frac{d_1}{k_e - g}. \qquad (16.8a)$$

Step 4. Equation 16.8a can be solved for k_e:

$$k_e = \frac{d_1}{p_0(1-f)} + g. \qquad (16.7)$$

Here f is the percentage cost of selling the issue, so $p_0 (1 - f) = p_n$ is the net price received by the firm. For example, if p_0 is \$10 and f is 10 percent, then the firm receives \$9 for each new share sold; hence p_n is \$9. (Equation 16.7 is strictly applicable only if future growth is expected to be constant.)

For Aubey Rents, the cost of new outside equity is computed as follows:

$$k_e = \frac{\$1}{\$20(1 - 0.10)} + 5\% = 10.55\%.$$

Investors require a return of $k_r = 10$ percent on Aubey's stock. However, because of flotation costs, Aubey must earn *more* than 10 percent on stock-financed investments to provide this 10 percent. Specifically, if Aubey Rents earns 10.55 percent on investments financed by new common stock issues, then earnings per share will not fall below previously expected earnings, the expected dividend can be maintained, the growth rate for earnings and dividends will be maintained, and (as a result of all this) the price per share will not decline. If Aubey earns less than 10.55 percent, then earnings, dividends, and growth will fall below expectations, causing the price of the stock to decline. Since the cost of capital is *defined* as the rate of return that must be earned to prevent the price of the stock from falling, we see that the company's cost of external equity, k_e, is 10.55 percent.[11]

Finding the Basic Required Rate of Return on Common Equity

It is obvious by now that the basic rate of return investors require on a firm's common equity, k_s, as developed in Chapter 14, is a most important quantity. This required rate of return is the cost of retained earnings, and it forms the basis for the cost of capital obtained from new stock issues. How is it estimated?

Although complicated procedures for making this estimation can be used, satisfactory estimates can be obtained in three ways:

1. Estimate the security market line (SML) as described in Chapter 14. Estimate the relative riskiness of the firm in question; then use the estimate to obtain the required rate of return on the firm's stock:

$$k_s = R_F + \rho.$$

11. The cost of external equity is sometimes defined as:

$$k_e = \frac{k_r}{1 - f}.$$

This equation is correct if the firm's expected growth rate is zero (see Equation 16.7). In other cases it tends to overstate k_e.

Under this procedure, the estimated cost of equity (k_s) will move up or down with changes in interest rates and in investor psychology.[12]

2. An alternative procedure, which should be used in conjunction with the one described above, is to estimate the basic required rate of return as follows:

   a. Assume that investors expect the past realized rate of return on the stock to be earned in the future, so the expected return is equal to $\overline{k}_s$.

   b. Assume that the stock is in equilibrium, with $k_s^* = \overline{k}_s$.

   c. Under these assumptions, the required rate of return can be estimated as equal to the past realized rate of return:

$$k_s^* = \overline{k}_s = \frac{d_1}{p_0} + \text{Past growth rate.}$$

Stockholder returns are derived from dividends and capital gains, and the total of the dividend yield plus the average growth rate over the past five to ten years can give an estimate of the total returns that stockholders expect in the future from a particular share of stock.

3. For "normal" companies in "normal" times, past growth rates can be projected into the future, and the second method will give satisfactory results. However, if the company's growth has been abnormally high or low, either because of its own unique situation or because of general economic conditions, then investors will not project the past growth rate into the future, so Method 2 will not yield a good estimate of k_s^*. In this case, g must be estimated in some other manner. Security analysts regularly make earnings growth forecasts, looking at such factors as projected sales, profit margins, and competitive factors. Someone making a cost of capital estimate can obtain such analysts' forecasts and use them as a proxy for the growth expectations of investors in general, combine g with the current dividend yield, and estimate $\overline{k}_s$ as

$$k_s^* = \frac{d_1}{p_0} + \text{Growth rate as projected by security analysts.}$$

Again, note that this estimate of k_s^* is based on the assumption that g is expected to remain constant in the future.

Based on our own experience in estimating equity capital costs, we recognize that both careful analysis and very fine judgments are required in this process. It would be nice to pretend that these judgments are unnecessary and to specify an easy, precise way of determining the exact cost of equity capital. Unfortunately, this is not possible. Finance is in large part a matter of judgment, and we simply must face this fact.

12. See Weston and Brigham, *Managerial Finance,* app. C to chap. 19, for illustrations of the use of the capital asset pricing model in calculating the cost of equity capital and the cost of capital for firms.

Effects of Risky Leverage

Effect of Leverage on the Cost of Equity

In Chapter 15, we used the Universal Machine Company case to demonstrate that for any given degree of business risk, the higher the debt ratio, the larger the measures of variability in earnings per share and return on equity. The higher the level of debt, the higher the fixed charges and the higher the probability of not being able to cover them. The inability to meet fixed charges may trigger a number of penalty clauses in the debt indentures (agreements) and lead to reorganization or bankruptcy (see Chapter 25), with attendant costs of attorneys and court proceedings. Even before such legal difficulties, the increasing risk of financial difficulties may result in the loss of key employees (who find positions with firms whose financial outlook is safer), in the reduced availability of goods from key suppliers, and in reduced financing.

The existence of substantial bankruptcy costs causes the relationship between leverage and the related risks of equity and debt to become curvilinear upward, thereby increasing the required returns on equity and debt. In this section we will analyze the effect on required returns on equity. Accordingly, the relationship between leverage and the required rates of return can be as set forth in Table 16.3.

In Chapter 14 we indicated that the required rate of return consisted of the riskless rate plus a risk premium: $k_s = R_F + \rho$. Here we divide ρ into two components, ρ_1 ("rho one"), a premium for business risk; and ρ_2, a premium required to compensate equity investors for the additional risk brought on by financial leverage. Expressed as an equation:

$$k_s = R_F + \rho_1 + \rho_2. \qquad (16.9)$$

The riskless rate of return, R_F, is a function of general economic conditions, Federal Reserve policy, and the like. The premium for business risk, ρ_1, is a function of the nature of the firm's industry, its degree of operating leverage, its diversification, and so on. Financial risk, ρ_2, depends on the degree of financial leverage employed.[13]

In Table 16.3 we illustrate how the magnitudes of business and financial risk can be measured in relation to leverage and then indicate their plausible impact on the required rates of return on equity.[14] The calculations of ρ_1^* and ρ_2^* are based on the assumptions of no substantial bankruptcy costs. ρ_1^* is simply the beta of an unlevered firm multiplied by the market risk premium, and ρ_2^* is ρ_1^* multiplied by B/S times $(1 - T)$—as measured in Chapter 15.

---

13. ρ_2 increases at an increasing rate with leverage because bankruptcy, as opposed to lower earnings, becomes an increasing threat as the debt ratio rises; and bankruptcy may have high costs of its own (see Chapter 25).
14. Keep in mind that throughout this analysis we are holding constant the firm's assets and the EBIT on these assets. We wish to consider the effect of leverage on the cost of capital *holding other things constant.*

**Table 16.3
Leverage, Risk Indexes, and the
Required Rates of Return on
Equity for Universal Machine
Company**

Leverage (Debt/Equity— B/S)	Without Bankruptcy Penalties[a]		With Bankruptcy Penalties[b]		Required Return on Equity	
					Without Bankruptcy Penalties[c]	With Bankruptcy Penalties[d]
	ρ_1^*	ρ_2^*	ρ_1	ρ_2		
0	6%	0%	6%	0%	12.00	12.00
0.25	6	0.75	6	0.75	12.75	12.75
0.43	6	1.29	6	1.29	13.29	13.29
0.67	6	2.01	6	3.51	14.01	15.51
1.00	6	3.00	6	6.00	15.00	18.00
1.50	6	4.50	6	11.86	16.50	23.86
4.00	6	12.00	6	33.54	24.00	45.54

[a]The columns are calculated as follows:

$$(k_M - R_F) = 0.05; \; \beta_u = 1.2. \quad \rho_1^* = \beta_u\,(k_M - R_F); \; \rho_2^* = (B/S)\,(1 - T)\,\rho_1^*.$$

[b]Calculations: This procedure involves modifying on a judgmental basis the basic equation for the relationship between the levered beta and the unlevered beta.

$$\rho_1 = \beta_u\,(k_M - R_F).$$

For ρ_2 we have:
$$\begin{aligned}
B/S &\leq 0.43 & \rho_2 &= (B/S)\,(1 - T)\,\rho_1. \\
B/S &= 0.67 & \rho_2 &= (0.5 + B/S)\,(1 - T)\,\rho_1. \\
B/S &= 1.00 & \rho_2 &= (1 + B/S)\,(1 - T)\,\rho_1. \\
B/S &= 1.50 & \rho_2 &= (1 + B/S)^{1.5}(1 - T)\,\rho_1. \\
B/S &= 4.00 & \rho_2 &= (1 + B/S)^{1.5}(1 - T)\,\rho_1.
\end{aligned}$$

[c]Calculations: $6\% + \rho_1^* + \rho_2^*$.
[d]Calculations: $6\% + \rho_1 + \rho_2$.

With bankruptcy costs, however, the indexes of financial risk are likely to increase at an increasing rate when leverage passes some critical point and become curvilinear upward as measured in Table 16.3, which is also graphed in Figure 16.1. The required rate of return on equity is 12 percent if the company uses no debt, but k_s^* increases after debt passes some critical level and is 23.86 percent if the debt to value ratio is as high as 60 percent.[15] With leverage beyond 60 percent, it is likely that the required cost of equity is so high that the funds for all practical purposes are not available.

15. This corresponds to a debt to equity ratio of 150 percent. In this example we assume that the risk-return tradeoff function has been estimated, perhaps in a subjective manner, by the financial manager. The precise specification of such risk-return functions is one of the more controversial areas of finance, and having attempted to measure them empirically ourselves, we can attest to the difficulties involved. However, even though the precise shape of the function is open to question, it is generally agreed (1) that the curve is upward sloping and (2) that some estimate, be it better or worse, is necessary if we are to obtain a cost of capital for use in capital budgeting. In this chapter our main concern is that the broad concepts be grasped.

**Figure 16.1
Illustrative Relationship between
the Cost of Equity and Financial
Leverage**

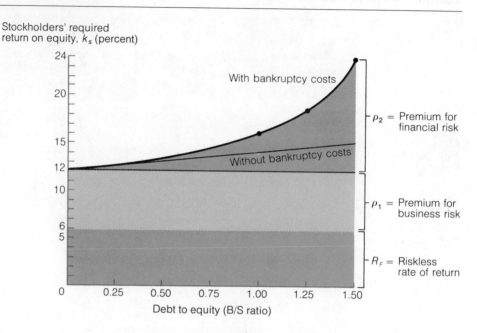

Stockholders' required
return on equity, k_s (percent)

Effect of Leverage on the Component Cost of Debt

The component cost of debt is also affected by leverage. The higher the leverage ratio, the higher the cost of debt. Further, the cost of debt can be expected to rise at an increasing rate with leverage. To see why this is so, we can again consider the Universal Machine Company example. The more debt the firm has, the higher the interest requirements; and the higher the interest charges, the greater the probability that earnings (EBIT) will not be sufficient to meet these charges. Creditors will perceive this increasing risk as the debt ratio rises, and they will begin charging a risk premium above the riskless rate, causing the firm's interest rate to rise. (Since creditors are risk averters and are assumed to have a diminishing marginal utility for money, they will demand that interest rates be increased to compensate for the increased risk.)

One other effect that may operate to raise interest rates at an increasing rate is the fact that a firm may need to use a variety of sources in order to borrow large amounts of funds in relation to its equity base. For example, a firm may be able to borrow from banks only up to some limit set by bank policy or bank examiner regulations. In order to increase its borrowings, the firm will have to seek other institutions, such as insurance companies and finance companies, that may demand higher interest rates than those charged by banks. Such an effect may tend to cause interest rates to jump whenever the firm is forced to find new lenders.

Table 16.4 shows the estimated relationships among leverage, the interest rate, and the after-tax cost of debt for Universal Machine Company. Assuming a 50 percent tax rate, the after-tax cost of debt is half the interest rate; these figures are also shown in Figure 16.2, where they are plotted against the debt ratio. In the example, Universal's cost of debt is constant until the debt ratio passes 20 percent or $2 million; then it begins to climb.

Table 16.4
Effect of Leverage on the Cost of Debt for Universal Machine Company

Leverage (Debt/Assets)	Interest Rate (k_b)	After-Tax Cost of Debt $k_b(1 - T)$
0%	10.0%	5.0%
20	10.0	5.0
30	10.8	5.4
35	11.0	5.5
40	13.0	6.5
50	16.0	8.0
60	27.0	13.5

Combining Debt and Equity: Weighted Average, or Composite, Cost of Capital

Debt and equity can be combined to determine Universal Machine's average, or composite, cost of capital; Table 16.5 shows the calculations used to determine the weighted average cost. The average cost, together with the component cost of debt and equity, is plotted against the debt ratio in Figure 16.3. Here the composite cost of capital is minimized when its debt ratio is approximately 35 percent, so Universal's optimal capital structure calls for about 35 percent debt and 65 percent equity.

Note that the average cost of capital curve is relatively flat over a fairly broad range. If Universal Machine's debt ratio is in the range of 20 to 40 percent, the average cost of capital cannot be lowered very much by moving to the optimal point. This appears to be a fairly typical situation, since almost any "reasonable" schedule for the component costs of debt and equity will produce a saucer-shaped average cost of capital schedule similar to that shown in Figure 16.3. This gives financial managers a large degree of flexibility in planning their financing programs, permitting them to sell debt one year and equity the next in order to take advantage of capital market conditions and to avoid high flotation costs associated with small security issues.

**Figure 16.2
After-tax Cost of Debt
for Universal Machine Company**

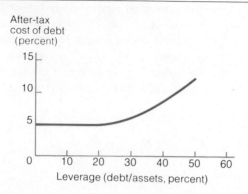

**Table 16.5
Calculation of Points on Average
Cost of Capital Curve (Percent),
or the Composite Cost of Capital
for Different Capital Structures
for Universal Machine Company**

		Percent of Total (1)	Component Costs (2)	Weighted, or Composite, Cost: $k = (1) \times (2) \div 100$ (3)[a]
0%	Debt	0	5.0	0.0
	Equity	100	12.0	12.0
		100		12.0
20%	Debt	20	5.0	1.0
	Equity	80	12.6	10.1
		100		11.1
30%	Debt	30	5.4	1.6
	Equity	70	12.9	9.0
		100		10.6
35%	Debt	35	5.5	1.9
	Equity	65	13.0	8.4
		100		10.3
40	Debt	40	6.5	2.6
	Equity	60	14.4	8.6
		100		11.2
50	Debt	50	8.0	4.0
	Equity	50	17.0	8.5
		100		12.5
60	Debt	60	13.5	8.1
	Equity	40	21.4	8.6
		100		16.7

[a] We divide by 100 to obtain percentages; figures are rounded to the nearest hundredth.

**Figure 16.3
Cost of Capital Curves for
Universal Machine Company**

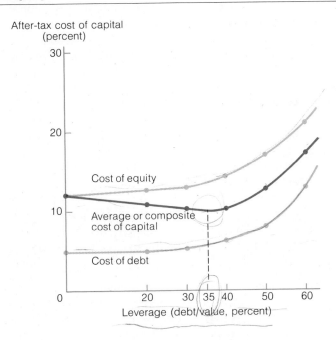

After-tax cost of capital (percent)

Cost of equity

Average or composite cost of capital

Cost of debt

Leverage (debt/value, percent)

Table 16.5 and Figure 16.3 are based on the assumption that the firm is planning to raise a given amount of new capital during the year. For a larger or smaller amount of new capital, some other cost figures may be applicable; the optimal capital structure may call for a different debt ratio, and the minimum average cost of capital (k) may be higher or lower.

Since interest on debt is deductible for tax purposes, the use of debt provides a tax shelter for some of the firm's cash flows. Hence the value of a firm increases with increases in debt if the only influence operating is the tax shelter effect of increased debt. But risks of rising bankruptcy costs will cause the value of a firm to fall at some level of increased leverage.

Bankruptcy costs take several forms. The most obvious are the legal, accounting, and other administrative costs associated with financial readjustments and legal proceedings. In addition, some costs of bankruptcy arise before the actual legal procedures of bankruptcy take place. As the operating performance of the firm deteriorates in relation to its fixed contractual obligations, or as the amount of debt increases in relation to the firm's equity for a given level of operating performance, the financial markets may become increasingly reluctant to provide additional financing. While these conditions deteriorate, a number of costs arise as a result of different degrees of financial inadequacy or failure on the part of the firm. These costs, in order of seriousness, include the following:

1. Financing under increasingly onerous terms, conditions, and rates, representing increased costs.
2. Loss of key employees. If the firm's prospects are unfavorable, able employees and executives will seek alternative employment.
3. Loss of suppliers of the most salable types of goods. The suppliers may fear that they will not be paid or that the customer will not achieve sales growth in the future.
4. Loss of sales due to lack of confidence on the part of customers that the firm will be around to stand behind the product.
5. Lack of financing under any terms, conditions, and rates to carry out favorable but risky investments because the overall prospects of the firm are not favorable in relation to its existing obligations.
6. Need to liquidate fixed assets to meet working capital requirements (forced reduction in the scale of operations).
7. Formal bankruptcy proceedings, with the incurrence of legal and administrative costs. In addition, a receiver will be appointed to conduct the firm's operations, and this may involve a disruption of operations.

The existence of both tax shelter benefits of corporate debt and increased risks of rising bankruptcy costs with increased leverage will cause the value of the firm to behave as depicted in Figure 16.4. As the amount of debt in the financial structure increases, the present value of tax savings will initially cause the market value of the firm to rise. (The slope of the line will be equal to the corporate tax rate.) However, at some point, bankruptcy costs will cause the market value of the firm to bend down from what it would be if the only influence were corporate income taxes. Possible bankruptcy costs may become so large that the indicated market value of the firm actually begins to turn down (Point C in Figure 16.4). This point represents the target leverage ratio at which the market value of the firm is maximized—the optimal financial structure.

Calculating the Marginal Cost of Capital for an Actual Company

The concepts and procedures discussed above can be tied together by applying them to an actual company—the Continental Container Company. Continental Container is a large firm with assets of over $950 million and sales of $1.5 billion in 1977. The analysis is made in late 1977 for use in planning for 1978 and for the three-year period 1978-1980. Dividends have been paid since 1923, even during the depression of the 1930s. On the basis of an indicated dividend rate of $2 and a current price of $33.50 a share, the dividend yield is 6 percent. Over the past ten years, earnings, dividends, and the price of the stock have grown at a rate of about 5 percent;

Figure 16.4
Influence of Debt on Market Value
of the Firm

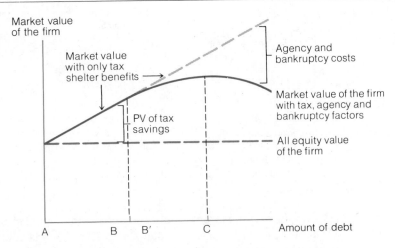

all indications are that the same rate of growth will be maintained in the foreseeable future.[16] Since internally generated funds provide sufficient equity, only the costs of internal equity (found in this case to be the 6 percent dividend yield plus the 5 percent growth rate, or a total of 11 percent) need be considered.

The average interest rate on Continental Container's outstanding debt is 4.5 percent, but much of this debt was issued in earlier years, when interest rates were much lower than they are now. Current market yields (in late 1977) on both long-term and short-term debt are about 8 percent, and approximately this amount will be associated with new debt issues. After a 48 percent income tax, the cost of debt is estimated to be 4.2 percent. The cost of preferred stock is stated to be 3.75 percent, but it was also issued when rates were low. On the basis of current market yields, the estimated cost of new preferred stock is 7.5 percent.

The right-hand side of Continental Container's balance sheet is given in Table 16.6. A large portion (24 percent) of the firm's funds are "free" in the sense that no interest is charged for them; accounts payable and accruals are in this class. Some argue that "free" capital should be included in the calculation of the overall cost of capital. Under certain circumstances this procedure is valid; usually, however, only "nonfree" capital need be con-

16. Earnings per share for 1964 were $2.25, while EPS for 1974 were $3.65. Dividing $3.65 by $2.25 gives 1.62, which is the CVIF for ten years at 5 percent from Table A.1. Thus EPS grew at a 5 percent rate over the ten-year period from 1964 through 1974. Dividends grew similarly, and security analysts are projecting a continuation of these rates.

**Table 16.6
Continental Container Company
Right-hand Side of Balance Sheet
(Millions of Dollars)**

	Amount	Percent	Nonfree Funds Only	
Payables and accruals	$186	19.4%		
Tax accruals	44	4.6		
Total "free" current funds	$230	24.0%		
Interest-bearing debt	$160	16.7%	$160	22%
Preferred stock	7	0.8	7	1
Common equity	560	58.5	560	77
Nonfree funds	$727	76.0%	$727	100%
Total financing	$957	100.0%		

sidered.[17] Of the target, or chosen, long-term capital structure, 22 percent is debt, 1 percent is preferred stock, and 77 percent is common equity. This means in effect that each $1 of new capital is raised as $.22 of debt, $.01 of preferred stock, and $.77 of common equity (retained earnings or new stock).

If management believes that some other capital structure is optimal, then other weights will be used. For the purpose of illustration it is assumed that the existing structure has been determined to be the optimal one. It is further assumed that Continental Container plans to raise $20 million during the current year. To maintain the target capital structure, this $20 million must be raised as follows: $4.4 million as debt, $200,000 as preferred stock, and $15.4 million as equity. (All equity is obtained in the form of retained earnings.) On the basis of these weights and the previously determined costs of debt, equity, and preferred stock, the calculations shown in Table 16.7 indicate that Continental Container's composite cost of new capital is 9.5 percent. As long as the company finances in the indicated manner and uses only retained earnings of equity, each dollar of new funds should cost this amount.

17. The primary justification for ignoring "free" capital is that in the capital budgeting process these spontaneously generated funds are netted out against the required investment outlay, then ignored in the cost of capital calculation. To illustrate: Consider a retail firm thinking of opening a new store. According to customary practice, the firm should (1) estimate the required outlay, (2) estimate the net receipts (additions to profits) from the new store, (3) discount the estimated receipts at the cost of capital, and (4) accept the decision to open the new store only if the net present value of the expected revenue stream exceeds the investment outlay. The estimated accruals, trade payables, and other costless forms of credit are deducted from the investment to determine the "required outlay" before making the calculation. Alternatively, "free" capital could be costed in, and working capital associated with specific projects could be added in when determining the investment outlay. In most instances, the two procedures will result in similar decisions.

**Table 16.7
Continental Container
Illustrative Calculation of
Average Cost of Capital:
$20 Million New Capital**

	Amount of Capital (1)	Proportion (2)	Component Cost (3)	Product (2) × (3) (4)
Debt	$ 4.4	22.0%	4.2%	0.0092
Preferred stock	0.2	1.0	7.5	0.0008
Common equity	15.4	77.0	11.0	0.0847
	$20.0	100.0%		$k = 0.0947 \approx 9.5\%$

**Marginal Cost of
Capital When
New Common
Stock Is Used**

In the preceding example we assumed that the company would finance only with debt, preferred stock, and *internally generated equity.* On this basis we found the weighted average cost of new capital (or the marginal cost of capital) to be 9.5 percent. What would have occurred, however, if the firm's need for funds had been so great that it was forced to sell new common stock? The answer is that its marginal cost of new capital would be increased. To show why this is so, we shall extend the Continental Container example.

First, suppose that during 1977 Continental Container had total earnings of $59 million available for common stockholders, paid $27 million in dividends, and retained $32 million. We know that to keep the capital structure in balance, the retained earnings should equal 77 percent of the net addition to capital, (the other 23 percent being debt and preferred stock). Therefore, the total amount of new capital that can be obtained on the basis of the retained earnings is

$$\text{Retained earnings} = \text{Percent equity} \times \text{New capital}$$

$$\text{New capital} = \frac{\text{Retained earnings}}{\text{Percent equity}}$$

$$= \frac{\$32 \text{ million}}{0.77} = \$41.6 \text{ million.}$$

Next, we note that 1 percent of the new capital, or about $400,000, should be preferred stock and that 22 percent, or $9.2 million, should be debt. In other words, Continental Container can raise a total of $41.6 million—$32 million from retained earnings, $9.2 million in the form of debt, and $400,000 in the form of preferred stock—and still maintain its target capital structure in exact balance.

If all financing up to $41.6 million is in the prescribed proportions, the composite cost of each dollar for new capital *up to $41.6 million* is still 9.5 percent, the previously computed weighted average cost of capital. In Table

431

16.7, we showed the calculation of the weighted average cost of raising $20 million; had we made the calculation for any other amount *up to $41.6 million,* the weighted average cost would also have been 9.5 percent. Each dollar of new capital costs 9.5 percent, so this is the marginal cost of capital.

As soon as the total of the required funds exceeds $41.6 million, however, Continental must begin relying on more expensive new common stock. Therefore, beyond this amount we must compute a new marginal cost of capital. Assuming Continental will incur a flotation cost on new equity issues equal to 10 percent, we can compute the cost of capital for funds over $41.6 million as shown in Table 16.8. According to Table 16.7, as long as the company raises no more than $41.6 million, its weighted average and marginal cost of new or incremental capital is 9.5 percent, but as we have shown in Table 16.8, every dollar over $41.6 million has a cost of 10 percent. Thus the marginal cost beyond $41.6 million is 10 percent.

**Table 16.8
Calculation of Continental
Container's Marginal Cost of
Capital Using External Common
Stock**

1. Find the cost of new equity:

$$\text{Cost of new common stock} = \frac{\text{Dividend yield}}{1 - \text{Flotation percentage}} + \text{Growth}$$

$$k_e = \frac{0.06}{0.90} + 5\% = 11.7\%.$$

2. Find a new weighted or composite cost of each dollar of new capital in excess of $41.6 million, using only new common stock for the equity component:

Proportion × Component cost = Product

Debt	22%	4.2%	0.0092
Preferred stock	1	7.5	0.0008
Equity (new)	77	11.7	0.0901
	100%	$k =$	0.1001 ≈ 10%

**Other Breaks in
the MCC
Schedule**

The marginal cost of capital schedule shows the relationship between the weighted average cost of each dollar raised *(k)* and the total amount of capital raised during the year, other things (such as the riskiness of the assets acquired) held constant. In the preceding section, we saw that Continental Container's MCC schedule increases at the point where the company's retained earnings are exhausted and it begins to use more expensive new common stock.

Actually, any time a component cost rises, a similar break will occur. For example, if Continental could obtain only $10 million of debt at 8 percent, with additional debt costing 9 percent, then this rise in k_b would produce a higher $k_b(1 - T)$, which in turn would lead to a higher k. Under the assumptions made thus far, the break would occur at $45.5 million, found as:

$$\text{Break in MCC schedule caused by rising debt cost} = \frac{\text{Amount of lower-cost debt}}{\text{Debt as percentage of capital raised}}$$

$$= \frac{\$10 \text{ million}}{0.22} = \$45.5 \text{ million.}$$

Suppose that only an additional $5 million over and above the first $10 million can be borrowed at 9 percent, after which the before-tax component cost of new debt rises to 10 percent. A new break will occur, this one at $68.2 million.

$$\frac{\text{Amount of lower-cost debt}}{\text{Debt/Total capital}} = \frac{\$10 \text{ million} + \$5 \text{ million}}{0.22} = \$68.2 \text{ million.}$$

Similar breaks could be caused by increases in the cost of preferred stock, higher common stock flotation costs as more stock is sold, and perhaps even a change in k_s, the basic required rate of return on the firm's common equity (as discussed in Chapter 14).[18]

In general, breaks in the MCC schedule occur whenever any component cost increases as a result of the volume of capital raised, and the breaking points can be calculated by the use of Equation 16.10:

$$\text{Break in MCC} = \frac{\text{Total amount of lower-cost capital for a given component}}{\text{Percentage of total capital represented by the component}}. \qquad \textbf{(16.10)}$$

If we determine that Continental Container will experience higher component costs for debt at $10 million and at $15 million, for preferred at $5 million, and for common equity at $32 million (when retained earnings are exhausted) and at $50 million, then Equation 16.10 can be used to compute breaks in the company's MCC schedule:

Point Where Break Occurs	Cause of Break	k in Interval before Break
$ 41.6 million	Shift from k_r to k_e	9.5%
45.5	Rising k_b	10.0
64.9	Rising k_e	10.6
68.2	Rising k_b	11.2
500.0	Rising k_{ps}	11.6

18. It has been argued that as a company sells more and more stock or other types of securities, it must attract investors who are less and less familiar with and impressed by the company and that the securities must thus be sold at lower prices and higher yields. This pressure can affect all securities, new and old. If the sale of additional stock permanently lowers the price of old stock, then the reduction in value must be assessed as a marginal cost of the new stock. This situation is said to exist for the utilities, whose huge recurrent issues of securities in recent years have been depressing the prices of their outstanding securities.

It is necessary to calculate a different MCC = k for the interval between each of the breaks in the MCC schedule. For example, we have already calculated the MCC from zero to $41.6 million as 9.5 percent and that from $41.6 to $45.5 million as 10 percent. The values of k for each interval shown above are plotted as the step-function MCC schedule in Figure 16.5(a).

This graph is highly idealized; in fact, the actual MCC curve looks much more like the one shown in Figure 16.5(b). Here the curve is flat until it reaches the vicinity of $41.6 million; it then turns up gradually and continues rising. It will go up gradually rather than suddenly because the firm will probably make small adjustments to its target debt ratio, its dividend payout ratio, the actual types of securities it uses, and so on. And the curve will continue to rise because, as more and more of its securities are put on the market during a fairly short period, it will experience more and more difficulty in getting the market to absorb the new securities.

Ordinarily, a firm will calculate its MCC schedule as a step-function similar to the one shown in Figure 16.5(a), then smooth it out by connecting the values of k shown in the middle of each interval. Recognition of the types of estimates and approximations that go into the step-function curve makes the smoothing process appear less arbitrary than it does at first.

In the earlier analysis, associated with Figure 16.3, we were investigating the influence of the financing mix or financial structure on the firm's cost of capital. The financing mix was varied, but the total amount of capital raised was not. Since a marginal cost is the increment in cost as the total amount of financing is increased, varying the financing mix while holding the total amount of financing constant means that the relevant cost of capital is the weighted average cost of capital (WACC). We can say either that no marginal cost of capital is involved or that the marginal cost of capital is equal to the WACC (symbolized by k).

In the present analysis, Figure 16.5 portrays the effects of increasing the total amount of new financing while holding the financing mix fixed at the optimal proportions. Over the flat segment of the MCC curve, the average cost of capital is equal to the marginal cost of capital. When the marginal cost of capital begins to rise, the curve that is an average cost in relation to the MCC lies below the MCC. (If nine people who are all six feet tall come into a room in sequence, the average and marginal height will be 6 feet. If the tenth person entering is 7 feet tall, the marginal height will be 7 feet, but the average height will be 6.1 feet.) We exhibit only the MCC in Figure 16.5 because we are analyzing the determination of the total capital budget for a firm; hence the MCC is relevant as the investment hurdle rate. But recall that we are holding the financing mix at its optimal proportions, so the MCC for each amount of new financing is also the WACC for the optimal mix of financing that minimizes the level of the MCC curve. For these reasons, we again use k as the symbol for the cost of capital along the MCC curve.

Figure 16.5
Relationship between Marginal
Cost of Capital and Amount of
Funds Raised

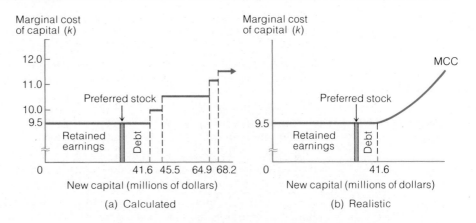

(a) Calculated (b) Realistic

Combining the
MCC and the
Investment
Opportunity
Schedules

Having developed the firm's MCC schedule and planned its financing mix so as to minimize the schedule, the financial manager's next task is to utilize the MCC in the capital budgeting process. How is this done? First, suppose that the k value in the flat part of the MCC schedule is used as the discount rate for calculating the NPV and that the total cost of all projects with NPV > 0 is less than the dollar amount at which the MCC schedule turns up. In this case, the value of k that was used is the correct one. For example, if Continental Container uses 9.5 percent as its cost of capital and finds that the acceptable projects total $41.6 million or less, then 9.5 percent is the appropriate cost of capital for capital budgeting.[19]

But suppose the acceptable projects total more than $41.6 million with a 9.5 percent discount rate. What do we do now? The most efficient procedure is given below.

Step 1. Calculate and plot the MCC schedule as shown in Figure 16.5.

Step 2. Ask the operating personnel to estimate the dollar volume of acceptable projects at a range of discount rates, say 14 percent, 13 percent, 12 percent, 11 percent, 10 percent, and 9 percent. There will thus be an estimate of the capital budget at a series of k values. For Continental Container, these values were estimated as follows:

19. We are, of course, abstracting from project risk; here we assume that the average riskiness of all projects undertaken is equal to the average riskiness of the firm's existing plant. Some projects may be more risky than average and therefore call for a risk-adjusted cost of capital greater than 9.5 percent, while others may be less risky than average and call for a cost of capital less than 9.5 percent.

Capital Budget (in Millions)	$20	$30	$40	$50	$60	$70
k	14%	13%	12%	11%	10%	9%

Step 3. Plot the capital budget points (k) as determined in Step 2 on the same graph as the MCC; this plot is labeled IRR in Figure 16.6.[20]

Step 4. The correct MCC for use in capital budgeting—assuming both the MCC and IRR curves are developed correctly—is the value at the intersection of the two curves, 10.4 percent. If this value of k is used to calculate NPVs, then projects totaling $56 million will have NPVs greater than zero. This is the capital budget that will maximize the value of the firm.

Dynamic Considerations

Conditions change over time; and when they do, the firm must make adjustments. First, the firm's individual situation may change. For example, as it grows and matures, its business risk may decline; this may in turn lead to an optimal capital structure that includes more debt. Second, capital market conditions may undergo a pronounced long-run change, making either debt or equity relatively favorable. This too may lead to a new optimal capital structure. Third, even though the long-run optimal structure remains unchanged, temporary shifts in the capital markets may suggest that the firm use either debt or equity, departing somewhat from the optimal capital structure, then adjust back to the long-run optimum in subsequent years. Fourth, the supply and demand for funds varies from time to time, causing shifts in the cost of both debt and equity and, of course, in the marginal cost of capital.

For example, by Mid-November 1978 the commercial bank prime rate had risen to 11 percent, and yields on long-term bonds were approaching 10 percent. Continental's cost of equity was about 14 percent. The equity to total asset ratio was moving down toward 50 percent for many companies. The effective tax rate was about 44 percent because of tax deferrals through the use of accelerated depreciation. Continental's cost of capital with a 60 percent equity ratio looked like this:

	Proportion	Cost	Product
Debt	39.0%	11(.56)	0.024
Preferred stock	1.0	10.0	0.001
Common equity	60.0	14.0	0.084
	100.0		$k = 0.109 \approx 11\%$

Thus, only one year later, Continental's cost of capital had risen by almost 1.5 percent. Some feel that an inflation rate of 6 to 8 percent in the U.S.

---

20. To see why the capital budget line, k, is a type of IRR curve, consider the following:
   1. The NPV of a project is zero if the project's IRR is equal to k.
   2. If no projects have NPV $\geq$ 0 at $k = 15\%$, then no projects have IRR $\geq 15\%$.
   3. If $20 million of projects have NPV $\geq$ 0 at $k = 14\%$, then these projects all have $14\% \leq$ IRR $\leq 15\%$.
   4. If the projects are completely divisible and if we examine very small changes in k, then we will have a continuous IRR curve. As it is, the curve labeled IRR in Figure 16.6 is an approximation. But the example does illustrate how an IRR curve can be developed even though a company uses the NPV capital budgeting method.

**Figure 16.6
Interfacing the MCC and IRR
Curves to Determine the Total
Capital Budget for a Given
Time Period**

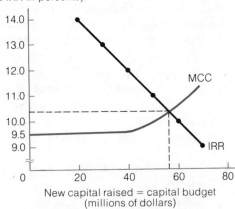

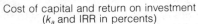

Cost of capital and return on investment
(k_a and IRR in percents)

New capital raised = capital budget
(millions of dollars)

economy will persist and that the cost of capital for most large companies
has moved to the 11 to 12 percent level. Yet, during almost all the first half
of 1977, the prime rate was around 6 percent. Because the financial markets
have fluctuated so widely in recent years, it is necessary for firms to reexamine their cost of capital periodically.

**Large Firms
versus Small
Firms**

Significant differences in capital costs exist between large and small firms.
These differences are especially pronounced for privately owned small
firms. The same concepts are involved, and the methods of calculating the
average and marginal cost of capital are similar; but some points of difference arise:

1. It may be difficult to obtain reasonable estimates of equity capital costs
   for small, privately owned firms.
2. Tax considerations are generally quite important for privately owned
   companies, since owner-managers may be in the top personal tax brackets. This factor can cause the effective after-tax cost of retained earnings to be considerably lower than the after-tax cost of new outside
   equity.
3. Flotation costs for new security issues, especially new stock issues, are
   much higher for small than for large firms (see Chapter 18).

Points 2 and 3 both cause the marginal cost curves for small firms to rise
rapidly once retained earnings are exhausted, and these relationships have
implications for the growth and development of large versus small firms.

Summary

In Chapter 14, the nature of the valuation process and the concept of expected rates of return were considered in some detail. The present chapter has used these valuation concepts to develop an average cost of capital for the firm. First, the cost of the individual components of the capital structure—debt, preferred stock, and equity—were analyzed. Next, these individual component costs were brought together to form an average, or composite, cost of capital. The effects of risky versus nonrisky debt were analyzed. Finally, the conceptual ideas developed in the first three sections were illustrated with an example of the cost of capital for an actual company—Continental Container Company.

The *cost of debt, $k_b (1 - T)$,* is defined as the interest rate that must be paid on new increments of debt capital multiplied by (1 − tax rate). The *preferred stock cost* to the company is the effective yield and is found as the annual preferred dividend divided by the net price the company receives when it sells new preferred stock. In equation form:

$$\text{Cost of preferred stock} = k_{ps} = \frac{\text{Preferred dividend}}{\text{Net price of preferred}}.$$

The *cost of common equity* is defined as the minimum rate of return that must be earned on equity-financed investments to keep the value of the existing common equity unchanged. This required rate of return is the rate of return that investors expect to receive on the company's common stock—the dividend yield plus the capital gains yield. Sometimes, we assume that investors expect to receive about the same rates of return in the future that they have received in the past; in this case, we can estimate the required rate of return on the basis of actual historical returns.

Equity capital comes from two sources—retained earnings and the sale of new issues of common stock. The basic required rate of return (k_r) is used for the cost of retained earnings. However, new stock has a higher cost because of flotation costs associated with the sale of stock. The cost of new common stock issues is computed as follows:

$$\text{Cost of new stock} = k_e = \frac{\text{Dividend yield}}{1 - \text{Flotation percentage}} + \text{Growth}.$$

New common stock is therefore more expensive than retained earnings.

If a firm has a high leverage ratio, increasing the proportion of debt will make the debt riskier because it increases the probability of bankruptcy. If bankruptcy costs are substantial, the value of the firm will rise, reach a peak, and then fall. The maximum point on this curve indicates a target debt ratio.

The first step in calculating the weighted average cost of capital, k, is to determine the cost of the individual capital components. The next step is to establish the proper set of weights to be used in the averaging process. Unless there is reason to think otherwise, the general assumption is that the present capital structure of the firm is at an optimum (where the optimum is the capital structure that will produce the minimum average cost of capital for raising a given amount of funds, or a minimum cost of incremental capital). The optimal capital structure varies from industry to industry, with more stable industries having optimal capital structures that call for the use of more debt than unstable industries.

The *marginal cost of capital schedule,* defined as the cost of each additional dollar raised during the current year, is of interest for two reasons. First, the firm should finance in a manner that minimizes the MCC schedule; therefore it must measure the MCC. Second, the MCC is the rate that should be used in the capital budgeting process. The firm should take on new capital projects only if their net present values are positive when evaluated at the marginal cost of capital.

The marginal cost of capital is constant over a range, then begins to rise. The rise is probably gradual rather than abrupt because firms make small adjustments in their target debt ratios, begin to use an assortment of securities, retain more of their earnings, and so on, as they reach the limit of internally generated equity funds.

Questions

16.1 Suppose that basic business risks to all firms in any given industry are similar.
   a. Would you expect all firms in each industry to have approximately the same cost of capital?
   b. How would the averages differ among industries?

16.2 Why are internally generated retained earnings less expensive than equity raised by selling stock?

16.3 Prior to the 1930s the corporate income tax was not very important, since the rates were fairly low. Also, prior to the 1930s preferred stock was much more important than it has been since that period. Is there a relationship between the rise of corporate income taxes and the decline in importance of preferred stock?

16.4 Describe how each of the following situations will affect the cost of capital to corporations in general.
   a. The federal government solves the problem of business cycles (that is, cyclical stability is increased).
   b. The Federal Reserve Board takes action to lower interest rates.
   c. The cost of floating new stock issues rises.

16.5 The firm's covariance is 0.014, the risk-free rate is 7 percent, the market risk premium ($\overline{k}_M = R_F$) is 5 percent, and the variance of the market returns is 1 percent.
   a. With no bankruptcy costs, what is the cost of capital, k, for an unlevered firm?
   b. What is the beta of the firm?

16.6 Assume that the information in Question 16.5 is all on an after-tax basis, that the corporate tax rate is 50 percent, and that the firm has a debt to equity ratio of 50 percent, with a debt cost of 10 percent.
  a. What is the new beta of the firm?
  b. What is its return on equity?
  c. What is the cost of capital for the levered firm?

16.7 An unlevered firm has a beta of 0.8. How much leverage can it employ if its corporate tax rate is 50 percent and it aims to have a beta of 1.2?

16.8 The formula $k_r = (d_1/p_0) + g$, where d_1 = expected current dividend, p_0 = the current price of a stock, and g = the past rate of growth in dividends, is sometimes used to estimate k_r, the cost of equity capital. Explain the implications of the formula.

16.9 What factors operate to cause the cost of debt to increase with financial leverage?

16.10 Explain the relationship between the required rate of return on common equity (k_s^*) and the debt ratio.

16.11 How will the various component costs of capital and the average cost of capital be likely to change if a firm expands its operations into a new, more risky industry?

16.12 The stock of XYZ Company is currently selling at its low for the year, but management feels that the stock price is only temporarily depressed because of investor pessimism. The firm's capital budget this year is so large that it is contemplating the use of new outside equity. However, management does not want to sell new stock at the current low price and is therefore considering a departure from its "optimal" capital structure by borrowing the funds it would otherwise have raised in the equity markets. Does this seem to be a wise move? Explain.

16.13 Explain the following statement: The marginal cost of capital is an average in some sense.

Problems

16.1 The Abbott Company is expected to grow at 9 percent per year. Abbott's common stock sells for $30 per share, and the company pays a dividend of $2.40 per share. What is its cost of equity capital?

16.2 The Crothers Company has a beta of 1.5. It has no debt in its capital structure.
  a. The expected market rate of return is 14 percent and the risk-free rate is 6 percent. What is the cost of equity capital for Crothers?
  b. Should Crothers accept a project that earns a rate of return of 15 percent and has a beta of 0.9?

16.3 The Graham Company's financing plans for next year include the sale of long-term bonds with a 9 percent coupon. The company believes it can sell the bonds at a price that will give a yield to maturity of 10 percent. If the tax rate is 40 percent, what is Graham's after-tax cost of debt?

16.4 The Iversen Company earns $5 per share. The expected year-end dividend is

$1.60, and price per share is $40. Iversen's earnings, dividends, and stock price have been growing at 8 percent per year, and this growth rate is expected to continue indefinitely. New common stock can be sold to net $38. What is Iversen's cost of retained earnings (required rate of return on internally financed equity)?

16.5 The Longwell Company is expected to pay a year-end dividend of $4.40. Longwell earns $7.70 per share, and its stock sells at $55 per share. Stock price, earnings, and dividends are expected to grow 6 percent per year indefinitely.

a. Calculate the stockholders' rate of return.

b. Assume that Longwell's additional retained earnings are reinvested at 9 percent rather than at the cost of capital. Also assume that this new growth rate is permanent, that dividends remain constant, and that the firm continues to earn the same rate of return on its original capital as it has in previous years. What will the price of the common stock be at the end of one year?

c. If the firm has a zero growth rate and pays out all its earnings as dividends, what is the stockholder's rate of return? (Use the original stock price in your calculations).

16.6 The Riley Company has $200 million total net assets at the end of 1978. It plans to increase its production machinery in 1979 by $50 million. Bond financing, at a 10 percent rate, will sell at par. Preferred will have an 11 percent interest payment and will be sold at a par value of $100. Common stock currently sells for $50 per share and can be sold to net $45 after flotation costs. There is $10 million of internal funding available from retained earnings. Over the past few years, dividend yield has been 6 percent and the firm's growth rate 8 percent. The tax rate is 40 percent. The present capital structure shown below is considered optimal:

Debt: 4% coupon bonds	$40,000,000	
7% coupon bonds	40,000,000	$ 80,000,000
Preferred stock		20,000,000
Common stock ($10 par)	$40,000,000	
Retained earnings	60,000,000	
Equity		100,000,000
		$200,000,000

a. How much of the $50 million must be financed by equity capital if the present capital structure is to be maintained?

b. How much of the equity funding must come from the sale of new common stock?

c. What is Riley's cost of equity for 1979?

d. What is Riley's incremental cost of capital for 1979?

16.7 The Tanner Company's cost of equity is 18 percent. Tanner's before-tax cost of debt is 12 percent, and its tax rate is 40 percent. Using the following balance sheet, calculate Tanner's after-tax weighted average cost of capital:

Assets		Liabilities	
Cash	$ 100	Accounts payable	$ 200
Accounts receivable	200	Accrued taxes due	200
Inventories	300	Long-term debt	400
Plant and equipment, net	1,800	Equity	1,600
Total assets	$2,400	Total liabilities	$2,400

16.8 Bennett Company is considering payment of a $1 per share dividend. Stockholders can invest dividends to earn 18 percent; investors are taxed at 30 percent, and the brokerage costs on reinvestment are 3.5 percent. What rate of return must Bennett earn on retained earnings to equate incremental internal earnings to what stockholders would receive externally?

16.9 You are planning to form a new company, and you can use several different capital structures. Investment bankers indicate that debt and equity capital will cost the following under different debt ratios (debt/total assets):

Debt Ratio	20% and Below	21 to 40%	41 to 50%	51 to 65%
Before-tax cost of debt	8%	9%	11%	14%
Cost of equity capital	12	13	18	25

a. Assuming a 40 percent tax rate, what is the after-tax weighted cost of capital for the following capital structures?

	(1)	(2)	(3)	(4)	(5)	(6)	(7)	(8)
Debt	0%	20%	21%	40%	41%	50%	51%	65%
Equity	100	80	79	60	59	50	49	35

b. Which capital structure minimizes the weighted average cost of capital?

16.10 On January 1, 1979, the total assets of the Rossiter Company were $60 million. By the end of the year total assets are expected to be $90 million. (Assume there is no short-term debt.) The firm's capital structure, shown below, is considered to be optimal:

Debt (6% coupon bonds)	$24,000,000
Preferred stock (at 7%)	6,000,000
Common equity	30,000,000
	$60,000,000

New bonds will have an 8 percent coupon rate and will be sold at par. Preferred stock will have a 9 percent rate and will also be sold at par. Common stock, currently selling at $30 a share, can be sold to net the company $27 a share. Stockholders' required rate of return, estimated to be 12 percent, consists of a dividend yield of 4 percent and an expected growth of 8 percent. Retained earnings are estimated to be $3 million (ignoring depreciation). The marginal corporate tax rate is 50 percent.

a. Assuming all asset expansion (gross expenditures for fixed assets plus related working capital) is included in the capital budget, what is the dollar amount of the capital budget (ignoring depreciation)?

b. To maintain the present capital structure, how much of the capital budget must be financed by equity?

c. How much of the new equity funds needed must be generated internally? How much externally?

d. Calculate the cost of each of the equity components.

e. At what level of capital expenditures will there be a break in the MCC schedule?

f. Calculate the MCC both below and above the break in the schedule.

g. Plot the MCC schedule. Also, draw in an IRR schedule that is consistent with the MCC schedule and the projected capital budget.

16.11 The Austen Company has the following capital structure as of December 31, 1979:

Debt (at 8%)		$12,000,000
Preferred (at 8¹/₂%)		4,000,000
Common stock	$ 4,000,000	
Retained earnings	12,000,000	
Common equity		16,000,000
Total capitalization		$32,000,000

Earnings per share have grown steadily from $0.93 in 1969 to $2 estimated for 1979. Expecting this growth to continue, the investment community applies a price/earnings ratio of 18 to yield a current market price of $36. Austen's last annual dividend was $1.25, and the company expects the dividend to grow at the same rate as earnings. The addition to retained earnings for 1979 is projected at $4 million; these funds will be available during the next budget year. The corporate tax rate is 50 percent.

Assuming that the capital structure relations set out above are maintained, new securities can be sold at the following costs:

Bonds: Up to and including $3 million of new bonds, 8 percent yield to investor on all new bonds

From $3.01 million to $6 million of new bonds, 8¹/₂ percent yield to investor on this increment of bonds

Over $6 million of new bonds, 10 percent yield to investor on this increment of bonds

Preferred: Up to and including $1 million of preferred stock, 8¹/₂ percent yield to investor on all new preferred stock

From $1.01 million to $2 million of preferred stock, 9 percent yield to investor on this increment of preferred stock

Over $2 million of preferred stock, 10 percent yield to investor on this increment of preferred stock

Common: Up to $4 million of new outside common stock, $36 a share less $2.50 a share flotation cost

Over $4 million of new outside common stock, $36 a share less $5 a share flotation cost on this increment of new common

a. At what dollar amounts of new capital will breaks occur in the MCC?
b. Calculate the MCC in the interval between each of these breaks; then plot the MCC schedule.
c. Discuss the breaking points in the marginal cost curve. What factors in the real world would tend to make the marginal cost curve smooth?
d. Assume now that Austen has the following investment opportunities:
  1. It can invest any amount up to $4 million at an 11 percent rate of return.
  2. It can invest an additional $8 million at a 10.2 percent rate of return.
  3. It can invest still another $12 million at a 9.3 percent rate of return. Thus Austen's total potential capital budget is $24 million. Determine the size of the company's optimal capital budget for the year.

CHAPTER **17** DIVIDEND POLICY AND
INTERNAL FINANCING

Dividend policy determines the division of earnings between payments to stockholders and reinvestment in the firm. Retained earnings are one of the most significant sources of funds for financing corporate growth, but dividends constitute the cash flows that accrue to stockholders. The factors that influence the allocation of earnings to dividends or retained earnings are the subject of this chapter.

Factors Influencing Dividend Policy

What factors determine the extent to which a firm will pay out dividends instead of retaining earnings? As a first step toward answering this question, we shall consider some of the factors that influence dividend policy.

Legal Rules Although state statutes and court decisions governing dividend policy are complicated, their essential nature can be stated briefly. The legal rules provide that dividends must be paid from earnings—either from the current year's earnings or from past years' earnings as reflected in the balance sheet account "retained earnings."

State laws emphasize three rules: (1) the net profits rule, (2) the capital impairment rule, and (3) the insolvency rule. The *net profits rule* provides that dividends can be paid from past and present earnings. The *capital impairment rule* protects creditors by forbidding the payment of dividends from capital. (Paying dividends from capital would be distributing the investment in a company rather than its earnings.)[1] The *insolvency rule* provides that corporations cannot pay dividends while insolvent. (*Insolvency* is here defined, in the bankruptcy sense, as liabilities exceeding assets; and to pay dividends under such conditions would mean giving stockholders funds that rightfully belong to the creditors.)

Legal rules are significant in that they provide the framework within which dividend policies can be formulated. Within their boundaries, however, financial and economic factors have a major influence on policy.

Liquidity Position Profits held as retained earnings (which show up on the right-hand side of the balance sheet) are generally invested in assets required for the conduct of the business. Retained earnings from preceding years are already invested in plant and equipment inventories and other assets; they are not held as cash. Thus, even if a firm has a record of earnings, it may not be able to pay cash dividends because of its liquidity position. Indeed, a growing firm, even a very profitable one, typically has a pressing need for funds. In such a situation the firm may elect not to pay cash dividends.

If this point is not clear, refer back to Table 4.1—the Walker-Wilson Com-

---

1. It is possible, of course, to return stockholders' capital; when this is done, however, it must be clearly stated as such. A dividend paid out of capital is called a *liquidating* dividend.

pany's balance sheet. The retained earnings account shows $400,000, but the cash account shows only $50,000. Since some cash must be retained to pay bills, it is clear that Walker-Wilson's cash position precludes a dividend of even $50,000.

Need to Repay Debt When a firm has sold debt to finance expansion or to substitute for other forms of financing, it is faced with two alternatives. It can refund the debt at maturity by replacing it with another form of security, or it can make provisions for paying off the debt. If the decision is to retire the debt, this will generally require the retention of earnings.

Restrictions in Debt Contracts Debt contracts, particularly when long-term debt is involved, frequently restrict a firm's ability to pay cash dividends. Such restrictions, which are designed to protect the position of the lender, usually state that (1) future dividends can be paid only out of earnings generated *after* the signing of the loan agreement (that is, they cannot be paid out of past retained earnings) and (2) that dividends cannot be paid when net working capital (current assets minus current liabilities) is below a specified amount. Similarly, preferred stock agreements generally state that no cash dividends can be paid on the common stock until all accrued preferred dividends have been paid.

Rate of Asset Expansion The more rapid the rate at which the firm is growing, the greater its needs for financing asset expansion. The greater the future need for funds, the more likely the firm is to retain earnings rather than pay them out. If a firm seeks to raise funds externally, natural sources are the present shareholders, who already know the company. But if earnings are paid out as dividends and are subjected to high personal income tax rates, only a portion of them will be available for reinvestment.

Profit Rate The rate of return on assets determines the relative attractiveness of paying out earnings in the form of dividends to stockholders (who will use them elsewhere) or using them in the present enterprise.

Stability of Earnings A firm that has relatively stable earnings is often able to predict approximately what its future earnings will be. Such a firm is therefore more likely to pay out a higher percentage of its earnings than is a firm with fluctuating earnings. The unstable firm is not certain that in subsequent years the hoped-for earnings will be realized, so it is likely to retain a high proportion of current earnings. A lower dividend will be easier to maintain if earnings fall off in the future.

Access to the Capital Markets A large, well-established firm with a record of profitability and stability of earnings has easy access to capital markets and other forms of external financing. A small, new, or venturesome firm, however, is riskier for potential investors. Its ability to raise equity or debt funds from capital markets is restricted, and it must retain more earnings to finance its operations. A well-established firm is thus likely to have a higher dividend payout rate than is a new or small firm.

Control Another important variable is the effect of alternative sources of financing on the control situation in the firm. As a matter of policy, some corporations expand only to the extent of their internal earnings. This policy is defended on the ground that raising funds by selling additional common stock dilutes the control of the dominant group in that company. At the same time, selling debt increases the risks of fluctuating earnings to the present owners of the company. Reliance on internal financing in order to maintain control reduces the dividend payout.

Tax Position of Stockholders The tax position of the corporation's owners greatly influences the desire for dividends. For example, a corporation closely held by a few taxpayers in high income tax brackets is likely to pay a relatively low dividend. The owners are interested in taking their income in the form of capital gains rather than as dividends, which are subject to higher personal income tax rates. However, the stockholders of a large, widely held corporation may be interested in a high dividend payout.

At times there is a conflict of interest in large corporations between stockholders in high income tax brackets and those in low tax brackets. The former may prefer to see a low dividend payout and a high rate of earnings retention in the hope of an appreciation in the capital stock of the company. The latter may prefer a relatively high dividend payout. The dividend policy in such firms may be a compromise between a low and a high payout—an intermediate payout ratio. If one group comes to dominate the company and sets, say, a low payout policy, those stockholders who seek income are likely to sell their shares over time and shift into higher-yielding stocks. Thus, to at least some extent, a firm's payout policy determines the type of stockholders it has—and vice versa. This has been called the "clientele influence" on dividend policy.

Tax on Improperly Accumulated Earnings In order to prevent wealthy stockholders from using the corporation as an "incorporated pocketbook" by which they can avoid high personal income tax rates, tax regulations applicable to corporations provide for a special surtax on improperly accumulated income. However, Section 531 of the Revenue Act of 1954 places the burden of proof on the Internal Revenue Service to justify penalty rates for accumulation of earnings. That is, earnings retention is justified unless the IRS can prove otherwise.

Dividend Policy Decisions

There is a widespread tendency of corporations to pursue a relatively stable dividend policy. Profits of firms fluctuate considerably with changes in the level of business activity, but as Figure 17.1 shows, dividends are more stable than earnings.

Most corporations seek to maintain a target dividend per share. However, dividends increase with a lag after earnings rise; that is, they are increased only after an increase in earnings appears clearly sustainable and relatively permanent. When dividends have been increased, strenuous efforts are made to maintain them at the new level. If earnings decline, the existing dividend generally is maintained until it is clear that an earnings recovery will not take place.

Figure 17.2 illustrates these ideas by showing the earnings and dividend patterns for the Walter Watch Company over a thirty-year period. Initially, earnings are $2 and dividends $1 a share, providing a 50 percent payout ratio. Earnings rise for four years, while dividends remain constant; thus the payout ratio falls during this period. During 1955 and 1956, earnings fall substantially; however, the dividend is maintained, and the payout ratio rises above the 50 percent target. During the period between 1956 and 1960, earnings experience a sustained rise. Dividends are held constant for a time, while management seeks to determine whether the earnings increase is permanent. By 1961, the earnings gains seem permanent, and dividends are raised in three steps to reestablish the 50 percent target payout. During

**Figure 17.1
Corporate Earnings after Taxes
and Dividends**

Figure 17.2
Dividends and Earnings Patterns
for the Walter Watch Company

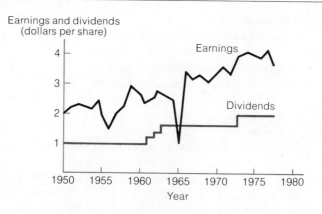

1965 a strike causes earnings to fall below the regular dividend; expecting the earnings decline to be temporary, management maintains the dividend. Earnings fluctuate on a fairly high plateau from 1966 through 1972, during which time dividends remain constant. A new increase in earnings induces management to raise the dividend in 1973 to reestablish the 50 percent payout ratio.

Rationale for Stable Dividends

Like the great majority of firms, Walter Watch keeps its dividend at a relatively steady dollar amount but allows its payout ratio to fluctuate. Why does it follow such a policy?

Consider the stable dividend policy from the standpoint of the stockholders as owners of the company. Their acquiescence with the general practice must imply that stable dividend policies lead to higher stock prices on the average than do alternative dividend policies. Is this a fact? Does a stable dividend policy maximize equity values for a corporation? There has been no truly conclusive empirical study of dividend policy, so any answer to the question must be regarded as tentative. On logical grounds, however, there is reason to believe that a stable dividend policy does lead to higher stock prices. First, investors can be expected to value more highly dividends they are more sure of receiving, since fluctuating dividends are riskier than stable ones. Accordingly, the same average amount of dividends received under a fluctuating dividend policy is likely to have a higher discount factor applied to it than is applied to dividends under a stable dividend policy. In the terms used in Chapter 16, this means that a firm with a stable dividend will have a lower required rate of return—or cost of equity capital—than one whose dividends fluctuate.

Second, many stockholders live on income received in the form of dividends. These stockholders are greatly inconvenienced by fluctuating dividends, and they will likely pay a premium for a stock with a relatively assured minimum dollar dividend.

A third advantage of a stable dividend from the standpoint of both the corporation and its stockholders is the requirement of legal listing. *Legal lists* are lists of securities in which mutual savings banks, pension funds, insurance companies, and other fiduciary institutions are permitted to invest. One of the criteria for placing a stock on the legal list is that dividend payments are maintained. Thus legal listing encourages pursuance of a stable dividend policy.

On the other hand, if a firm's investment opportunities fluctuate from year to year, should it not retain more earnings during some years in order to take advantage of opportunities when they appear and increase dividends when good internal investment opportunities are scarce? This line of reasoning leads to a recommendation for a fluctuating payout for companies whose investment opportunities are unstable. However, the logic of the argument is diminished by recognizing that it is possible to maintain a reasonably stable dividend by using outside financing, including debt, to smooth out the differences between the funds needed for investment and the amount of money provided by retained earnings.

Alternative Dividend Policies

Before considering dividend policy at a theoretical level, it is useful to summarize the three major types of dividend policies:

1. *Stable dollar amount per share.* The policy of a stable dollar amount per share, followed by most firms, is the policy implied by the words *stable dividend policy.*
2. *Constant payout ratio.* Very few firms follow a policy of paying out a constant percentage of earnings. Since earnings fluctuate, following this policy necessarily means that the dollar amount of dividends will fluctuate. For reasons discussed in the preceding section, this policy is not likely to maximize the value of a firm's stock. Before its bankruptcy, Penn Central Railroad followed the policy of paying out half its earnings: "a dollar for the stockholders and a dollar for the company," as one director put it.
3. *Low regular dividend plus extras.* The low regular dividend plus extras policy is a compromise between the first two. It gives the firm flexibility, but it leaves investors somewhat uncertain about what their dividend income will be. If a firm's earnings are quite volatile, however, this policy may well be its best choice.

The relative merits of these three policies can be evaluated better after a discussion of the residual theory of dividends, the topic covered in the next section.

Residual Theory of Dividends

The preceding chapters on capital budgeting and the cost of capital indicated that the cost of capital schedule and the investment opportunity schedule generally must be combined before the cost of capital can be established. In other words, the optimum capital budget, the marginal cost of capital, and the marginal rate of return on investment are determined *simultaneously*. This section examines the simultaneous solution in the framework of what is called the *residual theory of dividends.*[2] The theory draws on materials developed earlier in the book—capital budgeting and the cost of capital—and serves to provide a bridge between these key concepts.

The starting point in the theory is that investors prefer to have the firm retain and reinvest earnings rather than pay them out in dividends if the return on reinvested earnings exceeds the rate of return the investors can obtain on other investments of comparable risk. If the corporation can reinvest retained earnings at a 20 percent rate of return, while the best rate stockholders can obtain if they receive earnings in the form of dividends is 10 percent, then stockholders prefer to have the firm retain the profits.

Chapter 16 showed that the cost of equity capital obtained from retained earnings is an *opportunity cost* that reflects rates of return open to equity investors. If a firm's stockholders can buy other stocks of equal risk and obtain a 10 percent dividend plus capital gains yield, then 10 percent is the firm's cost of retained earnings. The cost of new outside equity raised by selling common stock is higher because of the costs of floating the issue.

Most firms have an optimum debt ratio that calls for at least some debt, so new financing is done partly with debt and partly with equity. Debt has a different, and generally lower, cost than equity, so the two forms of capital must be combined to find the *weighted average cost of capital.* As long as the firm finances at the optimum point (using an optimum amount of debt and equity) and uses only internally generated equity (retained earnings), its marginal cost of each new dollar of capital is minimized.

Internally generated equity is available for financing a certain amount of new investment; beyond this amount, the firm must turn to more expensive new common stock. At the point where new stock must be sold, the cost of equity and, consequently, the marginal cost of capital rise.

These concepts, which were developed in Chapter 16, are illustrated in

2. "Residual" implies *left over.* The residual theory of dividend policy implies that dividends are paid after internal investment opportunities have been exhausted.

Figure 17.3
The Marginal Cost of Capital

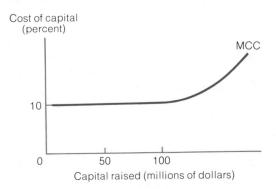

Figure 17.3. The firm has a marginal cost of capital of 10 percent so long as retained earnings are available; the marginal cost of capital begins to rise when new stock must be sold.

The hypothetical firm has $50 million of earnings and a 50 percent optimum debt ratio. It can make net investments (investments in addition to asset replacements financed from depreciation) up to $100 million—$50 million from retained earnings plus $50 million new debt supported by the retained earnings if it does not pay dividends. Therefore, its marginal cost of capital is constant at 10 percent for up to $100 million of capital. Beyond $100 million, the marginal cost of capital begins rising as the firm begins to use more expensive new common stock.

Suppose the firm's capital budgeting department draws up a list of investment opportunities, ranked in the order of each project's IRR, and plots them on a graph. The investment opportunity curves of three different years—one for a good year (IRR_1), one for a normal year (IRR_2), and one for a bad year (IRR_3)—are shown in Figure 17.4. IRR_1 shows that the firm can invest more money, and at higher rates of return, than it can when the investment opportunities are those given by IRR_2 and IRR_3.

The investment opportunity schedule is now combined with the cost of capital schedule in Figure 17.5. The point where the investment opportunity curve cuts the cost of capital curve defines the proper level of new investment. When investment opportunities are relatively poor, the optimum level of investment is $25 million; when opportunities are about normal, it is $75 million; and when opportunities are relatively good, it is $125 million.

Consider the situation where IRR_1 is the appropriate schedule. Suppose the firm has $50 million in earnings and a 50 percent target debt ratio, so it can finance $100 million ($50 million earnings plus $50 million debt) from

Figure 17.4
Investment Opportunities

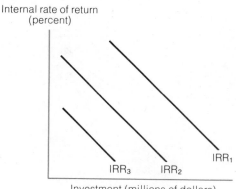

Internal rate of return
(percent)

IRR₃   IRR₂   IRR₁

Investment (millions of dollars)

retained earnings plus new debt *if it retains all its earnings*. If it pays out part of the earnings in dividends, then it will have to begin using expensive new common stock sooner, so the cost of capital curve will rise sooner. This suggests that under the conditions of IRR₁ the firm should retain all its earnings and actually sell some new common stock in order to take advantage of its investment opportunities. Its payout ratio would thus be zero percent.

Under the conditions of IRR₂, however, the firm should invest only $75 million. How should this investment be financed? First, notice that if it retains the full amount of its earnings, $50 million, it will need to sell only $25 million of new debt. However, by doing this, the firm will move away from its target capital structure. To stay on target, the firm must finance the required $75 million half by equity (retained earnings) and half by debt—that is, $37.5 million by retained earnings and $37.5 million by debt. If the firm has $50 million in total earnings and decides to retain and reinvest $37.5 million, it must distribute the residual $12.5 million to its stockholders. In this case, the payout ratio is 25 percent ($12.5 million divided by $50 million).

Finally, under the bad conditions of IRR₃, the firm should invest only $25 million. Because it has $50 million in earnings, it could finance the entire $25 million out of retained earnings and still have $25 million available for dividends. Should this be done? Under the assumptions, this would not be a good decision, because it would move the firm away from its target debt ratio. To stay in the 50-50 debt/equity position, the firm must retain $12.5 million and sell $12.5 million of debt. When the $12.5 million of retained earnings is subtracted from the $50 million of earnings, the firm is left with a residual of $37.5 million—the amount that should be paid out in dividends. In this case the payout ratio is 75 percent.

**Figure 17.5
Interrelationships among Cost of
Capital, Investment Opportunities,
and New Investment**

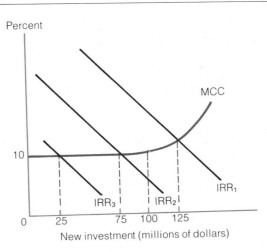

**Long-Run
Viewpoint**

A conflict apparently exists between the residual theory and the statement
made in an earlier section that firms should and do maintain reasonably stable cash dividends. How can this conflict be reconciled?

A firm may have a target capital structure without being at that target at
all times. In other words, it need not adjust its dividend each and every year.
Firms do have target debt ratios, but they also have a certain amount of flexibility; they can be moderately above or below the target debt position in
any year with no serious adverse consequences. This means that if an un-
usually large number of good investments are available in a particular year,
the firm does not necessarily have to cut its dividend to take advantage of
them; it can borrow somewhat more heavily than usual in that particular
year without getting its debt ratio too far out of line. Obviously, however,
this excessive reliance on debt cannot continue for too many years without
seriously affecting the debt ratio, necessitating either a sale of new stock or
a cut in dividends and an attendant increase in the level of retained earnings.

**High and Low
Dividend
Payout
Industries**

Some industries are experiencing rapid growth in the demand for their
products; this affords firms in the industries many good investment opportunities. Electronics, office equipment, and entertainment are examples of
such industries in recent years. Other industries have experienced much

slower growth and even declines. Examples of slow-growth industries are cigarette manufacturing and textiles. Still other industries are growing at about the same rate as the general economy; oil, autos, and banking are representative.

The theory suggests that firms in rapidly growing industries should generally have IRR curves that are relatively far to the right on graphs such as Figure 17.5; for example, Xerox, Polaroid, and IBM might have investment schedules similar to IRR_1. The tobacco companies, on the other hand, could be expected to have investment schedules similar to IRR_3; and IRR_2 might be appropriate for, say, Union Carbide.

Each of these firms would, of course, experience shifts in investment opportunities from year to year, but the curves would *tend* to be in about the same part of the graph. In other words, firms such as Xerox would tend to have more investment opportunities than money, so we would expect them to have zero (or very low) payout ratios. Reynolds Tobacco, on the other hand, would tend to have more money than good investments, so we would expect it to pay out a relatively high percentage of earnings in dividends. These companies do, in fact, conform with our expectations.

Conflicting Theories on Dividends

Two basic schools of thought on dividend policy have been expressed in the theoretical literature of finance. One school, associated with Myron Gordon and John Lintner, among others, holds that the capital gains expected to result from earnings retention are riskier than are dividend expectations. Accordingly, this school suggests that the earnings of a firm with a low payout ratio are typically capitalized at higher rates than the earnings of a high payout firm, other things held constant.

The other school, associated with Merton Miller and Franco Modigliani, holds that investors are basically indifferent to returns in the form of dividends or capital gains. When firms raise or lower their dividends, if their stock prices tend to rise or fall in like manner, does this prove that investors prefer dividends? Miller and Modigliani argue that it does not, that any effect a change in dividends has on the price of a firm's stock is related primarily to information about expected future earnings conveyed by a change in dividends. Recalling that corporate managements dislike cutting dividends. Miller and Modigliani argue that increases in cash dividends raise expectations about the level of future earnings—that they have favorable *information content*. In terms of Figure 17.2, Miller and Modigliani would say that Walter Watch's dividend increases in 1961, 1962, 1963, and 1973 had information content about future earnings—that they signaled to stockholders that management expected the recent earnings increases to be permanent.

Dividends are probably subject to less uncertainty than capital gains, but they are taxed at a higher rate. How do these two forces balance out? Some argue that the uncertainty factor dominates; others feel that the differential tax rate is the stronger force and causes investors to favor corporate retention of earnings; still others (and we put ourselves in this group) argue that it is difficult to generalize. Depending on the tax status and the current income needs of its set of stockholders (both brokerage costs and capital gains taxes make it difficult for individual stockholders to shift companies), as well as the firm's internal investment opportunities, the optimum dividend policy will vary from firm to firm. We thus place heavy emphasis on the "clientele effect."

Dividend Payments

Dividends are normally paid quarterly. For example, Liggett Group pays annual dividends of $2.50. In financial parlance we say that Liggett Group's regular quarterly dividend is 62.5 cents or that its regular annual dividend is $2.50. The management of a company such as Liggett Group conveys to stockholders, sometimes by an explicit statement in the annual report and sometimes by implication, an expectation that the regular dividend will be maintained if at all possible. Further, management conveys its belief that earnings will be sufficient to maintain the dividend.

Under other conditions, a firm's cash flows and investment needs may be too volatile for it to set a very high regular dividend. On the average, however, it needs a high dividend payout to dispose of funds not necessary for reinvestment. In such a case, the directors can set a relatively low regular dividend—low enough that it can be maintained even in low profit years or in years when a considerable amount of reinvestment is needed—and supplement it with an extra dividend in years when excess funds are available. General Motors, whose earnings fluctuate widely from year to year, has long followed the practice of supplementing its regular dividend with an extra dividend paid in addition to the regular fourth quarter dividend.

Payment Procedure

The actual payment procedure is of some importance, and the following is an outline of the payment sequence.

1. *Declaration date.* The directors meet, say, on November 15 and declare the regular dividend. On this date, they issue a statement similar to the following: "On November 15, 1978, the directors of the XYZ Company met and declared the regular quarterly dividend of 50 cents a share, plus an extra dividend of 75 cents a share, to holders of record on December 15, payment to be made on January 2, 1979."
2. *Holder-of-record date.* On December 15, the *holder-of-record-date,* the company closes its stock transfer books and makes up a list of the

shareholders as of that date. If XYZ Company is notified of the sale and transfer of some stock before December 16, the new owner receives the dividend. If notification is received on or after December 16, the old stockholder gets the dividend.

3. *Ex dividend date.* Suppose Irma Jones buys 100 shares of stock from Robert Noble on December 13. Will the company be notified of the transfer in time to list her as the new owner and thus pay her the dividend? To avoid conflict, the brokerage business has set up a convention of declaring that the right to the dividend remains with the stock until four days prior to the holder-of-record date; on the fourth day before the record date, the right to the dividend no longer goes with the shares. The date when the right to the dividend leaves the stock is called the *ex dividend date.* In this case, the ex dividend date is four days prior to December 15, or December 11. Therefore, if Jones is to receive the dividend, she must buy the stock by December 10. If she buys it on December 11 or later, Noble will receive the dividend. The total dividend, regular plus extra, amounts to $1.25, so the ex dividend date is important. Barring fluctuations in the stock market, we would normally expect the price of a stock to drop by approximately the amount of the dividend on the ex dividend date.

4. *Payment date.* The company actually mails the checks to the holders of record on January 2, the payment date.

Stock Dividends and Stock Splits

A significant aspect of dividend policy is stock dividends and stock splits. A *stock dividend* is paid in additional shares of stock instead of in cash and simply involves a bookkeeping transfer from retained earnings to the capital stock account.[3] In a *stock split* there is no change in the capital accounts; instead, a larger number of shares of common stock is issued. In a two-for-one split, stockholders receive two shares for each one previously held. The book value per share is cut in half; and the par, or stated, value per share of stock is similarly changed.

From a practical standpoint there is little difference between a stock dividend and a stock split. The New York Stock Exchange considers any distribution of stock totaling less than 25 percent of outstanding stock to be a stock dividend and any distribution of 25 percent or more a stock split.

---

3. The transfer from retained earnings to the capital stock account must be based on market value. In other words, if a firm's shares are selling for $100 and it has 1 million shares outstanding, a 10 percent stock dividend requires the transfer of $10 million (100,000 × $100) from retained earnings to capital stock. Stock dividends are thus limited by the size of retained earnings. The rule was put into effect to prevent the declaration of stock dividends unless the firm has had earnings. This is another in a long series of rulings designed to keep investors from being fooled by the practices of unscrupulous firms.

Since the two are similar, the issues outlined below are discussed in connection with both stock dividends and stock splits.

Price Effects

The results of a careful empirical study of the effects of stock dividends are available and can be used as a basis for observations on their price effects.[4] (The findings of the study are presented in Table 17.1.) When stock dividends were associated with a cash dividend increase, the value of the company's stock six months after the ex dividend date had risen by 8 percent. When stock dividends were not accompanied by cash dividend increases, stock values fell by 12 percent during the subsequent six-month period.

Table 17.1
Price Effects of Stock Dividends

	Prices at Selected Dates (in Percentages)		
	Six Months prior to Ex Dividend Date	At Ex Dividend Date	Six Months after Ex Dividend Date
Cash dividend increase	100	109	108
No cash dividend increase	100	99	88

These data seem to suggest that stock dividends are seen for what they are—simply additional pieces of paper—and that they do not represent true income. When they are accompanied by higher earnings and cash dividends, investors bid up the value of the stock. However, when they are not accompanied by such increases, the dilution of earnings and dividends per share causes the price of the stock to drop. The fundamental determinant is underlying earnings and dividend trends.

Effects on Extent of Ownership

Table 17.2 shows the effect of stock dividends on common stock ownership. Large stock dividends resulted in the largest percentage increases in stock ownership. The use of stock dividends increased share ownership by 25 percent on the average. For companies and industries that did not offer stock splits or stock dividends, the increase was only 5 percent. Furthermore, the degree of increase itself increased with the size of the stock dividend. This evidence suggests that regardless of the effect on the total market value of the firm, the use of stock dividends and stock splits effec-

---

4. C. A. Barker, "Evaluation of Stock Dividends," *Harvard Business Review* 36 (July–August 1958). Barker's study has been replicated several times in recent years, and his results are still valid.

**Table 17.2
Effect of Stock Dividends on
Stock Ownership**

	Percentage Increase in Ownership, 1950–1953
Stock dividend, 25% and over	30
Stock dividend, 5–25%	17
All stock dividends	25
No stock dividends or splits	5

Source: C. Austin Barker, "Evaluation of Stock Dividends," *Harvard Business Review* 36 (July–August 1958), pp. 99–114. Copyright © 1958 by the President and Fellows of Harvard College; all rights reserved.

tively increases stock ownership by lowering the price at which shares are traded to a more popular range.

Stock Repurchases as an Alternative to Dividends

Treasury stock is the name given to common stock that has been repurchased by the issuing firm, and the acquisition of treasury stock represents an alternative to the payment of dividends. If some of the outstanding stock is repurchased, fewer shares will remain oustanding; and assuming the repurchase does not adversely affect the firm's earnings, the earnings per share of the remaining shares will increase. This increase in earnings per share may result in a higher market price per share, so capital gains will have been substituted for dividends. These effects can be seen from the following example.

American Development Corporation (ADC) earned $4.4 million in 1978; of this amount, 50 percent, or $2.2 million, has been allocated for distribution to common shareholders. There are currently 1.1 million shares outstanding, and the market value is $20 a share. ADC can use the $2.2 million to repurchase 100,000 of its shares through a tender offer for $22 a share, or it can pay a cash dividend of $2 a share.[5]

---

5. Stock repurchases are commonly made in three ways. First, a publicly owned firm can simply buy its own stock through a broker on the open market. Second, it can issue a *tender* under which it permits stockholders to send in ("tender") their shares to the firm in exchange for a specified price per share. When tender offers are made, the firm generally indicates that it will buy up to a specified number of shares within a specified time period (usually about two weeks); if more shares are tendered than the company wishes to purchase, then purchases are made on a pro rata basis. Finally, the firm can purchase a block of shares from one large holder on a negotiated basis. If the latter procedure is employed, care must be taken to ensure that the single stockholder does not receive preferential treatment.

The effect of the repurchase on the EPS and market price per share of the remaining stock can be determined in the following way:

$$\text{Current EPS} = \frac{\text{Total earnings}}{\text{Number of shares}} = \frac{\$4.4 \text{ million}}{1.1 \text{ million}}$$
$$= \$4 \text{ per share.}$$

$$\text{Current P/E ratio} = \frac{\$20}{\$4} = 5 \text{ times.}$$

$$\begin{array}{l}\text{EPS after repurchase} \\ \text{of 100,000 shares}\end{array} = \frac{\$4.4 \text{ million}}{1 \text{ million}} = \$4.40 \text{ per share.}$$

$$\begin{array}{l}\text{Expected market price} \\ \text{after repurchase}\end{array} = (\text{P/E})\,(\text{EPS}) = (5)\,(\$4.40) = \$22 \text{ per share.}$$

It can be seen from this example that investors will receive benefits of $2 a share in any case, in the form of either a $2 cash dividend or a $2 increase in stock price. The result occurs because of the assumptions that (1) shares can be repurchased at $22 a share (2) EPS will remain unchanged, and (3) the P/E ratio will remain constant. If shares could be bought for less than $22, the operation would be even better for *remaining* stockholders, but the reverse would hold if ADC paid more than $22 a share. Furthermore, the P/E ratio might change as a result of the repurchase operation—rising if investors viewed it favorably, falling if they viewed it unfavorably. Some factors that might affect P/E ratios are considered next.

Advantages of Repurchases from the Stockholder's Viewpoint

Advantages to stockholders of repurchases include the following: Profits earned on repurchase are taxed at the capital gains rate, whereas dividend distributions are taxed at the stockholder's marginal tax rate. This is significant. For example, it has been estimated that, on the average, stockholders pay a tax of about 45 percent on marginal income. Since the capital gains tax rate is generally only half the ordinary tax rate, the typical shareholder clearly benefits if the distribution is in the form of a stock repurchase rather than a dividend (other things being equal).

The stockholder has a choice: sell or not sell. The person who receives a dividend has to accept the payment and pay the tax.

A qualitative advantage advanced by market practitioners is that repurchase can often remove a large block of stock overhanging the market.

Advantages of Repurchases from Management's Viewpoint

Advantages to management of repurchases include the following: Studies have shown that dividends are *sticky* in the short run because managements are reluctant to raise them if the new dividend cannot be maintained in the future. Hence, if the excess cash flow is thought to be only temporary, management may prefer to "conceal" the distribution in the form of share repurchases rather than to declare a cash dividend they believe cannot be maintained.

Repurchased stock can be used for acquisitions or released when stock options are exercised. Discussions with financial managers indicate that it is frequently more convenient and less expensive to use repurchased stock rather than newly issued stock for these purposes and when convertibles are converted or warrants exercised.

If directors have large holdings themselves, they may have especially strong preferences for repurchases rather than dividend payments because of the tax factor.

One interesting use of stock repurchases was Standard Products' strategy of repurchasing its own stock to thwart an attempted takeover. Defiance Industries attempted to acquire a controlling interest in Standard Products through a tender offer of $15 a share. Standard's management countered with a tender offer of its own at $17.25 a share, financed by $1.725 million in internal funds and by $3.525 million in long-term debt. This kept stockholders from accepting the outside tender offer and enabled Standard Products' management to retain control.

Repurchases can be used to effect large-scale changes in capital structure. For example, at one time American Standard had virtually no long-term debt outstanding. The company decided that its optimal capital structure called for the use of considerably more debt, but even if it financed *only* with debt it would have taken years to get the debt ratio up to the newly defined optimal level. So the company sold $22 million of long-term debt and used the proceeds to repurchase its common stock, thereby producing an instantaneous change in its capital structure.

Finally, treasury stock can be resold in the open market if the firm needs additional funds.

Disadvantages of Repurchases from the Stockholder's Viewpoint

Disadvantages to stockholders of repurchases include the following: Stockholders may not be indifferent to dividends and capital gains, and the price of the stock may benefit more from cash dividends than from repurchases. Cash dividends are generally thought of as being relatively dependable, and repurchases are not. Further, if a firm announces a regular, dependable repurchase program, the improper accumulation tax may become a threat.

The *selling* stockholders may not be fully aware of all the implications of a repurchase or may not have all pertinent information about the corporation's present and future activities. For this reason, firms generally announce a repurchase program before embarking on it.

The corporation may pay too high a price for the repurchased stock, to the disadvantage of remaining stockholders. If the shares are inactive, and if the firm seeks to acquire a relatively large amount of its stock, the price may be bid above a maintainable price and then fall after the firm ceases its repurchase operations.

By reducing the proportion of cash or marketable securities in the asset structure, the risk composition of the firm's assets and earnings may be increased. The P/E ratio may therefore drop.

Disadvantages of Repurchases from Management's Viewpoint

Disadvantages to management of repurchases include the following: Studies have shown that firms that repurchase substantial amounts of stock have poorer growth rates and investment opportunities than firms that do not. Thus some people feel that announcing a repurchase program is like announcing that management cannot locate good investment projects. One could argue that instituting a repurchase program should be regarded in the same manner as announcing a higher dividend payout, but if repurchases are regarded as indicating especially unfavorable growth opportunities, then they can have an adverse impact on the firm's image and on the price of its stock.

Repurchases may involve some risk from a legal standpoint. The SEC may raise serious questions if it appears that the firm is manipulating the price of its shares. Also, if the Internal Revenue Service can establish that the repurchases are primarily for the avoidance of taxes on dividends, then penalties may be imposed on the firm under the improper accumulation of earnings provision of the tax code. Actions have been brought against closely held companies under Section 531, but we know of no case where such an action has been brought against a publicly owned firm, even though some firms have retired over half their outstanding stock.

Conclusion on Stock Repurchases

When all the pros and the cons on stock repurchases are totaled, where do we stand? Our own conclusions can be summarized as follows: Repurchases on a regular, systematic, dependable basis (like quarterly dividends) are not feasible because of uncertainties about the tax treatment of such a program and about the market price of the shares, how many shares will be tendered, and so on. However, repurchases do offer some significant advantages over dividends, so the procedure should be given careful consideration on the basis of the firm's unique situation. They can be especially valuable to effect a significant shift in capital structure within a short period. Finally, repurchases may increase the riskiness of the firm's assets and earnings.

Summary

Dividend policy determines the extent of internal financing by a firm. The financial manager decides whether to release corporate earnings from the control of the enterprise. Because dividend policy may affect such areas as the financial structure, the flow of funds, corporate liquidity, stock prices, and investor satisfaction, it is clearly an important aspect of financial management.

In theory, once the firm's debt policy and cost of capital have been determined, dividend policy should automatically follow. Under our theoretical model, dividends are simply a residual after investment needs have been met; if the policy is followed and if investors are indifferent to receiving their investment returns in the form of dividends or capital gains, stockholders are better off than they are under any other possible dividend policy. However, the financial manager simply does not have all the information assumed in the theory, and judgment must be exercised.

As a guide to financial managers responsible for dividend policy, the following is a summary of the major economic and financial factors influencing dividend policy: (1) rate of growth and profit level, (2) stability of earnings, (3) age and size of firm, (4) cash position, (5) need to repay debt, (6) control, (7) maintenance of a target dividend, (8) tax position of stockholders, (9) tax position of the corporation (including improper accumulation considerations).

Some of the factors listed lead to higher dividend payouts and some to lower payouts. It is not possible to provide a formula that can be used to establish the proper dividend payout for a given situation; this is a task requiring the exercise of judgment. But the considerations summarized above provide a checklist for guiding dividend decisions.

Empirical studies indicate a wide diversity of dividend payout ratios not only among industries but also among firms in the same industry. Studies also show that dividends are more stable than earnings. Firms are reluctant to raise dividends in years of good earnings, and they resist dividend cuts as earnings decline. In view of investors' observed preference for stable dividends and of the probability that a cut in dividends is likely to be interpreted as forecasting a decline in earnings, stable dividends make good sense.

Neither stock dividends nor stock splits alone exert a major influence on prices. The fundamental determinant of the price of the company's stock is the company's earning power compared with the earning power of other companies. However, both stock splits and stock dividends can be used as effective instruments of financial policy. They are useful devices for reducing the price at which stocks are traded, and studies indicate that they tend to broaden the ownership of a firm's shares.

Stock repurchases have been used as an alternative to cash dividends. Although repurchases have significant advantages over dividends, they also have disadvantages; in particular, they necessarily involve greater uncertainty than cash dividends. Generalizations about stock repurchases are difficult; each firm has its unique problems and conditions, and repurchase policy must be formulated within the context of the firm's characteristics and circumstances as a whole.

Questions

17.1 As an investor, would you rather invest in a firm with a policy of maintaining (a) a constant payout ratio, (b) a constant dollar dividend per share, or (c) a constant regular quarterly dividend plus a year-end extra when earnings are sufficiently high or corporate investment needs are sufficiently low? Explain your answer.

17.2 How would each of the following changes probably affect aggregate payout ratios? Explain your answer.
   a. An increase in the personal income tax rate.
   b. A liberalization in depreciation policies for federal income tax purposes.
   c. A rise in interest rates.
   d. An increase in corporate profits.
   e. A decline in investment opportunities.

17.3 Discuss the pros and cons of having the directors formally announce what a firm's dividend policy will be in the future.

17.4 Most firms would like to have their stock selling at a high P/E ratio and have extensive public ownership (many different shareholders). Explain how stock dividends or stock splits may be compatible with these aims.

17.5 What is the difference between a stock dividend and a stock split? As a stockholder, would you prefer to see your company declare a 100 percent stock dividend or a two-for-one split?

17.6 In theory, if we had perfect capital markets, we would expect investors to be indifferent about whether cash dividends were issued or an equivalent repurchase of stock outstanding were made. What factors might in practice cause investors to value one over the other?

17.7 Discuss the statement: The cost of retained earnings is less than the cost of new outside equity capital. Consequently, it is totally irrational for a firm to sell a new issue of stock and to pay dividends during the same year.

17.8 Would it ever be rational for a firm to borrow money in order to pay dividends? Explain.

17.9 Unions have presented arguments similar to the following: "Corporations such as General Foods retain about half their profits for financing needs. If they financed by selling stock instead of by retaining earnings, they could cut prices substantially and still earn enough to pay the same dividend to their shareholders. Therefore, their profits are too high." Evaluate this statement.

Problems

17.1 The Arizona Engineering Company has $2 million of backlogged orders for its patented solar heating system. Management plans to expand production capacity by 30 percent with a $6 million investment in plant machinery. The firm wants to maintain a 45 percent debt to total asset ratio in its capital structure; it also wants to maintain its past dividend policy of distributing 20 percent of after-tax earnings. In 1978, earnings were $2.6 million. How much external equity must the firm seek at the beginning of 1979?

17.2 Warner Company expects next year's after-tax income to be $5 million. The firm's current debt-equity ratio is 80 percent. If Warner has $4 million of profitable investment opportunities and wishes to maintain its current debt-equity ratio, how much should it pay out in dividends next year?

17.3 After a 3 for 1 stock split, Nevada Company paid a dividend of $4. This represents an 8 percent increase over last year's pre-split dividend. Nevada Company's stock sold for $80 prior to the split. What was last year's dividend per share?

17.4 The following is an excerpt from a 1977 *Wall Street Journal* article:

General Motors Corp., confident of its outlook for auto sales and profit, boosted its quarterly dividend to $1 a share from 85 cents and declared a special year-end dividend of $2.25 a share. Both the quarterly and the special are payable Dec. 10 to stock of record Nov. 17.

The sizable fourth quarter payout, totaling $3.25 a share, is a record for any GM dividend in the final quarter. Last year, the No. 1 auto maker, buoyed by strong sales and sharply improved earnings, paid $3 a share in the fourth quarter.

The $3.25-a-share fourth quarter will bring GM's total cash dividend on common stock for 1977 to a record $6.80 a share, up from the previous record, set last year, of $5.55 a share.

Yesterday's action by GM directors underscored the wave of higher profit that most of the auto makers have been riding for almost two years. Moreover, in raising its quarterly dividend to $1 a share, GM indicated that it expects strong sales and earnings to continue into 1978. In announcing the board's action, Thomas A. Murphy, chairman, and Elliott M. Estes, president, said the dividends "reflect GM's strong earnings and capital position and our confidence in the fundamental strength of the U.S. economy and the automotive market."

The 85-cents-a-share quarterly dividend was instituted by GM in 1966; it was scaled back in 1974 when the auto industry entered a prolonged slump. The 85-cent rate was restored in the third quarter of 1976.[6]

a. Does GM appear to be following a stable dividend payout ratio or a policy of a stable dollar amount of dividends per quarter? What role do the fourth-quarter year-end "extras" perform in this policy?

b. Some authors have suggested that dividends have "announcement effects," performing the role of signaling investors that a change in under-

6. "General Motors Boosts Payout to $1 a Share," *Wall Street Journal,* November 8, 1977. Reprinted by permission of The Wall Street Journal, © Dow Jones & Company, Inc. 1977. All rights reserved.

lying earning power has taken place. Is there anything in the article relevant to the concept that dividend changes convey information to investors?

17.5 In 1977 the Vermont Company paid dividends totaling $1,125,000. For the past ten years, earnings have grown at a constant rate of 10 percent. After-tax income was $3,750,000 for 1977. However, in 1978, earnings were $6,750,000 with investment of $5,000,000. It is predicted that Vermont Company will not be able to maintain this higher level of earnings and will return to its previous 10 percent growth rate. Calculate dividends for 1978 if Vermont Company follows each of the following policies:
a. Its dividend payment is stable and growing.
b. It continues the 1977 dividend payout ratio.
c. It uses a pure residual dividend policy (30 percent of the $5,000,000 investment was financed with debt).
d. The investment in 1978 is financed 90 percent with retained earnings and 10 percent with debt. Any earnings not invested are paid out as dividends.
e. The investment in 1978 is financed 30 percent with external equity, 35 percent with debt, and 40 percent with retained earnings. Any earnings not invested are paid out as dividends.

17.6 Charleston Company stock earns $7 per share, sells for $30, and pays a $4 dividend per share. After a 2 for 1 split, the dividend will be $2.70 per share. By what percentage has the payout increased?

17.7 Cramer Company has 500,000 shares of common stock outstanding. Its capital stock account is $500,000, and retained earnings are $2 million. Cramer is currently selling for $10 per share and has declared a 10 percent stock dividend. After distribution of the stock dividend, what balances will the retained earnings and capital stock accounts show?

17.8 The directors of Northwest Lumber Supply have been comparing the growth of their market price with that of one of their competitors, Parker Panels. Their findings are summarized below.

Northwest Lumber Supply

Year	Earnings	Dividend	Payout	Price	P/E
1978	$4.30	$2.58	60%	$68	15.8
1977	3.85	2.31	60	60	15.6
1976	3.29	1.97	60	50	15.2
1975	3.09	1.85	60	42	13.6
1974	3.05	1.83	60	38	12.5
1973	2.64	1.58	60	31	11.7
1972	1.98	1.19	60	26	13.1
1971	2.93	1.76	60	31	10.6
1970	3.48	2.09	60	35	10.1
1969	2.95	1.77	60	30	10.2

Parker Panels

Year	Earnings	Dividend	Payout	Price	P/E
1978	$3.24	$1.94	60%	$70	21.6
1977	2.75	1.79	65	56	20.4
1976	2.94	1.79	61	53	18.0
1975	2.93	1.73	59	48	16.4
1974	2.90	1.65	57	44	15.2
1973	2.86	1.57	55	41	14.3
1972	2.61	1.49	57	35	13.4
1971	1.55	1.50	97	20	12.9
1970	2.24	1.50	67	34	15.2
1969	2.19	1.49	68	30	13.7

Both companies are in the same markets, and both are similarly organized (approximately the same degree of operating and financial leverage). Northwest has been consistently earning more per share; yet, for some reason, it has not been valued at as high a P/E ratio as Parker. What factors would you point out as possible causes for this lower market valuation of Northwest's stock?

17.9 General Industries has earnings this year of $16.5 million, 50 percent of which is required to take advantage of the firm's excellent investment opportunities. The firm has 206,250 shares outstanding, selling currently at $320 a share. Bruce Newton, a major stockholder (18,750 shares), has expressed displeasure with a great deal of managerial policy. Management has approached him with the prospect of selling his holdings back to the firm, and he has expressed a willingness to do this at a price of $320 a share. Assuming that the market uses a constant P/E ratio of 4 in valuing the stock, answer the following questions:
   a. Should the firm buy Newton's shares? Assume that dividends will not be paid on them if they are repurchased.
   b. How large a cash dividend should be declared?
   c. What is the final value of General Industries' stock after all cash payments to shareholders?

17.10 New Life Tobacco Company has for many years enjoyed a moderate but stable growth in sales and earnings. However, cigarette consumption and, consequently, New Life sales have been falling off recently, partly because of a national awareness of the dangers of smoking to health. Anticipating further declines in tobacco sales for the future, New Life management hopes eventually to move almost entirely out of the tobacco business and develop a new diversified product line in growth-oriented industries.

New Life has been especially interested in the prospects for pollution control devices. (Its research department has already done much work on problems of filtering smoke.) Right now, the company estimates that an investment of $24 million is necessary to purchase new facilities and begin operations on developing these products, but the investment could return about 18 percent within a short time. Other investment opportunities total $9.6 million and are expected to return about 12 percent.

The company has been paying a $2.40 dividend on its 6 million shares outstanding. The announced dividend policy has been to maintain a stable dollar dividend, raising it only when it appears that earnings have reached a new, permanently higher level. The directors might, however, change this policy if reasons for doing so are compelling. Total earnings for the year are $22.8 million, common stock is currently selling for $45, and the firm's current leverage ratio *(B/A)* is 45 percent. Current costs of various forms of financing are:

New bonds: 7%
New common stock sold at $45 to yield the firm: $41
Investors' required rate of return on equity: 9%
Tax rate: 50%

a. Calculate the marginal cost of capital above and below the point of exhaustion of retained earnings for New Life.
b. How large should the company's capital budget be for the year?
c. What is an appropriate dividend policy for the firm? How should the capital budget be financed?
d. How might risk factors influence New Life's cost of capital, capital structure, and dividend policy?
e. What assumptions, if any, do your answers to the above make about investors' preference for dividends versus capital gains—that is, regarding different *d/p* and *g* components of *k?*

PART 6 — LONG-TERM FINANCING

We are now at an advantageous point to review where we have been and to look ahead to where we are going. In Part 2 the techniques of financial analysis and forecasting were developed to provide a basis for projecting the needs for funds. These tools were especially vital for the discussion in Part 3 of working capital management, which requires adjustments by the firm to many continuous changes. Short-term financing decisions were also covered in that part. Part 4 considered longer-term investment decisions and led into Part 5, which provided a basis for decisions in the broad categories of equity and debt financing. Now, Part 6 considers the specific forms of long-term equity and debt financing the firm can employ. This will complete the treatment of the central topics of managerial finance. The final section, Part 7, will deal with a series of subjects providing new applications for concepts already developed.

18

CHAPTER   OBTAINING EXTERNAL
LONG-TERM FUNDS

An overview of the three broad sources of external funds used by business corporations is presented in Table 18.1. The sources are internal cash flows, short-term external funds, and long-term external funds. The first two categories of financing were discussed in previous chapters. The third is the subject of this chapter, which provides an overview of the market mechanisms for raising long-term funds. The overview is intended as a framework for the discussion of individual forms of long-term financing, which are presented in the remaining chapters of this section.

Table 18.1
Sources of Funds for Business
Corporations, 1972–1978
(Billions of Dollars)

Year	Internal Cash Flow		Short-Term External Funds		Long-Term External Funds		Total
	Amount	Percent	Amount	Percent	Amount	Percent	
1972	$ 87	60	$10	7	$47	33	$144
1973	102	57	32	18	45	25	179
1974	116	57	37	18	51	25	204
1975	120	76	−14	−9	51	33	157
1976	140	67	20	10	48	23	208
1977	153	55	31	23	51	22	235
1978	167	65	39	15	51	20	257

Source: Data based on Donald E. Woolley and Beverly Lowen, *Credit and Capital Markets, 1978* (New York: Bankers Trust Company, 1978), p. T26. Reprinted by permission.

The data in Table 18.1 show that long-term external financing is much smaller in magnitude than internal cash flows. It constitutes half or less of internal financing in any year. Long-term external financing is, however, larger and much more stable in amount than external short-term financing (which is a kind of balance-wheel, increasing when the economy is strong and decreasing during recessions). The percentage of long-term financing to total financing has declined between 1972 and 1978 because its absolute amount has remained constant while total financing has almost doubled. Nevertheless, long-term external financing represents a market of over $50 billion per year of net funds raised.

In making decisions about where and how to raise long-term funds, one important choice is between private sources and the public markets. Private financing represents funds obtained directly from one or a few individuals or financial institutions, such as banks, insurance companies, or pension funds. Public financing uses investment bankers to sell securities to a large number of investors—both individuals and financial institutions. In the 1800s, before the development of broad financial markets, business firms were financed by a few wealthy individuals. One of the economic contributions of investment banking was to bring the general public into such financing by assembling smaller amounts of funds from larger numbers of sources and making the total available to business firms. By the 1930s, large pools of funds had been accumulated in insurance companies, pension funds, and commercial banks. This resulted in an increase in direct financing that bypassed to some degree the use of investment banking. Since direct financing is less complicated than public financing, it will be covered first in the chapter. Then the nature of investment banking will be discussed.

Direct Financing

Two major forms of direct long-term financing are term lending by commercial banks and insurance companies and the private placement of securities with insurance companies and pension funds. *Term loans* are direct business loans with a maturity of more than one year but less than fifteen years and with provisions for systematic repayment (amortization during the life of the loan). *Private placements* are direct business loans with a maturity of more than fifteen years.[1] Approximately half of such placements have been in the form of long-term promissory notes.[2] The distinction is, of course, arbitrary. Private placement differs from the term loan only in its arbitrary maturity length; this distinction becomes even fuzzier when we discover that some private placements call for repayment of as much as 20 percent of the principal within five years and nearly 60 percent within ten years, "exclusive of repayments from optional and contingent sinking funds."[3] Thus term loans and private placements represent about the same kind of financing arrangements.

The total amount of bank term loans outstanding at the end of 1977 was $70 billion. Gross corporate debt sold publicly in 1978 is projected at $25 billion; the amount sold privately is projected at $18 billion (representing 72 percent of the amount of public offerings). Net public debt outstanding at the end of 1977 was estimated to be $237 billion; privately held debt outstanding was estimated to be $109 billion (almost half the publicly held corporate debt).[4] These data establish that direct financing represents a major portion of long-term financing of business firms.

The central question of interest to financial managers is: What are the ad-

1. This is the dividing line drawn by N. H. Jacoby and R. J. Saulnier, *Term Lending to Business* (New York: National Bureau of Economic Research, 1942), pp. 10-14, and app. B, pp. 143–147. See also the analysis in Avery B. Cohan, *Private Placements and Public Offerings* (Chapel Hill: School of Business Administration, University of North Carolina, 1961), pp. 2–5.
2. E. Raymond Corey, *Direct Placement of Corporate Securities* (Cambridge, Mass.: School of Business Administration, Harvard University, 1961), pp. 115–116.
3. Ibid., pp. 120–121.
4. Salomon Brothers, *Prospects for the Credit Markets in 1978* (New York: Salomon Brothers, 1978), pp. 22, 33.

vantages and disadvantages of these two major sources of financing? The considerations that make direct financing of interest to borrowers can be considered under the heading of demand factors. These include:

1. Term loans and private placements represent in part a shift by business firms from dependence on short-term bank borrowing to a greater utilization of longer-term financing. This shift helps businesses avoid the problem of unavailability of short-term loans during tight money periods.
2. Term loans and private placements were stimulated after 1934 by the increased cost and time involved in public offerings. The Securities Acts of 1933 and 1934 required that new financing go through a registration process and a twenty-day waiting period. Developing data for the SEC registration statements increased the cost of public flotations, particularly for issues of less than $1 million, because the fixed costs were spread over small amounts.
3. A public offering takes time to prepare. There are registration statements to be written, underwriting agreements to be made, and a possible two-to-three months waiting period before the offering can be made. A private placement or term loan can be taken care of in a matter of hours, especially where there is a continuing relationship between the insurance company or bank and the borrower.
4. If the securities of a public offering are widely held, it is more difficult to negotiate a modification in the indenture (loan agreement) provisions. If, for example, some of the terms of a direct loan have become onerous (not in the best interests of the borrower), the borrower can negotiate directly with the bank or the insurance company. It is much more difficult to contact thousands of bondholders to obtain agreement about modifying provisions of the bond issue.
5. The increased rates of corporate taxation in the 1930s made it more difficult for small and medium-sized firms to finance their growth with internal funds. It thus became necessary for them to turn to external sources, and direct longer-term loans represented one of these available sources. One study observes that "the most important characteristic of the private placement market is that it serves as the major source of long-term debt financing for smaller, less financially secure companies."[5] The supply of long-term funds increased in the early 1930s for various reasons, among them:
   a. Inauguration in 1933 of deposit insurance by the Federal Deposit Insurance Corporation reduced the likelihood of widespread runs on banks by depositors. The result was greater stability of the deposits in small banks as well as greater stability of the banks' own deposits in

---

5. E. Shapiro and C. R. Wolf, *The Role of Private Placements in Corporate Finance* (Cambridge, Mass.: Harvard Graduate School of Business Administration, 1972), p. 2.

the larger correspondent banks. This stability made it feasible for commercial banks to extend longer-term loans.

b. Also, because of the depressed business conditions in the early 1930s, commercial banks had excess reserves, and insurance companies were continuing to accumulate funds. Thus ample funds were available, and suppliers were looking for new ways of lending them.

c. The increase in pension funds and state and local retirement funds greatly augmented the money available for longer-term financing.

Characteristics of Term Loans and Private Placements

Most term loans are repayable on an amortized basis. Because this repayment, or amortization, schedule is a particularly important feature of such loans, it is useful to describe how it is determined. The purpose of amortization, of course, is to have the loan repaid gradually over its life rather than fall due all at once; this protects both the lender and the borrower against the possibility that the borrower will not make adequate provisions for retirement of the loan during its life. Amortization is especially important where the loan is for the purpose of purchasing a specific item of equipment; here the schedule of repayment will be geared to the productive life of the equipment, and payments will be made from cash flows resulting from use of the equipment.

To illustrate how the amortization schedule is determined, assume that a firm borrows $1,000 on a ten-year loan, that interest is computed at 8 percent on the declining balance, and that the principal and interest are to be paid in ten equal installments. What is the amount of each of the ten annual payments? To find this value we must use the present value concepts developed in Chapter 11.

First, notice that the lender advances $1,000 and receives in turn a ten-year annuity of a dollars each year. In Chapter 11 we saw that these receipts could be calculated as:

$$a = \frac{PV_{at}}{PVIF_a},$$

where:

a = the annual receipt.
PV_{at} = the present value of the annuity.
$PVIF_a$ = the appropriate interest factor (found in either Table 11.5 or Appendix Table A.4).

Substituting the $1,000 for PV_{at} and the interest factor for a ten-year, 8 percent annuity—6.710—for $PVIF_a$, we find:

$$a = \frac{\$1,000}{6.710} = \$149.$$

Therefore, if the firm makes ten annual installments of $149 each, it will have retired the $1,000 loan and provided the lender an 8 percent return on the investment.

Table 18.2 breaks down the annual payments into interest and repayment components and, in the process, proves that level payments of $149 will, in fact, retire the $1,000 loan and give the lender an 8 percent return. This breakdown is important for tax purposes, because the interest payments are deductible expenses to the borrower and taxable income to the lender.

Table 18.2
Term Loan Schedule

Year	Total Payment	Interest[a]	Amortization Repayment	Remaining Balance
1	$149	$80	$ 69	$931
2	149	74	75	856
3	149	68	81	775
4	149	62	87	688
5	149	55	94	594
6	149	48	101	493
7	149	39	110	383
8	149	31	118	265
9	149	21	128	137
10	149	11	138	—

[a] Interest for the first year is $0.08 \times \$1,000 = \$80$; for the second year, $0.08 \times \$931 = \$74$; and so on.

Other Characteristics

Maturity For commercial banks, the term loan runs five years or less (typically three years). For insurance companies, typical maturities have been five to fifteen years. This difference reflects the fact that liabilities of commercial banks are shorter term than those of insurance companies. Banks and insurance companies occasionally cooperate in their term lending. For example, if a firm (usually a large one) seeks a fifteen-year term loan, a bank may take the loan for the first five years and an insurance company for the last ten years.

Collateral Commercial banks require security on about 60 percent of the volume and 90 percent of the number of term loans made. They take as security mainly stocks, bonds, machinery, and equipment. Insurance companies also require security on nearly one-third of their loans, frequently using real estate as collateral on the longer-term ones.

Options In recent years institutional investors have increasingly taken compensation in addition to fixed interest payments on directly negotiated loans. The most popular form of additional compensation is an option to buy common stock, the option being in the form of detachable warrants permitting the purchase of the shares at stated prices over a designated period. (See Chapter 22 for more details on warrants.)

Terms of Loan Agreements

A major advantage of a term loan is that it assures the borrower of the use of the funds for an extended period. On a ninety-day loan, since the commercial bank has the option to renew or not renew, it has frequent opportunities to reexamine the borrower's situation. If it has deteriorated unduly, the loan officer simply does not renew the loan. On a term loan, however, the bank or insurance company has committed itself for a period of years. Because of this long-term commitment, restrictive provisions are incorporated into the loan agreement to protect the lender for the duration of the loan. The most important of these provisions (though by no means all of them) are listed below:

1. *Current ratio.* The current ratio must be maintained at some specified level—2½ to 1; 3 to 1; 3½ to 1—depending on the borrower's line of business. Net working capital must also be maintained at some minimum level.
2. *Additional long-term debt.* Typically, there are prohibitions against (a) incurring additional long-term indebtedness, except with the permission of the lender; (b) the pledging of assets; (c) the assumption of any contingent liabilities, such as guaranteeing the indebtedness of a subsidiary; and (d) the signing of long-term leases beyond specified amounts.
3. *Management.* The loan agreement may require (a) that any major changes in management personnel be approved by the lender; (b) that life insurance be taken out on the principals or key people in the business; and (c) that a voting trust be created or proxies be granted for a specified period to ensure that the management of the company will be under the control of the group on which the lender has relied in making the loan.
4. *Financial statements.* The lender will require the borrower to submit periodic financial statements for review.

Costs

Another major aspect of term loans is their cost. As with other forms of lending, the interest rate on these loans varies with the size of the loan and the quality of the borrower, reflecting also the fixed costs of making loans. Surveys show that on small term loans the interest rate may run up to 15 percent. On loans of $1 million and more, term loan rates have been close to the prime rate.

The interest rate may be fixed for the life of the loan, or it may vary. Often the loan agreement specifies that the interest rate will be based on the average of the rediscount rate in the borrower's Federal Reserve district during the previous three months—generally 1 or 2 percent above the rediscount rate.[6] It may also be geared to the published prime rate charged by New York City banks.

On private placements the interest rate generally runs from about ten to forty basis points higher than on comparable public issues. Thus, to some extent, the economies of using private placements are offset by their somewhat higher interest rate.

From the standpoint of the borrower, the advantages of direct financing are:

1. Much seasonal short-term borrowing can be dispensed with, thereby reducing the danger of nonrenewal of loans.
2. The borrower avoids the expenses of SEC registration and investment bankers' distribution.
3. Less time is required to complete arrangements for obtaining a loan than is involved in a bond issue.
4. Since only one lender is involved, rather than many bondholders, it is possible to modify the loan indenture.

The disadvantages to a borrower of direct financing are:

1. The interest rate may be higher on a term loan than on a short-term loan because the lender is tying up money for a longer period and therefore does not have the opportunity to review the borrower's status periodically (as is done with a short-term loan).
2. The cash drain is large. Since the loans provide for regular amortization or sinking fund payments, the company experiences a continuous cash drain. From this standpoint, direct loans are less advantageous than equity money (which never has to be repaid), a preferred stock without maturity, or even a bond issue without a sinking fund requirement.
3. Since the loan is a long-term commitment, the lender employs high credit standards, insisting that the borrower be in a strong financial position and have a good current ratio, a low debt-equity ratio, good activity ratios, and good profitability ratios.
4. The loan agreement has restrictions that are not found in a ninety-day note. (The reasons for the restrictions and their nature have already been explained.)
5. Investigation costs may be high. The lender stays with the company for a longer period. Therefore, the longer-term outlook for the company must be looked into, and the lender makes a more elaborate investigation than would be done for a short-term note. For this reason the lender may set a minimum on any loan (for example, $50,000) in order to recover the costs of investigating the applicant.

6. The rediscount rate is the rate of interest at which a bank can borrow from a Federal Reserve Bank.

In addition, there are some advantages to the public distribution of securities that are not achieved by term loans or private placement. These include:

1. The firm establishes its credit and achieves publicity by having its securities publicly and widely distributed. Because of this, it will be able to engage in future financing at lower rates.
2. The wide distribution of debt or equity may enable its repurchase on favorable terms at some subsequent date if the market price of the securities falls.

Thus direct long-term financing has both advantages and limitations. While it has grown to represent a substantial volume of financing, public financing of long-term funds still predominates and is likely to continue doing so. Therefore, the institutions for long-term public financing are discussed next.

Investment Banking

In the U.S. economy, saving is done by one group of persons and investing by another. (*Investing* is used here in the sense of actually putting money into plant, equipment, and inventory, not in the sense of buying securities.) Savings are placed with financial intermediaries who, in turn, make the funds available to firms wishing to acquire plants and equipment and to hold inventories.

One of the major institutions performing this channeling role is the *investment banking* institution. The term *investment banker* is somewhat misleading in that investment bankers are neither investors nor bankers. That is, they do not invest their own funds permanently; nor are they repositories for individuals' funds, as are commercial banks or savings banks. What, then, is the nature of investment banking?

The many activities of investment bankers can be described first in general terms and then with respect to specific functions. The traditional function of the investment banker has been to act as the middleman in channeling driblets of individuals' savings and funds into the purchase of business securities. The investment banker does this by purchasing and distributing the new securities of individual companies by performing the functions of underwriting, distribution of securities, and advice and counsel.

Underwriting

Underwriting is the insurance function of bearing the risks of adverse price fluctuations during the period in which a new issue of securities is being distributed. The nature of the investment banker's underwriting function can best be conveyed by example: A business firm needs $10 million. It selects an investment banker, holds conferences, and decides to issue $10 million of bonds. An underwriting agreement is drawn up. On a specific day, the investment banker presents the company with a check for $10 million (less commission). In return, the investment banker receives bonds in denominations of $1,000 each to sell to the public.

The company receives the $10 million before the investment banker has sold the bonds. Between the time the firm is paid the $10 million and the time the bonds are sold, the investment banker bears all the risk of market price fluctuations in the bonds. Conceivably, it can take the person days, months, or longer to sell bonds. If the bond market collapses in the interim, the investment banker carries the risk of loss on the sale of the bonds.

There have been dramatic instances of bond market collapses within one week after an investment banker has bought $50 million or $100 million of bonds. For example, in the spring of 1974 an issue of New Jersey Sporting Arena bonds dropped $140 per $1,000 bond during the underwriting period, costing the underwriters an estimated $8 million. The issuing firm, however, does not need to be concerned about the risk of market price fluctuations while the investment banker is selling the bonds, since it has received its money. One fundamental economic function of the investment banker, then, is to underwrite the risk of a decline in the market price between the time the money is transmitted to the firm and the time the bonds are placed in the hands of their ultimate buyers. For this reason, investment bankers are often called underwriters; they underwrite risk during the distribution period.

Distribution

The second function of the investment banker is marketing new issues of securities. The investment banker is a specialist who has a staff and organization to distribute securities and can therefore perform the physical distribution function more efficiently and more economically than can an individual corporation. A corporation that wished to sell an issue of securities would find it necessary to establish a marketing or selling organization—a very expensive and ineffective method of selling securities. The investment banker has a permanent, trained staff and dealer organization available to distribute securities. In addition, the investment banker's reputation for selecting good companies and pricing securities fairly builds up a broad clientele over time, and this further increases the efficiency with which securities can be sold.

Advice and Counsel

The investment banker, engaged in the origination and sale of securities, through experience becomes an expert adviser about terms and characteristics of securities that will appeal to investors. This advice and guidance is valuable. Furthermore, the person's reputation as a seller of securities depends on their subsequent performance. Therefore, investment bankers often sit on the boards of firms whose securities they have sold. In this way they can provide continuing financial counsel and increase the firm's probability of success.

Investment Banking Operation

Probably the best way to gain a clear understanding of the investment banking function is to trace the history of a new issue of securities.[7] Accordingly, this section describes the steps necessary to issue new securities.

Preunderwriting Conferences

First, the members of the issuing firm and the investment banker hold preunderwriting conferences at which they discuss the amount of capital to be raised, the type of security to be issued, and the terms of the agreement. Memorandums are written by the treasurer of the issuing company to the firm's directors and other officers describing proposals suggested at the conferences. Meetings of the board of directors of the issuing company are held to discuss the alternatives and to attempt to reach a decision.

At some point, the issuer enters an agreement with the investment banker that a flotation will take place. The investment banker then begins to conduct an underwriting investigation. If the company is proposing to purchase additional assets, the underwriter's engineering staff may analyze the proposed acquisition. A public accounting firm is called upon to make an audit of the issuing firm's financial situation and also helps prepare the registration statements in connection with these issues for the SEC.

A firm of lawyers is called in to interpret and judge the legal aspects of the flotation. In addition, the originating underwriter (who is the manager of the subsequent underwriting syndicate) makes an exhaustive investigation of the company's prospects.

When the investigations are completed but before registration with the SEC is made, an underwriting agreement is drawn up by the investment banker. Terms of the tentative agreement may be modified through discussions between the underwriter and the issuing company, but the final agreement will cover all underwriting terms except the price of the securities.

7. The process described here relates primarily to situations where the firm doing the financing picks an investment banker, then negotiates over the terms of the issue. An alternative procedure, used extensively only in the public utility industry, is for the selling firm to specify the terms of the new issue, then to have investment bankers bid for the entire new issue with *sealed bids*. The very high fixed costs that an investment banker must incur to investigate thoroughly the company and its new issue rule out sealed bids except for the largest issues. The operation described in this section is called *negotiated underwriting*. Competition is keen among underwriters, of course, to develop and maintain working relations with business firms.

Registration Statement

A registration statement then is filed with the SEC. The statutes set a twenty-day waiting period (which in practice may be shortened or lengthened by the SEC) during which the SEC staff analyzes the registration statement to determine whether there are any omissions or misrepresentations of fact. During the examination period, the SEC can file exceptions to the registration statement or can ask for additional information from the issuing company or the underwriters. Also during this period, the investment bankers are not permitted to offer the securities for sale, although they can print preliminary prospectuses with all the customary information except the offering price.

Pricing the Securities

The actual price the underwriter pays the issuer is not generally determined until the end of the registration period. There is no universally followed practice, but one common arrangement for a new issue of stock calls for the investment banker to buy the securities at a prescribed number of points below the closing price on the last day of registration. For example, in October 1977 the stock of Wilcox Chemical Company had a current price of $38 and had traded between $35 and $40 a share during the previous three months. The firm and the underwriter agreed that the investment banker would buy 200,000 new shares at $2.50 below the closing price on the last day of registration. The stock closed at $36 on the day the SEC released the issue, so the firm received $33.50 a share. Typically, such agreements have an escape clause that provides for the contract to be voided if the price of the securities falls below some predetermined figure. In the case of Wilcox, this "upset" price was set at $34 a share. Thus, if the closing price of the shares on the last day of registration had been $33.50, Wilcox would have had the option of withdrawing from the agreement.

This arrangement holds, of course, only for additional stock offerings of firms whose old stock was previously traded. When a company "goes public" for the first time, the investment banker and the firm negotiate a price in accordance with the valuation principles described in Chapter 14.

The investment banker has an easier job if the issue is priced relatively low, but the issuer of the securities naturally wants as high a price as possible. Some conflict on price therefore arises between the investment banker and the issuer. If the issuer is financially sophisticated and makes comparisons with similar security issues, the investment banker is forced to price close to the market.

Underwriting Syndicate

The investment banker with whom the issuing firm has conducted its discussions does not typically handle the purchase and distribution of the issue alone, unless the issue is a very small one. If the sums of money involved are large and the risks of price fluctuations are substantial, the investment banker forms a syndicate in an effort to minimize the amount of personal risk. A syndicate is a temporary association for the purpose of carrying out a specific objective. The nature of the arrangements for a syndicate in the underwriting and sale of a security through an investment banker can best be understood with the aid of Figure 18.1.

The managing underwriter invites other investment bankers to participate in the transaction on the basis of their knowledge of the particular kind of offering to be made and their strength and dealer contacts in selling securities of this type. Each investment banker has business relationships with other investment bankers and dealers and thus has a selling group composed of these people.

Some firms combine all these characteristics. For example, Merrill Lynch, Pierce, Fenner & Smith underwrites some issues and manages the underwriting of others. On still other flotations, it is invited by the manager to join in the distribution of the issue. It also purchases securities as a dealer, carries an inventory of those securities, and publishes lists of securities it has for sale. In addition to being a dealer, Merrill Lynch, of course, carries on substantial activity as a broker. An individual investment firm may also carry on all these functions.

There are also firms with a narrower range of functions—specialty dealers, specialty brokers, and specialty investment counselors. Thus, in the financial field, there is often specialization of financial functions. A *dealer* purchases securities outright, holds them in inventory, and sells them at whatever price can be gotten. The dealer may benefit from price appreciation or may suffer a loss on declines, as any merchandiser does. A *broker,* on the other hand, takes orders for purchases and transmits them to the proper exchange; the gain is the commission charged for the service.

Syndicates are used in the distribution of securities for three reasons:

1. A single investment banker may be financially unable to handle a large issue alone.
2. The originating investment banker may desire to spread the risk even if it is financially able to handle the issue alone.
3. The utilization of several selling organizations (as well as other underwriters) permits an economy of selling effort and expense and encourages nationwide distribution.

Participating underwriters and dealers are provided with full information on all phases of these financing transactions, and they share in the underwriting commission. Suppose that an investment banker buys $10 million worth of bonds to be sold at par, or $1,000 each. If he receives a two-point spread, he will buy the bonds from the issuer at 98; that is, he must pay the issuer $9.8 million for the issue of $10 million. Typically, on a two-point spread, the managing underwriter receives the first 0.25 percent for originat-

Figure 18.1
Diagram of Sales of $100 Million of Bonds
through Investment Bankers

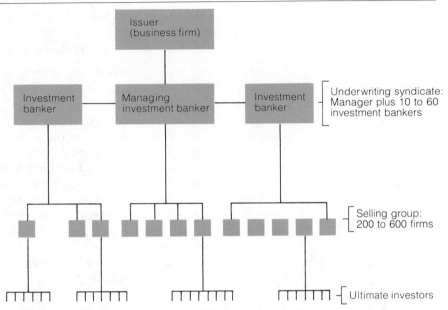

ing and managing the syndicate. Next, the entire underwriting group receives about 0.75 percent. Members of the selling group receive about 1 percent as a sales commission.

The manager of the underwriting group who makes a sale to an ultimate purchaser of the securities receives the 0.25 percent as manager, 0.75 percent as underwriter, and 1 percent as seller—the full 2 percent. If the manager wholesales some of the securities to members of the selling group who make the ultimate sale, they receive the 1 percent selling commission and the manager receives the other 1 percent for managing and underwriting the issue. If the issue is managed by one firm, underwritten by a second, and sold by a third, the 2 percent commission is divided, with 1 percent going to the selling firm, 0.75 percent to the underwriter, and 0.25 percent to the manager of the underwriting group.

Ordinarily, each underwriter's liability is limited to the agreed-upon commitment. For example, an investment banker who participates in a $20 million offering and agrees to see to it that $5 million of the securities are sold no longer is responsible after the $5 million of securities are sold.

Selling Group

The selling group is formed primarily for the purpose of distributing securities; it consists of dealers, who take relatively small participations from the members of the underwriting group. The underwriters act as wholesalers; members of the selling group act as retailers. The number of investment banking houses in a selling group depends partly on the size of the issue. A selling group may have as many as three hundred to four hundred dealers. The operation of the selling group is controlled by the *selling group agreement,* which usually covers the following major points.

1. *Description of the issue.* The description is set forth in a report on the issue—the prospectus—which fully describes the issue and the issuer.
2. *Concession.* Members of the selling group subscribe to the new issue at a public offering price less the *concession* given to them as a commission for their selling service. In the preceding example, this was 1 percent.
3. *Handling purchased securities.* The selling group agreement provides that no member of the selling group will be permitted to sell the securities below the public offering price. The syndicate manager invariably "pegs" the quotation in the market by placing continuous orders to buy at the public offering price. A careful record is kept of bond or stock certificate numbers so that repurchased bonds can be identified with the member of the selling group who sold them. The general practice is to cancel the commission on such securities and add brokerage costs incurred in the repurchase. Repurchased securities are then placed with other dealers for sale.[8]
4. *Duration of selling group.* The most common provision in selling group agreements is that the group has an existence of thirty days, subject to earlier termination by the manager. The agreement may be extended, however, for an additional eighty days by members representing 75 percent of the selling group.

Offering and Sale   After the selling group has been formed, the actual offering takes place. Publicity for the sale is given in advance of the offering date. Advertising material is prepared for release as soon as permissible. The actual day of the offering is chosen with a view to avoiding temporary congestion in the security market and other unfavorable events or circumstances.

The formal public offering is called "opening the books," an archaic term reflecting ancient customs of the investment banking trade. When the books are opened, the manager accepts subscriptions to the issue from both selling group participants and outsiders who wish to buy. If the demand is great, the books may be closed immediately and an announcement made that the issue is oversubscribed; the issue is said to "fly out the window." If the reception is weak, the books may remain open for an extended period.

---

8. Without these repurchase arrangements, members of the selling group could sell their share of the securities on the open market instead of to new purchasers. Since the pegging operation is going on, there will be a ready market for the securities; consequently, a penalty is necessary to avoid thwarting the syndicate operation.

Market Stabilization

During the period of the offering and distribution of securities, the manager of the underwriting group typically stabilizes the price of the issue. The duration of the price-pegging operation is usually thirty days. The price is pegged by placing orders to buy at a specified price in the market. The pegging operation is designed to prevent a cumulative downward movement in the price, which would result in losses for all members of the underwriting group. Since the manager of the underwriting group has the major responsibility, that person assumes the task of pegging the price.

If the market deteriorates during the offering period, the investment banker carries a substantial risk. For this reason, the pegging operation may not be sufficient to protect the underwriters. In one Pure Oil Company issue of $44 million convertible preferred stock, only $1 million of shares were sold at the $100 offering price. At the conclusion of the underwriting agreement, initial trading took place at $74, incurring for the investment bankers a loss of over $11 million ($43 million × 26 percent). In the Textron issue of June 1967, the offering was reduced from $100 million to $50 million because of market congestion, and 5 percent of the bonds still were unsold after the initial offering. Other such cases can be cited.

It has been charged that pegging the price during the offering period constitutes a monopolistic price-fixing arrangement. Investment bankers reply, however, that not to peg the price would increase the risk and therefore the underwriting cost to the issuer. On balance, it appears that the pegging operation has a socially useful function. The danger of monopolistic pricing is avoided, or at least mitigated substantially, by competitive factors. If an underwriter attempts to set a monopolistic price on a particular issue of securities, the investor can turn to thousands of other securities that are not price pegged. The degree of control over the market by the underwriter in a price-pegging operation seems negligible.

Costs of Flotation

The cost of selling new issues of securities is put into perspective in Table 18.3. The table summarizes recent data on costs of flotation compiled by the SEC. Two important generalizations can be drawn from these data:

1. The cost of flotation for common stock is greater than for preferred stock, and the costs of both are greater than the cost of flotation for bonds.
2. The cost of flotation as a percentage of the gross proceeds is greater for small issues than for large ones.

The explanations for these relationships are found in the amount of risk involved and in the job of physical distribution. Bonds are generally bought in large blocks by relatively few institutional investors, whereas stocks are bought by millions of individuals. For this reason the distribution job for

**Table 18.3
Costs of Flotation as a
Percentage of Proceeds for
Common Stock Issues,
1971–1975[a]**

Size of Issue (Millions of Dollars)	Underwriting				Rights with Standby Underwriting				Rights	
	Number	Compensation as a Percentage of Proceeds	Other Expenses as a Percentage of Proceeds	Total Cost as a Percentage of Proceeds	Number	Compensation as a Percentage of Proceeds	Other Expenses as a Percentage of Proceeds	Total Cost as a Percentage of Proceeds	Number	Total Cost as a Percentage of Proceeds
Under .50	0	—	—	—	0	—	—	—	3	8.99
.50–.99	6	6.96	6.78	13.74	2	3.43	4.80	8.24	2	4.59
1.00–1.99	18	10.40	4.89	15.29	5	6.36	4.15	10.51	5	4.90
2.00–4.99	61	6.59	2.87	9.47	9	5.20	2.85	8.06	7	2.85
5.00–9.99	66	5.50	1.53	7.03	4	3.92	2.18	6.10	6	1.39
10.00–19.99	91	4.84	0.71	5.55	10	4.14	1.21	5.35	3	0.72
20.00–49.99	156	4.30	0.37	4.67	12	3.84	0.90	4.74	1	0.52
50.00–99.99	70	3.97	0.21	4.18	9	3.96	0.74	4.70	2	0.21
100.00–500.00	16	3.81	0.14	3.95	5	3.50	0.50	4.00	9	0.13
Total/Avg	484	8.02	1.15	6.17	56	4.32	1.73	6.05	38	2.45

[a] Issues are included only if the company's stock was listed on the NYSE, AMEX, or regional exchanges prior to the offering; any associated secondary distribution represents less than 10 percent of the total proceeds of the issue, and the offering contains no other types of securities.
Source: From Clifford W. Smith, Jr., "Substitute Methods for Raising Additional Capital: Rights Offerings versus Underwritten Issues," *Journal of Financial Economics*, December 1977, Vol. 5, No. 3. By permission of North-Holland Publishing Company, Amsterdam.

common stock is harder and the expenses of marketing it are greater. Similarly, stocks are more volatile than bonds, so underwriting risks are larger for stock than for bond flotations.

Reasons for the variation in cost with the size of issue are also easily found. First, certain fixed expenses are associated with any distribution of securities: the underwriting investigation, the preparation of the registration statement, legal fees, and so on. Since these expenses are relatively large and fixed, their percentage of the total cost of flotation runs high on small issues. Second, small issues are typically those of relatively less well-known firms, so underwriting expenses may be larger than usual because the danger of omitting vital information is greater. Furthermore, the selling job is more difficult; salespeople must exert greater effort to sell the securities of less well-known firms. For these reasons the underwriting commission, as a percentage of the gross proceeds, is relatively high for small issues.

Flotation costs are also influenced by whether or not the issue is a "rights offering," and if it is, by the extent of the underpricing.[9] If rights are used, and if the underpricing is substantial, then the investment banker bears little risk of being unable to sell the shares. Further, very little selling effort is required in such a situation. These two factors enable a company to float new securities to its own stockholders at a relatively low cost. However, rights offerings without use of underwriters accounted for only 38 of the 578 issues sold (less than 7 percent) during the 1971–1975 period covered in Table 18.3.

Regulation of Security Trading

The operations of investment bankers, exchanges, and over-the-counter markets described in the previous sections of this chapter are significantly influenced by a series of federal statutes enacted during and after 1933. The financial manager is affected by these laws for several reasons:

1. Corporate officers are subject to personal liabilities.
2. The laws affect the ease and costs of financing and the behavior of the money and capital markets in which the corporation's securities are sold and traded.
3. Investors' willingness to buy securities is influenced by the existence of safeguards provided by these laws.

Securities Act of 1933

The first of the securities acts, the Securities Act of 1933, followed congressional investigations of the stock market collapse of 1929–1932. Motivating the act were (1) the large losses to investors, (2) the failures of many corpo-

---

9. "Rights offerings" involve the sale of stock to existing stockholders. This topic is discussed extensively in Chapter 19.

rations on which little information had been provided, and (3) the misrepresentations that had been made to investors.

The basic objective of the Securities Act of 1933 is to provide for both *full disclosure* of relevant information and a *record of representations.* The act seeks to achieve these objectives by the following means:

1. It applies to all interstate offerings to the public in amounts of $500,000 or more. (Some exemptions are government bonds and bank stocks.)
2. Securities must be registered at least twenty days before they are publicly offered. The registration statement provides financial, legal, and technical information about the company. A prospectus summarizes this information for use in selling the securities. If information is inadequate or misleading, the SEC will delay or stop the public offering. (Obtaining the information required to review the registration statement may result in a waiting period that exceeds twenty days.)
3. After the registration has become effective, the securities can be offered if accompanied by the prospectus. Preliminary, or "red herring," prospectuses can be distributed to potential buyers during the waiting period.
4. If the registration statement or prospectus contains misrepresentations or omissions of material facts, any purchaser who suffers a loss can sue for damages. Liabilities and severe penalties can be imposed on the issuer and its officers, directors, accountants, engineers, appraisers, and underwriters and on all others who participated in preparing the registration statement.

Securities Exchange Act of 1934

The Securities Exchange Act of 1934 extends the disclosure principle applied to new issues by the Securities Act of 1933 to trading in already issued securities (the "secondhand" securities market). It seeks to accomplish this by the following measures:

1. It establishes the Securities and Exchange Commission. (The Federal Trade Commission had been administering the Securities Act of 1933.)
2. It provides for registration and regulation of national securities exchanges. Companies whose securities are listed on an exchange must file reports similar to registration statements with both the SEC and the stock exchange and must provide periodic reports as well.
3. It establishes control over corporate "insiders." Officers, directors, and major stockholders of a corporation must file monthly reports of changes in holdings of the corporation's stock. Any short-term profits from such transactions are payable to the corporation.
4. It gives the SEC the power to prohibit manipulation by such devices as pools (aggregations of funds used to affect prices artificially), wash sales (sales among members of the same group to record artificial transaction prices), and pegging the market other than during stock flotations.

5. It gives the SEC control over the proxy machinery and practices.
6. It establishes control over the flow of credit into security transactions by giving the board of governors of the Federal Reserve System the power to control margin requirements.

Appraisal of Regulation of Security Trading

Why should security transactions be regulated? It can be argued that a great body of relevant knowledge is necessary to make an informed judgment of the value of a security. Moreover, security values are subject to many gyrations that influence stability and business conditions generally. Hence, social well-being requires that orderly markets be promoted. There are three primary objectives of regulation:

1. To protect amateur investors from fraud and to provide them with a basis for informed judgments.
2. To control the volume of bank credit to finance security speculation.
3. To provide orderly markets in securities.

Progress has been made on all three counts. There has been some cost in the increased time and expense involved in new flotations by companies, although the benefits seem worth their costs. The regulations are powerless to prevent investors from investing in unsound ventures or to prevent stock prices from skyrocketing during booms and plummeting during periods of pessimism. Still, requirements for increased information have been of value in preventing fraud and gross misrepresentations.

From the standpoint of the financial manager, regulation has a twofold significance. It affects both the costs of issuing securities and the riskiness of securities—and hence the rate of return investors require when they purchase stocks and bonds. As has been seen in previous chapters, these two factors have an important bearing on the firm's cost of capital and, through the capital budgeting process, on its investment decisions. Further, since business investment is a key determinant of employment and production in the economy, efficient capital markets have an important impact on all of society.

Summary

Longer-term obligations are sold directly to investors or through the investment banking distribution systems. Two major forms of direct financing are term lending by commercial banks and the private placement of securities with insurance companies and pension funds. Term loans and private placements represent similar financing arrangements. Their advantages are avoidance of SEC registration procedures, flexibility in renegotiation of terms, and the assurance of availability of financing provided by long-term arrangements as compared with short-term bank borrowing.

Ordinarily, direct loans are retired by systematic repayments (amortization payments) over the life of the loan. Security, generally in the form of a chattel mortgage on equipment, is often employed, although the larger, stronger companies are usually able to borrow on an unsecured basis. Commercial banks typically make small short-term loans; life insurance companies and pension funds grant larger, longer-term loans.

Like rates on other credits, the cost of direct loans varies with the size of the loan and the strength of the borrower. For small loans to small companies, rates may be as high as 15 percent; for large loans to large firms, they will probably be close to the prime lending rate. Since these loans run for long periods, during which interest rates can change radically, many of them have variable interest rates, with the rate set at a certain level above the prime rate or above the Federal Reserve rediscount rate. Often, direct loans include a "kicker" in the form of warrants to purchase the borrower's equity securities near the price prevailing at the time of the loan transaction.

Another aspect of direct loans is the series of *protective covenants* contained in most loan agreements. The lender's funds are tied up for a long period, and during this time the borrower's situation can change markedly. For self-protection, the lender includes in the loan agreement stipulations that the borrower will maintain the current ratio at a specified level, limit acquisitions of additional fixed assets, keep the debt ratio below a stated amount, and so on. These provisions are necessary from the lender's point of view, but they restrict the borrower's actions.

The investment banker provides middleman services to both the seller and the buyer of new securities, helping plan the issue, underwriting it, and handling the job of selling the issue to the ultimate investor. The cost of this service to the issuer is related to the magnitude of the total job that must be performed to place the issue. The investment banker must also look to the interests of the brokerage customers; if these investors are not satisfied with the banker's products, they will deal elsewhere.

Flotation costs are lowest for bonds, higher for preferred stock, and highest for common stock. Larger companies have lower flotation costs than smaller ones for each type of security, and most companies can cut their stock flotation costs by issuing the new securities to stockholders through rights offerings. (These offerings are discussed in Chapter 19.)

The financial manager should be familiar with the federal laws regulating the issuance and trading of securities, because they influence liabilities and affect financing methods and costs. Regulation of securities trading seeks (1) to provide information that investors can utilize as a basis for judging the merits of securities, (2) to control the volume of credit used in securities trading, and (3) to provide orderly securities markets. The laws do not, however, prevent either purchase of unsound issues or wide price fluctuations.

They raise the costs of flotation somewhat, but they also probably decrease the cost of capital by increasing public confidence in the securities markets.

Questions

18.1 State several advantages to a firm that lists its stock on a major stock exchange.

18.2 Would you expect the cost of capital of a firm to be affected if it changed its status from one traded over the counter to one traded on the New York Stock Exchange? Explain.

18.3 Evaluate the following statement: Buying stocks is in the nature of true investment; stock is purchased in order to receive a dividend return on the invested capital. Short selling, on the other hand, is fundamentally a form of gambling; it is simply betting that a stock's price will decline. Consequently, if we do not wish to see Wall Street turned into an eastern Las Vegas, all short selling should be forbidden.

18.4 Evaluate the following statement: The fundamental purpose of the federal security laws dealing with new issues is to prevent investors, principally small ones, from sustaining losses on the purchase of stocks.

18.5 Suppose two similar firms are each selling $10 million of common stock. The firms are of the same size, are in the same industry, have the same leverage, and so on—except that one is publicly owned and the other is closely held.
  a. Will their costs of flotation be the same?
  b. If the issue were $10 million of bonds, would your answer be the same?

18.6 Define these terms: *brokerage firm, underwriting group, selling group,* and *investment banker.*

18.7 Each month the Securities and Exchange Commission publishes a report of the transactions made by the officers and directors of listed firms in their own companies' equity securities. Why do you suppose the SEC makes this report?

18.8 The SEC forbids officers and directors to sell short the shares of their own companies. Why do you suppose this rule is on the books?

18.9 Prior to 1933, investment banking and commercial banking were both carried on by the same firm. In that year, however, the Banking Act required that these functions be separated. On the basis of your knowledge of investment banking and commercial banking, discuss the pros and cons of this forced separation.

18.10 Before entering a formal agreement, investment bankers carefully investigate the companies whose securities they underwrite; this is especially true of the issues of firms going public for the first time.
  a. Since the bankers do not themselves plan to hold the securities but intend to sell them to others as soon as possible, why are they so concerned about making careful investigations?
  b. Does your answer to the question have any bearing on the fact that investment banking is a very difficult field to break into? Explain.

18.11 a. If competitive bidding were required on all security offerings, would flotation costs be higher or lower?

b. Would the size of the issuing firm be material in determining the effects of required competitive bidding?

18.12 Since investment bankers price new issues in relation to outstanding issues, should a spread exist between the yields on the new and the outstanding issues? Discuss this matter separately for stocks and bonds.

18.13 What issues are raised by the increasing purchase of equities by institutional investors?

Problems

18.1 Your firm is planning to sell $1.5 million of bonds with a fifteen-year maturity. The going rate on debt of this quality and maturity is 10 percent. However, total costs of the underwriting have been estimated to be 10.5 percent of gross proceeds. Calculate the cost of this debt to your firm. (Hint: Let the coupon rate be 10 percent so the bonds will sell at face value; then solve for the IRR, which will make the future payments on the bond equal to face value less 10.5 percent—that is, to $895 per bond.)

18.2 If your firm sells preferred stock in the amount of $1.5 million, the total flotation expense will be about 11.5 percent of gross proceeds. If the going rate on preferred stock of the same quality as your firm's is 12 percent, what is the effective cost of the preferred stock issue? (Assume the stock will remain outstanding in perpetuity.)

18.3 The Algonquin Table Company was planning to issue $5 million of new common stock. In reaching the decision as to the form of offering, two alternatives were considered:

1. A rights offering, with out-of-pocket cost as a percentage of new capital at 1.4 percent.
2. An underwriting, with out-of-pocket cost as a percentage of new capital at 7.0 percent.

Algonquin chose the second alternative. Given the difference in cost, this choice seems paradoxical.

a. From Table 18.3, what proportion of issues this size are made by rights offerings instead of by underwriters?

b. Discuss the influence of other factors (in addition to direct costs cited) that must be taken into account in choosing between the two alternative methods of offering. In your answer consider the following as well as other factors that may occur to you:
1. Timing of receipt of flows
2. Risk
3. Other internal benefits and costs
4. Distribution
5. Effect on stock price.

18.4 Each of three companies is considering a new offering:

1. The Crown Company is in the paint manufacturing industry and has total assets of $30 million. It contemplates a new common stock issue of $1.5 million. It has determined that use of an underwriter will be desirable.
2. The Apache Company is in the "small aircraft" industry and has assets of $1 billion. It intends a $40 million offering using rights with a standby underwriting.
3. AT&T plans a $500 million common stock offering using rights and direct sale without use of an investment banker.

What will be the compensation costs as a percent of proceeds for each of the three companies? Explain the reasons for the differences in costs.

18.5 In March 1975, three executives of the Hughes Aircraft Company, one of the largest privately owned corporations in the world, decided to break away from Hughes and to set up a company of their own. The principal reason for this decision was capital gains; Hughes Aircraft stock is all privately owned, and the corporate structure makes it impossible for executives to be granted stock purchase options. Hughes's executives receive substantial salaries and bonuses, but this income is all taxable at normal tax rates, and no capital gains opportunities are available.

The three men, Jim Adcock, Robert Goddard, and Rick Aiken, have located a medium-size electronics manufacturing company available for purchase. All the stock of this firm, Baynard Industries, is owned by the founder, Joseph Baynard. Although the company is in excellent shape, Baynard wants to sell it because of his failing health. A price of $5.7 million has been established, based on a price/earnings ratio of 12 and annual earnings of $475,000. Baynard has given the three prospective purchasers an option to purchase the company for the agreed price; the option is to run for six months, during which time the three men are to arrange financing with which to buy the firm.

Adcock has consulted with Jules Scott, a partner in the New York investment banking firm of Williams Brothers and an acquaintance of some years' standing, to seek his assistance in obtaining the funds necessary to complete the purchase. Adcock, Goddard, and Aiken each have some money available to put into the new enterprise, but they need a substantial amount of outside capital. There is some possibility of borrowing part of the money, but Scott has discouraged this idea. His reasoning is, first, that Baynard Industries is already highly leveraged, and if the purchasers were to borrow additional funds, there would be a very severe risk that they would be unable to service this debt in the event of a recession in the electronics industry. Although the firm is currently earning $475,000 a year, this figure could quickly turn into a loss in the event of a few canceled defense contracts or cost miscalculations.

Scott's second reason for discouraging a loan is that Adcock, Goddard, and Aiken plan not only to operate Baynard Industries and seek internal growth but also to use the corporation as a vehicle for making further acquisitions of electronics companies. This being the case, Scott believes that it would be wise for the company to keep any borrowing potential in reserve for use in later acquisitions. Scott proposes that the three partners obtain funds to purchase Baynard Industries in accordance with the figures shown in the following table.

Baynard Industries

Price paid to Joseph Baynard				$5,700,000
(12 × $475,000 earnings)				
Authorized shares		$5,000,000		
Initially issued shares		1,125,000		
Initial distribution of shares:				
Adcock	100,000 shares at $1.00			$ 100.000
Goddard	100,000 shares at $1.00			100,000
Aiken	100,000 shares at $1.00			100,000
Williams Brothers	125,000 shares at $7.00			875,000
Public stockholders	700,000 shares at $7.00			4,900,000
	1,125,000			$6,075,000
Underwriting costs: 5% of $4,900,000		$ 245,000		
Legal fees, and so on, associated with issue		45,000		290,000
				$5,785,000
Payment to Joseph Baynard				5,700,000
Net funds to Baynard Industries				$ 85,000

Baynard Industries would be reorganized with an authorized 5,000,000 shares, with 1,125,000 to be issued at the time the transfer takes place and the other 3,875,000 to be held in reserve for possible issuance in connection with acquisitions. Adcock, Goddard, and Aiken would each purchase 100,000 shares at a price of $1 a share, the par value. Williams Brothers would purchase 125,000 shares at a price of $7. The remaining 700,000 shares would be sold to the public at a price of $7 a share.

Williams Brothers' underwriting fee would be 5 percent of the shares sold to the public, or $245,000. Legal fees, accounting fees, and other charges associated with the issue would amount to $45,000, for a total underwriting cost of $290,000. After deducting the underwriting charges and the payment to Baynard from the gross proceeds of the stock sale, the reorganized Baynard Industries would receive funds in the amount of $85,000, which would be used for internal expansion purposes.

As a part of the initial agreement, Adcock, Goddard, and Aiken each would be given options to purchase an additional 80,000 shares at a price of $7 a share for one year. Williams Brothers would be given an option to purchase an additional 100,000 shares at $7 a share in one year.

a. What is the total underwriting charge, expressed as a percentage of the funds raised by the underwriter? Does this charge seem reasonable in the light of published statistics on the cost of floating new issues of common stock?

b. Suppose that the three men estimate the following probabilities for the firm's stock price one year from now:

Price	Probability
$ 1	0.05
5	0.10
9	0.35
13	0.35
17	0.10
21	0.05

Assuming Williams Brothers exercises its options, calculate the following ratio (ignore time-discount effects):

$$\frac{\text{Gross profit to Williams Brothers}}{\text{Funds raised by underwriter}}$$

Disregard Williams Brothers' profit on the 125,000 shares it bought outright at the initial offering. Comment on the ratio.

c. Are Adcock, Goddard, and Aiken purchasing their stock at a "fair" price? Should the prospectus disclose the fact that they would buy their stock at $1 a share, whereas public stockholders would buy their stock at $7 a share?

d. Would it be reasonable for Williams Brothers to purchase its initial 125,000 shares at a price of $1?

e. Do you foresee any problems of control for Adcock, Goddard, and Aiken?

f. Would the expectation of an exceptionally large need for investment funds next year be a relevant consideration in deciding on the amount of funds to be raised now?

CHAPTER **19** COMMON STOCK

Common equity or, if unincorporated firms are being considered, partnership or proprietorship interests constitute the first source of funds to a new business and the base of support for borrowing by existing firms. Accordingly, our discussion of specific forms of long-term financing will begin with an analysis of common stock.

Apportionment of Income, Control, and Risk

The nature of equity ownership depends on the form of the business or organization. The central problem of such ownership revolves around an apportionment of certain rights and responsibilities among those who have provided the funds necessary for the operation of the business. The rights and responsibilities attaching to equity consist of positive considerations—income potential and control of the firm—and negative considerations—loss potential, legal responsibility, and personal liability.

General Rights of Holders of Common Stock

The rights of holders of common stock in a business corporation are established by the laws of the state in which the corporation is chartered and by the terms of the charter granted by the state. Charters are relatively uniform on many matters, including collective and specific rights.

Collective Rights Certain collective rights are usually given to the holders of common stock. Some of the more important rights allow stockholders (1) to amend the charter with the approval of the appropriate officials in the state of incorporation, (2) to adopt and amend bylaws, (3) to elect the directors of the corporation, (4) to authorize the sale of fixed assets, (5) to enter into mergers, (6) to change the amount of authorized common stock, and (7) to issue preferred stock, debentures, bonds, and other securities.

Specific Rights Holders of common stock also have specific rights as individual owners: (1) the right to vote in the manner prescribed by the corporate charter, (2) the right to sell their stock certificates (their evidence of ownership) and in this way to transfer their ownership interest to other persons, (3) the right to inspect the corporate books,[1] and (4) the right to share residual assets of the corporation on dissolution. (However, the holders of common stock are last among the claimants to the assets of the corporation.)

---

1. Obviously, a corporation cannot have its business affairs disturbed by allowing every stockholder to go through any records the stockholder wants to inspect. Furthermore, a corporation cannot wisely permit a competitor who buys shares of its common stock to look at all the corporation records. There must be, and there are, practical limitations to this right.

Apportionment of Income

Two important positive considerations are involved in equity ownership: income and control. The right to income carries the risk of loss. Control also involves responsibility and liability. In an individual proprietorship that uses funds supplied only by the owner, the owner has a 100 percent right to income and control and to loss and responsibility. As soon as the proprietor incurs debt, however, he or she has entered into contracts that limit the freedom to control the firm and to apportion the firm's income. In a partnership, these rights are apportioned among the partners in an agreed-upon manner. In the absence of a formal agreement, a division is made by state law. In a corporation, more significant issues arise concerning the rights of the owners.

Apportionment of Control

Through the right to vote, holders of common stock have legal control of the corporation. As a practical matter, however, in many corporations the principal officers constitute all, or a majority, of the members of the board of directors. In this circumstance the board may be controlled by the management rather than by the owners. However, numerous examples demonstrate that stockholders can reassert their control if they are dissatisfied with the corporation's policies. In recent years, proxy battles with the aim of altering corporate policies have occurred fairly often, and firms whose managers are unresponsive to stockholders' desires are subject to takeover bids by other firms.

As receivers of residual income, holders of common stock are frequently referred to as the ultimate entrepreneurs in the firm. They are the ultimate owners, and they have the ultimate control. Presumably the firm is managed on behalf of the holders of common stock, but there has been much dispute about the actual situation. The point of view has been expressed that the corporation is an institution with an existence separate from the owners, that it exists to fulfill certain functions for stockholders as only one among other important groups, such as workers, consumers, and the economy as a whole. While this view has some validity, ordinarily the officers of a firm are also large stockholders. In addition, more and more firms are relating officers' compensation to the firm's profit performance, either by granting executives stock purchase options or by giving them bonuses. These actions are, of course, designed to make managers' personal goals more consistent with those of the stockholders—to increase the firm's earnings and stock price.

Apportionment of Risk

Another consideration involved in equity ownership is risk. Because, on liquidation, holders of common stock are last in the priority of claims, the portion of capital they contribute provides a cushion for creditors if losses occur on dissolution. The equity to total assets ratio indicates the percentage by which assets may shrink in value on liquidation before creditors will incur losses.

For example, compare two corporations, A and B, whose balance sheets are shown in Table 19.1. The ratio of equity to total assets in Corporation A is 80 percent. Total assets will therefore have to shrink by 80 percent before creditors will lose money. By contrast, in Corporation B the extent by which assets will have to shrink in value on liquidation before creditors lose money is only 40 percent.

Table 19.1
Balance Sheets for Corporations A and B

	Corporation A			Corporation B	
		Debt	$ 20		Debt	$ 60
		Equity	80		Equity	40
Total assets $100		Total claims $100	Total assets $100		Total claims $100

Common Stock Financing

Before undertaking an evaluation of common stock financing, more of the important characteristics of such stock will be described: (1) the nature of voting rights, (2) the nature of the preemptive right, and (3) variations in the forms of common stock.

Nature of Voting Rights

For each share of common stock owned, the holder has the right to cast one vote at the annual meeting of stockholders or at such special meetings as may be called.

Proxy Provision is made for the temporary transfer of the right to vote by an instrument known as a *proxy*. The transfer is limited in its duration; typically it applies only to a specific occasion such as the annual meeting of stockholders.

The SEC supervises the use of the proxy machinery and frequently issues rules and regulations to improve its administration. SEC supervision is justified for at least two reasons:

1. If the proxy machinery is left wholly in the hands of management, there is a danger that the incumbent management will be self-perpetuated.
2. If it is made easy for minority groups of stockholders and opposition stockholders to oust management, there is a danger that they will gain control of the corporation for temporary advantages or to place their friends in management positions.

Cumulative Voting A method of voting that has come into increased prominence is cumulative voting. Cumulative voting for directors is required in twenty-two states, including California, Illinois, Pennsylvania, Ohio, and Michigan. It is permissible in eighteen, including Delaware, New York, and New Jersey. Ten states make no provision for it.

Cumulative voting permits multiple votes for a single director. For example, suppose six directors are to be elected. The owner of 100 shares can cast 100 votes for each of the six openings. Cumulatively, then, the stockholder has 600 votes. When cumulative voting is permitted, the stockholder can accumulate the votes and cast all of them for *one* director, instead of 100 each for *six* directors. Cumulative voting is designed to enable a minority group of stockholders to obtain some voice in the control of the company by electing at least one director to the board.

The nature of cumulative voting is illustrated by the use of the following formula:

$$req. = \frac{des.(n)}{\# + 1} + 1. \tag{19.1}$$

where:

$req.$ = number of shares required to elect a desired number of directors.
$des.$ = number of directors stockholder desires to elect.
  n = total number of shares of common stock outstanding and entitled to be voted.[2]
  $\#$ = total number of directors to be elected.

The formula can be made more meaningful by an example. The ABC company will elect six directors. There are fifteen candidates and 100,000 shares entitled to be voted. If a group desires to elect two directors, how many shares must it have?

$$req. = \frac{2 \times 100,000}{6 + 1} + 1 = 28,572.$$

Observe the significance of the formula. Here, a minority group wishes to elect one-third of the board of directors. It can achieve its goal by owning less than one-third the number of shares of stock.[3]

---

2. An alternative that may be agreed to by the contesting parties is to define *n* as the number of shares *voted,* not *authorized to be voted.* This procedure, which in effect gives each group seeking to elect directors the same percentage of directors as their percentage of the voted stock, is frequently followed. When it is used, a group that seeks to gain control with a minimum investment must estimate the percentage of shares that will be voted and then obtain control of more than 50 percent of that number.
3. Note also that at least 14,287 shares must be controlled to elect one director. Any number less than that constitutes a useless minority.

Alternatively, assuming that a group holds 40,000 shares of stock in the company, how many directors can it elect following the rigid assumptions of the formula? The formula can be used in its present form or can be solved for *des.* and expressed as:

$$des. = \frac{(req. - 1)(\# + 1)}{n}. \qquad (19.2)$$

Inserting the figures, the calculation is:

$$des. = \frac{39,999 \times 7}{100,000} = 2.8.$$

The 40,000 shares can thus elect two and eight-tenths directors. Since directors cannot exist as fractions, the group can elect only two directors.

As a practical matter, suppose that in the above situation the total number of shares is 100,000; hence 60,000 shares remain in other hands. The voting of all the 60,000 shares may not be concentrated. Suppose the 60,000 shares (cumulatively 360,000 votes) not held by the minority group are distributed equally among ten candidates—with 36,000 shares held by each candidate. If the minority group's 240,000 votes are distributed equally among each of six candidates, it can elect all six directors even though it does not have a majority of the stock.

Actually, it is difficult to make assumptions about how the opposition votes will be distributed. What is shown here is a good example of game theory. One rule in this theory is to assume that your opponents will do the worst they can do to you and to counter with actions to minimize the maximum loss. This is the kind of assumption followed in the formula. If the opposition concentrates its votes in the optimum manner, what is the best you can do to work in the direction of your goal? Other plausible assumptions can be substituted if there are sufficient facts to support alternative hypotheses about the opponents' behavior.

Preemptive Right   The preemptive right gives holders of common stock the first option to purchase additional issues of common stock. In some states, this right is made part of every corporate charter; in others, it is necessary to insert the right specifically in the charter.

The purpose of the preemptive right is twofold. First, it protects the power of control of present stockholders. If it were not for this safeguard, the management of a corporation under criticism from stockholders could prevent stockholders from removing it from office by issuing a large number of additional shares at a very low price and purchasing these shares itself. Management would thereby secure control of the corporation to frustrate the will of the current stockholders.

The second, and by far the more important, protection that the preemptive right affords stockholders concerns dilution of value. For example, assume that 1,000 shares of common stock, each with price of $100, are outstanding—making the total market value of the firm $100,000. An additional 1,000 shares are sold at $50 a share—a total of $50,000—thereby raising the market value of the firm to $150,000. When the total market value is divided by the new total shares outstanding, a value of $75 a share is obtained. Thus selling common stock at below market value will dilute the price of the stock and will be detrimental to present stockholders and beneficial to those who purchase the new shares. The preemptive right prevents such occurrences. (This point is discussed at length later in the chapter.)

Forms of Common Stock[4]

Classified Classified common stock was used extensively in the late 1920s, sometimes in ways that misled investors. During that period Class A common stock was usually nonvoting, and Class B was usually voting. Thus promoters could control companies by selling large amounts of Class A stock while retaining Class B stock.

In more recent years there has been a revival of Class B common stock for sound purposes. It is used by small, new companies seeking to acquire funds from outside sources. Class A common stock is sold to the public and typically pays dividends; its holders have full voting rights. Class B common stock is retained by the organizers of the company, but dividends are not paid on it until the company has established its earning power. By the use of this classified stock, the public can take a position in a conservatively financed growth company without sacrificing income.

Founders' Shares Founders' shares are somewhat like Class B stock except that they carry *sole* voting rights and typically do not confer the right to dividends for a number of years. Thus the organizers of the firm are able to maintain complete control of the operations in the firm's crucial initial development. At the same time, other investors are protected against excessive withdrawals of funds by owners.

---

4. Besides *common stock,* accountants also use the term *par value* to designate an arbitrary value assigned when stock is sold. When a firm sells newly issued stock, it must record the transaction on its balance sheet. For example, suppose a newly created firm commences operations by selling 100,000 shares at $10 a share, raising a total of $1 million. This $1 million must appear on the balance sheet. But what will it be called? One choice is to assign the stock a "par value" of $10 and label the $1 million "common stock." Another choice is to assign a $1 par value and show $100,000 ($1 par value × 100,000 shares) as "common stock" and $900,000 as "paid-in surplus." Still another choice is to disregard the term *par value* entirely—that is, use no-par stock—and record the $1 million as "common stock." Since the choice is quite arbitrary for all practical purposes, more and more firms are adopting the last procedure and abolishing the term *par value.* Because there are quite enough useful concepts and terms in accounting and finance, we heartily applaud the demise of useless ones such as this.

Evaluation of Common Stock as a Source of Funds

Thus far, the chapter has covered the main characteristics of common stock (frequently referred to as equity shares). Now it will appraise this type of financing from the viewpoint of the issuer and from a social viewpoint.

From the Viewpoint of the Issuer

Advantages There are several advantages to the issuer of financing with common stock:

1. Common stock does not entail fixed charges. If the company generates the earnings, it can pay common stock dividends. In contrast to bond interest, however, there is no legal obligation to pay dividends.
2. Common stock carries no fixed maturity date.
3. Since common stock provides a cushion against losses of creditors, the sale of common stock increases the creditworthiness of the firm.
4. Common stock can at times be sold more easily than debt. It appeals to certain investor groups because (a) it typically carries a higher expected return than does preferred stock or debt; and (b) since it represents the ownership of the firm, it provides the investor with a better hedge against inflation than does straight preferred stock or bonds. Ordinarily, common stock increases in value when the value of real assets rises during an inflationary period.[5]
5. Returns from common stock in the form of capital gains are subject to the lower personal income tax rates on capital gains. Hence the effective personal income tax rates on returns from common stock may be lower than the effective tax rates on the interest on debt.

Disadvantages Disadvantages to the issuer of common stock are:

1. The sale of common stock extends voting rights or control to the additional stock owners who are brought into the company. For this reason, among others, additional equity financing is often avoided by small and new firms, whose owner-managers may be unwilling to share control of their companies with outsiders.
2. Common stock gives more owners the right to share in income. The use of debt may enable the firm to utilize funds at a fixed low cost, whereas common stock gives equal rights to new stockholders to share in the net profits of the firm.

---

5. During the inflation of the last decade, the lags of product price increases behind the rise of input costs have depressed corporate earnings and increased the uncertainty of earnings growth, causing price/earnings multiples to fall.

3. As we saw in Chapter 18, the costs of underwriting and distributing common stock are usually higher than those for underwriting and distributing preferred stock or debt. Flotation costs for selling common stock are characteristically higher because (a) costs of investigating an equity security investment are higher than investigating the feasibility of a comparable debt security; and (b) stocks are more risky, which means equity holdings must be diversified, which in turn means that a given dollar amount of new stock must be sold to a greater number of purchasers than the same amount of debt.

4. As we saw in Chapter 16, if the firm has more equity or less debt than is called for in the optimum capital structure, the average cost of capital will be higher than necessary.

5. Common stock dividends are not deductible as an expense for calculating the corporation's income subject to the federal income tax, but bond interest is deductible. The impact of this factor is reflected in the relative cost of equity capital vis-à-vis debt capital.

From a Social Viewpoint

From a social viewpoint, common stock is a desirable form of financing because it renders business firms (a major segment of the economy) less vulnerable to the consequences of declines in sales and earnings. Common stock financing involves no fixed charges, the payment of which might force a faltering firm into reorganization or bankruptcy.

However, another aspect of common stock financing may have less desirable social consequences. Common stock prices fall in recessions, which represents a rise in the cost of equity capital. The rising cost of equity raises the overall cost of capital, which in turn reduces investment. This reduction further aggravates the recession. However, an expanding economy is accompanied by rising stock prices, and with rising stock prices comes a drop in the cost of capital. This in turn stimulates investment, which may add to a developing inflationary boom. In summary, a consideration of its effect on the cost of capital suggests that stock financing may tend to amplify cyclical fluctuations. Just how these opposing forces combine to produce a net effect is unknown, but the authors believe that the first is the stronger—that stock financing tends to stabilize the economy.

Use of Rights in Financing

If the preemptive right is contained in a firm's charter, then the firm must offer any new common stock to existing stockholders. If the charter does not prescribe a preemptive right, the firm has a choice of making the sale to its existing stockholders or to an entirely new set of investors. If it sells to the existing stockholders, the stock flotation is called a *rights offering.* Each stockholder is issued an option to buy a certain number of the new shares, and the terms of the option are contained on a piece of paper called a *right.* Each stockholder receives one right for each share of stock owned. The advantages and disadvantages of rights offerings are described in the following section.

Theoretical Relationships of Rights Offerings

Several issues confront the financial manager who is deciding on the details of a rights offering. The various considerations can be shown by the use of illustrative data on the Southeast Company, whose balance sheet and income statement are given in Table 19.2.

Southeast earns $4 million after taxes and has 1 million shares outstanding, so earnings per share are $4. The stock sells at 25 times earnings, or for $100 a share. The company plans to raise $10 million of new equity funds through a rights offering and decides to sell the new stock to shareholders for $80 a share. The questions now facing the financial manager are:

1. How many rights will be required to purchase a share of the newly issued stock?
2. What is the value of each right?
3. What effect will the rights offering have on the price of the existing stock?

Table 19.2
Southeast Company Financial Statements before Rights Offering

Partial Balance Sheet

	Total debt (at 5%)	$ 40,000,000
	Common stock	10,000,000
	Retained earnings	50,000,000
Total assets $100,000,000	Total liabilities and capital	$100,000,000

Partial Income Statement

Total earnings	$10,000,000
Interest on debt	2,000,000
Income before taxes	$ 8,000,000
Taxes (50% assumed)	4,000,000
Earnings after taxes	$ 4,000,000
Earnings per share (1 million shares)	$4
Market price of stock (price/earnings ratio of 25 assumed)	$100

Number of Rights Needed to Purchase a New Share

As already mentioned, Southeast plans to raise $10 million in new equity funds and to sell the new stock at a price of $80 a share. Dividing the subscription price into the total funds to be raised gives the number of shares to be issued:

$$\text{Number of new shares} = \frac{\text{Funds to be raised}}{\text{Subscription price}} = \frac{\$10,000,000}{\$80}$$

$$= 125,000 \text{ shares.}$$

The next step is to divide the number of new shares into the number of previously outstanding shares to get the number of rights required to subscribe to one share of the new stock. Note that stockholders always receive one right for each share of stock they own:

$$\frac{\text{Number of rights needed to}}{\text{buy a share of the stock}} = \frac{\text{Old shares}}{\text{New shares}} = \frac{1,000,000}{125,000} = 8 \text{ rights.}$$

Therefore, a stockholder will have to surrender eight rights plus $80 to receive one of the newly issued shares. If the subscription price had been set at $95 a share, 9.5 rights would have been required to subscribe to each new share; if the price had been set at $10 a share, only 1 right would have been needed.

Value of a Right

It is clearly worth something to be able to pay less than $100 for a share of stock selling for $100. The right provides this privilege, so it must have a value. To see how the theoretical value of a right is established, we continue with the example of the Southeast Company, assuming that it will raise $10 million by selling 125,000 new shares at $80 a share.

Notice that the *market value* of the old stock was $100 million: $100 a share times 1 million shares. (The book value is irrelevant.) When the firm sells the new stock, it brings in an additional $10 million. As a first approximation, assume that the market value of the common stock increases by exactly this $10 million. Actually, the market value of all the common stock will go up by more than $10 million if investors think the company will be able to invest these funds at a yield substantially in excess of the cost of equity capital, but it will go up by less than $10 million if investors are doubtful of the company's ability to put the new funds to work profitably in the near future.

Under the assumption that market value exactly reflects the new funds brought in, the total market value of the common stock after the new issue will be $110 million. Dividing this new value by the new total number of shares outstanding, 1.125 million, gives a new market value of $97.78 a share. Therefore, after the financing has been completed, the price of the common stock will have fallen from $100 to $97.78.

Since the rights give the stockholders the privilege of paying only $80 for a share of stock that will end up being worth $97.78—thereby saving them $17.78—is $17.78 the value of each right? The answer is no, because eight rights are required to buy one new share. The $17.78 must be divided by 8 to get the value of each right. In the example, each one is worth $2.22.

Ex Rights

The Southeast Company's rights have a very definite value, and this value accrues to the holders of the common stock. But what happens if stock is traded during the offering period? Who will receive the rights—the old owners or the new? The standard procedure calls for the company to set a *holder of record date* and for the stock to go *ex rights* after that date. If the stock is sold prior to the ex rights date, the new owner receives the rights; if it is sold on or after the ex rights date, the old owner receives them. For example, on October 15, Southeast Company announces the terms of the new financing; the company states that rights will be mailed out on December 1 to stockholders of record as of the close of business on November 15. Anyone buying the old stock on or before November 15 will receive the rights; anyone buying the stock on or after November 16 will *not* receive them. Thus November 16 is the *ex rights date;* before November 16 the stock sells *rights on.* In the case of Southeast Company, the rights-on price is $100, and the ex rights price is $97.78.

Formula Value of a Right

Rights on Equations have been developed for determining the value of rights without going through all the procedures described above. While the stock is still selling rights on, the value at which the rights will sell when they are issued can be found by use of the following formula:

$$\frac{\text{Value of}}{\text{one right}} = \frac{\text{Market value of stock, rights on} - \text{Subscription price}}{\text{Number of rights required to purchase 1 share} + 1}$$

$$v_r = \frac{p_0 - p^s}{\# + 1}, \tag{19.3}$$

where:

p_0 = the rights-on price of the stock.
p^s = the subscription price.
$\#$ = the number of rights required to purchase a new share of stock.
v_r = the value of one right.

Substituting the appropriate values for the Southeast Company:

$$v_r = \frac{\$100 - \$80}{8 + 1} = \frac{\$20}{9} = \$2.22.$$

This agrees with the value of the rights found by the step-by-step analysis.

509

Ex Rights Suppose you are a stockholder in the Southeast Company. When you return to the United States from a trip to Europe, you read about the rights offering in the newspaper. The stock is now selling ex rights for $97.78 a share. How can you calculate the theoretical value of a right? By using the following formula, which follows the logic described in preceding sections, you can determine the value of each right:

$$\frac{\text{Value of}}{\text{one right}} = \frac{\text{Market value of stock, ex rights} - \text{Subscription price}}{\text{Number of rights required to purchase 1 share}}$$

$$V_r = \frac{p_e - p^s}{\#} \qquad (19.4)$$

$$= \frac{\$97.78 - \$80}{8} = \frac{\$17.78}{8} = \$2.22.$$

Here, p_e is the ex rights price of the stock.[6]

Effects on Position of Stockholders

Stockholders have the choice of exercising their rights or selling them. If they have sufficient funds and want to buy more shares of the company's stock, they will exercise the rights. If they do not have the money or do not want to buy more stock, they will sell the rights. In either case, provided the formula value of the rights holds true, stockholders will neither benefit nor lose by the rights offering. This statement can be made clear by considering the position of an individual stockholder in the Southeast Company.

---

6. We developed Equation 19.4 directly from the verbal explanation given in the immediately preceding section. Equation 19.3 can thus be derived from Equation 19.4 as follows:

$$p_e = p_0 - v_r. \qquad (19.5)$$

Substituting Equation 19.5 into Equation 19.4:

$$V_r = \frac{p_0 - v_r - p^s}{\#} \qquad (19.6)$$

Simplifying Equation 19.6:

$$V_r = \frac{p_0 - p^s}{\#} - \frac{v_r}{\#}$$

$$V_r + \frac{v_r}{\#} = \frac{p_0 - p^s}{\#}$$

$$V_r\left(\frac{\# + 1}{\#}\right) = \frac{p_0 - p^s}{\#}$$

$$V_r = \frac{p_0 - p^s}{\#} \cdot \frac{\#}{\# + 1}$$

$$V_r = \frac{p_0 - p^s}{\# + 1}$$

The result is Equation 19.3.

The stockholder has eight shares of stock before the rights offering. Each share has a market value of $100, so the stockholder has a total market value of $800 in the company's stock. If, after the rights offering, he exercises his rights, he will be able to purchase one additional share at $80—a new investment of $80. His total investment will be $880; and he will own nine shares of the company's stock, which now has a value of $97.78 a share. The value of his stock will be $880, exactly what he has invested in it.

Alternatively, if he sells his eight rights, which have a value of $2.22 a right, he will receive $17.78. He will thus have his original eight shares of stock plus $17.78 in cash. But his original eight shares of stock now have a market price of $97.78 a share. The $782.22 market value of his stock plus the $17.78 in cash is the same as the $800 market value of stock with which he began.

From a purely mechanical or arithmetical standpoint, stockholders neither gain nor lose from the sale of additional shares of stock through rights. Of course, if they forget to exercise or sell the rights, or if the brokerage costs of selling are excessive, then they can suffer a loss. But the issuing firm generally makes special efforts to minimize brokerage costs and to allow enough time for the stockholder to take some action, so losses are minimal.

Oversubscription Privilege

Even though the rights are very valuable and should be exercised, some stockholders neglect to do so. Still, all the stock is sold because of the *oversubscription privilege* contained in most rights offerings. This privilege gives subscribing stockholders the right to buy, on a pro rata basis, all shares not taken in the initial offering. To illustrate: If Jane Doe owns 10 percent of the stock in Southeast Company, and if 20 percent of the rights offered by the company are not exercised (or sold) by the stockholders to whom they were originally given, then she can buy an additional 2.5 percent of the new stock.[7] Since this stock is a bargain—$80 for stock worth $97.78— Jane Doe and other stockholders will use the oversubscription privilege, thereby assuring the full sale of the new stock issue.

Relationship between Market Price and Subscription Price

We can now investigate the factors influencing the use of rights and, if they are used, the level at which the subscription price is set. The Southeast Company's articles of incorporation permit the firm to decide whether or not to use rights, depending on whether their use is advantageous to the firm and its stockholders. The financial vice-president of the company is considering three methods of raising the sum of $10 million:

7. Eighty percent of the stock was subscribed. Since Jane Doe subscribed to 10/80, or 12.5 percent, of the stock that was taken, she can obtain 12.5 percent of the unsubscribed stock. Therefore, her oversubscription allocation is 12.5 percent × 20 = 2.5 percent of the new stock.

1. The company could sell to the public, through investment bankers, additional shares at approximately $100 a share. The company would net approximately $96 a share; thus it would need to sell 105,000 shares in order to cover the underwriting commission.

2. The company could sell additional shares through rights, using investment bankers and paying a commission of 1 percent on the total dollar amount of the stock sold plus an additional $3/4$ percent on all shares unsubscribed and taken over by the investment bankers. Allowing for the usual market pressure when common stock is sold, the new shares would be sold at a 20 percent discount, or at $80. Thus 125,000 additional shares would be offered through rights. With eight rights, an additional share could be purchased at $80. Since stockholders are given the right to subscribe to any unexercised rights on a pro rata basis, only those shares not subscribed to on the original or secondary level are sold to the underwriters and subjected to the $3/4$ percent additional commission.

3. The company could sell additional shares through rights, at $10 a share, and not use investment bankers. The number of additional shares of common stock to be sold would be 1 million. For each right held, existing stockholders would be permitted to buy one share of the new common stock.

Method 1 uses investment bankers and no rights at all. In this circumstance the underwriting commission, or flotation cost, is approximately 4 percent. In Method 2, where rights are used with a small discount, the underwriting commission is reduced, because the discount removes much of the risk of not being able to sell the issue. The underwriting commission consists of two parts—1 percent on the original issue and an additional $3/4$ percent commission on all unsubscribed shares the investment bankers are required to take over and sell. Thus the actual commission ranges somewhere between 1 percent and $1 3/4$ percent. Under Method 3, the subscription price is $10 a share. With such a large concession, the company does not need to use investment bankers at all, because the rights are certain to have value and to be either exercised or sold. Which of the three methods is superior?

Method 1 provides a wider distribution of the securities sold, thereby lessening any possible control problems. The investment bankers assure that the company will receive the $10 million involved in the new issue, and they give the firm ongoing financial counsel. The company pays for these services in the form of underwriting charges. After the issue, the stock price should be approximately $100.

Under Method 2, by utilizing rights, the company reduces its underwriting expenses and the unit price per share (from $100 to $97.78). Some stockholders may suffer a loss because they neither exercise nor sell their rights. Existing stockholders will buy some of the new shares, so the distribution is likely to be narrower than under Method 1. Because of the underwriting contract, the firm is assured of receiving the funds sought. Finally, investors often like the opportunity to purchase additional shares through rights offerings; thus their use may increase stockholder loyalty.

Method 3 involves no underwriting expense and results in a substantial decrease in the unit price of shares. Initially, however, the shares are less widely distributed than under either of the other two methods. Method 3 also has a large stock-split effect, which results in a much lower final stock price per share than under either of the other two methods.[8] Many people feel that there is an optimal stock price—one that will produce a maximum total market value of the shares—and that this price is generally in the range of $30 to $60 a share. If this is the feeling of Southeast's directors, they may believe that Method 3 will permit them to reach the more desirable price range while at the same time reducing flotation costs on the new issue. However, since the rights have a substantial value, any stockholder who fails either to exercise or to sell them will suffer a serious loss.

The three methods are summarized in Table 19.3. The most advantageous method depends on the company's needs. For a company strongly interested in wide distribution of its securities, Method 1 is preferable. For a firm most interested in reducing the unit price of its shares and confident that the lower unit price will induce wide distribution, Method 3 is preferable. For a company whose needs are moderate in both directions, Method 2 may offer a satisfactory compromise. Whether rights will be used and the level of the subscription price both depend on the company's needs at a particular time.

**Table 19.3
Summary of Three Methods of
Raising Additional Money**

	Advantages	Disadvantages
Method 1	1. Wide distribution 2. Certainty of receiving funds	1. High underwriting costs
Method 2	1. Small underwriting costs 2. Low unit price of shares 3. Certainty of receiving funds 4. Increased stockholder loyalty	1. Narrow distribution 2. Losses to forgetful stockholders
Method 3	1. No underwriting costs 2. Substantial decrease in unit price of shares 3. Increased stockholder loyalty	1. Narrow distribution 2. Severe losses to forgetful stockholders

8. Stock splits are discussed in Chapter 17. Basically, a stock split is simply the issuance of additional shares to existing stockholders for *no* additional funds. Stock splits divide the "pie" into more pieces.

Exercise of Rights

Interestingly enough, it is expected that a small percentage of stockholders will neglect to exercise or to sell their rights. In a recent offering, the holders of $1\frac{1}{2}$ percent of General Motors common stock did not exercise their rights. The loss experienced by these stockholders was $1.5 million. In a recent AT&T issue, the loss to shareholders who neglected to exercise their rights was $960,000.

Market Price and Subscription Price

Measured from the registration date for the new issue of the security, the average percentage by which the subscription prices of new issues were below their market prices has been about 15 percent in recent years. Examples of price concessions of 40 percent or more can be observed in a small percentage of issues, but the most frequently encountered discounts are from 10 to 20 percent.

Effect on Subsequent Behavior of Market Price

It is often said that issuing new stock through rights will depress the price of the company's existing common stock. To the extent that a subscription price in connection with the rights offering is lower than the market price, there will be a "stock-split effect" on the market price of the common stock. With the prevailing market price of Southeast Company's stock at $100 and a $10 subscription price, the new market price will probably drop to about $55.

But whether, because of the rights offering, the actual new market price will be $55 or lower or higher is unknown. Again, empirical analysis of the movement in stock prices during rights offerings indicates that generalization is not practical. What happens to the market prices of the stock ex rights and after the rights trading period depends on the future earnings prospects of the issuing company.

Advantages of Use of Rights in New Financing

The preemptive right gives shareholders the protection of preserving their pro rata share in the earnings and control of the company. It also benefits the firm. By offering new issues of securities to existing stockholders, the firm increases the likelihood of a favorable reception for the stock. By their ownership of common stock in the company, investors have already evaluated the company favorably. They may, therefore be receptive to the purchase of additional shares, particularly when the following information is taken into account.

The shares purchased with rights are subject to lower margin requirements. For example, margin requirements since January 1974 have been 50 percent; in other words, people buying listed stocks must put up at least $50 of their own funds for every $100 of securities purchased. However, if shares of new stock issues are purchased with rights, only $25 per $100 of common stock purchased must be furnished by investors; they are permitted by law to borrow up to 75 percent of the purchase price. Furthermore, the absence of a clear pattern in the price behavior of the adjusted market price of the stocks and rights before, during, and after the trading period may enhance interest in the investment possibilities of the instruments.

These factors can offset the tendency toward a downward pressure on the price of the common stock occurring at the time of a new issue.[9] With the increased interest in (and advantages afforded by) the rights offering, the "true" or "adjusted" downward price pressure may actually be avoided.

A related advantage is that the issuer's flotation costs associated with a rights offering are lower than the cost of a public flotation. Costs referred to here are cash costs. For example, the flotation costs of common stock issues during the period 1971–1975 were 6.17 percent on public issues compared with 2.45 percent on rights offerings.[10]

The financial manager can obtain positive benefits from underpricing. Since a rights offering is a stock split to a certain degree, it causes the market price of the stock to fall to a level lower than it otherwise will be. But stock splits can increase the number of shareholders in a company by bringing the price of a stock down to a more attractive trading level. Furthermore, a rights offering may be associated with increased dividends for the stock owners.[11]

In general, a rights offering can stimulate an enthusiastic response from stockholders and from the investment market as a whole, with the result that opportunities for financing become more attractive to the firm. Thus the financial manager may be able to engage in common stock financing at lower costs and under more favorable terms.

Choosing among Alternative Forms of Financing	A pattern of analysis can be formulated for choosing among alternative forms of financing. This framework applies to the decision choices involved in evaluating the other major forms of financing covered: various forms of debt, preferred stock, lease financing, and financing in international markets, among others. Thus the pattern of analysis has broad applications.

9. The downward pressure develops because of an increase in the supply of securities without a necessarily equivalent increase in the demand. Generally it is a temporary phenomenon, and the stock tends to return to the theoretical price after a few months. Obviously, if the acquired funds are invested at a very high rate of return, the stock price benefits; if the investment does not turn out well, the stock price suffers.

10. C. W. Smith, Jr., "Substitute Methods for Raising Additional Capital: Rights Offerings versus Underwritten Issues," *Journal of Financial Economics* 5 (December 1977).

11. The increased dividends may convey information that the prospective earnings of the firm have improved and may result in a higher market price for the firm's stock.

The framework set forth brings together a number of topics that have already been treated. Risk aspects were covered in Chapters 5 and 15. Relative costs were covered in Chapters 14 and 16. Control was discussed earlier in this chapter.

To make the application of the concepts more concrete, a case example will be used as a vehicle for illustrating the procedures involved. Stanton Chemicals has estimated that it will need to raise $200 million for an expansion program. The company discusses with its investment bankers whether it should raise the $200 million through debt financing or through selling additional shares of common stock. The bankers are asked to make their recommendation to Stanton's board of directors using the following information on industry financial ratios and on the basis of the company's 1978 balance sheet (Table 19–4) and income statement (Table 19–5):

Chemical Industry Financial Ratios

Current ratio: 2.0 times
Sales to total assets: 1.6 times
Current debt to total assets: 30%
Long-term debt to net worth: 40%
Total debt to total assets: 50%
Coverage of fixed charges: 7 times
Net income to sales: 5%
Return on total assets: 9%
Net income to net worth: 13%

Table 19.4
Stanton Chemicals Company
Balance Sheet as of
December 31, 1978
(Millions of Dollars)

Assets		Liabilities		
Total current assets	$1,000	Notes payable (at 10%)	$300	
Net fixed assets	800	Other current liabilities	400	
		Total current liabilities		$ 700
		Long-term debt (at 10%)		300
		Total debt		$1,000
		Common stock, par value $1		100
		Paid-in capital		300
		Retained earnings		400
Total assets	$1,800	Total claims on assets		$1,800

Table 19.5
Stanton Chemicals Company
Income Statement for Year
Ended December 31, 1978
(Millions of Dollars)

	1978	Pro Forma after Financing
Total revenues	$3,000	$3,400
Depreciation expense	200	220
Other costs	2,484	2,820
Net operating income	$ 316	$ 360
Interest expense	60	
Net income before taxes	$ 256	
Income taxes (at 50%)	128	
Net income to equity	$ 128	

Stanton's dividend payout has averaged about 30 percent of net income. At present, its cost of debt is 10 percent and its cost of equity 14 percent. If the additional funds are raised by debt, the cost of debt will be 12 percent, and the cost of equity will rise to 16 percent. If the funds are raised by equity, the cost of debt will remain at 10 percent, and the cost of equity will fall to 12 percent; new equity will initially be sold at $9 per share.

Stanton's common stock is widely held; there is no strong control group. The market parameters are a risk-free rate of 6 percent and an expected return on the market of 11 percent. The debt will carry a maturity of ten years and will require a sinking fund of $20 million per year.

In their analysis of which form of financing should be chosen, the investment bankers consider the following factors:

Risk
1. Financial structure
2. Fixed charge coverage
3. Coverage of cash flow requirements
4. Level of beta

Relative costs
1. Effects on market value per share of common stock
2. Effects on cost of capital

Effects on control

The solution process proceeds as follows. First, the two forms of financing are examined with reference to the firm's risk as measured by its financial structure (see Table 19.6). Stanton fails to meet the industry standards on both the short-term and total debt ratios. If it finances with debt, its financial structure ratios will be further deficient. If it finances with equity, its long-term debt to net worth ratio will be strengthened, and it will meet the industry standard for the total debt to total asset ratio. Stanton should therefore seek to fund some short-term debt into longer-term debt in the future, and it should try to build up its equity base further from retained earnings.

Stanton's fixed charge coverage is analyzed next—in Table 19.7. The table shows that the company's fixed charge coverage is below the industry standard. The use of debt financing will further aggravate the weakness in this area. The use of equity financing will move the company toward the industry standard.

Table 19.6
Stanton Financial Structure
(Millions of Dollars)

| | Present | | Pro Forma | | | | Industry Standard |
| | | | Debt | | Equity | | |
	Amount	Percent	Amount	Percent	Amount	Percent	Percent
Current debt	$ 700	39	$ 700	35	$ 700	35	30
Long-term debt	300	17	500	25	300	15	20
Total debt	$1,000	56	$1,200	60	$1,000	50	50
Equity	800	44	800	40	1,000	50	
Total assets	$1,800	100	$2,000	100	$2,000	100	
Long-term debt to net worth		38		62		30	40

Table 19.7
Fixed Charge Coverage
(Millions of Dollars)

| | | Pro Forma | | Industry Standard |
	Present	Debt	Equity	
Net operating income	$316	$360	$360	
Interest expenses	60	84	60	
Coverage ratio	5.27	4.29	6.00	7.00

Stanton's cash flow coverage is analyzed in Table 19.8. To obtain the cash inflow, depreciation expense is added to net operating income. To obtain the cash outflow requirements, the before-tax sinking fund payment is added to the interest expenses. The sinking fund payments must be placed on a before-tax basis because they are not a tax-deductible expense.

The resulting cash flow coverage ratios appear satisfactory when measured against the industry standard of 3.00. However, this result has to be qualified by the recognition that a full analysis of cash flow coverage must consider other cash outflow requirements. These will include scheduled principal repayments on debt obligations, preferred stock dividends, payments under lease obligations, and probably some capital expenditures that

Table 19.8
Stanton's Cash Flow Coverage
(Millions of Dollars)

| | | Pro Forma | | |
	Present	Debt	Equity	Industry Standard
Net operating income	$316	$360	$360	
Depreciation expense	200	220	220	
Cash inflow	$516	$580	$580	
Interest expenses	60	84	60	
Sinking fund payments	20	40	20	
Before-tax sinking fund payments	40	80	40	
Cash outflow requirements	$100	$164	$100	
Cash flow coverage ratio	5.16	3.54	5.80	3.00

are regarded as essential for the continuity of the firm. Within the broader definition of cash outflow requirements, Stanton's cash flow coverage would undoubtedly be lowered.

The next consideration is the effect of the various forms of financing on the level of the firm's beta. As indicated earlier, Stanton's cost of equity is at present 14 percent. Using the security market line and additional data on the market parameters already provided, Stanton's present level of beta can be determined as follows:

$$k_s = R_F + (\bar{k}_M - R_F)\beta$$
$$0.14 = 0.06 + (0.11 - 0.06)\beta$$
$$\beta = 1.6 \text{ at present.}$$

Stanton's present level of beta is 1.6. As stated earlier, if the additional funds are raised by debt, the cost of equity will rise to 16 percent. The implied new beta will therefore be:

$$0.16 = 0.06 + (0.05)\beta$$
$$\beta = 2.0.$$

Stanton's beta will rise to 2 with debt financing. With equity financing, the cost of equity will fall to 12 percent. The implied new beta will thus be 1.2.

Four measures of risk have been used to assess the effect of choosing between equity financing and debt financing. Each measure has covered different aspects of risk and the results for Stanton have all pointed in the same direction. If debt financing is used, the financial structure ratios will be above the industry standards, the deficiency in the fixed charge coverage ratio will be further aggravated, and the cash flow coverage will move toward the industry standard (and by a broader measure may even fall below it). The existing 1.6 beta level is relatively high. The use of debt financing will push the beta level to 2, which is high for an industrial firm. The use of equity financing will move the beta level toward the average beta level of the market, which is 1. Clearly, therefore, from the standpoint of the four different measures of risk, equity financing is definitely the more favorable.

The next consideration is the relative costs of the different forms of financing. Relative costs are measured by the effects of each form of financing on the market value per share of common stock and by the effects on the firm's cost of capital. To apply these two criteria it is first necessary to calculate the amount of interest expense (in Table 19.9) for use in the income statements (Table 19.10).

Table 19.9
Calculation of the Amount of Debt Interest for Stanton
(Millions of Dollars)

Form of Debt	No Expansion		Expansion with Debt		Expansion with Equity	
	Amount	Rate	Amount	Rate	Amount	Rate
$300 million short-term notes payable	$30	10%	$36	12%	$30	10%
$300 million existing long-term debt	30	10	30	10	30	10
$200 million new long-term debt			24	12		
Total interest expense	$60		$90		$60	

The total amount of interest expense without expansion is $60 million. Interest expense will remain unchanged if the expansion is financed by equity funds. If the expansion is financed by long-term debt, the facts of the problem state that the cost of debt will rise to 12 percent. The opportunity cost of all debt funds is therefore 12 percent, and an argument can be made that all forms of debt should bear the higher 12 percent rate. However, the actual rate paid on the long-term debt will remain at 10 percent, while the short-term notes payable must be renewed periodically at the higher 12 percent rate (as shown in Table 19.9). If the expansion is financed by debt, the total interest expense will be $90 million. The total interest expense amounts needed for the income statements in Table 19.10 are now available.

Table 19.10
Stanton's Income Statements
(Millions of Dollars)

	No Expansion	Expansion with Debt	Expansion with Equity
Net operating income	$316	$360	$360
Interest expense	60	90	60
Net income before taxes	$256	$270	$300
Income taxes (at 50%)	128	135	150
Net income to equity	$128	$135	$150

With the information developed in the income statements, the market value of equity can be calculated (see Table 19.11).

The net income under each alternative is capitalized by the applicable cost of equity to obtain the total market value of equity. The price per share can also be determined. The total number of shares of common stock outstanding do not change with no expansion or with expansion financed by debt. The facts of the case stated that if equity were sold, the price would be $9 per share; the $200 of new financing divided by the $9 equals 22.2 million shares. Thus the total number of shares is 122.2 million (the original 100 million plus the additional 22.2 million). The indicated new price per share of common stock is obtained by dividing the total value of equity by the total number of shares of common stock outstanding. The resulting new price per share declines with expansion by debt financing and increases with expansion by equity financing—which means that equity financing is more favorable than debt financing. If debt financing were used, the criterion of maximizing share price would recommend that the expansion program not be adopted.

Table 19.11
Stanton's Market Value of Equity
(Millions of Dollars)

	No Expansion	Expansion with Debt	Expansion with Equity
Net income (NI)	$128	$135	$150
Cost of equity (k_s)	0.14	0.16	0.12
Value of equity (S)	$914	$844	$1,250
Number of shares	100	100	122.2
Price per share	$9.14	$8.44	$10.23

This result can be checked further by calculating the total market value of the firm (see Table 19.12). The total market value is obtained by adding the amount of debt to the market value of equity. It is increased by expansion with either debt or equity. However, as shown in Table 19.11, the market price per share of common stock is decreased by expansion with debt.

The main reason for calculating the total market value of the firm is to de-

Table 19.12
Stanton's Market Value
(Millions of Dollars)

	No Expansion	Expansion with Debt	Expansion with Equity
Market value of equity	$ 914	$ 844	$1,250
Amount of debt	600	800	600
Value of the firm	$1,514	$1,644	$1,850

termine the firm's capital structure proportions for use in the cost of capital calculations. The leverage ratios are calculated in Table 19.13.

The leverage ratio is increased if debt is employed but decreased if equity financing is employed. Using the capital structure proportions from Table 19.13, the weighted average cost of capital can be calculated:

$$
\begin{array}{llll}
 & k_b(1 - T)(B/V) & + & k_s(S/V) & = & k \\
\text{No expansion} & 0.10(0.5)(0.40) & + & 0.14(0.60) & = 0.020 + 0.084 = 10.4\% \\
\text{Expansion with debt} & 0.12(0.5)(0.49) & + & 0.16(0.51) & = 0.029 + 0.082 = 11.1\% \\
\text{Expansion with equity} & 0.10(0.5)(0.32) & + & 0.12(0.68) & = 0.016 + 0.082 = \ \ 9.8\%
\end{array}
$$

Expansion with debt will raise Stanton's cost of capital from 10.4 percent to 11.1 percent. Expansion with equity will lower the company's cost of capital from 10.4 percent to 9.8 percent. These results are consistent with the findings for the market value per share of common stock, where debt financing caused a decrease and equity financing an increase. Thus the cost of capital and market price per share of common stock criteria provide consistent findings.

**Table 19.13
Calculation of Stanton's
Leverage Ratios**

	No Expansion	Expansion with Debt	Expansion with Equity
Total debt	$ 600	$ 800	$ 600
Market value of the firm	$1,514	$1,644	$1,850
Debt to value ratio	0.40	0.49	0.32

The final item on the checklist of factors for evaluating alternative forms of financing is "effects on control." The problem states that the common stock is already widely held so that there is no control problem to militate against the use of equity financing.

The investment bankers summarize the evidence with respect to the two forms of financing as follows. Risks are already high and will be further increased if debt financing is used. As a result of this substantial increase in risk, the costs of both debt and equity funds will rise. With equity financing, the value per share of common stock is increased and the cost of capital reduced. There is no control issue. On the basis of all the factors considered, the common stock financing is recommended.

The Stanton case illustrates the application of a checklist of key factors to evaluate alternative forms of financing. Four measures of risk and several measures of costs to the firm (returns to investors) are employed. Relative costs of financing can be evaluated by reference to effects on market value per share of common stock, on the cost of capital, and on control of the firm. Thus the analysis is basically a risk-return evaluation and reflects a basic theme that runs through all of the chapters of this book.

Summary

The explanations of common stock financing and of the advantages and disadvantages of external equity financing compared with the use of preferred stock and debt provide a basis for making sound decisions when common stock financing is being considered by a firm.

Rights offerings can be used effectively by financial managers. If the new financing associated with the rights represents a sound decision—one likely to result in improved earnings for the firm—a rise in stock values will probably result. The use of rights will permit shareholders to preserve their positions or improve them. However, if investors feel that the new financing is not well advised, the rights offering may cause the price of the stock to decline by more than the value of the rights. Because rights offerings are directed to existing shareholders, their use can reduce the costs of floating the new issue.

A major decision for financial managers in a rights offering is to set the subscription price, or the amount of the concession from the existing market price of the stock. Formulas reflecting the static effects of a rights offering indicate that neither the stockholders nor the company gain or lose from the price changes. The rights offering has the effect of a stock split; that is, the level set for the subscription price reflects to a great degree the objectives and effects of a stock split.

The subsequent price behavior of the rights and the common stock in the associated new offering reflects the earnings and dividends prospects of the company as well as underlying developments in the securities markets. The new financing associated with the rights offering can be an indicator of prospective growth in the company's sales and earnings. The stock-split effects of the rights offering can be used to alter the company's dividend payments. The effects of these developments on the market behavior of the rights and the securities before, during, and after the rights trading period reflect the expectations of investors toward the outlook for the earnings of the firm.

A framework for decisions on choosing among various forms of financing is applied to the evaluation of common stock financing and can also be applied to the other forms of financing discussed in subsequent chapters.

Questions

19.1 By what percentage could total assets shrink in value on liquidation before creditors incur losses in each of the following cases:
   a. Equity to total asset ratio of 50 percent.
   b. Debt to equity ratio of 50 percent.
   c. Debt to total asset ratio of 40 percent.

19.2 How many shares must a minority group own in order to assure election of two directors if nine new directors will be elected and 200,000 shares are outstanding? Assume cumulative voting exists.

19.3 Should the preemptive right entitle stockholders to purchase convertible bonds before they are offered to outsiders?

19.4 What are the reasons for not letting officers and directors of a corporation make short sales in their company's stock?

19.5 It is frequently stated that the primary purpose of the preemptive right is to allow individuals to maintain their proportionate share of the ownership and control of a corporation.
   a. Just how important do you suppose this consideration is for the average stockholder of a firm whose shares are traded on the New York or the American stock exchange?
   b. Is the preemptive right likely to be of more importance to stockholders of closely held firms? Explain.

19.6 How would the success of a rights offering be affected by a declining stock market?

19.7 What are some of the advantages and disadvantages of setting the subscription price on a rights offering substantially below the current market price of the stock?

19.8 a. Is a firm likely to get wider distribution of shares if it sells new stock through a rights offering or directly to underwriters?
   b. Why would a company be interested in getting a wider distribution of shares?

Problems 19.1 The common stock of Arlington Development Company is selling for $32 a share on the market. Stockholders are offered one new share at a subscription price of $20 for every three shares held. What is the value of each right?

19.2 United Appliance Company common stock is priced at $40 a share on the market. Notice is given that stockholders can purchase one new share at a price of $27.50 for every four shares held.
   a. At approximately what market price will each right sell?
   b. Why will this be the approximate price?
   c. What effect will the issuance of rights have on the original market price?

19.3 Eileen Johnson has 600 shares of Fisher Industries. The market price per share is $81. The company now offers stockholders one new share at a price of $45 for every five shares held.
   a. Determine the value of each right.
   b. Assume that Johnson (1) uses 160 rights and sells the other 440, and (2) sells 600 rights at the ex rights market price you have calculated. Prepare a statement showing the changes in her position under the two assumptions.

19.4 As a shareholder of Younger Corporation, you are notified that for each seven shares you own you have the right to purchase one additional share at a price of $15. The current market price of Younger Stock is $63 per share.
   a. Determine the value of each right.

b. At the time of the offering your total assets consist of 490 shares of Younger stock and $1,500 in cash. Prepare a statement to show total assets before the offering and total assets after the offering if you exercise all the rights.

c. Prepare a statement to show total assets after the offering if you sell all the rights.

19.5 The Northridge Company has the following balance sheet and income statement:

**The Northridge Company
Balance Sheet before Rights
Offering**

		Total debt (6%)	$ 7,000,000
		Common stock (100,000 shares)	3,000,000
		Retained earnings	4,000,000
Total assets	$14,000,000	Total liabilities and capital	$14,000,000

**The Northridge Company
Income Statement**

Earning rate: 12% on total assets	
Total earnings	$1,680,000
Interest on debt	420,000
Income before taxes	$1,260,000
Taxes (50% rate assumed)	630,000
Earnings after taxes	$ 630,000
Earnings per share	$6.30
Dividends per share (56% of earnings)	$3.53
Price/earnings ratio	15 times
Market price per share	$94.50

The company plans to raise an additional $5 million through a rights offering; the additional funds will continue to earn 12 percent. The price/earnings ratio is assumed to remain at 15 times, the dividend payout will continue to be 56 percent, and the 50 percent tax rate will remain in effect. (Do not attempt to use the formula given in the chapter. Additional information is given here that violates the "other things constant" assumption inherent in the formula.)

a. Assuming subscription prices of $25, $50, and $80 a share:
1. How many additional shares of stock will have to be sold?
2. How many rights will be required to purchase one new share?
3. What will be the new earnings per share?
4. What will be the new market price per share?
5. What will be the new dividend per share if the dividend payout ratio is maintained?

b. What is the significance of the results?

19.6 As one of the minority shareholders of the Belmont Corporation, you are dissatisfied with the current operations of the company. You feel that if you could gain membership on the company's board of directors, you could persuade the company to make improvements. The problem is that current management controls 75 percent of the stock, you control only 7 percent, and the balance is held by other minority shareholders. There is a total of 500,000 voting shares. Ten directors will be elected at the next annual stockholder meeting.

   a. If voting is noncumulative, can you elect yourself director?
   b. Suppose you are able to persuade all the minority shareholders that you should be elected. If voting is noncumulative, can they elect you?
   c. If voting is cumulative, can you elect yourself director?
   d. What percent of the minority shares other than your own will you need to have voted for you to be certain of election?
   e. What is the number of directors the minority shareholders can elect with certainty?

19.7 The Frost Crop Food Company is engaged principally in the business of growing, processing, and marketing a variety of frozen vegetables. A major company in this field, it produces and markets high quality food at premium prices.

   During each of the past several years the company's sales have increased and the needed inventories have been financed from short-term sources. The officers have discussed the idea of refinancing their bank loans with long-term debt or common stock. A common stock issue of 310,000 shares sold at this time (present market price $72 a share) will yield $21 million after expenses. The same sum can be raised by selling twelve-year bonds with an interest rate of 8 percent and a sinking fund to retire the bonds over their twelve-year life. (See financial ratios and statements below.)

   a. Should Frost Crop Food refinance the short-term loans? Why?
   b. If the bank loans should be refinanced, what factors should be considered in determining which form of financing to use?

Food Processing Industry
Financial Ratios

Current ratio: 2.2 times
Sales to total assets: 2.0 times
Sales to inventory: 5.6 times
Average collection period: 22.0 days
Current debt/total assets: 25–30%
Long-term debt/total assets: 10–15%
Preferred/total assets: 0.5%
Net worth/total assets: 60–65%
Profits to sales: 2.3%
Net profits to total assets: 4.0%
Profits to net worth: 8.4%
Expected growth rate of earnings and dividends: 6.5%

**Frost Crop Food Company
Consolidated Balance Sheet as
of March 31, 1978
(Millions of Dollars)[a]**

Current assets	$141	Accounts payable	$12	
Fixed plant and equipment	57	Notes payable	36	
Other assets	12	Accruals	15	
		Total current liabilities		$ 63
		Long-term debt (at 5%)		63
		Preferred stock		9
		Common stock (par $6)	$12	
		Retained earnings	63	
		Net worth		75
Total assets	$210	Total claims on assets		$210

[a] The majority of harvesting activities do not begin until late April or May.

**Frost Crop Food Company
Consolidated Income Statement
for Year Ended March 31
(Millions of Dollars)**

	1975	1976	1977	1978
Net sales	$225.0	$234.6	$292.8	$347.1
Cost of goods sold	146.1	156.6	195.3	230.4
Gross profit	$ 78.9	$ 78.0	$ 97.5	$116.7
Other expenses	61.8	66.0	81.0	88.5
Operating income	$ 17.1	$ 12.0	$ 16.5	$ 28.2
Other income (net)	−3.3	−4.2	−5.7	−9.3
Earnings before tax	$ 13.8	$ 7.8	$ 10.8	$ 18.9
Taxes	7.2	3.3	5.4	9.6
Net profit	$ 6.6	$ 4.5	$ 5.4	$ 9.3
Preferred dividend	0.3	0.3	0.3	0.3
Earnings available to common stock	$ 6.3	$ 4.2	$ 5.1	$ 9.0
Earnings per share	$3.15	$2.10	$2.55	$4.50
Cash dividends per share	$1.29	$1.44	$1.59	$1.80
Price range for common stock:				
High	$66.00	$69.00	$66.00	$81.00
Low	$30.00	$42.00	$51.00	$63.00

19.8 In 1975, Inland Steel was planning an expansion program. It estimated that it would need to raise an additional $200 million. Inland discussed with its investment banker whether to raise the $200 million through debt financing or through selling additional shares of common stock. The banker's recommendation was based on the following background information. The dividend payout has averaged about 50 percent of net income. The cost of debt is 10 percent, and the cost of equity is 14 percent. If the additional funds are raised by debt, the cost of debt will be 12 percent and the cost of equity will rise to 16 percent. If the additional funds are raised by equity, the cost of debt will remain at 10 percent, and the cost of equity will fall to 12 percent. Equity will be sold at $9 per share. (See also the steel industry standards and Inland's balance sheet and income statement below.)

a. Make a financial risk analysis using financial structure ratios and the fixed charge coverage ratio.
b. Complete the pro forma income statements under the two forms of financing.
c. Calculate the market value of equity and the indicated market price per share before and after financing by the two methods.
d. Calculate the value of the firm and the B/S, B/V, and S/V percentages.
e. Calculate the weighted cost of capital at present and under the two financing alternatives.
f. Recommend the best form of financing for Inland.

Steel Industry Standards

Long-term debt to shareholder's equity: 30%
Shareholder's equity to total assets: 55%
Fixed charges coverage: 7 times
Current ratio: 2.1 times
Return on net worth: 11%

Inland Steel
Balance Sheet as of December
31, 1975 (Millions of Dollars)

Assets			Liabilities		
Total current assets	$ 600		Notes payable (at 10%)	$100	
Net fixed assets	1,200		Other current liabilities	100	
			Total current liabilities		$ 200
			Long-term debt (at 10%)		500
			Other liabilities		300
			Total debt		$1,000
			Common stock, par value $1		100
			Paid-in capital		300
			Retained earnings		400
Total assets	$1,800		Total claims on assets		$1,800

**Inland Steel
Income Statement for Year
Ended December 31, 1975
(Millions of Dollars)**

	Current Year	With Expansion, Pro Forma
Total revenues	$2,000	$2,400
Net operating income	316	360
Interest expense	60	————
Net income before taxes	$ 256	————
Income taxes (at 50%)	128	————
Net income to equity	$ 128	————

19.9 Allied Chemists has experienced the following sales, profit, and balance sheet patterns. Identify the financial problem that has developed, and recommend a solution for it.

**Allied Chemists Financial Data,
1968–1977 (Millions of Dollars)**

Income Statements	1968	1969	1970	1971	1972	1973	1974	1975	1976	1977
Sales	$100	$140	$180	$200	$240	$400	$360	$440	$480	$680
Profits after tax	10	14	18	20	24	40	36	44	48	68
Dividends	8	10	12	12	14	20	20	28	36	48
Retained earnings	$ 2	$ 4	$ 6	$ 8	$ 10	$ 20	$ 16	$ 16	$ 12	$ 20
Cumulative retained earnings	$ 2	$ 6	$ 12	$ 20	$ 30	$ 50	$ 66	$ 82	$ 94	$114

Balance Sheets	1968	1969	1970	1971	1972	1973	1974	1975	1976	1977
Current assets	$ 20	$ 30	$ 40	$ 50	$ 60	$100	$ 80	$110	$120	$160
Net fixed assets	30	40	50	50	60	100	100	110	120	180
Total assets	$ 50	$ 70	$ 90	$100	$120	$200	$180	$220	$240	$340
Trade credit	$ 8	$ 12	$ 16	$ 18	$ 20	$ 36	$ 30	$ 40	$ 40	$120
Bank credit	8	12	20	20	26	58	28	40	40	40
Other	2	10	12	12	14	16	16	18	16	16
Total current liabilities	$ 18	$ 34	$ 48	$ 50	$ 60	$110	$ 74	$ 98	$ 96	$176
Long-term debt	0	0	0	0	0	10	10	10	20	20
Total debt	$ 18	$ 34	$ 48	$ 50	$ 60	$120	$ 84	$108	$116	$196
Common stock	30	30	30	30	30	30	30	30	30	30
Retained earnings	2	6	12	20	30	50	66	82	94	114
Net worth	$ 32	$ 36	$ 42	$ 50	$ 60	$ 80	$ 96	$112	$124	$144
Total claims on assets	$ 50	$ 70	$ 90	$100	$120	$200	$180	$220	$240	$340

CHAPTER 20   FIXED INCOME SECURITIES:
DEBT AND PREFERRED STOCK

There are many classes of fixed income securities: long term and short term, secured and unsecured, marketable and nonmarketable, participating and nonparticipating, senior and junior, and so on. Different classes of investors favor different classes of securities, and tastes change over time. An astute financial manager knows how to "package" securities at a given point in time to make them attractive to the maximum number of potential investors, thereby keeping the cost of capital to a minimum. This chapter deals with the two most important types of long-term, fixed-income securities—bonds and preferred stocks.

Instruments of Long-Term Debt Financing

An understanding of long-term forms of financing requires some familiarity with technical terminology. The discussion of long-term debt therefore begins with an explanation of several important instruments and terms.

Bond

Most people have had some experience with short-term promissory notes. A *bond* is simply a long-term promissory note.

Mortgage

A *mortgage* represents a pledge of designated property for a loan. Under a *mortgage bond,* a corporation pledges certain real assets as security for the bond. A mortgage bond is therefore secured by real property.[1] The pledge is a condition of the loan.

Debenture

A *debenture* is a long-term bond that is *not* secured by a pledge of any specific property. However, like other general creditor claims, it is secured by any property not otherwise pledged.

Indenture

The long-term relationship between the borrower and the lender of a long-term promissory note is established in a document called an *indenture.* In the case of an ordinary sixty- or ninety-day promissory note, few developments are likely to occur in the life or affairs of the borrower that will endanger repayment. The lender looks closely at the borrower's current position, because current assets are the main source of repayment. A bond, however, is a long-term contractual relationship between the bond issuer

---

1. There is also the *chattel mortgage,* which is secured by personal property; but this is generally an intermediate-term instrument. *Real property* is defined as real estate—land and buildings. *Personal property* is defined as any other kind of property, including equipment, inventories, and furniture.

and the bondholder; over this extended period the bondholder has cause to worry that the issuing firm's position may change materially.

In the ordinary common stock or preferred stock certificate or agreement, the details of the contractual relationship can be summarized in a few paragraphs. The bond indenture, however, can be a document of several hundred pages that discusses a large number of factors important to the contracting parties, such as: (1) the form of the bond and the instrument; (2) a complete description of property pledged; (3) the authorized amount of the bond issue; (4) detailed protective clauses, or *covenants,* which usually include limits on indebtedness, restrictions on dividends, and a sinking fund provision; (5) a minimum current ratio requirement; and (6) provisions for redemption or call privileges.

Trustee

Bonds are not only of long duration but also, usually, of substantial size. Before the rise of large aggregations of savings through insurance companies or pension funds, no single buyer was able to buy an issue of such size. Bonds were therefore issued in denominations of $1,000 each and were sold to a large number of purchasers. To facilitate communication between the issuer and the numerous bondholders, a trustee was appointed to represent the bondholders. The trustee is still presumed to act at all times for the protection of the bondholders and on their behalf.

Any legal person, including a corporation, is considered competent to act as a trustee. Typically, however, the duties of the trustee are handled by a department of a commercial bank.

Trustees have three main responsibilities:

1. They certify the issue of bonds. This duty involves making certain that all the legal requirements for drawing up the bond contract and the indenture have been carried out.
2. They police the behavior of the corporation in its performance of the responsibilities set forth in the indenture provisions.
3. They are responsible for taking appropriate action on behalf of the bondholders if the corporation defaults on payment of interest or principal.

It is said that in many corporate bond defaults in the early 1930s, trustees did not act in the best interests of the bondholders. They did not conserve the assets of the corporation effectively, and often they did not take early action, thereby allowing corporation executives to continue their salaries and to dispose of assets under conditions favorable to themselves but detrimental to the bondholders. In some cases, assets pledged as security for the bonds were sold, and specific security was thus no longer available. The result in many instances was that holders of mortgage bonds found themselves more in the position of general creditors than of secured bond-holders.

As a consequence of such practices, Congress passed the Trust Indenture Act of 1939 in order to give more protection to bondholders. The act provides (1) that trustees must be given sufficient power to act on behalf of bondholders; (2) that the indenture must fully disclose rights and responsibilities and must not be deceptive; (3) that bondholders can make changes in the indenture; (4) that prompt, protective action be taken by the trustees for bondholders if default occurs; (5) that an arm's-length relationship exist between the issuing corporation and the trustee, and (6) that the corporation must make periodic reports to its trustee to enable that person to carry out the protective responsibilities.

Call Provision

A *call provision* gives the issuing corporation the right to call in the bond for redemption. The provision generally states that the company must pay an amount greater than the par value of the bond; this additional sum is defined as the *call premium.* The call premium is typically equal to one year's interest if the bond is called during the first year, and it declines at a constant rate each year thereafter. For example, the call premium on a $1,000 par value, twenty-year, 6 percent bond is generally $60 if called during the first year, $57 if called during the second year (calculated by reducing the $60, or 6 percent, premium by one-twentieth), and so on.

The call privilege is valuable to the firm but potentially detrimental to the investor, especially if the bond is issued in a period when interest rates are thought to be cyclically high. The problem for investors is that the call privilege enables the issuing corporation to substitute bonds paying lower interest rates for bonds paying higher ones. Consider a simple example of consols (bonds with no maturity). Suppose consols are sold to yield 10 percent when interest rates are high. If interest rates drop so that the consols yield 8 percent, the value of the bond theoretically could rise to $1,250. Suppose the issuing firm can call the bond by paying a $100 premium. The investor receives $1,100 for a bond whose market value will otherwise be $1,250. The callability of the bond will probably prevent its rising to the full $1,250 in the marketplace.

This disadvantage of the call privilege to the investor is supported by empirical data. Studies indicate that when interest rate levels are high, new issues of callable bonds must bear yields from 0.25 percent to 0.50 percent higher than the yields of noncallable bonds. If callability is deferred for five years (that is, if the issuer cannot exercise the call privilege until the bond has been outstanding for at least five years), in periods of relatively high interest rates, the yields for long-term bonds with five years of call deferment are about 0.13 percent lower than the yields for similar bonds that can be called immediately. During periods of relatively low interest rates, the discount for five years of deferment drops to about 0.04 percent from yields on fully callable bonds.[2] (The procedures for calculating when it is advantageous for the corporation to call or refund a bond or preferred stock issue are presented later in the chapter.)

Sinking Fund

A *sinking fund* is a provision that facilitates the orderly retirement of a bond issue (or, in some cases, preferred stock issue). Typically, it requires the firm to buy and retire a portion of the bond issue each year. Sometimes the stipulated sinking fund payment is tied to the current year's sales or earnings, but usually it is a mandatory fixed amount. If it is mandatory, a failure to meet the payment causes the bond issue to be thrown into default and can lead the company into bankruptcy. Obviously, then, a sinking fund can constitute a dangerous cash drain on the firm.

In most cases the firm is given the right to handle the sinking fund in either of two ways:

1. It can call a certain percentage of the bonds at a stipulated price each year (for example, 2 percent of the original amount at a price of $1,050). The actual bonds to be called, which are numbered serially, are determined by a lottery.
2. It can spend the funds provided by the sinking fund payment to buy the bonds on the open market. The firm will do whichever results in the greatest reduction of outstanding bonds for a given expenditure. Therefore, if interest rates have risen (and the price of the bonds has fallen), the firm will choose the open market alternative. If interest rates have fallen (and bond prices have risen), it will elect the option of calling bonds.

The call provision of the sinking fund at times works to the detriment of bondholders. If, for example, the bond carries a 7 percent interest rate, and if yields on similar securities are 4 percent, the bond will sell for well above par. A sinking fund call at par thus greatly disadvantages some bondholders. On balance, securities that provide for a sinking fund and continuing redemption are likely to be offered initially on a lower yield basis than are securities without such a fund. Since sinking funds provide additional protection to investors, sinking fund bonds are likely to sell initially at higher prices; hence, they have a lower cost of capital to the issuer.

Funded Debt

Funded debt is simply long-term debt. A firm planning to "fund" its floating debt will replace short-term securities by long-term securities. *Funding*

---

2. See F. C. Jen and J. E. Wert, "The Effects of Call Risk on Corporate Bond Yields," *Journal of Finance* 22 (December 1967); and G. Pye, "The Value of Call Deferment on a Bond: Some Empirical Results," *Journal of Finance* 22 (December 1967).

does not imply placing money with a trustee or other repository; part of the jargon of finance, it simply means "long term."[3]

Secured Bonds

Secured long-term debt can be classified according to (1) the priority of claims, (2) the right to issue additional securities, and (3) the scope of the lien.

Priority of Claims

A senior mortgage has prior claims on assets and earnings. Senior railroad mortgages, for example, have been called the "mortgages next to the rail," implying that they have the first claim on the land and assets of the railroad corporations. A junior mortgage is a subordinate lien, such as a second or third mortgage. It is a lien or claim junior to others.

Right to Issue Additional Securities

Mortgage bonds can also be classified with respect to the right to issue additional obligations pledging already encumbered property.

In the case of a *closed-end mortgage,* a company cannot sell additional bonds (beyond those already issued) secured by the property specified in the mortgage. For example, assume that a corporation with plant and land worth $5 million has a $2 million mortgage on these properties. If the mortgage is closed end, no more bonds having first liens on this property can be issued. Thus a closed-end mortgage provides security to the bond buyer. The ratio of the amount of the senior bonds to the value of the property is not increased by subsequent issues.

If the bond indenture is silent on this point, it is called an *open-end mortgage.* Its nature can be illustrated by referring to the example cited above. Against property worth $5 million, bonds of $2 million are sold. If an additional first mortgage bond of $1 million is subsequently sold, the property has been pledged for a total of $3 million of bonds. If, on liquidation, the property sells for $2 million, the original bondholders will receive 67 cents on the dollar. If the mortgage has been closed end, they would have been fully paid.

Most characteristic is the *limited open-end mortgage.* Its nature can be indicated by continuing the example. A first mortgage bond issue of $2 million, secured by the property worth $5 million, is sold. The indenture provides that an additional $1 million worth of bonds—or an additional amount

3. Tampa Electric Company provides a good example of funding. This company has a continuous construction program. Typically, it uses short-term debt to finance construction expenditures. However, once short-term debt has built up to about $75 million, the company sells a stock or bond issue, uses the proceeds to pay off its bank loans, and starts the cycle again. The high flotation costs of small security issues make this process desirable.

of bonds up to 60 percent of the original cost of the property—can be sold. Thus the mortgage is open only to a certain point.

Scope of the Lien

Bonds can also be classified with respect to the scope of their lien. A lien is granted on certain specified property. When a *specific lien* exists, the security for a first or second mortgage is a specifically designated property. On the other hand, a *blanket mortgage* pledges all real property currently owned by the company. Real property includes only land and those things affixed thereto; thus a blanket mortgage is not a mortgage on cash, accounts receivables, or inventories, which are items of personal property. A blanket mortgage gives more protection to the bondholder than does a specific mortgage because it provides a claim on all real property owned by the company.

Unsecured Bonds

Debentures

The reasons for a firm's use of unsecured debt are diverse. Paradoxically, the extremes of financial strength and weakness may give rise to its use. Also, tax considerations and great uncertainty about the level of the firm's future earnings have given rise to special forms of unsecured financing. A *debenture* is an unsecured bond and, as such, provides no lien on specific property as security for the obligation. Debenture holders are therefore general creditors whose claim is protected by property not otherwise pledged. The advantage of debentures from the issuer's standpoint is that the property is left unencumbered for subsequent financing. However, in practice, the use of debentures depends on the nature of the firm's assets and its general credit strength.

A firm whose credit position is exceptionally strong can issue debentures; it simply does not need specific security. However, the credit position of a company may be so weak that it has no alternative to the use of debentures; all its property may already be encumbered. The debt portion of American Telephone & Telegraph's vast financing program since the end of World War II has been mainly through debentures. AT&T is such a strong institution that it does not have to provide security for its debt issues.

Debentures are also issued by companies in industries where it is not practical to provide a lien through a mortgage on fixed assets. Examples of such companies are large mail order houses and finance companies, which characteristically do not have large fixed assets in relation to their total assets. The bulk of their assets is in the form of inventory or receivables, neither of which is satisfactory security for a mortgage lien.

Subordinated Debentures

The term *subordinate* means below or inferior. Thus *subordinated debt* has claims on assets after unsubordinated debt in the event of liquidation. Debentures can be subordinated to designated notes payable—usually bank loans—or to any or all other debt. In the event of liquidation or reorganization, the debentures cannot be paid until senior debt *as named in the indenture* has been paid. Senior debt typically does not include trade accounts payable. How the subordination provision strengthens the position of senior debt holders is shown in Table 20.1.

Table 20.1
Illustration of Bankruptcy
Payments to Senior Debt, Other
Debt, and Subordinated Debt

Financial Structure	Book Value (1)	Percent of Total Debt (2)	Initial Allocation (3)	Actual Payment (4)	Percent of Original Claim Satisfied (5)
$200 available for claims on liquidation					
Bank debt	$200	50%	$100	$150	75%
Other debt	100	25	50	50	50
Subordinated debt	100	25	50	0	0
Total debt	$400	100%	$200	$200	50%
Net worth	300				0
Total	$700				29%
$300 available for claims on liquidation					
Bank debt	$200	50%	$150	$200	100%
Other debt	100	25	75	75	75
Subordinated debt	100	25	75	25	25
Total debt	$400	100%	$300	$300	75%
Net worth	300				0
Total	$700				43%

Steps: 1. Express each type of debt as a percentage of total debt (Column 2).
2. Multiply the debt percentages (Column 2) by the amount available to obtain the initial allocations (Column 3).
3. The subordinated debt is subordinate to bank debt. Therefore, the initial allocation to subordinate debt is added to the bank debt allocation until it has been exhausted or until the bank debt is finally paid off (Column 4).

Where $200 is available for distribution, the subordinated debt has a claim on 25 percent of $200, or $50. However, this claim is subordinated only to the bank debt (the only senior debt) and is added to the $100 claim of the bank. As a consequence, 75 percent of the bank's original claim is satisfied.

Where $300 is available for distribution, the $75 allocated to the subordinated debt is divided into two parts; $50 goes to the bank, and the other $25 remains for the subordinated debt holders. In this situation, the senior bank debt holders are fully paid off, 75 percent of other debt is paid, and only 25 percent of subordinated debt is paid.

Subordination is frequently required. Alert credit managers of firms supplying trade credit or commercial bank loan officers typically insist on subordination, particularly where debt is owed to the principal stockholders or officers of a company. Often, subordinated debentures are also convertible into the common stock of the issuing company.

In comparison to subordinated debt, preferred stock suffers from the disadvantage that its dividends are not deductible as an expense for tax purposes. Subordinated debentures have been referred to as being like a special kind of preferred stock, the dividends of which *are* deductible as an expense for tax purposes. Subordinated debt has therefore become an increasingly important source of corporate capital.

The reasons for the use of subordinated debentures are clear. They offer a great tax advantage over preferred stock; yet they do not restrict the borrower's ability to obtain senior debt, as would be the case if all debt sources were on an equal basis.

The use of subordinated debentures is further stimulated by periods of tight money, when commercial banks tend to require a greater equity base for short-term financing. These debentures provide a greater equity cushion for loans from commercial banks or other forms of senior debt. Their use also illustrates the development of hybrid securities that emerge to meet the changing situations that develop in the capital market.

Income Bonds

Income bonds typically arise from corporate reorganizations, and they pay interest only if income is actually earned by the company. A company that has gone through reorganization has been in difficult financial circumstances; thus interest is not a fixed charge. The principal, however, must be paid when due.

Income bonds are like preferred stock in that management is not required to pay interest if it is not earned. However, they differ from preferred stock in that (1) if interest has been earned, management is required to pay it, and (2) interest paid on income bonds is deductible for income tax purposes while preferred dividends are not.

The main characteristic and distinct advantage of the income bond is that interest is payable only if the company achieves earnings. Since earnings calculations are subject to differing interpretations, the indenture of the income bond carefully defines income and expenses. If it did not, litigation might result.

Some income bonds are cumulative indefinitely (if interest is not paid, it "accumulates" and must be paid at some future date); others are cumulative for the first three to five years, after which they become noncumulative.

Income bonds usually contain sinking fund provisions to provide for their retirement. The annual payments to the sinking funds range between $1/2$ and 1 percent of the face amount of the original issue. Because the sinking fund payment requirements are typically contingent on earnings, a fixed cash drain on the company is avoided.

Sometimes income bonds are convertible; there are sound reasons for this if they arise out of a reorganization. Creditors who receive income bonds in exchange for defaulted obligations have a less desirable position than they had previously. Since they have received something based on an adverse and problematical forecast of the company's future, it is appropriate that if the company does prosper, income bondholders are entitled to participate. When income bonds are issued in situations other than reorganization, the convertibility feature is likely to make the issue more attractive to prospective bond buyers.

Typically, income bondholders do not have voting rights when the bonds are issued. Sometimes bondholders are given the right to elect some specified number of directors if interest is not paid for a certain number of years.

Characteristics of Long-Term Debt

From the viewpoint of long-term debt holders, debt is good in regard to risk, has limited advantages in regard to income, and is weak in regard to control. To elaborate:

1. In the area of risk, debt is favorable because it gives the holder priority both in earnings and in liquidation. Debt also has a definite maturity and is protected by the covenants of the indenture.
2. In the area of income, the bondholder has a fixed return; except in the case of income bonds, interest payments are not contingent on the company's level of earnings. However, debt does not participate in any superior earnings of the company, and gains are limited in magnitude. Bondholders actually suffer during inflationary periods. A twenty-year, 6 percent bond pays $60 of interest each year. Under inflation, the purchasing power of this $60 is eroded, causing a loss in real value to the bondholder.[4] Frequently, long-term debt is callable. If bonds are called, the investor receives funds that must be reinvested to be kept active.
3. In the area of control, the bondholder usually does not have the right to vote. However, if the bonds go into default, then bondholders in effect take control of the company.

From the viewpoint of long-term debt issuers there are several advantages and disadvantages to bonds. The advantages are:

1. The cost of debt is definitely limited. Bondholders do not participate in superior profits (if earned).

---

4. Recognizing this fact, investors demand higher interest rates during inflationary periods. This point was discussed in Chapter 2.

2. Not only is the cost limited, but typically the expected yield is lower than that of common stock.
3. The owners of the corporation do not share their control when debt financing is used.
4. The interest payment on debt is deductible as a tax expense.
5. Flexibility in the financial structure of the corporation can be achieved by inserting a call provision in the bond indenture.

The disadvantages are:

1. Debt is a fixed charge; if the earnings of the company fluctuate, it may be unable to meet the charge.
2. As seen in Chapter 14, higher risk brings higher capitalization rates on equity earnings. Thus, even though leverage is favorable and raises earnings per share, the higher capitalization rates attributable to leverage may drive the common stock value down.
3. Debt usually has a fixed maturity date, and the financial officer must make provision for repayment of the debt.
4. Since long-term debt is a commitment for a long period, it involves risk. The expectations and plans on which the debt was issued may change, and the debt may prove to be a burden. For example, if income, employment, the price level, and interest rates all fall greatly, the prior assumption of a large amount of long-term debt may have been an unwise financial policy. The railroads are always given as an example in this regard. They were able to meet their ordinary operating expenses during the 1930s but were unable to meet the heavy financial charges they had undertaken earlier, when their prospects looked more favorable than they turned out to be.
5. In a long-term contractual relationship, the indenture provisions are likely to be much more stringent than they are in a short-term credit agreement. Hence the firm may be subject to much more disturbing and crippling restrictions than if it had borrowed on a short-term basis or had issued common stock.
6. There is a limit on the extent to which funds can be raised through long-term debt. Generally accepted standards of financial policy dictate that the debt ratio shall not exceed certain limits. When debt goes beyond these limits, its cost rises rapidly.

Decisions on the Use of Long-Term Debt

When a number of methods of long-term financing are being considered, the following conditions favor the use of long-term debt:

1. Sales and earnings are relatively stable, or a large increase in future sales and earnings is expected to provide a substantial benefit from the use of leverage.

2. A substantial rise in the price level is expected in the future, making it advantageous for the firm to incur debt that will be repaid with cheaper dollars.
3. The existing debt ratio is relatively low for the line of business.
4. Management thinks the price of the common stock in relation to that of bonds is temporarily depressed.
5. Sale of common stock would involve problems of maintaining the existing control pattern in the company.

Decisions about the use of debt can also be considered in terms of the average cost of capital curve, as developed in Chapter 16: Firms have optimal capital structures, or perhaps optimal ranges, and the average cost of capital is higher than it need be if the firm uses other than an optimal amount of debt. The factors listed above all relate to the optimal debt ratio; some cause the optimal ratio to increase, and others cause it to decrease.

Whenever the firm contemplates raising new outside capital and chooses between debt and equity, it implicitly makes a judgment about its actual debt ratio in relation to the optimal ratio. For example, consider Figure 20.1, which shows the assumed shape of the Longstreet Company's average cost of capital schedule. If Longstreet plans to raise outside capital, it must make a judgment about whether it is presently at Point A or Point B. If it decides that it is at A, it should issue debt; if it believes that it is at B, it should sell new common stock. This, of course, is a judgment decision; but all the factors discussed in this chapter must be considered in a qualitative way as well as on the basis of the formal analysis presented in Chapter 16.

Nature of Preferred Stock

Preferred stock has claims and rights ahead of common stock but behind all bonds. The preference may be a prior claim on earnings, a prior claim on assets in the event of liquidation, or a preferential position with regard to both earnings and assets.

The hybrid nature of preferred stock becomes apparent when we try to classify it in relation to bonds and common stock. The priority feature and the (generally) fixed dividend indicate that preferred stock is similar to bonds. Payments to preferred stockholders are limited in amount, so that common stockholders receive the advantages (or disadvantages) of leverage. However, if the preferred dividends are not earned, the company can forego paying them without danger of bankruptcy. In this characteristic, preferred stock is similar to common stock. Moreover, failure to pay the stipulated dividend does not cause default of the obligation, as does failure to pay bond interest.

In some types of analysis, preferred stock is treated as debt. This occurs, for example, when the analysis is being made by a *potential stockholder*

Figure 20.1
The Longstreet Company's
Average Cost of Capital Schedule

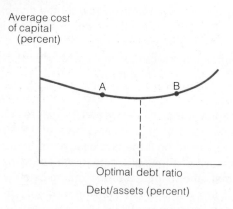

considering the earnings fluctuations induced by fixed charge securities. Suppose, however, that the analysis is by a *bondholder* studying the firm's vulnerability to failure brought on by declines in sales or income. Since the dividends on preferred stock are not a fixed charge (in the sense that failure to pay them represents a default of an obligation), preferred stock represents a cushion; it provides an additional equity base. For *stockholders,* it is a leverage-inducing instrument much like debt. For *creditors,* it constitutes additional net worth. Preferred stock can therefore be treated as either debt or equity, depending on the nature of the problem under consideration.[5]

Major Provisions of Preferred Stock Issues

Because the possible characteristics, rights, and obligations of any specific security vary so widely, a point of diminishing returns is quickly reached in a descriptive discussion of the different kinds of securities. As economic circumstances change, new kinds of securities are manufactured. Their number and variety are limited chiefly by the imagination and ingenuity of the managers formulating the terms of the issues. It is not surprising, then, that preferred stock can be found in many forms. The following sections will look at the main terms and characteristics in each case and examine the possible variations in relation to the circumstances in which they could occur.[6]

5. Accountants generally include preferred stock in the equity portion of the capital structure. But preferred is very different from common equity.
6. Much of the data in this section is taken from a study by Donald E. Fischer and Glenn A. Wilt, Jr., "Non-convertible Preferred Stocks as a Financing Instrument," *Journal of Finance* 23 (September 1968).

Priority in Assets and Earnings

Many provisions in a preferred stock certificate are designed to reduce the purchaser's risk in relation to the risk carried by the holder of common stock. Preferred stock usually has priority with regard to earnings and assets. Two provisions designed to prevent undermining this priority are often found. The first states that, without the consent of the preferred stockholders, there can be no subsequent sale of securities having a prior or equal claim on earnings. The second seeks to keep earnings in the firm. It requires a minimum level of retained earnings before common stock dividends are permitted. In order to assure the availability of liquid assets that can be converted into cash for the payment of dividends, the maintenance of a minimum current ratio may also be required.

Par Value

Unlike common stock, preferred stock usually has a par value; this value is a meaningful quantity. First, the par value establishes the amount due the preferred stockholders in the event of liquidation. Second, the preferred dividend is frequently stated as a percentage of the par value. For example, J. I. Case's preferred stock outstanding has a par value of $100 and a stated dividend of 7 percent of par. (It would, of course, be just as appropriate for the Case preferred stock to state simply that the annual dividend is $7; on many preferred stocks the dividends are stated in this manner rather than as a percentage of par value.)

Cumulative Dividends

A high percentage of dividends on preferred stocks is cumulative—that is, all past preferred dividends must be paid before common dividends can be paid. The cumulative feature is therefore a protective device. If the preferred stock were not cumulative, preferred and common stock dividends could be passed by for a number of years. The company could then vote a large common stock dividend but only the stipulated payment to preferred stock. Suppose that preferred stock with a par value of $100 carried a 7 percent dividend and that the company did not pay dividends for several years, thereby accumulating funds that would enable it to pay in total about $50 in dividends. It could pay a single $7 dividend to the preferred stockholders and a $43 dividend to the common stockholders. Obviously, this device could be used to evade the preferred position that the holders of preferred stock have tried to obtain. The cumulative feature prevents such evasion.[7]

Large arrearages on preferred stock make it difficult to resume dividend payments on common stock. To avoid delays in beginning common stock dividend payments again, a compromise arrangement with the holders of common stock is likely to be worked out. A package offer is one possibility;

---

7. Note, however, that compounding is absent in most cumulative plans. In other words, the arrearages themselves earn no return.

for example, a recapitalization plan may provide for an exchange of shares. The arrearage will be wiped out by the donation of common stock with a value equal to the amount of the preferred dividend arrearage, and the holders of preferred stock will thus be given an ownership share in the corporation. In addition, resumption of current dividends on the preferred may be promised. Whether these provisions are worth anything depends on the future earnings prospects of the company.

The advantage to the company of substituting common stock for dividends in arrears is that it can start again with a clear balance sheet. If earnings recover, dividends can be paid to the holders of common stock without making up arrearages to the holders of preferred stock. The original common stockholders, of course, will have given up a portion of their ownership of the corporation.

Convertibility

Approximately 40 percent of the preferred stock that has been issued in recent years is convertible into common stock. For example, 1 share of a particular preferred stock could be convertible into 2.5 shares of the firm's common stock at the option of the preferred shareholder. (The nature of convertibility will be discussed in Chapter 22.)

Some Infrequent Provisions

Some of the other provisions occasionally encountered in preferred stocks include the following:

1. *Voting rights.* Sometimes preferred stockholders are given the right to vote for directors. When this feature is present, it generally permits the preferred stockholders to elect a *minority* of the board, say three out of nine directors. The voting privilege becomes operative only if the company has not paid the preferred dividend for a specified period, say six, eight, or ten quarters.
2. *Participating.* A rare type of preferred stock is one that participates with the common stock in sharing the firm's earnings. The following factors generally relate to participating preferred stocks: (a) the stated preferred dividend is paid first—for example, $5 a share; (b) next, income is allocated to common stock dividends up to an amount equal to the preferred dividend—in this case, $5; and (c) any remaining income is shared equally between the common and preferred stockholders.
3. *Sinking fund.* Some preferred issues have a sinking fund requirement. When they do, the sinking fund ordinarily calls for the purchase and retirement of a given percentage of the preferred stock each year.
4. *Maturity.* Preferred stocks almost never have maturity dates on which they must be retired. However, if the issue has a sinking fund, this effectively creates a maturity date.

5. *Call provision.* A call provision gives the issuing corporation the right to call in the preferred stock for redemption, as for bonds. If it is used, the call provision generally states that the company must pay an amount greater than the par value of the preferred stock, the additional sum being defined as the *call premium.* For example, a $100 par value preferred stock might be callable at the option of the corporation at $108 a share.

Evaluation of Preferred Stock

There are both advantages and disadvantages to selling preferred stock. Among the advantages are:

1. In contrast to bonds, the obligation to make fixed interest payments is avoided.
2. A firm wishing to expand because its earning power is high can obtain higher earnings for the original owners by selling preferred stock with a limited return rather than by selling common stock.
3. By selling preferred stock, the financial manager avoids the provision of equal participation in earnings that the sale of additional common stock would require.
4. Preferred stock also permits a company to avoid sharing control through participation in voting.
5. In contrast to bonds, it enables the firm to conserve mortgageable assets.
6. Since preferred stock typically has no maturity and no sinking fund, it is more flexible than bonds.

Among the disadvantages are:

1. Characteristically, preferred stock must be sold on a higher yield basis than that for bonds.[8]
2. Preferred stock dividends are not deductible as a tax expense, a characteristic that makes their cost differential very great in comparison with that of bonds.
3. As shown in Chapter 16, the after-tax cost of debt is approximately half

8. Historically, a given firm's preferred stock generally carried higher rates than its bonds because of the preferred's greater risk from the holder's viewpoint. However, as is noted below, the fact that preferred dividends are largely exempt from the corporate income tax has made preferred stock attractive to corporate investors. In recent years, high-grade preferreds on average have sold on a lower yield basis than high-grade bonds. Fischer and Wilt, in "Non-convertible Preferred Stocks as a Financing Instrument," found that in 1965 bonds had a yield 0.39 percentage points *above* preferred stocks. Thus a very strong firm could sell preferreds to yield about 0.3 percent less than bonds. As an example, on March 27, 1973, AT&T sold a preferred issue that yielded 7.28 percent to an investor. On that same date, AT&T bonds yielded 7.55 percent, or 0.27 percent more than the preferred. The tax treatment accounted for this differential; the *after-tax* yield was greater on the preferred stock than on the bonds.

the stated coupon rate for profitable firms. The cost of preferred, how-ever, is the full percentage amount of the preferred dividend.[9]

In fashioning securities, the financial manager needs to consider the investor's point of view. Frequently it is asserted that preferred stocks have so many disadvantages to both the issuer and the investor that they should never be issued. Nevertheless, preferred stock is issued in substantial amounts. Preferred stock provides the following advantages to the investor:

1. It provides reasonably steady income.
2. Preferred stockholders have a preference over common stockholders in liquidation; numerous examples can be cited where the preference position of holders of preferred stock saved them from losses incurred by holders of common stock.
3. Many corporations (for example, insurance companies) like to hold preferred stocks as investments because 85 percent of the dividends received on these shares is not taxable.

Preferred stock also has some disadvantages to investors:

1. Although the holders of preferred stock bear a substantial portion of ownership risk, their returns are limited.
2. Price fluctuations in preferred stock are far greater than those in bonds; yet, yields on bonds are frequently higher than those on preferred stock.
3. The stockholders have no legally enforceable right to dividends.
4. Accrued dividend arrearages are seldom settled in cash comparable to the amount of the obligation that has been incurred.

Recent Trends

Because of the nondeductibility of preferred stock dividends as a tax expense, many companies have retired their preferred stock. Often debentures or subordinated debentures are offered to preferred stockholders in exchange, since the interest on the debentures is deductible as a tax expense.

When the preferred stock is not callable, the company must offer terms of exchange sufficiently attractive to induce the preferred stockholders to agree to the exchange. Characteristically, bonds or other securities in an amount somewhat above the recent value of the preferred stock are issued in exchange. Sometimes bonds equal in market value to the preferred stock are issued along with additional cash or common stock to provide an extra inducement to the preferred stockholders. At other times the offer is bonds

---

9. By far the most important issuers of nonconvertible preferred stocks are the utility companies. For these firms, taxes are an expense for rate-making purposes—that is, higher taxes are passed on to the customers in the form of higher prices—so tax deductibility is not an important issue. This explains why utilities issue about 85 percent of all nonconvertible preferreds.

equal to only a portion of the current market value of the preferred with an additional amount represented by cash or common stock that will bring the total offered the preferred stockholder to something over the preferred market value as of a recent date.

U.S. Steel's replacement of its 7 percent preferred stock in 1965 is a classic illustration of these exchange patterns. U.S. Steel proposed that its 7 percent preferred stock be changed into $4^5/_8$ percent thirty-year bonds at a rate of $175 principal amount of bonds for each preferred share. On August 17, 1965, when the plan was announced, the preferred stock was selling at $150. U.S. Steel also announced that the conversion would increase earnings available to common stock by $10 million yearly, or 18 cents a share at 1965 federal income tax rates; this was sufficient inducement to persuade the company to give the preferred stockholders the added $25 a share.

Decision Making on the Use of Preferred Stock

As a hybrid security, preferred stock is favored by conditions that fall between those favoring common stock and those favoring debt. When a firm's profit margin is high enough to more than cover preferred stock dividends, it is advantageous to employ leverage. However, if the firm's sales and profits are subject to considerable fluctuation, the use of debt with fixed interest charges may be unduly risky. Preferred stock can offer a happy compromise. Its use is strongly favored if the firm already has a debt ratio that is high in relation to the reference level maximum for the line of business.

Relative costs of alternative sources of financing are always important considerations. When the market prices of common stocks are relatively low, the costs of common stock financing are relatively high (see Chapter 14). The costs of preferred stock financing follow interest rate levels more than common stock prices; in other words, when interest rates are low, the cost of preferred stock is also likely to be low. When the cost of fixed income instruments, such as preferred stock, are low and the costs of variable value securities, such as common stock, are high, the use of preferred stock is favored. Preferred stock may also be the desired form of financing whenever the use of debt will involve excessive risk but the issuance of common stock will result in problems of control for the dominant ownership group in the company.

Rationale for Different Classes of Securities

At this point, the following questions are likely to come to mind: Why are there so many different forms of long-term securities? Why is anybody ever willing to purchase subordinated bonds or income bonds? The answers to both questions can be made clear by reference to Figure 20.2. The now

**Figure 20.2
The Longstreet Company's Risk
and Expected Returns on Different
Classes of Securities**

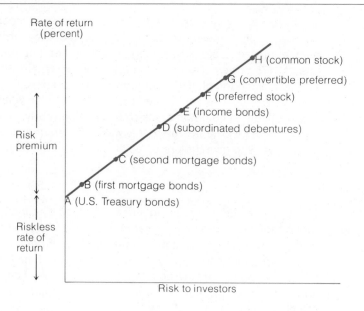

familiar tradeoff function is drawn to show the risk and expected returns for the various securities of the Longstreet Company. Longstreet's first mortgage bonds are slightly more risky than U.S. Treasury bonds and sell at a slightly higher expected return. The second mortgage bonds are yet more risky and have a still higher expected return. Subordinated debentures, income bonds, and preferred stocks all are increasingly risky and have increasingly higher expected returns. Longstreet's common stock, the riskiest security the firm issues, has the highest expected return of any of its offerings.

Why does Longstreet issue so many different classes of securities? Why not just offer one type of bond plus common stock? The answer lies in the fact that different investors have different risk-return tradeoff preferences, so if the company's securities are to appeal to the broadest possible market, Longstreet must offer as many as investors seem to want. Used wisely, a policy of selling differentiated securities can lower a firm's overall cost of capital below what it would be if it issued only one class of debt and common stock.

Refunding a Bond or a Preferred Stock Issue

Suppose a company sells bonds or preferred stock at a time when interest rates are relatively high. Provided the issue is callable, as many are, the company can sell a new issue of low-yielding securities if and when interest rates drop and use the proceeds to retire the high-rate issue. This is called a *refunding operation.*[10]

The decision to refund a security issue is analyzed in much the same manner as a capital budgeting expenditure. The costs of refunding—the investment outlay—are (1) the call premium paid for the privilege of calling the old issue and (2) the flotation costs incurred in selling the new issue. The annual receipts, in the capital budgeting sense, are the interest payments saved each year; for example, if interest expense on the old issue is $1 million while that on the new issue is $700,000, the $300,000 saving constitutes the annual benefit.

In analyzing the advantages of refunding, the recommended procedure is the net present value method—discounting the future interest savings back to the present and comparing the discounted value with the cash outlays associated with the refunding. In the discounting process, the after-tax cost of the new debt, not the average cost of capital, is used as the discount factor. The reason for this is that there is relatively little risk to the savings; their value is known with relative certainty (which is quite unlike most capital budgeting decisions). The following case illustrates the calculations needed in a refunding decision.

As discussed in Chapters 8 and 23, interest rate levels peaked cyclically in the autumn of 1974, when the rates on new issues of AAA corporate bonds exceeded 10 percent. By December 1976 these yields had declined to almost 8 percent, representing a swing of approximately 200 basis points. The last half of 1976 was characterized by a substantial activity in refunding of bond and preferred stock issues at lower interest rates. A moderate increase in interest rates occurred during the early part of January 1977, but refundings continued to be attractive. Also, interest rates were considered to be near their cyclical lows. Illustrative of the bond refunding activity that occurred in 1976–1977 is the South Carolina Electric & Gas Company's $30 million First and Refunding Mortgage Bond issue of February 17, 1977, at an 8 3/8 percent interest rate, maturing March 1, 2007.[11] The net proceeds from the sale of these bonds were applied to the redemption of Carolina's First and Refunding Mortgage Bonds, 9 7/8 percent series, due in the year

---

10. For an excellent discussion of refunding, see O. D. Bowlin, "The Refunding Decision," *Journal of Finance* 21 (March 1966); for an analysis in the Modigliani-Miller framework, see A. R. Ofer and R. A. Taggert, "Bond Refunding: A Clarifying Analysis," *Journal of Finance* 32 (March 1977).
11. This is an actual refunding operation based on the company prospectus dated February 17, 1977, and information obtained on the old issue from *Moody's Public Utilities,* 1977.

2000 at a redemption price of 107.04 percent of the principal amount plus accrued interest to the date of redemption at April 1, 1977.

The relevant data on the old issue and on the new refunding issue are summarized below:

	Old Issue	New Issue
Face amount	$30,000,000	$30,000,000
Interest rate	$9^7/_8\%$	$8^3/_8\%$
Life of bond	30 years	30 years
Maturity date	June 1, 2000	March 1, 2007
Total issue proceeds	$29,700,000	$29,918,100
Flotation costs	$600,000	$262,500
Net proceeds of sale	$29,100,000	$29,655,600

Step 1. What is the investment outlay required to refund the issue? There are four components to the required investment outlay; the call premium on the old issue, flotation costs on the new issue, flotation costs on the old issue, and additional interest expense.

a. Call premium:

The call premium is 7.04 percent of face value as given by the bond indenture on the old issue. Since this is a tax deductible expense, the actual cost is reduced by the company's tax rate of 40 percent.

$$\text{Before-tax call premium} = \text{Call rate} \times \text{Face amount}$$
$$\$2,112,000 = 0.0704 \times \$30,000,000.$$
$$\text{After-tax call premium} = \text{Before-tax call premium} \times (1 - \text{Tax rate})$$
$$\$1,267,200 = \$2,112,000 \times (1 - 0.40).$$

Although South Carolina Electric & Gas must expend $2.112 million on the call premium, this is a deductible expense. Since the company is in a 40 percent tax bracket, it saved $844,800 in taxes. The after-tax cost of the call is therefore only $1,267,200.

b. Flotation costs on new issue:

Total flotation costs are $262,500. For tax purposes, costs are amortized over the life of the new bond, or thirty years. Assuming straight-line amortization, the annual tax deduction is given by:

$$\text{Annual tax deduction} = \frac{\text{Flotation costs}}{\text{Life of bond (new issue)}}$$
$$\$8,750 = \frac{\$262,500}{30}.$$

Since South Carolina E & G is in the 40 percent tax bracket, it has a tax saving of $3,500 a year ($8,750 × 0.40) for thirty years. This is an annuity of $3,500 for thirty years. The present value of the annuity is found by discounting at the after-tax cost of the new debt issue. The after-tax cost of debt is the before-tax interest rate times one minus the tax rate (8.375 × 0.60), or 5 percent.

$$\text{PV of tax saving} = \text{PVIF}_a \times \text{Annual after-tax saving}$$
$$= 15.373 \times \$3,500$$
$$= \$53,805.$$

Net after-tax effect on new flotation cost is:

New flotation costs	$262,500
PV of tax savings	53,805
Net cost	$208,695

c. Flotation costs on old issue:

The old issue has an unamortized flotation cost of $460,000 (23/30 × $600,000). This can be recognized immediately as an expense, thus creating an after-tax savings of $184,000. The firm will, however, lose a deduction of $20,000 a year for twenty-three years, or an after-tax benefit of $8,000 a year. The present value of this loss benefit, discounted at 5 percent is:

$$\text{PV of lost benefit} = \text{PVIF}_a \times \$8,000$$
$$= 13.488 \times \$8,000$$
$$= \$107,906.$$

The net after-tax effect of old flotation costs is:

Tax savings on old flotation costs	($184,000)
PV of lost benefit	107,906
Net after-tax effect of old flotation costs	($76,084)

d. Additional interest:

The old bond will not be retired until one month after the new bond is issued. Thus there will be a period of one month when interest is accruing on both bonds. During this period, the proceeds of the new issue are invested in short-term Treasury bills to earn 4.5 percent.

One month "extra" interest on new issue:

$$\text{Face amount} \times \tfrac{1}{12} \times 8.375\% = \text{Before-tax interest costs}$$
$$\$30,000,000 \times \tfrac{1}{12} \times 0.08375 = \$209,375.$$

One-month income from Treasury bill investment:

$$\$29,655,600 \times \tfrac{1}{12} \times 0.045 = \$111,209.$$

Net after-tax interest cost:

$$(\text{Interest cost} - \text{Interest revenue}) \times (1 - \text{Tax rate}) = \text{Cost}$$
$$(\$209,375 - \$111,209)(1 - 0.4) = \$58,900.$$

e. Total after-tax investment:

The total investment outlay required to refund the bond issue is thus:

Call premium	$1,267,200
Flotation cost, new	208,695
Flotation cost, old	−76,096
Additional interest	58,900
Total investment	$1,458,699

Step 2. What are the annual savings?

a. Old bond interest after tax:

$$\text{Face amount} \times \text{Interest rate} \times (1 - \text{Tax rate}) = \text{Interest}$$
$$\$30,000,000 \times 0.09875 \times (1 - 0.4) = \$1,777,500.$$

b. New bond interest after tax:

$$\$30,000,000 \times 0.08375 \times (1 - 0.4) = \underline{\$1,507,500.}$$

c. Annual savings:

$$\$\ 270,000$$

Step 3. What is the present value of the savings?

a. Twenty-three years PV of annuity factor at 5 percent = 13.488.

b. PV of $270,000 a year for twenty-three years:

$$13.488 \times \$270,000 = \$3,641,760.$$

Step 4. Conclusion: Since the present value of the receipts ($3,641,760) exceeds the required investment ($1,458,699), the issue should be refunded.

Two other points should be mentioned. First, since the $270,000 savings is an essentially riskless investment, its present value is found by discounting at the firm's least risky rate—its after-tax cost of debt. Second, since the refunding operation is advantageous to the firm, it must be disadvantageous to bondholders; they must give up their 9⅞ percent bond and reinvest in one yielding 8⅜ percent. This points out the danger of the call provision to bondholders and explains why, at any given time, bonds without a call provision command higher prices than callable bonds.[12]

Summary

A *bond* is a long-term promissory note. A *mortgage bond* is secured by real property. An *indenture* is an agreement between the firm issuing the bond and the numerous bondholders, represented by a *trustee*.

Secured long-term debt differs with respect to (1) the priority of claims, (2) the right to issue additional securities, and (3) the scope of the lien provided. These characteristics determine the amount of protection provided to

---

12. See Jen and Wert, "Effects of Call Risk on Corporate Bond Yields"; and Pye, "Value of Call Deferment on a Bond."

the bondholder by the terms of the security. Giving investors more security will induce them to accept a lower yield but will restrict the future freedom of action of the issuing firm.

The main classes of unsecured bonds are (1) *debentures,* (2) *subordinated debentures,* and (3) *income bonds.* Holders of debentures are unsecured general creditors. Subordinated debentures are junior in claim to bank loans. Income bonds are similar to preferred stock in that interest is paid only when earned.

The characteristics of long-term debt determine the circumstances under which it will be used when alternative forms of financing are under analysis. The cost of debt is limited, but it is a fixed obligation. Bond interest is an expense deductible for tax purposes. Debt carries a maturity date and may require sinking fund payments to prepare for extinguishing the obligation. Indenture provisions are likely to include restrictions on the freedom of action of the firm's management.

The nature of long-term debt encourages its use under the following circumstances:

1. Sales and earnings are relatively stable.
2. Profit margins are adequate to make leverage advantageous.
3. A rise in profits or the general price level is expected.
4. The existing debt ratio is relatively low.
5. Common stock price/earnings ratios are low in relation to the levels of interest rates.
6. Control considerations are important.
7. Cash flow requirements under the bond agreement are not burdensome.
8. Restrictions of the bond indenture are not onerous.

Although seven of the eight factors may favor debt, the eighth can swing the decision to the use of equity capital. The list of factors is thus simply a checklist of things to be considered when deciding on bonds versus stock; the actual decision is based on a judgment about the relative importance of the several factors.

The characteristics of preferred stock vary with the requirements of the situation under which it is used. However, certain patterns tend to remain. Preferred stocks usually have priority over common stocks with respect to earnings and claims on assets in liquidation. Preferred stocks are usually cumulative; they have no maturity but are sometimes callable. They are typically nonparticipating and offer only contingent voting rights.

The advantages to the issuer are limited dividends and no maturity. These advantages may outweigh the disadvantages of higher cost and nondeductibility of the dividends as an expense for tax purposes. But their acceptance by investors is the final test of whether they can be sold on favorable terms.

Companies sell preferred stock when they seek the advantages of financial leverage but fear the dangers of the fixed charges on debt in the face of potential fluctuations in income. If debt ratios or the cost of common stock financing are relatively high, the advantages of preferred stock are reinforced.

The use of preferred stock has declined significantly since the advent of the corporate income tax because preferred dividends are not deductible for income tax purposes, while bond interest payments are deductible. In recent years, however, there has been a strong shift back to a new kind of preferred stock—convertible preferred, used primarily in connection with mergers. If the stockholders of the acquired company receive cash or bonds, they are required to pay capital gains taxes on any gains they realize. If convertible preferred stock is given to the selling stockholders, this constitutes a tax-free exchange of securities. The selling stockholders can obtain a fixed income security and at the same time postpone the payment of capital gains taxes.

If a bond or preferred stock issue was sold when interest rates were higher than they are at present, and if the issue is callable, it may be profitable to call the old issue and refund it with a new, lower-cost issue. An analysis similar to capital budgeting is required to determine whether a refunding operation should be undertaken.

Questions

20.1 A sinking fund is set up in one of two ways:
  a. The corporation makes annual payments to the trustee, who invests the proceeds in securities (frequently government bonds) and uses the accumulated total to retire the bond issue on maturity.
  b. The trustee uses the annual payments to retire a portion of the issue each year, either calling a given percentage of the issue by a lottery and paying a specified price per bond or buying bonds on the open market, whichever is cheaper.
  Discuss the advantages and disadvantages of each procedure from the viewpoint of both the firm and the bondholders.

20.2 Since a corporation often has the right to call bonds at will, do you believe individuals should be able to demand repayment at any time they so desire? Explain.

20.3 What are the relative advantages and disadvantages of issuing a long-term bond during a recession versus during a period of prosperity?

20.4 Missouri Pacific's 4 3/4 percent income bonds due in 2020 are selling for $770, while the company's 4 1/4 percent first mortgage bonds due in 2005 are selling for $945. Each has a $1,000 par value. Why do the bonds with the lower coupon sell at a higher price?

20.5 When a firm sells bonds, it must offer a package of terms acceptable to potential buyers. Included in this package are such features as the issue price, the coupon interest rate, the term of maturity, and sinking fund provisions. The package itself is determined through a bargaining process between the firm and the investment bankers who handle the issue. What particular features would you, as a corporate treasurer, be especially interested in having, and which would you be most willing to give ground on, under each of the following conditions:

a. You believe that the economy is near the peak of a business cycle.

b. Long-run forecasts indicate that your firm may have heavy cash inflows in relation to cash needs during the next five to ten years.

c. Your current liabilities are presently low, but you anticipate raising a considerable amount of funds through short-term borrowing in the near future.

20.6 Bonds are less attractive to investors during periods of inflation because a rise in the price level reduces the purchasing power of the fixed interest payments and of the principal. Discuss the advantages and disadvantages to a corporation of using a bond whose interest payments and principal would increase in direct proportion to increases in the price level (an inflation-proof bond).

20.7 If preferred stock dividends are passed for several years, the preferred stockholders are frequently given the right to elect several members of the board of directors. In the case of bonds that are in default on interest payments, this procedure is not followed. Why does the difference exist?

20.8 Preferred stocks are found in almost all industries, but one industry is the really dominant issuer of preferred shares. What is this industry, and why are firms in it so disposed to using preferred stock?

20.9 If the corporate income tax were abolished, would this raise or lower the amount of new preferred stock issued?

20.10 Investors buying securities have some expected or required rate of return in mind. Which would you expect to be higher—the required rate of return (before taxes) on preferred stocks or that on common stocks:

a. for individual investors?

b. for corporate investors (for example, insurance companies)?

20.11 Do you think the before-tax required rate of return is higher or lower on very high grade preferred stocks or on bonds:

a. for individual investors?

b. for corporate investors?

20.12 For purposes of measuring a firm's leverage, should preferred stock be classified as debt or as equity? Does it matter if the classification is being made (a) by the firm itself, (b) by creditors, or (c) by equity investors?

Problems

20.1 Several years ago your father purchased a farm adjacent to his existing farm. The deal was financed partly by a long-term mortgage loan requiring payments of $21,909 per year (including interest and principal) for twenty more years and with a contract interest rate of 10 percent. Your father is considering refinancing the loan because current rates for similar loans have dropped to 8 percent. He is hesitant to refund the mortgage, however, because there is a prepayment penalty of six months' interest on the unpaid balance. Further, about 4 percent of the loan amount will be required for set-up fees for a new loan. Because of other write-offs, your father pays no income taxes. Should your father refinance the loan? (Hint: Begin by finding the unpaid balance of the existing loan, which is equal to the present value of the remaining payments, discounted at the contract interest rate.)

20.2 Three years ago your firm issued some eighteen-year bonds with 10.5 percent coupon rates and a 10 percent call premium. You have called these bonds. The bonds originally sold at their face value of $1,000.

a. Compute the realized rate of return for investors who purchased the bonds when they were issued.

b. Given the rate of return in Part a, did investors welcome the call? Explain.

20.3 Carson Electronics, a leading manufacturer of electronics, is planning an expansion program. It has estimated that it will need to raise an additional $100 million. Carson is discussing with its investment banker the alternatives of raising the $100 million through debt financing or through selling additional shares of common stock.

The prevailing cost of Aaa debt is 8 percent, while the prevailing cost of Baa debt is 9.6 percent. New equity would be sold at $10 per share. The corporate tax rate is 50 percent. Below are the industry's financial ratios, (followed by Carson's balance sheet and income statement):

Electronics Industry Financial Ratios

Current ratio: 2.1 times
Sales to total assets: 1.8 times
Current debt to total assets: 30%
Long-term debt to net worth: 40%
Total debt to total assets: 50%
Coverage of fixed charges: 7 times
Net income to sales: 5%
Return on total assets: 9%
Net income to net worth: 12%

**Carson Electronics
Balance Sheet as of
December 31, 1978
(Millions of Dollars)**

Assets			Liabilities		
Total current assets	$	600	Total current liabilities	$200	
Net fixed assets		400	Long-term debt (at 8%)	100	
			Total debt		$ 300
			Common stock, par value $1		100
			Additional paid-in capital		200
			Retained earnings		400
Total assets		$1,000	Total claims on assets		$1,000

Carson Electronics
Income Statement for Year
Ended December 31, 1978
(Millions of Dollars)

Total revenues	$2,000
Net operating income	248
Interest expense	8
Net income before taxes	$ 240
Income taxes (at 50%)	120
Net income to equity	$ 120

a. Estimate Carson Electronics' cost of equity capital by using the security market line. The risk-free rate is 6 percent, the expected return on the market is 11 percent, and the beta based on Carson's present leverage is 1.2.

b. What is the value of Carson's total equity? What is its indicated price per share?

c. On the basis of a cost of debt of 8 percent and the cost of equity that you have calculated, determine the weighted average cost of capital for Carson at the present time. (The company has no short-term interest-bearing debt.)

d. If Carson finances its expansion by the use of debt, calculate the new financial structure and coverage relationships, and present your conclusion on whether the new debt issue will be risky or relatively risk-free. (Assume that the same percentage of net operating income is earned on the increase in assets as was earned on the total assets before the financing.)

e. If Carson finances with debt, the cost of debt will be 8 percent, while the cost of equity will reflect the rise in β to 1.25. If the company finances with equity, the cost of debt will be 8 percent, while the cost of equity will reflect a drop in beta to 1.19. Compare the cost of equity under the two methods of financing.

f. Under each of the two methods of financing, what will be the total value of the equity, and what will be the new value per share of common stock?

g. Under the same assumptions as in the preceding questions, calculate the value of the firm under the two methods of financing.

h. Compare the weighted cost of capital under the two methods of financing.

i. Summarize your recommendation about which form of financing Carson should employ for raising the additional $100 million.

20.4 The Longmont Corporation has a $600,000 long-term bond issue outstanding. This debt has an additional ten years to maturity and bears a coupon interest rate of 9 percent. The firm now has the opportunity of refinancing the debt with ten-year bonds at a rate of 7 percent. Further declines in the interest rate are unanticipated. The bond redemption premium (call premium) on the old bond would be $30,000; issue cost on the new would be $20,000. If tax effects are ignored, should the firm refund the bonds?

20.5 In late 1978 the Coaltown Gas & Electric Company sought to raise $6 million to refinance current preferred stock issues at a lower rate. The company could have sold additional debt at 9 percent, preferred stock at 8.84 percent, or common stock at $50 a share. How should the company have raised the money? Relevant financial information is provided below:

Public Utilities Financial Ratios

Current ratio: 1.0 times
Interest earned (before taxes): 4.0 times
Sales to total assets: 0.3 times
Average collection period: 28.0 days
Current debt/total assets: 5–10%
Long-term debt/total assets: 45–50%
Preferred/total assets: 10–15%
Common equity/total assets: 30–35%
Earnings before interest and taxes to total assets: 8.9%
Profits to common equity: 12.1%
Expected growth in earnings and dividends: 4.5%

Coaltown Gas & Electric Company Balance Sheet as of July 31, 1978 (Millions of Dollars)

Assets		Liabilities	
Cash	$ 0.75	Current liabilities	$ 3.00
Receivables	1.50	Long-term debt (at 8%)	27.00
Material and supplies	1.20	Preferred stock (at 10%)	6.00
Total current assets	$ 3.45	Common stock, $25 par value	11.25
		Capital surplus	6.60
Net property	56.55	Retained earnings	6.15
Total assets	$60.00	Total claims	$60.00

Coaltown Gas & Electric Company Income Statement for Year Ended July 31, 1978 (Millions of Dollars)

Operating revenues	$18.9000
Operating expenses	10.7570
Earnings before interest and taxes	$ 8.1430
Interest deduction	2.1600
Earnings before taxes	$ 5.9830
Income taxes (at 50%)	2.9915
Earnings after taxes	$ 2.9915
Preferred dividends	0.6000
Net income available to common	$ 2.3915
Earnings per share =	$ 5.31
Expected dividends per share =	$ 4.25

20.6 The Ellis Corporation plans to expand assets by 25 percent. It can finance the expansion with straight debt or with common stock. The interest rate on the debt would be 12 percent. Ellis's current balance sheet and income statement are shown below.

**Ellis Corporation
Balance Sheet as of
December 31, 1978
(Thousands of Dollars)**

Assets		Liabilities	
		Debt (at 10%)	$300
		Common stock, $1 par (100,000 shares outstanding)	100
		Retained earnings	400
Total assets	$800	Total claims	$800

**Ellis Corporation Income
Statement for Year Ended
December 31, 1978
(Thousands of Dollars)**

Sales	$2,300
Total costs (excluding interest)	2,070
Net operating income	$ 230
Debt interest	30
Income before taxes	$ 200
Taxes (at 50%)	100
Net income	$ 100

Earnings per share: $\frac{\$100,000}{100,000} = \$1$

Price/earnings ratio = 10[a]

Market price = P/E × EPS = 10 × 1 = $10

[a] The P/E ratio is the market price per share divided by earnings per share. It represents the amount of money an investor is willing to pay for $1 of current earnings. The higher the riskiness of a stock, the lower its P/E ratio, other things held constant.

If Ellis Corporation finances the $200,000 expansion with debt, the rate on the incremental debt will be 12 percent, and the price/earnings ratio of the common stock will drop to nine times. If the expansion is financed with equity, the new stock will sell for $8 per share, the rate on debt will be 10 percent, and the price/earnings ratio will remain at ten times. (The opportunity cost of debt is 12 percent. However, use the 10 percent rate, on the debt already on the balance sheet, because this is the rate actually being paid.)

a. Assume that net income before interest and taxes (EBIT) is 10 percent of sales. Calculate EPS at sales levels of $0, $600,000, $2,400,000, $2,800,000, $3,000,000, $3,600,000 and $4,800,000 for financing with (1) debt and (2) common stock. Assume no fixed costs of production.

b. Make a breakeven chart for EPS, and indicate the breakeven point in sales (that is, where EPS using bonds equals EPS using stock).

c. Using the price/earnings ratio, calculate the market value per share of common stock for each sales level for both the debt and the equity financing.

d. Make a breakeven chart of market value per share using data from Part c, and indicate the breakeven point.

e. If the firm follows the policy of seeking to maximize (1) EPS or (2) market price per share, which form of financing should be used?

f. The probability estimates of future sales are: 5 percent chance of $0; 10 percent chance of $600,000; 20 percent chance of $2,400,000; 30 percent chance of $2,800,000; 20 percent chance of $3,000,000; 10 percent chance of $3,600,000; and 5 percent chance of $4,800,000. Calculate expected values for EPS, market price per share, the standard deviation, and the coefficient of variation for each alternative.

g. What other factors should be taken into account in choosing between the two forms of financing?

h. Would it matter if the presently outstanding stock was all owned by the final decision maker—the president—and that this represented his entire net worth? Would it matter if he was compensated entirely by a fixed salary? Would it matter if he had a substantial number of stock options?

CHAPTER **21** LEASE FINANCING

Firms are generally interested in using buildings and equipment. One way of obtaining their use is to buy them, but an alternative is to lease them. Prior to the 1950s, leasing was most often associated with real estate—land and buildings—but today it is possible to lease virtually any kind of fixed asset. The following quotation from *Fortune* will give an idea of the importance of equipment leasing (leases for real estate increase the significance of this financing technique):

Capital equipment with an original cost of somewhat more than $60 billion is now on lease in the U.S. to corporations, institutions, and governments. New equipment worth over $11 billion was leased last year, and it accounted for about 14 percent of all business investment in capital equipment. Overall, the volume of leasing is expanding by around 20 percent a year. If leasing continues to grow at its recent rate, by 1977 about one-fifth of all new capital equipment put in use by business will be leased.[1]

In a number of respects, leasing is quite similar to borrowing. However, while debt or equity financing, as part of a general pool of financing sources, cannot be associated with specific assets, leasing is typically identified with such assets.

Leasing provides for the acquisition of assets and their "complete financing" simultaneously. Its advantage over debt is that the lessor has a better position than a creditor if the user firm experiences financial difficulties. If the lessee does not meet the lease obligations, the lessor has a stronger legal right to take back the asset because the lessor still legally owns the asset. A creditor, even a secured creditor, encounters costs and delays in recovering assets that have been directly or indirectly financed. Since the lessor has less risk than other financing sources used in acquiring assets, the riskier the firm seeking financing, the greater the reason for the supplier of financing to formulate a leasing arrangement rather than a loan. While banks, which provide term loans as well as leases, may prefer leases or shift to them for risky applicants, the extent to which this differential risk position accounts for the growth of leasing activity is not known.

Types of Leases

Conceptually, as shown below, leasing is similar to borrowing and therefore provides financial leverage. Leases take several different forms, the most important of which are sale and leaseback, service, and straight financial. These three major types of leases are described below.

Sale and Leaseback

Under a sale and leaseback arrangement, a firm owning land, buildings, or equipment sells the property to a financial institution and simultaneously

1. Peter Vanderwicken, "The Powerful Logic of the Leasing Boom," *Fortune,* November 1973, p. 136.

executes an agreement to lease the property back for a certain period under specific terms. If real estate is involved, the financial institution is generally a life insurance company; if the property consists of equipment and machinery, the financial institution can be an insurance company, a commercial bank, or a specialized leasing company.

Note that the seller, or *lessee,* immediately receives the purchase price put up by the buyer, or *lessor.* At the same time, the seller-lessee retains the use of the property. This parallel is carried over to the lease payment schedule. Under a mortgage loan arrangement, the financial institution receives a series of equal payments just sufficient to amortize the loan and to provide the lender with a specified rate of return on investment. Under a sale and leaseback arrangement, the lease payments are set up in the same manner. The payments are sufficient to return the full purchase price to the financial institution in addition to providing it with some return on its investment.

Service Leases

Service, or operating, leases include both financing and maintenance services. IBM is one of the pioneers of the service lease contract; computers and office copying machines, together with automobiles and trucks, are the primary types of equipment involved. The leases ordinarily call for the lessor to maintain and service the leased equipment, and the costs of this maintenance are either built into the lease payments or contracted for separately.

Another important characteristic of the service lease is that it is frequently not fully amortized. In other words, the payments required under the lease contract are *not* sufficient to recover the full cost of the equipment. Obviously, however, the lease contract is written for considerably less than the expected life of the leased equipment, and the lessor expects to recover the cost either in subsequent renewal payments or on disposal of the equipment.

A final feature of the service lease is that it frequently contains a cancellation clause giving the lessee the right to cancel the lease and return the equipment before the expiration of the basic agreement. This is an important consideration for the lessee, who can return the equipment if technological developments render it obsolete or if it simply is no longer needed.

Financial Leases

A strict financial lease is one that does not provide for maintenance services, is not cancellable, and is fully amortized (that is, the lessor receives rental payments equal to the full price of the leased equipment). The typical arrangement involves the following steps:

1. The firm that will use the equipment selects the specific items it requires and negotiates the price and delivery terms with the manufacturer or distributor.

563

2. Next, the user firm arranges with a bank or leasing company for the latter to buy the equipment from the manufacturer or distributor, simultaneously executing an agreement to lease the equipment from the financial institution. The terms call for full amortization of the financial institution's cost, plus a return of from 6 to 12 percent a year on the unamortized balance. The lessee generally has the option to renew the lease at a reduced rental on expiration of the basic lease but does not have the right to cancel the basic lease without completely paying off the financial institution.

Financial leases are almost the same as sale and leaseback arrangements, the main difference being that the leased equipment is new and the lessor buys it from a manufacturer or a distributor instead of from the user-lessee. A sale and leaseback can thus be thought of as a special type of financial lease.

Internal Revenue Service Requirements for a Lease

The full amount of the annual lease payments is deductible for income tax purposes—provided the Internal Revenue Service agrees that a particular contract is a genuine lease and not simply an installment loan called a lease. This makes it important that the lease contract be written in a form acceptable to the IRS. Following are the major requirements for bona fide lease transactions from the standpoint of the IRS:

1. The term must be less than thirty years; otherwise the lease is regarded as a form of sale.
2. The rent must represent a reasonable return to the lessor—in the range of 7 to 12 percent on the investment.
3. The renewal option must be bona fide, and this requirement can best be met by giving the lessee the first option to meet an equal bona fide outside offer.
4. There must be no repurchase option; if there is, the lessee should merely be given parity with an equal outside offer.

Accounting for Leases

In November 1976 the Financial Accounting Standards Board issued its Statement of Financial Accounting Standards No. 13, *Accounting for Leases.* Like other FASB statements, the standards set forth must be followed by business firms if their financial statements are to receive certification by auditors. FASB No. 13 has implications both for the utilization of leases and for their accounting treatment. The elements of FASB No. 13 most relevant for financial analysis of leases are summarized below.

For some types of leases, FASB No. 13 requires that the obligation be capitalized on the asset side of the balance sheet with a related lease obligation on the liability side. Since the treatment depends on the type of lease, the criteria for classification are first set forth. A lease is classified as a capital lease if it meets one or more of four Paragraph 7 criteria:

1. The lease transfers ownership of the property to the lessee by the end of the lease term.
2. The lease gives the lessee the option to purchase the property at a price sufficiently below the expected fair value of the property that the exercise of the option is highly probable.
3. The lease term is equal to 75 percent or more of the estimated economic life of the property.
4. The present value of the minimum lease payments exceeds 90 percent of the fair value of the property at the inception of the lease. The discount factor to be used in calculating the present value is the implicit rate used by the lessor or the lessee's incremental borrowing rate, whichever is lower. (Note that the lower discount factor represents a higher present value factor and therefore a higher calculated present value for a given pattern of lease payments. It thus increases the likelihood that the 90 percent test will be met and that the lease will be classified as a capital lease.)

From the standpoint of the lessee, if a lease is not a capital lease, it is classified as an operating lease. From the standpoint of the lessor, four types of leases are defined: (1) sales-type leases, (2) direct financing leases, (3) leveraged leases, and (4) operating leases representing all leases other than the first three types. Sales-type leases and direct financing leases meet one or more of the four Paragraph 7 criteria and both of the two Paragraph 8 criteria, which are:

1. Collectibility of the minimum lease payments is reasonably predictable.
2. No important uncertainties surround the amount of unreimbursable costs yet to be incurred by the lessor under the lease.

Sales-type leases give rise to profit (or loss) to the lessor—the fair value of the leased property at the inception of the lease is greater (or less) than its cost of carrying amount. Sales-type leases normally arise when manufacturers or dealers use leasing in marketing their products. Direct financing leases are leases other than leveraged leases for which the cost of carrying amount is equal to the fair value of the leased property at the inception of the lease. Leveraged leases are direct financing leases in which substantial financing is provided by a long-term creditor on a nonrecourse basis with respect to the general credit of the lessor.

Accounting by Lessees

For operating leases, rentals must be charged to expense over the lease term, with disclosures of future rental obligations in total as well as by each of the following five years. For lessees, capital leases are to be capitalized and shown on the balance sheet both as a fixed asset and a noncurrent obligation. Capitalization represents the present value of the minimum lease payments minus that portion of lease payments representing executory costs such as insurance, maintenance, and taxes to be paid by the lessor (including any profit return in such charges). The discount factor is as described in Paragraph 7 (4)—the lower of the implicit rates used by the lessor and the incremental borrowing rate of the lessee.

The asset must be amortized in a manner consistent with the lessee's normal depreciation policy for owned assets. During the lease term, each lease payment is to be allocated between a reduction of the obligation and the interest expense to produce a constant rate of interest on the remaining balance of the obligation. Thus, for capital leases, the balance sheet includes the items in Table 21.1.

**Table 21.1
Company X Balance Sheet**

Assets	December 31, 1977	1976	Liabilities	December 31, 1977	1976
			Current:		
Leased property under capital leases, less accumulated amortization	XXX	XXX	Obligations under capital leases	XXX	XXX
			Noncurrent:		
			Obligations under capital leases	XXX	XXX

In addition to the balance sheet capitalization of capital leases, substantial additional footnote disclosures are required for both capital and operating leases. These include a description of leasing arrangements, an analysis of leased property under capital leases by major classes of property, a schedule by years of future minimum lease payments (with executory and interest costs broken out for capital leases), and contingent rentals for operating leases.

FASB No. 13 sets forth requirements for capitalizing capital leases and for standardizing disclosures by lessees for both capital leases and operating leases. Lease commitments therefore do not represent "off–balance sheet" financing for capital assets, and standard disclosure requirements make general the footnote reporting of information on operating leases. Hence, the argument that leasing represents a form of financing that lenders may not take into account in their analysis of the financial position of firms seeking financing will be even less valid in the future than it is now.

It is unlikely that sophisticated lenders were ever fooled by off–balance sheet leasing obligations. However, the capitalization of capital leases and the standard disclosure requirements for operating leases will make it easier for general users of financial reports to obtain additional information on firms' leasing obligations. Hence, the requirements of FASB No. 13 are useful. Probably, the extent of use of leasing will remain substantially unaltered, since the particular circumstances that have provided a basis for its use in the past are not likely to be greatly affected by the increased disclosure requirements.

Cost Comparison between Lease and Purchase

For an understanding of the possible advantages and disadvantages of lease financing, the cost of leasing must be compared with the cost of owning the equipment.[2] To make the leasing versus owning cost comparison clear, the lessor's point of view will be explored. Assume the following:

I = cost of an asset = $20,000.

Dep = the annual economic and tax depreciation charge.

k = the appropriate cost of capital or the competitive risk-adjusted return of the project associated with the asset = 10%.

T = the lessor's corporate tax rate = 40%.

N = the economic life and tax depreciation life of the asset = 5 years.

NPV_{LOR} = the net present value of the lease-rental income from the assets to the lessor.

With the above facts, the equilibrium lease rental rate in a competitive market of lessors can be calculated. What has been posed is a standard capital budgeting question. What cash flow return from the use of an asset will earn the applicable cost of capital? The investment or cost of the capital budgeting project is $- I$. The return is composed of two elements: the cash inflow from the lease rental and the tax shelter from depreciation. The discount factor is the weighted cost of capital reflecting the appropriate debt leverage applicable to the kinds of equipment being leased. These factors represent the basic capital budgeting analysis discussed in Chapter 12. Consistent with the foregoing analysis, the equation to solve for the uniform annual lease rental rate, L_t, is Equation 21.1.

$$NPV_{LOR} = -I + \sum_{t=1}^{N} \frac{L_t(1-T) + TDep_t}{(1+k)^t}$$
$$= -I + (PVIF_a)[L_t(1-T) + TDep_t]. \qquad \textbf{(21.1)}$$

Given the above facts and assuming straight-line depreciation, the solution to Equation 21.1 is shown in the following equation. The competitive market assumption constrains the net present value of the lessor in the equation to

2. The materials on the financial analysis of leasing reflect collaborative research by Fred Weston and Larry Y. Dann, who provided valuable insights.

zero. Hence, the NPV of the lessor in Equation 21.1 is set equal to zero, and the following equation is solved for the competitive equilibrium rental rate:

$$0 = -\$20,000 + \sum_{t=1}^{5} \frac{L_t(1-0.4)+0.4(\$4,000)}{(1.1)^t}$$

$$3.791(0.6L_t) = \$20,000 - 3.791(\$1,600)$$

$$0.6L_t = \$13,934.4/3.791$$

$$L_t = \$6,126.$$

Under the facts assumed, at an equilibrium rental of $6,126 the lessor companies earn their cost of capital of 10 percent.

Next, the position of the asset user is viewed. The user faces the decision of whether to lease the asset or to own it. The new symbols and facts are:

NPV_0 = the net present value to the user if the firm owns the assets.

NPV_L = the net present value to the user if the firm leases the assets.

F_t = the marginal product value of the asset to a specific user firm or the cash flow benefits from the use of the capital assets (excluding depreciation effects) = $6,126.

k = the cost of capital to the user firm reflecting the risk in use when the marginal value product of the machine varies systematically with the return on total wealth = 10%.

First consider the results if the user is the owner of the equipment. The user's position is exactly the same as the lessor's. The user's leverage position and therefore the weighted average cost of capital are the same as for the leasing company. The formula is exactly the same as Equation 21.1, except that the cash flows represent the marginal product value of the equipment used. Thus these benefits are indicated as F_t rather than L_t. The expression for determining the net present value of owning is set forth in Equation 21.2:

$$NPV_0 = \sum_{t=1}^{N} \frac{F_t(1-T)}{(1+k)^t} - I + \sum_{t=1}^{N} \frac{TDep_t}{(1+k)^t} \qquad (21.2)$$

$$= -I + (PVIF_a)[F_t(1-T) + TDep_t].$$

The first term represents the net cash flows from the use of the asset; these are the same whether the asset is leased or owned. If the asset is owned, it is purchased at the cost of the asset, which is I. The third term in Equation 21.2 represents the benefits that the owner of the asset will have through the tax shelter effect of the depreciation outlays. Equation 21.2 can be used to calculate the net present value of owning the asset. The calculation is shown in the following equation:

$$NPV_0 = -\$20,000 + 3.791[\$6,126(0.6) + \$4,000(0.4)]$$
$$= -\$20,000 + 3.791(\$5,275.6)$$
$$= 0.$$

Next, the user's alternative of leasing the equipment is considered. The net present value of leasing is determined by taking the net present value of the net benefits from the use of the assets and calculating their present value over the life of the lease. From this is deducted the annual lease rental payments made by the lessee.[3] This is expressed formally in Equation 21.3:

$$NPV_L = \sum_{t=1}^{N} \frac{F_t(1-T)}{(1+k)^t} - \sum_{t=1}^{N} \frac{L_t(1-T)}{(1+k)^t} \qquad (21.3)$$
$$= (PVIF_a)[F_t(1-T) - L_t(1-T)].$$

Using the facts of the case as set forth above and assuming that F_t, the cash benefits from the use of the capital assets, is equal to $6,126, Equation 21.3 can be solved as follows:

$$NPV_L = 3.791[\$6,126(1-T) - \$6,126(1-T)]$$
$$= 0.$$

The result is the same as that for the user as owner and the lessor. The zero net present values reflect equilibrium in the equipment leasing market as well as in the equipment user's market.[4]

However, it would not be unreasonable to have the particular uses to which users put the equipment represent some disequilibrium gains. For example, if the benefits from the use of the equipment by particular users with some special advantages were $6,500 per year, the net present value of owning would be shown as follows:

$$NPV_0 = -\$20,000 + 3.791[\$6,500(0.6) + \$4,000(0.4)]$$
$$= -\$20,000 + 3.791(\$5,500)$$
$$= -\$20,000 + \$20,850.5$$
$$= \$850.5.$$

3. The actual pattern of payment on leases is different from the equal annual payment schedule assumed in the above analysis. Typically, monthly payments are required at the start to initiate the leasing contract. In fact, the payment patterns vary greatly, depending on the requirements of the lessee and the circumstances of the lessor. The solution framework set forth in the text is sufficiently flexible to be used for whatever pattern of payments agreed on in the leasing contract.

4. A more complete development of the reasons for these indifference results is presented in recent articles. See Merton H. Miller and Charles W. Upton, "Leasing, Buying, and the Cost of Capital Services," and Wilbur G. Lewellen, Michael S. Long, and John J. McConnell, "Asset Leasing in Competitive Capital Markets," both in *Journal of Finance* 31 (June 1976).

The net present value if the user leases the equipment is shown as follows:

$$NPV_L = 3.791[\$6,500(0.6) - \$6,126(0.6)]$$
$$= 3.791(\$3,900 - \$3,675.6)$$
$$= 3.791(\$224.4)$$
$$= \$850.7.$$

Again, the indifference result between user ownership and leasing is found. A sound method of analyzing leasing versus owning must obtain this indifference result unless some specific market imperfections can be identified to account for differences. Such imperfections include differences in the applicable tax rates for the lessor versus user firm, differences in the amount of tax subsidies available, and differences in transactions costs.

Next, consider the use of accelerated depreciation. In Appendix 12A, Table A12.1 provides in convenient form the present value of depreciation for the sum-of-years'-digits and the double declining balance methods of depreciation over a range of values of the cost of capital. In the present example, the sum-of-years'-digits method of depreciation will be illustrated with the cost of capital of 10 percent for five years. The depreciation factor of .806 can be read directly from Table A12.1. To utilize the depreciation factor the cash inflow factors in the last term of Equation 21.1 are separated into two parts, as shown below:

$$NPV_{LOR} = -I + \sum_{t=1}^{N} \frac{L_t(1-T)}{(1+k)^t} + \sum_{t=1}^{N} \frac{T\,Dep_t}{(1+k)^t}, \tag{21.1a}$$

from which the calculations can be made. The next equation utilizes the data from the illustrative example used throughout this discussion. However, instead of straight line depreciation, the present value factor for the sum-of-years'-digits method of depreciation—.806 for the 10 percent cost of capital for the five-year life of the asset—is used. Then the equation is solved for the uniform annual lease-rental rate required by the lessor in order to earn a cost of capital of 10 percent:

$$NPV_{LOR} = -\$20,000 + \sum_{t=1}^{N} \frac{L_t(0.6)}{(1.1)^t} + \sum_{t=1}^{N} \frac{TDep_t}{(1+k)^t}$$
$$= -\$20,000 + 3.791(0.6L) + 0.4(\$20,000)(0.806)$$
$$3.791(0.6L) = \$20,000 - \$6,448$$
$$0.6L = \$13,552/3.791$$
$$0.6L = \$3,575$$
$$L = \$5,958.$$

The resulting uniform annual lease-rental charge required by the lessor in order to earn the cost of capital of 10 percent is $5,958. Note that this is lower than the lease-rental required for the lessor to earn the cost of capital when straight line depreciation was used. The reason is that with accelerated depreciation the tax shelter comes in larger amounts in the earlier years, when the present value factors are higher. Thus, since the amount of tax shelter is increased, and since under competitive conditions the lease-rental moves to the level at which lessors earn their cost of capital, the lease-rental is reduced.

If the benefits of accelerated depreciation were not available to the user firm, the net present value from owning would remain at $850.[5] But, as shown below, the net present value from leasing is $1,233 if the leasing firms can utilize accelerated depreciation, and competition results in their passing these tax advantages on in the form of lower lease-rental charges. This illustrates the kind of market frictions that can result in an advantage to leasing as compared to owning an asset. Specific frictions of this kind must be brought in to a previous equilibrium result to establish whether leasing or owning is advantageous to the user firm.

In the present illustration, if the user firm can also utilize the benefits of accelerated depreciation, the indifference result will again obtain. Therefore, the effects of accelerated depreciation on the user firm that leases or buys the asset can be examined. When the user firm leases the asset, Equation 21.3 is unchanged; the lower rental rate is simply inserted for the L_t in the equation. The result is as follows:

$$\text{NPV}_L = 3.791(\$6,500)(0.6) - \$5,958(0.6)(3.791)$$
$$= \$14,785 - \$13,552$$
$$= \$1,233.$$

The net present value to the lessee now is $1,233, which is higher than the net present value when straight line depreciation was being used.

Next, consider the position of the user firm that owns the asset. In this case, Equation 21.2 is used again. However, now the sum-of-the-years'-digits depreciation factor, as shown in the last term of the following equation, is used:

$$\text{NPV}_0 = 3.791(\$6,500)(0.6) - \$20,000 + 0.4(\$20,000)(0.806)$$
$$= \$14,785 - \$20,000 + \$6,448$$
$$= \$1,233.$$

The net present value of owning is $1,233, which was exactly the net present value of leasing. Thus the effect of accelerated depreciation is to provide larger tax shelters. Given competitive conditions among lessors, this results

---

5. This could occur if the user firm had tax loss carryovers that rendered the accelerated depreciation benefits of no benefit to it.

in a lower rental rate and a higher net present value of using the asset, regardless of whether the use is achieved through leasing (renting) or through buying and owning. But again, assuming competitive financial markets, the terms on which leasing versus owning are available to the user firm result in no advantage to one form of acquiring the use of the assets as compared with another. Only when some form of friction in the markets results in more favorable terms to lessees than to user-owners is there an advantage to leasing.

Alternative Approaches to Leasing Decisions

Cost of Debt as the Discount Factor

Different points of view exist on the formulation of the appropriate framework for leasing decisions. Indeed, there has been considerable disagreement on the appropriate discount rate to be used in the analysis. Thus far the chapter has utilized the cost of capital applicable to the risk of the project.

An alternative view is that of using the after-tax cost of debt as the discount factor on the ground that leasing is a substitute for borrowing. That is, if one form of borrowing is being compared with another form of borrowing, it is argued that the cost of debt can be used in comparing the costs. If this were true, the only elements to be compared would be the interest costs and interest tax shields. But since other elements, such as the costs of ownership to both the lessor and user-owner, and other types of tax shields, such as depreciation, enter into the analysis, the comparison to be made must involve more than one form of borrowing versus another.

Although leasing is an alternative to debt financing, debt financing itself requires an equity base. Hence a weighted marginal cost of capital should be used to discount the differential cash flows involved in leasing versus owning an asset. Nevertheless, some widely respected people in the field argue for using the after-tax cost of debt as the discount factor. This approach will be illustrated so the reader can see the nature of its application.

The previous illustration will be continued with the cost of debt used as the discount factor. The lease-rental rate under competitive conditions in the leasing market was determined to be $6,126 per year. The cost of leasing can be determined by discounting the lease payments at the after-tax cost of debt. Assuming a cost of debt of 10 percent and a uniform stream of payments as before, the present value of the cost of leasing can be expressed compactly.[6] It is:

6. We emphasize again that a wide variety of payment patterns can be encountered in leasing. Among them are: (1) requiring the first payment or the first and last payments in advance; (2) starting with high payments, then scaling them down to lower ones; (3) starting with low payments and increasing them toward the end of the lease payment; and (4) requiring a balloon payment at some point. But since these are mechanical matters in the calculation, we shall assume the simplest pattern to focus on the central conceptual matters involved.

$$\text{Present value of the cost of leasing} = \sum_{t=1}^{N} \frac{L_t(1-T)}{[1+k_b(1-T)]^t} \quad \textbf{(21.4)}$$

Equation 21.4 consists of the lease payments minus the tax shield on them. If the cost of debt, k_b, is 10 percent, its after-tax cost is 6 percent, since the tax rate is 40 percent. Inserting the numerical values gives:

$$\text{Present value of the cost of leasing} = \sum_{t=1}^{5} \frac{\$6,126(0.6)}{(1.06)^t}$$

$$= \$3,675.6(4.212) = \$15,482.$$

The conventional analysis of the cost of owning formulates the cost in a "borrow-own" framework. It is assumed that the alternative to leasing is to borrow the full amount of the value of the asset—$20,000 in our example. Then a schedule of debt payments is made in order to determine the amount of the annual interest charges. The procedure is illustrated in Table 21.2.

It is assumed that the loan of $20,000 is paid off at a level annual amount that covers annual interest charges plus amortization of the principal. The amount is an annuity that can be determined by the use of the present value of an annuity formula, shown in Equation 21.5:

$$\$20,000 = \sum_{t=1}^{N} \frac{a_t}{(1+k_b)^t} \quad \textbf{(21.5)}$$

$$a_t = \frac{\$20,000}{(\text{PVIF}_a)}$$

$$a_t = \frac{\$20,000}{3.791} = \$5,276.$$

Solving Equation 21.5 for the level annual annuity results in $5,276, which represents the principal plus interest payments set forth in Column 3 of Table 21.2. The sum of these five annual payments is shown to be $26,380,

Table 21.2
Schedule of Debt Payments

End of Year (1)	Balance of Principal Owed at End of Year (2)	Principal plus Interest Payments (3)	Annual Interest [10% × (2)] (4)	Reduction of Principal (5)
1	$20,000	$ 5,276	$2,000	$ 3,276
2	16,724	5,276	1,672	3,604
3	13,120	5,276	1,312	3,964
4	9,156	5,276	916	4,360
5	4,796	5,276	480	4,796
Totals		$26,380	$6,380	$20,000

which represents repayment of the principal of $20,000 plus the sum of the annual interest payments. The interest payments of each year are determined by multiplying Column 2, the balance of principal owed at the end of the year, by 10 percent, the assumed cost of borrowing. The sum of the annual interest payments does, in fact, equal the total interest of $6,380 obtained by deducting the principal of $20,000 from the total of the five annual payments shown in Column 3.

A schedule of cash outflows for the borrow-own alternative is then developed to determine the present value of the after-tax cash flows. This is illustrated in Table 21.3.

The analysis of cash outflows begins with a listing of the loan payments, as shown in Column 2. Next, the annual interest payments from Table 21.2 are listed in Column 3. Since straight line depreciation is assumed, the annual depreciation charges are $4,000 per year, as shown in Column 4. The tax shelter to the owner of the equipment is the sum of the annual interest plus depreciation multiplied by the tax rate. The amounts of the annual tax shield are shown in Column 5. Column 6 is cash flow after taxes, obtained by deducting Column 5 from Column 2.

Table 21.3
Schedule of Cash Outflows:
Borrow-Own

End of Year (1)	Loan Payment (2)	Annual Interest (3)	Depreciation (4)	Tax Shield [(3) + (4)].4 (5)	Cash Flows after Taxes [(2) − (5)] (6)	Present Value Factor (at 6%) (7)	Present Value of Cash Flows (8)
1	$ 5,276	$2,000	$ 4,000	$ 2,400	$ 2,876	0.943	$ 2,712
2	5,276	1,672	4,000	2,269	3,007	0.890	2,676
3	5,276	1,312	4,000	2,125	3,151	0.840	2,647
4	5,276	916	4,000	1,966	3,310	0.792	2.622
5	5,276	480	4,000	1,792	3,484	0.747	2,603
Totals	$26,380	$6,380	$20,000	$10,552	$15,828		$13,260

Since the cost of borrowing is 10 percent, its after-tax cost with a 40 percent tax rate is 6 percent. The present value factors at 6 percent are listed in Column 7. They are multiplied by the after-tax cash flows to obtain Column 8, the present value of after-tax cash flows.

The total of Column 8 represents the present value of the after-tax cost of the borrow-own alternative. This amount is compared with the $15,482 obtained as the present value of the cost of leasing. The borrow-own alternative is shown to involve a cost that is lower than the cost of leasing by $2,222.

The usual explanation for this difference is that under the borrow-own alternative the annual interest expenses are higher in the early years, when the present value factors are higher. This provides a larger tax shield in the earlier years and is said to result in a lower cost under the borrow-own alternative.

However, this method of analysis is suspect because it utilizes the data from the example in which there was no advantage to leasing versus owning consistent with competitive market equilibrium conditions. Since the use of the after-tax cost of debt as the discount factor produces something other than this indifference result, its underlying theoretical validity is suspect. In addition, as a practical matter, the terms of the lease payments will not necessarily be an equal annual amount. The annual lease payments can readily be increased in the earlier years and decreased in the later years to result in the same present value of after-tax cost of leasing as for the borrow-own alternative.

The framework is sufficiently broad and flexible to accommodate various choices of the discount rate to be employed in the valuation relationships. If, for example, someone prefers to substitute the cost of debt for the weighted marginal cost of capital, this can be done. However, the symmetry of the lessor's and lessee's position, which is generally agreed to be necessary for a correct analysis, will not be possible to achieve if the cost of debt is used as the discount factor. Clearly, a 100 percent debt ratio for the lessor firm is not realistic, so a weighted cost to reflect some use of equity is required. By symmetry, the use of the cost of debt alone is inappropriate for analyzing the lessee's position.

Use of an Internal Rate of Return Analysis

A related second approach to analyzing the cost of leasing versus other sources of financing utilizes the internal rate of return. In this approach the cost of leasing is the internal rate of return or discount rate that equates the present value of leasing payments—net of their tax shields plus the tax shields for depreciation and the investment tax credit that would be obtained if the asset were purchased—with the cost of the asset. In this method the cost of leasing includes not only the after-tax lease payments but the investment tax credit foregone and the depreciation tax deductions that otherwise would have been obtained if the asset had been purchased.

The cost of the asset avoided by leasing is treated as a cash inflow, while the costs of leasing just described are treated as cash outflows. A column of cash flows after taxes is calculated; it begins with a positive figure—the cost of the asset avoided—and then moves to negative figures representing the costs of leasing. A rate of discount that equates the negative cash flows with the positive cash flows in the column (10 percent in our example) is then determined.

The discount rate is taken as a measure of the after-tax cost of lease financing. In the procedure, this after-tax cost is then compared with the after-tax cost of debt financing. In our example, the after-tax cost of debt financing is 6 percent, so the 10 percent after-tax cost of leasing is more expensive.

One of the advantages claimed for the approach is that it avoids the problem of having to determine a discount rate. However, this claim is illusory. The internal rate of return approach to the leasing comparison is fundamentally no different from the after-tax cost of debt method described in the previous section. When the discount rate, which is treated as the after-tax cost of lease financing, is compared with the after-tax cost of debt financing, the implication is that the relevant measure for comparison is the after-tax cost of debt financing rather than the firm's cost of capital. Since leasing involves the acquisition of an asset as well as its financing, and since it generally provides "complete financing" that substitutes for a normal mix of financing, many financial managers believe that the appropriate discount factor to apply to lease payments is the firm's cost of capital. For this reason, It can be argued that the calculation of the discount factor, called the after-tax cost of lease financing, based on leasing payments should be compared with the firm's cost of capital rather than with its cost of debt. Hence, the internal rate of return analysis does not avoid the problem of selecting the appropriate discount rate.

Additional Influences on the Leasing versus Owning Decision

A number of other factors can influence the user firm's costs of leasing versus owning capital assets. These include:

(1) different costs of capital for the lessor versus the user firm, (2) financing costs higher in leasing, (3) differences in maintenance costs, (4) the benefits of residual values to the owner of the assets, (5) the possibility of reducing obsolescence costs by the leasing firms, (6) the possibility of increased credit availability under leasing, (7) more favorable tax treatment, such as more rapid write-off, and (8) possible differences in the ability to utilize tax reduction opportunities. A number of arguments exist with respect to the advantages and disadvantages of leasing, given these factors. Many of the arguments carry with them implicit assumptions; thus their applicability to real world conditions is subject to considerable qualifications.

Different Costs of Capital for the Lessor versus the User Firm

It can be argued that if the leasing company has a lower cost of capital than the user firm, the result in competitive markets will be a lease-rental whose costs to the user are lower than the costs of owning. This follows in a straightforward way from the type of financial analysis made in Equations 21.1 to 21.3. But under what circumstances will the cost of capital be different for the leasing firm and the user firm? To answer this question, the basic risks involved in using capital assets must be considered. It has been demonstrated that two broad types of risks are present.

One risk is that an asset's economic depreciation will vary in some systematic way with the level of the economy from the rate of depreciation expected when the lease rental rate is determined. That is, the risk is that the agreed upon lease payments, which are based on expected depreciation, will be insufficient to cover the subsequent realized depreciation. This risk is borne by the owner, whether it is a leasing firm or a user-buyer.

The other risk is associated with F_t, the uncertain future net cash flows to be derived from employing the capital services of the asset. This risk is borne by the leasing company if the lease contract is cancellable at any time with no penalty, borne by the user firm if the lease contract is noncancellable over the life of the asset, and shared by them under any contractual arrangement between these two extremes. But competitive capital markets will ensure that the implicit discount rate in the leasing arrangement, as negotiated, will reflect the allocation of the risks under the particular sharing arrangement specified. Under the standard price equals marginal cost condition of competitive markets, it is the project's cost of capital that is the relevant discount rate. Hence it is difficult to visualize why the risk in use of a capital asset will be different whether the asset is owned by a leasing company or by the user firm.[7]

Another possibility is that the user firm may have a lower cost of capital than the leasing company. This possibility has been evaluated as follows: "It is true that such a company, looking only at the conventional formulas, might find it profitable to buy rather than rent. But it would find it even more profitable, under those circumstances, to enter the leasing business."[8] This would eliminate any divergence.

Under competitive market conditions, it is unlikely that the disequilibrium conditions implied by the different costs of capital will long persist. The supply of financial intermediaries of the leasing kind will either increase or decrease to restore equilibrium in the benefits by a user firm from leasing versus owning an asset.

Financing Costs Higher in Leasing

A similar view is that leasing always involves higher implicit financing costs. This argument is also of doubtful validity. First, when the nature of the lessee as a credit risk is considered, there may be no difference. Second, it is difficult to separate the money costs of leasing from the other services embodied in a leasing contract. If, because of its specialized operations, the leasing company can perform nonfinancial services such as maintenance of

7. Miller and Upton, "Leasing, Buying, and the Cost of Capital Services."
8. Ibid., p. 767.

the equipment at a lower cost than the lessee or some other institution can perform them, then the effective cost of leasing may be lower than the cost of funds obtained from borrowing or other sources. The efficiencies of performing specialized services may thus enable the leasing company to operate by charging a lower total cost than the lessee would have to pay for the package of money plus services on any other basis.

Differences in Maintenance Costs

Another argument frequently encountered is that leasing may be less expensive because no explicit maintenance costs are involved. But this is because the maintenance costs are included in the lease-rental rate. The key question is whether the maintenance can be performed at a lower cost by the lessor or by an independent firm that specializes in performing maintenance on capital assets of the type involved. Whether the costs will differ if supplied by one type of specialist firm rather than another is a factual matter depending on the industries and particular firms involved.

Residual Values

One important point that must be mentioned in connection with leasing is that the lessor owns the property at the expiration of the lease. The value of the property at the end of the lease is called the *residual value.* Superficially, it appears that where residual values are large, owning is less expensive than leasing. However, even this apparently obvious advantage of owning is subject to substantial qualification. On leased equipment, the obsolescence factor may be so large that it is doubtful whether residual values will be of a great order of magnitude. If these values appear favorable, competition between leasing companies and other financial sources, as well as competition among leasing companies themselves, will force leasing rates down to the point where the potentials of residual values are fully recognized in the leasing contract rates. Thus, the existence of residual values is unlikely to result in materially lower costs of owning.

However, in decisions about whether to lease or to own land, the obsolescence factor is involved only to the extent of deterioration in areas with changing population or use patterns. In a period of optimistic expectations about land values, there may be a tendency to overestimate their rates of increase. As a consequence, the current purchase of land may involve a price so high that the probable rate of return on owned land will be relatively small. Under this condition, leasing may well represent the more economical way of obtaining the use of land. Conversely, if the probable increase in land values is not fully reflected in current prices, it will be advantageous to own the land.

Thus it is difficult to generalize about whether residual value considerations are likely to make the effective cost of leasing higher or lower than the cost of owning. The results depend on whether the individual firm has opportunities to take advantage of overoptimistic or overpessimistic evaluations of future value changes by the market as a whole and whether the firm or market is correct on average.

Obsolescence Costs

Another popular notion is that leasing costs will be lower because of the rapid obsolescence of some kinds of equipment. If the obsolescence rate on equipment is high, leasing costs must reflect that rate. Thus, in general terms, it can be argued that neither residual values nor obsolescence rates can basically affect the cost of owning versus leasing.

However, it is possible that certain leasing companies are well equipped to handle the obsolescence problem. For example, the Clark Equipment Company is a manufacturer, reconditioner, and specialist in materials handling equipment, with its own sales organization and system of distributors. This may enable Clark to write favorable leases for equipment. If the equipment becomes obsolete to one user, it may be satisfactory for other users with different materials handling requirements, and Clark is well situated to locate the other users. The situation is similar in computer leasing.

This illustration indicates how a leasing company, by combining lending with other specialized services, may reduce the social costs of obsolescence and increase effective residual values. By such operations the total cost of obtaining the use of such equipment is reduced. Possibly other institutions that do not combine financing and specialist functions (such as manufacturing, reconditioning, servicing, and sales) may, in conjunction with financing institutions, perform the overall functions as efficiently and at as low cost as do integrated leasing companies. However, this is a factual matter depending on the relative efficiency of the competing firms in different lines of business and different kinds of equipment.

Increased Credit Availability

Two possible situations that give leasing an advantage to firms seeking the maximum degree of financial leverage may exist. First, it is frequently stated that firms wishing to purchase a specific piece of equipment can obtain more money for longer terms under a lease arrangement than under a secured loan agreement. Second, leasing may not have as much of an impact on future borrowing capacity as does borrowing to buy the equipment.

This point is illustrated by the balance sheets of two hypothetical firms, A and B, in Table 21.4. Initially, the balance sheets of both firms are identical, with both showing debt ratios of 50 percent. Next, each company decides to acquire assets costing $100. Firm A borrows $100 to make the purchase, so an asset and a liability go on its balance sheet, and its debt ratio is increased to 75 percent. Firm B leases the equipment. The lease may call for fixed charges as high as or even higher than the loan, and the obligations assumed under the lease can be equally or more dangerous to other credi-

Table 21.4
Balance Sheet Effects of Leasing

Before Asset Increase Firms A and B			After Asset Increase Firm A			Firm B		
Total		Debt	$ 50	Total		Debt	$150	Total		Debt	$ 50

Before Asset Increase — Firms A and B:

		Debt	$ 50
Total		Equity	50
assets	$100	Total	$100

After Asset Increase — Firm A:

		Debt	$150
Total		Equity	50
assets	$200	Total	$200

Firm B:

		Debt	$ 50
Total		Equity	50
assets	$100	Total	$100

tors; but the fact that its reported debt ratio is lower may enable Firm B to obtain additional credit from other lenders. The amount of the annual rentals is shown as a note to Firm B's financial statements, so credit analysts are aware of it; but evidence suggests that many of them will still give less weight to Firm B's lease than to Firm A's loan.

This illustration indicates quite clearly a weakness of the debt ratio. If two companies are being compared, and if one leases a substantial amount of equipment, then the debt ratio as calculated here does not accurately show their relative leverage positions.[9]

Rapid Write-off

If the lease is written for a period that is much shorter than the depreciable life of the asset, with renewals at low rentals after the lessor has recovered costs during the basic lease period, then the deductible depreciation is small in relation to the deductible lease payment in the early years. In a sense, this amounts to a very rapid write-off, which is advantageous to the lessee. However, the Internal Revenue Service correctly disallows as deductions lease payments under leases that (1) call for a rapid amortization of the lessor's costs and (2) have a relatively low renewal or purchase option.

Differences in Tax Rates or Tax Subsidies

Frequently there is an advantage to leasing versus buying when the tax rates of the lessor firm are lower than those of the user firm. In this situation, competition among leasing firms results in reduced lease-rental rates to the user firms. Similarly, if the user firm is unable to use tax subsidies such as investment tax credits, it may be advantageous for a leasing firm to

9. Three comments are appropriate here. First, financial analysts sometimes attempt to reconstruct the balance sheets of firms such as B by capitalizing the lease payments—that is, estimating the value of both the lease obligation and the leased assets and transforming B's balance sheet into one comparable to A's. Second, as indicated in Chapter 4, lease charges are included in the fixed charge coverage ratio; and this ratio is approximately equal for Firms A and B, thereby revealing the true state of affairs. Thus it is unlikely that lenders will be fooled into granting more credit to a company with a lease than to one with a conventional loan having terms similar to those of the lease. Third, FASB No. 13 provides for including capital leases in the firm's balance sheet.

organize itself in such a way that it can utilize the tax shelters from tax subsidies.

For example, the investment tax credit (discussed in Chapter 3) can be taken only if the firm's profits and taxes exceed a certain level. If a firm is unprofitable, or if it is expanding so rapidly and generating such large tax credits that it cannot use them all, then it may be profitable for it to enter a lease arrangement. In this situation, the lessor (a bank or leasing company) can take the credit and give the lessee a corresponding reduction in lease charges. In recent years, railroads and airlines have been large users of leasing for this reason, as have industrial companies faced with similar situations. Anaconda, for example, financed most of the cost of a $138 million aluminum plant built in 1973 through a lease arrangement.[10] Anaconda had suffered a $356 million tax loss when Chile expropriated its copper mining properties, and the carry-forward of this loss would hold taxes down for years. Thus it could not use the tax credit associated with the new plant. By entering a lease arrangement, the company was able to pass the tax credit on to the lessors, who in turn gave it lower lease payments than would have existed under a loan arrangement. Anaconda's financial staff estimated that financial charges over the life of the plant would be $74 million less under the lease arrangement than under a borrow-and-buy plan.

Incidentally, the Anaconda lease was set up as a "leveraged lease."[11] A group of banks and Chrysler Corporation provided about $38 million of equity and were the owner-lessors. They borrowed the balance of the required funds from Prudential, Metropolitan, and Aetna—large life insurance companies. The banks and Chrysler received not only the investment tax credit but also the tax shelter associated with accelerated depreciation on the plant. Such leveraged leases, often with wealthy individuals seeking tax shelters acting as owner-lessors, are an important part of the financial scene today and help explain why leasing has reached a total volume of over $60 billion.

Summary

Leasing has long been used in connection with the acquisition of equipment by railroad companies. In recent years, it has been extended to a wide variety of equipment.

The most important forms of lease financing are: (1) sale and leaseback, in which a firm owning land, buildings, or equipment sells the property and simultaneously executes an agreement to lease it for a certain period under

10. Vanderwicken, "Powerful Logic of the Leasing Boom," pp. 136–140.
11. Technically, a leveraged lease is one in which the financial intermediary (a bank or other lessor) uses borrowed funds to acquire the assets it leases.

specific terms; (2) service leases or operating leases, which include both financing and maintenance services, are often cancellable, and call for payments under the lease contract that may not fully recover the cost of the equipment; and (3) financial leases, which do not provide for maintenance services, are not cancellable, and do fully amortize the cost of the leased asset during the basic lease contract period.

To understand the possible advantages and disadvantages of lease financing, the cost of leasing an asset must be compared with the cost of owning it. In the absence of major tax advantages and other "market imperfections," there should be no advantage to either leasing or owning an asset when the project's weighted cost of capital is used as the discount factor in the analysis. But when the cost of debt is used as the discount factor, the "indifference result" is not obtained. The conceptual reason for using the cost of capital rather than the cost of debt in analyzing leasing versus owning is that any form of debt requires an equity base that should be taken into account in determining the applicable discount factor. (However, because of the widespread use of the cost of debt as the discount factor, this procedure is also illustrated.)

The recommended procedure is to first use the cost of capital to obtain the result of no advantage to either leasing or owning. Then a wide range of factors that may influence the indifference result can be introduced. These possible influences include tax differences, differences in maintenance costs, different costs of capital for the lessor and the user firm, differences in obsolescence, and differences in the contractual positions in leasing versus other forms and sources of financing. Whether these other factors will actually give an advantage or disadvantage to leasing depends on the facts and circumstances of each transaction analyzed.

Questions

21.1 Discuss this statement: The type of equipment best suited for leasing has a long life in relation to the length of the lease, is a removable, standard product that could be used by many different firms, and is easily identifiable. In short, it is the kind of equipment that could be repossessed and sold readily. However, we would be quite happy to write a ten-year lease on paper towels for a firm such as General Motors.

21.2 Leasing is often called a hedge against obsolescence. Under what conditions is this actually true?

21.3 Is leasing in any sense a hedge against inflation for the lessee? For the lessor?

21.4 One alleged advantage of leasing is that it keeps liabilities off the balance sheet, thus making it possible for a firm to obtain more leverage than it otherwise could. This raises the question of whether both the lease obligation and the asset involved should be capitalized and shown on the balance sheet. Discuss the pros and cons of capitalizing leases and related assets.

21.5 A firm is seeking a term loan from a bank. Under what conditions would it want a fixed interest rate, and under what conditions would it want the rate to fluctuate with the prime rate?

21.6 Under what conditions would a "balloon note," or a loan that is not fully amortized, be advantageous to a borrower?

Problems

21.1 a. The Clarkton Company produces industrial machines, which have five-year lives. Clarkton is willing to either sell the machines for $30,000 or to lease them at a rental that, because of competitive factors, yields a return to Clarkton of 12 percent—its cost of capital. What is the company's competitive lease rental rate? (Assume straight line depreciation, zero salvage value, and $T = 40$ percent.)

b. The Stockton Machine Shop is contemplating the purchase of a machine exactly like those rented by Clarkton. The machine will produce net benefits of $10,000 per year. Stockton can buy the machine for $30,000 or rent it from Clarkton at the competitive lease rental rate. Stockton's cost of capital is 12 percent, and $T = 40$ percent. Which alternative is better for Stockton?

c. If Clarkton's cost of capital is 9 percent and competition exists among lessors, solve for the new equilibrium rental rate. Will Stockton's decision be altered?

21.2 The Nelson Company is faced with the decision of whether it should purchase or lease a new forklift truck. The truck can be leased on an eight-year contract for $6,951.42 a year, or it can be purchased for $26,000. The lease includes maintenance and service. The salvage value of the truck after eight years is $2,000. The company uses straight line depreciation. If the truck is purchased, service and maintenance charges (deductible costs) will be $500 per year. The company can borrow at 10 percent and has a 40 percent marginal tax rate and 12 percent cost of capital.

a. Analyze the lease versus purchase decision using the firm's cost of capital of 12 percent as the discount factor.

b. Make the analysis using the after-tax cost of debt as the discount factor.

c. Compare your results.

21.3 The Bradley Steel Company seeks to acquire the use of a rolling machine at the lowest possible cost. The choice is either to lease one at $17,142 annually or to purchase one for $54,000. The company's cost of capital is 14 percent, and its tax rate is 40 percent. The machine has an economic life of six years and no salvage value. The company uses straight line depreciation. Which is the less costly method of financing?

21.4 The Scott Brothers Department Store is considering a sale and leaseback of its major property, consisting of land and a building, because it is thirty days late on 80 percent of its accounts payable. The recent balance sheet of Scott Brothers is shown on the next page:

Scott Brothers Department Store
Balance Sheet as of
December 31, 1975
(Thousands of Dollars)

Assets		Liabilities	
Cash	$ 288	Accounts payable	$1,440
Receivables	1,440	Bank loans (at 8%)	1,440
Inventories	1,872	Other current liabilities	720
Total current assets	$3,600	Total current debt	$3,600
Land	1,152	Common stock	1,440
Building	720	Retained earnings	720
Fixtures and equipment	288		
Net fixed assets	2,160		
Total assets	$5,760	Total claims	$5,760

Profit before taxes in 1975 is $36,000; after taxes, $20,000. Annual depreciation charges are $57,600 on the building and $72,000 on the fixtures and equipment. The land and building could be sold for a total of $2.8 million. The annual net rental will be $240,000.

a. How much capital gains tax will Scott Brothers pay if the land and building are sold? (Assume all capital gains are taxed at the capital gains tax rate; that is, disregard such items as recepture of depreciation, tax preference treatment, and so on.)

b. Compare the current ratio before and after the sale and leaseback if the after-tax net proceeds are used to "clean up" the bank loans and to reduce accounts payable and other current liabilities.

c. If the lease had been in effect during 1975, what would Scott Brothers' profit for 1975 have been?

d. What are the basic financial problems facing Scott Brothers? Will the sale and leaseback operation solve them?

21.5 According to a prospectus dated April 18, 1978, Itel Corporation, a leasing company, raised $100 million. The data in the prospectus indicated the following capital sources and costs of financing:

	Amount (in Millions)
Senior debt (at 9%)	$460
Subordinated debt (at 10%)	15
Preferred stock (at 9.6%)	65
Equity (at 15% at book)	120
Total assets	$660

Itel's effective tax rate in recent years has approximated 10 percent. Itel had 9.1 million shares of common stock outstanding with an average price of $20 per share.

a. Calculate Itel's weighted cost of capital using equity at book weights (before and after taxes).
b. Do the same, using market value for equity.
c. Would you expect Itel to use its cost of debt or its weighted cost of capital in pricing out its proposals when it bids on new leasing business?

CHAPTER 22 WARRANTS
AND CONVERTIBLES

Thus far the discussion of long-term financing has dealt with the nature of common stock, preferred stock, various types of debt, and leasing. It has also explained how offering common stock through the use of rights can facilitate low-cost stock flotations. This chapter will show how the financial manager, through the use of warrants and convertibles, can make the company's securities attractive to an even broader range of investors. Therefore, it is important to understand the characteristics of these two types of securities.[1]

Warrants

A *warrant* is an option to buy a stated number of shares of stock at a specified price. For example, Trans Pacific Airlines has warrants outstanding that give the warrant owners the right to buy one share of TPA stock at a price of $22 for each warrant held. Warrants generally expire on a certain date (TPA's warrants on December 1, 1981), although some have perpetual lives.

Formula Value of a Warrant

Warrants have a calculated, or formula, value and an actual value, or price, that is determined in the marketplace. The formula value is found by use of the following equation:

$$\text{Formula value} = \begin{pmatrix} \text{Market price of} \\ \text{common stock} \end{pmatrix} - \begin{pmatrix} \text{Option} \\ \text{price} \end{pmatrix} \times \begin{pmatrix} \text{Number of shares each} \\ \text{warrant entitles owner} \\ \text{to purchase} \end{pmatrix}.$$

For instance, a TPA warrant entitles the owner to purchase one share of common stock at $22 a share. If the market price of the common stock is $64.50, the formula price of the warrant is obtained as follows:

$$(\$64.50 - \$22) \times 1.0 = \$42.50.$$

The formula gives a negative value when the stock is selling for less than the option price. For example, if TPA stock is selling for $20, the formula value of the warrants is − $2. This makes no sense, so the formula value is defined as zero when the stock is selling for less than the option price.

Actual Price of a Warrant

Generally, warrants sell above their formula values. When TPA stock was selling for $64.50, the warrants had a formula value of $42.50 but were selling at a price of $46.87. This represents a premium of $4.37 above the formula value.

A set of TPA stock prices, together with actual and formula warrant val-

---

1. Additional aspects of these and other forms of options are treated in J. Fred Weston and Eugene F. Brigham, *Managerial Finance*, 6th ed. (Hinsdale, Ill.: Dryden Press, 1978), app. A to chap. 16.

ues, is given in Table 22.1 and plotted in Figure 22.1. At any stock price below $22, the formula value of the warrant is zero; beyond $22, each $1 increase in the price of the stock brings with it a $1 increase in the formula value of the warrant. The actual market price of the warrant lies above the formula value at each price of the common stock. Notice, however, that the premium of market price over formula value declines as the price of the common stock increases. For example, when the common sold for $22 and the warrants had a zero formula value, their actual price, and the premium, was $9. As the price of the stock rises, the formula value of the warrants matches the increase dollar for dollar, but for a while the *market price* of the warrant climbs less rapidly and the premium declines. The premium is $9 when the stock sells for $22 a share, but it declines to $1 by the time the stock price has risen to $75 a share. Beyond this point the premium seems to be constant.

Table 22.1
Formula and Actual Values of
TPA Warrants at Different Market
Prices

	Value of Warrant		
Price of Stock	Formula Price	Actual Price	Premium
$ 0.00	$ 0.00	Not available	—[a]
22.00	0.00	$ 9.00	$9.00
23.00	1.00	9.75	8.75
24.00	2.00	10.50	8.50
33.67	11.67	17.37	5.70
52.00	30.00	32.00	2.00
75.00	53.00	54.00	1.00
100.00	78.00	79.00	1.00
150.00	128.00	Not available	—[a]

[a] Cannot be calculated.

Why does this pattern exist? The answer lies in the speculative appeal of warrants; they enable a person buying securities to gain a high degree of personal leverage. To illustrate: Suppose TPA warrants always sell for exactly their formula value, and suppose you are thinking of investing in the company's common stock at a time when it is selling for $25 a share. If you buy a share and the price rises to $50 in a year, you will make a 100 percent capital gain. However, if you buy the warrants at their formula value ($3 when the stock sells for $25), your capital gain will be $25 on a $3 investment, or 833 percent. At the same time, your total loss potential with the warrant is only $3, while the potential loss from the purchase of the stock is $25. The huge capital gains potential, combined with the loss limitation, is

**Figure 22.1
Formula and Actual Values of TPA
Warrants at Different Common
Stock Prices**

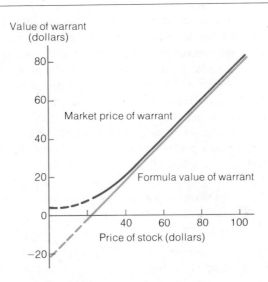

clearly worth something—and the exact amount it is worth to investors is the amount of the premium.[2]

But why does the premium decline as the price of the stock rises? The answer is that both the leverage effect and the loss protection feature decline at high stock prices. For example, if you are thinking of buying TPA stock at $75 a share, the formula value of the warrants is $53. If the stock price doubles to $150, the formula value of TPA warrants goes from $53 to $128. The capital gain on the stock is still 100 percent, but the gain on the warrant declines from 833 percent to 142 percent. Moreover, the loss potential on the warrant is much greater when it is selling at high prices. These two factors—the declining leverage impact and the increasing danger of losses—explain why the premium diminishes as the price of the common stock rises.

In the past, warrants have generally been used by small, rapidly growing firms as "sweeteners" when selling either debt or preferred stocks. Since such firms are frequently regarded by investors as highly risky, their bonds can be sold only if they are willing to accept extremely high rates of interest and very restrictive indenture provisions, to offer warrants, or to make the bonds convertible. In April 1970, however, AT&T raised $1.57 billion by sell-

---

2. However, a $3 decline in the stock price produces only a 12 percent loss if the stock is purchased but a 100 percent loss if the warrant is bought and it declines to its formula value.

ing bonds with warrants. This was the largest financing of any type ever undertaken by a business firm, and it marked the first use of warrants by a large, strong corporation.[3] It can safely be anticipated that other large firms will follow AT&T's lead.[4]

Giving warrants along with bonds enables investors to share in the company's growth if it does, in fact, grow and prosper; therefore, investors are willing to accept a lower bond interest rate and less restrictive indenture provisions. A bond with warrants has some characteristics of debt and some of equity. It is a hybrid security that provides the financial manager with an opportunity to expand the mix of securities, appealing to a broader group of investors and possibly lowering the firm's cost of capital.

Warrants can also bring in additional funds. The option price is generally set 15 to 20 percent above the market price of the stock at the time of the bond issue. If the firm does grow and prosper, and if its stock price rises above the option price at which shares can be purchased, warrant holders will surrender their warrants and buy stock at the stated price. There are several reasons for this:

1. Warrant holders will surrender warrants and buy stock if the warrants are about to expire with the market price of the stock above the option price.
2. Warrant holders will surrender and buy as just mentioned if the company raises the dividend on the common stock. No dividend is earned on the warrant, so it provides no current income. However, if the common stock pays a high dividend, it provides an attractive dividend yield. This induces warrant holders to exercise their option to buy the stock.
3. Warrants sometimes have stepped-up option prices. For example, Textron has warrants outstanding that had an exercise price of $10 per share until May 1, 1979, at which time the option price rose to $11.25. It will continue at that level until the expiration date of the warrants on May 1, 1984.

One desirable feature of warrants is that they generally bring in additional funds only if such funds are needed. If the company grows and prospers, causing the price of the stock to rise, the warrants are exercised and bring in needed funds. If the company is unsuccessful and cannot profitably employ additional money, the price of its stock will probably not rise sufficiently to induce exercise of the options.

3. It is interesting to note that before the AT&T issue, the New York Stock Exchange had a policy against listing warrants. The NYSE's stated policy was that warrants could not be listed because they were "speculative" instruments rather than "investment" securities. When AT&T issued warrants, however, the exchange changed its policy and agreed to list warrants that met certain specifications.
4. In fact, the number of warrants listed on the New York Stock Exchange increased to thirty-five by the end of 1977. See *1978 Fact Book* (New York: New York Stock Exchange, 1978), p. 34.

Convertibles   *Convertible securities* are bonds or preferred stocks that are exchangeable
into common stock at the option of the holder and under specified terms
and conditions. The most important of the special features relates to how
many shares of stock a convertible holder receives by converting. This feature is defined as the *conversion ratio,* and it gives the number of shares of
common stock the holder of the convertible receives on surrender of the
security. Related to the conversion ratio is the *conversion price*—the effective price paid for the common stock when conversion occurs. In effect, a
convertible is similar to a bond with an attached warrant.

The relationship between the conversion ratio and the conversion price is
illustrated by Adams Electric Company convertible debentures, issued at
their $1,000 par value in 1975. At any time prior to maturity on July 1, 1995, a
debenture holder can turn in the bond and receive in its place 20 shares of
common stock; therefore, the conversion ratio is 20 shares for 1 bond. The
bond has a par value of $1,000, so the holder is giving up this amount on
conversion. Dividing the $1,000 by the 20 shares received gives a conversion
price of $50 a share:

$$\text{Conversion price} = \frac{\text{Par value of bond}}{\text{Shares received}} = \frac{\$1,000}{20} = \$50.$$

The conversion price and conversion ratio are established at the time the
convertible bond is sold. Generally, these values are fixed for the life of the
bond, although sometimes a stepped-up conversion price is used. Litton Industries' convertible debentures, for example, were convertible into 12.5
shares until 1972, and they can be exchanged into 11.76 shares from 1972
until 1982 and into 11.11 shares from 1982 until they mature in 1987. The
conversion price thus started at $80 and will rise to $85, then to $90. Litton's
convertibles, like most, are callable at the option of the company.

Another factor that may cause a change in the conversion price and ratio
is a standard feature of almost all convertibles—the clause protecting the
convertible against dilution from stock splits, stock dividends, and the sale
of common stock at low prices (as in a rights offering). The typical provision
states that no common stock can be sold at a price below the conversion
price and that the conversion price must be lowered (and the conversion
ratio raised) by the percentage amount of any stock dividend or split. For
example, if Adams Electric had a two-for-one split, the conversion ratio
would automatically be adjusted to forty and the conversion price lowered
to $25. If this protection was not contained in the contract, a company could
completely thwart conversion by the use of stock splits and dividends. Warrants are similarly protected against dilution.

Like warrant option prices, the conversion price is characteristically set
from 15 to 20 percent above the prevailing market price of the common

stock at the time the convertible issue is sold. Exactly how the conversion price is established can best be understood after examining some of the reasons why firms use convertibles.

Advantages of Convertibles

Convertibles offer advantages to corporations as well as to individual investors. The most important of these advantages are discussed below.

A "Sweetener" When Selling Debt A company can sell debt with lower interest rates and less restrictive covenants by giving investors a chance to share in potential capital gains. Convertibles, like bonds with warrants, offer this possibility.

The Sale of Common Stock at Higher than Prevailing Prices Many companies actually want to sell common stock, not debt, but feel that the price of the stock is temporarily depressed. Management may know, for example, that earnings are depressed because of a strike but that they will snap back during the next year and pull the price of the stock up with them. To sell stock now would require giving up more shares to raise a given amount of money than management thinks is necessary. However, setting the conversion price 15 to 20 percent above the present market price of the stock will require giving up 15 to 20 percent fewer shares when the bonds are converted than would be required if stock was sold directly.

Notice, however, that management is counting on the stock's price rising above the conversion price to make the bonds actually attractive in conversion. If the stock price does not rise and conversion does not occur, then the company is saddled with debt.

How can the company be sure that conversion will occur when the price of the stock rises above the conversion price? Characteristically, convertibles have a provision that gives the issuing firm the opportunity of calling the convertible at a specified price. Suppose the conversion price is $50, the conversion ratio is twenty, the market price of the common stock has risen to $60, and the call price on the convertible bond is $1,050. If the company calls the bond (by giving the usual notification of twenty days), bondholders can either convert into common stock with a market value of $1,200 or allow the company to redeem the bond for $1,050. Naturally, bondholders prefer $1,200 to $1,050, so conversion occurs. The call provision therefore gives the company a means of forcing conversion, provided that the market price of the stock is greater than the conversion price.

Low-Cost Capital during a Construction Period Another advantage from the standpoint of the issuer is that a convertible issue can be used as a temporary financing device. During the years 1946 through 1957, AT&T sold $10 billion of convertible debentures. By 1959, about 80 percent of these convertible debentures had been converted into common stock. AT&T did not want to sell straight debt in that amount because its financial structure would have been unbalanced. On the other hand, if it had simply issued large amounts of common stock periodically, there would have been price pressure on its stock because the market is slow to digest large blocks of stock.

By using convertible debentures, which provided for a lag of some six to nine months before they were convertible into common stock, AT&T received relatively cheap money to finance growth. Transmission lines and telephone exchange buildings must first be built to provide the basis for installing phones. While AT&T was building such installations, these investments were not earning any money. Therefore, it was important for the company to minimize the cost of money during the construction period. After six to nine months had elapsed and the installations had been translated into telephones that were bringing in revenues, AT&T was better able to pay the regular common stock dividend.

Disadvantages of Convertibles

From the standpoint of the issuer, convertibles have one possible disadvantage. Although the convertible bond does give the issuer the opportunity to sell common stock at a price 15 to 20 percent higher than it could otherwise be sold, if the stock greatly increases in price, the issuer may find that it would have been better off if it had waited and simply sold the common stock. Further, if the company truly wants to raise equity capital, and if the price of the stock declines after the bond is issued, then it is stuck with debt.

Analysis of Convertible Debentures

A convertible security is a hybrid, having some of the characteristics of common stocks and some of bonds or preferred stocks.[5] Investors expect to earn an interest yield as well as a capital gains yield. Moreover, the corporation recognizes that it incurs an interest cost and a potential dilution of equity when it sells convertibles. This section will develop a theoretical model to combine these two cost components and then will discuss the conditions under which convertibles should be used.

Model of Convertible Bonds

Since an investor who purchases a convertible bond expects to receive interest plus capital gains, the total expected return is the sum of these two parts. The expected interest return is dependent primarily on the bond's

5. For further analysis of the issues treated in this section, see E. F. Brigham, "An Analysis of Convertible Debentures: Theory and Some Empirical Evidence," *Journal of Finance* 21 (March 1966).

coupon interest rate and the price paid for the bond, while the expected capital gains yield is dependent basically on (1) the relationship between the stock price at the time of issue and the conversion price and (2) the expected growth rate in the price of the stock. These two yield components will now be discussed.

Think of the graph in Figure 22.2 as showing the *ex ante,* or expected, relationships, starting now at Year $t = 0$ and projecting events into the future. (The symbols used in Figure 22.2 and the remainder of this chapter are listed in Table 22.2.)

Call Price and Maturity Value The hypothetical bond is a new issue that can be purchased for $M = \$1,000$; this initial price is also the par (and maturity) value. The bond is callable at the option of the corporation, with the call price originating at $V_0 = \$1,040$, somewhat above par, and declining linearly over the twenty-year term to maturity to $M'' = \$1,000$ at maturity.

Value in Conversion At any point in time, the bond can be converted to stock; the value of the stock received on conversion is defined as the *conversion value* of the bond. The original conversion value (C_0) is established by multiplying the market price of the stock at the time of issue by the number of shares into which the bond can be converted (the conversion ratio). The stock price is expected to grow at a certain rate (g), causing the conversion value curve (C_t) to rise at this same rate. This establishes the curve C_t, which shows the expected conversion value at each point in time. All of this is expressed by Equation 22.1:

$$C_t = p_0(1 + g)^t \#, \tag{22.1}$$

**Figure 22.2
Model of a Convertible Bond**

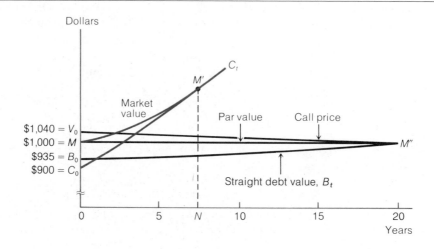

**Table 22.2
Summary of Symbols Used in
Chapter 22**

B_t = straight debt value of a bond at time t.

c = dollars of interest paid each year ($\$40 = 4$ percent of M).

C_N = conversion value = $p_0(1 + g)^N$#.

C_t = conversion value at time t.

g = expected rate of growth of the stock's price.

k_b = market rate of interest on equivalent risk, nonconvertible debt issues.

k_c = internal rate of return, or expected yield, on the convertible.

M = price paid for the bond.

M' = market value of the convertible bond when its conversion value becomes equal to its market value.

M'' = maturity value.

N = number of years bond is expected to be held.

= conversion ratio, or number of shares received on conversion.

p_c = conversion price = M/#.

p_0 = current market price of the stock.

t = number of years since date of issue.

t^* = number of years remaining until maturity = original term to maturity.

T = marginal corporate income tax rate.

V_0 = original call price of an option.

where:

C_t = conversion value at time t.

p_0 = initial price of the common stock = $\$45$ per share.

g = expected rate of growth of the stock's price = 4 percent.

= conversion ratio, or number of shares received on conversion = 20.

The initial conversion value of the bond, when $t = 0$, is simply $\$45 \times 20$, or $\$900$. One year later it is expected to be $\$45 \,(1.04)(20) = \$936$; after two years it is expected to rise to $\$973.44$; and so on. Thus the expected conversion value curve, C_t, is a function of the expected growth in the price of the stock.

Bond Value In addition to its value in conversion, the bond also has a straight debt value, B_t, defined as the price at which the bond would sell in any year t if it did not have the conversion option. At each point in time, B_t is determined by Equation 22.2:

$$B_t = \sum_{j=1}^{t^*} \frac{c}{(1 + k_b)^j} + \frac{M''}{(1 + k_b)^{t^*}},\qquad (22.2)$$

where:

t = number of years since date of issue.

t^* = number of years remaining until maturity = original term to maturity (20 years) minus t.

595

j = time subscript from 1 to t^*.

k_b = market rate of interest on equivalent risk, nonconvertible debt issues = $4\frac{1}{2}$ percent. (Note that k_b > coupon interest on the convertible.)

c = dollars of interest paid each year; $40 = 4 percent of M.

M'' = maturity value.

Equation 22.2 is used to calculate the bond value, B_t, from each point t to the maturity date. To illustrate the use of the equation, B_t will be calculated at $t = 0$ and $t = 8$. First, note that $t = 0$ is the point in time when the bond is issued, while $t = 8$ means the bond is 8 years old and has 12 years remaining to maturity. So, for B_0, the summation term refers to an annuity of $40 per year for $t^* = 20 - 0 = 20$ years; while for B_8, the summation represents a 12-year annuity—$t^* = 20 - 8 = 12$ years:

$$B_0 = \sum_{j=1}^{20} \frac{\$40}{(1.045)^j} + \frac{\$1,000}{(1.045)^{20}}$$

$$= \$40\,(13.026) + \$1,000\,(0.416)$$

$$= \$521.04 + \$416 = \$937.04.$$

$$B_8 = \sum_{j=1}^{12} \frac{\$40}{(1.045)^j} + \frac{\$1,000}{(1.045)^{12}}$$

$$= \$40\,(9.124) + \$1,000\,(0.591)$$

$$= \$364.96 + \$591 = \$955.96.$$

Thus B_t rises over time, and $B_{20} = \$1,000$.[6]

Market Value Floor The convertible will never sell below its value as a straight bond. If it did, investors interested in buying debt instruments would see it as a bargain, start buying the bonds, and drive their value up to B_t. Similarly, the convertible can never sell below its conversion value. If it did, investors interested in the stock would buy the bonds, convert, and obtain shares at a bargain price; but they would drive the price of the convertible up to C_t in the process. Thus the lines C_0C_t and B_0M'' in Figure 22.2 serve as floors below which the market price of the bond cannot fall. The higher of these two floors dominates, with the dark, discontinuous curve B_0XC_t forming the *effective market value floor*.

6. In Equation 22.2, bond values are calculated at the beginning of each period, just after the last interest payment has been made. Most bonds (convertible and nonconvertible alike) are actually traded on the basis of a basic price, determined as in Equation 22.2, plus interest accrued since the last payment date. Thus, a person who bought this bond a few days before the end of Year 20 would pay approximately $1,000 plus $40 accrued interest, and the invoice from the broker would indicate these two components.

Expected Market Value Ordinarily, convertibles sell at premiums over their bond and conversion value floors. For the illustrated bond, the expected market value is represented in Figure 22.2 by the curve MM', which lies above the effective floor (B_0XC_t) over most of the range but converges with B_0XC_t in Year N. The rationale behind this price action is developed in the following two sections.

Why the Market Value Exceeds the B_0XC_t Floor The spread between MM' and B_0XC_t, which represents the premium marginal investors are willing to pay for the conversion option, can be explained in several ways.[7] First, since the convertible bond can be converted into common stock if the company prospers and the stock price rises, it usually commands a premium over its value as straight debt (that is, the right of conversion has a positive value). Second, the convertible bond usually commands a premium over its conversion value because investors are able to reduce their risk exposure by holding convertibles. To illustrate: Suppose someone buys the hypothetical bond for $1,000. At the time, it is convertible into 20 shares of stock with a market price of $45, giving a conversion value of $900. If the stock market turns sharply down and the stock price falls to $22.50 per share, the stock investor will suffer a 50 percent loss in value. The price of a convertible bond, however, will fall from $1,000 to the bond value floor $(B_0M''$ in Figure 22.2), which is at least $937. Hence, holding the convertible entails less risk than holding common stock, and this too causes convertibles to sell at a premium above their conversion value.[8]

Why the Market Value Approaches the Conversion Value The MM' curve in Figure 22.2 rises less rapidly than the C_0C_t curve, indicating that the market value approaches the conversion value as the conversion value increases. This is caused by three separate factors. First, and probably most important, the bondholders realize that the issue is callable; if it is in fact called, they have the option of either surrendering for redemption or converting. In the former case, they receive the call price; in the latter, they receive stock with a value designated by C_t. If the market price of the bond is above both these values, the holder is in danger of a potential loss in

7. Marginal investors, often called "the market," are defined as those just willing to hold the bond at its going price. These investors are, in fact, the ones who actually determine the level of the bond's price.
8. Two institutional factors may also contribute to convertibles' premiums. First, margin requirements are typically lower for convertibles than for stock; thus investors can speculate with less money in the convertible market than in the stock market. Second, certain institutional investors, such as life insurance companies, have more freedom to invest in convertibles than in stocks; so if these institutions want to invest in stocks to a greater extent than their regulators permit, they can expand stock holdings "through the back door" with convertibles.

wealth in the event of a call; this fact prevents wide spreads between MM' and B_0XC_t whenever the market value exceeds the call price.

The second factor driving MM' toward C_0C_t is related to the loss protection characteristic of convertibles. Barring changes in the interest rate on the firm's straight debt securities, the potential loss on a convertible is equal to the spread between MM' and B_0M''. Since this spread increases at high conversion values, the loss potential also increases, causing the premium attributable to the loss protection to diminish.

The third factor causing the gap between MM' and C_0C_t to close has to do with the relationship between the yield on a convertible and that on the common stock for which it can be exchanged. The yield on most common stocks consists of two components: a dividend yield and an expected capital gain yield. (The next section will show that convertibles also have two yield components, one from interest payments and one from capital gains.) After some point, the expected capital gain is the same for both instruments, but the current yield on the bond declines in comparison with that on the common stock because dividends on stocks whose prices are rising are typically also rising, while interest payments are fixed. This causes the gap between M' and C_0C_t to close and would eventually lead to a negative premium except for the fact that voluntary conversion occurs first.

Expected Rate of Return on a Convertible

The purchaser of a convertible generally expects the price of the stock to rise, the conversion value to rise with the stock, and the conversion to take place after some period of time, say N years. Thus the purchaser expects first to receive a series of interest payments of $\$c$ per year for N years and then to have stock with a value equal to $C_N = p_0(1 + g)^N\#$. The expected rate of return on the convertible, k_c, is found by solving for it in Equation 22.3:

$$M = \sum_{t=1}^{N} \frac{c}{(1 + k_c)^t} + \frac{C_N}{(1 + k_c)^N},$$ (22.3)

where:

$M =$ maturity value (and par value). Note also that M is the price paid for the bond.
$c =$ dollars of interest received per year.
$C_N =$ conversion value $= p_0(1 + g)^N\#$.
$N =$ number of years bond is expected to be held.
$k_c =$ internal rate of return, or expected yield, on the convertible.

The equation is purely definitional; it simply states that if an investor pays M dollars for a convertible bond, holds it for N years, and receives a series of interest payments plus a terminal value, then the return on the investment will be equal to k_c.[9]

The *ex ante* yield on a convertible (k_c) is probabilistic—dependent on a set of variables subject to probability distributions and hence itself a random variable. It is possible, however, to define each of the determinants of k_c in terms of its mean expected value; $E(g)$, for example, is the expected value of the growth rate in the stock's price over N years. For simplicity, $E(g)$ and other random variables are shortened to g, C_N, and so on. With the variables defined in this manner, it is possible to work sequentially to determine C_N from Equation 22.5, developed shortly, then to use C_N in Equation 22.3 to find a value of k_c (the return on a convertible bond) that makes Equation 22.3 hold. The determinants of C_N are (1) the corporation's policy in regard to calling the bond to force conversion; or (2) the investor's decision to hold the bond until it is called, to sell it, or to convert voluntarily. Corporate call policy and investor cash-out policy are therefore examined in the next two sections.

Corporate Call Policy Corporations issuing convertible bonds generally have policies regarding just how far up the C_0C_t curve they will allow a bond to go before calling to force conversion. These policies range from calling as soon as the company is "sure" conversion will take place (this generally means a premium of about 20 percent over the par value) to never calling at all. If the policy is never to issue a call, however, the firm generally relies on the dividend-interest differential to cause voluntary conversion.

It is apparent that call policy has a direct influence on the expected number of years a convertible will remain outstanding and therefore on the value of C_N found by Equation 22.3. Naturally, expectations about call policy influence the expected rate of return on a convertible bond. Because of this, the issuing firm must take investor expectations into account. A policy in the apparent short-run interest of the corporation may penalize the investor with such a low effective actual yield that the firm will have difficulties when it subsequently attempts to market additional securities.[10] (This point is illustrated in one of the problems at the end of the chapter.)

9. Three simplifications are made in this analysis. First, taxes are ignored. Second, the problem of reinvestment rates is handled by assuming that all reinvestment is made at the internal rate of return. Third, it is assumed that bondholders do not hold stock after conversion; they cash out, as do institutional investors precluded from holding common stock.

10. Some firms seek to encourage *voluntary conversion* rather than call to force conversion. One way of doing this is to include a provision for periodic stepped-up conversion prices; for example, Litton Industries' conversion price goes up every three years (so the number of shares received upon conversion goes down), and this stimulates voluntary conversion at the step-up date provided the conversion value of the bond is above the straight debt value. In addition, voluntary conversion occurs when the dividend yield on stock received on conversion exceeds the interest yield on the convertibles.

Investor Cash-Out Policy Investor cash-out policy is similar to corporate call policy in that it sets a limit on how far up the C_0C_t curve investors are willing to ride. The decision is influenced by the interest-dividend relationship, by investors' aversion to risk (recall that risk due to a stock price decline increases as one moves up the C_0C_t curve), and by investors' willingness to hold securities providing low current yields. In general, it appears that investors are willing to ride higher up C_0C_t, given the dividend-interest relationship, than the firm is willing to let them ride; hence, corporate call policy generally supersedes investor cash-out policy.

Years the Bond Is Held

As already discussed, the path of the conversion value curve is traced out by Equation 22.1:

$$C_t = p_0(1 + g)^t \; \#. \tag{22.1}$$

Recognizing that $\# = M/p_c$, where p_c is defined as the initial conversion price of the shares, Equation 22.1 can be rewritten as:

$$C_t = \frac{p_0}{p_c} (1 + g)^t M. \tag{22.4}$$

Setting Equation 22.4 equal to the C_N defined by corporate policy (in this case, $1,200 if a 20 percent premium is used) results in:

$$C_N = \frac{p_0}{p_c} (1 + g)^N M = \$1,200 \tag{22.5}$$

$$\$1,200 = \frac{\$45}{\$50} (1.04)^N \$1,000 = \$900 \, (1.04)^N$$

$$\frac{\$1,200}{\$900} = 1.333 = (1.04)^N.$$

The 1.333 is the CVIF for the compound sum of $1 growing at 4 percent for N years. In the 4 percent column of Table A.1, the factor 1.333 lies between the seventh and eighth years, so $N \approx 7\frac{1}{2}$ years.

This value of N (rounded to eight years for simplicity), together with the other known data, can now be substituted into Equation 22.3:

$$M = \sum_{t=1}^{N} \frac{c}{(1 + k_c)^t} + \frac{p_0(1 + g)^N \;\#}{(1 + k_c)^N} \tag{22.3}$$

$$\$1,000 = \sum_{t=1}^{8} \frac{c}{(1 + k_c)^t} + \frac{\$45 \, (1.04)^8 20}{(1 + k_c)^8}$$

$$= \$40(\text{PVIF}_a) + \$1,232(\text{PVIF}).$$

Using the interest factors for 6 percent:

$$PV = \$40(6.210) + \$1,232(0.627)$$

$$= \$248 + \$772 = \$1,020 > \$1,000.$$

Therefore, k_c is a little larger than 6 percent. Using interest factors for 7 percent:

$$PV = \$239 + \$717 = \$956 < \$1,000.$$

Thus, k_c is between 6 and 7 percent. Interpolating, $k_c = 6.3$ percent, so someone purchasing this convertible for $1,000 can expect to obtain a return of 6.3 percent on the investment.

Decisions on the Use of Warrants and Convertibles

The Winchester Company, an electronic circuit and component manufacturer with assets of $12 million, illustrates a situation where convertibles are useful. Winchester's profits were depressed as a result of its heavy expenditures on research and development for a new product. This situation had held down the growth rate of earnings and dividends; the price/earnings ratio was only 18 times, as compared with an industry average of 22. At the then current $2 earnings per share and P/E of 18, the stock was selling for $36 a share. The Winchester family owned 70 percent of the 300,000 shares outstanding, or 210,000 shares. It wanted to retain majority control but could not buy more stock.

The heavy R & D expenditures had resulted in the development of a new type of printed circuit that management believed would be highly profitable. To build and equip new production facilities, $5 million was needed; and profits would not start to flow into the company for some eighteen months after construction on the new plant was started. Winchester's debt amounted to $5.4 million, or 45 percent of assets—well above the 25 percent industry average. Debt indenture provisions restricted the company from selling additional debt unless the new debt was subordinate to that outstanding.

Investment bankers informed J. H. Winchester, Jr., the financial vice-president, that subordinated debentures could not be sold unless they were convertible or had warrants attached. Convertibles or bonds with warrants could be sold with a 5 percent coupon interest rate if the conversion price or warrant option price was set at 15 percent above the market price of $36—that is, at $41 a share. Alternatively, the investment bankers were willing to buy convertibles or bonds with warrants at a $5\frac{1}{2}$ percent interest rate and a 20 percent conversion premium, or a conversion (or exercise) price of $43.50. If the company wanted to sell common stock directly, it could net $33 a share.

Which of the alternatives should Winchester have chosen? If common stock were to be used, the company would have to sell 151,000 shares ($5 million divided by $33). Combined with the 90,000 shares held outside the family, this would amount to 241,000 shares versus the Winchester holdings of 210,000; thus the family would lose majority control if common stock were to be sold.

If the 5 percent convertibles or bonds with warrants were to be used and the bonds converted or the warrants exercised, 122,000 new shares would have been added. Combined with the old 90,000, the outside interest would then be 212,000, so again the Winchester family would lose majority control. However, if the 5½ percent convertibles or bonds with warrants were to be used, then, after conversion or exercise, only 115,000 new shares would be created. In this case the family would have 210,000 shares versus 205,000 for outsiders; absolute control would be maintained.

In addition to assuring control, using the convertibles or warrants also would benefit earnings per share in the long run. The total number of shares would be less because fewer new shares would have to be issued to get the $5 million; thus earnings per share would be higher. Before conversion or exercise, however, the firm had a considerable amount of debt outstanding. Adding $5 million would raise the total debt to $10.4 million against new total assets of $17 million, so the debt ratio would be over 61 percent versus the 25 percent industry average. This could have been dangerous. If delays were encountered in bringing the new plant into production, if demand did not meet expectations, if the company experienced a strike, if the economy went into a recession, the company would be extremely vulnerable because of the high debt ratio.

Under these circumstances, Winchester decided to sell the 5½ percent convertible debentures. Two years later, earnings climbed to $3 a share, the P/E ratio went to 20, and the price of the stock rose to $60. The bonds were called, but conversion of course occurred. After conversion, debt amounted to approximately $5.5 million against total assets of $17.5 million (some earnings had been retained), so the debt ratio was down to a more reasonable 31 percent.

Convertibles were chosen rather than bonds with warrants for the following reason. If a firm has a high debt ratio and its near-term prospects are favorable, it can anticipate a rise in the price of its stock and thus be able to call the bonds and force conversion. Warrants, on the other hand, have a stated life; and even if the price of the firm's stock rises, the warrants may not be exercised until near their expiration date.[11] If, subsequent to the favorable period (during which convertibles can be called), the firm encounters less favorable developments and the price of its stock falls, the warrants may lose their value and may never be exercised. The heavy debt burden will then become aggravated. Therefore, the use of convertibles gives the

---

11. To our knowledge, no company has ever issued a "callable" warrant—one that the issuer would call for exercise under specific conditions. We recently recommended to a company that it consider issuing perpetual, but callable, warrants. These could be called to force exercise if the price of the stock exceeded the exercise price by, say, 30 percent; otherwise they would have no expiration date. Such warrants would probably be viewed with favor by investors afraid of warrants that might expire valueless, and they would still give the company control over the warrants similar to that over convertibles.

firm greater control over the timing of future capital structure changes. This factor is of particular importance to the firm if its debt ratio is already high in relation to the risks of its line of business.

Reporting Earnings If Convertibles or Warrants Are Outstanding

Firms with convertibles or warrants outstanding are required to report earnings per share in two ways: (1) *primary EPS,* which in essence is earnings available to common stock divided by the number of shares actually outstanding, and (2) *fully diluted EPS,* which shows what EPS would be if all warrants had been exercised or convertibles converted prior to the reporting date. For firms with large amounts of option securities outstanding, there can be a substantial difference between the two EPS figures. The purpose of the provision is, of course, to give investors more information on the firm's profit position.

Summary

Both warrants and convertibles are forms of options used in financing business firms. Their use is encouraged by an economic environment combining prospects of both boom or inflation and depression or deflation. The senior position of the securities protects against recessions, and the option feature offers the opportunity for participation in rising stock prices.

Both the convertibility privilege and warrants are used as "sweeteners." The option privileges they grant can make it possible for small companies to sell debt or preferred stock that otherwise cannot be sold. For large companies, the "sweeteners" result in lower costs of the securities sold. In addition, the options provide for the future sale of the common stock at prices higher than can be obtained at present. The options thereby permit the delayed sale of common stock at more favorable prices.

The conversion of bonds by their holders does not ordinarily bring additional funds to the company. However, the exercise of warrants does provide such funds. The conversion of securities results in reduced debt ratios, and the exercise of warrants strengthens the equity position but leaves the debt or preferred stock on the balance sheet. In comparing convertibles to senior securities carrying warrants, a firm with a high debt ratio should choose convertibles, while a firm with a moderate or low debt ratio should probably employ warrants.

In the past, larger and stronger firms tended to favor convertibles over bonds with warrants, so most warrants have been issued by smaller, weaker concerns. AT&T's use of warrants in its $1.57 billion 1970 financing has caused other large firms to reexamine their positions on warrants, and we anticipate that warrants will come into increasing use in the years ahead.

Questions

22.1 Why do warrants typically sell at prices greater than their formula values?

22.2 Why do convertibles typically sell at prices greater than their formula values (the higher of the conversion value or straight debt value)? Would you expect the percentage premium on a convertible bond to be more or less than that on a warrant? (The percentage premium is defined as the market price minus the formula value, divided by the market price.)

22.3 What effect does the trend in stock prices (subsequent to issue) have on a firm's ability to raise funds (a) through convertibles and (b) through warrants?

22.4 If a firm expects to have additional financial requirements in the future, would you recommend that it use convertibles or bonds with warrants? Why?

22.5 How does a firm's dividend policy affect each of the following:
   a. The value of long-term warrants
   b. The likelihood that convertible bonds will be converted
   c. The likelihood that warrants will be exercised

22.6 Evaluate the following statement: Issuing convertible securities represents a means by which a firm can sell common stock at a price above the existing market.

22.7 Why do corporations often sell convertibles on a rights basis?

Problems

22.1 A convertible bond has a face value of $1,000 and a 10 percent coupon rate. It is convertible into stock at $50; that is, each bond can be exchanged for twenty shares. The current price of the stock is $43 per share.
   a. If the price per share grows at 6 percent per year for five years, what will the approximate conversion value be at the end of five years?
   b. If dividends on the stock are presently $2 per share, and if these also grow at 6 percent per year, will bondholders convert after five years, or will they tend to hold onto their bonds? Explain.
   c. If the bonds are callable at a 10 percent premium, about how much would you lose per bond if the bonds were called before you converted? (Assume the same conversion value as in Part a above, at the end of five years.)

22.2 Warrants attached to a bond entitle the bondholder to purchase one share of stock at $10 per share. Compute the approximate value of a warrant if:
   a. The market price of the stock is $9 per share
   b. The market price of the stock is $12 per share
   c. The market price of the stock is $15 per share
   d. Each warrant entitles you to purchase two shares at $10, and the current price of the stock is $15 per share

22.3 The Garnet Lumber Company's capital consists of 24,000 shares of common stock and 8,000 warrants, each good for buying 3 shares of common at $30 a share. The warrants are protected against dilution (that is, the subscription price is adjusted downward in the event of a stock dividend or if the firm sells common stock at less than the $30 exercise price). The company issues rights to buy 1 new share of common for $25 for every 4 shares. With the stock selling rights on at $35, compute:

a. The theoretical value of the rights before the stock sells ex-rights

b. The new subscription price of the warrants after the rights issue

22.4 The Ironhill Manufacturing Company was planning to finance an expansion in the summer of 1978. The principal executives of the company were agreed that an industrial company such as theirs should finance growth by means of common stock rather than debt. However, they felt the price of the company's common stock did not reflect its true worth, so they were desirous of selling a convertible security. They considered a convertible debenture but feared the burden of fixed interest charges if the common stock did not rise in price to make conversion attractive. They decided on an issue of convertible preferred stock.

The common stock was selling at $48 a share. Management projected earnings for 1979 at $3.60 a share and expected a future growth rate of 12 percent a year. It was agreed by the investment bankers and management that the common stock would sell at 13.3 times earnings, the current price/earnings ratio.

a. What conversion price should be set by the issuer?

b. Should the preferred stock include a call price provision? Why?

22.5 Quality Photocopy has the following balance sheet:

Balance Sheet 1

Current assets	$125,000	Current debt (free)	$ 50,000
Net fixed assets	125,000	Common stock, par value $2	50,000
		Retained earnings	150,000
Total assets	$250,000	Total claims	$250,000

a. The firm earns 18 percent on total assets before taxes (with a 50 percent tax rate); 25,000 shares are outstanding. What are earnings per share?

b. If the price/earnings ratio for the company's stock is 16 times, what is the market price of the company's stock?

c. What is the book value of the company's stock? Sales and financing needs of the firm are expected to double in the next few years. The firm decides to sell debentures to meet these needs. It is undecided, however, whether to sell convertible debentures or debentures with warrants. The new balance sheet is as follows:

Balance Sheet 2

Current assets	$250,000	Current debt	$100,000
Net fixed assets	250,000	Debentures	150,000
		Common stock, par value $2	50,000
		Retained earnings	200,000
Total assets	$500,000	Total claims	$500,000

The convertible debentures will pay 7 percent interest and will be convertible into 40 shares of common stock for each $1,000 debenture. The debentures with warrants will carry an 8 percent coupon and entitle each holder of a $1,000 debenture to buy 25 shares of common stock at $50.

d. Assume that convertible debentures are sold and that all are later converted. Show the new balance sheet, disregarding any changes in retained earnings.

Balance Sheet 3

	Current debt	_____
	Debentures	_____
	Common stock, par value $2	_____
	Paid-in capital	_____
	Retained earnings	_____
Total assets _____	Total claims	_____

e. Complete the firm's income statement after the debentures have all been converted:

Income Statement 1

Net income after all charges except debenture interest and before taxes (18% of total assets)	_____
Debenture interest	_____
Federal income tax (at 50%)	_____
Net income after taxes	_____
Earnings per share after taxes	_____

f. Assume that instead of convertibles, debentures with warrants were issued. Assume further that the warrants were all exercised. Show the new balance sheet figures:

Balance Sheet 4

	Current debt	_____
	Debentures	_____
	Common stock, par value $2	_____
	Paid-in capital	_____
	Retained earnings	_____
Total assets _____	Total claims	_____

g. Complete the firm's income statement after the debenture warrants have all been exercised:

Income Statement 2

Net income after all charges except debenture interest
and before taxes _____
Debenture interest _____
Taxable income _____
Federal income tax _____
Net income after taxes _____
Earnings per share after taxes _____

22.6 The Printomat Company has grown rapidly during the past five years. Recently its commercial bank has urged the company to consider increasing permanent financing. Its bank loan under a line of credit has risen to $175,000, carrying 7 percent interest. Printomat has been thirty to sixty days late in paying trade creditors.

Discussions with an investment banker have resulted in the suggestion to raise $350,000 at this time. Investment bankers have assured the company that the following alternatives will be feasible (ignoring flotation costs):
1. Sell common stock at $7.
2. Sell convertible bonds at a 7 percent coupon, convertible into common stock at $8.
3. Sell debentures at a 7 percent coupon, each $1,000 bond carrying 125 warrants to buy common stock at $8.

Additional information is given in the company's balance sheet and income statement below:

Printomat Company Balance Sheet

		Current liabilities	$315,000
		Common stock, par $1	90,000
		Retained earnings	45,000
Total assets	$450,000	Total liabilities and capital	$450,000

Printomat Company Income Statement

Sales	$900,000
All costs except interest	810,000
Gross profit	$ 90,000
Interest	10,000
Profit before taxes	$ 80,000
Taxes (at 50%)	40,000
Profit after taxes	$ 40,000
Shares	90,000
Earnings per share	$0.44
Price/earnings ratio	17 times
Market price of stock	$7.48

Larry Anderson, the president, owns 70 percent of Printomat's common stock and wishes to maintain control of the company; 90,000 shares are outstanding.

a. Show the new balance sheet under each alternative. For alternatives 2 and 3, show the balance sheet after conversion of the debentures or exercise of warrants. Assume that half the funds raised will be used to pay off the bank loan and half to increase total assets.

b. Show Anderson's control position under each alternative, assuming that he does not purchase additional shares.

c. What is the effect on earnings per share of each alternative if it is assumed that profits before interest and taxes will be 20 percent of total assets?

d. What will be the debt ratio under each alternative?

e. Which of the three alternatives would you recommend to Anderson? Explain.

22.7 Continental Chemical Company is planning to raise $25 million by selling convertible debentures. Its stock is currently selling for $50 per share ($P_0 = $50). The stock price has grown in the past, and is expected to grow in the future, at the rate of 5 percent per year. Continental's current dividend is $3 per share, so investors appear to have an expected (and required) rate of return of 11 percent ($k = D/P_0 + g = \$3/\$50 + 5\%$) on investments as risky as the company's common stock. Continental's tax rate is 50 percent.

Continental recently sold nonconvertible debentures that yield 7 percent. Investment bankers have informed the treasurer that he can sell convertibles at a lower interest yield; they have offered him these two choices:

A. $P_c = \$55.55$ (# = 18)
   $C = \$60$ (6% coupon yield)
   $M = \$1,000$
   25-year maturity

B. $P_c = \$62.50$ (# = 16)
   $C = \$65$ (6½% coupon yield)
   $M = \$1,000$
   25-year maturity

In each case, the bonds are not callable for two years; but thereafter they are callable at $1,000. Investors do not expect the bonds to be called unless $C_t = \$1,266$; but they do expect the bonds to be called if $C_t = \$1,266$.

a. Determine the expected yield on Bond A (that on Bond B is 8.5 percent).

b. Do the terms offered by the investment bankers seem consistent? Which bond would an investor prefer? Which would Continental's treasurer prefer?

c. Suppose the company decided on Bond A but wanted to step up the conversion price from $55.55 to $58.82 after ten years. Should this stepped-up conversion price affect the expected yield and the other terms on the bonds?

d. Suppose, contrary to investors' expectations, Continental called the bonds after two years. What would the *ex post* effective yield be on Bond A? Would this early call affect the company's credibility in the financial markets?

e. Sketch out a rough graph similar to Figure 22.2 for Continental. Use the graph to illustrate what would happen to the wealth position of an investor who bought Continental bonds the day before the announcement of the unexpected two-year call.

f. Suppose the expected yield on the convertible had been less than that on straight debt (actually, it was higher). Would this appear logical? Explain.

PART 7 INTEGRATED TOPICS IN FINANCIAL MANAGEMENT

The final four chapters take up important but somewhat specialized topics that draw on the concepts developed in earlier sections. Chapter 23 introduces dynamics into the decision process by showing how financial managers react to changing conditions in the capital markets. Chapter 24 deals with the growth of firms through mergers and holding companies and the reasoning behind this development. Until now, the text has dealt with growing and successful firms. However, many firms face financial difficulties, and the causes of and possible remedies for these difficulties are discussed in Chapter 25. International aspects of managerial finance have been treated in a number of places, and some additional important areas are covered in Chapter 26, the final chapter of the book.

CHAPTER
POLICY

TIMING OF FINANCIAL

Although the timing of financial policy has always been important, the new inflationary environment has caused timing to take on greater significance than ever before. Since the mid-1960s, the U.S. economy has experienced a series of "credit crunches," during which the costs of financing have risen substantially. Minimizing the need to raise capital during these crunches is important. Also, a key question facing financial managers is whether financing costs will return to lower levels in the reasonably near future or whether the upward trends in recent years will continue. How this question is resolved will greatly influence the costs, amounts, and types of capital raised by business firms.

In an inflationary environment, changes in asset requirements are magnified by rising price levels; financial managers must consider this when planning their requirements. Also, when analyzing prospective returns from capital assets, they must realize that the prices of similar capital assets will increase substantially in future years. Finally, since it is exceedingly difficult to raise the requisite amount of funds in an inflationary environment, they must consider the problem of how to meet future maturing obligations.

Significance to Financial Management

The significance of financial timing is suggested by the following quotation from *Business Week:*

Even a modest increase in monetary restraint will be hard for most companies to handle. Ever since the end of the last year's credit drought, companies have worked hard to rebuild liquidity.

However, there's a "difference between actual and desired liquidity," says an economist for a major New York City Bank, "and companies haven't succeeded in loosening up balance sheets."

In contrasting money market conditions that lie ahead with 1966, economists stress the expected impact of inflation itself. During late 1966, the wholesale price index remained relatively stable. But if price increases get larger in coming months, interest rates are almost sure to climb.

"People who borrow under conditions of sharp inflation are willing to pay any amount for money," says Milton Friedman of the University of Chicago, "and people who lend ask high rates to protect themselves from loss of purchasing power." If the Fed doesn't tighten, Friedman expects prices to rise by at least 5 percent and possibly 7 percent during 1968 and predicts that interest rates will be in the 9 percent to 10 percent range.[1]

Friedman's forecast was subsequently borne out. But financial managers have also had to face another problem—fluctuating interest rates. These rates have fluctuated very sharply over the past decade, although the trend

1. "Is a Money Crunch on Its Way?" *Business Week,* September 29, 1967, p. 36.

in yields has generally been upward. In 1969 and early 1970, when inflationary expectations were strong and bank credit expansion was curtailed, market rates reached the highest levels in U.S. history. Then, during 1970 and early 1971, as economic activity slowed and monetary policy eased, interest rates dropped more sharply than in most earlier periods of decline. In 1974, under the stimulus of double-digit inflation, new records were set; major corporations and the U.S. government paid record amounts for long-term debt, and the prime rate hit a new high of 12 percent late in that year. Interest rates then were reduced in an attempt to reverse the economic decline that began in the fourth quarter of 1974. On December 22, 1976, the prime rate was reduced to 6 percent by the Chase Manhattan Bank, but most banks held their prime rate at $6^{1}/_{4}$ percent.

Financial managers are divided on the questions of whether major fluctuations in money costs will continue to occur and whether interest rates will continue their upward trend. Experience suggests that both possibilities should be taken into account in financial planning. Accordingly, this chapter first analyzes cyclical patterns in the costs of financing and then reviews the nature of monetary and fiscal policies, focusing on the implications of these policies for future patterns in the cost of external financing.

Historical Patterns in Interest Rate Movement

Interest rates are usually expressed in terms of percentages, but the percentages can be readily translated into dollar amounts. For example, a 7 percent per year interest rate represents the cost of interest per year per $100 borrowed. The price of funds fluctuates, as shown in Figure 23.1, which presents the relationship between long- and short-term interest rates since the turn of the century.

A number of features are revealed by the pattern of this relationship. First, it is clear that interest rates fluctuate widely over the years. The period from 1900 to 1930 was one of relatively high interest rates, while the period from 1930 to the early 1950s was one of relatively low interest rates. Since 1960, interest rate levels have moved up.

Second, although most of the time short-term interest rates are lower than long-term rates, there are times when they are higher. The period from 1900 to 1930 was unusual in that short-term interest rates were almost always higher than long-term rates. However, since then, short-term interest rates have been higher than long-term rates only during periods of tight money conditions.

Third, while short-term interest rates fluctuate widely, long-term interest rates for any given time period move within a narrower range. The greater volatility of short-term rates is seen dramatically in Figure 23.2, which presents the relationship between short-term interest rates and bond yields from 1970 to 1978. During this time corporate AAA bond yields fluctuated

Figure 23.1
Long- and Short-Term Interest Rates

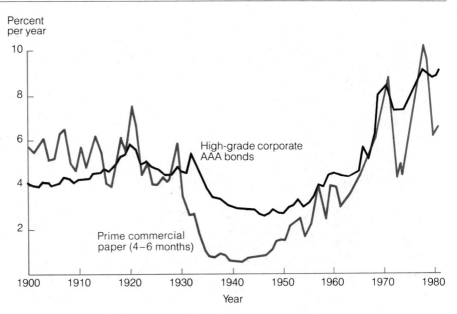

Sources: *Federal Reserve Historical Chart Book, Financial and Business Statistics,* 1977; and
Federal Reserve Bulletin, May 1978.

mainly within a range of 7 to 9 percent, while short-term interest rates fluctuated from about 3 to 9 percent. Some sharp movements occurred over relatively short periods of time. For example, between February 1972 and July 1973 the Treasury bill rate moved from a little over 3 percent to almost 9 percent. The increase was almost 200 percent over the level that existed at the beginning of the period. Then, between mid-1974 and mid-1975 the Treasury bill rate dropped from about 9 percent to almost 5 percent, a decline of almost 50 percent within a year.

Thus swings of 100 percent or more in short-term interest rates are not unusual. Financial managers therefore must take into account both the wide swings in the cost of what they are responsible for acquiring and the shifts in the patterns between short-term and long-term interest rates.

The movements in the levels of interest rates reflect fluctuations in the supply and demand for what is variously termed *funds, credit,* or *loanable funds.* These fluctuations in turn reflect changes in economic conditions as influenced by shifts in government policy. When economic activity is strong and expanding, the demand for funds is likely to increase relative to their supply. Expansion in economic activity is therefore likely at some point to be associated with the rise in interest rates. If, for any of a number of

Figure 23.2
Interest Rates and Bond Yields

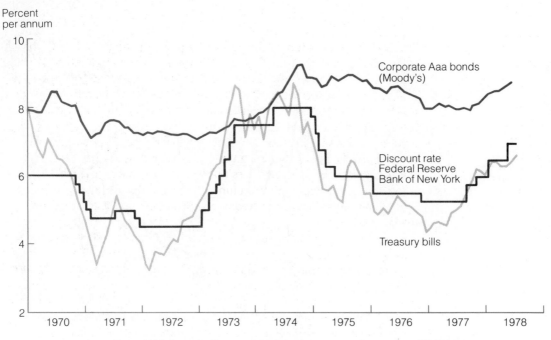

Source: U.S. Council of Economic Advisers, *Economic Indicators,* June 1978, p. 30.

reasons, the level of economic activity peaks and begins to decline, interest rates are likely to fall. Their further decline will be encouraged by Federal Reserve and federal budget policies that increase the available amount of funds. Thus both fundamental economic conditions and government policies influence interest rate levels.

Since the mid-1960s, underlying expectations of inflation related to expansionary government monetary and fiscal policies have exerted an upward push on the general level of interest rates. This influence of anticipated inflation on interest rates reflects the desire of the recipients of any form of income to determine the value of their income in real terms after adjusting for changes in the purchasing power of the currency unit. Those who receive interest payments in return for making their funds available for others' use also seek to evaluate what they will receive after adjustments have been made for the purchasing power of the currency unit. As a consequence, if lenders as a group expect inflation, the supply price of funds in nominal terms will rise so that after adjustments for inflation the underlying productivity of investment funds will be realized. Thus, while it is generally difficult to forecast future interest rate levels, if we expect the future rate of inflation to be high, we can also expect interest rates to fluctuate around a relatively high level.

Interest Rates as an Index of Availability of Funds

The data on fluctuations in short- and long-term interest rates in Figures 23.1 and 23.2 demonstrate that the cost of capital is one of the most volatile inputs purchased by firms. While the cost variations associated with interest rate fluctuations are substantial, the greatest significance of interest rates is their role as an index of the availability of funds. A period of high interest rates reflects tight money, which in turn is associated with tight reserve positions at commercial banks. At such times interest rates rise. However, since there are conventional limits on interest rates, a larger quantity of funds is demanded by borrowers than banks are able to make available. Banks therefore begin to ration funds among prospective borrowers by continuing lines of credit to traditional customers and restricting loans to new borrowers.

Small firms characteristically have greater difficulty than large ones in obtaining financing during periods of tight money; and even among large borrowers, the bargaining position of the financial institutions is stronger. It is a lender's rather than a borrower's market. Consequently, the cost is higher and the conditions in all loan agreements are more restrictive when the demand for funds is high. For small- and medium-sized firms, a period of rising interest rates may mean difficulty in obtaining any financing at all.

Periods of tight money have a particularly strong impact on utilities and other heavy industries, state and local governments, and the housing and construction sectors. (The heavy long-term investments in these areas cause the impact of interest rates on profitability to be especially significant.) During the credit crunch of 1974, funds became virtually unavailable to these sectors. Utility companies were forced to reduce planned expansions, state and local financing became difficult, and housing and construction declined substantially. The tightness of monetary conditions in the late autumn of 1977 again affected these sectors.

Costs of Different Kinds of Financing over Time

As mentioned earlier, interest rates vary widely over time. In addition, the relative costs of debt, preferred stock, and equity fluctuate. Data on these relative costs are presented in Figure 23.3, which shows that earnings/price ratios have fluctuated from 16 percent to 7 percent.[2] During the 1960s, E/P ratios averaged about 6 percent, ranging from 4.7 to 6.7 percent. However, in the 1970s, the rising costs of capital associated with inflation drove stock

2. An earnings/price ratio, the reciprocal of a P/E ratio, does not measure exactly the cost of equity capital, but it does indicate *trends* in this cost. In other words, when earnings/price ratios are high, the cost of equity capital tends to be high, and vice versa.

617

Figure 23.3
Long-Term Security Yields

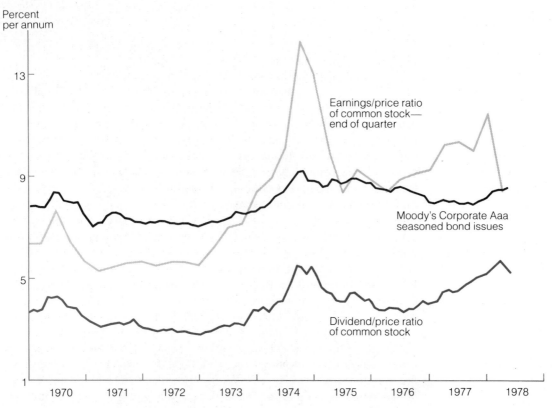

Source: Board of Governors of the Federal Reserve System, *Federal Reserve Monthly Chart Book*,
June 1978, p. 69.

prices down and E/P ratios up to over 11 percent in 1974 and 1978. Yields
on bonds have fluctuated to a much lesser extent. Furthermore, since bonds
and preferred stocks both provide a stable, fixed income to investors, they
are close substitutes for each other and their yields closely parallel each
other.[3]

3. Preferred stock yields are not shown in Figure 23.3 because they have been very close to AAA corporate bond yields (lower by five to fifty basis points during the period covered by the figure). Historically, bond yields have tended to be lower than preferred stock yields, because bonds have priority over
preferred stocks and, hence, are less risky. However, preferred stock dividends are largely tax exempt
to corporate owners, so after-tax yields (to corporations) are considerably higher than those on bonds.
Of the dividends received by a corporate stockholder, 85 percent are tax exempt to the receiver,
whereas interest income is fully taxable. During the 1960s, certain corporations (insurance companies,
savings and loans, mutual savings banks) that had previously paid very low taxes became subject to
higher taxes. These firms bought preferred stocks, thereby pushing preferred stock before-tax yields
below those of bonds in the late 1960s and early 1970s.

The pronounced decline in earnings/price ratios that began in the early 1950s resulted largely from investors' increasing awareness of the growth potential in common stock earnings, dividends, and stock prices. The economy was strong during this period, and security analysts and investors became aware of the importance of the g component in the expected rate of return equation $k_s = d/p + g$. A recognition of the dangers of inflation and of its effect on fixed income securities was driving bond and preferred stock yields up, further closing the gap between interest rates and earnings/price ratios.

Characteristic Patterns in Cost of Money

Figure 23.4 depicts in a general way the relationship of gross national product (GNP) to interest rates. Short-term interest rates show the widest amplitude of swings. Since long-term interest rates are *averages* of short-term rates, they are not as volatile as the short-term rates; that is, short-term rates move more quickly and fluctuate more than long-term rates. The cost of debt funds tends to coincide with movements in general business conditions both at the peak and at the trough.

The cost of equity funds can best be approximated by expected equity yields—dividends plus capital gains. To understand the behavior of equity yields, one must analyze the behavior of earnings, dividends, and stock prices. Corporate earnings are highly volatile; they lead the business cycle on both the upturn and the downturn—and dividends follow earnings. Prices of common stocks anticipate changes in corporate earnings. Prices of equities are also influenced by money market conditions. Owing to the gradual tightening in money market conditions as expansion continues, bond yields rise and attract money out of stocks and into bonds, causing the prices of equities to turn down before corporate profits reach their peak. Hence, the cost of equity financing turns up because firms receive lower prices for the stocks they sell.[4] In other words, the cost of equity capital begins to rise in the later stages of the business cycle.

---

4. Chapter 14 showed that, at least conceptually, stock prices can be determined by the following equation:

$$p = \frac{d}{k_s - g},$$

where:

p = the price of a share of stock.

d = the dividend on the stock.

k_s = the required rate of return on the stock (or the cost of equity capital).

g = the expected growth rate.

Since stocks and bonds compete with each other for investors' funds, if monetary policy drives interest rates up, k_s will likewise rise, and p will decline.

Figure 23.4
Relationship of Gross National
Product to Interest Rates

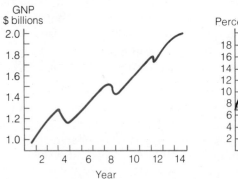
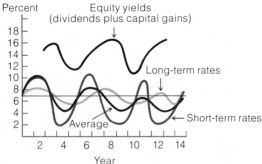

The relationships illustrated in Figure 23.4 represent generalizations that provide a frame of reference for the financial manager; they are not intended as precise guidelines. A basic requirement for sound financial management is the ability to make judgments about future economic and financial conditions that will affect both financial timing and the forms and sources of financing used. The next section seeks to provide a foundation for evaluating trends in financial markets.

Interest Rate Forecasts

Within the framework of general economic and financial patterns, short-term interest rate patterns and forecasts can be analyzed through the use of flow of funds accounts. These accounts, summarized in Table 23.1, depict the behavior of the major kinds of suppliers and demanders of funds. By projecting the sources and uses of funds in different categories, the direction of the pressure on interest rates can be estimated.[5]

Table 23.1 can be used in the following way. Historical patterns can be established to show uses and sources of funds in relation to the growth of the economy as a whole (as measured by GNP). In any particular year, if the demand for funds grows faster than the supply in relation to historical patterns, interest rates are likely to rise. The extra funds are supplied by the commercial banking system—the pivot in the financial mechanism. Whenever the demand for funds must be met by drawing on the commercial banking system to a greater than normal degree, interest rates rise.

Another significant statistic in the table is the rise in the supply of funds

---

5. Compilations of studies of this kind are facilitated by the flow of funds data developed by the Federal Reserve System and published monthly in the *Federal Reserve Bulletin*.

**Table 23.1
Brief Summary of Supply and
Demand in U.S. Credit Markets
(Annual Net Increases in
Amounts Outstanding—
Billions of Dollars)**

	1971	1972	1973	1974	1975	1976	1977	1978[a]
Realized Net Demands								
Privately held mortgages	44.3	68.8	68.7	42.8	40.2	72.0	94.0	97.0
Corporate and foreign bonds	25.6	19.9	14.2	29.1	39.1	39.1	33.8	36.2
Business loans and open market paper	7.6	27.8	49.3	53.3	−13.7	13.5	47.8	59.0
Consumer and other loans	17.0	24.2	28.2	12.9	10.2	32.6	45.2	50.5
Privately held Treasury and agency debt	21.7	27.5	21.6	29.4	87.8	75.5	72.6	84.2
State and local debt	21.7	12.8	14.1	14.5	16.3	17.1	29.7	21.2
Total demand for credit	137.9	181.0	196.1	182.0	179.9	249.8	323.1	348.1
Invested Net Supply								
Thrift institutions	41.2	47.1	36.0	25.6	53.4	68.8	79.8	75.8
Insurance and pension funds	12.8	14.9	19.5	29.6	40.8	46.9	55.9	58.8
Investment companies	0.5	1.6	1.6	1.9	3.7	4.6	5.3	5.8
Other investing institutions	12.1	13.5	17.2	5.1	−3.6	5.0	18.4	18.8
Commercial banks	50.9	73.3	77.6	59.8	31.0	64.0	78.4	93.3
Various other (primarily money market) investors[b]	25.3	11.2	4.8	21.2	19.0	32.0	53.4	50.2
Residual: Households direct	−4.9	19.4	39.4	38.8	35.6	28.5	31.9	45.4
Total supply of credit	137.9	181.0	196.1	182.0	179.9	249.8	323.1	348.1

[a] Preliminary figures.
[b] Consists of business corporations, state and local governments, and foreign investors.
Source: Henry Kaufman and James McKeon, *Prospects for the Credit Markets in 1978* (New York: Salomon Brothers, 1977), Table 1. Reprinted by permission.

from "Residual: Households direct"; funds from this source increased greatly between 1972 and 1973. Because of restrictive Federal Reserve policies, the ability of the commercial banks and other financial institutions to supply funds was held back in relation to demand. This produced high interest rates, which induced individuals, businesses, and others to make their surplus funds available to borrowers. The supply of funds was thereby augmented from nonbanking sources but only at substantially higher interest rates. By this test, a firming of interest rates during 1978 was also indicated.

Most longer-term predictions for the financial market call for continued high interest rates with only moderate declines of short duration from time to time. The causes are diverse, but a major factor is the efforts of governments throughout the world to achieve full employment and high growth rates. A worldwide capital shortage has resulted.

The outlook for continued price level increases and high interest rates has had a number of effects on corporate financial policy. Table 23.2 presents the uses and sources of corporate funds for the period 1963 to 1978, expressed as a percentage of the annual net increases. Dramatic fluctuations

**Table 23.2
Selected Components of Uses
and Sources of Corporate Funds,
1963–1977
(Percentages of Annual Net
Increases)**

	1963	1968	1971	1972	1973	1974	1975	1976	1977[a]	1978[b]
Uses										
Total physical investment	81%	97%	83%	79%	87%	93%	79%	80%	81%	86%
Net trade and consumer credit	6	4	2	6	4	4	c	4	5	5
Other	13	−1	15	15	9	3	21	16	14	9
Total uses	100%	100%	100%	100%	100%	100%	100%	100%	100%	100%
Sources										
Retained earnings	22%	8%	11%	12%	10%	1%	15%	22%	15%	12%
Depreciation	53	52	49	46	44	47	58	47	46	45
Internal cash generation	75%	60%	60%	58%	54%	48%	73%	69%	61%	57%
Bank loans	6	12	3	9	18	19	−9	c	9	12
Mortgage debt	d	5	10	13	12	9	7	7	7	8
Other	d	8	1	3	4	7	2	6	8	8
Net new bond issues	7	12	16	9	7	14	20	13	11	11
Net new stock issues	c	3	10	8	5	3	7	5	4	4
Total external sources	25%	40%	40%	42%	46%	52%	27%	31%	39%	43%
Total sources	100%	100%	100%	100%	100%	100%	100%	100%	100%	100%

[a] Estimated figures.
[b] Preliminary figures.
[c] Less than 1 percent.
[d] Not available.
Source: Based on materials in Henry Kaufman and James McKeon, *Prospects for the Credit Markets
in 1978* (New York: Salomon Brothers, 1977), Table 3B. Reprinted by permission.

have taken place in the role of internal financing. Total internal cash generation declined from 75 percent of total sources in 1963 to 48 percent in 1974.
In 1977 and 1978 internal cash generation again accounted for more than
half of total sources.

Another significant change has been an increase in the use of external
long-term financing from stocks and bonds. New common stock financing
rose from negligible amounts in 1963 to 10 percent in 1971 and has been stable at about 5 percent since 1975. The use of common stock financing to
strengthen the equity position of firms was even greater in certain industries
and for some individual firms. Long-term bond financing likewise grew from
7 percent in 1963 to 20 percent by 1975. It remained relatively high—at
something over 10 percent—for both 1976 and 1977.

These relations are further emphasized in Table 23.3. Part 1 of the table
presents data on gross proceeds (total funds raised before using part of the
cash proceeds to retire obligations previously outstanding). Part 2 presents
data on net proceeds after refundings and other adjustments. Part 3 an-

**Table 23.3
Long-Term Corporate Capital by
Type, 1963–1978**

	1963	1968	1972	1973	1974	1975	1976	1977	1978[a]
1. Gross Proceeds of Bond and Stock Financing (Percentages)									
Straight debt, public	42%	42%	57%	54%	73%	72%	59%	56%	57%
Straight debt, private	53	29	35	42	23	25	38	43	42
Convertible debt for cash	3	17	8	3	2	3	2	1	1
Convertible debt in mergers	2	12	[b]	1	2	[b]	1	[b]	[b]
Total bonds	100%	100%	100%	100%	100%	100%	100%	100%	100%
Total bonds	91%	79%	68%	67%	84%	80%	79%	80%	81%
Total stocks	9	21	32	33	16	20	21	20	19
Total bonds and stocks	100%	100%	100%	100%	100%	100%	100%	100%	100%
2. Net Proceeds of Bond and Stock Financing (Percentages)									
Straight debt, public	41%	48%	70%	79%	84%	82%	69%	67%	69%
Straight debt, private	55	19	28	27	15	17	30	33	31
Convertible debt	4	33	2	−6	1	1	1	[b]	[b]
Total bonds	100%	100%	100%	100%	100%	100%	100%	100%	100%
Total bonds	104%	107%	60%	60%	86%	76%	74%	75%	77%
Total stocks	−4	−7	40	40	14	24	26	25	23
Total bonds and stocks	100%	100%	100%	100%	100%	100%	100%	100%	100%
3. Analysis of Convertible Bond Offerings (Annual Net Increases in Amounts Outstanding—Billions of Dollars)									
Total convertibles	$0.5	$5.6	$2.3	$0.9	$1.1	$1.6	$1.4	$0.6	$0.6
Less convertibles called, retired, or converted	0.3	1.0	2.0	1.7	0.7	1.2	1.1	0.5	0.6
Called, retired, or converted as a percentage of total	60%	18%	87%	189%	64%	75%	79%	83%	100%
Yearly net convertible debt	0.2	4.6	0.3	−0.8	0.4	0.4	0.3	0.1	0.0
Cumulative outstanding[c]	0.2	11.5	20.1	19.3	19.7	20.1	20.4	20.5	20.5

[a] Preliminary figures.
[b] Less than 1 percent.
[c] Cumulative 1963 through 1977.
Source: Based on material in Henry Kaufman and James McKeon, *Prospects for the Credit Markets in 1978*
(New York: Salomon Brothers, 1977), Tables 3A and 3C. Reprinted by permission.

alyzes some patterns in convertible debt financing. These data indicate, as expected, a changing pattern of financing as interest rates rose during the 1960s and 1970s:

1. Stock financing as a percentage of long-term external financing almost quadrupled on a gross basis and rose from −4 percent to +40 percent on a net basis, then declined to the 25 percent range.
2. Bond financing on a gross basis dropped from over 90 percent to under 70 percent of the total, then rose to 80 percent.
3. Between 1963 and 1968, private placement of debt dropped from over

half of total long-term debt financing to as low as 24 percent on a gross basis and to as low as 15 percent on a net basis, then rising again. The fluctuations in the private placement of debt reflect the periodic impact of tight money on the financing demands placed on insurance companies, a major source of direct placement of financing.

4. With the onset of inflation in 1966 the use of convertible debt increased substantially, representing 17 percent of gross financing in 1968. In subsequent years, however, the use of convertibles moderated. Their reduced attractiveness may reflect the relatively weak stock market after 1967.

5. Convertible debt issued in mergers rose from less than 2 percent before 1967 to over 10 percent in 1968, but in the 1970s it declined to 1 percent or less.

6. The percentage of convertible debt reduced by conversion into stock was relatively high in 1963, declined substantially in 1968, and thereafter again increased significantly.

7. The cumulative total of net convertible debt outstanding rose from $11.5 billion in 1968 to $20.5 billion by 1978. It is clear that the increased uncertainties about the rate of inflation and the increased difficulties of forecasting interest rate patterns during this period led to the greater use of hybrid forms of financing—debt with equity participation such as convertibles or warrants. The percentage of direct loans with such equity sweeteners, or interest adjustment provisions, is reported to be even higher than that for public flotations for which data are available.

8. The credit stringency that reached a climax in May 1970 with the Penn Central bankruptcy led to a massive effort to restructure corporate balance sheets. Long-term financing accounted for about 84 percent of total external financing in 1970, versus an average of 62 percent for the five years prior to 1969.[6] The use of net short-term external financing sources, including bank loans and commercial paper, actually declined by $500 million during the first quarter of 1971. Thus short-term debt was repaid as longer-term debt and equity were used to improve corporate liquidity.

9. Internal cash generation peaked at 75 percent of total financing in 1963. After dropping to a low of 48 percent in 1974, it shot up to 73 percent during the recession of 1975, when bank loans declined. The percentage of financing requirements that can be covered from internal sources has been dropping since 1975.

Data on recent trends in preferred stock offerings are presented in Table 23.4. By far the largest sources of offerings are the utilities: electric power, water, gas, and telephone. The new issue preferred stock volume was re-

6. Richard L. Gady, "Recent Patterns in Corporate Financing," *Economic Commentary* (Federal Reserve Bank of Cleveland), June 14, 1971.

**Table 23.4
Recent Trends in the Volume of
New Preferred Stock Offerings,
by Type of Issue and Issuer, in
Historical Perspective
(Billions of Dollars)**

	1971	1972	1973	1974	1975	12 Months Ending Nov. 1976
Utility (excluding telephone)	1.9	2.4	1.9	2.0	2.5	2.1
Telephone	1.4	0.7	1.2	0.1	0.1	0.1
Manufacturing and mining	0.3	0.2	0.1	0.1	0.6	0.5
Financial and real estate	a	a	0.1	a	0.1	0.2
Other	a	a	a	a	0.1	a
Total	3.7	3.4	3.3	2.3	3.5	2.9
Memo: Public offerings	3.6	2.4	2.4	1.7	3.1	2.5
Private placements	0.1	1.0	0.9	0.5	0.4	0.4

Note: Columns may not add to totals due to rounding.
a Less than $50 million.
Source: *Comments on Credit,* Salomon Brothers, April 1, 1977, p. 4. Reprinted by permission.

duced in 1976 because the Bell System was out of the market that year. Other utilities also issued common stock rather than preferred stock during 1976. However, the volume of industrial and financial preferreds remained high, as did the volume of private placements.

Thus the interactions of the higher rates of inflation since 1966 and fluctuating interest rate levels have produced changing patterns of financial policies in business firms.

Implications of Interest Rate Patterns for Financial Timing

Variations in the cost of money and in its availability are likely to continue to be of great significance to financial managers. The importance of sound financial timing is underscored by past mistakes and future uncertainties.

A question that continues to challenge financial managers is whether interest rates, which appeared to have bottomed in late 1976 at levels above their previous 1971 lows, will keep moving upward. In terms of cyclical movements, long-term financing appeared attractive in 1976, and interest rates firmed during 1978. However, if interest rates in later years again move to the lower levels experienced in previous decades, the 1976 financing will have locked companies into high-cost, long-term capital.

Easy answers to financial questions are not available, and uncertainties have given rise to new forms and patterns of financing, as documented throughout this book. Even though definitive answers to the questions cannot be given, financial executives must make decisions—and therefore judgments—about these issues.

Summary

Financial managers have at least some flexibility in their operations. Even if a firm has a target debt/assets ratio, it can deviate from this target to some extent in a given year to take advantage of favorable conditions in either the bond or the stock market. Similarly, even if the firm has a target ratio of long-term to short-term debt, it can vary from this target if market conditions suggest that the action is appropriate.

To form a basis for making sound decisions with respect to financial timing, data covering both cyclical and long-term trends have been analyzed. Uncertainties about the future have increased in recent years, with a resultant increase in the importance of sound financial timing. Moreover, attempts to deal with an increasing level of uncertainty in the economy have given rise to innovations in financing techniques and patterns. Some important changes in financing that have developed in response to changes in the economy, especially in the money and capital markets, are:

1. Long-term financing has increased in comparison with the use of short-term commercial bank financing. Bond flotations in the capital markets have risen to record levels.
2. Public flotations of equity issues have increased substantially.
3. A large increase in debt ratios has occurred in response to the inflationary environment. From 1966 to 1977 the ratio of debt to assets for all manufacturing companies rose from 33 to 47 percent.[7]
4. An increase has occurred in the use of equity participations in the form of convertibles or warrants.
5. Insurance companies and other institutional lenders have virtually ceased to provide credit to small- and medium-sized borrowers on a straight debt basis. For business loans, warrants are usually required, while on mortgages, supplementary payments based on a percentage of gross or net income are stipulated in loan contracts.
6. Since larger firms have greater access to the financial markets, an increase in the volume of trade credit has occurred, with larger firms increasing their extension of credit to smaller ones.
7. New equity issues have taken place with each cyclical recovery in stock prices. In the middle and late stages of business recoveries, short-term financing has increased. After economic downturns, when interest rates have been reduced, corporations have increasingly utilized long-term financing to decrease the ratio of short-term financing to long-term financing. As equity prices have recovered during the early stages of business upswings, business firms have sought to strengthen their leverage positions by selling new equity issues.

---

7. Federal Trade Commission, *Quarterly Financial Report,* Fourth Quarter 1966 and Fourth Quarter 1977, April 10, 1978.

These developments indicate that trends in the money and capital markets are of increasing importance to financial managers. The changes have been so massive that innovations in the forms of financing have been stimulated Thus financial policies have not only been broadened but have taken on greater importance in the overall management of business firms.

Questions

23.1 Discuss the statement: It makes good sense for a firm to fund its floating debt, because this relieves the possibility that it will be called upon to pay off debt at an awkward time. From the standpoint of cost, however, it is always cheaper to use short-term debt than long-term debt.

23.2 Historical data indicate that more than twice as much capital is raised yearly by selling bonds than by selling common stocks. Does this indicate that corporate capital structures are becoming overburdened with debt?

23.3 Is the Federal Reserve's tight money policy restraining the country's economic growth? Discuss the pros and cons from the corporation's viewpoint.

23.4. Why do interest rates on different types of securities vary widely?

23.5 What does GNP represent? Why are its levels and growth significant to the financial manager?

23.6 When are short-term interest rates higher than long-term rates? What is indicated if short-term rates are high in relation to long-term rates for a prolonged period of time (such as twenty years) in a given country?

23.7 During a period of ten years, the price level in a particular country doubled. But during the following ten years, the price level was relatively stable. Discuss the effects on interest rates during the two ten-year periods.

Problems

23.1 A number of aspects of the timing of financing were treated in a *Business Week* article, excerpted here:

> For a variety of reasons—higher capital spending, the accumulation of inventories, rising interest rates, or the simple hedging of their bets—many corporate treasurers are rushing to their bankers to line up loans. Significantly, even some blue-chip companies that have been relying on commercial paper now show signs of returning to banks for at least part of their short-term cash.
>
> Although banks generally have plenty of money available . . . they are trying to make more loans at floating interest rates.[8]

a. Why was business borrowing from commercial banks expected to increase during the second half of 1978?

b. What are floating rate loans?

c. Why did banks want to use floating rate instead of fixed rate loans in 1978?

8. "The Corporate Rush to Borrow," *Business Week*, June 12, 1978, pp. 56–57.

    d. Why didn't the commercial banks shift completely to floating rate notes by mid-1978?

    e. What were some of the reasons large firms began shifting from the commercial paper market to bank borrowing during the latter half of 1978?

23.2 In July 1975, as the economy in general was emerging from the 1973–1974 downturn and Video Industries Corporation's business was resuming its strong growth in sales, Sam Lincoln, the treasurer, concluded that the firm would require more working capital financing during the year ending June 30, 1976. Given the historical and pro forma income statements and balance sheets of the Video Industries Corporation, how should its financing needs be met? Explain. (Although the $1.6 million pro forma financial requirements are shown in the long-term section of the balance sheet, they can be met with either long- or short-term funds.)

**Video Industries Corporation
Income Statements for Years
Ended June 30, 1975, and June
30, 1976 (Millions of Dollars)**

	1975	Pro Forma 1976
Sales, net	$20.0	$28.0
Cost of sales	16.0	20.0
Gross profit	$ 4.0	$ 8.0
Operating expenses	2.0	3.0
Operating profit	$ 2.0	$ 5.0
Other income, net	0.4	0.2
Profit before taxes	$ 2.4	$ 5.2
Taxes	1.2	2.6
Net profit after taxes	$ 1.2	$ 2.6
Dividends	0.2	0.4
To retained earnings	$ 1.0	$ 2.2

**Video Industries Corporation
Balance Sheets as of June 30,
1975, and June 30, 1976
(Millions of Dollars)**

Assets	1975	Pro Forma 1976	Liabilities and Capital	1975	Pro Forma 1976
Cash	$0.4	$ 1.2	Accounts payable	$0.6	$ 1.0
Receivables	1.6	2.4	Accruals	0.2	0.4
Inventories	2.0	3.2	Reserves for taxes	1.2	1.6
Total current assets	$4.0	$ 6.8	Total current liabilities	$2.0	$ 3.0
Fixed assets, net	2.0	4.0	Additional financing needed	0	1.6
Total assets	$6.0	$10.8	Common stock, $10 par	2.0	2.0
			Retained earnings	2.0	4.2
			Total liabilities and capital	$6.0	$10.8

23.3 Drake Manufacturing Company has decided to undertake a two-part capital expansion program, from which no benefits will accrue until both phases are completed. As treasurer, it is your responsibility to examine the various sources of funds available to finance each phase. The first phase will cost $5 million and will be undertaken immediately. It is anticipated that the company will begin the second phase, which also has an estimated cost of $5 million, approximately one year from now. The estimate for the second phase includes an adjustment for the rate of inflation, which is expected to increase from the current rate of 7 percent to approximately 9 percent at the end of the coming year. Drake's common stock is widely held and is traded on the over-the-counter market. Drake's balance sheet, income statement, and market information for the last fiscal year are given here:

**Drake Manufacturing Company
Balance Sheet as of
December 31, 1976
(Millions of Dollars)**

Assets		Liabilities and Capital	
Cash	$ 2.0	Accounts payable	$ 5.0
Accounts receivable (net)	10.0	Accruals	2.4
Inventory	20.0	Current portion of long-term debt	2.0
Total current assets	$32.0	Total current liabilities	$ 9.4
		Long-term debt (at 7%)	16.0
		Common stock ($10 par)	21.5
		Paid-in capital	13.0
Net property, plant and equipment	50.0	Retained earnings	22.1
Total assets	$82.0	Total liabilities	$82.0

**Drake Manufacturing Company
Income Statement for Year
Ending December 31, 1976
(Millions of Dollars)**

Sales	$150.00	
Gross margin	60.00	
Operating expenses	39.00	
Operating income	21.00	
Interest	1.26	Earnings per share (EPS) = $4.59
Pretax earnings	$ 19.74	Dividends per share (DPS) = $1.60
Taxes (at 50%)	9.87	Price/earnings (P/E) ratio = 10 times
Net income	$ 9.87	Market price = $45.90

After a thorough review of the situation and discussions with several banks and underwriters, you conclude that the following options are open to Drake (note, however, that in any given year, only one source of funds can be used):

1. Short-term debt to cover Phases 1 and 2 of the construction program, then a refund of this debt with any of the long-term methods (noted in Item 2) at the end of the construction period.
2. Long-term financing now for Phase 1 of the construction program, then additional financing next year for Phase 2. The long-term financing methods available are bank term loans, debentures, and common stock.
3. Long-term financing now to cover both phases of the expansion program, using one of the methods outlined in Item 2 to raise $10 million.

A review of the February 24, 1977 *Wall Street Journal* indicates that the following interest rates are now prevailing:

Bank Loans

Prime bank rate	6.75%
Revolving loan	8.75
Long-term	9.25

Commercial Paper

90–119 days	5.93%
4–6 months	6.27

U.S. Treasury Securities

3 months	4.93%
6 months	5.33
1 year	5.78

Corporate Bonds (20 Years)

Aa	8.8%

Your analysis of the economy shows that economic activity began showing strong signs of improvement about two months ago, following a long period of sluggishness. You also notice that, according to the 2/24/77 *Wall Street Journal,* the average P/E ratio for Dow Jones Industrials is 13.1, compared to 8.6 less than one year ago.

You are concerned about the effect the additional financing will have on Drake's EPS and market price, since the benefits from the expansion will not begin to be realized for about three years. You also wish to maintain a strong, liquid balance sheet. The maximum acceptable ratio of long-term debt to total long-term capital is 33 percent. Discussions with underwriters have indicated that a stock issue could be sold at the current market price. However, the discussion of a public or private debt issue (and the rating for a public issue of bonds) was not conclusive. Management believed that a public bond issue would probably be rated A. As treasurer, you are requested to analyze the situation completely and to support what you feel is the optimum financing plan and timing.

23.4 a. A manufacturing firm with $60 million of assets judges that it is at the beginning of a three-year growth cycle. It has a total debt to assets ratio of 16 percent, and it expects sales and net earnings to grow at a rate of 10 percent a year and stock prices to rise 30 percent a year over the three-year period. The firm will need $6 million at the beginning of the three-year period and another $3 million by the middle of the third year. It is at the beginning of a general business upswing, when money and capital costs are what they generally are after about a year of recession and at the beginning of an upswing. By the middle of the third year, money and capital costs will show their characteristic pattern near the peak of an upswing. How should the firm raise the $6 million and the $3 million?

b. An aerospace company with sales of $25 million a year needs $5 million to finance expansion. It has a debt to total assets ratio of 65 percent; and its common stock, which is widely held, is selling at a price/earnings ratio of twenty-five times. It is comparing the sale of common stock and convertible debentures. Which do you recommend? Explain.

c. A chemical company has been growing steadily. To finance a growth of sales from $40 million a year to $50 million over a two-year period, it needs $2 million in additional equipment. When additional working capital needs are taken into account, the total additional financing required during the first year is $5 million. Profits will rise by 50 percent after the first ten months. The stock is currently selling at twenty times earnings. The company can borrow on straight debt at $7\frac{1}{2}$ percent or with a convertibility or warrant "sweetener" for $\frac{3}{4}$ percent less. The present debt to total assets ratio is 25 percent. Which form of financing should it employ?

23.5 Evaluate the timing decision associated with a recent issue of corporate bonds.

a. From an issue of the *Wall Street Journal* published within the most recent thirty-day period, in the pages that describe new issues of stock and bonds sold to the public, identify a public issue of corporate bonds that came to market (were issued) the preceding day. Record information identifying the issuer, the date of the issue, the amount of the issue, and its maturity, coupon rate, price, yield to maturity, rating, and any other stated terms, along with the degree of success of the first day's sales. (Much of this information can be found in the "tombstone" advertisement for the issue. Somewhere in the immediately surrounding pages will be a paragraph or a very short statement about the issue, its rating, and the way it was received by the market.)

b. In the most recent monthly issue of the *Federal Reserve Bulletin (FRB)*, locate in the index the item "Interest Rates: Bond and Stock Yields," and in that table, under "Corporate Bonds," locate the column headed "Total." Record the yields under "Total" for each of the last fifteen months reported; also record the yield reported for each of the five years preceding the monthly data.

1. Plot these data.
2. Indicate the yield for your new issue, as determined in Part a, on this graph.

c. Briefly explain what has happened to long-term corporate interest rates in general in the interim between the most recent *FRB* data and the date of your new issue in Part a. Given the current state of the economy, what is the outlook for interest rates over the next six months to one year?

d. Discuss the percentage interest cost incurred by the issuer of your bonds and the timing of the new issue.

CHAPTER **24** EXTERNAL GROWTH:
MERGERS AND HOLDING COMPANIES

Growth is vital to the well-being of a firm. Without it, the business cannot attract able management because it cannot give recognition in promotions or offer challenging, creative activity. And without able executives, the firm is likely to decline and die. Much of the previous material dealing with analysis, planning, and financing has a direct bearing on the financial manager's potential contribution to the firm's growth. This chapter focuses on strategies for promoting growth.

Merger activity has played an important part in the growth of U.S. firms, and financial managers are required both to appraise the desirability of prospective mergers and to participate directly in evaluating the companies involved in them.[1] Consequently, it is essential that the study of financial management provide the background necessary for effective participation in merger negotiations and decisions.

Financial managers also need to be aware of the broad significance of mergers. Despite the heightened merger activities in the 1920s, again after World War II, and during the 1960s, recent merger movements have neither approached the magnitude nor had the social consequences of those that took place from 1890 to 1905. During this period, more than two hundred major combinations were effected, resulting in the concentration that has characterized the steel, tobacco, and other important industries. Regardless of the business objectives and motives of merger activity, its social and economic consequences must also be taken into account.

While the frenzied merger movement of the 1960s peaked in the last two years of that decade, it resumed its surge in 1977 and 1978. In 1977 there were 2,224 mergers, and the number in 1978 was expected to rise by 5 percent to 2,335.[2] While the replacement costs of fixed assets have continued to rise with inflation, market values are often below book values based on historical costs. Companies seeking to add capacity can do so by buying companies at market prices well below the current replacement costs of the assets acquired. Also, the decline in the international value of the U.S. dollar makes acquisition of U.S. companies by foreign companies "cheap" when expressed in foreign currencies whose value has risen compared to the U.S. dollar.

A sharp increase has occurred in tender offers, in which acquiring firms make their offers to buy directly to the stockholders at a premium price above current market price. The total $20 billion value of 1969 mergers was closely approached or exceeded during each of the years 1977 and 1978. Illustrative of the large mergers in recent years are the twelve listed in Table 24.1.

1. As we use the term, *merger* means any combination that forms one economic unit from two or more previous ones. For legal purposes there are distinctions among the various ways these combinations can occur, but the emphasis here is on fundamental business and financial aspects of mergers or acquisitions.
2. "The Matchmaker," *Wall Street Journal,* August 8, 1978, p. 1.

**Table 24.1
Twelve Major Mergers in
1976–1977**

Acquiring Company	Acquired Company	Value of Transaction (in Millions)
General Electric	Utah International	$2,170
Atlantic Richfield	Anaconda	536
R. J. Reynolds	Burmah Oil & Gas	520
J. Ray McDermott	Babcock & Wilcox	510
Gulf Oil	Kewanee Industries	440
Getty Oil	Mission; Skelly Oil	356
Champion International	Hoerner Waldorf	351
Pepsico	Pizza Hut	313
Continental Group	Richmond	293
Nestlé	Alcon Laboratories	268
Marathon Oil	Pan Ocean Oil	265
ITT	Carbon Industries	264
Total		$6,286

Source: "The Great Takeover Binge," *Business Week,* November 14, 1977, p. 177.

Mergers versus Internal Growth

Many of the objectives of size and diversification can be achieved either by internal growth or by external growth through acquisitions and mergers. In the post–World War II period, considerable diversification was achieved by many firms through external acquisition. Some financial reasons for utilizing external acquisition instead of internal growth to achieve diversification are discussed below.

Financing

Sometimes it is possible to finance an acquisition when it is not possible to finance internal growth. Building a large steel plant, for example, involves a large investment. Steel manufacturing capacity can be acquired in a merger through an exchange of stock more cheaply than it can be obtained by buying the facilities themselves. Sellers are often more willing to accept the purchaser's stock in payment for the facilities sold than are investors in a public offering, and the use of stock reduces cash requirements for the acquisition of assets.

Market Capitalization Rates

While it is not strictly an operating factor, the fact that the earnings of larger economic units are frequently capitalized at lower rates and hence produce higher market values has stimulated many mergers. The securities of larger firms have better marketability; these firms are more able to diversify and thus reduce risks, and they are generally better known. All these factors

635

lead to lower required rates of return and higher price/earnings ratios. As a result, the market value of consolidated firms may be greater than the sum of their individual values, even if there is no increase in aggregate earnings. To illustrate: Three companies may each be earning $1 million and selling at ten times earnings, for a total market value of $30 million. When these companies combine, the new company may obtain a stock exchange listing or may take other action to improve the price of its stock. If so, the price/earnings ratio may rise to fifteen, in which case the market value of the consolidated firm will be $45 million.[3]

The major reason for the increase in takeovers in 1976–1977 is that the replacement values of corporate assets have been rising with inflation while inflation has depressed real earnings, the result being lower stock prices. It has been estimated that by the late 1970s the replacement costs of corporate net assets (for nonfarm, nonfinancial corporations) were about 25 percent higher than the market values of the corporate securities representing ownership of the corporate assets.[4] Because selling prices of products have been based on the historical costs of assets, the prospective returns on new investments at current, higher replacement costs have been unattractively low. With the market values of other companies substantially below their replacement costs, acquisitions provide the opportunity of higher returns than would be earned by investments in physical assets either in the firm's own line of business or in new areas.

Taxes

Without question, the high level of taxation was a factor stimulating merger activity in the postwar period. Studies have indicated that taxes appear to have been a major reason for the sale of about one-third of the firms acquired by merger. In some cases, inheritance taxes precipitated these sales; in others, the advantage of buying a company with a tax loss provided the motivation.

Terms of Mergers

For every merger actually consummated, a number of other potentially attractive combinations fail during the negotiating stage. Negotiations may be broken off when it is revealed that the companies' operations are not compatible or when the parties are unable to agree on the merger terms. The most important of these terms is the price to be paid by the acquiring firm.

---

3. The market capitalization rate is related to the cost of equity, as discussed in Chapter 16. A lower capitalization rate results in a lower cost of capital. Therefore, the same actions that raise the market value of the equity also lower the firm's cost of new capital.
4. "The Great Takeover Binge," *Business Week*, November 14, 1977, p. 179.

Effects on Price and Earnings

A merger carries the potential for either favorable or adverse effects on earnings, on market prices of shares, or on both. Previous chapters have shown that investment decisions should be guided by the effects on market values, and these effects should in turn be determined by the probable effects on future earnings and dividends. Future events are difficult to forecast, however, so stockholders, as well as managers, attribute great importance to the immediate effects on earnings per share of a contemplated merger. Company directors will often state, "I do not know how the merger will affect the market price of the shares of my company, because so many forces influencing market prices are at work. But the effect on earnings per share can be seen directly."

An example will illustrate the effects of a proposed merger on earnings per share and thus suggest the kinds of problems likely to arise. Assume the following facts for two companies:

	Company A	Company B
Total earnings	$20,000	$50,000
Number of shares of common stock	5,000	10,000
Earnings per share of stock	$4	$5
Price/earnings ratio per share	15 times	12 times
Market price per share	$60	$60

Suppose the firms agree to merge, with B, the surviving firm, acquiring the shares of A by a one-for-one exchange of stock. The exchange ratio is determined by the market prices of the two companies. Assuming no increase in earnings, the effects on earnings per share are shown in the following tabulation:

	Shares of Company B Owned after Merger	Earnings per Share Before Merger	Earnings per Share After Merger
A's stockholders	5,000	$4	$4.67
B's stockholders	10,000	5	4.67
Total	15,000		

Since total earnings are $70,000, and since a total of 15,000 shares will be outstanding after the merger has been completed, the new earnings per share will be $4.67. Earnings will increase by 67 cents for A's stockholders, but they will decline by 33 cents for B's.

The effects on market values are less certain. If the combined company sells at Company A's price/earnings ratio of 15, the market value per share of the new company will be $70. In this case, shareholders of both companies will have benefited. This result comes about because the combined earnings are now valued at a multiplier of 15, whereas prior to the merger one portion of the earnings was valued at a multiplier of 15 and another portion at a multiplier of 12. If, on the other hand, the earnings of the new company are valued at B's multiplier of 12, the indicated market value of the shares will be $56; and the shareholders of each company will have suffered a $4 dilution in market value.

Because the effects on market value per share are less certain than those on earnings per share, the impact of earnings per share tends to be given great weight in merger negotiations. The following analysis thus emphasizes effects on earnings per share while recognizing that maximizing market value is a valid rule of investment decisions.

As shown below, if a merger takes place on the basis of earnings, neither earnings dilution nor earnings appreciation will take place:

	Shares of Company B Owned after Merger	Earnings per Old Share	
		Before Merger	After Merger
A's stockholders	4,000	$4	$4
B's stockholders	10,000	5	5
Total	14,000		

It is clear that the equivalent earnings per share after the merger are the same as before the merger.[5] The effect on market values, however, will depend on whether the 15-times multiplier of A or the 12-times multiplier of B prevails.

Of the numerous factors affecting the valuation of the constituent companies in a merger, all must ultimately be reflected in the companies' earnings per share, or market price. Hence, all the effects on the earnings position or wealth position of stockholders are encompassed by the above example.

Quantitative Factors Affecting Terms of Mergers

Five factors have received the greatest emphasis in arriving at merger terms: (1) earnings and the growth of earnings, (2) dividends, (3) market values, (4) book values, and (5) net current assets. Analysis is typically based on the per share values of the foregoing factors. The relative importance of each factor and the circumstances under which each is likely to be the most influential determinant in arriving at terms will vary. The nature of these influences is described below.

---

5. On the basis of earnings, the exchange ratio is 4:5; that is, Company A's shareholders receive four shares of B stock for each five shares of A stock they own. Earnings per share of the merged company are $5. But, since A's shareholders now own only 80 percent of the number of their old shares, their equivalent earnings per *old* share are the same $4. For example, if one of A's stockholders formerly held 100 shares, that person will own only 80 shares of B after the merger; and the total earnings will be 80 × $5 = $400. Dividing the $400 total earnings by the number of shares formerly owned, 100, gives the $4 per *old* share.

Earnings and Growth Rates Both expected earnings and capitalization rates as reflected in P/E ratios are important in determining the values that will be established in a merger. The analysis necessarily begins with historical data on the firms' earnings; their past growth rates, probable future trends, and variability are important determinants of the earnings multiplier, or P/E ratio, that will prevail after the merger.

How future earnings growth rates affect the multiplier can be illustrated by extending the preceding example. First, high P/E ratios are commonly associated with rapidly growing companies. Since Company A has the higher P/E ratio, it is reasonable to assume that its earnings will grow more rapidly than those of Company B. Suppose A's expected growth rate is 10 percent and B's is 5 percent. Looking at the proposed merger from the viewpoint of Company B and its stockholders, and assuming that the exchange ratio is based on present market prices, it can be seen that B will suffer a dilution in earnings when the merger occurs. However, B will be acquiring a firm with more favorable growth prospects; hence, its earnings after the merger should increase more rapidly than before. In this case, the new growth rate is assumed to be a weighted average of the growth rates of the individual firms—weighted by their respective total earnings before the merger. In the example, the new expected growth rate is 6.43 percent.

With the new growth rate it is possible to determine just how long it will take Company B's stockholders to regain the earnings dilution—that is, how long it will take earnings per share to revert back to their position before the merger. This can be determined graphically from Figure 24.1.[6] Without the merger, B will have initial earnings of $5 a share, and these earnings will grow at a rate of 5 percent a year. With the merger, earnings will drop to $4.67 a share, but the rate of growth will increase to 6.43 percent. Under these conditions, the earnings dilution will be overcome after five years; from the fifth year on, B's earnings will be higher, assuming the merger is consummated.

This same relationship can be developed from the viewpoint of the faster growing firm, for which there is an immediate earnings increase but a reduced rate of growth. Working through the analysis shows the number of years before the earnings accretion will be eroded.

It is apparent that the critical variables are (1) the respective rates of

6. The calculation could also be made algebraically by solving for N in the following equation:

$$E_1(1 + g_1)^N = E_2(1 + g_2)^N,$$

where:

E_1 and E_2 = earnings before and after the merger, respectively.

g_1 and g_2 = the growth rates before and after the merger, respectively.

N = the breakeven number of years.

Figure 24.1
Effect of Merger on Future
Earnings

growth of the two firms; (2) their relative sizes, which determine the actual
amount of the initial earnings per share dilution or accretion, as well as the
new weighted average growth rate; (3) the firms' P/E ratios; and (4) the exchange ratio. These factors interact to produce the resulting pattern of earnings per share for the surviving company. It is possible to generalize the relationships somewhat; for the immediate purposes, it is necessary simply to
note that in the bargaining process the exchange ratio is the variable that
must be manipulated in an effort to reach a mutually satisfactory earnings
pattern.[7]

7. Certain companies, especially the conglomerates, are reported to have used mergers to produce a
   "growth illusion" designed to increase the prices of their stocks. When a high P/E ratio company buys
   a low P/E ratio company, the earnings per share of the acquiring firm rise *because* of the merger. Thus
   mergers can produce growth in reported earnings for the acquiring firm. This growth by merger in turn
   can cause the acquiring firm to keep its high P/E ratio. With this ratio, the conglomerates can seek new
   low P/E merger candidates and thus continue to obtain growth through mergers. The chain is broken
   if (1) the rate of merger activity slows, or (2) the P/E ratio of the acquiring firm falls. In 1968 and 1969
   several large conglomerates reported profit declines caused by losses in certain of their divisions.
   This reduced the growth rate in EPS, which in turn led to a decline in the P/E ratio. A change in tax
   laws and antitrust suits against some conglomerate mergers also made it more difficult to consummate
   favorable mergers. These factors, along with tight money and depressed conditions in some industries, caused a further reduction in the P/E ratio and compounded the firms' problems. The net result
   was a drastic revaluation of conglomerate share prices, with such former favorites as LTV falling from
   a high of $169 to $7.50 and Litton Industries from $115 to $6.75.

Dividends Because they represent the actual income received by stock-holders, dividends can influence the terms of merger. As Chapter 17 suggests, however, dividends are likely to have little influence on the market price of companies with a record of high growth and high profitability. Some companies have not yet paid cash dividends but command market prices representing a high multiple of current earnings. For example, some non−dividend paying companies with high price/earnings ratios reported in the *Wall Street Journal* in 1977 were Continental Materials with a price/earnings ratio of 113, Ranger Oil with 58, and Viatech with 100. However, for utility companies and for companies in industries where growth rates and profitability have declined, the dollar amount of dividends paid can have a relatively important influence on the market price of the stock. Dividends can therefore influence the terms on which these companies will be likely to trade in a merger.[8]

Market Values The price of a firm's stock reflects expectations about its future earnings and dividends, so current market values are expected to have a strong influence on the terms of a merger. However, the value placed on a firm in an acquisition is likely to exceed its current market price for a number of reasons:

1. If the company is in a depressed industry, its stockholders are likely to overdiscount the dismal outlook for the company. This will result in a very low current market price.
2. The prospective purchaser may be interested in the company for the contribution that it will make to the purchaser's company. Thus the acquired company may be worth more to an informed purchaser than it is in the general market.
3. Stockholders are offered more than current market prices for their stock as an inducement to sell.

For these reasons, the offering price is usually in the range of 10 to 20 percent above the market price before the merger announcement.

Book Value per Share Book value is generally considered to be relatively unimportant in determining the value of a company, since it represents only the historical investments made in the company—investments that may have little relation to current values or prices. At times, however, especially when it substantially exceeds market value, book value may well have an impact on merger terms. Book value is an index of the amount of physical facilities made available in the merger. Despite a past record of low earning

---

8. If a company that does not pay dividends on its stock is seeking to acquire a firm whose stockholders are accustomed to receiving dividends, the exchange can be on a convertibles for common stock basis. This will enable the acquired firm's stockholders to continue receiving income.

power, it is always possible that, under effective management, a firm's assets may once again achieve normal earning power, in which case the market value of the company will rise. Because of the potential contribution of physical properties to improved future earnings, book value may have an influence on actual merger terms.

Net Current Assets per Share Net current assets (current assets minus current liabilities) per share are likely to have an influence on merger terms because they represent the amount of liquidity that can be obtained from a company in a merger. In the postwar textile mergers, net current assets were very high, and this was one of the characteristics making textile companies attractive to the acquiring firms. By buying a textile company, often with securities, an acquiring company was in a position to look for still other merger candidates, paying for new acquisitions with the just-acquired liquidity. Similarly, if an acquired company is debt-free, the acquiring firm may be able to borrow the funds required for the purchase, using the acquired firm's assets and earning power to pay off the loan after the merger or to provide security for renewing or even increasing the borrowing.[9]

Relative Importance of Quantitative Factors Attempts have been made to determine statistically the relative weights assigned to each of the above factors in actual merger cases. These attempts have been singularly unsuccessful. In one case, one factor seems to dominate; in another, some other determinant appears most important. This absence of consistent patterns among the quantitative factors suggests that qualitative forces are also at work.

Qualitative Influences: Synergy

Sometimes the most important influence on the terms of a merger is a business consideration not reflected at all in historical quantitative data. A soundly conceived merger is one in which the combination produces what may be called a *synergistic,* or "two-plus-two-equals-five," effect. By the combination, more profits are generated than could be achieved by the sum of the individual firms operating separately.

To illustrate: In the merger between Merck and Company and Sharp and Dohme, it was said that each company complemented the other in an important way. Merck had a good reputation for its research organization; Sharp and Dohme had an effective sales force. The combination of these two pharmaceutical companies added strength to both. Another example is the merger between Carrier Corporation and Affiliated Gas Equipment. The

---

9. By the same token, a firm seeking to *avoid* being acquired may reduce its liquid position and use up its borrowing potential.

merger enabled the combined company to provide a complete line of air-conditioning and heating equipment. The merger between Hilton Hotels and Statler Hotels led to economies in the purchase of supplies and materials. One Hilton executive estimated that the savings accruing simply from the combined management of the Statler Hotel in New York and Hilton's New York Hotel amounted to $700,000 a year. The bulk of the savings was in laundry, food, advertising, and administrative costs.

The qualitative factors may also reflect other influences. The merger or acquisition may enable a company that lacks general management ability to obtain it from the other company. Another factor may be the acquisition of a technically competent scientific or engineering staff if one of the companies has fallen behind in the technological race. In such a situation, the company needing the technical competence possessed by the other firm may be willing to pay a substantial premium over previous levels of earnings, dividends, market values, or book values of the acquired firm.

The purpose of the merger may be to develop a production capability a firm does not possess. Some firms are strong in producing custom-made items with high performance characteristics; yet on entering new markets, these firms must make use of mass production techniques. If a firm has had no such experience, this skill may have to be obtained by means of a merger. Another firm may need to develop an effective sales organization. For example, some of the companies previously oriented to the defense market, such as those in aerospace, found that they had only a limited industrial sales organization; merger was the solution to the problem.

The foregoing are the kinds of qualitative considerations that may have an overriding influence on the actual terms of merger, and the value of such contributions is never easy to quantify. The all-encompassing question, of course, is how the factors will affect the contribution of each company to future earnings per share in the combined operation. The historical data and qualitative considerations described, in addition to judgment and bargaining, combine to determine merger terms.

Holding Companies

In 1889, New Jersey became the first state to pass a general incorporation law permitting corporations to be formed for the sole purpose of owning the stocks of other companies. This law was the origin of the holding company. The Sherman Act of 1890, which prohibits combinations or collusion in restraint of trade, gave an impetus to holding company operations as well as to outright mergers, because companies could do as one company what they were forbidden to do as separate companies.

Many of the advantages and disadvantages of holding companies are no more than the advantages and disadvantages of large-scale operations already discussed in connection with mergers and consolidations. Whether a company is organized on a divisional basis or with the divisions kept as separate companies does not affect the basic reasons for conducting a large-scale, multiproduct, multiplant operation. However, the holding company form of large-scale operations has different advantages and disadvantages from those of completely integrated divisionalized operations.

Advantages of Holding Companies

Control with Fractional Ownership Through a holding company operation, a firm can buy 5, 10, or 50 percent of the stock of another corporation. Such fractional ownership may be sufficient to give the acquiring company effective working control of or substantial influence over the operations of the company in which it has acquired ownership. Working control is often considered to entail more than 25 percent of the common stock, but it can be as low as 10 percent if the stock is widely distributed. Also, control on a very slim margin can be held through friendship with large stockholders outside the holding company group. Sometimes holding company operations represent the initial stages of transforming an operating company into an investment company, particularly when the operating company is in a declining industry. When an industry's sales begin to decline permanently and the firm begins to liquidate its operating assets, it may use the liquid funds to invest in industries having a more favorable growth potential.

Isolation of Risks Because the various operating companies in a holding company system are separate legal entities, the obligations of any one unit are separate from those of the other units. Catastrophic losses incurred by one unit are therefore not transmitted as claims on the assets of the other units.

Although this is the customary generalization of the nature of a holding company system, it is not completely valid. In extending credit to one of the units of a holding company system, an astute financial manager or loan officer will require a guarantee or a claim on the assets of all the elements in the system. To some degree, therefore, the assets in the various elements are joined. The advantage remains to the extent that catastrophes occurring to one unit are not transmitted to the others.

Approval Not Required A holding company group that seeks to obtain effective working control of a number of companies may quietly purchase a portion of their stock. The operation is completely informal, and the permission or approval of the stockholders of the acquired company or companies is not required. Thus the guiding personalities in a holding company operation are not dependent on negotiations and approval of the other interest groups in order to obtain their objectives. This feature of holding company operations has, however, been limited somewhat by the recent SEC actions described later in the chapter.

Disadvantages of Holding Companies

Partial Multiple Taxation Provided the holding company owns at least 80 percent of a subsidiary's voting stock, Internal Revenue regulations permit the filing of consolidated returns, in which case dividends received by the parent are not taxed. However, if less than 80 percent of the stock is owned, returns cannot be consolidated, although 85 percent of the dividends received by the holding company can be deducted. With a tax rate of 46 percent, this means that the effective tax on intercorporate dividends is 6.9 percent. This partial double taxation somewhat offsets the benefits of holding company control with limited ownership, but whether the penalty of 6.9 percent of dividends received is sufficient to offset the advantages is a matter that must be decided in individual situations.[10]

Ease of Enforced Dissolution In the case of a holding company operation that falls into disfavor with the U.S. Department of Justice, it is relatively easy to require dissolution of the relationship by disposal of stock ownership; for instance, in the late 1950s du Pont was required to dispose of its 23 percent stock interest in General Motors Corporation, acquired in the early 1920s. Because there was no fusion between the corporations, there were no difficulties, from an operating standpoint, in requiring the separation of the two companies. However, if complete amalgamation had taken place, it would have been much more difficult to break up the company after so many years, and the likelihood of forced divestiture would have been reduced.

Risks of Excessive Pyramiding While pyramiding magnifies profits if operations are successful, as was seen in the financial leverage analysis, it also magnifies losses. The greater the degree of pyramiding, the greater the degree of risk involved in any fluctuations in sales or earnings. This potential disadvantage of pyramiding operations through holding companies is discussed in the next section.

Leverage in Holding Companies

The problem of excessive leverage is worthy of further note, for the degree of leverage in certain past instances has been truly staggering. For example, in the 1920s, Samuel Insull and his group controlled electric utility operating companies at the bottom of a holding company pyramid by a one-twentieth of 1 percent investment. As a ratio, this represents 1/2,000. In other words, $1 of capital at the top holding company level controlled $2,000 of assets at the operating level. A similar situation existed in the railroad field. It has

10. The 1969 Tax Reform Law also empowers the Internal Revenue Service to prohibit the deductibility of debt issued to acquire another firm where the following conditions hold: (1) the debt is subordinated to a "significant portion" of the firm's other creditors; (2) the debt is convertible or has warrants attached; (3) the debt/assets ratio exceeds 67 percent; and (4) on a pro forma basis, the times interest earned ratio is less than 3. The IRS can use discretion in invoking this power.

645

been stated that Robert R. Young, with an investment of $254,000, obtained control of the Allegheny system, consisting of total operating assets of $3 billion.

The nature of leverage in a holding company system and its advantages and disadvantages are illustrated by the hypothetical example developed in Table 24.2.[11] As in the previous example, although this case is hypothetical, it illustrates actual situations. Half of the operating company's Class B common stock is owned by Holding Company 1; in fact, it is the only asset of Holding Company 1. Holding Company 2 holds as its total assets half of the Class B common stock of Holding Company 1. Consequently, $1,000 of Class B common stock of Holding Company 2 controls $2 million of assets at the operating company level. Further leverage could, of course, have been postulated in this situation by setting up a third company to own Class B common stock of Holding Company 2.

**Table 24.2
Leverage in a Holding Company
System**

Operating Company			
Total assets	$2,000,000	Debt	$1,000,000
		Preferred stock	150,000
		Common stock: Class A[a]	650,000
		Common stock: Class B	200,000
	$2,000,000		$2,000,000
Holding Company 1			
Class B common stock of		Debt	$ 50,000
operating company	$100,000	Preferred stock	10,000
		Common stock: Class A[a]	30,000
		Common stock: Class B	10,000
	$100,000		$100,000
Holding Company 2			
Class B common stock of Holding		Debt	$2,000
Company 1	$5,000	Preferred stock	1,000
		Common stock: Class A[a]	1,000
		Common stock: Class B	1,000
	$5,000		$5,000

[a] Class A common stock is nonvoting.

Table 24.3 shows the results of holding company leverage on gains and losses at the top level. In the first column, it is assumed that the operating company earns 12 percent before taxes on its $2 million of assets; in the second column it is assumed that the return on assets is 8 percent. The operating and holding companies are the same ones described in Table 24.2.

11. Corrections in computations were supplied by Dr. Narendra C. Bhandari, University of Baltimore.

**Table 24.3
Results of Holding Company
Leverage on Gains and Losses**

	Earnings before Interest and Taxes	
	12%	8%
Operating Company		
Earnings before interest and taxes	$240,000	$160,000
Less interest on debt (at 4%)	40,000	40,000
Earnings after interest	$200,000	$120,000
Less tax (at 50%)	100,000	60,000
After-tax earnings available for stockholders	$100,000	$ 60,000
Less: Preferred stock (at 5%)	7,500	7,500
Common stock (at 8%)	52,000	52,000
Earnings available to Class B common stock	$ 40,500	$ 500
Dividends to Class B common stock (by management decision)	40,000	500
Transferred to retained earnings	$ 500	$ 0
Holding Company 1		
Earnings before interest and taxes (received from the operating company)	$ 20,000	$ 250
Less 85% of dividends received	17,000	212
Intercorporate dividends subject to tax, before interest	$ 3,000	$ 38
Less interest on debt (at 4%)	2,000	2,000
Before-tax earnings	$ 1,000	[a]
Less tax (at 50%)	500	0
After-tax earnings	$ 500	$ 0
Amount of untaxed dividend	$ 17,000	[b]
After-tax earnings available to stockholders	$ 17,500	$ 0
Less: Preferred stock (at 5%)	500	0
Class A common stock (at 8%)	2,400	0
Earnings available to Class B common stock	$ 14,600	$ 0
Less dividends to Class B common stock (by management decision)	10,000	0
Transferred to reserves	$ 4,600	$ 0
Holding Company 2		
Earnings before interest and taxes (received from Holding Company 1)	$ 5,000	
Less 85% of dividends received	4,250	
Intercorporate dividends subject to tax, before interest	$ 750	
Less interest on debt (at 4%)	80	
Before-tax earnings	$ 670	
Less tax (at 50%)	335	
After-tax earnings	$ 335	
Amount of untaxed dividends	4,250	
After-tax earnings available to stockholders	$ 4,585	
Less: Preferred stock (at 5%)	50	
Class A common stock (at 8%)	80	
Earnings available to Class B common stock	$ 4,455	
Percentage return on Class B common stock	445.5%	

[a] Loss.
[b] The available amount ($250) is used up by part of the interest charges

A return of 12 percent on the operating assets of $2 million represents a total profit of $240,000. The debt interest of $40,000 is deducted from this amount, and the 50 percent tax rate applies to the remainder. The amount available to common stock after payment of debt interest, preferred stock dividends, and an 8 percent return to the nonvoting Class A common stock is $40,500. Assuming a $40,000 dividend payout, Holding Company 1, on the basis of its 50 percent ownership of the operating company, earns $20,000. If the same kind of analysis is followed through, the amount available to Class B common stock in Holding Company 2 is $4,455. This return is on an investment of $1,000, and it represents a return on the investment in Class B common stock of Holding Company 2 of about 445 percent. The power of leverage in a holding company system can indeed be great.

On the other hand, if a decline in revenues causes the pretax earnings to drop to 8 percent of the total assets of the operating company, the results will be disastrous. The amount earned under these circumstances will be $160,000. After deducting the bond interest, the amount subject to tax will be $120,000, and the tax will be $60,000. The after-tax but before-interest earnings will be $100,000. The total prior charges will be $99,500, leaving $500 available to Class B common stock. If all earnings are paid out in dividends to Class B common stock, the earnings of Holding Company 1 will be $250. This is not enough to meet the debt interest. The holding company system will thus be forced to default on the debt interest of Holding Company 1 and, of course, Holding Company 2.

This example illustrates the potential for tremendous gains in a holding company system. It also illustrates that a small earnings decline on the assets of the operating companies will be disastrous.

Tender Offers

In a tender offer, one party—generally a corporation seeking a controlling interest in another corporation—asks the stockholders of the firm it is seeking to control to submit, or "tender," their shares in exchange for a specified price. The price is generally stated as so many dollars per share of acquired stock, although it can be stated in terms of shares of stock in the acquiring firm. Tender offers have been used for a number of years, but the pace greatly accelerated after 1965 and peaked in 1976 and 1977.

If one firm wishes to gain control over another, it typically seeks approval for the merger from the other firm's management and board of directors. An alternative approach is the "bear hug"; in this approach, a company mails a letter to the directors of the takeover target announcing the acquisition proposal and requiring the directors to make a quick decision on the bid. If approval cannot be obtained, the acquiring company can appeal directly to stockholders by means of the tender offer, unless the management and directors of the target firm hold enough stock to retain control. The technique of going directly to the shareholders has been called a "Saturday night special.'' The term implies that a gun has been aimed at the directors, since, if the shareholders respond favorably to the tender offer, the acquiring company will gain control and have the power to replace the directors who have not cooperated in their takeover efforts.

During 1967, congressional investigations were conducted to obtain information that could be used to legislate controls over tender offers. The reasons for the investigations were (1) the frequency of tender offers, (2) the thought that the recent merger trend was leading to ''too much concentration'' in the economy, and (3) the feeling that tender offers were somehow ''unfair'' to the managements of the firms acquired through this vehicle. A law placing tender offers under full SEC jurisdiction became effective on July 29, 1968. Disclosure requirements written into the statute include the following:

1. The acquiring firm must give the management of the target firm and the SEC thirty days' notice of its intentions to make the acquisition.
2. When substantial blocks are purchased through tender offers or through open market purchases—that is, on the stock exchange—the beneficial owner of the stock must be disclosed, together with the name of the party putting up the money for the transaction. Usually the stock is in the ''street'' name of the brokerage house that acts on behalf of the real (beneficial) owner.

In addition to the new powers granted to the SEC to require disclosure of takeover intentions, certain tactics to prevent takeover can be used by the intended target. More than thirty states have adopted antitakeover laws that can delay tender offers so that an alternative can be pursued. The takeover target may also utilize other legal tactics, such as court suits alleging that antitrust laws and other regulatory guidelines are being violated. Such tactics may forestall a takeover. For example, when Anderson, Clayton, & Co. made a bid for Gerber Products Co., the latter instituted a number of legal suits. After five months of legal maneuvers on both sides, Anderson, Clayton dropped its bid in September 1977. In another case, because Marshall Field threatened antitrust actions and announced its own acquisition program, Carter, Hawley, Hale dropped its 1978 takeover attempt. The Hart-Scott-Rodino Act of 1976, amending the antitrust laws, contains a provision that requires premerger notification to the FTC of large mergers. This provision became effective in July 1978.

As a consequence of the disclosure requirements in connection with intended tender offers, competition among bidders in takeover efforts may cause the acquisition price to rise well above the market price of the stock before the initial tender offer. This can be illustrated by a few examples.

The first example is Tenneco's acquisition of Kern County Land Company. Kern was a relatively old, conservatively managed company whose assets consisted largely of oil properties and agricultural land, together with some manufacturing subsidiaries. Many informed investors believed that Kern's assets had a potential long-run value in excess of its current market price. Occidental Petroleum, a relatively aggressive company, investigated Kern's assets and decided to make a tender offer for the company. At that time, Kern's market price on the New York Stock Exchange was about $60 a share, while the price Occidental decided to offer Kern's stockholders was $83.50 a share. According to Kern's management, Occidental's management got in touch with them over a weekend and informed them that the tender offer would be made the following Monday.

Kern's management resisted the offer. Because Occidental's published statements indicated that it felt Kern's undervalued position was partly the result of an unimaginative management, Kern's management anticipated being replaced in the event that Occidental effected the takeover. Naturally, they resisted the takeover. Kern's president wrote a letter to stockholders condemning the merger and published the letter as an advertisement in the *Wall Street Journal*. His position was that Kern's stock was certainly valuable and that it was worth more than had been offered by Occidental Petroleum.

How would Kern County's stockholders react to this exchange? In the first place, the stock had been selling at about $60 a share, and now they were offered $83.50 a share. With this differential, stockholders would certainly accept the tender unless Kern's management could do something to keep the price above $83.50. What Kern did was to obtain "marriage proposals" from a number of other companies. Kern's management reported to the newspapers—while Occidental's tender offer was still outstanding—that it had received a number of proposals calling for the purchase of Kern's stock at a price substantially in excess of $83.50.

The offer Kern's management finally accepted—and presumably the one giving Kern's stockholders the highest price—was from Tenneco Corporation. Tenneco offered one share of a new $5.50 convertible preferred stock for each share of Kern's stock. At the time of Tenneco's offer, the market value of this convertible preferred was estimated at about $105 a share. Further, Kern's stockholders would not have to pay capital gains tax on this stock at the time of the exchange. (Had they accepted Occidental's offer, the difference between $83.50 and the cost of their stock would be taxable income to Kern's stockholders.) According to newspaper reports, Tenneco planned to keep Kern's existing management after the merger was completed. When the Kern-Tenneco merger was completed, Tenneco owned the Kern stock and thus became a holding company, with Kern being one of its operating subsidiaries.

If the takeover company bids too low initially, it may stimulate a bidding contest. But if it makes the initial bid at a substantial premium over the prevailing market price of the takeover target, it may be criticized by its stockholders for having paid an excessive amount. Both situations have occurred, so a difficult challenge is posed in formulating the right takeover bid. Examples are provided by dramatic episodes that occurred during 1977.

United Technologies (UT) bid $42 per share in March 1977 for Babcock & Wilcox (BW), whose common stock was then selling for less than $35 per share. UT is a producer of aircraft engines, rocket motors and engines, automotive and space equipment, helicopters, elevators, escalators, and other industrial equipment. BW was mainly in steam generating equipment, such as the massive boilers used in both fossil fuel and nuclear powered turbine generator systems. In addition, it produced pollution control equipment and other equipment for the handling and transfer of heat. UT's 1976 sales were $5.2 billion, while BW's 1976 sales were $1.7 billion. Shortly after UT's tender offer, J. Ray McDermott & Co. (JRM) entered the contest. JRM, smaller than either of the other two companies, with sales of $1.2 billion in 1976, was mainly in the engineering, fabrication, and installation of facilities for the production of oil and gas. By May 1977, JRM announced that it had bought nearly 9 percent of BW's stock on the open market. BW proceeded to take legal action against both takeover rivals. In August 1977, UT upped its bid for BW to $48. Shortly thereafter, JRM bid $55, which the BW directors urged its shareholders to accept. A complicated series of counterbids ensued, with JRM winning the competition for a final price of $65 a share, nearly double the pre-tender market price.

In an example of a bid that might have been too high, Kennecott Copper was motivated by the fear of becoming a takeover target itself. In accordance with a requirement by the FTC of divestiture of Peabody Coal, Kennecott had agreed to a sale to a group of companies for $1.2 billion to be paid in installments. Since Kennecott was in the process of becoming cash rich as it received installment payments for the purchase price, it wanted to utilize the cash. It sought to avoid being acquired by a company that might use debt to buy Kennecott and then use the cash flowing into Kennecott to pay off the debt. Kennecott is an integrated producer of metals (mainly copper) and mineral products with 1976 sales of slightly under $1 billion.

Eaton Corporation (formerly Eaton Yale & Towne), with 1976 revenues of $1.8 billion, had, in early November 1977, made an offer of $47 per share for the stock of the Carborundum Company, then selling at $33.25 per share. Eaton produces locks and other security systems as well as automotive parts and components. Carborundum, a leading producer of carbon products, other abrasives, and refractory and electric products, had 1976 revenues of $614 million. In mid-November 1977, Kennecott made an offer to Carborundum of $66 per share. On November 17, 1977, it was announced that the directors of both companies had unanimously approved the offer. Some stockholders stated that they were stunned by this "squandering of

Kennecott's cash." Others praised Kennecott for avoiding the "ridiculous newspaper auction that marked the Babcock & Wilcox battle." The reader is invited to judge the appropriateness of the $66 price paid by Kennecott.

Summary

Growth is vital to the well-being of a firm. Without it the firm cannot attract able management because it cannot give recognition in promotions and challenging creative activity. Mergers have played an important part in the growth of firms, and since financial managers are required both to appraise the desirability of a prospective merger and to participate in evaluating the respective companies involved in it, the chapter has been devoted to the terms of merger decisions.

The most important term to be negotiated in a merger arrangement is the price the acquiring firm will pay for the acquired one. The most important *quantitative* factors influencing the terms of a merger are (1) current earnings, (2) current market prices, (3) book values, and (4) net working capital. Qualitative considerations may suggest that *synergistic,* or "two-plus-two equals-five," effects may be present to a sufficient extent to warrant paying more for the acquired firm than the quantitative factors suggest. Recently, the current replacement values of corporate stock have exceeded the market values of related corporate securities.

In mergers, one firm disappears. However, an alternative is for one firm to buy all or a majority of the common stock of another and to run the acquired firm as an operating subsidiary. When this occurs, the acquiring firm is said to be a *holding company.* A number of advantages arise when a holding company is formed, among them:

1. It may be possible to control the acquired firm with a smaller investment than necessary for a merger.
2. Each firm in a holding company is a separate legal entity, and the obligations of any unit are separate from the obligations of the other units.
3. Stockholder approval is required before a merger can take place. This is not necessary in a holding company situation.

There are also some disadvantages to holding companies, among them:

1. If the holding company does not own 80 percent of the subsidiary's stock and does not file consolidated tax returns, it is subject to taxes on 15 percent of the dividends received from the subsidiary.
2. The leverage effects possible in holding companies can subject the company to magnification of earnings fluctuations and related risks.
3. The antitrust division of the U.S. Department of Justice can much more easily force the breakup of a holding company situation than it can bring about the dissolution of two completely merged firms.

Questions

24.1 The number of mergers tends to fluctuate with business activity, rising when GNP rises and falling when GNP falls. Why does this relationship exist?

24.2 A large firm has certain advantages over a smaller one. What are some of the financial advantages of large size?

24.3 What are some of the potential benefits that can be expected by a firm that merges with a company in a different industry?

24.4 Distinguish between a holding company and an operating company. Give an example of each.

24.5 Which appears to be riskier—the use of debt in the holding company's capital structure or the use of debt in the operating company's capital structure? Explain.

24.6 Is the public interest served by an increase in merger activity? Give both pro and con arguments.

24.7 Is the book value of a company's assets considered the absolute minimum price to be paid for a firm? Explain. Is there any value that qualifies as an absolute minimum? Explain.

24.8 Discuss the situation where Midwest Motors calls off merger negotiations with American Data Labs because the latter's stock price is overvalued. What assumption concerning dilution is implicit in the above situation?

24.9 There are many methods by which a company can raise additional capital. Can a merger be considered a means of raising additional equity capital? Explain.

24.10 A particularly difficult problem regarding business combinations has been whether to treat the new company as a purchase or as a pooling of interests.
   a. What criteria can be used to differentiate between these two forms of business combinations?
   b. As a stockholder in one of the firms, would you prefer a purchase or a pooling arrangement? Explain.
   c. Which combination would you prefer if you were a high-ranking manager in one of the firms?

24.11 Question 24.10 discusses purchase and pooling arrangements. Why is it important to distinguish between these two combination forms?

24.12 Are the negotiations for merger agreements more difficult if the firms are in different industries or in the same industry? If they are about the same size or quite different in size? If the ages of the firms are about the same or if they are very different? Explain.

24.13 How would the existence of long-term debt in a company's financial structure affect its valuation for merger purposes? Could the same be said for any debt account regardless of its maturity? Explain.

24.14 During 1964–1965, the Pure Oil Company was involved in merger negotiations with at least three other firms. The terms of these arrangements varied from a transfer of stock to a direct cash purchase of Pure Oil. Discuss the relative advantages to a corporation of paying for an acquisition in cash or in stock.

24.15 In late 1968 the SEC and the New York Stock Exchange each issued sets of rulings on disclosure of information that, in effect, required that firms disclose that they have entered into merger discussions as soon as they start such discussions. Since the previous procedure had been to delay disclosure until it was evident that there was a reasonably good expectation the merger would actually go through (and not to bring the matter up at all if the merger died in the early stages), it can safely be predicted that, in a statistical sense, a larger percentage of prospective mergers will be "abandoned" in the future than in the past.

a. Why do you suppose the new rulings were put into effect?

b. Will the new rulings have any adverse effects? Explain.

Problems

24.1 The Brunner Company has agreed to merge with the Powell Company. The shareholders of Powell have agreed to accept half a share of Brunner for each of their Powell shares. The new company will have a P/E ratio of 40. Following is additional information about the merging companies.

	Brunner	Powell
P/E ratio	56	7
Shares outstanding	2,500,000	500,000
Earnings	$1,750,000	$700,000
Earnings per share	$.70	$1.40
Market value per share	$39.20	$9.80

a. After Brunner and Powell merge, what will the new price per share be?

b. Calculate the dollar and percent accretion in EPS for Brunner.

c. Calculate the dollar and percent dilution in EPS for Powell.

d. What is the effect on market price for each?

24.2 The Morris Company has agreed to merge with the Kingston Company. The following is information about the two companies prior to their merger:

	Kingston	Morris
Total earnings	$1,000,000	$750,000
Shares outstanding	1,000,000	250,000
P/E ratio	20 times	18 times

a. The Kingston Company will buy the Morris Company with a 4-for-1 exchange of stock. Combined earnings will remain at the premerger level. What will be the effect on EPS for premerger Kingston stockholders?

b. What will be the effect on EPS for the Morris Company stockholders?

c. Assuming that Kingston has been growing at 20 percent a year and Morris at 5 percent, what is the expected growth rate? (There are no synergistic effects.)

24.3 Melton Company and Kelly Company merge on the basis of market values. Melton Company acquires Kelly Company with a three-for-one exchange of stock. Following are data for the two companies:

	Melton	Kelly
Total earnings	$100,000,000	$1,000,000
Shares outstanding	80,000,000	800,000
Expected growth rate in earnings	10%	25%
P/E ratio	8 times	24 times

a. What is the new EPS for the premerger Melton and Kelly stockholders?
b. If Melton's P/E ratio rises to 15, what is its new market price?
c. What merger concept does this problem illustrate?

24.4 Hempler Company merges with Rider Company on the basis of market values. Hempler pays one share of convertible preferred stock with a par value of $100 and an interest rate of 6 percent (convertible into Hempler's common stock at two shares, or $60) for each four shares of Rider Company. Following are more data:

	Hempler	Rider
Total earnings	$1,000,000	$400,000
Common shares outstanding	200,000	80,000
Expected growth rate in earnings	18%	6%
Dividends per share	$1.80	$1.80
P/E ratio	12 times	6 times
Dividend yield	3%	6%

a. Is the dividend return to Rider shareholders changed?
b. 1. What are the new EPS and market price of Hempler if the P/E ratio remains at 12 times?
   2. What are the new EPS and market price on a fully diluted basis?
c. Why might Rider Company shareholders agree to the acquisition?

24.5 You are given the following balance sheets:

Rocky Mountain Services Company Consolidated Balance Sheet (Millions of Dollars)

Cash	$1,500	Borrowings	$1,125
Other current assets	1,125	Common stock	1,875
Net property	1,875	Retained earnings	1,500
Total assets	$4,500	Total claims on assets	$4,500

White Lighting Company Balance Sheet (Millions of Dollars)

Cash	$375	Net worth	$750
Net property	375		
Total assets	$750	Total net worth	$750

a. The holding company, Rocky Mountain, buys the operating company, White Lighting, with "free" cash of $750 million. Show the new consolidated balance sheet for Rocky Mountain after the acquisition.

b. Instead of buying White Lighting, Rocky Mountain buys Conner Company with free cash of $1.125 billion. Conner's balance sheet follows:

Conner Company Balance Sheet (Millions of Dollars)

Cash	$ 750	Borrowings	$ 750
Net property	1,125	Net worth	1,125
Total assets	$1,875	Total claims on assets	$1,875

Show the new consolidated balance sheet for Rocky Mountain after acquisition of Conner.

c. What are the implications of your consolidated balance sheets for measuring the growth of firms resulting from acquisitions?

24.6 Southern Realty Company is a holding company owning the entire common stock of Bryant Company and Sunther Company. The balance sheet as of December 31, 1978, for each subsidiary is identical with the following one:

Balance Sheet as of December 31, 1978 (Millions of Dollars)

Current assets	$ 7.50	Current liabilities	$ 1.25
Fixed assets, net	5.00	First mortgage bonds (at 9%)	2.50
		Preferred stock (at 7%)	2.50
		Common stock	5.00
		Retained earnings	1.25
Total assets	$12.50	Total claims on assets	$12.50

Each operating company earns $1.375 million annually before taxes and before interest and preferred dividends. A 50 percent tax rate is assumed.

a. What is the annual rate of return on each company's net worth (common stock plus retained earnings)?

b. Construct a balance sheet for Southern Realty Company based on the following assumptions: (1) The only asset of the holding company is the common stock of the two subsidiaries, carried at par (not book) value. (2) The holding company has $1.2 million of 8 percent coupon debt and $2.8 million of 6 percent preferred stock.

24.7 To meet its growth objectives, Proxmire Manufacturing is planning to expand by acquisition. It has two potential candidates, Apex Corporation and Allied Engineering. The latest balance sheet for Proxmire is given below, along with certain statistical data for all three companies. Assume that the pretax cost of new debt to Proxmire is 9 percent, that its cost of equity is 10 percent, and that it has an effective tax rate of 50 percent.

**Proxmire Manufacturing Balance
Sheet as of December 31, 1976
(Thousands of Dollars)**

Current assets	$120,000	Current liabilities		$ 50,000
Net fixed assets	150,000	Long-term debt (at 9%)		70,000
		Common equity		150,000
Total	$270,000	Total		$270,000

	EPS	DPS	Growth Rate	Market Price	Shares Outstanding
Proxmire	$3.00	$1.80	6%	$45.00	5,000,000
Apex	2.00	0.50	7.5	50.00	2,000,000
Allied	4.00	3.00	2	42.00	3,000,000

a. Based on the above information, determine an appropriate price for Proxmire to pay for each acquisition candidate. Proxmire computes the value of an acquisition candidate's stock using the constant growth model, based on the target company's growth rate and projected dividends. It uses its own marginal cost of capital as the minimum required rate of return.

b. Given that Proxmire is forced to make a tender offer for each of the two candidates at 20 percent above their current market value, compute the following:

   1. The exchange ratio based on a stock offering.

   2. Proxmire's new earnings growth rate for next year after the acquisition of each company—Apex and Allied.

   3. Proxmire's new EPS following each acquisition.

c. Chart Proxmire's growth in EPS for the next ten years with and without each acquisition to illustrate the dilution effect of the purchase price computed in Part b.

Appendix 24A Financial Accounting Policies in Mergers	After merger terms have been agreed upon, the financial manager must be familiar with the accounting principles for recording the financial results of the merger and for reflecting the initial effect on the earnings of the surviving firm. The financial statements of the survivor in a merger must follow the SEC's regulations. These regulations follow the recommendations of professional accounting societies on combinations, but interpretations of actual situations require much financial and economic analysis.

On August 2, 1970, the eighteen-member Accounting Principles Board (APB) of the American Institute of Certified Public Accountants issued Opinion 16, dealing with guidelines for corporate mergers, and Opinion 17, dealing with goodwill arising from mergers. The recommendations, which became effective October 31, 1970, modify and elaborate previous pronouncements on the "pooling of interests" and "purchase" methods of accounting for business combinations. For reasons that will become clear later in this section, corporate managements generally prefer pooling. Six broad tests are used to determine whether the conditions for the pooling of interest treatment are met. If all of them are met, then the combination is, in a sense, a "merger among equals," and the *pooling of interests* method can be employed. The six tests are:

1. The acquired firm's stockholders must maintain an ownership position in the surviving firm.
2. The basis for accounting for the assets of the acquired entity must remain unchanged.
3. Independent interests must be combined, each entity must have had autonomy for two years prior to the initiation of the plan to combine, and no more than 10 percent ownership of voting common stock can be held as intercorporate investments.
4. The combination must be effected in a single transaction; contingent payouts are not permitted in poolings but can be used in purchases.
5. The acquiring corporation must issue only common stock with rights identical to its outstanding voting common stock in exchange for substantially all the voting common stock of the other company (*substantially* is defined as 90 percent).
6. The combined entity must not intend to dispose of a significant portion of the assets of the combining companies within two years after the merger.

In contrast, a *purchase* involves (1) new owners, (2) an appraisal of the acquired firm's physical assets and a restatement of the balance sheet to reflect these new values, and (3) the possibility of an excess or deficiency of consideration given up vis-à-vis the book value of equity. Point 3 refers to the creation of goodwill. In a purchase, the excess of the purchase price paid over the book value (restated to reflect the appraisal value of physical assets) is set up as goodwill, and capital surplus is increased (or decreased) accordingly. In a pooling of interests, the combined total assets after the merger represent a simple sum of the asset contributions of the constituent companies.

In a *purchase,* if the acquiring firm pays more than the acquired net worth, the excess is associated either with tangible depreciable assets or with goodwill. Asset write-offs are deductible, but goodwill written off is not deductible for tax purposes, even though the new recommendations require that goodwill be written off over some reasonable period but no longer than forty years. This requires a write-off of at least 2.5 percent a year of the amount of goodwill arising from a purchase. Therefore, if a merger is treated as a purchase, reported profits will be lower than if it is handled as a pooling of interests. This is one of the reasons that pooling is popular among acquiring firms.

Previous to the issuance of APB Opinion 16, another stimulus to pooling was the opportunity to dispose of assets acquired at depreciated book values, selling them at their current values and recording subsequent profits on sales of assets. Opinion 16 attempted to deal with this practice by the requirement that sales of major portions of assets not be contemplated for at least two years after the merger has taken place. For example, suppose Firm A buys Firm B, exchanging stock worth $100 million for assets worth $100 million but carried at $25 million. After the merger, A could, before the change in rules, sell the acquired assets and report the difference between book value and the purchase price, or $75 million, as earned income. Thus mergers could be used in still another way to create an illusion of profits and growth.

Financial Treatment of a Purchase

The financial treatment of a purchase can best be explained by use of a hypothetical example.[1] The Mammoth Company has just purchased the Petty Company under an arrangement known as a *purchase.* The facts are as given in Table A24.1, which also shows the financial treatment. The illustration conforms to the general nature of a purchase. Measured by total assets, the Mammoth Company is twenty times as large as Petty, while its total earnings are fifteen times as large. The terms of the purchase are one share of Mammoth for two shares of Petty, based on the prevailing market value of their shares of common stock. Thus, in terms of Mammoth's stock, Mammoth is giving to Petty's stockholders $30 of market value and $7 of book value for each share of Petty stock. Petty's market value is $30 a share, its book value is $3 a share, and the fair value of the equity is $6,000.[2] The total market value of Mammoth paid for Petty is $60,000. The goodwill involved can be calculated as follows:

Value given by Mammoth	$60,000
Fair value of net worth of Petty purchased	6,000
Goodwill	$54,000

The $54,000 goodwill represents a debit in the adjustments column and is carried to the pro forma balance sheet. The pro forma balance sheet is obtained by simply adding the balance sheets of the constituent companies, together with adjustments.

A total value of $60,000 has been given by Mammoth for a book value of $6,000. This amount represents, in addition to the debt, a payment of $1,000 for the common stock of Petty, $5,000 for the retained earnings, and $54,000

---

1. The material in this section is technical and is generally covered in accounting courses.
2. Under purchase accounting, the acquiring company "should allocate the cost of an acquired company to the assets acquired and liabilities assumed" (APB Opinion No. 16, p. 318, par. 87). A specific procedure is set forth. First, all identifiable assets acquired should be assigned a portion of the cost of the acquired company, normally equal to their fair (market or appraised) values at date of acquisition. Second, the excess of the cost of the acquired company over the sum of the amounts assigned to net assets should be recorded as goodwill. The sum of fair market values assigned may exceed the cost of the acquired company. If so, values otherwise assignable to noncurrent assets should be reduced by a proportionate part of the excess. If noncurrent assets are reduced to zero and some excess still remains, it should be set up as a deferred credit.

**Table A24.1
Financial Treatment of a
Purchase**

	Mammoth Company	Petty Company	Adjustments Debit	Adjustments Credit	Pro Forma Balance Sheet
Assets					
Current assets	$ 80,000	$ 4,000			$ 84,000
Other assets	20,000	2,000			22,000
Net fixed assets	100,000	4,000			104,000
Goodwill			$54,000		54,000
Total assets	$200,000	$10,000			$264,000
Liabilities and Net Worth					
Current liabilities	$ 40,000	$ 4,000			$ 44,000
Long-term debt	20,000				20,000
Common stock	40,000	1,000	1,000	4,000	44,000
Capital surplus	20,000			56,000	76,000
Retained earnings	80,000	5,000	5,000		80,000
Total liabilities and net worth	$200,000	$10,000	$60,000	$60,000	$264,000
Explanation					
Par value per share, common stock	$4	$0.50			
Number of shares outstanding	10,000	2,000			
Book value per share	$14	$3			
Total earnings	$30,000	$2,000			
Earnings per share	$3	$1			
Price/earnings ratio	20 times	30 times			
Market value per share	$60	$30			

for goodwill. The corresponding credit is the 1,000 shares of Mammoth given in the transaction at their par value of $4 a share, resulting in a credit of $4,000. The capital surplus of Mammoth is increased by $56,000 ($60,000 paid minus $4,000 increase in common stock). The net credit to the net worth account is $54,000, which balances the net debit to the asset accounts. When these adjustments are carried through to the pro forma balance sheet, total assets are increased from the uncombined total of $210,000 to a new total of $264,000. Total tangible assets, however, still remain $210,000.

The effects on earnings per share for stockholders in each company are shown below:

Total earnings (before write-off of goodwill)	$32,000
Amortization of goodwill	1,350
Total net earnings	$30,650
Total shares	11,000
Earnings per share	$2.79
For Petty shareholders:	
New earnings per share	$1.40
Before-purchase earnings per share	1.00
Accretion per share	$0.40

For Mammoth shareholders:

Before-purchase earnings per share	$3.00
New earnings per share	2.79
Dilution per share	$0.21

Total earnings represent the combined earnings of Mammoth and Petty. Mammoth believes that the value reflected in goodwill will be permanent, but under APB Opinion 17, it is required to write off the goodwill account over a maximum of forty years. The annual charge of $1,350 is the goodwill of $54,000 divided by 40. The total amount of net earnings is therefore $30,650.

The total shares are 11,000 because Mammoth has given one share of stock for every two shares of Petty previously outstanding.[3] The new earnings per share are therefore $2.79. The calculation of earnings accretion or dilution proceeds on the same principles as the calculations set forth earlier. The results require two important comments, however.

Although the earnings accretion per share for Petty is 40 cents, the earnings dilution per share for Mammoth is relatively small, only 21 cents a share. The explanation is that the size of Mammoth is large in relation to that of Petty. This example also illustrates a general principle: When a large company acquires a small one, it can afford to pay a high multiple of earnings per share of the smaller company. In the present example, the price/earnings ratio of Petty is 30, whereas that of Mammoth is 20. If the acquiring company is large in relation to the acquired firm, it can pay a substantial premium and yet suffer only small dilution in its earnings per share.

It is, however, unrealistic to assume that the same earnings on total assets will result after the merger. After all, the purpose of the merger is to achieve something that the two companies could not have achieved alone. When Philip Morris & Company purchased Benson & Hedges (the maker of Parliament, a leading filter-tip brand), it was buying the ability and experience of Benson & Hedges. By means of this merger, Philip Morris was able to make an entry into the rapidly growing filter cigarette business more quickly than it could otherwise have done. The combined earnings per share were expected to rise.

In the Mammoth-Petty illustration, the earnings rate on the tangible assets of Mammoth is 15 percent and on the total assets of Petty is 20 percent. Assume that the return on total tangible assets of the combined companies rises to 20 percent. The 20 percent of tangible assets of $210,000 equals $42,000; less the amortization of goodwill over forty years at $1,350 per year, the total is $40,650 net earnings. With the same total shares of 11,000 outstanding, the new earnings per share will be $3.70. Thus there will be an

---

3. After the one-for-two exchange, Petty shareholders have only half as many shares as before the merger.

accretion of 85 cents for the Petty shareholders and an accretion of 70 cents for the Mammoth shareholders.

This illustrates another general principle: If the purchase of a small company adds to the earnings of the consolidated enterprise, earnings per share may increase for both participants in the merger. Even if the merger results in an initial dilution in earnings per share of the larger company, it may still be advantageous. The initial dilution can be regarded as an investment that will have a payoff at some future date in terms of increased growth in earnings per share of the consolidated company.

Treatment of Goodwill

In a purchase, goodwill is likely to arise; since it represents an intangible asset, its treatment is subject to the exercise of judgment. It will therefore be useful to set out a few generalizations on good practice in the treatment of goodwill.

1. When goodwill is purchased, it should not be charged to surplus immediately on acquisition. Instead it should be written off against income and should go through the income statement. Since goodwill is to be written off against income, it is not appropriate to write it off entirely on acquisition, because this will be of such magnitude that distortion of earnings for that year will result.
2. The general view is not to write off purchased goodwill by charges to capital surplus. Purchased goodwill is supposed to represent and to be reflected in a future rise of income. It should therefore be written off against income rather than against capital surplus.
3. When goodwill is purchased, an estimate should be made of its life. Annual charges based on the estimated life should then be made against income to amortize the goodwill over the estimated period of its usefulness.
4. Intangibles must be written off over a maximum of forty years according to APB Opinion 17.

When goodwill is purchased, it should be treated like any other asset. It should be written off to the extent that the value represented by any part of it has a limited life, as is likely to be the situation. In a free enterprise economy, the existence of high profits represented by superior earning power attracts additional resources into that line of business. The growth of capacity and the increase in competition are likely to erode the superior earning power over time.

Financial Treatment of Pooling of Interests

When a business combination is a pooling of interests rather than a purchase, the accounting treatment is simply to combine the balance sheets of the two companies. Goodwill will not ordinarily arise in the consolidation.

The financial treatment can be indicated by another example, which reflects the facts as they are set forth in Table A24.2. In order to focus on the critical issues, the balance sheets are identical in every respect. However, a difference in the amount and rate of profit after interest of the two companies is indicated.

Book value per share is $10. The amount of profit after interest and taxes is $42,000 for Company A and $21,000 for Company B. Earnings per share are therefore $3.50 and $1.75, respectively. The price/earnings ratio is 18 for A and 12 for B, so the market price of stock is $63 for A and $21 for B. The net working capital per share is $4.17 in each instance. The dividends per share are $1.75 for A and $0.875 for B.

Table A24.2
Financial Treatment of Pooling
of Interests

	Company A	Company B	Net Adjustments on A's Books Debit	Net Adjustments on A's Books Credit	Acquiring Company A's New Balance Sheets and Earnings If the Exchange Basis Is 2/1	Acquiring Company A's New Balance Sheets and Earnings If the Exchange Basis Is 3/1
Current assets	$100,000	$100,000			$200,000	$200,000
Fixed assets	100,000	100,000			200,000	200,000
Total assets	$200,000	$200,000			$400,000	$400,000
Current liabilities	$ 50,000	$ 50,000			$100,000	$100,000
Long-term debt	30,000	30,000			60,000	60,000
Total debt	80,000	80,000			160,000	160,000
Common stock, par value $5	60,000	60,000	$30,000[a] $40,000[b]		90,000	80,000
Capital surplus	50,000	50,000		$30,000[a] $40,000[b]	130,000	140,000
Retained earnings	10,000	10,000			20,000	20,000
Total claims on assets	$200,000	$200,000			$400,000	$400,000
			Ratios A/B			
Number of shares of stock	12,000	12,000			18,000	16,000
Book value	$10	$10	1.0			
Amount of profit after interest and taxes	$42,000	$21,000			$63,000	$63,000
Earnings per share	$3.50	$1.75	2.0		$3.50	$3.94
Price/earnings ratio	18	12				
Market price of stock	$63	$21	3.0			
Net working capital per share	$4.17	$4.17	1.0			
Dividends per share	$1.75	$0.875	2.0			

					Shareholders' New EPS A	Shareholders' New EPS B
Exchange ratio no. 1: Earnings basis	2/1					
Equivalent earnings per share (new basis)					$3.50	$1.75
Exchange ratio no. 2: Price basis	3/1					
Equivalent earnings per share (new basis)					$3.94	$1.31

[a] 2/1 ratio basis.
[b] 3/1 ratio basis.

663

Assume that the terms of the merger will reflect either (1) earnings or (2) market price per share. In both cases it is assumed that A is the acquiring and surviving firm. If A buys B on the basis of earnings, it exchanges half a share of A's common stock for one share of B's common stock. The total number of shares of A's common stock that will be outstanding after the acquisition is 18,000, of which 6,000 will be held by the old stockholders of B. The new earnings per share in the now larger Firm A will be the total earnings of $63,000 divided by 18,000, which equals $3.50 per share. Thus the earnings per share for A remain unchanged. The old shareholders of B now hold half a share of A for each share of B held before the acquisition. Hence, their equivalent earnings per share from their present holdings of A shares are $1.75, the same as before the acquisition. The stockholders of both A and B have experienced no earnings dilution or accretion.

When the terms of exchange are based on market price per share, the terms of acquisition will be the exchange of one-third share of A stock for one share of B stock. The number of A shares is increased by the 4,000 exchanged for the 12,000 shares of B. The combined earnings of $63,000 are divided by 16,000 shares to obtain an increase in A's earnings per share to $3.94, which represents an earnings accretion of 44 cents per share for the A shareholders. The old B shareholders now hold one-third share of A for each share of B held before the acquisition. Their equivalent earnings are now $3.94 divided by 3, or $1.31, representing an earnings dilution of 44 cents per share.

The adjustment to the common stock account in surviving Firm A's balance sheet reflects the fact that only 6,000 shares of A are used to buy 12,000 shares of B when the acquisition is made on the basis of earnings. The decrease of 6,000 shares times the par value of $5 requires a net debit of $30,000 to the common stock account of A ($60,000 + $60,000 − $30,000 = $90,000) with an offsetting increase of $30,000 in the capital surplus account of Firm A ($50,000 + $50,000 + $30,000 = $130,000). When the exchange is made on the basis of market values, only 4,000 shares of A are needed to acquire the 12,000 shares of B. Hence, the net decrease in the common stock account of A is $40,000, with an offsetting increase of the same amount in A's capital surplus.

The general principle is that when the terms of merger are based on the market price per share, and the price/earnings ratios of the two companies are different, earnings accretion and dilution will occur. The company with a higher P/E ratio will have earnings accretion; the company with the lower P/E ratio will suffer earnings dilution. If the sizes of the companies are greatly different, the effect on the larger company will be relatively small, whether in dilution or accretion. The effect on the smaller company will be large.

CHAPTER   FAILURE,
REORGANIZATION, AND LIQUIDATION

Thus far the text has dealt with issues associated mainly with the growing, successful enterprise. Not all businesses are so fortunate, however, so this chapter will examine financial difficulties—their causes and their possible remedies. The material is significant for the financial manager of successful, as well as potentially unsuccessful, firms. The successful firm's financial manager must know the firm's rights and remedies as a creditor and must participate effectively in efforts to collect from financially distressed debtors. The financial manager of a less successful firm must know how to handle the firm's affairs if financial difficulties arise. Such understanding can often mean the difference between loss of ownership of the firm and rehabilitation of it as a going enterprise.

Some dramatic major bankruptcies have occurred in recent years. Most notable was the huge Penn Central Company, which involved total assets at the end of 1969 of almost $7 billion and total debts outstanding of over $4 billion. The W. T. Grant bankruptcy was also of substantial magnitude, involving $1.2 billion of assets. A number of bankruptcies have raised questions of impropriety. Illustrative is the Equity Funding Company bankruptcy, which involved writing up fictitious life insurance.

The instabilities of the early 1970s involved large commercial banks as well as nonfinancial enterprises. The Franklin National Bank, which failed in 1974, had reached an asset size of $5 billion and was the twentieth largest of the nation's more than 14,000 FDIC-insured banks. In the same year, the Beverly Hills Bancorp went into bankruptcy. Earlier, the U.S. National Bank of San Diego had to be taken over by the FDIC, and questions of fraud were raised in connection with its prior management. Even large foreign banks ran into difficulties in 1974. The failure of Bankhaus I. D. Herstatt, one of Germany's largest private banks, sent shock waves through the international money markets.

The Firm's Life Cycle

The life cycle of an industry or firm is often depicted as an S-shaped curve, as shown in Figure 25.1. Although the figure is an oversimplification, it does provide a useful framework for analysis. The hypothesis represented by the four-stage life cycle concept is based on a number of assumptions—competent management in the growth periods and insufficient management foresight prior to the decline phase. Obviously, one of management's primary goals is to prolong Phase B and to completely forestall Phase D; many firms are apparently successful in these endeavors. If an industry experiences the period of decline, financial readjustment problems will arise, affecting most firms in the industry. Furthermore, specific events—for example, a prolonged strike, a fire inadequately covered by insurance, or a bad decision on a new product—may result in business failure.

Figure 25.1
Hypothetical Life Cycle of a Firm

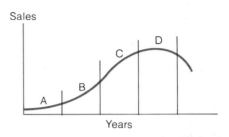

Failure

Failure can be defined in several ways, and some failures do not necessarily result in the collapse and dissolution of a firm.

Economic Failure

Failure in an economic sense usually signifies that a firm's revenues do not cover its costs. It can also mean that the rate of earnings on its historical cost of investment is less than the firm's cost of capital. It can even mean that the firm's actual returns have fallen below its expected returns. There is no consensus on the definition of failure in an economic sense.

Financial Failure

Although *financial failure* is a less ambiguous term than *economic failure,* even it has two generally recognized aspects. A firm can be considered a failure if it cannot meet its current obligations as they fall due, even though its total assets may exceed its total liabilities. This is defined as *technical insolvency.* A firm is a failure, or *bankrupt,* if its total liabilities exceed a fair valuation of its total assets (that is, if the "real" net worth of the firm is negative).

Hereafter, when the word *failure* is used, it will mean both technical insolvency and bankruptcy.

Causes of Failures

Different studies assign the causes of failure to different factors. Dun & Bradstreet compilations assign these causes as follows:[1]

Cause of Failure	Percentage of Total
Neglect	2.0
Fraud	1.5
Disaster	.9
Management incompetence	93.1
Unknown	2.5

1. *The Failure Record, 1972* (New York: Dun & Bradstreet, 1973).

A number of other studies of failures can be generalized into the following groups:[2]

Cause of Failure	Percentage of Total
Unfavorable industry trends	20
Management incompetence	60
Catastrophes	10
Miscellaneous	10

Both classifications include the effects of recessions but place the resulting failures in the category of managerial incompetence. This method is logical; managements should be prepared to operate in environments in which recessions occur and should frame their policies to cope with downturns as well as to benefit from business upswings. Managements also should anticipate unfavorable industry trends.

A number of financial remedies are available to management when it becomes aware of the imminence or occurrence of insolvency. These remedies are described in the remainder of the chapter.

The Failure Record[3]

How widespread is business failure? Is it a rare phenomenon, or does it occur fairly often? In recent times, about ten thousand to twelve thousand firms a year have failed, but they represent less than one-half of 1 percent of all business firms. The failure rate rises during recession periods, when the economy is weakened and credit is tightened. (Among the large and well-known companies that have gone bankrupt during the 1970s are the Penn Central Transportation Company, Dolly Madison Industries, Four Seasons Nursing Centers, King Resources Company, Farrington Manufacturing Company, and W. T. Grant.)

Often, mergers or government intervention are arranged as alternatives to outright bankruptcy. Thus, in recent years, the Federal Home Loan Bank System has arranged the mergers of several very large "problem" savings and loan associations into sound institutions, and the Federal Reserve System has done the same thing for banks. Several government agencies, principally the U.S. Department of Defense, arranged to bail out Lockheed in 1970 to keep it from failing. The merger of Douglas Aircraft and McDonnell in the late 1960s was designed to prevent Douglas's failure. Similar instances could be cited for the securities brokerage industry in the late 1960s and early 1970s.

2. See studies referred to in A. S. Dewing, *The Financial Policy of Corporations,* vol. 2 (New York: Ronald Press, 1953), chap. 28.
3. This section draws heavily from Edward I. Altman, *Corporate Bankruptcy in America* (Lexington, Mass.: Heath Lexington Books, 1972).

Why do government and industry seek to prevent the bankruptcy of larger firms? Three of the many reasons are (1) to prevent an erosion of confidence (in the case of financial institutions), (2) to maintain a viable supplier, and (3) to avoid disrupting a local community. Also, bankruptcy is an expensive process, so even when the public interest is not at stake, private industry has strong incentives to prevent it. The costs of bankruptcy, as well as alternatives to it, are discussed in subsequent sections.

Extension and Composition

Extension and composition are discussed together because they both represent voluntary concessions by creditors. *Extension* postpones the date of required payment of past-due obligations. *Composition* voluntarily reduces the creditors' claims on the debtor. Both are intended to keep the debtor in business and to avoid court costs. Although creditors must absorb a temporary loss, the debtor's recovery is often greater than if one of the formal procedures had been followed; and the hope is that a stable customer will emerge.

Procedure

A meeting of the debtor and the creditors is held. At the meeting, the creditors appoint a committee consisting of four or five of the largest creditors and one or two of the smaller ones. The meeting is typically arranged and conducted by an adjustment bureau associated with local credit managers' associations or by a trade association.

After the first meeting, if it is judged that the case can be worked out, the bureau assigns investigators to make an exhaustive report. The bureau and the creditors' committee use the facts of the report to formulate a plan for adjustment of the claims. Another meeting between the debtor and the creditors is then held in an attempt to work out an extension or composition, or a combination of the two. Subsequent meetings may be required to reach final agreements.

Necessary Conditions

At least three conditions are usually necessary to make an extension or a composition feasible:

1. The debtor must be a good moral risk.
2. The debtor must show ability to make a recovery.
3. General business conditions must be favorable to recovery.

Extension

Creditors prefer an extension because it provides for payment in full. The debtor buys current purchases on a cash basis and pays off the past-due balance over an extended time. In some cases, creditors may agree not only to extend the time of payment but also to subordinate existing claims to new debts incurred in favor of vendors extending credit during the period of the extension.

Of course, the creditors must have faith that the debtor will solve the problems. But because of the uncertainties involved, they will want to exercise controls over the debtor while waiting for their claims to be paid. For example, the creditors' committee may insist that an assignment (turnover of assets) to it be executed, to be held in escrow in case of default. If the debtor is a corporation, the committee may require that stockholders transfer their stock certificates into an escrow account until the repayment called for under the extension has been completed. The committee may also designate a representative to countersign all checks, and it may obtain security in the form of notes, mortgages, or assignment of accounts receivable.

Composition

In a composition, a pro rata cash settlement is made. Creditors receive from the debtor a uniform percentage of the obligations—in cash. The cash received is taken as full settlement of the debt, even though the ratio may be as low as 10 percent. Bargaining occurs between the debtor and the creditors over the savings that result from avoiding bankruptcy: administration costs, legal fees, investigating costs, and so on. In addition to avoiding these costs, the debtor avoids the stigma of bankruptcy and thus may be induced to part with most of the savings that result from avoiding the bankruptcy.

Combination Settlement

Often the bargaining process results in a compromise involving both an extension and a composition. For example, the settlement may provide for a cash payment of 25 percent of the debt and six future installments of 10 percent each. Total payment thereby aggregates to 85 percent. Installment payments are usually evidenced by notes, and creditors also seek protective controls.

Appraisal of Voluntary Settlements

The advantages of voluntary settlements are informality and simplicity. Investigative, legal, and administrative expenses are held to a minimum. The procedure is the most economical and results in the largest return to creditors.

One possible disadvantage is that the debtor is left in control of the business. This situation may involve legal complications or erosion of assets still operated by the debtor. However, numerous controls are available to give the creditors protection.

A second disadvantage is that small creditors may take a nuisance role in that they may insist on payment in full. As a consequence, settlements typically provide for payment in full for claims under $50 or $100. If a composition is involved, and all claims under $50 are paid, all creditors will receive a base of $50 plus the agreed-on percentage of the balance of their claims.

Reorganization in General

Reorganization is a form of extension or composition of the firm's obligations. However, the legal formalities are much more involved than the procedures thus far described. Regardless of the legal procedure followed, reorganization processes have several features in common:

1. The firm is insolvent either because it is unable to meet cash obligations as they come due or because claims on the firm exceed its assets. Hence, some modifications in the nature or amount of the firm's obligations must be made. A scaling down of terms or amounts must be formulated. This procedure may represent scaling down fixed charges or converting short-term debt into long-term debt.
2. New funds must be raised for working capital and for property rehabilitation.
3. The operating and managerial causes of difficulty must be discovered and eliminated.

The procedures involved in effecting a reorganization are highly legalistic and, in fact, thoroughly understood only by attorneys who specialize in bankruptcy and reorganization. This section will therefore discuss only the general principles involved.

In essence, a reorganization is a composition, a scaling down of claims. In any composition, two conditions must be met:

1. The scaling down must be fair to all parties.
2. In return for the sacrifices, successful rehabilitation and profitable future operation of the firm must be feasible.

These are the standards of fairness and feasibility, which are analyzed further in the next section.

Financial Decisions in Reorganization

When a business becomes insolvent, a decision must be made whether to dissolve the firm through liquidation or to keep it alive through reorganization. Fundamentally, this decision depends on a determination of the value of the firm if it is rehabilitated versus the value of the sum of the parts if it is dismembered.

Liquidation values depend on the degree of specialization of the capital assets used in the firm and, hence, their resale value. In addition, liquidation itself involves costs of dismantling, including legal costs. Of course, successful reorganization also involves costs. Typically, better equipment must be installed, obsolete inventories must be disposed of, and improvements in management must be made. Often the greater indicated value of the firm in reorganization compared with its value in liquidation is used to force a compromise agreement among the claimants, even when they feel that their relative position has not been treated fairly in the reorganization plan.

Both the SEC and the courts are called upon to determine the fairness and feasibility of proposed plans of reorganization.[4] In developing standards of fairness in connection with such reorganizations, the courts and the SEC have adhered to two precedent setting court decisions.[5]

Standards of Fairness

The basic doctrine of fairness states that claims must be recognized in the order of their legal and contractual priority. Junior claimants such as common stockholders can participate only to the extent that they make an additional cash contribution to the reorganization of the firm.

Carrying out this concept of fairness involves the following steps:

1. An estimate of future sales must be made.
2. An analysis of operating conditions must be made so the future earnings on sales can be estimated.
3. A determination of the capitalization rate to be applied to these future earnings must be made.
4. The capitalization rate must be applied to the estimated future earnings to obtain an indicated value of the company's properties.
5. Provision for distribution to the claimants must be made.

Example of Reorganization and Standards of Fairness

The meaning and content of these procedures can be set out by the use of an actual example of reorganization—that of R. Hoe and Company, Inc.[6] The company was incorporated in 1909 and went public in 1924. Principally involved in the production of printing presses and saws and other wood-cutting products, the company operated successfully until after 1965.[7]

At that point sales began growing at an accelerating rate. The rapid growth of sales and profits was accompanied by a rise in the price of Hoe common

---

4. The federal bankruptcy laws specify that reorganization plans be worked out by court-appointed officials and be reviewed by the SEC.
5. Case v. Los Angeles Lumber Products Co., 308 U.S. 106 (1939) and Consolidated Rock Products Co. v. duBoise, 213 U.S. 510 (1940). Securities and Exchange Commission, Seventeenth Annual Report (Washington, D.C.: Government Printing Office, 1951), p. 130.
6. This material is based on the Securities and Exchange Commission Corporate Reorganization Release No. 319, September 8, 1976.
7. The early presses were made of wood, and R. Hoe began to manufacture saws to cut the wood.

stock from $2 per share in 1965 to $48 per share in 1968. But the rapid sales growth put a strain on the company's working capital. To remedy this, the firm issued new common stock in 1967 and 1968. In April 1969 it arranged additional financing in the form of a loan at high interest from James Talcott, Inc.

By this point the situation had already begun to deteriorate. Despite the new capital, Hoe continued having difficulty meeting its obligations. Not long after the loan from Talcott, the American Stock Exchange (ASE) suspended trading of Hoe stock because the company had failed to file audited financial statements for the previous year on a timely basis. Subsequently, Hoe reported a decline in earnings for 1968 and a loss for the first quarter of 1969. Trade creditors reacted by demanding payment on past-due accounts before shipping new supplies. The withdrawal of trade credit resulted in Hoe filing a petition on July 7, 1969, to reorganize under Chapter X of the Bankruptcy Act.

The bankruptcy trustee who was appointed was forced to deal with some urgent problems. Immediate working capital needs to continue the saw operation were met by renegotiation of contracts with printing press customers. The press operation was based on job orders from customers; but, because of the bankruptcy, no new orders were being received. By October 18, 1974, the trustee had formulated and then filed with the court a reorganization plan that was subsequently analyzed by the SEC. By court order, in 1975 the press business was sold for stock and notes to Wood Industries (a public company), and the loan from Talcott Industries was settled for about $1 million.

Table 25.1 shows the R. Hoe balance sheet as of December 30, 1975—

**Table 25.1
R. Hoe and Company, Inc.,
Balance Sheet as of
December 31, 1975
(Thousands of Dollars)**

Assets		Liabilities	
Cash and equivalent	$ 3,139	Current liabilities	$ 483
Receivables	925	Debts granted administration status	148
Inventory	3,476	Priority claims (taxes and wages)	390
Net plant	1,307	Unsecured claims	8,719
Investment in Wood Industries, Inc.	633	Total liabilities	$ 9,740
Other assets unrelated to saw division		Class A stock (436,604 shares, $15	
operations	826	liquidating value)	6,549
		Dividends in arrears on Class A stock	5,392
		Common stock (1,933,462 shares outstanding)	781
		Retained earnings deficit	−12,156
		Total stockholder equity	566
Total assets	$10,306	Total liabilities and equity	$10,306

after settlement of the court orders. The trustee proposed an internal plan of reorganization under which Hoe would continue to operate the saw manufacturing business. New capitalization would consist only of 2.87 million shares of common stock. The plan was based on a valuation of the firm of $15,095,000, payable to all creditors and to Class A stockholders. The valuation and plan are detailed in Table 25.2

**Table 25.2
R. Hoe and Company, Inc.,
Trustee Valuation and Plan
(Thousands of Dollars)**

Valuation

Going concern value of saw division	$ 9,688
Excess cash	2,609
Excess inventory	—
Nonoperating assets at present value	1,958
Value of tax-free carry-forward	2,840
Gross amount available for claims	$17,095
Less trustee administrative costs	−2,000
Available for claims after trustee costs	$15,095

Priority claims paid in cash:

Debts granted administrative status	$390	
Priority claims	148	
Interest on priority claims	215	
Total paid in cash		753
Available for remainder of claims		$14,342

Plan (Remainder of Claims Based on Shares Valued at $5)

		New Shares		
	Amount of Claims	Number of Shares	Value	Percent of Shares
Unsecured claims	$ 8,719			
Interest on unsecured claims	4,190			
Total	$12,909	2,581,800	$12,909	90
Class A stockholders (436,604 shares)	11,941	286,600	1,433	10
Total value	$24,850	2,868,400	$14,342	100

All priority claims and trustee fees were to be paid in full with cash. Unsecured claims consisting primarily of current liabilities that existed prior to bankruptcy would receive 1 share of common stock for each $5 of claims. Class A stockholders would receive 1 share for each 1.523 shares of existing stock. Common stockholders would receive nothing, since the value of the firm was insufficient to meet creditors' claims, and Class A stock had a liquidation preference of $15 per share plus dividends in arrears.

In evaluating the proposal from the standpoint of fairness, the Securities and Exchange Commission began with an analysis of the prospective value of the company (Table 25.3). The SEC evaluated it at $2.4 million higher than

Table 25.3
R. Hoe and Company, Inc.,
SEC Evaluation of Fairness

Valuation (Thousands of Dollars)	Trustee Valuation	SEC Valuation
Going concern value of saw division	$ 9,688	$10,800
Excess cash	2,609	3,475
Excess inventory	—	1,000
Nonoperating assets at present value	1,958	1,536
Value of tax loss carry-forward	2,840	2,470
Gross amount available for claims	$17,095	$19,281
Less trust administration costs	2,000	1,848
Net value	$15,095	$17,433

the trustee had—primarily because of differences in beliefs about working capital needs and the going concern value of the firm. To determine going concern value, the trustee had used a P/E ratio of 11.7; but the SEC felt 12 would be more appropriate. The SEC also estimated future annual income at slightly higher than the trustee's estimate—$900,000 compared to $875,000.

Because of these differences, the SEC felt that the trustee's plan did not meet the standard of fairness. It therefore proposed an amended plan, under which the allocation to Class A stockholders would be increased, and unsecured creditors would receive 1 share of new common stock for each $5 value of claims (a total of 2.58 million shares)—the same as under the trustee's plan. (See Table 25.4.) The allocation to Class A stockholders was increased because of the SEC's higher estimated value of the firm. Under the new plan, Class A stockholders would receive 1 share for each 0.579 shares of their Class A stock. Again, common stockholders would receive nothing, since the value of the firm was insufficient to meet preferential claims.

Table 25.4
SEC Amended Plan
(Thousands of Dollars)

	Amount of Claim	New Shares Number of Shares	New Shares Value	New Shares Percent of Shares
Unsecured claims:				
Principal	$ 8,719			
Interest	4,190			
Total	$12,909	2,581,800	$12,909	77
Class A stockholders:				
436,604 shares	$11,941	754,200	$ 3,771	23
Total value	$24,850	3,336,000	$16,680	100

Priority claims of $753,000 were to be paid per the trustee's plan.

Standard of Feasibility

The primary test of feasibility is that the fixed charges on the income of the corporation after reorganization are amply covered by earnings or, if a value is established for a firm that is to be sold, that a buyer can be found at that price. Adequate coverage of fixed charges for a company that is to continue in operation generally requires an improvement in earnings or a reduction of fixed charges, or both.

Among the actions that will have to be taken to improve the earning power of the company are the following:

1. Where the management has been inefficient and inadequate for the task, new talents and abilities must be brought into the company.
2. If inventories have become obsolete, they must be disposed of and the operations of the company streamlined.
3. Sometimes the plant and the equipment of the firm must be modernized before it can operate and compete successfully on a cost basis.
4. Reorganization may also require an improvement in production, marketing, advertising, and other functions to enable the firm to compete successfully.
5. It is sometimes necessary to develop new products so the firm can move from areas where economic trends have become undesirable into areas where the growth and stability potential is greater.

Application of Feasibility Tests

Referring again to the R. Hoe and Company, the SEC observed that the company's failure had come about as the result of management attempts to expand the company faster than prudent working capital management would permit. With the sale of the printing press division by court order in 1975, the firm was left with the profitable saw division.

In the SEC's judgment, the critical element in the viability of the saw division was sufficient cash to carry out the SEC's plan and to provide adequate working capital. Under this plan, it was hoped that Hoe would emerge from Chapter X with normal current liabilities incident to its business and a simple and conservative capital structure, consisting only of current liabilities and common stock. Based on the December 31, 1975, balance sheet in Table 25.1, cash and equivalents would be $3,139,000 minus the $753,000 paid to priority claims, or a total of $2,386,000. This is nearly five times the $483,000 level of then-current liabilities.

Among the assets of the new company would be an estimated $633,000 investment in stock and notes of Wood Industries. Because the fairness and feasibility of the plan depended in part on Wood's performance, the SEC analyzed that investment and determined that, since the stock was publicly traded, market value over the recent past provided the best indication of real value. By this method the value determined by the SEC was somewhat below the trustee's estimate.

Liquidation Procedures

Liquidation of a business occurs when the firm is worth more dead than alive. Assignment is a liquidation procedure that does not go through the courts, although it can be used to achieve full settlement of claims on the debtor. Bankruptcy is a legal procedure, carried out under the jurisdiction of special courts, in which a firm is formally liquidated and creditors' claims are completely discharged.

Assignment

Assignment (as well as bankruptcy) takes place when the debtor is insolvent and the possibility of restoring profitability is so remote that the enterprise should be dissolved. Assignment is a technique for liquidating a debt and yielding a larger amount to the creditors than is likely to be achieved in formal bankruptcy.

Technically, there are three classes of assignments: (1) common-law assignment, (2) statutory assignment, and (3) assignment plus settlement.

Common-Law Assignment Common law provides for an assignment whereby a debtor transfers the title to assets to a third person, known as an assignee or trustee. This person is instructed to liquidate the assets and to distribute the proceeds among the creditors on a pro rata basis.

Typically, an assignment is conducted through the adjustment bureau of the local credit managers' association. The assignee may liquidate the assets through a bulk sale—a public sale through an auctioneer. The auction is preceded by advertising so there will be a number of bids. Liquidation may also be by a piecemeal auction sale conducted on the premises of the assignor by a competent, licensed auctioneer. On premises sales are particularly advantageous in the liquidation of large machine shops of manufacturing plants.

The common-law assignment, as such, does not discharge the debtor's obligations. If a corporation goes out of business and does not satisfy all its claims, there will still be claims against it; but in effect the corporation has ceased to exist. The people who have been associated with it can organize another corporation free of the debts and obligations of the previous one. Under a common-law assignment, the assignee, in drawing up the checks to pay the creditors, should write on each check the requisite legal language to make the payment a complete discharge of the obligation. The legal requirements for this process are technical and best carried out with the aid of a lawyer, but a statement that endorsement of the check represents acknowledgment of full payment for the obligation is essential.

Statutory Assignment Statutory assignment is similar in concept to common-law assignment. Legally, it is carried out under state statutes regulating assignment; technically, it requires more formality. The debtor executes an instrument of assignment, which is recorded and thereby provides notice to all third parties. The proceedings are handled under court order; the court appoints an assignee and supervises the proceedings, including the sale of the assets and the distribution of the proceeds. As with the common-law assignment, debtors are not automatically discharged from the balance of the obligations. They can discharge themselves, however, by printing the requisite statement on the settlement checks.

Assignment Plus Settlement Both the common-law and the statutory assignment may take place with recognition and agreement beforehand by the creditors that it will represent a complete discharge of obligation. Normally, the debtor communicates with the local credit managers' association. The association's adjustment bureau arranges a meeting of all the creditors, and a trust instrument of assignment is drawn up. The adjustment bureau is designated to dispose of the assets, which are sold through regular trade channels, by bulk sales, by auction, or by private sales. The creditors typically leave all responsibility for the liquidation procedure with the assignee—the adjustment bureau.

Having disposed of the assets and obtained funds, the adjustment bureau then distributes the proceeds pro rata among the creditors, designating on the check that this is in full settlement of the claims on the debtor. Ordinarily, a release is not agreed upon before the execution of the assignment. Instead, after full examination of the facts, the creditors' committee usually recommends granting a release following the execution of the assignment. If releases are not forthcoming, the assignor can, within four months of the date of the assignment, file a voluntary petition in bankruptcy. In this event, the assignment is terminated and the assignee must account for the assets, report to the trustee and the referee in bankruptcy, and deliver to the trustee all assets in the estate. (Usually, by that time, assets have been reduced to cash.)

Assignment has substantial advantages over bankruptcy. Bankruptcy through the courts involves much time, legal formalities, and accounting and legal expenses. Assignment saves the costs of bankruptcy proceedings, and it may save time as well. Furthermore, an assignee usually has much more flexibility in disposing of property than does a bankruptcy trustee. Assignees may be more familiar with the normal channels of trade; and since they take action quickly, before the inventories become obsolete, they may achieve better results.

Bankruptcy

Although the bankruptcy procedures need improvement, the Federal Bankruptcy Acts represent some major achievements:

1. They provide safeguards against fraud by the debtor during liquidation.
2. Simultaneously, they provide for an equitable distribution of the debtor's assets among the creditors.
3. Insolvent debtors can discharge all their obligations and start new businesses unhampered by a burden of prior debt.

Prerequisites for Bankruptcy

The debtor can file a voluntary petition of bankruptcy; but if the debtor files an involuntary petition, three conditions must be met:

1. The total debts of the insolvent must be $1,000 or more.
2. If the debtor has fewer than twelve creditors, any single creditor can file the petition if the amount owed is $500 or more. If there are twelve or more creditors, the petition must be signed by three or more of them, each having provable total claims of at least $500.
3. Within the four preceding months, the debtor must have committed one or more of the following six acts of bankruptcy.

Acts of Bankruptcy

The six acts of bankruptcy can be summarized briefly:

1. *Concealment or Fraudulent Conveyance.* Concealment constitutes the hiding of assets with intent to defraud creditors. Fraudulent conveyance is transfer of property to a third party without adequate consideration and with intent to defraud creditors.
2. *Preferential Transfer.* A preferential transfer is the transfer of money or assets by an insolvent debtor to a creditor, giving that creditor a greater portion of the claim than other creditors would receive on liquidation.
3. *Legal Lien or Distraint.* If an insolvent debtor permits any creditor to obtain a lien on the property and fails to discharge the lien within thirty days, or if the debtor permits a landlord to distrain (to seize property that has been pledged as security for a loan) for nonpayment of rent, that person has committed an act of bankruptcy. By obtaining a lien, creditors can force an insolvent but obdurate debtor into bankruptcy.
4. *Assignment.* An act of bankruptcy likewise exists if a debtor makes a general assignment for the benefit of creditors. Again, this enables creditors who have become distrustful of the debtor in the process of assignment to transfer the proceeds to a bankruptcy court. As a matter of practice, creditors in common-law assignments typically require that a debtor execute a formal assignment document to be held in escrow and to become effective if informal and voluntary settlement negotiations fail. In the event of failure, the assignment becomes effective, and the creditors have the right to bring the case into bankruptcy court.
5. *Appointment of Receiver or Trustee.* If an insolvent debtor permits the ap-

pointment of a receiver or a trustee to take charge of the property, the debtor has committed an act of bankruptcy. In this event, the creditors can remove a receivership or an adjustment proceeding to a bankruptcy court.

6. *Admission in Writing.* A debtor who admits in writing an inability to pay the debts and a willingness to be judged bankrupt has committed an act of bankruptcy. The reason for this sixth act of bankruptcy is that debtors are often unwilling to engage in voluntary bankruptcy because it carries the stigma of avoidance of obligations. Sometimes, therefore, negotiations with a debtor reach an impasse. Admission in writing is one of the methods of forcing the debtor to commit an act of bankruptcy and of moving the proceedings into a bankruptcy court, where the debtor will no longer be able to reject all plans for settlement.

Adjudication and the Referee

On the filing of the petition of involuntary bankruptcy, a subpoena is served on the debtor. There is usually no contest by the debtor, and the court adjudges the person bankrupt. On adjudication, the case is transferred by the court to a referee in bankruptcy, generally a lawyer appointed for a specified term by the judge of the bankruptcy court to act in the judge's place after adjudication.

In addition, on petition of the creditors, the referee in voluntary proceedings or the judge in involuntary proceedings can appoint a receiver, who serves as the custodian of the debtor's property until the appointment of a trustee. This arrangement was developed because a long period elapses between the date of the filing of a petition in bankruptcy and the election of a trustee at the first creditors' meeting. To safeguard the creditors' interests during this period, the court, through either the referee or the judge, can appoint a receiver in bankruptcy, who has full control until the trustee is appointed.

First Creditors' Meeting: Election of Trustee

At the first meeting of the creditors, a trustee is elected. If different blocks of creditors have different candidates for trustee, the election may become drawn out. Frequently, the trustee will be the adjustment bureau of the local credit managers' association. At this first meeting the debtor may also be examined for the purpose of obtaining necessary information.

Subsequent Procedure

The trustee and the creditors' committee act to convert all assets into cash. The trustee sends a letter to people owing the debtor money, warning that all past-due accounts will result in instant suit if immediate payment is not made. Appraisers are appointed by the courts to set a value on the property. With the advice of the creditors' committee and authorization of the referee, the merchandise is sold by approved methods. As in an assignment, auctions may be held.

Without the consent of the court, property cannot be sold at less than 75 percent of the value set by the court-appointed appraisers. Cash received from the disposition of the property is used first to pay all expenses associated with the bankruptcy proceedings and then to pay any remaining funds to the claimants.

Final Meeting and Discharge

The trustee who has completed the liquidation and has sent out all the claimants' checks makes an accounting, which is reviewed by the creditors and the referee. The bankruptcy is then discharged, and the debtor is released from all debts.

If the hearings before the referee indicate the probability of fraud, the FBI is required to undertake an investigation. If fraud was not committed and the bankruptcy is discharged, the debtor is again free to engage in business. Since business is highly competitive in many fields, the debtor will probably not have great difficulty in obtaining credit again. Under the National Bankruptcy Act, however, a debtor cannot be granted a discharge more often than once every six years.

Priority of Claims on Distribution of Proceeds

The order of priority of claims in bankruptcy is as follows:

1. Costs of administering and operating the bankruptcy estate.
2. Wages due workers if earned within three months prior to the filing of the petition in bankruptcy, the amount not to exceed $600 per person.
3. Taxes due federal, state, county, or any other government agencies.
4. Secured creditors, with the proceeds of the sale of specific property pledged for a mortgage.
5. General or unsecured creditors—the claim consisting of the remaining balances after payment to secured creditors from the sale of specific property and including trade credit, bank loans, and debenture bonds. Holders of subordinated debt fall into this category, but they must turn over required amounts to the holders of senior debt.
6. Preferred stockholders.
7. Common stockholders.

An example will illustrate how this priority of claims works out. The balance sheet of a bankrupt firm is shown in Table 25.5. Assets total $90 million, and claims are those indicated on the right-hand side of the balance sheet. The subordinated debentures are subordinated to the notes payable to commercial banks.

Assume that the firm's assets are sold. These assets, shown in the balance

Table 25.5
Bankrupt Firm Balance Sheet
(Millions of Dollars)

Current assets	$80.0	Accounts payable	$20.0
Net property	10.0	Notes payable (due bank)	10.0
		Accrued wages (1,400 at $500 each)	0.7
		U.S. taxes	1.0
		State and local taxes	0.3
		Current debt	$32.0
		First mortgage	$ 6.0
		Second mortgage	1.0
		Subordinated debentures[a]	8.0
		Long-term debt	$15.0
		Preferred stock	$ 2.0
		Common stock	26.0
		Capital surplus	4.0
		Retained earnings	11.0
		Net worth	$43.0
Total assets	$90.0	Total claims	$90.0

[a] Subordinated to $10 million notes payable to the First National Bank.

sheet, are greatly overstated; they are worth much less than the $90 million at which they are carried. The following amounts are realized on liquidation:

Current assets	$28,000,000
Net property	5,000,000
Total assets	$33,000,000

The order of priority of payment of claims is shown by Table 25.6. Fees and expenses of administration are typically about 20 percent of gross proceeds, and in this example they are assumed to be $6 million. Next in priority are wages due workers, which total $700,000. The total amount of taxes to be paid is $1.3 million. Thus far, the total of claims paid for the $33 million is $8 million. The first mortgage is then paid from the net proceeds of $5 million from the sale of fixed property, leaving $20 million available to the general creditors.

The claims of the general creditors total $40 million. Since $20 million is available, each claimant will receive 50 percent of the claim before the subordination adjustment. This adjustment requires that the holders of subordinated debentures turn over to the holders of the notes to which they are subordinated all amounts received until the notes to which they are subordinated are satisfied. In this situation, the claim of the holders of notes payable is $10 million, but only $5 million is available; the deficiency is therefore $5 million. After transfer of $4 million by the holders of subordinated debentures, there remains a deficiency of $1 million, which will be unsatis-

Table 25.6
Bankrupt Firm's Order of Priority
of Claims (Millions of Dollars)

Distribution of Proceeds on Liquidation

1. Proceeds of sale of assets	$33.0
2. Fees and expenses of administration of bankruptcy	6.0
3. Wages due workers earned three months prior to filing of bankruptcy petition	0.7
4. Taxes	1.3
5. Available after priority payments	$25.0
6. First mortgage, paid from sale of net property	5.0
7. Available to general creditors	$20.0

Claims of General Creditors

Class of Creditor	Claim (1)	Application of 50 Percent (2)	After Subordination Adjustment (3)	Percentage of Original Claims Received (4)
Unsatisfied portion of first mortgage	$1.0	$0.5	$ 0.5	92
Unsatisfied portion of second mortgage	1.0	0.5	0.5	50
Notes payable	10.0	5.0	9.0	90
Accounts payable	20.0	10.0	10.0	50
Subordinated debentures	8.0	4.0	0	0
	$40.0	$20.0	$20.0	56

Notes: 1. Column 1 is the claim of each class of creditor. Total claims equal $40 million.
2. Line 7 in the upper section of the table shows that $20 million is available. This sum divided by the $40 million of claims indicates that general creditors will receive 50 percent of their claims shown in Column 1.
3. The debentures are subordinated to the notes payable; $4 million is transferred from debentures to notes payable in Column 3.
4. Column 4 shows the results of dividing the Column 3 figure by the original amount given in Table 25.5 except for first mortgage, where $5 million paid on sale of property is included. The 56 percent total figure includes the first mortgage transactions, that is: ($20,000,000 + $5,000,000) ÷ ($40,000,000 + $5,000,000) = 56%.

fied. Note that 90 percent of the bank claim will be satisified, whereas only 50 percent of other unsecured claims will be satisfied. These figures illustrate the usefulness of the subordination provision to the security to which the subordination is made. Since no other funds remain, the claims of the holders of preferred and common stocks are completely wiped out.

The order of priority can be altered by special subordination agreements. For example, in the W. T. Grant bankruptcy during the mid-1970s, the commercial banks had agreed to subordinate their loans to the amounts payable to trade creditors in order to induce suppliers of W. T. Grant to continue the flow of merchandise to the company. As a consequence, of the $400 million that appeared to be realizable from W. T. Grant, the order of priority seemed to be the following. First in line were the holders of the $24 million worth of senior debentures. Second, because of an unusual lien arrangement, came trade creditors, with $110 million owed. Third were the banks, which subordinated to the trade creditors $300 million of their $640 million loan to Grant along with an additional $90 million loaned after the filing for reorganization. Next came junior debenture holders, with claims of $94 million. Last in line were the holders of unsecured debt, including $300 million in landlord claims and utility bills. In addition, it was estimated that administrative costs of the reorganization would total $30 million. There was also an unresolved Internal Revenue Service claim of $60 million plus interest. Further, there would be legal fees estimated to run into the millions that would assume a priority status.[8]

Studies of the proceeds in bankruptcy liquidations reveal that unsecured creditors receive, on the average, about 15 cents on the dollar. Consequently, where assignment to creditors is likely to yield more, assignment is to be preferred to bankruptcy.

Summary

The major cause of a firm's failure is incompetent management. Bad managers should, of course, be removed as promptly as possible; if failure has occurred, a number of remedies are open to the interested parties.

The first question to be answered is whether the firm is better off dead or alive—whether it should be liquidated and sold off piecemeal or rehabilitated. Assuming the decision is made that the firm should survive, it must be put through what is called a reorganization. Legal procedures are always costly, especially in the case of a business failure. Therefore, if it is at all possible, both the debtor and the creditors are better off if matters can be handled on an informal basis rather than through the courts. The informal procedures used in reorganization are (1) extension, which postpones the date of settlement, and (2) composition, which reduces the amount owed.

If voluntary settlement through extension or composition is not possible, the matter is thrown into the courts. If the court decides on reorganization rather than liquidation, it will appoint a trustee (1) to control the firm going through reorganization and (2) to prepare a formal plan of reorganization. The plan, which must be reviewed by the SEC, must meet the standards of fairness to all parties and feasibility in the sense that the reorganized enterprise will stand a good chance of surviving instead of being thrown back into the bankruptcy courts.

8. "Dividing What's Left of Grant's," *Business Week*, March 1, 1976, p. 21.

The application of standards of fairness and feasibility can help determine the probable success of a particular plan for reorganization. The concept of fairness involves the estimation of sales and earnings and the application of a capitalization rate to the latter to determine the appropriate distribution to each claimant.

The feasibility test examines the ability of the new enterprise to carry the fixed charges resulting from the reorganization plan. The quality of management and the company's assets must be assured. Production and marketing may also require improvement.

Finally, where liquidation is treated as the only solution to the debtor's insolvency, the creditors should attempt procedures that will net them the largest recovery. Assignment of the debtor's property is the cheaper and the faster procedure. Furthermore, there is more flexibility in disposing of the property and thus providing larger returns. Bankruptcy provides formal procedures in liquidation to safeguard the debtor's property from fraud and to assure equitable distribution to the creditors. The procedure is long and cumbersome. Moreover, the debtor's property is generally poorly managed during bankruptcy proceedings unless the trustee is closely supervised by the creditors.

Questions

25.1 Discuss this statement, giving both pros and cons: A certain number of business failures is a healthy sign. If there are no failures, this is an indication (a) that entrepreneurs are overly cautious, hence not as inventive and as willing to take risks as a healthy, growing economy requires; (b) that competition is not functioning to weed out inefficient producers; or (c) that both situations exist.

25.2 How can financial analysis be used to forecast the probability of a given firm's failure? Assuming that such analysis is properly applied, will it always predict failure? Explain.

25.3 Why do creditors usually accept a plan for financial rehabilitation rather than demand liquidation of the business?

25.4 Would it be possible to form a profitable company by merging two companies, both of which are business failures? Explain.

25.5 Distinguish between a reorganization and a bankruptcy.

25.6 Would it be a sound rule to liquidate whenever the liquidation value is above the value of the corporation as a going concern? Discuss.

25.7 Why do liquidations usually result in losses for the creditors or the owners, or both? Would partial liquidation or liquidation over a period of time limit their losses? Explain.

25.8 Are liquidations likely to be more common for public utility, railroad, or industrial corporations? Why?

Problems   25.1 The financial statements of the Hamilton Publishing Company for 1978 are
shown below:

Hamilton Publishing Company
Balance Sheet,
December 31, 1978
(Thousands of Dollars)

Current assets	$130,000	Current liabilities	$ 53,000
Investments	40,000	Advance payments for subscriptions	78,000
Net fixed assets	200,000	Reserves	8,000
Goodwill	14,000	$8 preferred stock, $100 par	
		(1,500,000 shares)	150,000
		$9 preferred stock, no par	
		(100,000 shares, callable at $110)	11,000
		Common stock, $1.50 par	
		(8,000,000 shares)	12,000
		Retained earnings	72,000
Total assets	$384,000	Total claims	$384,000

Hamilton Publishing Company
Income Statement for Year
Ended December 31, 1978
(Thousands of Dollars)

Operating income		$194,400
Operating expenses		172,800
Earnings before income tax		21,600
Income tax (at 50 percent)		10,800
Income after taxes		10,800
Dividends on $8 preferred stock	$12,000	
Dividends on $9 preferred stock	900	12,900
Income available for common stock		−$2,100

A recapitalization plan is proposed in which each share of $8 preferred
stock will be exchanged for a share of $2 preferred (stated value $20), plus
$80 of stated principal in 8 percent subordinated income debentures with
par value $1,000. The $9 preferred will be retired from cash.
a. Show the pro forma balance sheet (in thousands of dollars) giving effect
to the recapitalization and showing the new preferred at its stated value
and the common stock at par value.
b. Present the pro forma income statement (in thousands of dollars).
c. How much does the firm increase income available to common stock by
the recapitalization?
d. How much less are the required pretax earnings after the recapitalization
compared to before the change? (Required earnings are the amount
necessary to meet fixed charges, debenture interest, and preferred dividends.)
e. How is the debt to net worth position of the company affected by the recapitalization?
f. Would you vote for the recapitalization if you were a holder of the $8 pre-
ferred stock?

25.2 The Accurate Instrument Company produces precision instructions. The company's products, designed and manufactured according to specifications set out by its customers, are highly specialized. Declines in sales and increases in development expenses in recent years resulted in a large deficit at the end of 1978 (see the balance sheet and income statement below):

Accurate Instrument Company
Balance Sheet as of
December 31, 1978
(Thousands of Dollars)

Current assets	$375	Current liabilities	$450
Fixed assets	375	Long-term debt (unsecured)	225
		Capital stock	150
		Retained earnings (deficit)	−75
Total assets	$750	Total claims	$750

Accurate Instrument Company
Sales and Profits, 1975–1978
(Thousands of Dollars)

Year	Sales	Net Profit after Tax before Fixed Charges
1975	$2,625	$262.5
1976	2,400	225.0
1977	1,425	−75.0
1978	1,350	−112.5

Independent assessment led to the conclusion that the company would have a liquidation value of about $600,000. As an alternative to liquidation, management concluded that a reorganization was possible with the investment of an additional $300,000. Management was confident of the company's eventual success and stated that the additional investment would restore earnings to $125,000 a year after taxes and before fixed charges. The appropriate multiplier to apply is eight times. Management is negotiating with a local investment group to obtain the additional $300,000. If the funds are obtained, the holders of the long-term debt will be given half the common stock in the reorganized firm in place of their present claims.

Should the creditors agree to the reorganization, or should they force liquidation of the firm?

25.3 During the past several months, the American Industrial Products Company has had difficulty meeting its current obligations. Attempts to raise additional working capital have failed. To add to AIP's problems, its principal lenders, The First National Bank and the General Insurance Company, have been placing increased pressure on it because of its continued delinquent loan payments and apparent lack of fiscal responsibility.

The First National Bank is first mortgage holder on AIP's production facility and has a $1 million, unsecured revolving loan with AIP that is past due and on which certain restrictive clauses have been violated. The General Insurance Company is holding $5 million of AIP's subordinated debentures, which are subordinate to the notes payable.

Because of the bank's increasing concern for the long-term future of AIP, it has attached $750,000 of AIP's deposits. This action has forced the company into either reorganization or bankruptcy.

General Insurance has located a large manufacturing company that is interested in taking over AIP's operations. This company has offered to assume the $8 million mortgage, pay all back taxes, and pay $4.3 million in cash for the company.

AIP's estimated sales for 1978 are $20 million, its estimated earnings are $1,294,000, and its capitalization factor is 10 times. The company's balance sheet as of December 31, 1978 is given below:

American Industrial Products Company Balance Sheet as of December 31, 1978 (Thousands of Dollars)

Assets		Liabilities	
Current assets	$ 3,000	Accounts payable	$ 2,000
Net property, plant, and equipment	12,000	Taxes	200
Other assets	2,800	Notes payable to bank	250
		Other current liabilities	1,350
		Total current liabilities	$ 3,800
		Mortgage	8,000
		Subordinated debentures	5,000
		Common stock	1,000
		Paid-in capital	2,000
		Retained earnings	−2,000
Total assets	$17,800	Total liabilities and stockholders' equity	$17,800

a. Given all the data and the fact that AIP cannot be reorganized internally, show the effect of the reorganization plan on claims of AIP's creditors.
b. Based on the information in the paragraph preceding the balance sheet, test for the standard of fairness.
c. Comment on the actions of the bank in offsetting AIP's deposits.
d. Do you feel the bank and the insurance company were right in not advancing AIP additional money?

CHAPTER

INTERNATIONAL BUSINESS FINANCE

Introduction International financial developments are having an increased effect on people because all parts of the world are now more closely linked together than ever before. Communications throughout the world take place within a matter of minutes or even seconds. Jet airplanes can take people anywhere within a matter of hours. Realignment of the relative values of different countries' currencies is continually occurring. These international financial developments have been helpful to some and harmful to others. Although the relationships are complex, the fundamentals presented here will provide a basis for understanding the new opportunities and threats that result from the increasingly dynamic international environment.

The changes in currency values that have taken place since 1965 are set forth in Table 26.1, which compares the values in relation to the U.S. dollar for two countries whose currencies have increased in strength and two whose currencies have declined in strength over recent years. In August 1971 the major countries of the world departed from a policy of fixed exchange rates. But, even before this formal recognition of realignment in currency values, changes had already been taking place. For years the ratio of the Japanese yen to the U.S. dollar was 360 to 1. By mid-1978 the number of yen required to equal one dollar had dropped to 186. The value of the yen in

Table 26.1
Number of Foreign Currency
Units per U.S. Dollar

	1965	1970	1971	1972	1973	1974	1975	1976	1977	August 11, 1978
Japan X	360.90	357.60	314.80	302.00	280.00	300.95	305.15	292.80	240.00	185.94
E	0.00277	0.00280	0.00318	0.00331	0.00357	0.00332	0.00328	0.00342	0.00417	0.005378
Index	100	101	115	119	129	120	118	123	150	194
W. Germany X	4.00	3.65	3.27	3.20	3.70	2.41	2.62	2.36	2.11	1.97
E	0.2500	0.2740	0.3058	0.3125	0.2703	0.4150	0.3817	0.4237	0.4739	0.5072
Index	100	110	122	125	108	166	153	169	190	203
Mexico X	12.50	12.50	12.50	12.50	12.50	12.50	12.50	20.00	22.70	22.83
E	0.08	0.08	0.08	0.08	0.08	0.08	0.08	0.05	0.0440	0.0438
Index	100	100	100	100	100	100	100	62	55	55
Brazil X	0.89	2.47	5.64	6.22	6.22	7.44	9.07	12.35	16.05	18.35
E	1.1236	0.4049	0.1773	0.1608	0.1608	0.1344	0.1102	0.0810	0.0623	0.0545
Index	100	36	16	14	14	12	10	7	6	5

X = number of LCs (foreign currency units) per dollar.
E = value of one LC (foreign currency unit) in dollars.
Index: 1965 = 100.
Source: International Monetary Fund, *International Financial Statistics,* monthly issues, and *Wall Street Journal,* August 14, 1978.

This chapter utilizes materials developed jointly with Bart W. Sorge in J. Fred Weston and Bart W. Sorge, *International Managerial Finance* (Homewood, Ill.: Richard D. Irwin, 1972); and J. Fred Weston and Bart W. Sorge, *Guide to International Financial Management* (New York: McGraw-Hill, 1977).

relation to the dollar has increased by 94 percent since 1965. Similarly, the value of the German mark was four marks to the dollar, but by mid-1978 it had dropped to about two marks to the dollar. Thus the dollar value of the mark increased from approximately 25 cents to 50 cents—an increase of 100 percent.

For Mexico and Brazil, however, the changes have been in the opposite direction. During the 1960s the Mexican peso was worth 8 cents, and its ratio to the U.S. dollar was 12.5 to 1. In 1976 the peso was allowed to float against the dollar, and by mid-1978 the ratio of the peso to the dollar had moved up to 22.83. Thus the value of the peso had shrunk to slightly over 4 cents, a decline of almost 50 percent from its previous value. For years Brazil has had a policy of periodically adjusting the value of its cruzeiro. Through these successive adjustments, in mid-1978 the value of the cruzeiro in relation to the dollar was only 5 percent of what it had been in 1965.

Thus changes in currency values in relation to the dollar have been very substantial—and in both directions. Almost every business firm has experienced some of the effects of these changes on its operations. Its inputs may include imported materials, and its products may be exported or become part of an exported product. Some large companies have earned more than half their profits abroad. Even for smaller companies it is not uncommon to find that, if international sales can be developed to about one-fourth of total sales, then earnings from foreign sales or operations are likely to be as high as 40 to 50 percent of total earnings. International operations often enable the smaller firm to achieve better utilization of its investment in fixed plant and equipment.

The Development of an International Firm

A firm generally develops its international activities through an evolutionary process. Different areas of each firm are engaged in international activities in different degrees. The steps in the progression from a domestic to a multinational firm may differ among individual firms, but a general pattern can be observed. The existence or the development of a strong competitive product for domestic sales is a prerequisite for international operations. A firm must have a management team capable of developing and producing a strong, quality product to be able to cope with the many new environmental factors and uncertainties that will be encountered in international operations. A firm that cannot make it in the domestic market is even less likely to make it in the international market. Furthermore, a firm that is successful on a domestic basis is more likely than others to be able to obtain the financing required to achieve involvement in international operations.

Importing raw materials or parts may bring international exposure to the firm, since import contacts create interest in potential outlets for foreign sales. Exporting through brokers is a recommended first step if the firm's sales personnel have little experience in export sales and if the goods sold require a knowledge of foreign markets. A firm that exports large industrial machines may attempt to make sales directly since it is dealing with buyers whose needs it fully understands. But a firm selling a consumer nondurable good, such as a food product, needs to develop an understanding of the purchase habits and requirements of the consumers in foreign countries. It may also have to make use of a complex and different form of distribution system. Hence its first step is likely to be through brokers.

When a satisfactory volume of sales has been achieved, the firm may establish a foreign branch sales office, which will enable it to achieve more direct contacts overseas and to keep in closer touch with foreign market developments. The foreign sales office also locates technical service personnel closer to the firm's customers, which enables them to respond promptly when needed.

For a number of reasons, a firm may subsequently begin to consider establishing a production operation abroad. For example, before the U.S. automobile market became receptive to small cars, companies such as General Motors and Ford began producing more compact cars in foreign countries, where higher gasoline prices and narrower streets and roads created a much earlier market for such cars.

However, because of strong controls by some foreign governments, licensing often has to precede foreign sales as well as foreign production operations. Where licensing is essential because of foreign government regulations, its advantages and disadvantages must be evaluated. One of the advantages is that it can shift a wide range of problems from the domestic firm to its foreign licensee. Another advantage is that since the domestic firm is not required to make an additional investment, the net cash flows from licensing may represent a very high return on the incremental investment to the U.S. firm. From the long-term point of view, however, licensing has serious disadvantages. A firm producing highly technical products involving unique manufacturing processes may have to impart confidential know-how or information to the licensee, which can become a competitor when the license expires. For this reason a firm may seek to work out a partial ownership position with the licensee so that it can continue to participate in the long-term profits from the operation.

Joint venture is another form of participation in foreign operations that may precede the establishment of foreign subsidiaries. Indeed, it may be required by government regulations and restrictions. For example, some countries do not permit foreign firms to engage in manufacturing operations, limiting them to joint ventures as minority investors. Joint ventures can be of value in helping obtain the local goodwill and support necessary for the success of the operation. They also enable smaller firms to expand abroad with a small investment and to share the risk with foreign investors.

But joint ventures can also produce conflicts of interest and a possible loss of control for the U.S. firm.

Ultimately, the U.S. firm may seek to establish wholly-owned manufacturing branch plants or subsidiaries abroad, since administration and control are easier without the complication of local partners and maximum security of business methods and know-how is achieved. Wholly-owned manufacturing facilities are possible in most developed countries and in some developing countries.

The development of international operations is shown in Table 26.2, which indicates how a firm progresses from export and import sales activities to become an international company financed by sales of equity as well as by debt issues in countries throughout the world. However, this sequence is not always followed. A small firm with limited international experience that sells to countries characterized by considerable uncertainty may be limited to export and import activity. On the other hand, a large firm with well-established products in the United States, with long experience in international operations, and with a broad range of experienced management personnel may ultimately have wholly-owned foreign subsidiaries. Even before a firm is established abroad, it may finance abroad. After it is established abroad, its equity shares are likely to be widely owned by foreign nationals, particularly in countries where it conducts business operations.

**Table 26.2
The Development Process for
Multinational Operations**

1. Development of a strong product for domestic sales
2. Importation of some products
3. Use of export brokers
4. Direct export selling
5. Branch sales office abroad
6. Licensing
7. Licensing with joint venture
8. Joint venture
9. Wholly-owned manufacturing subsidiary
10. Multinational management organization
11. Multinational ownership of equity securities

Now that the methods by which a firm can become involved in international operations have been sketched, some of the specific decision areas will be dealt with. Although many business firms do not regard themselves as involved in international operations, they are nevertheless affected by international developments—developments that affect their cost of labor (for example, if prices of imports rise, the U.S. cost of living will rise, triggering wage increases) and material inputs, the prices of the products sold, and the sources of competition in the sale of products. The most pervasive influence, however, is that of fluctuating foreign exchange rates.

Impact of Exchange Rate Fluctuations

A fundamental difference between international business finance and domestic business finance is that international transactions and investments are conducted in more than one currency. For example, when a U.S. firm sells goods to a French firm, the U.S. firm usually wants to be paid in dollars and the French firm usually expects to pay in francs. Because of the existence of a foreign exchange market in which individual dealers and many banks trade, the buyer can pay in one currency and the seller can receive payment in another.

Since different currencies are involved, a rate of exchange must be established between them. The conversion relationship of the currencies is expressed in terms of their price relationship. If foreign exchange rates did not fluctuate, it would make no difference whether firms dealt in dollars or any other currency. However, since exchange rates do fluctuate, firms are subject to exchange rate fluctuation risks if they have a net asset or net liability position in a foreign currency. When net claims exceed liabilities in a foreign currency, the firm is said to be in a "long" position, because it will benefit if the value of the foreign currency rises. When net liabilities exceed claims in regard to foreign currencies, the firm is said to be in a "short" position, because it will gain if the foreign currency declines in value.

Because of the risks of exchange rate fluctuations, transactions have developed in a forward, or futures, foreign exchange market. This market enables a firm to hedge in an attempt to reduce the risk. Individuals also speculate by means of transactions in the forward market. Forward contracts are normally for a thirty-, sixty-, or ninety-day period, although special contracts for longer periods can be arranged by negotiation.

The cost of this protection is the premium or discount of the forward contract over the current spot rate, which varies from 0 to 2 or 3 percent per year for currencies that are considered reasonably stable. For currencies undergoing devaluation in excess of 4 to 5 percent per year, the required discounts may be as high as 15 to 20 percent per year. When it is probable that future devaluations may exceed 20 percent per year, forward contracts are usually unavailable.

The magnitude of the premium or discount required depends on the forward expectations of the financial communities of the two countries involved and on the supply and demand conditions in the foreign exchange market. Since members of the financial communities are usually well-informed about the expected forward exchange values of their respective currencies, the premiums or discounts quoted are very closely related to the probable occurrence of changes in the exchange rates. As a result, the forward market is chiefly used as protection against *unexpected* changes in the foreign exchange value of a currency.

Risk Position of the Firm in Foreign Currency Units

The risk position of a firm in relation to possible fluctuations in foreign exchange rates can be clarified by referring to expected receipts or obligations in foreign currency units. If a firm is expecting receipts in foreign currency units (if it is "long" in the foreign currency units), its risk is that the value of the foreign currency units will fall (devaluing the foreign currency in relation to the dollar). If a firm is expecting to have obligations in foreign currency units (if it is "short" in the foreign currency units), its risk is that the value of the foreign currency will rise and it will have to buy the currency at a higher price.

Methods of Dealing with the Risk of a Decline in Foreign Currency Values

A brief example will illustrate methods of taking protective action against a decline in the value of a foreign currency. On September 1, 1978, the USP Company makes a sale of goods to a foreign firm; it will receive LC 380,000 (payment in local or foreign currency units) on December 1, 1978. The USP Company has incurred costs in dollars and wishes to make definite the amount of dollars it will receive on December 1. It is considering three alternatives to deal with the risk of exchange rate fluctuation. The first alternative is to enter the forward market to sell LC 380,000 for dollars at the ninety-day forward rate quoted on September 1, 1978. The company can then utilize the LC 380,000 it receives on December 1, 1978, to pay for the dollars it has contracted to buy at the ninety-day forward rate. Under this arrangement the company will receive a definite amount in dollars in December as determined by the forward rate on September 1.

The second alternative is to borrow now from a foreign bank the LC amount such that the principal plus interest will equal what the company will be receiving on December 1. The interest rate paid is 28 percent. By borrowing, the company will receive the LCs immediately, and with the LCs it can immediately purchase dollars at the September spot rate. It can then invest the dollars received in the United States at an 8 percent interest rate. When the company receives the LC 380,000 in December, it can use the funds to liquidate the local currency loan incurred in September. (The effective tax rate in both countries is 40 percent.)

The third alternative is to make no attempt to cover the exchange risk involved in waiting the three months for receipt of the LC 380,000. Under this alternative, the USP Company will convert the LC 380,000 into dollars at whatever spot rate prevails on December 1, 1978.

The three alternatives will be analyzed for a pattern of actual spot and forward exchange rates on September 1, 1978, and the expected spot rate on December 1, 1978. First to be considered is the pattern of rates characteristic of countries subject to currency devaluation:

	September 1, 1978
Spot rate of foreign currency units per $1	LC 1.90
Ninety-day forward rate	LC 2.00

	December 1, 1978
Expected future spot rate	LC 2.10

The three alternatives can now be analyzed. The first alternative involves entering a forward contract in which the USP Company sells LC 380,000 for dollars at a rate of 2 LC to $1. Therefore, the company has contracted to receive $190,000. At the spot rate, it would have received $200,000, so a reduction of expected sales revenue of $10,000 has been incurred, providing a tax shelter of $4,000. Thus total receipts and taxes saved amounts to $194,000.

Under the second alternative, the USP Company borrows LC from a bank in the foreign country; the amount of LC plus interest equals the LC 380,000 that will be received in December. The company will have to pay interest at 28 percent on the loan obtained from the foreign bank. Since the loan is for ninety days, or one-fourth of a year, the 28 percent is divided by 4 to obtain 7 percent, which is then multiplied by $(1 - T)$, for a total of 4.2 percent, the after-tax interest rate. Since

$$1.042 \ X = LC \ 380,000,$$
$$X = LC \ 364,683.$$

At the spot exchange rate, the proceeds from the LC 364,683 divided by 1.90 equal $191,938; and this amount can be invested in the U.S. to earn an 8 percent annual rate for ninety days, or 2 percent times $(1 - T)$, which equals 1.2 percent. The proceeds of $191,938 times 1.012 equal $194,241. On December 1, 1978, USP will receive the LC 380,000, which it will use to repay the LC 380,000 principal plus interest on its LC loan.

Under the third alternative, on December 1, 1978, the LC 380,000 will be converted into dollars at the spot rate then in effect. This represents LC 380,000 divided by 2.10, or $180,952. The expected $180,952 involves a reduction in taxable sales revenue of $19,048, so net proceeds with the tax shelter are $180,952 plus 0.4 ($19,048), which equals $188,571.

The net proceeds received under the three alternatives are:

1. Sell LC in forward market for dollars $194,000
2. Borrow LC and repay from LC received in future   194,241
3. Receive dollars based on spot rate when LC funds received   188,571

Under the assumptions of this example, the second alternative provides the greatest amount of funds. But different degrees of uncertainty are associated with each of the three alternatives. The dollars to be received under the first two alternatives are certain, while those under the third are not.

Before the fact, it is not possible to state definitely which alternative will yield the largest number of dollars on December 1, 1978. It depends on the future level of the spot rate on that date. Suppose that the actual spot rate on December 1, 1978, turns out to be exactly what it was on September 1, 1978. In this situation, the first two alternatives will be unchanged, but for the third alternative, 380,000 divided by 1.90 equals $200,000—making it the best choice. But under the original assumptions, the third alternative was the worst choice. Thus doing nothing under the new set of assumed data turns out to be the best course of action, although it is clearly the riskiest. The use of the forward market or borrowing and investing through the money markets will sometimes yield lower net proceeds than will taking no protective actions whatsoever, but having an unprotected position with respect to foreign exchange rate fluctuations is the greatest risk.

Using the forward market or borrowing is a form of insurance taken out to protect against unexpected fluctuations in foreign exchange rates. Like other forms of insurance, the protection involves a cost. But the situation is similar to that of buying fire insurance on your house. You could save the money if you could be sure that a fire were not going to occur. If you have paid fire insurance for several years and no fire has occurred, you could have saved money by not buying the fire insurance. But you paid the money to protect against the loss that would have taken place if the unexpected fire had occurred. Similarly, the cost of forward hedging or borrowing is a form of insurance premium paid to avoid even larger losses.

Protection against Rising Values of Foreign Currencies

When a foreign currency is rising in value, the U.S. firm has a risk exposure if it is in a short position with respect to the foreign currency. This means that if the firm has payments to be made in foreign currency units or has liabilities outstanding that are expressed in such units, a rise in the value of the foreign currency unit will require that more dollars be used to buy it after it has risen in value. Or, to put it another way, if the firm has future obligations that are expressed in foreign currency units, its risk exposure is from the potential rise in the value of those units.

To illustrate: On September 1, 1978, the INT Corporation made a purchase of goods from a foreign firm that will require the payment of LC 380,000 on December 1, 1978. The corporation wishes to make definite the amount of dollars it will need to pay the LC 380,000 on that date. The foreign firm is in a country whose currency has been rising in relation to the dollar in recent years. The tax rate in both countries is 40 percent. The observed pattern of foreign exchange rates is as follows:

	September 1, 1978
Spot rate of foreign currency units per $1	LC 2.10
Ninety-day forward rate	LC 2.00
	December 1, 1978
Expected future spot rate	LC 1.90

The INT Corporation considers the three alternatives discussed earlier to deal with the risk of exchange rate fluctuations. However, the *direction* of actions is now different. The first alternative is to enter the forward market to *buy* LC 380,000 for dollars at the ninety-day forward rate in effect on September 1, 1978. The corporation can then utilize the LC 380,000 it will receive under the forward contract on December 1, 1978, to meet the obligations it has incurred to make a payment of LC 380,000 on that date.

The second alternative is to borrow an amount in dollars to exchange into LCs to buy foreign securities that, with interest, will equal LC 380,000 on December 1, 1978. The interest rate paid in the United States is 12 percent; the interest earned in the foreign country is 8 percent.

The third alternative is to make no attempt to cover the risk involved in waiting for three months to pay the foreign currency obligation in the amount of LC 380,000. Under this alternative, the corporation will need sufficient dollars to equal LC 380,000 at whatever spot rate prevails on December 1, 1978.

The effects of the three alternatives can be analyzed. The first alternative involves entering a forward contract in which the INT Corporation buys LC 380,000 for dollars at a rate of LC 2 to $1. Therefore, the corporation will spend $190,000 to meet the future foreign currency obligation in the amount of LC 380,000. At the spot rate, it would have had to make a payment of 380,000 divided by 2.10, or $180,952, which is $9,048 less than the $190,000. This increase in expenses represents a tax shelter, at the 40 percent tax rate, of $3,619. The $190,000 expended on the forward contract minus the tax shelter of $3,619 is equal to $186,381, which represents the net after-tax costs of meeting the foreign currency obligation of LC 380,000 due on December 1, 1978.

Under the second alternative, the INT Corporation borrows dollars from a bank in the United States in an amount which, with foreign income, will total LC 380,000 when the foreign obligation becomes due on December 1, 1978. The amount it borrows is:

$$(2.10) \ (1 + [0.08 \div 4]0.6)X = LC \ 380,000$$
$$(2.10) \ (1.012)X = LC \ 380,000$$
$$2.1252X = LC \ 380,000$$
$$X = \$178,807.$$

Adding the interest expense, the total cost is 1.018 ($178,807) = $182,025.

Under the third alternative, on December 1, 1978, the LC 380,000 will be obtained by the use of dollars converted into the foreign currency at the spot rate then in effect. This will represent LC 380,000 divided by 1.90, or $200,000. However, under the September 1 spot rate, INT Corporation will have needed a dollar outlay of only $180,952 (LC 380,000 divided by 2.10). Therefore, the firm will have incurred an opportunity loss of $19,048, which will result in a tax shelter of 0.4($19,048), or $7,619.20. Hence, the after-tax costs are $192,381.

The amount of dollars to be paid under the three alternatives are:

1. Buy LC in forward market $186,381
2. Borrow in the United States and invest in foreign country 182,025
3. Pay dollars for LC based on expected future spot rate 192,381

Under the assumptions of this example, the second alternative involves the smallest outlay in dollars to meet the LC 380,000 obligation due on December 1, 1978. The dollars that will have to be paid under the first and second alternatives are certain; under the third alternative, the total proceeds are uncertain. Before the fact, it is not possible to state definitely which alternative will cost the least amount of dollars to meet the obligation due on December 1, 1978. It depends on the future level of the spot rate on that date. For example, suppose that the actual spot rate on December 1 turns out to be exactly what it was on September 1. In that case the net cost of using the third alternative for arranging to meet the future LC obligation will be dollars based on the December 1, 1978, spot rate of LC 2.10— $180,952.

The third alternative is best here, while under the original assumptions it was the worst. But taking no protective action is clearly the riskiest method.

Monetary Balance

Firms must take protective actions not only in regard to future expected receipts or obligations but also against a long or short position in foreign currencies resulting from the balance sheet position of their foreign subsidiaries. In the example of USP Company, the sale of the goods for LC 380,000 represented an accounts receivable for the three months until the obligation was paid. Suppose, however, that the number of LCs per $1 had risen from 1.90 to 2.00. At 1.90 LCs per $1, the accounts receivable would have been worth $200,000 in U.S. currency. But at the lower value of the LCs, 2 LC to $1, the accounts receivable would have been worth only $190,000. This represents a before-tax loss of $10,000 in the dollar value of the receivables.

Conversely, in the INT Corporation example, the firm had an accounts payable of LC 380,000. If the change in the LC value had been an upward one, from LC 2.00 to LC 1.90 per $1, the firm would have had a loss because the accounts payable expressed in dollars would have increased by $10,000. Hence the concept of monetary balance comes into consideration. *Monetary balance* involves avoiding either a net receivable or a net payable position. Monetary assets and liabilities are those items whose value, expressed in local currency, does not change with devaluation or revaluation. To illustrate:

Monetary Assets	Monetary Liabilities
Cash	Accounts payable
Marketable securities	Notes payable
Accounts receivable	Tax liability reserve
Tax refunds receivable	Bonds
Notes receivable	Preferred stock
Prepaid insurance	

What is referred to as a firm's monetary position is another way of stating the firm's position with regard to real assets. For example, the basic balance sheet equation can be written as follows:

Monetary assets + Real assets = Monetary liabilities + Net worth.

Consider the following pattern of relationships:

	Monetary Assets	+	Real Assets	=	Monetary Liabilities	+	Net Worth
Firm A: Monetary creditor	$6,000		$4,000		$4,000		$6,000
Firm B: Monetary debtor	4,000		6,000		6,000		4,000

Firm A is a monetary creditor because its monetary assets exceed its monetary liabilities; its net worth position is negative with respect to its investment coverage of net worth by real assets. In contrast, Firm B is a monetary debtor because it has monetary liabilities that exceed its monetary assets; its net worth coverage by investment in real assets is positive. Thus the monetary creditor can be referred to as a firm with a negative position in real assets and the monetary debtor as a firm with a positive position in real assets. From the foregoing we can see that the following relationships are equivalent:

Firm A	(Long position in foreign currency)	≡	Monetary creditor	≡	Monetary assets exceed monetary liabilities	≡	Negative position in real assets	≡	Balance of receipts in foreign currency less obligations in foreign currency is *positive*

Firm B	(Short position in foreign currency)	≡	Monetary debtor	≡	Monetary liabilities exceed monetary assets	≡	Positive position in real assets	≡	Balance of receipts in foreign currency less obligations in foreign currency is *negative*

Thus, if Firm A has a long position in a foreign currency, on balance it will be receiving more funds in foreign currency, or it will have a net monetary asset position that exceeds its monetary liabilities in that currency. The opposite holds for Firm B, which is in a short position with respect to a foreign currency. Hence the analysis with respect to a firm with net future receipts or net future obligations can be applied also to a firm's balance sheet position. A firm with net receipts is a net monetary creditor. Its foreign exchange rate risk exposure is having a net receipts position in a foreign currency that is vulnerable to a decline in value.

Conversely, a firm with future net obligations in foreign currency is in a net monetary debtor position. The foreign exchange risk exposure it faces is the possibility of an increase in the value of the foreign currency. The alternative methods of protection against foreign exchange fluctuations discussed earlier apply to the short or long balance sheet position a firm may have with respect to foreign currency.

In addition to the specific actions of hedging in the forward market or borrowing and lending through the money markets, other business policies can help the firm achieve a balance sheet position that minimizes the foreign exchange rate risk exposure to either currency devaluation or currency revaluation upward. Specifically, in countries whose currency values are likely to fall, local management of subsidiaries should be encouraged to follow these policies:

1. Never have excessive idle cash on hand. If cash accumulates, it should be used to purchase inventory or other real assets.
2. Attempt to avoid granting excessive trade credit or trade credit for extended periods. If accounts receivable cannot be avoided, an attempt should be made to charge interest high enough to compensate for the loss of purchasing power.
3. Wherever possible, avoid giving advances in connection with purchase orders unless a rate of interest is paid by the seller on these advances from the time the subsidiary—the buyer—pays them until the time of delivery, at a rate sufficient to cover the loss of purchasing power.
4. Borrow local currency funds from banks or other sources whenever these funds can be obtained at a rate of interest no higher than U.S. rates adjusted for the anticipated rate of devaluation in the foreign country.

5. Make an effort to purchase materials and supplies on a trade credit basis in the country in which the foreign subsidiary is operating, extending the final date of payment as long as possible.

The opposite policies should be followed in a country where a revaluation upward in foreign currency values is likely to take place. All these policies are aimed at a monetary balance position in which the firm is neither a monetary debtor nor a monetary creditor. Some firms take a more aggressive position. They seek to have a net monetary debtor position in a country whose exchange rates are expected to fall and a net monetary creditor position in a country whose exchange rates are likely to rise. Since exchange rate risk protection, as well as the conduct of international operations, requires international financing, this topic is considered next.

International Financing

The general principles affecting financing decisions are the same for international financing as for domestic financing. However, the variables affecting international financing decisions are expanded, and the number of financing methods and sources are increased. The forms and sources of financing are similar in the different countries of the world, but important differences provide new pitfalls and additional opportunities. A wider range of alternatives must be evaluated in both quantitative and qualitative terms in choosing among alternative sources, forms, and localities of international financing. Financing in an international setting makes use of the increasingly important international financing markets—the Eurocurrency and Eurobond markets. The facilities of private lending institutions are augmented substantially by international lending agencies, national development banks, and other government agencies performing important functions in financing operations and projects.

Some financing operations are distinctive to international business finance. A form of commercial bank financing widely used in Europe is represented by overdrafts. An overdraft agreement permits a customer to draw checks up to some specified maximum limit in excess of the checking account balance. In contrast to U.S. practice, European overdrafts are provided for in previous loan agreements and have widespread use in normal banking relations.

Another form of financing—one that was until recent years much more widespread in Europe than in the United States—is the use of discounting "trade bills" in both domestic and foreign transactions. The increased use of banker's acceptances in the United States has been associated with the growth of the movement of goods in international trade.

A third variation from U.S. financing practices found in Europe is the broad participation of commercial banks in medium- and long-term lending activities. In Europe, commercial banks carry on considerable activities of the kind that would be described as investment banking operations in the United States. This difference results from a legal requirement in the United States. The Banking Act of 1933 required the divestiture of investment banking operations by commercial banks.

A fourth practice distinctive to international financing relates to arbi-loans and link financing, both of which represent forms of equalizing the supply of and demand for loanable funds in relation to sensitive interest rate levels among different countries. Under arbi-loans, or international interest arbitrage financing, a borrower obtains loans in a country where the supply of funds is relatively abundant. The borrowed funds are then converted into another foreign currency needed by the firm. Simultaneously, the borrower enters into a forward exchange contract to protect itself on the reconversion of the new foreign currency into the original foreign currency that will be required at the time the loan must be repaid. Commercial banks are typically involved in arbi-loan transactions both as lenders and as intermediaries in the foreign exchange trading.

In link financing the commercial banks take an even more direct role. A lender bank in the U.S., for example, deposits funds with a bank in Mexico, the borrower's country, where interest rates are higher. This deposit may be earmarked for the specified borrower. The lender, of course, is expected to hedge its position in the foreign exchange markets, since it will be repaid in the currency of the country in which the bank deposit was made. The U.S. bank receives a rate that provides an interest differential after all additional expenses, such as the cost of hedging, are taken into consideration. The Mexican bank receives a commission for handling the transaction.

Expanding Role of U.S. Commercial Banks and Investment Bankers

Commercial banks have long performed an important role in export and import financing. They have increased the number of their foreign branches and have expanded their foreign operations and lending activities. They have also participated in consortiums with foreign merchant banks (banks that specialize in business lending) and investment banks for the conduct of all forms of international financing services.

Through their Edge Act corporations, by which they can make equity investments, commercial banks have participated for many years in the financing of international operations. Edge Act subsidiaries were provided for by amendments in 1916 and 1919 to the Federal Reserve Act of 1913. The amendments give U.S. commercial banks the authority to enter international markets and engage in certain operations that are prohibited in the United States. Edge Act subsidiaries can conduct all forms of international banking; they can issue or confirm letters of credit, finance foreign trade, engage in spot and foreign exchange transactions, and so on. Through these foreign banking subsidiaries and affiliates, direct investments in the form of both debt and equity can be made in commercial and industrial firms.

U.S. investment banking firms have actively participated in arranging Eurocurrency financing, mainly for their U.S. customers. They have developed joint participation activities with foreign merchant banks and with foreign investment banking houses. They have established offices in foreign countries and have participated in international underwriting groups that have developed the Eurobond market.

Commerical banks have become especially active in international project financing. This type of financing involves large investment projects, usually joint ventures between government and private enterprise that are financed by international and government sources as well as by private sources, often through a Eurodollar bank syndicate. International project financing is characterized by large investments for development activities such as the opening of a new mine, major drilling or exploration, or the establishment of a major chemical or pharmaceutical complex. Normally there is more than one major equity owner of the project company itself. The equity owners collectively possess or arrange for the requisite operating, technical, marketing, and financial strengths needed for the project's success.

International project financing generally involves relatively high debt leverage. Since the projects provide output for international markets, debt is issued in several currencies. The sources of debt are commercial banks, export credit agencies, suppliers, product purchasers, international lending agencies, regional or national development banks, and local governments.

International investment bankers serve as project financial advisers, fitting together the various types of financing needed to meet the project's requirements. Each transaction typically includes various covenants related directly to the characteristics of the project.[1]

The Eurodollar System

The Eurodollar system, which operates as an international money market, was developed in the early 1950s as banks accepted interest-bearing deposits and currencies other than their own. Most of the early activity occurred in Europe, where the predominant foreign currency used was the dollar (whose stability gave it the status of an international currency). Since the system is now worldwide, including many different currencies, it is often called the Eurocurrency system.

The flow process of the Eurodollar market can be illustrated as follows. A European firm holds a dollar deposit in a New York bank. It can hold the dollars in the form of a dollar deposit claim on its European bank by drawing a check on the New York bank and making a deposit in the European

---

1. For a more complete discussion, see Robert L. Huston, "Project Financing," in *Treasurer's Handbook*, ed. J. Fred Weston and M. G. Goudzwaard (Homewood, Ill.: Dow Jones–Irwin, 1976).

bank. The European bank can in turn make loans to other customers. Except for holding fractional reserves against its dollar deposit liabilities, the European bank has served as an intermediary in transferring the dollar balances in the United States from its depositors to its borrowers. Yet, its depositors still hold claims in dollars.

The Eurobanks, including the foreign branches of many U.S. banks, accept Eurodollar deposits and loan out these funds. The transactions involve large amounts, and the spread between the interest rates on loans and the interest paid on deposits is usually small. This is a fast-action market in which most transactions are arranged over the phone or through cables, with the confirming documents sent later by mail.

Eurodollar loans are typically in multiples of $1 million and have maturities ranging from thirty days to five to seven years. If the borrower is known to the bank, a loan of less than a year can be arranged quickly. Eurodollar loans are typically unsecured, but there may be restrictions of other kinds placed on the borrowing activities of the firm receiving the loan. One form of Eurodollar loan is the floating rate revolving loan, sometimes referred to as a revolver or a roll-over credit. The rate on the loan is quoted as the percentage above the London interbank offer rate (LIBO), and it reflects the rates on liquid funds that move among the money markets of the developed nations. The floating rate provision dampens borrowing based on speculation on future interest rates. Prime borrowers typically pay from three-fourths of 1 percent over the LIBO (for seven to eight year maturities) to three-eighths of 1 percent over the LIBO (for five-year maturities). Lines of credit are typically established for a given period not to exceed twelve months and can be renegotiated at the end of the period. There is usually a commitment fee of one-fourth of 1 percent to one-half of 1 percent on the unused portion of the line of credit. The Eurocurrency system contributes to increasing and redistributing the world supply of international reserves or liquid resources. It represents an important addition to the development of a competitive and unified international money market.

Eurobonds represent the longer-term range of maturities in the Eurocurrency market. They are offered for sale in more than one country through international syndicates of underwriting and selling banks, and they are typically denominated in a strong currency, such as the German mark. The U.S. dollar continues to be used despite fluctuations in its value because it is a principal transaction currency. A large pool of Eurodollars is also available. Sometimes Eurobonds are denominated for repayment in multiple currencies. The creditor can request payment of the interest and principal in any predetermined currency at a previously established parity.

Convertible Eurobonds were stimulated by the entry of U.S. firms into financing through the Eurobond market. The convertible Eurobonds of U.S. firms have the advantage of carrying relatively low interest rates. Also, the market is broad so that larger amounts can be sold. This represents a method of internationalizing the ownership of the common stock of U.S. multi-national corporations that have large direct investments and operations in foreign countries. For the foreign investors the convertible Eurobonds have the advantage of a fixed rate of interest plus potential capital gains.

The Eurobond market has helped internationalize the local character of the capital markets in individual European countries by underwriting the sales of their securities to investors in a number of European countries. The market contributes to the international financial adjustment process by stimulating the outflow of funds from countries with balance of payments surpluses (such as Germany).

Working Capital Management in International Enterprise

International cash management involves minimizing the exposure of foreign-located funds to foreign exchange rate risk and avoiding prohibitions on the movement of funds from one country to another. Funds denominated in a foreign currency, particularly that of developing countries, are potentially subject to a decrease in value in terms of the home currency. The financial manager who hopes to avoid foreign exchange rate risk and prohibitions against the international movement of funds must continually assess political and economic trends in the countries of operation in order to anticipate changes that can have a detrimental effect.

The general principles that apply to the management of cash on an international basis are very similar to those used successfully by many firms on a domestic basis. Multinational firms try to speed up the collection of cash by having bank accounts in the banking system of each country. In many countries, customers pay their bills by requesting their bank or postal administration to deduct the amount owed from their account and to transfer it to the other firm's account.

Multinational commercial banks, particularly those that have branches or affiliates in a large number of countries, can be very helpful to multinational firms. Several of the larger U.S. multinational commercial banks have foreign departments whose sole purpose is to help U.S. multinational firms solve their problems of international cash management. An international bank can speed the flow of funds of a multinational firm and thereby decrease the exposure of these funds to foreign exchange rate risk. It can suggest the routing of the transfers as well as the national currency to be used. While in the United States the average time between the initiation and completion of a financial transaction is two to three days, the time interval for foreign transactions can be as long as two or three weeks. The long delays tie up large amounts of funds unnecessarily and should be avoided. In this area, the multinational commercial banks are particularly helpful, since they can transfer funds from one country to another (providing government restrictions do not interfere) on a same-day basis if they have branches or affiliates in the two countries involved.

Increasingly, the arena for business finance is the global market. At the start of each day, the corporate treasurer determines whether to borrow or to lend in the international financial market. The investment decisions are made in both domestic and foreign countries.

The financial manager of the multinational corporate enterprise must consider the form and extent of protection against currency fluctuations on sales and purchases. If the firm has surplus cash, the financial manager must compare the returns from investing in the domestic money market with those from investing in the international market. Similarly, if short-term financing needs arise, the manager must make comparisons between domestic and foreign financing sources. Among the considerations are the advantages and disadvantages of using the impersonal international financial markets versus those of developing long-term financing relations with international commercial banks or financial groups in the U.S., London, Paris, Zurich, Bonn, and Tokyo.

Summary

A firm generally develops its international activities through an evolutionary process. First, it needs to develop a strong competitive product for domestic sales. Then it may start to export through a broker. When foreign sales increase, it may open a foreign branch sales office. Finally, it may establish a wholly-owned manufacturing plant or subsidiary in the foreign country. If the foreign government places restrictions on foreign investments or imports, licensing or joint ventures may be the only feasible ways of doing business in the foreign country.

International business transactions are conducted in more than one currency. If a firm is expecting receipts in foreign currency units, its risk is that the value of the foreign currency units will fall. If it has obligations to be paid in foreign currency units, its risk is that the value of the foreign currency will rise. To reduce foreign exchange risk, firms can engage in transactions in the forward foreign exchange market. They can also borrow at current spot exchange rates the amount of local currency needed for future transactions. These two forms of hedging are essentially insurance and therefore involve costs.

Firms also take protective action against long or short positions in foreign currencies resulting from the balance sheet position of their foreign subsidiaries. Monetary assets and liabilities are those items whose value, expressed in local currency, does not change with devaluation or revaluation. A firm seeks to have a net monetary creditor position in a country whose exchange rates are expected to rise and a net monetary debtor position in a country whose exchange rates are expected to fall. A monetary debtor position can be created by investing all excess cash, granting as little trade credit as possible, avoiding advances, and borrowing funds. A monetary creditor position can be developed by holding cash or cash equivalents, such as foreign securities, and by having receivables due in the foreign currency.

International financing broadens the range of fund sources. These sources include international and government institutions, Eurocurrency and Eurobond markets, overdrafts from European banks, discounted trade bills, and arbi-loans and link financing. Edge Act subsidiaries permit commercial banks to enter international markets and engage in operations from which they are prohibited in the United States. U.S. commercial banks and investment banking firms have become very active in international financing and related services.

International cash management involves minimizing exposure of foreign-located funds to exchange rate risks and avoiding restrictions on the movement of funds from one country to another. International banks provide many services that facilitate effective international working capital management by multinational firms.

Questions

26.1 What has been the impact of advances in the technology of transportation and communication on international trade and finance?

26.2 Why is the ratio of foreign earnings to a firm's total earnings likely to be greater than the ratio of its foreign sales to total sales?

26.3 If a firm has difficulty developing a product that will sell in the local domestic market, is it likely to have greater success in a foreign market? Explain.

26.4 What are the advantages and disadvantages to a firm of licensing the production of its products to foreign firms?

26.5 What are the pros and cons of engaging in a joint venture rather than establishing a wholly-owned foreign subsidiary?

26.6 What are monetary assets and liabilities (as contrasted with "real" or non-monetary assets and liabilities)?

26.7 What are arbi-loans and link financing?

26.8 What are some of the services provided by U.S. commercial banks to firms engaged in international operations or financing?

26.9 What are some of the services provided by U.S. investment banking firms to U.S. business firms engaged in international operations or financing?

26.10 What is the Eurocurrency system, and what economic functions does it perform?

26.11 Describe some major characteristics of Eurodollar loans.

26.12 In what respects are domestic working capital management and international working capital management similar and different?

26.13 What services can the multinational commercial bank perform to help the U.S. multinational operating firm solve its problems of international cash management?

26.14 What are some of the reasons that U.S. firms engage in financing abroad?

Problems

26.1 The Whitley Company's subsidiary has monetary assets of LC 800,000 and monetary liabilities of LC 1,000,000. Calculate the gain or loss of the parent under the following two states of the world:
   a. There has been a devaluation; the local currency has dropped from 20 LC per $1 to 25 LC per $1.
   b. There has been a revaluation; the local currency has appreciated from 20 LC per $1 to 15 LC per $1.

26.2 The Ravel Company exports a substantial amount of cosmetics each year and therefore has a great part of its assets invested in LC receivables. Monetary assets are LC 30,000,000, while monetary liabilities are LC 10,000,000. Calculate any gains or losses under the following two states of the world:
   a. There is a revaluation from 4 LC per $1 to 3 LC per $1.
   b. There is a devaluation from 4 LC per $1 to 5 LC per $1.

26.3 The Ajax Company's international transfer of funds amounts to about $2 million monthly. Presently the average transfer time is ten days. It has been proposed that the transfer of funds be turned over to one of the larger international banks, which can reduce the transfer time to an average of two days. A charge of one-half of 1 percent of the volume of transfer has been proposed for this service. In view of the fact that the firm's opportunity cost of funds is 12 percent, should this offer be accepted?

26.4 The MNC Corporation has a number of subsidiaries located in various Asian countries. These subsidiaries collect the equivalent of $500,000 each month, and the funds are transferred to the company's cash center in Hong Kong. The average transfer time has been fourteen days. An international bank, eager to solicit business from MNC, has offered to handle the transfer of these funds at a guaranteed average transfer time of not more than two days. The company's opportunity cost is 15 percent.
   a. How much is this service worth to the company?
   b. What are the advantages and disadvantages of the arrangement?

26.5 Davidson International's principal manufacturing plant in Europe is located in Paris. In-transfer and temporarily idle funds have been routed to and through this office. However, since forward market quotations on the French franc have been weakening lately, the manager of the international division is planning to reroute temporarily idle cash funds to the office of the company's German subsidiary. The company has been protecting itself by entering into forward ninety-day contracts to purchase dollars with French francs at an annual discount of 5 to 6 percent. By comparison, ninety-day forward contracts can be obtained to buy dollars with West German marks at a premium in relation to the present spot rate of 1.5 percent. Short-term interest rates in France are 7.5 percent and in West Germany approximately 7 percent.

   a. Should West Germany become the transfer center of the firm's international funds flow? What would be the cost or benefit of any change that might be suggested?

   b. What requirements for an international financial center are considered important in locating a cash concentration center in a particular city? Why?

26.6 The Kory Company has made a sale of construction equipment to a foreign firm and will receive LC 11,000,000 on May 31, 1979. The company has incurred all its expenses in dollars and needs to know the definite dollar amounts that it will receive on May 31, 1979. The effective tax rate in both countries is 40 percent, and the expected future spot rate is 12 LC per dollar. The director of finance at Kory Company is considering three options to deal with the foreign exchange risk:

   a. To enter the forward market to sell LC 11,000,000 for dollars at the ninety-day forward rate quoted on March 1, 1979, which is 11 LC per dollar. Under this arrangement the Kory Company will receive a definite amount in dollars in May as determined by the forward rate on March 1, 1979.

   b. To borrow on March 1, 1979, from a foreign bank an amount in local currency (LC) plus interest that will equal the amount the Kory Company will be receiving on May 31, 1979. The interest rate on the loan would be 32 percent. By borrowing, the company will receive LCs and, with the LCs received, can immediately purchase dollars at the March 1, 1979, spot rate, which is LC 10 per dollar. The dollars received can be invested in the United States at an interest rate of 12 percent. When the company receives the LC 11,000,000 on May 31, 1979, it can liquidate the local currency loan plus interest.

   c. To make no attempt to cover the exchange risk involved in waiting the three months for receipt of the LC 11,000,000. Under the third alternative the company will convert the LC 11,000,000 into dollars at the spot rate of LC 12 per dollar that is expected to prevail on May 31, 1979.

   Which alternative should be chosen?

26.7 Rework Problem 26.6 assuming a foreign interest rate of 60 percent. Which alternative is the most attractive now? Explain.

26.8 On March 1, 1979, the Burrows Company bought from a foreign firm electronic equipment that will require the payment of LC 900,000 on May 31, 1979. The spot rate on March 1, 1979, is LC 10 per dollar; the expected future spot rate is LC 8 per dollar; and the ninety-day forward rate is LC 9 per dollar. The U.S. interest rate is 12 percent, and the foreign interest rate is 8 percent. The tax rate for both countries is 40 percent. The Burrows Company is considering three alternatives to deal with the risk of exchange rate fluctuations:

   a. To enter the forward market to buy LC 900,000 at the ninety-day forward rate in effect on May 31, 1979.

b. To borrow an amount in dollars to buy the LC at the current spot rate. This money is to be invested in government securities of the foreign country; with the interest income, it will equal LC 900,000 on May 31, 1979.

c. To wait until May 31, 1979, and buy LCs at whatever spot rate prevails at that time.

Which alternative should the Burrows Company follow in order to minimize its cost of meeting the future payment in LCs? Explain.

APPENDIX A INTEREST TABLES

Table A.1
Compound Sum of $1:
$$CVIF = (1 + r)^N$$

Period	1%	2%	3%	4%	5%	6%	7%	8%	9%	10%	12%	14%	15%	16%	18%	20%	24%	28%	32%	36%
1	1.0100	1.0200	1.0300	1.0400	1.0500	1.0600	1.0700	1.0800	1.0900	1.1000	1.1200	1.1400	1.1500	1.1600	1.1800	1.2000	1.2400	1.2800	1.3200	1.3600
2	1.0201	1.0404	1.0609	1.0816	1.1025	1.1236	1.1449	1.1664	1.1881	1.2100	1.2544	1.2996	1.3225	1.3456	1.3924	1.4400	1.5376	1.6384	1.7424	1.8496
3	1.0303	1.0612	1.0927	1.1249	1.1576	1.1910	1.2250	1.2597	1.2950	1.3310	1.4049	1.4815	1.5209	1.5609	1.6430	1.7280	1.9066	2.0972	2.3000	2.5155
4	1.0406	1.0824	1.1255	1.1699	1.2155	1.2625	1.3108	1.3605	1.4116	1.4641	1.5735	1.6890	1.7490	1.8106	1.9388	2.0736	2.3642	2.6844	3.0360	3.4210
5	1.0510	1.1041	1.1593	1.2167	1.2763	1.3382	1.4026	1.4693	1.5386	1.6105	1.7623	1.9254	2.0114	2.1003	2.2878	2.4883	2.9316	3.4360	4.0075	4.6526
6	1.0615	1.1262	1.1941	1.2653	1.3401	1.4185	1.5007	1.5869	1.6771	1.7716	1.9738	2.1950	2.3131	2.4364	2.6996	2.9860	3.6352	4.3980	5.2899	6.3275
7	1.0721	1.1487	1.2299	1.3159	1.4071	1.5036	1.6058	1.7138	1.8280	1.9487	2.2107	2.5023	2.6600	2.8262	3.1855	3.5832	4.5077	5.6295	6.9826	8.6054
8	1.0829	1.1717	1.2668	1.3686	1.4775	1.5938	1.7182	1.8509	1.9926	2.1436	2.4760	2.8526	3.0590	3.2784	3.7589	4.2998	5.5895	7.2058	9.2170	11.703
9	1.0937	1.1951	1.3048	1.4233	1.5513	1.6895	1.8385	1.9990	2.1719	2.3579	2.7731	3.2519	3.5179	3.8030	4.4355	5.1598	6.9310	9.2234	12.166	15.916
10	1.1046	1.2190	1.3439	1.4802	1.6289	1.7908	1.9672	2.1589	2.3674	2.5937	3.1058	3.7072	4.0456	4.4114	5.2338	6.1917	8.5944	11.805	16.059	21.646
11	1.1157	1.2434	1.3842	1.5395	1.7103	1.8983	2.1049	2.3316	2.5804	2.8531	3.4785	4.2262	4.6524	5.1173	6.1759	7.4301	10.657	15.111	21.198	29.439
12	1.1268	1.2682	1.4258	1.6010	1.7959	2.0122	2.2522	2.5182	2.8127	3.1384	3.8960	4.8179	5.3502	5.9360	7.2876	8.9161	13.214	19.342	27.982	40.037
13	1.1381	1.2936	1.4685	1.6651	1.8856	2.1329	2.4098	2.7196	3.0658	3.4523	4.3635	5.4924	6.1528	6.8858	8.5994	10.699	16.386	24.758	36.937	54.451
14	1.1495	1.3195	1.5126	1.7317	1.9799	2.2609	2.5785	2.9372	3.3417	3.7975	4.8871	6.2613	7.0757	7.9875	10.147	12.839	20.319	31.691	48.756	74.053
15	1.1610	1.3459	1.5580	1.8009	2.0789	2.3966	2.7590	3.1722	3.6425	4.1772	5.4736	7.1379	8.1371	9.2655	11.973	15.407	25.195	40.564	64.358	100.71
16	1.1726	1.3728	1.6047	1.8730	2.1829	2.5404	2.9522	3.4259	3.9703	4.5950	6.1304	8.1372	9.3576	10.748	14.129	18.488	31.242	51.923	84.953	136.96
17	1.1843	1.4002	1.6528	1.9479	2.2920	2.6928	3.1588	3.7000	4.3276	5.0545	6.8660	9.2765	10.761	12.467	16.672	22.186	38.740	66.461	112.13	186.27
18	1.1961	1.4282	1.7024	2.0258	2.4066	2.8543	3.3799	3.9960	4.7171	5.5599	7.6900	10.575	12.375	14.462	19.673	26.623	48.038	85.070	148.02	253.33
19	1.2081	1.4568	1.7535	2.1068	2.5270	3.0256	3.6165	4.3157	5.1417	6.1159	8.6128	12.055	14.231	16.776	23.214	31.948	59.567	108.89	195.39	344.53
20	1.2202	1.4859	1.8061	2.1911	2.6533	3.2071	3.8697	4.6610	5.6044	6.7275	9.6463	13.743	16.366	19.460	27.393	38.337	73.864	139.37	257.91	468.57
21	1.2324	1.5157	1.8603	2.2788	2.7860	3.3996	4.1406	5.0338	6.1088	7.4002	10.803	15.667	18.821	22.574	32.323	46.005	91.591	178.40	340.44	637.26
22	1.2447	1.5460	1.9161	2.3699	2.9253	3.6035	4.4304	5.4365	6.6586	8.1403	12.100	17.861	21.644	26.186	38.142	55.206	113.57	228.35	449.39	866.67
23	1.2572	1.5769	1.9736	2.4647	3.0715	3.8197	4.7405	5.8715	7.2579	8.9543	13.552	20.361	24.891	30.376	45.007	66.247	140.83	292.30	593.19	1178.6
24	1.2697	1.6084	2.0328	2.5633	3.2251	4.0489	5.0724	6.3412	7.9111	9.8497	15.178	23.212	28.625	35.236	53.108	79.496	174.63	374.14	783.02	1602.9
25	1.2824	1.6406	2.0938	2.6658	3.3864	4.2919	5.4274	6.8485	8.6231	10.834	17.000	26.461	32.918	40.874	62.668	95.396	216.54	478.90	1033.5	2180.0
26	1.2953	1.6734	2.1566	2.7725	3.5557	4.5494	5.8074	7.3964	9.3992	11.918	19.040	30.166	37.856	47.414	73.948	114.47	268.51	612.99	1364.3	2964.9
27	1.3082	1.7069	2.2213	2.8834	3.7335	4.8223	6.2139	7.9881	10.245	13.110	21.324	34.389	43.535	55.000	87.259	137.37	332.95	784.63	1800.9	4032.2
28	1.3213	1.7410	2.2879	2.9987	3.9201	5.1117	6.6488	8.6271	11.167	14.421	23.883	39.204	50.065	63.800	102.96	164.84	412.86	1004.3	2377.2	5483.8
29	1.3345	1.7758	2.3566	3.1187	4.1161	5.4184	7.1143	9.3173	12.172	15.863	26.749	44.693	57.575	74.008	121.50	197.81	511.95	1285.5	3137.9	7458.0
30	1.3478	1.8114	2.4273	3.2434	4.3219	5.7435	7.6123	10.062	13.267	17.449	29.959	50.950	66.211	85.849	143.37	237.37	634.81	1645.5	4142.0	10143.
40	1.4889	2.2080	3.2620	4.8010	7.0400	10.285	14.974	21.724	31.409	45.259	93.050	188.88	267.86	378.72	750.37	1469.7	5455.9	19426.	66520.	*
50	1.6446	2.6916	4.3839	7.1067	11.467	18.420	29.457	46.901	74.357	117.39	289.00	700.23	1083.6	1670.7	3927.3	9100.4	46890.	*	*	*
60	1.8167	3.2810	5.8916	10.519	18.679	32.987	57.946	101.25	176.03	304.48	897.59	2595.9	4383.9	7370.1	20555.	56347.	*	*	*	*

*FVIF > 99,999.

Table A.2
Present Value of $1:
$PVIF = (1 + r)^{-N}$

Period	1%	2%	3%	4%	5%	6%	7%	8%	9%	10%	12%	14%	15%	16%	18%	20%	24%	28%	32%	36%
1	.9901	.9804	.9709	.9615	.9524	.9434	.9346	.9259	.9174	.9091	.8929	.8772	.8696	.8621	.8475	.8333	.8065	.7813	.7576	.7353
2	.9803	.9612	.9426	.9246	.9070	.8900	.8734	.8573	.8417	.8264	.7972	.7695	.7561	.7432	.7182	.6944	.6504	.6104	.5739	.5407
3	.9706	.9423	.9151	.8890	.8638	.8396	.8163	.7938	.7722	.7513	.7118	.6750	.6575	.6407	.6086	.5787	.5245	.4768	.4348	.3975
4	.9610	.9238	.8885	.8548	.8227	.7921	.7629	.7350	.7084	.6830	.6355	.5921	.5718	.5523	.5158	.4823	.4230	.3725	.3294	.2923
5	.9515	.9057	.8626	.8219	.7835	.7473	.7130	.6806	.6499	.6209	.5674	.5194	.4972	.4761	.4371	.4019	.3411	.2910	.2495	.2149
6	.9420	.8880	.8375	.7903	.7462	.7050	.6663	.6302	.5963	.5645	.5066	.4556	.4323	.4104	.3704	.3349	.2751	.2274	.1890	.1580
7	.9327	.8706	.8131	.7599	.7107	.6651	.6227	.5835	.5470	.5132	.4523	.3996	.3759	.3538	.3139	.2791	.2218	.1776	.1432	.1162
8	.9235	.8535	.7894	.7307	.6768	.6274	.5820	.5403	.5019	.4665	.4039	.3506	.3269	.3050	.2660	.2326	.1789	.1388	.1085	.0854
9	.9143	.8368	.7664	.7026	.6446	.5919	.5439	.5002	.4604	.4241	.3606	.3075	.2843	.2630	.2255	.1938	.1443	.1084	.0822	.0628
10	.9053	.8203	.7441	.6756	.6139	.5584	.5083	.4632	.4224	.3855	.3220	.2697	.2472	.2267	.1911	.1615	.1164	.0847	.0623	.0462
11	.8963	.8043	.7224	.6496	.5847	.5268	.4751	.4289	.3875	.3505	.2875	.2366	.2149	.1954	.1619	.1346	.0938	.0662	.0472	.0340
12	.8874	.7885	.7014	.6246	.5568	.4970	.4440	.3971	.3555	.3186	.2567	.2076	.1869	.1685	.1372	.1122	.0757	.0517	.0357	.0250
13	.8787	.7730	.6810	.6006	.5303	.4688	.4150	.3677	.3262	.2897	.2292	.1821	.1625	.1452	.1163	.0935	.0610	.0404	.0271	.0184
14	.8700	.7579	.6611	.5775	.5051	.4423	.3878	.3405	.2992	.2633	.2046	.1597	.1413	.1252	.0985	.0779	.0492	.0316	.0205	.0135
15	.8613	.7430	.6419	.5553	.4810	.4173	.3624	.3152	.2745	.2394	.1827	.1401	.1229	.1079	.0835	.0649	.0397	.0247	.0155	.0099
16	.8528	.7284	.6232	.5339	.4581	.3936	.3387	.2919	.2519	.2176	.1631	.1229	.1069	.0930	.0708	.0541	.0320	.0193	.0118	.0073
17	.8444	.7142	.6050	.5134	.4363	.3714	.3166	.2703	.2311	.1978	.1456	.1078	.0929	.0802	.0600	.0451	.0258	.0150	.0089	.0054
18	.8360	.7002	.5874	.4936	.4155	.3503	.2959	.2502	.2120	.1799	.1300	.0946	.0808	.0691	.0508	.0376	.0208	.0118	.0068	.0039
19	.8277	.6864	.5703	.4746	.3957	.3305	.2765	.2317	.1945	.1635	.1161	.0829	.0703	.0596	.0431	.0313	.0168	.0092	.0051	.0029
20	.8195	.6730	.5537	.4564	.3769	.3118	.2584	.2145	.1784	.1486	.1037	.0728	.0611	.0514	.0365	.0261	.0135	.0072	.0039	.0021
25	.7798	.6095	.4776	.3751	.2953	.2330	.1842	.1460	.1160	.0923	.0588	.0378	.0304	.0245	.0160	.0105	.0046	.0021	.0010	.0005
30	.7419	.5521	.4120	.3083	.2314	.1741	.1314	.0994	.0754	.0573	.0334	.0196	.0151	.0116	.0070	.0042	.0016	.0006	.0002	.0001
40	.6717	.4529	.3066	.2083	.1420	.0972	.0668	.0460	.0318	.0221	.0107	.0053	.0037	.0026	.0013	.0007	.0002	.0001	*	*
50	.6080	.3715	.2281	.1407	.0872	.0543	.0339	.0213	.0134	.0085	.0035	.0014	.0009	.0006	.0003	.0001	*	*	*	*
60	.5504	.3048	.1697	.0951	.0535	.0303	.0173	.0099	.0057	.0033	.0011	.0004	.0002	.0001	*					

*The factor is zero to four decimal places.

Table A.3
Sum of an Annuity for $1 for N Years

$$CVIF_a = \frac{(1+r)^N - 1}{r}$$

Number of Periods	1%	2%	3%	4%	5%	6%	7%	8%	9%	10%	12%	14%	15%	16%	18%	20%	24%	28%	32%	36%
1	1.0000	1.0000	1.0000	1.0000	1.0000	1.0000	1.0000	1.0000	1.0000	1.0000	1.0000	1.0000	1.0000	1.0000	1.0000	1.0000	1.0000	1.0000	1.0000	1.0000
2	2.0100	2.0200	2.0300	2.0400	2.0500	2.0600	2.0700	2.0800	2.0900	2.1000	2.1200	2.1400	2.1500	2.1600	2.1800	2.2000	2.2400	2.2800	2.3200	2.3600
3	3.0301	3.0604	3.0909	3.1216	3.1525	3.1836	3.2149	3.2464	3.2781	3.3100	3.3744	3.4396	3.4725	3.5056	3.5724	3.6400	3.7776	3.9184	4.0624	4.2096
4	4.0604	4.1216	4.1836	4.2465	4.3101	4.3746	4.4399	4.5061	4.5731	4.6410	4.7793	4.9211	4.9934	5.0665	5.2154	5.3680	5.6842	6.0156	6.3624	6.7251
5	5.1010	5.2040	5.3091	5.4163	5.5256	5.6371	5.7507	5.8666	5.9847	6.1051	6.3528	6.6101	6.7424	6.8771	7.1542	7.4416	8.0484	8.6999	9.3983	10.146
6	6.1520	6.3081	6.4684	6.6330	6.8019	6.9753	7.1533	7.3359	7.5233	7.7156	8.1152	8.5355	8.7537	8.9775	9.4420	9.9299	10.980	12.135	13.405	14.798
7	7.2135	7.4343	7.6625	7.8983	8.1420	8.3938	8.6540	8.9228	9.2004	9.4872	10.089	10.730	11.066	11.413	12.141	12.915	14.615	16.533	18.695	21.126
8	8.2857	8.5830	8.8923	9.2142	9.5491	9.8975	10.259	10.636	11.028	11.435	12.299	13.232	13.726	14.240	15.327	16.499	19.122	22.163	25.678	29.731
9	9.3685	9.7546	10.159	10.582	11.026	11.491	11.978	12.487	13.021	13.579	14.775	16.085	16.785	17.518	19.085	20.798	24.712	29.369	34.895	41.435
10	10.462	10.949	11.463	12.006	12.577	13.180	13.816	14.486	15.192	15.937	17.548	19.337	20.303	21.321	23.521	25.958	31.643	38.592	47.061	57.351
11	11.566	12.168	12.807	13.486	14.206	14.971	15.783	16.645	17.560	18.531	20.654	23.044	24.349	25.732	28.755	32.150	40.237	50.398	63.121	78.998
12	12.682	13.412	14.192	15.025	15.917	16.869	17.888	18.977	20.140	21.384	24.133	27.270	29.001	30.850	34.931	39.580	50.894	65.510	84.320	108.43
13	13.809	14.680	15.617	16.626	17.713	18.882	20.140	21.495	22.953	24.522	28.029	32.088	34.351	36.786	42.218	48.496	64.109	84.852	112.30	148.47
14	14.947	15.973	17.086	18.291	19.598	21.015	22.550	24.214	26.019	27.975	32.392	37.581	40.504	43.672	50.818	59.195	80.496	109.61	149.23	202.92
15	16.096	17.293	18.598	20.023	21.578	23.276	25.129	27.152	29.360	31.772	37.279	43.842	47.580	51.659	60.965	72.035	100.81	141.30	197.99	276.97
16	17.257	18.639	20.156	21.824	23.657	25.672	27.888	30.324	33.003	35.949	42.753	50.980	55.717	60.925	72.939	87.442	126.01	181.86	262.35	377.69
17	18.430	20.012	21.761	23.697	25.840	28.212	30.840	33.750	36.973	40.544	48.883	59.117	65.075	71.673	87.068	105.93	157.25	233.79	347.30	514.66
18	19.614	21.412	23.414	25.645	28.132	30.905	33.999	37.450	41.301	45.599	55.749	68.394	75.836	84.140	103.74	128.11	195.99	300.25	459.44	700.93
19	20.810	22.840	25.116	27.671	30.539	33.760	37.379	41.446	46.018	51.159	63.439	78.969	88.211	98.603	123.41	154.74	244.03	385.32	607.47	954.27
20	22.019	24.297	26.870	29.778	33.066	36.785	40.995	45.762	51.160	57.275	72.052	91.024	102.44	115.37	146.62	186.68	303.60	494.21	802.86	1298.8
21	23.239	25.783	28.676	31.969	35.719	39.992	44.865	50.422	56.764	64.002	81.698	104.76	118.81	134.84	174.02	225.02	377.46	633.59	1060.7	1767.3
22	24.471	27.299	30.536	34.248	38.505	43.392	49.005	55.456	62.873	71.402	92.502	120.43	137.63	157.41	206.34	271.03	469.05	811.99	1401.2	2404.6
23	25.716	28.845	32.452	36.617	41.430	46.995	53.436	60.893	69.531	79.543	104.60	138.29	159.27	183.60	244.48	326.23	582.62	1040.3	1850.6	3271.3
24	26.973	30.421	34.426	39.082	44.502	50.815	58.176	66.764	76.789	88.497	118.15	158.65	184.16	213.97	289.49	392.48	723.46	1332.6	2443.8	4449.9
25	28.243	32.030	36.459	41.645	47.727	54.864	63.249	73.105	84.700	98.347	133.33	181.87	212.79	249.21	342.60	471.98	898.09	1706.8	3226.8	6052.9
26	29.525	33.670	38.553	44.311	51.113	59.156	68.676	79.954	93.323	109.18	150.33	208.33	245.71	290.08	405.27	567.37	1114.6	2185.7	4260.4	8233.0
27	30.820	35.344	40.709	47.084	54.669	63.705	74.483	87.350	102.72	121.09	169.37	238.49	283.56	337.50	479.22	681.85	1383.1	2798.7	5624.7	11197.9
28	32.129	37.051	42.930	49.967	58.402	68.528	80.697	95.338	112.96	134.20	190.69	272.88	327.10	392.50	566.48	819.22	1716.0	3583.3	7425.6	15230.2
29	33.450	38.792	45.218	52.966	62.322	73.639	87.346	103.96	124.13	148.63	214.58	312.09	377.16	456.30	669.44	984.06	2128.9	4587.6	9802.9	20714.1
30	34.784	40.568	47.575	56.084	66.438	79.058	94.460	113.28	136.30	164.49	241.33	356.78	434.74	530.31	790.94	1181.8	2640.9	5873.2	12940.	28172.2
40	48.886	60.402	75.401	95.025	120.79	154.76	199.63	259.05	337.88	442.59	767.09	1342.0	1779.0	2360.7	4163.2	7343.8	22728.	69377.	*	*
50	64.463	84.579	112.79	152.66	209.34	290.33	406.52	573.76	815.08	1163.9	2400.0	4994.5	7217.7	10435.	21813.	45497.	*	*	*	*
60	81.669	114.05	163.05	237.99	353.58	533.12	813.52	1253.2	1944.7	3034.8	7471.6	18535.	29219.	46057.	*	*	*	*	*	*

*CVIFA > 99,999

Table A.4
Present Value of $1 Received Annually:

$$PVIF_a = \frac{1 - (1 + r)^{-N}}{r}$$

Number of payments	1%	2%	3%	4%	5%	6%	7%	8%	9%	10%	12%	14%	15%	16%	18%	20%	24%	28%	32%
1	0.9901	0.9804	0.9709	0.9615	0.9524	0.9434	0.9346	0.9259	0.9174	0.9091	0.8929	0.8772	0.8696	0.8621	0.8475	0.8333	0.8065	0.7813	0.7576
2	1.9704	1.9416	1.9135	1.8861	1.8594	1.8334	1.8080	1.7833	1.7591	1.7355	1.6901	1.6467	1.6257	1.6052	1.5656	1.5278	1.4568	1.3916	1.3315
3	2.9410	2.8839	2.8286	2.7751	2.7232	2.6730	2.6243	2.5771	2.5313	2.4869	2.4018	2.3216	2.2832	2.2459	2.1743	2.1065	1.9813	1.8684	1.7663
4	3.9020	3.8077	3.7171	3.6299	3.5460	3.4651	3.3872	3.3121	3.2397	3.1699	3.0373	2.9137	2.8550	2.7982	2.6901	2.5887	2.4043	2.2410	2.0957
5	4.8534	4.7135	4.5797	4.4518	4.3295	4.2124	4.1002	3.9927	3.8897	3.7908	3.6048	3.4331	3.3522	3.2743	3.1272	2.9906	2.7454	2.5320	2.3452
6	5.7955	5.6014	5.4172	5.2421	5.0757	4.9173	4.7665	4.6229	4.4859	4.3553	4.1114	3.8887	3.7845	3.6847	3.4976	3.3255	3.0205	2.7594	2.5342
7	6.7282	6.4720	6.2303	6.0021	5.7864	5.5824	5.3893	5.2064	5.0330	4.8684	4.5638	4.2883	4.1604	4.0386	3.8115	3.6046	3.2423	2.9370	2.6775
8	7.6517	7.3255	7.0197	6.7327	6.4632	6.2098	5.9713	5.7466	5.5348	5.3349	4.9676	4.6389	4.4873	4.3436	4.0776	3.8372	3.4212	3.0758	2.7860
9	8.5660	8.1622	7.7861	7.4353	7.1078	6.8017	6.5152	6.2469	5.9952	5.7590	5.3282	4.9464	4.7716	4.6065	4.3030	4.0310	3.5655	3.1842	2.8681
10	9.4713	8.9826	8.5302	8.1109	7.7217	7.3601	7.0236	6.7101	6.4177	6.1446	5.6502	5.2161	5.0188	4.8332	4.4941	4.1925	3.6819	3.2689	2.9304
11	10.3676	9.7868	9.2526	8.7605	8.3064	7.8869	7.4987	7.1390	6.8052	6.4951	5.9377	5.4527	5.2337	5.0286	4.6560	4.3271	3.7757	3.3351	2.9776
12	11.2551	10.5753	9.9540	9.3851	8.8633	8.3838	7.9427	7.5361	7.1607	6.8137	6.1944	5.6603	5.4206	5.1971	4.7932	4.4392	3.8514	3.3868	3.0133
13	12.1337	11.3484	10.6350	9.9856	9.3936	8.8527	8.3577	7.9038	7.4869	7.1034	6.4235	5.8424	5.5831	5.3423	4.9095	4.5327	3.9124	3.4272	3.0404
14	13.0037	12.1062	11.2961	10.5631	9.8986	9.2950	8.7455	8.2442	7.7862	7.3667	6.6282	6.0021	5.7245	5.4675	5.0081	4.6106	3.9616	3.4587	3.0609
15	13.8651	12.8493	11.9379	11.1184	10.3797	9.7122	9.1079	8.5595	8.0607	7.6061	6.8109	6.1422	5.8474	5.5755	5.0916	4.6755	4.0013	3.4834	3.0764
16	14.7179	13.5777	12.5611	11.6523	10.8378	10.1059	9.4466	8.8514	8.3126	7.8237	6.9740	6.2651	5.9542	5.6685	5.1624	4.7296	4.0333	3.5026	3.0882
17	15.5623	14.2919	13.1661	12.1657	11.2741	10.4773	9.7632	9.1216	8.5436	8.0216	7.1196	6.3729	6.0472	5.7487	5.2223	4.7746	4.0591	3.5177	3.0971
18	16.3983	14.9920	13.7535	12.6593	11.6896	10.8276	10.0591	9.3719	8.7556	8.2014	7.2497	6.4674	6.1280	5.8178	5.2732	4.8122	4.0799	3.5294	3.1039
19	17.2260	15.6785	14.3238	13.1339	12.0853	11.1581	10.3356	9.6036	8.9501	8.3649	7.3658	6.5504	6.1982	5.8775	5.3162	4.8435	4.0967	3.5386	3.1090
20	18.0456	16.3514	14.8775	13.5903	12.4622	11.4699	10.5940	9.8181	9.1285	8.5136	7.4694	6.6231	6.2593	5.9288	5.3527	4.8696	4.1103	3.5458	3.1129
25	22.0232	19.5235	17.4131	15.6221	14.0939	12.7834	11.6536	10.6748	9.8226	9.0770	7.8431	6.8729	6.4641	6.0971	5.4669	4.9476	4.1474	3.5640	3.1220
30	25.8077	22.3965	19.6004	17.2920	15.3725	13.7648	12.4090	11.2578	10.2737	9.4269	8.0552	7.0027	6.5660	6.1772	5.5168	4.9789	4.1601	3.5693	3.1242
40	32.8347	27.3555	23.1148	19.7928	17.1591	15.0463	13.3317	11.9246	10.7574	9.7791	8.2438	7.1050	6.6418	6.2335	5.5482	4.9966	4.1659	3.5712	3.1250
50	39.1961	31.4236	25.7298	21.4822	18.2559	15.7619	13.8007	12.2335	10.9617	9.9148	8.3045	7.1327	6.6605	6.2463	5.5541	4.9995	4.1666	3.5714	3.1250
60	44.9550	34.7609	27.6756	22.6235	18.9293	16.1614	14.0392	12.3766	11.0480	9.9672	8.3240	7.1401	6.6651	6.2492	5.5553	4.9999	4.1667	3.5714	3.1250

APPENDIX B ANSWERS TO SELECTED END-OF-CHAPTER PROBLEMS

We present here answers to selected end-of-chapter problems. For the most part, the answers are only the final ones (or those at intermediate steps) to the more complex problems. Within limits, these answers are useful for students who want to see if they are on the right track to solving the problems. The primary limitation is that some problems may have more than one solution, depending on which of several equally plausible assumptions are made in working them. Also, many of the problems involve explanations as well as numerical calculations, and these are not given here.

2.1 a. 1. 25% gain   2. 34% gain   3. 46% gain
     b. 1. 23% loss   2. 34.6% loss   3. 50.1% loss

2.2 a. 1. 33.8% loss   2. 50% loss   3. 71.6% loss
     b. 1. 16.2% gain   2. 21.4% gain   3. 28.3% gain

2.3 d. 50%

3.1 a. $8,300   b. 22%   c. 20.75%

3.2 a. $9,400   b. 22%   c. 20.89%

3.3 a. $26,340   b. 26.34%

3.4 a. 20%, 20%   b. 48%, 34.5%   c. 48%, 46.65%   d. 48%, 47.99%

3.5 $24,300

3.6 1970, 1971, 1972, 1973—all 0; 1974, $10,500; 1975, $3,000; 1976, −$6,000; 1977, $3,000; 1978, −$13,500

3.7 1974, 1975—both 0; 1976, $6,100; 1977, $20,100; 1978, $4,000

3.8 a. $7,882.50   b. $7,792.50

3.9 $10,362.50

3.10 $16,280

3.11 $4,728

		1	2
3.12	a. Corporation	$1,201	$1,801
	Proprietorship	$1,221	$1,924
	c. Corporation	$801	
	Proprietorship	$810	

3.13	a. Corporation	$ 9,622	$13,722	$18,122
	Proprietorship	$11,870	$23,780	$33,780

4.1 $200,000

4.2 Total assets $67,200

4.5 Return on total assets 4.68%

5.1 a. −$14,000, $34,000   b. BEP 13,750   c. DOL −56
     DOL 4.24   DOL 2.34

5.2 a. −$40,000, $80,000   b. BEP 6,000   c. COL −5, DOL 4
     d. BEP 4,800   e. BEP 6,000

5.3 a. −$25,000, $50,000   b. BEP 5,000   c. CBEP 1,000

5.4 b. Sources, Uses $381

5.5 a. BEPS 200   1,200   b. $130   c. $25,000   d. $100, $16,000

6.1 $66,500

6.2 $106,250

6.4 Additional financing needed $970,000

6.6 b. $414,000   d. 1. $216,000; $546,000   2. $532,800; $334,800
     3. $330,000

6.8 a. 12%   b. 27%   c. 5.4%   d. 18%   e. 11.9%

7.1 b. $737,000 $655,200 or 88.9%

7.2 a. Denby 82.4%   Korman 16.0%   All 58.2%

7.4 Ending cash balance, June 1979 $255

8.1 a. 6%, 6%, 7%, 7%   b. 5.827%, 5.827%, 6.128%, 6.903%

8.4 Aggressive 11.3%; Average 10.4%; Conservative 8.8%

8.5 b. EBIT to Assets

	Aggressive	Between	Conservative
Strong	29%	48%	36%
Average	20	38	28
Weak	11	28	20

9.1 20.99%

9.2 a. $2,450,000   b. $196,000   c. $16,333

9.3 a. C_3 $22,800 C_4 ($1,800) C_5 ($64,800)
    b. C_3 $40,800 C_4 $7,200 C_5 ($28,800)

9.4 b. 4 days   c. Bank's $750,000   Own records ($3,250,000)

9.5 a. $9,000   b. $4,163   c. $916   d. $3,921

9.6 a. 4,000   b. 75   c. 16,000

9.7 a. 4,500   b. 89   c. 18,000   d. 0.4   e. 0.4   f. (0.8)
    g. (0.8)

10.1 a. 24.24%   b. 14.69%   c. 22.27%   d. 24.49%   e. 12.12%

10.2 1. 12%   2. 12.5%   3. 11.8%

10.4 Line of credit $59,728; Field warehousing $49,375

10.5 a. 57%, 34%, 29%

10.6 a. $300,000

10.7 a. $125,000; $122,360   b. 10.0%; 8.98%

11.1 $1,004

11.2 4.64 million tons

11.3 8 years

11.4 a. $875.48   b. $999.60   c. $1,297.85

11.5 $7,477.51

11.6 $59,237.81

11.7 a. 12%   b. $748.52   c. $906.55

11.8

	1	2
a.	8%	8%
b.	$1,259.71	$1,244.52
c.	8%	7.56%
d.	8%	7.56%

11.9 a. $5,000   b. $56,369.98

11.10 8%

11.11 8%

11.12 7%

11.13 15%

11.14 a. Year 6 $2,700,000

11.15 a. PVA = $5.062;   PVB = $5,216

11.16 a. 6th year $2.70   b. $6.00   c. $10   d. $16

11.17 a. $100,020

11.18 8.32%

11.19 a. 8%

11.20 $73,998

11.22 a. $140,350

12.1   Truck $2,027.50, 20%   Pulley $5,587.50, 24%

12.2   Gas $4,118, 20%   Electric $5,147, 20%

12.3   b. $58,200

12.4 $17,245

12.5 $44,175

12.6   a. $720,000   b. $160,000   c. $100,000   d. −$51,340

12.7   a. $36,407.50   b. 44,815

12.8   a. −$3,266.45   b. −$1,588.65   c. $411.35   d. $3,519.60

12.9   a.

	0%	6%	10%	20%
Orchard	$70,000	31,790	11,970	−$24,160
Mining	$40,000	22,200	12,240	−$7,720

        b. O 12.86%   M 15.78%

13.1   a. $\overline{NPV} = \$10,175$ $\overline{IRR} = 14\%$ b. Prob (good) = 0.7

13.2   a. $\overline{F}_A = \$4,500$ $\overline{F}_B = \$5,100$ b. $NPV_A = \$6,691.50$
        $NPV_B = \$7,750.20$

13.3   5 years: −$207.60; 8 years: $8,546; 10 years: $13,406

13.4   e. Prob (good) = 41%

13.5   a. $CV_A = 0.242$ $CV_B = 0.421$
        b. $k_A = 8.42\%$ $k_B = 10.21\%$

13.6   8%, 10%, 14%

13.7   a. 15%,   b. $211.20

13.8

	k_A^*	k_B^*
Based on CV	14%	18%
Based on SML	15	12

14.1

	A	B
a.	$1,154.42	$1,249.25
b.	1,073.61	1,114.69

14.2

	C	D
a.	$571.77	$558.68
b.	424.53	417.61

14.3   10%, 8%, 6.67%

14.4   14%, 5%

14.5   a. $1,125   b. $750   c. $1,000

14.6   a. $2.00   b. $4.27, $6.25, $10.60, $28.00   c. undefined,
        negative   d. 2.135, 3.125, 5.300, 14.000

14.7   a. $53.00

14.8   a. 6.8%, 8%, 10%, 12%

15.1 B/TA 50%, $k_s = .168$

15.4   a. 0.99, 1.18, 1.28, 1.38, 1.57
        b. 10.95%, 11.9%, 12.4%, 12.9%, 13.85%

15.5   b. Debt $\overline{EPS}$ = $3.160   Equity $\overline{EPS}$ = $2.90

15.6   a. OL = 1.5   FL = 1.45   CLE = 2.18

	EPS	CLE
b. Bonds	$1.23	3.90
Stock	1.38	2.91

16.1   17%

16.2   a. 18%   b. 13.2%

16.3   6%

16.4   12%

16.5   a. 14%   b. $43.56   c. 14%

16.6   a. $25,000,000   b. $15,000,000   c. 14.7%, 14%, 14.42%
        d. 10.7%

16.7   15.84%

16.8   12.2%

16.9   b. 40% debt ratio

16.10   a. $30,000,000   b. $15,000,000   c. $3,000,000; $12,000,000

17.1 $1,220,000

17.2 $2,760,000

17.3 $11.11

17.5   a. $1,650,000   b. $2,025,000   c. $3,250,000
        d. $2,250,000   e. $4,750,000

17.6   35%

17.7 $1,500,000 $1,000,000

17.9   b. $12   c. $352

18.1   11.5%

18.2   13.6%

19.1 $3

19.2   a. $2.50

19.3   a. $6

19.4   a. $6

19.5   a. $25   1. 200,000   2. 0.5   3. $3.10   4. $46.50
        5. $1.74

19.6   c. 45,456   d. 11.6%   e. 2

19.8   c, e.

	No Expansion	Debt	Equity
Market value of equity	$914	$825	$1,250
Price per share	$9.14	$8.25	$10.23
Cost of capital	10.4%	11.1%	9.8%

20.1   NPV = $11,782

20.2   a. 13.8%

20.3   a. 12%   b. $S = $1,000 $p_0 = $10   c. 11.27%
        g, h.

	Debt Financing	Equity Financing
V_L	$1,248	$1,208
k (market weights)	10.93%	11.29%
k (book weights)	10.75%	11.50%

20.4   NPV ≈ $34,300

21.1   a. $9,870   b. Cost = $21,348   c. $8,853

21.2   a. 0   b. NAL = ($6,244)

21.3   NAL = 0

21.4   a. Capital gains tax = $278,400   b. 1/1 vs. 3.3/1

21.5   a. 7.58%   b. 8.21%

22.1   a. $1,150.60   c. $50.60

22.2   a. ($1)   b. $2   c. $5   d. $10

22.3   a. $2   b. $28

22.7   a. 8.9%   d. 6%

24.1   a. $35.60   b. $.19   27%   c. ($.955)   (68%)

24.2   a. (12.5%)   b. +16.7%   c. 13.5%

24.3   a. $1.23   b. $18.45

24.4

	1. Not Diluted	2. Fully Diluted
EPS	$6.40	$5.83
Market	$76.80	$69.96

24.6   a. 6.4%

24.7   a. Apex $45.00   Allied $45.67

25.1   c. +$5.1 million   d. $15.6 million

26.1   a. +$2,000   b. ($3,333.33)

26.2   a. +$1,666,666   b. ($1,000,000)

26.3   % yield = 0.267%

26.4   a. .5%

	Forward Market	Borrow-Invest	No Cover
26.6	$1,040,000	$1,068,511	$989,999.60
26.7		1,027,339	
26.8	96,000	90,534	103,500.00

GLOSSARY

Abandonment Value The amount that can be realized by liquidating a project before its economic life has ended.

Accelerated Depreciation Depreciation methods that write off the cost of an asset at a faster rate than the write-off under the straight line method. The three principal methods of accelerated depreciation are: sum-of-years'-digits, double declining balance, and units of production.

Accruals Continually recurring short-term liabilities. Examples are accrued wages, accrued taxes, and accrued interest.

Aging Schedule A report showing how long accounts receivable have been outstanding. It gives the percent of receivables not past due and the percent past due by, for example, one month, two months, or other periods.

Amortize To liquidate on an installment basis; an amortized loan is one in which the principal amount of the loan is repaid in installments during the life of the loan.

Annuity A series of payments of a fixed amount for a specified number of years.

Arbitrage The process of selling overvalued and buying undervalued assets so as to bring about an equilibrium where all assets are properly valued. One who engages in arbitrage is called an arbitrager.

Arrearage Overdue payment; frequently, omitted dividends on preferred stocks.

Assignment A relatively inexpensive way of liquidating a failing firm that does not involve going through the courts.

Balloon Payment The final payment, larger than preceding payments, on a debt that is not fully amortized.

Bankruptcy A legal procedure for formally liquidating a business, carried out under the jurisdiction of courts of law.

Beta Coefficient A measure of the extent to which the returns on a given stock move with the stock market.

Bond A long-term debt instrument.

Book Value The accounting value of an asset. The book value of a share of common stock is equal to the net worth (common stock plus retained earnings) of the corporation divided by the number of shares of stock outstanding.

Breakeven Analysis An analytical technique for studying the relationships among fixed cost, variable cost, and profits. A breakeven chart graphically depicts the nature of breakeven analysis. The breakeven point represents the volume of sales at which total costs equal total revenues (that is, profits equal zero).

Business Risk The basic risk inherent in a firm's operations. Business risk plus financial risk resulting from the use of debt equals total corporate risk.

Call (1) An option to buy (or "call") a share of stock at a specified price within a specified period. (2) The process of redeeming a bond or preferred stock issue before its normal maturity.

Call Premium The amount in excess of par value that a company must pay when it calls a security.

Call Price The price that must be paid when a security is called. The call price is equal to the par value plus the call premium.

Call Privilege A provision incorporated into a bond or a share of preferred stock that gives the issuer the right to redeem (call) the security at a specified price.

Capital Asset An asset with a life of more than one year that is not bought and sold in the ordinary course of business.

Capital Budgeting The process of planning expenditures on assets whose returns are expected to extend beyond one year.

Capital Gains Profits on the sale of capital assets held for six months or more.

Capital Losses Losses on the sale of capital assets.

Capital Market Line A graphic representation of the relationship between risk and the required rate of return on an efficient portfolio.

Capital Markets Financial transactions involving instruments with maturities greater than one year.

Capital Rationing A situation where a constraint is placed on the total size of the capital investment during a particular period.

Capital Structure The permanent long-term financing of the firm represented by long-term debt, preferred stock, and net worth. (Net worth consists of capital, capital surplus, and retained earnings.) Capital structure is distinguished from financial structure, which includes short-term debt plus all reserve accounts.

Capitalization Rate A discount rate used to find the present value of a series of future cash receipts; sometimes called discount rate.

Carry-back; Carry-forward For income tax purposes, losses that can be carried backward or forward to reduce federal income taxes.

Cash Budget A schedule showing cash flows (receipts, disbursements, and net cash) for a firm over a specified period.

Cash Cycle The length of time between the purchase of raw materials and the collection of accounts receivable generated in the sale of the final product.

Certainty Equivalents The amount of cash (or rate of return) people would require with certainty to make them indifferent between this certain sum (or rate of return) and a particular uncertain, risky sum (or rate of return).

Characteristic Line A linear least-squares regression line that shows the relationship between an individual security's return and returns on the market. The slope of the characteristic line is the beta coefficient.

Chattel Mortgage A mortgage on personal property—not real estate. A mortgage on equipment would be a chattel mortgage.

Coefficient of Variation Standard deviation divided by the mean: CV.

Collateral Assets that are used to secure a loan.

Commercial Paper Unsecured, short-term promissory notes of large firms, usually issued in denominations of $1 million or more. The rate of interest on commercial paper is typically somewhat below the prime rate of interest.

Commitment Fee The fee paid to a lender for a formal line of credit.

Compensating Balance A required minimum checking account balance that a firm must maintain with a commercial bank. The required balance is generally equal to 15 to 20 percent of the amount of loans outstanding. Compensating balances can raise the effective rate of interest on bank loans.

Composite Cost of Capital A weighted average of the component costs of debt, preferred stock, and common equity. Also called the weighted average cost of capital, it usually reflects the cost of each additional dollar raised, not the average cost of all capital the firm has raised throughout its history *(k)*.

Composition An informal method of reorganization that voluntarily reduces creditors' claims on the debtor firm.

Compound Interest An interest rate that is applicable when interest in succeeding periods is earned not only on the initial principal but also on the accumulated interest of prior periods. Compound interest is contrasted to simple interest, in which returns are not earned on interest received.

Compounding The arithmetic process of determining the final value of a payment or series of payments when compound interest is applied.

Conditional Sales Contract A contract for the financing of new equipment that calls for paying off the loan in installments over a one- to five-year period. The seller retains title to the equipment until payment has been completed.

Consolidated Tax Return An income tax return that combines the income statements of several affiliated firms.

Continuous Compounding (Discounting) As opposed to discrete compounding, interest is added continuously rather than at discrete points in time.

Conversion Price The effective price paid for common stock when the stock is obtained by converting either convertible preferred stocks or convertible bonds. For example, if a $1,000 bond is convertible into twenty shares of stock, the conversion price is $50 ($1,000/20).

Conversion Ratio, or Conversion Rate The number of shares of common stock that can be obtained by converting a convertible bond or share of convertible preferred stock.

Convertibles Securities (generally bonds or preferred stocks) that are exchangeable at the option of the holder for common stock of the issuing firm.

Correlation Coefficient A measure of the degree of relationship between two variables.

Cost of Capital The discount rate that should be used in the capital budgeting process.

Coupon Rate The stated rate of interest on a bond.

Covariance The correlation between two variables multiplied by the standard deviation of each.

Covenant A protective clause contained in a loan agreement. Covenants are designed to protect the lender and include such items as limits on total indebtedness, restrictions on dividends, minimum current ratio, and similar provisions.

Cumulative Dividends A protective feature on preferred stock that requires all past preferred dividends to be paid before any common dividends are paid.

Cutoff Point In the capital budgeting process, the minimum rate of return on acceptable investment opportunities.

Debenture A long-term debt instrument that is not secured by a mortgage on specific property.

Debt Ratio Total debt divided by total assets.

Decision Tree A device for setting forth graphically the relationships between decisions and chance events.

Default The failure to fulfill a contract, generally by not paying interest or principal on debt obligations.

Degree of Leverage The percentage increase in profits resulting from a given percentage increase in sales. The degree of leverage can be calculated for financial leverage, operating leverage, or a combination of the two.

Devaluation The process of reducing the value of a country's currency in terms of other currencies; for example, the British pound might be devalued from $2 to $1.60 in terms of dollars.

Discount Rate The interest rate used in the discounting process; sometimes called the capitalization rate.

Discounted Cash Flow Techniques Methods of ranking investment proposals. Included are the internal rate of return method, the net present value method, and the profitability index or benefit/cost ratio.

Discounting The process of finding the present value of a series of future cash flows. Discounting is the reverse of compounding.

Discounting of Accounts Receivable Short-term financing whereby accounts receivable are used to secure the loan. The lender does not buy the accounts receivable but simply uses them as collateral for the loan. Also called assigning accounts receivable.

Dividend Yield The ratio of the current dividend to the current price of a share of stock.

du Pont System A system of analysis designed to show the relationships among return on investment, asset turnover, and the profit margin.

EBIT Acronym for "earnings before interest and taxes."

Economical Ordering Quantity (EOQ) The optimum (least cost) quantity of merchandise that should be ordered.

EPS Acronym for "earnings per share."

Equity The net worth of a business, consisting of capital stock, capital (or paid-in) surplus, earned surplus (or retained earnings), and occasionally, certain net worth reserves, Common equity is that part of the total net worth belonging to the common stockholders. Total equity includes net worth belonging to preferred stockholders. The terms common stock, net worth, and common equity are frequently used interchangeably *(S)*.

Exchange Rate The rate at which one currency can be exchanged for another; for example, $2 may be exchangeable for one British pound.

Excise Tax A tax on the manufacture, sale, or consumption of specified commodities.

Ex Dividend Date The date on which the right to the current dividend no longer accompanies a stock. (For listed stock, the ex dividend date is four working days prior to the date of record.)

Exercise Price The price that must be paid for a share of common stock when it is bought by exercising a warrant.

Expected Return The rate of return a firm expects to realize from an investment. The expected return is the mean value of the probability distribution of possible returns.

Ex Rights Date The date on which stock purchase rights are no longer transferred to the purchaser of the stock.

Extension An informal method of reorganization in which the creditors voluntarily postpone the date of required payment on past-due obligations.

External Funds Funds acquired through borrowing or by selling new common or preferred stock.

Factoring A method of financing accounts receivable under which a firm sells its accounts receivable (generally without recourse) to a financial institution (the factor).

Field Warehousing A method of financing inventories in which a "warehouse" is established at the place of business of the borrowing firm.

Financial Accounting Standards Board (FASB) A private (nongovernment) agency that functions as an accounting standards-setting body.

Financial Intermediation Financial transactions that bring savings surplus units together with savings deficit units so that savings can be redistributed to their most productive uses.

Financial Lease A lease that does not provide for maintenance services, is not cancellable, and is fully amortized over its lifetime.

Financial Leverage The ratio of total debt to total assets. There are other measures of financial leverage, especially ones that relate cash inflows to required cash outflows. In this book, the debt/total asset ratio is generally used to measure leverage.

Financial Markets Transactions in which the creation and transfer of financial assets and financial liabilities take place.

Financial Risk That portion of total corporate risk, over and above basic business risk, that results from using debt.

Financial Structure The entire right-hand side of the balance sheet—the way in which a firm is financed.

Fisher Effect The increase in the nominal interest rates over real (purchasing power adjusted) interest rates reflecting anticipated inflation.

Fixed Charges Costs that do not vary with the level of output, especially fixed financial costs such as interest, lease payments, and sinking fund payments.

Float The amount of funds tied up in checks that have been written but are still in process and have not yet been collected.

Floating Exchange Rates Exchange rates that are allowed to move up and down according to supply and demand. Exchange rates can be fixed by government policy ("pegged") or allowed to "float." When market forces are allowed to function, exchange rates are said to be floating.

Flotation Cost The cost of issuing new stocks or bonds.

Funded Debt Long-term debt.

Funding The process of replacing short-term debt with long-term securities (stocks or bonds).

General Purchasing Power Reporting A proposal by the FASB that the current values of nonmonetary items in financial statements be adjusted by a general price index.

Goodwill Intangible assets of a firm established by the excess of the price paid for the going concern over its book value.

Holding Company A corporation operated for the purpose of owning the common stocks of other corporations.

Hurdle Rate In capital budgeting, the minimum acceptable rate of return on a project; if the expected rate of return is below the hurdle rate, the project is not accepted. The hurdle rate should be the marginal cost of capital.

Improper Accumulation Earnings retained by a business for the purpose of enabling stockholders to avoid personal income taxes.

Income Bond A bond that pays interest only if the current interest is earned.

Incremental Cost of Capital The average cost of the increment of capital raised during a given year.

Indenture A formal agreement between the issuer of a bond and the bondholders.

Insolvency The inability to meet maturing debt obligations.

Interest Factor (IF) Numbers found in compound interest and annuity tables.

Internal Financing Funds made available for capital budgeting and working capital expansion through the normal operations of the firm; internal financing is approximately equal to retained earnings plus depreciation.

Internal Rate of Return (IRR) The rate of return on an asset investment. The internal rate of return is calculated by finding the discount rate that equates the present value of future cash flows to the cost of the investment.

Intrinsic Value That value which, in the mind of the analyst, is justified by the facts. It is often used to distinguish between the true value of an asset (the intrinsic value) and the asset's current market price.

Investment Banker A banker who underwrites and distributes new investment securities; more broadly, a banker who helps business firms obtain financing.

Investment Tax Credit A specified percentage of the dollar amount of new investments in each of certain categories of assets that business firms can deduct as a credit against their income taxes.

Legal List A list of securities in which mutual savings banks, pension funds, insurance companies, and other fiduciary institutions are permitted to invest.

Leverage Factor The ratio of debt to total assets.

Lien A lender's claim on assets that are pledged for a loan.

Line of Credit An arrangement whereby a financial institution (bank or insurance company) commits itself to lend up to a specified maximum amount of funds during a specified period.

Liquidity The state of a firm's cash position and ability to meet maturing obligations.

Listed Securities Securities traded on an organized security exchange.

Lockbox Plan A procedure used to speed up collections and reduce float.

Margin—Profit on Sales The profit margin is the percentage of after-tax profit to sales.

Margin—Securities Business The buying of stocks or bonds on credit, known as buying on margin.

Marginal Cost The cost of an additional unit. The marginal cost of capital is the cost of an additional dollar of new funds.

Marginal Efficiency of Capital A schedule showing the internal rate of return on investment opportunities.

Marginal Revenue The additional gross revenue produced by selling one additional unit of output.

Merger Any combination that forms one company from two or more previously existing companies.

Money Market Financial market in which funds are borrowed or lent for short periods (less than one year). The money market is distinguished from the capital market, which is the market for long-term funds.

Mortgage A pledge of designated property as security for a loan.

Net Present Value (NPV) Method A method of ranking investment proposals. The NPV is equal to the present value of future returns, discounted at the marginal cost of capital, minus the present value of the cost of the investment.

Net Worth The capital and surplus of a firm—capital stock, capital surplus (paid-in capital), earned surplus (retained earnings), and occasionally, certain reserves. For some purposes, preferred stock is included; generally, net worth refers only to the common stockholders' position.

Nominal Interest Rate The contracted or stated interest rate, undeflated for price level changes.

Normal Probability Distribution A symmetrical, bell-shaped probability function.

Objective Probability Distributions Probability distributions determined by statistical procedures.

Operating Leverage The extent to which fixed costs are used in a firm's operation. Breakeven analysis is used to measure the extent to which operating leverage is employed.

Opportunity Cost The rate of return on the best alternative investment available. It is the highest return that will not be earned if the funds are invested in a particular project. For example, the opportunity cost of not investing in Bond A yielding 8 percent might be 7.99 percent, which could be earned on Bond B.

Options Contracts that give their holder the right to buy or sell an asset at a predetermined exercise price for a given period of time.

Ordinary Income Income from the normal operations of a firm. Operating income specifically excludes income from the sale of capital assets.

Organized Security Exchanges Formal organizations having tangible, physical locations. Organized exchanges conduct an auction market in designated (listed) investment securities. The New York Stock Exchange is an organized exchange.

Overdraft System A system where a depositor can write checks in excess of the balance, with the bank automatically extending a loan to cover the shortage.

Over-the-Counter Market All facilities that provide for trading in unlisted securities—that is, those not listed on organized exchanges. Most over-the-counter business is conducted by telephone.

Par Value The nominal or face value of a stock or bond.

Payback Period The length of time required for the net revenues of an investment to return the cost of the investment.

Payout Ratio The percentage of earnings paid out in the form of dividends.

Pegging A market stabilization action taken by the manager of an underwriting group during the offering of new securities, accomplished by continually placing orders to buy at a specified price in the market.

Perpetuity A stream of equal future payments expected to continue forever.

Pledging of Accounts Receivable Short-term borrowing from financial institutions where the loan is secured by accounts receivable. The lender may physically take the accounts receivable but typically has recourse to the borrower; also called discounting of accounts receivable.

Pooling of Interest An accounting method of combining the financial statements of firms that merge. Under the pooling-of-interest procedure, the assets of the merged firms are simply added to form the balance sheet of the surviving corporation. This method is different from the "purchase" method, where goodwill is put on the balance sheet to reflect a premium (or discount) paid in excess of book value.

Portfolio Effect The extent to which the variation in returns on a combination of assets (a portfolio) is less than the sum of the variations of the individual assets.

Portfolio Theory Theory used in selection of optimal portfolios—portfolios that provide the highest possible return for any specified degree of risk.

Preemptive Right A provision contained in the corporate charter and bylaws that gives holders of common stock the right to purchase on a pro rata basis new issues of common stock (or securities convertible into common stock).

Present Value (PV) The value today of a future payment, or stream of payments, discounted at the appropriate discount rate.

Price/Earnings (P/E) Ratio The ratio of price to earnings. Faster growing or less risky firms typically have higher P/E ratios than either slower growing or riskier firms.

Prime Rate The lowest rate of interest commercial banks charge very large, strong corporations.

Pro Forma A projection. A pro forma financial statement is one that shows how the actual statement will look if certain specified assumptions are realized. Pro forma statements can be either future or past projections. An example of a backward pro forma statement is one that, when two firms are planning to merge, shows what their consolidated financial statements would have looked like if they had been merged in preceding years.

Profit Center A unit of a large, decentralized firm that has its own investments and for which a rate of return on investment can be calculated.

Profit Margin The ratio of after-tax profits to sales.

Profitability Index (PI) The present value of future returns divided by the present value of the investment outlay.

Progressive Tax A tax that requires a higher percentage payment on higher incomes. The personal income tax in the United States, which is at the rate of 14 percent on the lowest increments of income to 70 percent on the highest increments, is progressive.

Prospectus A document issued for the purpose of describing a new security issue. The Securities and Exchange Commission (SEC) examines prospectuses to ensure that statements contained therein are not false and misleading.

Proxy A document giving one person the authority or power to act for another. Typically, the authority in question is the power to vote shares of common stock.

Pure (or Primitive) Security A security that pays off $1 if one particular state of the world occurs and pays off nothing if any other state of the world occurs.

Put An option to sell a specific security at a specified price within a designated period.

Rate of Return The internal rate of return on an investment, calculated by finding the discount rate that equates the present value of future cash flows to the cost of the investment.

Recourse Arrangement An arrangement under which, if a firm sells its accounts receivable to a financial institution, then, if the accounts receivable cannot be collected, the selling firm must repurchase the account from the financial institution.

Rediscount Rate The rate of interest at which a bank can borrow from a Federal Reserve Bank.

Refunding Sale of new debt securities to replace an old debt issue.

Regression Analysis A statistical procedure for predicting the value of one variable (dependent variable) on the basis of knowledge about one or more other variables (independent variables).

Reinvestment Rate The rate of return at which cash flows from an investment are reinvested. The reinvestment rate may or may not be constant from year to year.

Reorganization The restructuring of a financially troubled firm. When a firm goes through reorganization, its assets are restated to reflect their current market value, and its financial structure is restated to reflect any changes on the asset side of the statement. Under a reorganization the firm continues in existence; this is in contrast to bankruptcy, where the firm is liquidated and ceases to exist.

Replacement Cost Accounting A requirement under SEC Release No. 190 (1976) that large companies disclose the replacement costs of inventory items and depreciable plant.

Required Rate of Return The rate of return that stockholders expect to receive on common stock investments.

Residual Value The value of leased property at the end of the lease term.

Retained Earnings That portion of earnings not paid out in dividends. The figure that appears on the balance sheet is the sum of the retained earnings for each year throughout the company's history.

Right A short-term option to buy a specified number of shares of a new issue of securities at a designated subscription price.

Rights Offering A securities flotation offered to existing stockholders.

Risk The probability that actual future returns will be below expected returns, measured by standard deviation or coefficient of variation of expected returns.

Risk-Adjusted Discount Rate The discount rate applicable for a particular risky (uncertain) stream of income; the riskless rate of interest plus a risk premium appropriate to the level of risk attached to the particular income stream.

Risk Premium The difference between the required rate of return on a particular risky asset and the rate of return on a riskless asset with the same expected life.

Sale and Leaseback An operation whereby a firm sells land, buildings, or equipment to a financial institution and simultaneously executes an agreement to lease the property back for a specified period under specific terms.

Salvage Value The value of a capital asset at the end of a specified period. It is the current market price of an asset being considered for replacement in a capital budgeting problem.

Securities and Exchange Commission (SEC) The federal agency that supervises the operation of securities exchanges and related aspects of the securities business and with which a registration statement must be filed on new issues of securities.

Securities, Junior Securities that have lower priority in claims on assets and income than other securities (senior securities). For example, preferred stock is junior to debentures, but debentures are junior to mortgage bonds. Common stock is the most junior of all corporate securities.

Securities, Senior Securities having claims on income and assets that rank higher than certain other securities (junior securities). For example, mortgage bonds are senior to debentures, but debentures are senior to common stock.

Security Market Line A graphic representation of the relation between the required return on a security and the product of its risk times a normalized market measure of risk. Risk-return relationships for individual securities or investments.

Selling Group A group of stockbrokerage firms formed for the purpose of distributing a new issue of securities; part of the investment banking process.

Sensitivity Analysis Simulation analysis in which key variables are changed and the resulting change in the rate of return is observed. Typically, the rate of return is more sensitive to changes in some variables than it is to changes in others.

Service Lease A lease under which the lessor maintains and services the asset.

Short Selling Selling a security that is not owned by the seller at the time of the sale. The seller borrows the security from a brokerage firm and must at some point repay the brokerage firm by buying the security on the open market.

Simulation A technique whereby probable future events are simulated on a computer. Estimated rates of return and risk indexes can be generated.

Sinking Fund A required annual payment designed to amortize a bond or a preferred stock issue. The sinking fund can be held in the form of cash or marketable securities, but more generally the money put into it is used each year to retire some of the securities in question.

Small Business Administration (SBA) A government agency organized to aid small firms with their financing and other problems.

Standard Deviation A statistical measurement of the variability of a set of observations from the mean of the distribution (σ).

State Preference Model A framework in which decisions are based on probabilities of payoffs under alternative states of the world.

Stock Dividend A dividend paid in additional shares of stock rather than in cash. These dividends involve a transfer from retained earnings to the capital stock account; therefore, they are limited by the amount of retained earnings.

Stock Split An accounting action to increase the number of shares outstanding; for example, in a 3-for-1 split, shares outstanding are tripled and each stockholder receives three new shares for each one formerly held. Stock splits involve no transfer from surplus to the capital account.

Subjective Probability Distributions Probability distributions determined through subjective procedures without the use of statistics.

Subordinated Debenture A bond having a claim on assets only after the senior debt has been paid off (in the event of liquidation).

Subscription Price The price at which a security can be purchased in a rights offering.

Surtax A tax levied in addition to the normal tax. For example, the normal corporate tax rate is 22 percent, but a surtax of 26 percent is added to the normal tax on all corporate income exceeding $25,000.

Synergy A situation where the whole is greater than the sum of its parts. In a synergistic merger, the postmerger earnings exceed the sum of the separate companies' premerger earnings.

Systematic Risk The part of a security's risk that cannot be eliminated by diversification.

Tangible Assets Physical assets, as opposed to intangible assets such as goodwill and the stated value of patents.

Tender Offer An offer by one firm to buy the stock of another, with the firm going directly to the stockholders, frequently over the opposition of the management of the firm whose stock is being sought.

Term Loan A loan with a maturity greater than one year, generally obtained from a bank or an insurance company. Term loans are usually amortized.

Trade Credit Interfirm debt arising through credit sales and recorded as an account receivable by the seller and as an account payable by the buyer.

Treasury Stock Common stock that has been repurchased by the issuing firm.

Trust Receipt An instrument acknowledging that the borrower holds certain goods in trust for the lender. Trust receipt financing is used in connection with the financing of inventories for automobile dealers, construction equipment dealers, appliance dealers, and other dealers in expensive durable goods.

Trustee The representative of bondholders who acts in their interest and facilitates communication between them and the issuer. Typically these duties are handled by a department of a commercial bank.

Underwriting (1) The entire process of issuing new corporate securities. (2) The insurance function of bearing the risk of adverse price fluctuations during the period in which a new issue of stock or bonds is being distributed.

Underwriting Syndicate A syndicate of investment firms formed to spread the risk associated with the purchase and distribution of a new issue of securities. The larger the issue, the more firms typically are involved in the syndicate.

Unlisted Securities Securities that are traded in the over-the-counter market.

Unsystematic Risk That part of a security's risk associated with random events. Unsystematic risk can be eliminated by proper diversification.

Utility Theory A body of theory dealing with the relationships among money income, utility (or happiness), and the willingness to accept risks.

Warrant A long-term option to buy a stated number of shares of common stock at a specified price. The specified price is generally called the exercise price.

Weighted Cost of Capital A weighted average of the component costs of debt, preferred stock, and common equity. Also called the composite cost of capital.

Working Capital A firm's investment in short-term assets—cash, short-term securities, accounts receivable, and inventories. Gross working capital is a firm's total current assets. Net working capital is current assets minus current liabilities. If the term working capital is used without further qualification, it generally refers to gross working capital.

Yield The rate of return on an investment; the internal rate of return.

INDEX

Accelerated depreciation, 40–41, 56–59, 313
present value of, 313–317
present value tables for, 314
Accept-reject decisions, 287, 290, 293–294
Accounts payable financing, 228–231
Accounts receivable management, 210–216
and cash discounts, 213
and collections, 213
credit policy of, 213–216
credit standards for, 210–212
credit terms in, 212–213
Acquisitions. See Mergers
Activity ratios, 67, 71–74
Aging schedule, 73
Allocation of resources, 19–20
American Stock Exchange, 22–23
Amortization, 71
of financial leases, 563
of long-term loans, 474, 476
Annuity, 261
future value of, 261
present value of, 261–263
Assignment, in liquidation, 677–678
Auction markets, 23
Average collection period, 72

Balance sheet, 63–65
ratios for, 67–78
Banker's acceptances, 31, 237
Bankruptcy, 678–684
actions resulting in, 678–680
priority of claims in, 681–684
voluntary versus involuntary, 679
Beta coefficient, 339–343
and financial leverage, 386–394
of portfolio, 332–338
Bonds, 531–541
call provisions of, 533
characteristics of, 539–540
decisions on use of, 540–541
refunding of, 549–552
secured, 535–536
sinking fund, 534
unsecured, 536–539
valuation of, 355–360
Breakeven analysis, 106–119
and breakeven point in dollars, 111–112
and cash breakeven, 117–119
limitations of, 119
nonlinear, 108–109
operating leverage in, 112–117
Budgeting, 149–151
cash, 153–156

external uses of, 165
nature of the process of, 149–151
problems of, 158
regression method of, 157
use of, 158–159
variable or flexible, 156–158
Business risk, 381

Call option, 533
Call premium, 533
Call provision, 533–534
Capital asset pricing model, 338–343
assumptions of, 338
and beta coefficient, 339–343
and capital market line, 353–355
example of, 342–343
and expected return on investment, 333–335
market price of risk in, 335–336
and required return on investment, 353–355
risk-adjusted discount rate in, 339–340
and risk-return tradeoff, 335–336
Capital budgeting, 281–308
accept-reject decisions in, 295–296
administrative details of, 286
application of, 284–286
capital rationing and, 304–307
and conflicting rankings from NPV and IRR, 288–295
differences between NPV and IRR methods of, 295–298
discounted cash flow techniques of, 288, 290–292
economic basis of, 283–284
evaluating investment proposals in, 285–287
importance of, 281–283
independent investments and, 287
internal rate of return method of, 288–295
marginal cost of capital of, 428–437
methods for ranking proposals in, 288–295
mutually exclusive investments and, 286–287
net operating cash flow of, 288–289
net present value method of, 288, 290–292
payback method of, 288–290
project evaluation in 298–304
reinvestment assumption of, 298
uncertainty and, 319–347
worksheet for, 304–305
Capital components, 411–413
Capital gains tax, 41–42, 48

Capital impairment rule, 446
Capital losses taxation, 42, 43
Capital market line, 335–336
Capital markets, 19
Capital rationing, 304–307
Capital structure, 381
effects of on valuation, 515–523
Carry-back and carry-forward, 44–45
Cash budgeting, 153–156
Cash discounts,
and accounts receivable, 210–214
trade credit, as type of, 198–199
Cash flow cycle, 128–131
Cash management, 197–209
check clearing and, 200
compensating balances and, 204–205
and cost, 203–204
and float, 201–203
forecasting cash flows, as aspect of inventory problem, 221–222
and lockbox plan, 200
and minimum cash balance, 204–205
overdraft system of, 206
precautionary motive in, 197
speculative motive in, 197
and trade discounts, 198–199
transactions motive in, 197
Certificate of deposit, 30
Coefficient of variation, as a measure of risk, 325–326
Collateral on financing, 236–245, 477
Commercial banks, 19
forms of loans of, 231–234
short-term financing by, 231–237
Commercial paper, 31–32, 236–237
Common stock, 499–523
advantages and disadvantages of, 505–506
control of, 500
cost of, 419–421
cost of new equity of, 419–420
cumulative voting for, 502–503
election of directors for, 501–503
forms of, 504
income of, to stockholders, 500
market price of, 365–366
preemptive right of, 503–504
and proxy, 501–503
rate of return of, 361–365
rights offerings of, 506–515
rights of holders of, 499–501
risk-bearing, 500–501
and social viewpoint, 506
source of funds for, 505–506
valuation of, 361–365, 372–379
voting rights of holders of, 501–503
Compensating balances, 232–233
Composition of creditor claims, 669–671

Compound interest, 255–257
Compound value of annuity, 261
Convertible securities, 591–601
　advantages and disadvantages of,
　　592–593, 601–603
　effect of on reported earnings, 603
　expected rate of return of, 598
　pricing of, 593–601
　valuation of, 593–601
Corporate income tax, 39–46
Corporate tax tables, 40
Corporation, characteristics of, 51
Cost of capital, 411–439
　capital asset pricing model and,
　　438–443
　capital structure and, 411
　common stock and, 419–421
　components of, 411–425
　debt and, 413–415
　dynamics of, 436–437
　external equity and, 419–420
　investment opportunity schedule for,
　　435–437
　leverage and, 422–425
　marginal, 428–437
　MM approach to, 472–479
　preferred stock and, 415–416
　retained earnings and, 417–419
　security market line and, 420–421
　tax adjustments for, 416
　weighted average of, 425–428
Cost of common stock, 419–421
　effect of leverage on, 422–425
Cost of debt, 413–415
　effect of leverage on, 422–425
Cost of equity and security market line,
　420–421
Cost of external equity, 419–420
Cost of money, 619–620
Cost of new equity, 419–420
Cost of preferred stock, 415–416
Cost of retained earnings, 417–419
Credit policy, 213–216
Cumulative dividends, 543
Cumulative voting, 502–503
Current asset management,
　and accounts receivable management,
　　210–216
　and cash management, 197–209
　and cost of trade discounts, 229
　and inventory management, 216–222
　risk-return tradeoff in, 187–189
Current liabilities, 67–69
Current ratio, 67–68

Debentures, 531, 536
Debt, 20

cost of, 413–415
Debt/equity ratio, 69–70
Debt ratio, 69–70
Debt securities, 531–541
Debt service coverage ratio, 71
Decentralized firm, control of, 159–162
Decision trees, 327–329
Depreciation,
　and cash flows, 120–121
　life of, 60
　tax consequences of, 40–43, 56–59
Depreciation methods, accelerated,
　40–41
Discounted cash flow, in capital budget-
　ing, 289, 291–292
Discounted interest, 233
Discounted value of annuity, 261–263
Discount rate, 21
Dividend income, 43, 49
Dividend payments, procedure for,
　457–458
Dividend payout ratio, 451
Dividend policy, 446–465
　alternative of, 451–452
　conflicting theories of, 451
　factors influencing, 446–450
　long-run viewpoint of, 450
　payout ratio of, 451
　residual theory of, 452–455
　stable, rationale for, 450–451
　stock dividends and, 458–460
　stock repurchase and, 460–463
　stock splits and, 458–460
Double declining balance depreciation,
　57–58
Du Pont system, 79–81, 159–162
　defined, 79
　as means of control, 159–162

Economic order quantity, 218–221
Effective interest rate, 233
Efficient portfolios, 335
Eurodollars, 32–34, 704–706
Exchange rate fluctuations, 694
Expectations theory of interest rates,
　179–180
Ex-rights, 509–510
Extension, by creditors, 669–670
External equity, cost of, 419–420
External funds, needed, 131–137
　effect of inflation on, 135–137

Factoring accounts receivable, 238–241
Failure, 667–669
　causes of, 667–668

extension and compositions of,
　669–671
　and historical experience, 668–669
Fairness principle, in reorganization,
　672–676
Fair value, 352
Feasibility principle, in reorganization,
　672–676
Federal funds, 29–30
Federal Reserve System, 21
Finance companies, 19
Finance function, 3–11
　departmental organization and, 11
Financial decisions, 11–12
Financial forecasting, 128–142
　external funds needs and, 131–137
　linear regression and, 137–141
　percent of sales method of, 131–137,
　　139–140
　scatter diagram method of, 137–140
Financial institutions, 20
Financial intermediation, 19–20
Financial lease, 563–564
Financial leverage, 381–404
　degree of, 396–397
　versus operating leverage, 395–399
Financial management, 3
　changing role of, 9–11, 513–514
Financial markets, 17–20
Financial planning and control, 149–166
　budgeting and, 149–162
　in decentralized firm, 159–162
　du Pont system of, 159–162
　ROI control in, 159–162
Financial policy, timing of, 613–626
Financial ratios, 63–89
　and credit analysis, 86–87
　and Dun & Bradstreet industry aver-
　　ages, 83–85
　limitations of, 87–88
Financial risk, measurement of, 319–332
Financial statements, 63–67
Financial structure,
　breakeven analysis of, 394–395
　effects of on valuation, 388–394
　factors influencing, 400–404
　variations of, 399–400
Financing, 131
　alternative sources of, 388–394,
　　515–523
　and interest rate fluctuations, 179
　international, 702
　and long- versus short-term debt, 177,
　　181
　refunding risk in, 182
　risk-return tradeoff in, 388–394
　short-term versus long-term, 177
Financing sources, 19–20

Financing, using rights, 514–515
Financing of working capital, 174
Firm life cycle, 666–667
Fiscal policy, 21–22
Fixed assets, turnover of, 73–74
Fixed charge coverage of, 71
Float management, 201–203
Flotation costs, 415, 487–489
Foreign currency units, 695–698
Funded debt, 534–535
Future value, 255–257
Future value of annuity, 261

Goals of the firm, 4–8
Going concern value, 351
Goodwill treatment in mergers, 662
Gordon model, 373–379

Holding companies, 643–652
  advantages and disadvantages of,
    644–645
  and leverage, 645–648

Improper accumulation, 45–46
Income bonds, 538–539
Income statement, 65
Indenture, 531
Indifference curves, for risk and return,
    335–337
Inflation,
  effects of on financial margins, 9–11
  effects of on financial ratios, 95–108
  effects of on financial statements,
    10–11
  effects of on financing needs, 10
  effects of on interest rates, 10
  effects of on required returns,
    162–165
  and general purchasing power report-
    ing, 102–104
Installment loan, 234
Interest compounding, 255–257
Interest factor, 255–275
  annual accumulation of future sum as,
    264
  annual receipts from annuity as,
    264–265
  appropriate rate of, for discounting,
    265, 272–273
  compounding of, 255–257
  and compound value of annuity, 261
  determining the interest rate of, 265
  future value of annuity and, 261

interpolation of, 265–266
opportunity cost of, 272–273
present value of, 257–259
present value of annuity of, 261–263
risk premiums included in, 181–182
semiannual and other compounding
  period of, 268–271
Interest rate risk, 358
Interest rates, 179–182, 233
  discounted, 233
  expectations theory of, 179–180
  forecasts of, 182–186, 620–625
  historical patterns of, 614–617
  long- versus short-term rates of,
    179–182
  regular, 233
  term structure of, 178–182
Internal rate of return method of capital
    budgeting, 288–295
International business finance, 690–711
  and dealing with exchange rate fluc-
    tuations, 695
  and development of an international
    firm, 691–694
  exchange rate risks of, 694–695
  and international financing, 702–705
  and net monetary position, 699–702
  and working capital management,
    706–707
Inventory, 216–222
  EOQ model of, 218–221
  inflation's impact on, 97–99
  turnover ratio of, 72
Inventory lien, 243–245
Inventory management, 216–222
  and carrying cost, 216–221
  decision models of, 218–221
  and determining inventory size,
    216–217
  and economic order quantity, 218–221
  and finished goods inventory, 216
  and ordering cost, 218–221
  and raw materials inventory, 216
  and safety stocks, 219–221
  and work-in-process inventory, 216
Investment banking, 19, 480–487
  distribution function of, 481
  and international financing, 703
  process of, 482–487
  underwriting function of, 480–481
Investment decisions under uncertainty,
    319–344
Investment opportunity schedule,
    435–437
Investment tax credit, 41

Joint venture—international, 692

Lease financing, 562–582
  advantages of, 567–572, 576–581
  cost of debt as the discount factor in,
    572–575
  versus purchase, 567–572
  using internal rate of return, 575–576
Leases,
  accounting for, 564–567
  net present value of, 567–572
  tax treatments of, 564, 580–581
  types of, 563–564
Leverage, 395–399
  combination, 397–399
  effect of, on cost of capital, 422–425
  relation of financial to operating,
    395–399
Leverage ratios, 67, 69–71
Life insurance companies, 19
Line of credit financing, 232
Liquidation, 677–678
  assignment, 667–678
  value, 351
Liquidity ratios, 67–69
Listed securities, 26
Listed stock, 26
Lockbox plan, 200
Long-term debt, 32, 531–541
  advantages and disadvantages of
    bond as, 531
  call provisions of, 533–534
  debenture, as form of, 531, 536
  funded, 534–535
  income bonds, as type of, 538–539
  indenture, as type of, 531–532
  mortgage, as type of, 531
  refunding, 549–552
  secured, 535–536
  sinking fund for, 534
  subordinated debentures, as types of,
    536–538
  trustee for, 532–533
  unsecured, 536–539

Marginal cost of capital, 428–437
  investment opportunity schedule of,
    435–437
  and using new equity, 431–432
Margin trading, 28–29
Marketable securities, 206–209
  security portfolio selection of,
    207–208
Market equilibrium, 364–365
Market price of risk, 335–336
Market stabilization, 487
Market value, 351–352
Maximization objectives, 5–7

Mergers, 635–643
  accounting for, 657–664
  financing of, 635
  pooling of interest in, 662–663
  and purchase accounting, 659–662
  quantitative aspects of, 638–642
  synergistic effects of, 642–643
  terms of and treatment of goodwill in,
    636–643
  treatment of goodwill in, 662
Modigliani-Miller valuation model,
  372–379
Monetary balance—international,
  699–702
Money markets, 19–20
Mortgage, 531
Multinational business finance, 690–708

Net present value, 257–259
  and capital budgeting, 288, 290–292
  and leases, 567–572
Net working capital, 173
New York Stock Exchange, 22–23

Open market operations, 21
Operating leverage, 112–117, 395–399
Over-the-counter markets, 24–25

Partnership, 50–51
Payback method, 288–290
Pension funds, 19
Perpetual bonds, 356–357
Personal income tax, 46–49
  deductions for, 46–48
  tables for, 48
Pooling of interests, 662–663
Portfolio, 334
  efficient, 335
  measuring riskiness of, 332–338
  opportunities for, 334–335
  optimal, 337
Portfolio risk, 332–338
  beta coefficient and, 353–355
  correlation of, 333
  covariance of, 353–355
Preemptive rights, 503–504
Preferred stock, 541–548
  advantages and disadvantages of,
    545–547
  convertibility of, 543
  cost of, 415–416
  cumulative dividends on, 543
  par value of, 543
  priority in assets and earnings of, 543

provisions of, 542–545
  and refunding, 549–552
  valuation of, 360–361
Present value, 257–259, 261–263
  of annuity, 261–263
Primary markets for securities, 22
Prime rate loans, 31
Priority of claims, in bankruptcy,
  681–684
Profitability ratios, 67, 74–75
Profit margin on sales, 74–75
Profit maximization, 5–7
Profit planning, 106–124
Proprietorship, 49–53
Proxy voting, 501–503
Purchase treatment of mergers, 659–662

Quick ratio, 68–69

Ratio analysis, 63–89
Refunding of debt or preferred stock,
  182–184, 549–552
Registration statement, 483
Reorganization, 671–676
  fairness and feasibility in, 672–676
Replacement cost accounting, 99–102
Required rate of return, 353–355
  on common stock, 364–365, 420–421
Retained earnings,
  cost of, 417–419
  statement of, 65–66
Reserve requirements, 21
Return on net worth, 75
Return on total assets, 74–75
Rights,
  advantages of, in new financing,
    514–515
  effects of, on stockholder position,
    510–514
  exercise of, 514
  ex-rights date of, 509–510
  market value of, 511–514
  relationship of to common stock, 508
  and rights-on, 509
  stock split effect on, 458–460
  over subscription, 511
  use of, 514–515
  valuation of, 508–510
Risk, 5, 319–323
  analysis of, 319–323
  interest rate of, 358
  and leverage, 381–404, 422–425
  measurement of, 319–332
  probability distribution of, 319–320
Risk-return tradeoff, 11–12, 182–189,
  335–337

Safety stocks, 219–221
Sale and lease back, 562–563
Satisficing, 6–7
Savings and loan associations, 19
Secondary markets, 22
Securities,
  flotation cost of, 415, 487–489
  listed, 26
  listed versus unlisted, 24–25
  and long-term debt, 531–541
  margin trading of, 28–29
  market stabilization of, 487
  preferred stock as, 541–548
  pricing of issue of, 483
  and refunding, 182–184, 549–552
  registration statement for, 483
  selling short, 28–29
  underwriting, 480–481
Securities acts, 489–491
Securities markets, 22–29
  benefits of, 23–24
  over-the-counter, 24–25
  third and fourth, 25
Security market line, 338–343, 353–355,
  420–421
Selling group, 485–486
Sensitivity analysis, 327
Short selling, 28–29
Short-term financing, 228–246
  accounts payable as type of, 228–231
  from commercial banks, 231
  with commercial paper, 236–237
  compensating balances and, 232–233
  factoring as type of, 238–241
  inventory lien, as type of, 243–245
  net credit concept of, 230–231
  and security, 237–238
  trade credit, as type of, 228–231
  trust receipt and, 242
  warehousing as type of, 242–245
Sinking fund, 534
Small business,
  and cost of capital, 437
  organizational forms of, 49–51
  sole proprietorship as form of, 49–50
  tax rates lower for, 39–40
Social responsibility, 7–8
Sole proprietorship, 49–50
Sources and uses of funds, 119–123
  and depreciation, 120–121
Spontaneous financing, 131–137
Standard deviation, as measure of risk,
  324–325
Stock, 20
Stock dividends, 458–460
Stock exchanges, 23–29
Stock repurchase, 460–463
Stock splits, 458–460

Straight line depreciation, 57
Subordinated debentures, 536–538
Sum-of-years'-digits depreciation, 58
Supernormal growth and valuation,
    375–376
Synergy, 642–643

Tax environment, 39–55
    and corporate income tax, 39–46
    and depreciation, 40–41, 42–43,
        56–59
    and fiscal policy, 21–22
    and form of organization, 49–53
    and investment tax credit, 41
    and personal deductions, 46–48
    and personal income tax, 46–49
    and tax loss carry-back and carry-for-
        ward, 44–45
Tender offers, 648–652
Term loans, 474–480
    characteristics, 476–478
    cost of, 478–480
Term structure of interest rates, 179–182
    expectations theory of, 179–180
Trade credit, 228–231
    advantages of, 230–231
    cash discount, as form of, 229
Treasury stock, 460–463
Trend analysis, 77–79
Trustee, 532–533

Trust receipt, 242
Turnover ratio, 74

Uncertainty,
    and decision trees, 327–329
    and investment decisions, 319–344
    measures of project risk, 319–332
    and portfolio risk, 332–338
    and probability distribution, 319–320
    and riskiness over time, 326–327
    sensitivity analysis of, 327
    simulation of, 330–332
    and standard deviation as a measure
        of risk, 324–325
Underwriting, 480–481
Units of production in depreciation,
    58–59
Utility maximization, 7

Valuation, 351–368
    of bonds, 355–360
    of book versus market value, 351–352
    of capital structure, 515–523
    of common stock, 361–365
    of expected dividends, 372–373
    Gordon model of, 373–375
    of liquidation versus going concern,
        351
    of market equilibrium, 364–365

of market versus fair value, 352
multi-period stock valuation models of,
    372–379
of normal growth, 373–375
of perpetual bonds, 356–357
of preferred stock, 360–361
of required rate of return, 353–355,
    364–365
and security market line, 353–355
of short-term bonds, 357–358
of supernormal growth, 375–376
of yield to maturity, 358–360
of zero growth, 373
Variable budgets, 156–158

Warehouse financing, 242–245
Warrants, 587–590, 601–603
    reported earnings for, 603
    valuation of, 587–590
Wealth maximization, 5–7
Weighted average cost of capital,
    425–428
Working capital, 173–191
    concept of, 174–177
    current asset policy of, 187–189
    international, 706

Yield to maturity, 358–360

Frequently Used Symbols in Essentials of Managerial Finance

a	periodic level payment or annuity
b	proportion of net income (NI) retained by the firm
B	the market value of the firm's debt
β (beta)	beta of a security, a measure of its riskiness
c	coupon payment for a bond
CV	coefficient of variation
$CVIF$	compound value interest factor
$CVIF_a$	compound value interest factor for an annuity
d	dividend payment per share of common equity
D	total dividend payments of the firm for common equity
Dep	depreciation
EPS	earnings per share; also e
F	net after-tax cash flows for capital budgeting analysis of projects
g	growth rate or growth factor
i	interest rate
I	amount of investment
k	in general, the discount factor; more specifically, the weighted average cost of capital
k_b	cost of debt
k_c	cost of a convertible issue
k_j	returns to firm j or on security j
k_s	cost of common equity for the levered firm
k_{ps}	cost of senior equity, e.g., preferred stock
k_u	cost of capital for the unlevered firm
k_M	return on the market portfolio
λ (lambda)	slope of the security market line $= (\bar{k}_M - R_F)/\sigma^2_M$
n	number of shares outstanding
N	life of a project; also terminal year of decision or planning horizon
p	price of a security
P	sales price per unit of product sold
P_s	probability for state of the world s
$PVIF$	present value interest factor
$PVIF_a$	present value interest factor for an annuity
Q	quantity produced or sold
r	rate of return on new investments; also internal rate of return (IRR)
R_F	risk-free rate of interest
s	subscript referring to alternative states of the world
S	market value of a firm's common equity
σ (sigma)	standard deviation
σ^2	variance
t	time period
T	the marginal corporate income tax rate
TR	total revenues $\equiv$ sales $\equiv PQ$
V	market value of a firm
w	weights in capital structure or portfolio proportions
X	net operating income of the firm; also equals EBIT $\equiv$ NOI